ARTHURIAN
LITERATURE
IN THE
MIDDLE AGES

KING ARTHUR

Parisian tapestry, The Cloisters Museum. *c.* 1400

ARTHURIAN
LITERATURE
IN THE
MIDDLE AGES

A Collaborative History

EDITED BY

ROGER SHERMAN LOOMIS

OXFORD
AT THE CLARENDON PRESS

Oxford University Press, Amen House, London E.C.4

GLASGOW NEW YORK TORONTO MELBOURNE WELLINGTON
BOMBAY CALCUTTA MADRAS KARACHI KUALA LUMPUR
CAPE TOWN IBADAN NAIROBI ACCRA

FIRST PUBLISHED 1959
REPRINTED LITHOGRAPHICALLY IN GREAT BRITAIN
BY LOWE & BRYDONE, PRINTERS, LTD., LONDON
FROM CORRECTED SHEETS OF THE FIRST EDITION
1961

PREFACE

THE monumental *Evolution of Arthurian Romance from the Beginnings down to the Year 1300*, published by James Douglas Bruce in 1923, was a prodigious feat of erudition and synthesis, all the more remarkable since it was accomplished single-handed. It has proved a boon to all investigators of the subject, and that it has by no means lost its value is proved by the many references to it in the present work. Nevertheless, since by design it stopped with the year 1300, it left many significant developments untouched; it dealt very sketchily with the early stages and the Welsh material; and, though it evinced a sincere desire to be fair to all sides on controversial issues, there have been many critics who could not accept Bruce's conclusions. Inevitably, too, in the thirty-five years which have passed new editions and fresh evidence have made necessary a reconsideration of crucial problems and a new survey of the vast field.

In 1951 Professor Frappier of the Sorbonne, Professor Vinaver of the University of Manchester, and the present editor, now Professor Emeritus of Columbia University, canvassed the practicability of such a new survey, and, though foreseeing difficulties, decided that the effort should be made. Since no one person could read all the original texts short of a lifetime, and even a group of three or four could hardly master the scholarly commentary in any less time, the only feasible plan required a much larger group of collaborating scholars. As a matter of fact, thirty scholars have been enlisted in the enterprise and are represented in this book.

An inevitable consequence is some unevenness and disproportion in the treatment of the various topics. Critics may justly complain that certain chapters might well be expanded, and that others are too rich in detail. For such defects the editor must accept the major responsibility, but at the same time he may plead that there are limits to the authority which he may exercise over the contributors: they have their rights which he is bound to respect. In some cases, moreover, what may be regarded as an excessive allotment of space can be defended. One of the chief defects of Bruce's book was the all too cursory and superficial handling of the Welsh material and its influence—a defect for which only the advances in Welsh scholarship in these later years have provided a remedy. Much of this scholarship, however, has remained inaccessible except to those who can read Welsh. If the chapters devoted to the elucidation of the Welsh texts seem too long, it may be replied that here for the first time one may find in English a comprehensive and authoritative treatment of this obscure but fundamental material.

The chapter on the origin of the Grail legends may invite similar criticism, but if it were to be sharply cut down it would consist of flat statements unsupported by detailed evidence and utterly lacking in cogency. A problem so intricate and so many-sided demands a full and carefully documented answer.

Moreover, if there are marked differences in emphasis between the chapters, it should be remembered that the nature of the topics treated varies greatly, so that the method of approach and the points chosen for stress in one chapter would be quite inappropriate in another. As to differences of opinion, they are not only to be expected but they serve the useful purpose of reminding the reader that these issues are not closed.

Indeed, the editor instructed contributors to give their own opinions on debated questions and the reasons therefor, supplying references, however, to divergent views. In a few cases where the divergent views seemed to merit a fuller statement, it has been provided at the editor's request. In no instance has he sought to impose his own opinions, and each chapter after editorial revision has been submitted to its author for approval and correction. Parry's unfortunate death made necessary an exception to this procedure, though not to the principle that the opinions expressed are the author's.

The editor has, however, considered it his duty and prerogative to reduce or recast certain chapters, subject to the author's consent; to eliminate plain errors of fact or reference where they have been detected; to exercise some discretion in the expansion or curtailment of the footnote references; and to fit the chapters together by introductions and cross-references.

The bibliographical apparatus is necessarily selective. Antiquated editions and obsolete theories have generally been disregarded. Erudite readers will doubtless discover that some books and articles which they consider significant have been omitted. Some of these omissions are due to the interval between the submission of manuscript and the date of publication. But fortunately bibliographical guides to Arthurian literature abound: Bruce for the period up to 1922; the two bibliographies of critical Arthurian literature (1922–9, 1930–5), edited by Parry and by Parry and Schlauch and published by the Modern Language Association; the bibliographies published annually in the June numbers of the *Modern Language Quarterly* since 1940 and covering the period beginning 1936; and the *Bulletin Bibliographique de la Société Internationale Arthurienne*, which began to appear in 1949.

It remains for the editor to beg the pardon of the contributors and readers for his shortcomings; to express his regret that the death of Dr. Dorothy Everett prevented her supplying the chapter on Layamon which she had promised; to thank the twenty-nine scholars who have so generously given their time and expert knowledge to this enterprise and who have accepted with remarkable good nature the intervention of the editorial hand.

ROGER SHERMAN LOOMIS

CONTENTS

LIST OF PLATES

The Editor wishes to express his gratitude to the Curators of the Cloisters Museum
and the Victoria and Albert Museum and to the Curators of Manuscripts of the
Bibliothèque Nationale, the Bodleian Library, the Yale University Library, and the
Pierpont Morgan Library for permission to use illustrations from their collections,
as well as to Mrs. Lucy Kingsley Porter for the use of her photograph of the Modena
archivolt.

LIST OF ABBREVIATIONS

ADA	*Anzeiger für deutsches Altertum*
AR	*Archivum Romanicum*
Archiv	*Archiv für das Studium der neueren Sprachen*
BBCS	*Bulletin of the Board of Celtic Studies*
BBSIA	*Bulletin Bibliographique de la Société Internationale Arthurienne*
Beiträge	*Beiträge zur Geschichte der deutschen Sprache und Literatur*
Bruce	J. D. Bruce, *The Evolution of Arthurian Romance from the Beginnings to 1300* (Baltimore, Göttingen, 1923; reprinted New York, 1927).
CFMA	*Classiques Français du Moyen Âge*
DF	*Deutsche Forschungen*
DVLG	*Deutsche Vierteljahrschrift für Literaturwissenschaft und Geistesgeschichte*
EC	*Études Celtiques*
EETS	Early English Text Society, Original Series
EETSES	Early English Text Society, Extra Series
ELH	*English Literary History*
ESt	*Englische Studien*
Faral	E. Faral, *La Légende Arthurienne*, première partie (Paris, 1929)
GGA	*Göttingische gelehrte Anzeigen*
GSLI	*Giornale Storico della Letteratura Italiana*
JEGP	*Journal of English and Germanic Philology*
Loomis, *Arthurian Tradition*.	R. S. Loomis, *Arthurian Tradition and Chrétien de Troyes* (New York, 1949)
Loomis, *Wales*.	R. S. Loomis, *Wales and the Arthurian Legend* (Cardiff, 1956)
MA	*Moyen Âge*
MedAev	*Medium Aevum*
MLN	*Modern Language Notes*
MLQ	*Modern Language Quarterly*
MLR	*Modern Language Review*
MP	*Modern Philology*
Neo	*Neophilologus*
PMLA	*Publications of the Modern Language Association of America*
R	*Romania*
RB	*Revue Belge de Philologie et d'Histoire*
RC	*Revue Celtique*
RES	*Review of English Studies*
RF	*Romanische Forschungen*
RP	*Romance Philology*
RR	*Romanic Review*

SATF	*Société des Anciens Textes Français*
SM	*Studi Medievali*
SP	*Studies in Philology*
Spec	*Speculum*
SR	*Studj Romanzi*
THSC	*Transactions of the Honourable Society of Cymmrodorion*
Tijd	*Tijdschrift voor Nederlandse Taal- en Letterkunde*
ZCP	*Zeitschrift für celtische Philologie*
ZDA	*Zeitschrift für deutsches Altertum*
ZDP	*Zeitschrift für deutsche Philologie*
ZFSL	*Zeitschrift für französische Sprache und Literatur*
ZRP	*Zeitschrift für romanische Philologie*

PROLOGUE

EW people, except professional students of the subject, have any realization of the prodigious vogue of Arthurian romance and pseudo-history in Western Christendom during the Middle Ages. British readers think it quite natural that a British hero should be celebrated in the Welsh *Mabinogion* and in Malory's English book; most of them would be surprised to learn that three of the Welsh tales and nearly the whole of the *Morte d'Arthur* were derived, either directly or indirectly, from French sources, that, in fact, France produced a far larger bulk of Arthurian literature than England. This is the more startling when one considers the rivalry and intermittent hostility between the two kingdoms from 1154 to 1453. Strange that for three centuries the most eminent literary men of France were dedicating their talents to the glorification of an alien potentate who, it was claimed, had killed King Frollo of Gaul and subjugated his people! The wars and quarrels of Charlemagne and his peers lost favour in 'la douce France', while the exploits of Arthur and his knights in love and tournament seized and held the imagination till the Middle Ages themselves were spent.

It was mainly from France that the Matter of Britain, as it was called, spread through the Low Countries, Denmark, Germany, Switzerland, Bohemia, Italy, Sicily, Spain, and Portugal. Even in Cyprus we find French knights as early as 1223 amusing themselves with a Round Table in imitation of Arthur's banquets and joustings. The greatest poets of medieval Germany could find no more congenial subjects than the loves of Tristan and Isolt and Parzival's quest of the Grail, while Dante was evidently familiar with the romance of Lancelot. Thanks chiefly to Geoffrey of Monmouth, Merlin was revered for his mantic powers from Sicily to Iceland, and the prophecies concocted for him in 1135 were still taken seriously enough in Germany nearly 500 years later as to be published in 1608. Translations of Arthurian texts into Greek, Hebrew, and Irish have come down to us.

Students of medieval literature must be struck by two characteristics of this Matter of Britain—its novelty and its inconsistency. With the exception of some few borrowings from the Matter of France and obvious imitations of certain stylistic adornments of the Latin classics, nothing quite like the romantic fiction of the Arthurian cycle had appeared on the continent of Europe before. The element of the supernatural, particularly as it appears in the stories of Arthur's birth, passing, and survival and in the earliest forms of the Grail legend, has no antecedents in French literature. Though to us the fairy world of Morgain la Fée and the enchantments of Merlin may seem worn and threadbare, in twelfth-century France and England they were something quite new. Moreover, when one attempts to survey this international literature, one discovers that it is a mass of inconsistencies. One has only to sample a representative portion of it in Malory's book or to compare his account of the Grail quest with that of Wolfram von Eschenbach in order to realize that consistency, harmony, fixity are not its outstanding qualities.

Such a vast and peculiar literature has provoked and continues to provoke much speculation. What was the secret of its fascination, so pervasive and so persistent? Who were Arthur, Lancelot, Gawain, Tristan? Who were Guenevere, Isolt, the Lady of the Lake? Did any of them ever live? Were there legends about them in Wales, and have these been preserved? To what extent, if any, did these Welsh legends supply personages and plots to the romancers of England and the Continent? Was Geoffrey of Monmouth's successful hoax the starting-point of Arthur's startling rise to popularity?

Added to these obvious and basic questions, there are all the complex and often baffling problems of the interrelationship between texts. From these, in turn, arise problems of originality and servility, purpose and meaning. Some recent commentators would have it that all the major romances of the Arthurian cycle were written to convey not only the lessons and the ideas plainly expressed or obviously implied but also arcane symbolisms, so that scarcely a name, a number, a colour, or a weapon but was intended to convey a message to the initiates. On the other hand, there are scholars who protest that the typical romancer was no Dante, not even a minor one, and warn against the temptation to extract significances from narratives which the author's contemporaries and even the author himself never dreamed of. Then there are conflicting views as to the artistic values of this or that work, divergent estimates of the taste, the constructive skill, and technique of the author.

No one scholar can be expected to deal with so huge and so complex a body of literature in so many languages. The task has been divided to take advantage of the special knowledge possessed by a number of scholars. There are, to be sure, some disadvantages in such a distribution of labour. Single authorship, if it were possible, would have produced greater consistency and cohesion and better proportioning. The problems have not all been solved, and there will be criticism of some of the solutions proposed. But the reader will find in the following chapters a survey of this imposing body of medieval fiction in as clear a light as modern knowledge and a variety of contemporary specialists can throw upon it.

THE ARTHUR OF HISTORY

KENNETH HURLSTONE JACKSON

Dᴵᴰ King Arthur ever really exist? The only honest answer is, 'We do not know, but he may well have existed.' The nature of the evidence is such that proof is impossible. There is a certain amount of early material dealing with him, but the difficulty lies in distinguishing what is, if anything, history from what is legend. Most scholars would agree that the Arthur of Geoffrey of Monmouth is not historical at all. Similarly the Arthur in *Culhwch and Olwen*, and the other early Welsh literary sources discussed elsewhere in this book, is clearly a figure of folktale. Certain early legendary texts older than Geoffrey which mention Arthur are written in Latin, which has given them a spurious air of historicity by contrast with obviously fanciful material in Welsh like *Culhwch*. Hence, it is as well to clear these legends out of the way before discussing sources which may reasonably be regarded as historical.

The *Mirabilia* of Nennius's early ninth-century *Historia Brittonum* has two tales of Arthur. One describes a cairn in Breconshire called *Carn Cabal*, the topmost stone of which bore a footprint made by Arthur's dog Cabal while hunting the pig Troit. The other tells of the marvellous tomb of Arthur's son Amr[1] beside the source of the Amr—the Gamber in Hereford-shire. Both show that the Arthur story had already impressed itself on the landscape, in the form of 'local legends', at least as early as the beginning of the ninth century. Nothing else is known of Amr apart from a mention in *Gereint*, but the other tale proves the existence already of one of the central episodes in the Celtic legend of Arthur. None of this is history, however. In some late eleventh- and early twelfth-century Latin Lives of Welsh saints[2] he appears as a king or chief, usually troublesome to the saint at first but afterwards overcome by a miracle. These anecdotes run true to a form common in Lives of early Celtic saints, where wicked kings are miraculously discomfited, repent, and grant lands or other gifts to the Church. Why is Arthur so treated in these Lives, when in other contemporary material he had already become the popular hero later exploited by Geoffrey?

[1] The readings *Troynt* and *Anir* of the Harleian recension are certainly wrong.

[2] Relevant passages collected in E. K. Chambers, *Arthur of Britain* (London, 1927), pp. 243 ff., 262 ff.; and in Faral, i. 236–44. See also Tatlock in *Spec*, xiv (1939), 345–65; C. G. Loomis, ibid., viii (1933), 478 ff.; N. K. Chadwick in *Scottish Gaelic Studies*, vii (1953), 115–83.

B

Some have thought of a genuine tradition derived from parties opposed to the Arthur of history, which is scarcely probable considering the nature of these documents; others of monkish writers seeking to discredit the hero of apparently semi-pagan tales. One may suggest that the monks themselves regarded such stories as little better than worthless fairy-tales, but saw that to introduce such a hero in the stock part of the Recalcitrant King would give prestige to their own heroic saints. Hence the Arthur they describe is the typical one of early Welsh legend, overcoming monsters, having super-natural adventures with his warriors Cai and Bedwyr, and the rest. It is idle to look here for history.

Having set aside these pre-Geoffrey Latin references to Arthur and ig-noring a few others as being trivial, or taken from Nennius,[1] we are left with little indeed, but that little of prime importance. The name *Arthur* is un-questionably derived from *Artorius*, not rare in the history of Rome since it was the title of the *gens Artoria*. Like the many other Latin names adopted by the natives, it must have passed into British during or soon after the period of Roman rule. We know of one Artorius who really lived in Britain, an officer called Lucius Artorius Castus, apparently a Dalmatian, who led the VIth Legion on an expedition to Armorica in the middle of the second cen-tury.[2] He is much too early for our Arthur, and we need not suppose with Thurneysen[3] that the name was hereditary in Arthur's family because some ancestor had served under him; but the fact that he resided in Britain does prove that his name was known in Roman Britain.

Next, Gildas, who wrote about 540, perhaps somewhere in the west Mid-lands or in Wales, tells[4] how after a struggle of varying outcome the Britons finally defeated their enemies (the Saxons are meant) at the siege of *Mons Badonicus*, in the year of his own birth, after which there had been peace. He seems to say that the battle took place forty-four years before he wrote, though this is not certain; and though the exact date has been much disputed, it must have been not far from 500.[5] This suits remarkably the known history of southern England, from which it appears that the Anglo-Saxon pene-tration of the south-east during the first half-century of the invasion was stopped about 500, when it had reached the borders of Salisbury Plain in Berkshire and Hampshire, and was not resumed until another half-century later.[6] Mount Badon must be somewhere in this area, and Badbury near

---

[1] See Chambers, op. cit., pp. 242, 249 ff. On Nennius see N. K. Chadwick in *Studies in the Early British Church* (Cambridge, 1958), pp. 37–46, Ed.

[2] K. Malone in *MP*, xxii (1924–5), 367 ff.

[3] *ZCP*, xx (1933–6), 136–7.

[4] *De Excidio Britanniae*, chap. 26.

[5] R. G. Collingwood, J. N. L. Myres, *Roman Britain and the English Settlements* (Oxford, 1937), pp. 460 f.; A. G. Brodeur, 'Arthur, Dux Bellorum', *University of California Publications in English*, iii, no. 7 (1939), 237–84.

[6] Cf. K. H. Jackson, *Language and History in Early Britain* (Edinburgh, 1953), pp. 199 f., 202 f.

Swindon, Badbury Hill near Faringdon, or Badbury Rings near Blandford are possible sites.[1] This decisive victory was credited to Arthur already by Nennius's time, and would account well for his fame as the supreme conqueror of the English. The fact that Gildas does not mention him has been urged as a serious objection, but the argument has little force. Gildas was preaching a sermon against his contemporaries, not writing a detailed history of his father's generation, and it is his general practice to avoid mentioning personal names.[2] Besides, what English bishop, castigating the vices of his compatriots about 1860, would be so clumsy as to allude to 'the battle of Waterloo, *which was won by the Duke of Wellington*'?

There follows what may well be one of the most convincing pieces of evidence for a historical Arthur. The Welsh elegy *Gododdin*, attributed to the late sixth-century poet Aneirin, has been pretty well proved to be genuine and to date, at least in its original form, from about 600.[3] In lines 1241–2 of Ifor Williams's edition it is said of a certain hero that 'he glutted (?) black ravens on the rampart of the city, though he was not Arthur'; that is, he slew many and did heroic deeds, so that his valour was second only to Arthur's.[4] Arthur is treated here as a famous historical chief; Aneirin might easily have known personally old men who had met Arthur in their boyhood, if the generally accepted dates for his *floruit* are right. Unfortunately there are interpolations in the *Gododdin*, and it is impossible to prove that this is not one of them. Otherwise the historicity of Arthur would be established beyond doubt.

An important point in favour of a historical Arthur is the fact that we know of at least four, perhaps five, people called Arthur hailing from the Celtic areas of the British Isles who were born in the latter part of the sixth century and early in the seventh, whereas the name is unknown before (except for Arthur himself) and very rare later.[5] Some national figure called Arthur must surely have existed at this time or a generation or two before, after whom they were all named, either directly or because their fathers or grandfathers had been. It is specially significant that Aedán mac Gabráin, king of Scottish Dál Riada, who had British connexions, christened one of

[1] Cf. Chambers, op. cit., pp. 197 ff. The fact that the element *Bad-* here is an Anglo-Saxon personal name (*Badda*), not a British name, is not a serious objection, since a British *Din Badon*, 'Hill-Fort of Badon', would inevitably be identified by the English with their *Baddanburg*.

[2] J. E. Lloyd, *History of Wales*, 3rd ed. (London, 1939), i. 125, n. 5.

[3] Ed. I. Williams, *Canu Aneirin* (Cardiff, 1938), pp. xiv ff.; review by K. H. Jackson in *Antiquity*, xiii (1939), 25 ff.

[4] A. G. van Hamel's unhappy struggle with this passage in *Neo*, xxviii (1943), 218 ff., may best be passed over in silence.

[5] See, e.g. Thurneysen, *ZCP*, xx. 134–5; Bruce, i. 6; Chambers, op. cit., pp. 169 f.; H. M. and N. K. Chadwick, *Growth of Literature* (Cambridge, 1932), i. 161. Arthur son of Petr would have been born about 570. The fifth would be the Arthur who is given as a grandson of Aedán mac Gabráin in the *Senchus fer nAlban* (see A. O. Anderson, *Early Sources of Scottish History* [Edinburgh, 1922], i, p. cli), if he were not probably a doublet of Aedán's son, who is significantly omitted.

his sons Arthur about 570 (and perhaps a grandson), since he headed what was meant to be a massive attempt to drive the English out of Northumbria.

Our fullest apparently historical reference to Arthur is contained in chapter 56 of Nennius's *Historia Brittonum*. It tells us that after the death of Hengist his son Octha came from northern Britain and settled in Kent, whence come the kings of Kent; the Anglo-Saxon Chronicle dates the accession of Æsc, apparently the same person, in 488. Nennius continues: 'tunc Arthur pugnabat contra illos in illis diebus cum regibus Brittonum, sed ipse erat dux bellorum'. By *illos* he seems to mean the 'Saxons' under Octha. He then gives a list of the twelve victories won by Arthur. Some of the sites are quite unidentifiable, though a great deal of nonsense has been written in the attempt to identify them.[1] The last is *Mons Badonis*, evidently somewhere in Wessex as we have seen. *Urbs Legionis* is certainly Chester, and *silva Celidonis* or *Coit Celidon* is quite as certainly the forest later known to the Welsh as *Coed Celyddon*, a memory of the *Silva Caledoniae* of the ancients, apparently thought of, however, as lying somewhere in Strathclyde. The *regio Linnuis*, where four battles on an unidentified river *Dubglas* were fought, is probably Lindsey in Lincolnshire. The *Mons Breguoin* substituted by the 'Vatican recension' (compiled 944) for the *Mons Agned* of the older recensions may perhaps be High Rochester in the Cheviots,[2] though since the name is lacking in the earlier sources, and what seems to be the same battle is ascribed elsewhere to Urien,[3] it may be an interpolation. The 'ostium fluminis quod dicitur Glein' may possibly refer to the Northumberland or the Lincolnshire river Glen, but this is highly uncertain. The remainder are entirely unknown.[4] Of the battle at *Castellum Guinnion* Nennius says that Arthur there carried on his shoulders the image of the Virgin Mary, through whose virtue and that of Jesus Christ the pagans were routed that day; and of Badon he tells us that 960 men were slain on that one day by Arthur himself.

Before discussing this passage it will be convenient to mention the two remaining early 'historical' references to Arthur, in the *Annales Cambriae*, which were put together in their present form in the middle of the tenth century but may have been first compiled early in the ninth.[5] Where we can check this, it is a sober historical document using good sources, not an annal-

---

[1] K. H. Jackson in *MP*, xliii (1945), 44 ff. I should like to take this opportunity of noting that the name (*Traith*) *Tribruit* may mean rather 'The Many-Coloured Strand' (cf. I. Williams in *BBCS*, xi [1943], 95); and that the supposed connexion with Myrddin has been disproved by A. O. H. Jarman, *Ymddiddan Myrddin a Thaliesin* (Cardiff, 1951), pp. 36 f., so that all reason to place the battle in Scotland disappears.

[2] See Jackson in *Antiquity*, xxiii (1949), 48 f.   [3] *Book of Taliesin*, p. 61, ll. 16 f.

[4] J. Marx is mistaken in saying that Lot's attempt at identifications 'conserve une valeur de premier ordre' (*Légende Arthurienne et le Graal* [Paris, 1952], p. 49, n. 3). Where they differ from the above they are worthless, like all Lot's essays in Celtic philology.

[5] Cf. H. M. and N. K. Chadwick, op. cit. i. 158 f., and N. K. Chadwick in *Studies in the Early British Church*, pp. 46–65.

ized fiction. The first entry, 516, runs, 'The battle of Badon, in which Arthur bore the cross of our Lord Jesus Christ three days and three nights on his shoulders, and the Britons were victorious'; and the second, 537, 'The Battle of Camlann, in which Arthur and Medraut fell'. It is not known how these dates were calculated, but 516 is probably too late,[1] by as much as ten or fifteen years, so that the same may be true of 537. If Badon was fought about 500, and if Arthur really won eleven great victories before that, beginning perhaps in or after 488 (see above), he is hardly likely to have been born later than about 465, which would make him seventy-two at his last fight in 537, so that about 522–7 is more probable. It is sometimes asserted that the first of these entries has no value because it derives from Nennius.[2] But the second proves that the compiler knew Arthurian material not quoted by Nennius, and the differences from Nennius's account of Badon are more marked than the likenesses (a cross not an image, the battle Badon not Guinnion, and three days instead of one). It is obvious that the compiler used information closely allied to but different from Nennius's source,[3] and this makes it especially valuable; besides, the second entry is the only early reference to Camlann and to Arthur's fatal battle with Medraut, later known as Modred. Camlann is unknown, though Crawford's identification with Birdoswald is ingenious and by no means impossible.[4]

Immediately following the 'Arthuriana' in Nennius is the section we may call the 'Northern History', into which a number of 'Saxon Genealogies' have been clumsily interpolated. It was once thought that all this was compiled in 679 or 685, perhaps from even older sources. These dates have been demolished by Lot,[5] and it is now known that the 'Saxon Genealogies' derive from a collection put together in Mercia in 796; and it is probable that the source of the 'Northern History' was a lost northern British document giving a brief account of the sixth- and seventh-century Northumbrian kings based on the Moore Memoranda and the first four books of Bede, and not older than 737.[6] The monk who drew this up added various names and events from British tradition, perhaps from annals or entries in a Paschal Table going back at least to the seventh century[7] and related to the similar Strathclyde

---

[1] Cf. n. 5, p. 2.

[2] e.g. Bruce, i. 11; C. H. Stevenson in *English Historical Review*, xvii (1902), 633, &c. Contrast H. M. and N. K. Chadwick, op. cit. i. 149, 154 f.

[3] William of Malmesbury (c. 1125) says that Arthur routed 900 of the enemy single-handed, relying on the image of the mother of the Lord which he had sewn on his arms. This suggests that he knew the traditions represented by the *Annales Cambriae* as well as Nennius. See Chambers, op. cit., p. 250.

[4] O. G. S. Crawford in *Antiquity*, ix (1935), 289; but cf. K. H. Jackson in *MP*, xliii (1945), 56; J. E. Lloyd in *BBCS*, xi (1944), 158.

[5] F. Lot, *Nennius et l'Historia Brittonum* (Paris, 1934), p. 79, n. 2.

[6] See Lot, op. cit., pp. 71 ff., and P. Hunter Blair in C. Fox and B. Dickins, *Early Cultures of North-West Europe* (Cambridge, 1950), pp. 245 ff. Lot's date 774 is wrong.

[7] *Cunedag* in chap. 62 certainly and *Atbret* in chap. 65 probably come from a seventh-century

source of the eighth century which seems to lie behind the *Annales Cambriae*.[1]
Nennius incorporated this almost whole in his *Historia* as the 'Northern
History', extracting from it various British notes which he interpolated in
the 'Saxon Genealogies'. It has sometimes been assumed that the 'Arthuriana'
are part of the 'Northern History'.[2] If so, this would put them into the
seventh century, perhaps little more than a century later than Arthur's death,
and would give them great authority. Unfortunately it is improbable that
they are part of it. The source of the 'Northern History' evidently began its
account of Northumbria with Ida, doubtless because Bede and the Moore
Memoranda did so, and Nennius plainly added the 'Arthuriana' as a transition between the story of Hengist and the time of Ida. It is significant that
when the *genealogiae Saxonum* (meaning both the 'Northern History' and the
'Saxon Genealogies') were omitted from the so-called 'Nennian' recension
at the request of Beulan the 'Arthuriana' were retained, evidently being regarded as no part of the northern section. It is probable that it was Nennius
himself who prefixed the 'Arthuriana' to it.

It has been claimed[3] that the words 'tunc Arthur pugnabat', &c., quoted
above, form two 'Commodian' hexameters, and that the whole chapter may
come from an old British work on Arthur in Latin verse. But even allowing
for the fact that 'Commodian' covers a multitude of metrical sins, it is entirely
foreign to the Celtic tradition to write narrative in Latin verse, and there is
not the slightest evidence that the Britons ever composed Latin chronicle
poems. A Latin original would surely have taken the form of annals, and the
'Arthuriana' do not look as if they were derived from annals. Others think
the 'Arthuriana' are taken from a Welsh source, whether in prose or verse,
oral or written. There is some internal evidence for this. 'In ostium fluminis
Glein' is not a very natural Latin expression, whereas *in Oper Glein* would
be normal Old Welsh; besides, for what this is worth, neither river Glen has
an *ostium* whereas both have an *oper* ('confluence' *or* 'river-mouth', Latinized
wrongly here in the second sense?). 'In litore fluminis, quod vocatur Tribruit', 'on the river-strand[4] which is called Tribruit', is obviously a translation of *Traith Tribuit*, and the Vatican recension comments, 'which we call
[i.e. in Welsh] Traith Tribuit'. It is certain that *urbs Legionis* is a Latinization of *Cair Legion*, and likely that *castellum Guinnion* renders some *Din
Guinnion* unknown to us. Scholars have noted that when Nennius says
Arthur carried the image of the Virgin on his shoulders he may have had

---

written source; see Jackson, *Language and History*, pp. 458 and 48, n. 2. Nicknames like *Flesaur*
are obviously contemporary, and the names *Lin Garan* and *Birdei* unquestionably derive from a written
Strathclyde document.

[1] See H. M. and N. K. Chadwick, op. cit. i. 146 ff., especially 148, and cf. ibid., pp. 156 f.

[2] Cf. Thurneysen in *ZDP*, xxviii (1896), 85, 87; Bruce, i. 9; contrast Chambers, op. cit., pp. 15 f.

[3] Brodeur, op. cit., pp. 253 f.

[4] Cf. K. H. Jackson in *MP*, xliii (1945), 51 f.

scuit, 'shield', in his original, and misread it as *scuid*, 'shoulder'. This would be more conclusive if we knew that the Britons bore devices on their shields in the fifth century, and especially if the *Annales Cambriae* did not also give 'shoulders', which suggests an established tradition.

The Chadwicks have pointed the way to Nennius's probable source.[1] They note the early Welsh catalogue poem on the expeditions of the seventh-century king Cadwallon, which lists fifteen by name.[2] An even closer parallel is to be found in the very old poem on Cynan Garwyn,[3] who lived at the end of the sixth century. It runs in part: 'A battle was made for on the Wye, spears innumerable, the men of Gwent were killed with bloody blade; a battle in great fair Anglesey, it was surely praised, steeds and hosts crossing the Menai; a battle on the hill of Dyfed, Aergol in flight.' Another such[4] describes the battles of Urien, the sixth-century King of Rheged: 'A battle at the ford of Dumbarton, . . . a battle in the cells [or 'huts'] of Brewyn' (perhaps Arthur's Breguoin, see above), and so on. Elsewhere in the same manuscript there is a panegyric on Urien's son Owain,[5] naming his battles, and a similar poem on his contemporary Gwallawg.[6] It is probable therefore that Nennius had before him a written text, or knew an oral version, of a Welsh poem cataloguing Arthur's deeds in similar vein; the references to the image of the Virgin and the number of those slain by Arthur might well have been included, like the comments in the poems described. Indeed the figure 960 looks very like a corruption of the sort of number that was traditional in Welsh eulogistic verse; 120 was commonly the size of a chief's war-band, and an army consisting of three such bands would be quite natural. The British army of Gododdin is given usually as 300, or 300 with 3 chiefs, i.e. 3 war-bands of 100 plus a leader. Probably the original figure was *dccccix*, 3 times 303, misread by Nennius as *dccclx*. Besides the catalogue poem, he may also have had variant traditions about Arthur, in verse or prose; his note 'id est Cat Coit Celidon' on the battle 'in silva Calidonis' suggests that the name was familiar to him from elsewhere, and quite possibly the *Annales Cambriae* derived their information from some such variant source. That independent traditions of this kind existed in the tenth century is shown by the glosses in the Vatican recension, such as 'quem nos Cat Bregion appellamus'.

Such a catalogue poem is most unlikely to have been contemporary with Arthur or nearly contemporary. The Welsh language did not yet exist in Arthur's day, when Late British had not yet lost its final syllables and composition vowels, which means that verse composed at that time would have

---

[1] Op. cit. i. 155.
[2] Trans. W. F. Skene, *Four Ancient Books of Wales* (Edinburgh, 1868), i. 433 ff.
[3] Trans. ibid., pp. 447 f.
[4] Trans. ibid., pp. 350 f.
[5] Trans. ibid., pp. 363 ff.
[6] Trans. ibid., pp. 337 f.

lost its metric construction and disintegrated a couple of generations later.[1] This is very probably the reason why we neither have nor know of any Welsh poetry older than about the last third of the sixth century. We must think rather of some antiquarian poem on the long-dead hero, dating from between the late sixth and the late eighth centuries, based on earlier traditions, and analogous therefore to the poem on Cadwallon's expeditions, which is also clearly much later than his day. Our antiquarian panegyric poet may only have known that Arthur won twelve victories,[2] not the names of all of them or indeed of any, and he may have filled up what he did not know from other historical or legendary battles (or other events) of which he had vaguely heard. Thus Chester may be a faint memory of the battle of Chester of 613 or 616, a Welsh defeat; Coed Celyddon is a favourite place in Welsh tradition; Brewyn was doubtless a victory of Urien's, not Arthur's; and Badon might be known to him only from Gildas and therefore without the name of the general. Apart from Badon, only Traeth Tryfrwyd (Traith Tribruit) is associated with Arthur in later story. If, instead, Nennius himself was the compiler of our list, the above would apply to him;[3] after all, he, or a near source of his, seems to have done the same with the tradition learned from Gildas that there were twenty-eight *civitates* in Roman Britain.[4] The peculiar distribution of the identifiable names (Glein perhaps in Northumberland or Lincolnshire, Coed Celyddon in Strathclyde, Chester in the west Midlands, Brewyn possibly in the Cheviots, Badon in Wessex, and—in the *Annales Cambriae*—Camlann perhaps in Cumberland) strongly suggests a list which some early antiquarian built up at random from dim reminiscences of past events, doubtless in the honest belief that they were really battles of Arthur's; though naturally some may come from genuine tradition, especially Badon, the crowning victory. A mere forger would probably have picked well-known places, as Geoffrey of Monmouth always did,[5] though what was unfamiliar to Geoffrey in the twelfth century and is to us in the twentieth need not have been so to a Welsh poet in the seventh or to Nennius in the early ninth.

Two theories have been advanced in the attempt to prove that in spite of their wide dispersal, the battles are all genuinely Arthur's. According to one, Arthur was a general appointed by the chiefs of the still sub-Roman province to a rank representing that of the earlier *Comes Britanniae*,[6] the supreme

[1] See K. H. Jackson, *Language and History*, pp. 690 ff.

[2] So Lot, op. cit., p. 70, remarking that twelve is a suspicious number, and that the author failed to produce a full twelve. But the last point is surely an argument for the genuineness of the nine which are given.

[3] Cf. H. M. and N. K. Chadwick, op. cit. i. 162; Crawford, op. cit., p. 279; Lloyd, *History of Wales*, i. 126, n. 6.   [4] See Jackson in *Antiquity*, xii (1938), 52 ff.

[5] Cf. R. Thurneysen, in *ZCP*, xx. 134; R. G. Collingwood, op. cit., p. 322.

[6] Cf. J. Rhŷs, *Celtic Britain*, 2nd ed. (London, 1884), pp. 97 ff., 236 f.; *Studies in the Arthurian Legend* (Oxford, 1891), p. 7.

Roman commander whose duty it had been to defend the province anywhere where his presence was necessary, and whose troops were predominantly cavalry. This theory was prompted by Nennius's phrase 'cum regibus Brittonum, sed ipse erat dux bellorum', which was interpreted as a title analogous to *Comes Britanniae* and to that of the *Dux Britanniarum*, his lieutenant in northern Britain. The Latin is held to mean that Arthur was an inferior elected as general; 'along with the *kings* of the Britons, but *he* was (only) Dux Bellorum'. It is noted that St. Germanus is *dux belli* at the Halleluiah victory in Bede's *De Temporum Ratione*, and that in chapter 47 of the Vatican recension of Nennius (which derives here from Bede) Germanus was 'dux belli contra Saxones una voce factus'. But it is surely doubtful whether the phrase implies a high official rank. Nennius's words might well mean 'along with the (other) kings of the Britons, but *he* was their *leader* in the battles'. The words *dux belli* may not be a title at all but simply a description, 'commander in the battle'; compare the fact that in Bede's account of the Halleluiah victory[1] elsewhere, where he quotes Constantius, Germanus is *dux proelii*, not *belli*.[2] However that may be, the idea that Arthur was a latter-day *Comes Britanniae* was ingeniously urged by Collingwood, in an argument which it would be an understatement to call 'imaginative'.[3] The assumption of the high sub-Roman officer, fighting in widely scattered parts of Britain and employing the latest cavalry tactics,[4] is shown to be unfounded by the comparison[5] with the activities of Cadwallon, King of North Wales and no Roman, who besieged Edwin of Northumbria in Priestholm in 629, defeated and killed him near Doncaster in 633, captured York, ravaged Northumbria, killed Osric of Deira and Eanfrith of Bernicia, and was himself slain by Oswald in 634 near Hexham by the Wall.

The second hypothesis referred to is the popular notion that Arthur was a chief of the North: this has been rather discredited in the eyes of Celticists by the philological excesses of some of its supporters and their partiality in argument. The view is that since some of the names of his battles are certainly northern (really only one, Coed Celyddon), and one or two others may be, all or most of them must be—including, for some writers, even Badon— or must be made to be. This is easily done, by counting Chester as being in the North, and by identifications of the Macedon = Monmouth order, such

---

[1] *Historia Ecclesiastica*, i. 20.

[2] 'Germanus ducem se proelii profitetur', which seems to mean simply that Germanus took it on himself to captain his side; similarly 'dux belli . . . una voce factus' may well imply 'unanimously elected commander *ad hoc*'.

[3] Op. cit., pp. 321 ff. The characteristic heroic theme that Arthur himself killed vast numbers is surprisingly rationalized by Collingwood. The whole hypothesis, a seductive one typical of a certain enthusiastic approach to Celtic historical sources, makes large bricks with very little straw.

[4] Collingwood admits that Arthur as leader of a band of mounted knights is unknown before Geoffrey; it is of course a Norman concept.

[5] Cf. H. M. and N. K. Chadwick, op. cit. i. 162.

as *Linnuis* = *Lennox*, *Breguoin* = *Brougham*, *Mons Agned* = *Eamont*, and so on; for such authorities the correctness of these equations is 'evident' if the places concerned are northern. The idea is that the suspicion arising from the wide dispersal of the battles is misplaced since they are not in fact widely dispersed—though Lennox and Chester are over 200 miles apart! The difficulty that Arthur was fighting the 'Saxons' (as Nennius clearly shows, and specifically the Kentish men), and there were none near Chester or in the North in Arthur's time, is 'met' by supposing that it was really the Picts and Scots, and by stressing Nennius's story that Octha and Ebissa settled temporarily somewhere south of the Forth before coming to Kent.[1] But no amount of ingenuity can make Badon, the most probably genuine of them all, anything but a battle against the Saxons or Jutes in southern England. There might be something in all this, of course. A British leader in the last years of the fifth century could have fought the Picts in Strathclyde, and conceivably the English in Northumbria if we regard it as plausible that an early immigrant body was planted by their British hosts in Lothian as a defence against the Picts,[2] and later abandoned this ungrateful task, turned against the Britons, and joined their kinsmen in Kent. If so, the fact of a British campaign against them in the North might become almost totally forgotten by Nennius's time apart from one or two meaningless names, when it was eclipsed by their later presence in the South and by the glorious victory of Badon. But we ought to remember that this is a pure hypothesis, and above all should guard against trying to force philological evidence into supporting it.

Nothing is certain about the historical Arthur, not even his existence; however, there are certain possibilities, even probabilities. There may have been a supreme British commander of genius in the late fifth century who bore the Roman-derived name of Arthur, though it would be wrong to deduce anything about his background from the name. There is little reason to think that he held any definite sub-Roman office, whether *Dux Bellorum* or otherwise, and his supposed cavalry tactics are an illusion. If we grant his existence, it seems certain that his enemies were the English, and not indeed impossible that he also fought the Picts and perhaps traitorous Britons too; but there is no ground for holding that he belonged exclusively or even predominantly to the North, whereas there is definite reason to think his greatest victory was in Wessex. The period of his campaigns seems to have been the last decade of the fifth century, culminating about 500. He may have been killed about twenty years later, possibly in one of the civil conflicts alluded to by Gildas.[3] He was still vividly remembered towards the end of

---

[1] *Historia Brittonum*, chap. 38.

[2] Cf. Gildas, *De Excidio*, chap. 23: 'Saxones . . . in insulam ad retundendas Aquilonales gentes intromitterentur.'

[3] *De Excidio*, chap. 26.

the sixth century, when boys were named after him and heroes compared to him. His deeds were told in traditional Welsh oral literature, and at some time in the next two centuries may have been briefly related in a panegyric poem by an antiquarian who had heard that he won twelve victories, and knew perhaps some, but probably not all, of their real names. Badon is the most likely to be genuinely his, because it seems to have been a triumph which impressed itself deeply upon the minds of the Britons; it was fought against the English, apparently in Wessex. Nennius summarized this Welsh poem or Welsh tradition in Latin. He could hardly have *invented* Arthur himself, for Nennius was no Geoffrey; he was not capable of creating a character out of nothing at all. The *Annales Cambriae* likewise drew on Welsh traditions of a semi-historical nature, closely connected with but already divergent from those which reached Nennius. Meanwhile the historical general was already being evolved in popular story towards the miraculous 'emperor' of the later Arthurian legend.

ARTHUR IN EARLY WELSH VERSE

KENNETH HURLSTONE JACKSON

'EARLY' means here poetry of the native Welsh tradition older than the time of Geoffrey of Monmouth; or, if not demonstrably older than the late twelfth or first half of the thirteenth century, evidently uninfluenced by him. A word must be said about the character of early Welsh literature, as this has been constantly misinterpreted by certain Arthurian scholars. In the twelfth century the Welsh were the inheritors of a flourishing vernacular literary tradition which can be traced back for some six centuries. Part of this consisted of prose tales of popular entertainment, full of folk-lore, legend, and traces of pagan mythology; and part of popular verse of a varied nature, including poems dealing with genuine historical characters and events of the past, this verse having quite often taken the form of embellishments in a narrative which was chiefly in prose. Such tales and poems were learned and recited, new ones composed, and the tradition handed on mainly orally by professional entertainers called *cyfarwyddiaid* (sing. *cyfarwydd*). They were men of comparatively low standing in the literary hierarchy, dealing only with these semi-popular entertainments, and to judge from what remains of their repertoire the influence of Latin learning upon them was negligible. Doubtless they could not read Latin, and their training in their own vernacular tradition was such that Latin influences stood little chance of penetrating it. Many people do not sufficiently appreciate how entirely alien twelfth-century Latin prose and verse, with its elaborate, frigid rhetoric and its 'literary' treatment, must have been to such a popular yet firmly established body of entertainment; and the result has been the notion, preposterous to the Celtic scholar, that the Welsh material derives from Geoffrey of Monmouth instead of *vice versa*. Thus the poems in the Black Book of Carmarthen in the National Library, Aberystwyth (manuscript of *c.* 1200), put into the mouth of Myrddin are completely natural in early Welsh literature; they deal with the same person and setting as Geoffrey's Merlinus, but there is nothing in them which betrays a Latin origin or even Latin influence, as such influence in Welsh always betrays itself when it does occur. The attitude to these questions of scholars like Bruce, Faral, and Tatlock, part of a reaction against the excessive claims of an earlier generation, is itself already out of date.

The evidence that a poem is independent of Geoffrey is therefore partly a matter of style. It may also be linguistic. In some cases spellings and forms occur, or a significant aggregate of such forms, which Celticists would agree make it probable that the poem was copied from a manuscript, or goes back to a time, before the middle of the twelfth century. Unfortunately the Welsh language was changing so slowly at this period, and our knowledge of the chronology of its changes is so meagre, for lack of enough dated texts before 1200, that it is rarely possible to give anything like a precise dating. Still, the study of the history of the Welsh language has advanced considerably of recent years, largely owing to the work of Sir Ifor Williams, and we are better off in this respect than scholars of a generation ago.

The references to Arthur in early Welsh poetry are few.[1] The *Verses on the Graves of the Heroes* in the Black Book of Carmarthen, apparently extracted from various sources, say of him only 'An eternal wonder (*anoeth*) is the grave of Arthur', meaning perhaps that no one knew anything of his burial. The same manuscript has a poem on the sixth-century king of Dumnonia, Geraint son of Erbin, though the poem must be of a later date; another version is found in the Red Book of Hergest at Jesus College, Oxford (manuscript of *c.* 1400), varying from the Black Book text in a way natural to the oral tradition of the *cyfarwyddiaid*. It celebrates a battle at a place called Llongborth,[2] and the eighth verse in the Black Book says: 'In Llongborth I saw [Red Book: 'there were killed'] belonging to Arthur bold men who hewed with steel; the emperor, the ruler in the toil of battle.' Neither text states that Arthur was present,[3] but his men were evidently regarded as fighting on Geraint's side. Finally, the Black Book contains a dialogue in verse between Gwynn son of Nudd and Gwyddneu Garanhir naming certain sixth-century heroes, and one of the two says: 'I have been where Llacheu son of Arthur, wonderful in songs, was killed, when ravens croaked over gore.' Arthur's son Llacheu appears in a number of obscure references in early Welsh literature, including *Culhwch and Olwen* and a poem discussed below, but nothing of any significance is known about him. It is evident that he belongs to the same milieu of legend and marvel as Arthur's other son Amr mentioned in Chap. 1. In the same way Arthur himself is referred to several times in poems of various early dates in the Book of Taliesin (manuscript of *c.* 1275), but little more than the bare name appears.

There are two important poems in early Welsh which deal more fully with Arthur than this. One is no. XXXI in the Black Book and the other

---

[1] Most of the early references in Welsh verse were published by Rhŷs in his introduction to Malory's *Morte d'Arthur*, Everyman's Lib. 1. xix–xxv, but his translations, first published in 1893–4, must be revised in the light of later knowledge. The Welsh texts may also be found in W. F. Skene, *Four Ancient Books of Wales* (Edinburgh, 1868), but here the translations are even less dependable.

[2] In the Red Book text Geraint is said to have been killed there, but this is an inferior reading.

[3] Skene's translation (op. cit. i. 267), 'In Llongborth I saw Arthur', is incorrect.

no. XXX in the Book of Taliesin. Both are of uncertain date but probably older than the Norman period. Both unquestionably draw on the same mass of popular legend and mythology as *Culhwch* and the *Four Branches of the Mabinogi*; characters are referred to in both poems who are more or less prominent in those sources. The Black Book poem is a dialogue between Arthur and his gatekeeper Glewlwyd (familiar in *Culhwch*).[1] Glewlwyd asks who is at the gate and Arthur replies 'Arthur and Cai the Fair'. 'Who travels with you?' asks Glewlwyd, and Arthur names and describes them and their deeds. There are obscurities, but the general picture is fairly clear. Arthur's men are 'Mabon son of Modron, servant of Uthr Pendragon;[2] Custaint son of Banon and Gwynn Godyfrion; my servants were stiff in asserting their customs. Manawydan son of Llyr, profound was his counsel, Manawyd brought pierced shields from Tryfrwyd[3] [or 'from battle']; Mabon son of Mellt, he made blood stain the grass, and Anwas the Winged and Llwch Windy-Handed (?) [*Llawwynnawg*]; they were helping at Eidyn [Edinburgh] on the borders. . . . Cai pleaded with them while he hewed them down; though Arthur (only) played, the blood flowed, in the hall of Afarnach fighting with a hag. He pierced Pen Palach ['Cudgel-Head'?] in the dwellings of Dissethach; on the mountain of Eidyn he fought with Dogheads. . . . They fell by hundreds before Bedwyr of the four-pronged spear (?) on the strands of Tryfrwyd fighting with Garwlwyd.' Arthur continues with the praises of Cai and Bedwyr, and adds 'Before the kings of Emrys I saw Cai in haste. . . . Cai the Fair and Llacheu, they used to make battles. . . . In the heights of Ystafngwn (?) Cai pierced nine witches; Cai the Fair went to Anglesey to destroy lions; his shield was polished against Palug's Cat. When people ask who pierced Palug's Cat, nine score fierce ones (?) fell as its food, nine score chiefs' (here the poem breaks off).

In this curious jumble, among names like Custaint son of Banon, Afarnach, Pen Palach, Dissethach, Garwlwyd, and Ystafngwn, which are quite unknown elsewhere, we see a number of characters known in early Welsh legend. Precedence is given to Cai, and then to Bedwyr, as in *Culhwch*. Mabon son of Modron is also familiar, and Gwynn Godyfrion, Mabon son of Mellt, Anwas (Henwas) the Winged, and Llwch Windy-Handed (?) are found in that story, and Arthur's son Llacheu appears there, as already noted. Manawydan is, of course, one of the chief characters in the *Four Branches*,

---

[1] For a possible reflection of this situation in the Modena sculpture, where a porter stands in a gateway blocking the entrance to Arthur and his knights, see R. S. Loomis, *Arthurian Tradition*, pp. 237-9.

[2] Loth tried to do away with the personage of Uthr Pendragon as being an invention of Geoffrey of Monmouth (e.g. *RC*, xlix [1932], 132 ff.). See, however, Jarman in *Llên Cymru*, ii (1952), 127 f., where he is rehabilitated; also Parry in *Spec*, xiii (1938), 276 f.

[3] This may be a reference to the battle on the strand of Tryfrwyd mentioned below, but the meaning is uncertain; a third possibility for 'eis tull o trywruid' is 'pierced stained shields' (*eis* = 'ribs' is less satisfactory).

and both he and Mabon son of Modron belong ultimately to the realm of mythology. There is one reference, perhaps two, to the strands of Tryfrwyd which Nennius gives as the tenth in his list of Arthur's battles,[1] and (Gwrgi) Garwlwyd who seems to be the enemy there is mentioned in the Triads as an oppressor of the Cymry, apparently a Northerner.[2] Edinburgh 'on the borders' (i.e. of Britain and Pictland), and Arthur's Seat described as the abode of a mysterious tribe of Cynocephali,[3] hint at some lost tale of Arthur's men fighting monsters in Scotland. The hag in the hall of Afarnach may be the same as the Black Witch whom Arthur playfully cut in two to get her blood, in *Culhwch*. It is possible that 'Emrys' is Gildas's Ambrosius Aurelianus, though if so he is in strange company here. The nine witches remind one of the Nine Witches of Gloucester in *Peredur*. The remainder refers to the killing of the destructive monster Palug's Cat, whose story is told in the Triads.[4] In all this Arthur is the leader of a band of wonderful monster-slaying heroes, just as in *Culhwch* and the *Mirabilia* of Nennius, the typical Arthur of pre-Norman Welsh story; and tantalizing echoes of tales now lost can be faintly heard.

An even more peculiar legend is hinted at in the early poem called *The Spoils of Annwfn*, no. XXX in the Book of Taliesin.[5] There may have been a historical poet Taliesin in the sixth century, but if so, as with Arthur, a mass of strange fiction accumulated about him, telling how he underwent numerous transformations and acquired mystic knowledge. The texts involved are of various dates; among them are several very obscure poems in the Book of Taliesin in which the poet is made to boast of his own esoteric knowledge, of the reincarnations he has gone through, and of his adventures with the heroes of ancient Welsh myth and story. *The Spoils of Annwfn* is one of these, probably of pre-Norman date. It seems to describe a disastrous expedition undertaken by Arthur and his men, in his ship Prydwenn, to a certain city[6] called by various descriptive names, evidently representing Annwfn, the Celtic Otherworld (once, by a Christianizing confusion, referred to as Hell), which is apparently conceived of here, now as the overseas island usual in Celtic literature, now as a twilight underworld as elsewhere

---

[1] See above, p. 4, n. 1, and p. 6.

[2] 'Three chiefs of Deira and Bernicia, and they were three poets and three sons of Disyfndawd, who did the three fortunate slaughters; (one was) Diffeidell son of Disyfndawd, who killed Gwrgi Garwlwyd, and this man used to kill an enemy every day among the Cymry and two every Saturday, so as not to kill one on Sunday'; White Book Triads, *Y Cymmrodor*, vii (1884), 127.

[3] *Language*, xvii (1941), 249 ff.

[4] Loth, *Mabinogion*, 2nd ed., ii. 272, 289. This monster is believed to have survived as the Chapalu in the French romances. See Freymond's article in *Beiträge zur romanischen Philologie, Festgabe für G. Gröber* (Halle, 1899), pp. 311 ff.

[5] On the Book of Taliesin see I. Williams, *Lectures on Early Welsh Poetry* (Dublin, 1944), pp. 49–65.

[6] Perhaps instead of 'city' the word *caer* should be rendered 'fortress', since it often denotes a hill fort, Roman fort, or medieval castle.

in Welsh. The purpose of the expedition seems to have been the carrying off of the magic cauldron of the Otherworld. The relevant parts of the poem run as follows: (Stanza 1) '. . . Well-equipped was the prison of Gwair in Caer Siddi [i.e. 'the Faery City'], according to the story of Pwyll and Pryderi; no one before him went into it, into the heavy grey chain, it was a trusty servant who guarded him [or, 'the heavy grey chain which held him, faithful youth']; and in the presence of the Spoils of Annwfn dolefully he sang; and our bardic prayer shall last till Doomsday. Three shiploads of Prydwenn we went thither; except seven, none returned from Caer Siddi.' (Stanza 2) 'I am of fair fame, [my] song was heard in the four-cornered four-sided city; my first saying, it is from the cauldron that it was spoken; by the breath of nine maidens it was kindled. The cauldron of the Chief of Annwfn, what is its nature? Blue round its rim, and pearls; it will not boil the food of a coward, it has not been [so] destined. A flashing deadly sword [or, 'the sword of Lluch Lleawg'] was sought [?] from it, and in a fierce hand [or, 'in the hand of Lleminawg'] it was left; and before the gateway of Hell lamps were burning. And when we went with Arthur, a famous task, except seven none returned from Caer Feddwid ['the City of Carousal'].' (Stanza 3) 'I am of fair fame, [my] song is heard. In the four-cornered city, the mighty defence of the island, noonday is confused with jet-blackness. Sparkling wine was their drink in the presence of their retinue. Three shiploads of Prydwenn we went on the sea; except seven, none returned from Caer Rigor ['the City of ——'?]'. (Stanza 4) 'I, lord of letters, do not deserve [to deal with] mean men; beyond Caer Wydr ['the City of Glass'] they did not see the valour of Arthur. Three score hundred men stood upon the wall, it was difficult to talk with their watchman. Three shiploads of Prydwenn went with Arthur; except seven, none returned from Caer Goludd ['the Inward City?'].' The next two stanzas end with much the same words about the expedition with Arthur from which only seven returned, the city being called by the unintelligible titles Caer Fandwy and Caer Ochren.

The Celtic Otherworld is referred to again under the name Caer Siddi in another poem (no. XIV) belonging to the same group in the Book of Taliesin,[1] and the description amplifies the picture: 'Well-appointed is my chair in Caer Siddi, sickness and old age do not afflict him who is in it: Manawyd and Pryderi know it. Three organs round the fire play before it, and around its corners are the streams of the ocean; and the fruitful fountain which is above it, sweeter than white wine is the drink in it.'

The story of the raid on the Otherworld appears again in euhemerized form in *Culhwch*. Arthur and his men sail for Ireland in Prydwenn to fetch away the cauldron of Diwrnach. It is refused them, Bedwyr seizes it, Llenlleawg the Irishman (apparently one of the British party) kills Diwrnach

---

[1] For text and translation by Rhŷs see his *Celtic Folklore* (Oxford, 1901), ii. 678.

and his men with Arthur's sword Caledfwlch, and the raiders return home in triumph with the cauldron. That the cauldron of Diwrnach is really the same as the cauldron of the Otherworld is made probable by the reference to it in the list of the 'Thirteen Treasures of the Island of Britain' as 'The Cauldron of Tyrnoc [*or* 'of Dyrnawg'] the Giant; if meat was put in it for a coward it would never boil it enough, and if it was put in for a brave man it would quickly boil it enough.' The source of this is sixteenth century (the oldest known copy of the list, fifteenth century, merely calls it 'The Cauldron of Dyrnwch'), but it looks as if it derived from the original tale on which the poem and *Culhwch* independently draw. The latter has turned the Otherworld island into Ireland. The reference to the sword in the poem may connect with Llenlleawg's use of Caledfwlch in *Culhwch*; and if the translations 'the sword of Lluch Lleawg' and 'in the hand of Lleminawg' are correct, these, together with Llenlleawg, do look, as R. S. Loomis has proposed,[1] like a corruption of the name appearing in *Culhwch* and in the Black Book poem as Llwch (or Lloch) Llawwynnawg, 'Llwch the Windy-Handed' (?). One may even suggest that a story of how Arthur obtained his wonderful sword is concealed here; namely, that his man Llwch brought it away as one of the 'Spoils of the Otherworld'.

The city raided is unquestionably the Celtic Otherworld. Annwfn means this, and Caer Siddi implies it, not to mention the other names. The description of Caer Siddi in poem **XIV**, where sickness and old age are unknown, where there is music and marvellous drink, and where the Otherworld divinities Manawydan and Pryderi dwell, proves this; 'Taliesin' claims that his inspiration is of Otherworldly origin by placing his bardic chair there. In poem **XXX** the 6,000 men on the walls of the Glass City, whose sentinel would not speak when addressed, is a motif found elsewhere in Celtic sources, the earliest being in Nennius;[2] an attack is made on this island tower of glass and its unresponsive defenders, with results fatal to all but a few of the attackers. Scholars recognize that this theme represents the Otherworld. The Cauldron of the Chief of the Otherworld (*Penn Annwfn*, i.e. Pwyll) is obviously one of the well-known Celtic cauldrons of inspiration and plenty, and here also apparently a testing-talisman. The nine maidens who tended it are another familiar motif, reminding one of the nine witches already mentioned, the nine sorceress-priestesses of the island of Sena described by Pomponius Mela,[3] and the nine sorceress-queens of Insula Pomorum who received Arthur there after Camlann.[4] The reference to Gwair is obscure, but there was evidently some lost tale of his imprisonment on an Otherworld island, hinted at in the

---

[1] *PMLA*, lvi. 914–16. See his full and very valuable treatment of the 'Spoils of Annwn', loc. cit., pp. 887–936, and Loomis, *Wales*, pp. 131–78.

[2] *Historia Brittonum*, chap. 13.

[3] *Chorographia*, iii. 6, 48.

[4] *Vita Merlini*, vss. 908 ff.

triads where he is one of the Three Noble Prisoners of Britain; it has been suggested that Lundy Island, *Ynys Wair* in Welsh ('the Island of Gwair'), was regarded as the scene of this imprisonment,[1] and it may be that it was popularly thought of as an Otherworld island, like the Isle of Man and others including Grassholm, which in *Branwen* is the scene of an Otherworld feast partaken of by Manawydan, Pryderi, and Taliesin. 'The Story of Pwyll and Pryderi' suggests that the imprisonment of Gwair was told of in some early version of the *Four Branches* which has not survived. *The Spoils of Annwfn* and *Culhwch* bear witness, then, to some legend about a raid by Arthur and his men on the Otherworld, in which a magic cauldron and perhaps Arthur's wonderful sword were carried off to Britain. To follow the possible reflexes of this story in continental romance is beyond the scope of this chapter; the case has been ably argued by R. S. Loomis.[2]

Another Arthurian poem, probably of early origin, is the so-called dialogue of Arthur and Gwenhwyfar, discussed by Evan Jones[3] and Mary Williams;[4] the latter gives a convenient translation. The oldest manuscript is of the sixteenth century, and the language as it stands is not early, but shows a number of late rhymes. However, the texts vary in a way suggesting a considerable history of oral transmission, and Ifor Williams has demonstrated[5] the startling modernizations often made by scribes in this very type of poetry; and it may well be some centuries older than the sixteenth. Jones has proposed that the attribution to Arthur is incorrect, and that it is really a conversation between Melwas and Gwenhwyfar and probably also Cai; the context is clearly the abduction of Gwenhwyfar by Melwas as told in Caradoc's *Vita Gildae* (before 1136).[5] The mistaken title made the poem unintelligible in the past, but the present writer suggests that it has not been properly interpreted even yet. To understand it one must compare the story of the abduction of Guenièvre (= Gwenhwyfar) by Meleagant (= Melwas) in Chrétien's *Lancelot*. Meleagant appears at Arthur's court and challenges him to entrust the queen to the escort of one of his knights, saying that he will await the pair in a wood and decide by combat whether he will surrender to Arthur the captives that he holds. Keu (= Cai) demands the right to escort the queen to the wood; Meleagant wounds him and abducts Guenièvre. We may propose that in the Welsh poem Melwas comes to Arthur's court and seats himself below the salt; Arthur inquires who he is; he replies that he is Melwas from 'Ynys Wydrin' ('the Isle of Glass', the *Ynis Gutrin* and *Urbs Vitrea* of Caradoc); Arthur says that he does not pour wine for a man who will not fight. There follows a dialogue, perhaps between Melwas and Gwenhwyfar, the latter speaking on behalf of Cai, or perhaps between

[1] Rhŷs, *Celtic Folklore*, ii. 679.   [2] Cf. p. 17, n. 1.
[3] *BBCS*, viii (1936), 203 ff.   [4] *Spec*, xiii (1938), 38 ff.
[5] *BBCS*, ii (1925), 270 ff., 281 ff.   [5] See below, p. 178.

Melwas and Cai with interventions by Gwenhwyfar, in which Melwas is pitted against Cai in a contest of boasting. Gwenhwyfar only partly recognizes Melwas, but thinks she has seen him before at his court in Devon (compare the fact that Melwas is King of Somerset in Caradoc); this suggests that in the original story Arthur and Gwenhwyfar had visited Melwas's lands and he fell in love with her there. The poem ends with a challenge and fight between Melwas and Cai. We must remember that this type of poetry was probably regularly interspersed with passages of narrative prose giving the setting of the verse, and that it was the custom of the scribes to omit the prose parts when copying their manuscripts. Since the date of the poem is uncertain it is impossible to say whether this story comes directly from an original Welsh tale which in various forms reached Caradoc and the French romancers, or whether it represents a secondary readoption of a French version, comparable to the stories of Owein, Peredur, and Gereint in the *Mabinogion*. The first is perhaps the more likely.

Finally, mention should be made of the *Dialogue of Arthur and the Eagle*, another poem found only in late manuscripts, though Ifor Williams has brilliantly shown[1] that it is likely to be as old as the twelfth century. In it, Arthur meets an eagle sitting in a tree; it reveals itself as the spirit of his dead nephew Eliwlad the son of Madog son of Uthr. The religious dialogue which follows is of no interest here, but the occurrence of these names in a poem as old as, or at least independent of, Geoffrey, and the fact that the scene is in Cornwall and that the eagle can still address Arthur as 'chief of the battalions of Cornwall', just as in *Culhwch*, is worthy of note.

[1] *BBCS*, ii. 269 ff.

3

THE WELSH MYRDDIN POEMS

A. O. H. JARMAN

IN the preceding chapter reference has been made to Myrddin, the Welsh prophet, who as Merlin was destined to be drawn into the Arthurian orbit. In medieval Wales numerous mantic poems were ascribed to his authorship. He was also the central character of a legend of which the fragmentary remains are found embedded among other material in some six poems contained in manuscripts dating from the end of the twelfth to the middle of the fifteenth century. Three of these poems, the *Afallennau* (*Apple-trees*), the *Hoianau* (*Greetings, Little Pig*), and *Ymddiddan Myrddin a Thaliesin* (*The Dialogue of Myrddin and Taliesin*), are found in the Black Book of Carmarthen (*c.* 1200), and two, *Cyfoesi Myrddin a Gwenddydd ei Chwaer* (*The Conversation of Myrddin and his Sister Gwenddydd*) and *Gwasgargerdd Fyrddin yn y Bedd* (*The Song Uttered by Myrddin in the Grave*), in the Red Book of Hergest (*c.* 1400). Many later texts of all these poems occur and there are also earlier texts, both dated *c.* 1300, of the *Gwasgargerdd* and of a portion of the *Cyfoesi*.[1] The sixth poem, *Peirian Faban* (*Commanding Youth*), is found in a fifteenth-century manuscript, Peniarth 50.[2]

All these poems, except *Ymddiddan Myrddin a Thaliesin*, are prophecies and deal with the early history of the Welsh and their later struggles against the Normans and the English. Some of the historical references contained in them can be dated with fair exactitude, and it is certain that most of the stanzas in their present form were composed after the beginning of the Norman invasion of Wales. The vaticinations are uttered by Myrddin, who is presented as a figure of the sixth century in North Britain and made to refer at some length to the circumstances in which he was endowed with the gift of prophecy. These references preserve a substantial portion of the original legend. In the *Afallennau*, for instance, there are three stanzas which are entirely free of vaticination and which occur together in all the early texts. They probably contain the oldest material of the Myrddin legend in the Welsh language and may be regarded as the nucleus around which the *Afallennau* poem grew. It is now believed that the crystallization of much early

---

[1] The earliest text of the *Gwasgargerdd* is found in Peniarth 12 and has been published by E. Phillimore in *Y Cymmrodor*, vii. 89. An incomplete text of the *Cyfoesi*, found in Peniarth 3, has been published by Ifor Williams in *BBCS*, iv. 114.

[2] For text see *BBCS*, xiv. 104.

Welsh legend into verse form occurred during the ninth century and it is possible that between 850 and 1050 a poem on the Myrddin legend was composed of which these three stanzas are a remnant. In them Myrddin speaks as a madman leading a wretched existence in the Caledonian Forest, or Coed Celyddon, and while he meditates on his present misery his memory dwells on his former happiness and on the disaster which changed the course of his life. The stanzas contain some linguistic obscurities, but in the following rendering I have attempted to follow the sense as closely as possible:[1]

> Sweet-apple tree which grows in a glade,
> Its peculiar power hides it from the men of Rhydderch;
> A crowd by its trunk, a host around it,
> It would be a treasure for them, brave men in their ranks.
> Now Gwenddydd loves me not and does not greet me
> — I am hated by Gwasawg, the supporter of Rhydderch —
> I have killed her son and her daughter.
> Death has taken everyone, why does it not call me?
> For after Gwenddolau no lord honours me,
> Mirth delights me not, no woman visits me;
> And in the battle of Arfderydd my torque was of gold
> Though today I am not treasured by one of the colour of swans.
>
> Sweet-apple tree with gentle flowers
> Which grows hidden in the woodlands;
> I have heard tidings since early in the day
> That Gwasawg the supporter of . . . has been angered,
> Twice, thrice, four times in one day.
> O Jesus! would that my death had come
> Before I became guilty of the death of the son of Gwenddydd.
>
> Sweet-apple tree which grows on a river bank,
> The steward, approaching it, will not succeed in obtaining its fine fruit;
> While I was in my right mind I used to have at its foot
> A fair wanton maiden, one slender and queenly.
> For ten and forty years, in the wretchedness of outlawry,
> I have been wandering with madness and madmen.
> After goodly possessions and pleasing minstrels
> Now I suffer want with madness and madmen.
> Now I sleep not, I tremble for my lord,
> My sovereign Gwenddolau, and my fellow-countrymen.
> After enduring sickness and grief in the Forest of Celyddon
> May I be received into bliss by the Lord of Hosts.

It is clear that these three stanzas contain the debris of a legend concerned

---

[1] For Welsh text see J. Gwenogvryn Evans, *Black Book of Carmarthen* (Pwllheli, 1907), pp. 49. 15–51. 7.

with Myrddin and Gwenddydd, Rhydderch and Gwasawg, Gwenddolau
and the battle of Arfderydd. The part played by Gwasawg in the legend is
obscure, but Myrddin's attitude towards Rhydderch and Gwenddolau is
further clarified by a few references in the *Hoianau*. This is a poem of twenty-
five stanzas, each beginning with a greeting to the little pig which was
Myrddin's sole companion in the forest. It wears a less archaic aspect than the
Afallennau and consists almost entirely of twelfth-century vaticinations, but
some of the stanzas contain legendary material. In one of these Myrddin is
made to say:[1]

> O little pig, I do not sleep easily
> From the agitation of the sorrow which is upon me;
> For ten and forty years I have suffered pain,
> My appearance is woeful.

> I have seen Gwenddolau, a glorious prince,
> Gathering booty from every border;
> Beneath the brown earth now he is silent,
> First of the kings of the North, greatest in generosity.

Thus Myrddin bewails the death of his former overlord Gwenddolau. Of
Rhydderch he speaks bitterly in another stanza:[2]

> Little does Rhydderch Hael know tonight in his feast
> What sleeplessness I suffered last night;
> Snow up to my hips among the forest wolves,
> Icicles in my hair, spent is my splendour.

Other more casual references describe Rhydderch as a huntsman and as *ruyf-
adur fit*,[3] 'defender of the Faith'. This of course is the historical Rhydderch
ap Tudwal, usually known as Rhydderch Hael (the Generous), king of
Dumbarton in Brythonic Scotland towards the end of the sixth century, who
is mentioned in Adamnan's *Life of St. Columba*,[4] in the *Historia Brittonum* of
Nennius,[5] in the pedigrees contained in Harleian MS. 3859,[6] and, more
prominently, in the twelfth-century *Life of St. Kentigern* by Joceline of
Furness,[7] a work which like the Welsh *Hoianau*, preserves traditions of him
as a huntsman and as a protector of Christianity. Of Gwenddolau nothing is
known from any early historical source, though his pedigree is given in a
thirteenth-century manuscript.[8] It is clear, however, that he was believed to

---

[1] Evans, *Black Book of Carmarthen*, p. 53. 9–13, 16–19.
[2] Ibid., pp. 56. 15–57. 3.   [3] Ibid., p. 52. 11.
[4] William Reeves, *Life of St. Columba . . . written by Adamnan* (Edinburgh, 1874), p. 123.
[5] T. Mommsen, *Monumenta Germaniae Historica: Chronica Minora saec. iv, v, vi, vii*, vol. iii,
fasc. i (Berlin, 1894), p. 206.
[6] *Y Cymmrodor*, ix. 173.
[7] A. P. Forbes, *Lives of St. Ninian and St. Kentigern* (Edinburgh, 1874).
[8] W. F. Skene, *Four Ancient Books of Wales* (Edinburgh, 1868), ii. 454.

have fallen at the battle of Arfderydd, and this is explicitly stated in a line
of the *Cyfoesi* referring to 'the death of Gwenddolau in the slaughter of
Ar[f]derydd'.[1] The date of this battle is given in the *Annales Cambriae* as
573.[2] Since Myrddin refers in the *Afallennau* and *Hoianau* to Gwenddolau
as his sovereign lord, and expresses his abhorrence and fear of Rhydderch and
his men, it is reasonable to conclude that Arfderydd was a battle at which
Rhydderch defeated and slew Gwenddolau. It is also obvious that for Myrddin the defeat was a personal disaster of the first magnitude, for since that
day he has endured fifty years of outlawry and madness in the Forest of
Celyddon, hunted or thinking himself hunted by Rhydderch and his followers. The traditions current in Wales concerning this battle are reflected,
though in a somewhat confused form, in Geoffrey of Monmouth's *Vita
Merlini*,[3] according to which a war was fought between Guennolous on the
one hand and Rodarchus and Peredurus on the other. The fighting caused
the deaths of three brothers of Merlinus, King of Dyfed in south-west Wales,
as a result of which the latter lost his reason and fled to the woods. These
names, of course, are Geoffrey's Latinizations of the Welsh Gwenddolau,
Rhydderch, Peredur, Myrddin. The account in the *Vita Merlini* of the
events which brought about Myrddin's madness seems to bear some relation
to a statement in a thirteenth-century manuscript of the *Annales Cambriae*
that the battle of Arfderydd was fought between the sons of Eliffer and
Gwenddolau son of Ceidio, in which battle Gwenddolau fell and 'Merlinus'
became insane.[4] It will be noted that this account does not mention Rhydderch. The sons of Eliffer, however, were traditionally Gwrgi and Peredur,
both of whom died in 580 according to the *Annales Cambriae*,[5] and it is clear
that the latter of these is identical with Geoffrey's Peredurus. These references to the sons of Eliffer probably represent a late confusion of the personnel
of the legend, for neither Gwrgi nor Peredur is mentioned in any of the
Welsh poems, and it is unlikely that they had any place in the original story
of Myrddin. They seem, however, to have figured in a saga, now lost, concerning the battle of Arfderydd, in which the madness of Myrddin may at
one time have been merely an incident. The remains of this saga, as of many
others, have been preserved in the Welsh triads.[6] But it is a striking fact that

[1] J. Gwenogvryn Evans, *Poetry in the Red Book of Hergest* (Llanbedrog, 1911), col. 577. 27; also
577. 31; 578. 38.
[2] *Y Cymmrodor*, ix. 155.
[3] Ed. J. J. Parry, *University of Illinois Studies in Language and Literature*, vol. x, no. 3 (1925).
See Chap. 8 below.
[4] J. Williams (Ab Ithel), *Annales Cambriae* (London, 1860), p. 5: 'Bellum armterid (inter filios
Elifer et Guendoleu filium Keidiau; in quo bello Guendoleu cecidit: Merlinus insanus effectus est).'
[5] *Y Cymmrodor*, ix. 155.
[6] J. Rhŷs and J. Gwenogvryn Evans, *Text of the Mabinogion and Other Welsh Tales from the Red
Book of Hergest* (Oxford, 1887), pp. 301, 303, 305; Skene, *Four Ancient Books*, ii. 460, 462; *BBCS*,
xii. 13 f.; O. Jones, E. Williams, and W. O. Pughe, *Myvyrian Archaiology of Wales* (Denbigh, 1870),
p. 391.

Myrddin is not once mentioned in any of those which deal with the battle of Arfderydd.ˑ

It is not clear from the *Afallennau* what Gwenddydd's relationship to Myrddin was, but in both the text and the title of the *Cyfoesi* she is described as his sister. In the *Vita Merlini* Ganieda (Geoffrey's Latinization of Gwenddydd) is both Merlinus's sister and wife of Rodarchus. For the latter relationship there is no warrant in the Welsh poems, although according to the *Afallennau* both Rhydderch and Gwenddydd seem to belong to the party hostile to Myrddin. The *Cyfoesi* is a long poem, consisting mainly of vaticinations which span the space of six or seven centuries. Although certain portions are probably older than others, the whole of the poem is in the form of question and answer, Myrddin uttering the prophecies in reply to Gwenddydd's interrogations. The questions and answers are frequently confined to the last line of the stanza while the first two lines contain formal and stereotyped greetings or descriptions. There are several references to the fall of Gwenddolau at Arfderydd and to Myrddin's lapse into insanity, but the legendary content of the *Cyfoesi* differs somewhat from that of the *Afallennau* and the *Hoianau*. The most striking difference is the changed attitude of Myrddin and Gwenddydd towards each other. Myrddin's bitter complaint in the *Afallennau* that Gwenddydd does not love him and does not greet him is now replaced by a relationship of amity and concord. The death of Gwenddydd's son is not once mentioned, neither is there any reference to Gwasawg, the forest of Celyddon, the apple-tree, or the pigling. In the *Cyfoesi* Myrddin is an altogether more dignified figure, and although the earliest portions of the poem need not be dated later than the nucleus of the *Afallennau*, it represents a stage in the development of the theme of Myrddin the prophet out of the original legend. Myrddin is not now tormented by fear of Rhydderch Hael and his followers but rather he is able to prophesy the time of Rhydderch's death.

The amount of legend contained in the other three Myrddin poems is small. The *Gwasgargerdd*, purporting to be a prophecy uttered by Myrddin from his grave, has obscure references to Gwasawg, Gwenddydd, and the 'mountain madmen', and in the second and third stanzas Myrddin describes himself as the 'son of Morfryn' and also mentions the honourable position which he formerly enjoyed. The *Ymddiddan*, a poem in the form of a dialogue between Myrddin and Taliesin, seems to combine reflections by these two seers on two distinct events. The first twenty-two lines do not belong to the Myrddin legend but embody traditions concerning an attack made, or believed to have been made, by Maelgwn Gwynedd on the kingdom of Dyfed in the first half of the sixth century. The remainder of the poem is a prophecy in general terms about the battle of Arfderydd, and the action in Dyfed is referred to as a preparation for the great northern engagement. It also mentions 'Cynfelyn' (Drwsgl?), the 'seven sons of Eliffer', and 'seven score generous ones' who became mad and perished in the forest of Celyddon. These references suggest that the author of the poem derived his material from the saga of Arfderydd rather than from the more particular legend of Myrddin.[1] Finally, amidst some interesting vaticination, there are echoes of the Myrddin legend in *Peirian Faban*, including references to Gwenddydd, Rhydderch, Gwenddolau, and Gwasawg. The poem, however, adds nothing to our knowledge of the content of the legend.

In the legend of Myrddin as preserved in the Welsh texts we have remnants of the elaboration by early story-tellers of the well-known folk-lore theme of the 'wild man of the woods'.[2] In fact not only Wales but also Scotland and Ireland possess literary forms of the legend which are quite clearly related and which help to supply each other's deficiencies. In Scotland the twelfth-century *Life of St. Kentigern* by Joceline speaks of a certain *homo fatuus* named Laloecen (Laloicen) who lived at the court of king 'Rederech' and who, after the death of the saint, prophesied correctly that both the king and another of the great ones of the land would follow him within a year.[3] Two other stories about this madman are found in a fifteenth-century manuscript, Brit. Mus. Titus A. xix,[4] where his name is regularly given in the form Lailoken (or Lailochen). The first of these stories, *Lailoken and Kentigern*, states that St. Kentigern met in a deserted place with a certain naked, hairy madman named Lailoken, said by some to have been 'Merlin' (*Merlynum*), who declared that, being unworthy to undergo punishment for his sins among men, he had been condemned to suffer in solitude in the company of the beasts. He added that he had been the cause of the deaths of all the persons slain in the battle fought 'on the plain between Lidel and Carwannok', and that during the battle the heavens opened and a voice accused him of his crime and announced that he would have his abode among the beasts of the forest until the day of his death. When he looked up at the sky he saw a vision of intolerable splendour, countless troops of warriors brandishing their fiery lances and scintillating weapons at him. Thereupon he was seized by an evil spirit and driven to the forest. Having given this account of himself, Lailoken leapt from the saint's presence and fled to his wonted haunts in the woods. Later he made several other appearances and ultimately begged Kentigern to give him the Sacrament, declaring that he was about to die a triple death. After some hesitation the saint granted his request and the same day the shepherds of King Meldred waylaid him and beat him with cudgels and stones and then cast him into the river Tweed, where his body was pierced by a stake,

---

[1] See my edition of this poem, *Ymddiddan Myrddin a Thaliesin* (Cardiff, 1951), in which, p. 53, I suggest 1050–1100 as the date of its composition.

[2] See R. Bernheimer, *Wild Men in the Middle Ages* (Cambridge, Mass., 1952).

[3] Forbes, *Kentigern*, p. 241.

[4] For the text see Ward in *R*, xxii. 514–25.

thus fulfilling his prophecy by killing him in three ways at once. The other story, *Lailoken and Meldred*, tells how Lailoken was made captive by King Meldred and subsequently revealed to him that his queen, whose name is not given, had been guilty of adultery. The murder of Lailoken some years later by Meldred's shepherds was a revenge planned by the queen, and it is probable that this story was added to *Lailoken and Kentigern* as an explanation of the account given there of the circumstances of the madman's death.

There can be no doubt of the correctness of the view quoted in *Lailoken and Kentigern* that Lailoken was identical with Merlin (or Myrddin). Admittedly there are differences between the two. Myrddin is not associated with a saint in the Welsh poems, nor do these refer to such accretions to the original legend as the story of the exposure of the adulterous queen and the prophecy of the triple death.[1] It may be observed that both these themes occur in the *Vita Merlini* but that in Geoffrey's poem the guilty queen is Ganieda, sister of Merlinus and wife of Rodarchus, and that the triple death is prophesied by Merlinus of a boy brought by Ganieda to discredit her brother. The vision in the heavens is also absent from the Welsh poems but it is noteworthy that Giraldus Cambrensis states in his *Itinerarium Cambriae* that Merlinus Celidonius lost his reason when, having been placed between two opposing armies in battle, he saw a sight horrible beyond measure in the sky above him and fled thence to spend the rest of his life in the forest.[2] The general correspondence between Myrddin and Lailoken is, however, evident. Both are wild men of the woods living in the Scottish Lowlands towards the end of the sixth century, both have lost their reason in battle and are tormented by a sense of guilt, and both have the gift of prophecy. Both have relationships with King Rhydderch and foretell his death. The name Lailoken or Laloecen, preserved by Scottish tradition, can be equated with the Welsh form *llallogan*,[3] used in the *Cyfoesi* to describe Myrddin. Moreover, it was the reference in the text of *Lailoken and Kentigern* to the battle fought 'in campo qui est inter Lidel et Carwannok' that led W. F. Skene to establish the now generally accepted identification of Arfderydd with Arthuret, about eight miles north of Carlisle. Skene used the abridgement of *Lailoken and Kentigern* contained in Bower's *Scotichronicon*, in which the name Carwannok appears as Carwanolow. This name, which is the modern Carwinley, probably stands for *Caer Wenddolau*, 'Gwenddolau's fort'. The occurrence of the name Arthuret, which is clearly the Welsh Arfderydd, in the vicinity of Liddel Water and Carwinley fairly clinches the identity of the Myrddin of the Welsh poems with the Lailoken of Scottish tradition.[4]

---

[1] On the theme of the triple death see K. H. Jackson's paper in *Essays and Studies Presented to Professor Eoin MacNeill* (Dublin, 1940), p. 535, and J. J. Parry in *Spec*, v (1930), 2.

[2] J. F. Dimock, *Giraldi Cambrensis Opera* (London, 1868), vi. 133.

[3] For a discussion of the word see *BBCS*, ix. 8.

[4] On the identification of Arfderydd with Arthuret see Skene, *Chronicles of the Picts and Scots*

In Irish literature the legend of the wild man of the woods is found attached to the name of Suibne Geilt, legendary King of Dál nAraide, who was reputed to have lost his reason in the famous battle of Moira (Magh Rath) in 673. His story is contained in a cycle of three medieval tales, *Fled Dúin na nGéd* (*The Feast of Dún na nGéd*), *Cath Maige Rátha* (*The Battle of Moira*), and *Buile Shuibne* (The Frenzy of Suibne). The first two of these texts[1] describe the causes and events of the battle of Moira while the third[2] is concerned solely with the fate of Suibne and the life he led in the woodlands after his lapse into madness. Among the causes of the battle was the insult which Congal Claen, King of Ulster, believed himself to have received when the silver dish and goose-egg placed before him as part of his entertainment by Domnall son of Aed, High King of Ireland, suddenly changed into a wooden dish and a hen-egg, an incident which calls to mind the statement of one of the Welsh triads that the battle of Arfderydd was one of the Three Frivolous Battles because it was fought on account of the lark's nest.[3] Suibne was one of Congal's supporters, standing in the same relationship to him as Myrddin to Gwenddolau, and shortly before the battle commenced we are told that he laid violent hands on Saint Rónán and killed one of his clerics. When the fighting began, terror and madness seized him and he fled through the air like a bird, ultimately settling in a yew-tree. The acquirement by Suibne of the power of levitation is a feature which differentiates him from his Welsh counterpart Myrddin. Much of his life as a wild man was spent on the tops of the trees, and one day while in such a position in Tír Conaill he was observed by Domnall, the victor of Moira, who with his men approached the tree and tried to persuade Suibne to descend from it. But, in the words of the *Buile Shuibne*,[4] 'when Suibne heard the shout of the multitude and the tumult of the great army, he ascended from the tree towards the rainclouds of the firmament' and fled. This incident may help to explain

(Edinburgh, 1867), p. xciii; *Four Ancient Books*, i. 65; *Proceedings of the Antiquarian Society of Scotland*, vi. 91 (quoted by Forbes, *Kentigern*, p. 360). In *Arthurian Localities* (Edinburgh, 1869), pp. 68–70, J. S. Stuart Glennie claimed to have arrived independently at the same conclusions as Skene. *Arthuret* appears as *Artureth, Arturet, Artured* in the twelfth, thirteenth, and fourteenth centuries, and medieval forms of Carwinley are *Karwindelhou, Karwendelowe, Kaerwyndlo, Carwendlow*, &c. See Armstrong, Mawer, Stenton, and Dickins, *Place-Names of Cumberland*, English Place-Name Society, xx (Cambridge, 1950), part i, pp. 51–53; cf. also part iii (1952), pp. xvii–xviii.

   [1] Both were edited with an English translation by O'Donovan, *The Banquet of Dún na nGédh and the Battle of Mag Rath* (Dublin, 1848). The text of the *Fled* has also been published, with variant readings, by Marstrander in *Videnskabs-Selskabets Skrifter*, ii, Hist-Filos. Klasse, 1909, no. 6, and the same scholar has published the text, with translation, of the first recension of *Cath Maige Rátha* in *Ériu*, v. 226–47. Suibne is not mentioned in this version of the tale. For summaries of the two stories see Myles Dillon, *Cycles of the Kings* (Oxford, 1946), pp. 56–68.

   [2] Edited, with translation, for the ITS by J. G. O'Keeffe, *Buile Suibhne* (London, 1913). For a summary see Dillon, op. cit., pp. 68–74; also Dillon, *Early Irish Literature* (Chicago, 1948), pp. 94–100.

   [3] O. Jones, E. Williams, and W. O. Pughe, *Myvyrian Archaiology of Wales*, p. 391.

   [4] *Buile Suibhne*, p. 17.

the original role of the apple-tree in the Welsh *Afallennau*. In the first of the stanzas translated above Myrddin declares that the apple-tree's 'peculiar power hides it from the men of Rhydderch', that 'there is a crowd by its trunk, a host around it', and 'that it would be a treasure for them, brave men in their ranks'. Here Rhydderch, Myrddin's persecutor, corresponds to Domnall. It is possible that in the original Welsh legend Myrddin, having taken refuge in a tree (not necessarily an apple-tree), was seen by Rhydderch's men and surrounded. If like Suibne he possessed the power of levitation he would be safe, but the Welsh forms of the legend contain no evidence that he did. This feature may, however, have been present during an early phase of the legend and may then have been lost. If this can be assumed, then a protection of another kind would be needed to preserve him from capture. At first perhaps he merely hid himself among the branches, but in the course of time the tree itself developed the quality of invisibility, which Myrddin was also able to acquire as long as he remained upon it. At a later stage the tree became an apple-tree whose fruit contributed a solid element to Myrddin's sylvan diet and when the legend became a subject for poetry an address to the tree by the wild man was used as the opening phrase of each stanza. According to these invocations the apple-tree remained 'hidden from the men of Rhydderch', or 'hidden in the Forest of Celyddon' or 'hidden in the woodlands', and it must have been on account of this property that the *maer* or steward was unable to obtain its fine fruit. This probably was Rhydderch's steward, who either in actual fact or in Myrddin's imagination had been sent to deprive the latter of his means of sustenance.

The apple-tree also acquired other associations. For instance, in the last two stanzas of the Black Book text of the *Afallennau* it is stated that it will remain hidden until the coming of the two sons of prophecy, Cynan and Cadwaladr, to deliver the Welsh from their bondage. Again, in the third of the stanzas translated above, the apple-tree is associated by Myrddin with the happiness of former days before his lapse into madness, when he used to have at its foot 'a fair wanton maiden, one slender and queenly'. There is another stanza also which contains a reference to this theme, or one nearly related:

> Sweet-apple tree which grows beyond Rhun,
> I had engaged in combat at its foot for the satisfaction of a maiden
> With my shield on my shoulder and my sword on my thigh.[1]

Here again the tense of the verb implies a time long past. There was a widespread erotic development of the theme of the wild man during the Middle Ages, but his amatory adventures invariably happened to him as a wild man rather than during any antecedent period.[2] It is true that both Suibne and

---

[1] Evans, *Black Book of Carmarthen*, p. 49. 8–10.

[2] See the chapter on 'The Erotic Connotations' in Bernheimer, *Wild Men in the Middle Ages*, pp. 121–75.

Geoffrey's Merlinus in the *Vita Merlini* have wives, whom they leave behind when they take to the woods. On the other hand, the Lailoken stories contain no such theme and on the whole it seems improbable that the wild man had had previous relationships with a lady in the earliest forms of the legend. In any case, if the original role of the apple-tree has been correctly described above, its association with the ardours of Myrddin's youth must have been a fairly late development. In the *Vita Merlini* Merlinus meets with another madman who has lost his reason through eating poisoned apples which had been intended for Merlinus himself by a woman whom he had formerly loved and then rejected. The inclusion of this incident in the poem suggests that Geoffrey had heard tales of Myrddin's earlier adventures during the first half of the twelfth century.

In a recent study of the legend of Suibne Geilt James Carney has suggested that 'in the tale . . . as originally told the din of battle, the carnage, and a vision in the sky were alone the causes of his madness'.[1] Similarly in the Welsh legend it is probable that Myrddin's relationships with Rhydderch and Gwenddydd and Gwasawg, and the theme of his responsibility for having caused the death of Gwenddydd's son, were additions to the original tale, though at a much earlier stage than the erotic development described above. It is also fairly certain that in the early northern form of the legend the wild man was not known as Myrddin but as Lailoken or Laloecen. The name Myrddin does not occur in any northern source and the probability is, as Phillimore argued in 1890, that it was evolved in Wales out of the place-name Caer-fyrddin (Carmarthen), just as the personal names Efrog and Lleon were evolved out of Caer-efrog and Caer-lleon.[2] The name Caerfyrddin, of course, consists of the word *caer*, 'a fort', prefixed to the form assumed in Welsh by the Brythonic *Moridunon*, 'sea-fort'.[3] *Caer* in Welsh place-names is frequently followed by a personal name and it is quite reasonable to suppose that at an early date popular fancy had fashioned an eponymous personage Myrddin out of the second element in Caer-fyrddin. When the tale of Lailoken migrated to Wales during the seventh or eighth century it became attached to this shadowy figure and appropriated his name, while at the same time retaining its northern geographical setting.[4] This explains the

[1] *Éigse: A Journal of Irish Studies*, vi. 90; this was also O'Keeffe's view, *Buile Suibhne*, xxxiv. For a critique of some of the points made by Carney see a note by K. H. Jackson in *Éigse*, vii. 112.

[2] See notes by Phillimore in *Y Cymmrodor*, xi. 46–48.

[3] The form *Maridunon* is given by Ptolemy, see A. Holder, *Alt-Celtischer Sprachschatz* (Leipzig, 1891–1913), p. 427. See also *Y Cymmrodor*, xi. 25; Ifor Williams, *Breuddwyd Maxen*, 2nd ed. (Bangor, 1920), p. 27.

[4] It is, of course, difficult to suggest an exact dating for these developments. Probably the earliest reference to Myrddin is that found in *Armes Prydein*, a political poem contained in the Book of Taliesin (*c.* 1275) but dated by Ifor Williams *c.* 930, *Lectures on Early Welsh Poetry* (Dublin, 1944), p. 54; see also his edition of the poem (Cardiff, 1955), p. xvii. Myrddin is also mentioned in the *Gododdin*, see Ifor Williams, *Canu Aneirin* (Cardiff, 1938), p. 188. The manuscript is dated *c.* 1250 but the

fact that, although in the majority of the poems we have been discussing Myrddin inhabits the Caledonian Forest in Scotland, in *Ymddiddan Myrddin a Thaliesin* he seems to be speaking on behalf of the traditional heroes of Dyfed in South Wales. Geoffrey of Monmouth's work reflects the same confusion, for while in his *Historia Regum Britanniae* he discovered his Merlin at Carmarthen and described him as a grandson of a king of Dyfed, later in the *Vita Merlini*, although continuing to associate his hero with Dyfed by styling him King of the Demetae, he sent him in his madness to the Caledonian Forest and used material of northern origin extensively throughout the poem.[1]

In this chapter an analysis has been attempted of the legendary material contained in the Welsh Myrddin poems. In their present form these poems are without doubt fragmentary and it is probable that the original legend could be reconstructed much more fully by a comparative analysis of all the material contained in the Welsh, Scottish, and Irish sources. The complications which stemmed from Geoffrey's two widely differing portrayals of Merlin, and the great magician's subsequent career in literatures other than Welsh, will be covered in later chapters.

name, written *Mirdyn*, reflects the orthography of an earlier period. It is difficult to say whether this reference derives from a source older than 930.

[1] For a discussion of the discrepancy between Geoffrey's two portrayals of Merlin see H. M. and N. K. Chadwick, *Growth of Literature*, i (Cambridge, 1932), pp. 123–32, and below, Chap. 8.

4

CULHWCH AND OLWEN AND *RHONABWY'S DREAM*

IDRIS LLEWELYN FOSTER

BETWEEN 1838 and 1849 Lady Charlotte Guest published the text and a translation of eleven Welsh tales under the title of *The Mabinogion from the Llyfr Coch o Hergest, and Other Welsh Manuscripts*.[1] For this task she had the help of the best-known Welsh scholars of her day, and her natural and felicitous style soon established the popularity of the work. Though she and others have entertained mistaken notions as to the meaning of the word *mabinogion*, it is now settled that it is a modern plural form of the medieval Welsh word *mabinogi*, which corresponds in meaning to the French *enfance*, the story of a hero's youth from conception and birth to early manhood.[2] The manuscripts from which the word *mabinogi* is taken apply it only to the first four tales of Lady Guest's collection—*Pwyll, Branwen, Manawydau*, and *Math*, which are called *Branches of the Mabinogi*—and show that the word must have been broadened to include episodes in which the hero is no longer young. It is inexact to speak of the other tales as *mabinogion*, though there is no other term so convenient. Five of them come within the Arthurian orbit since Arthur is a prominent figure in each. Of these, two show almost no trace of continental or Anglo-Norman contamination, almost no sign of the pervasive influence of French romance. *Culhwch and Olwen* and *Rhonabwy's Dream* may be considered as the unadulterated products of Welsh narrative art—unadulterated except in so far as there is a tincture of Irish and Cornish tradition and a use of widespread folk-tale formulas.

Culhwch is one of the most important texts for the study of the Arthurian cycle because of its date, its multifarious sources, its kinship with early and late Irish fiction, the roll-call of heroes associated with Arthur, and the foreshadowing of themes which recur in later non-Celtic romances. Besides its importance for the scholar, and in spite of some defects of inconsistency and incoherence, it possesses the charm which Matthew Arnold claimed for it when he quoted the description of Olwen:[3] 'More yellow was her hair than

---

[1] Lady Guest's translation was expurgated to suit Victorian taste and is now superseded, but her notes are still useful. The best translations now available are that by Joseph Loth, 2nd ed. (Paris, 1913), and that by Gwyn Jones and Thomas Jones, Everyman's Library (1949).

[2] Cecile O'Rahilly, *Ireland and Wales* (London, 1924), pp. 101–3; Ifor Williams, *Pedeir Keinc y Mabinogi* (Cardiff, 1930), pp. xlii–liii; Gruffydd in *THSC*, 1912–13, pp. 39 f.

[3] *On the Study of Celtic Literature* (London, 1867), p. 160. Arnold quoted from Lady Guest's translation; for a more accurate one see *Mabinogion*, trans. Jones and Jones, pp. 110 f.

the flower of the broom, and her skin was whiter than the foam of the wave, and fairer were her hands and her fingers than the blossoms of the wood-anemone amidst the spray of the meadow fountains.' This quality, also exemplified in the spirited description of Culhwch's ride to Arthur's court, is balanced by a sort of grim humour, as in the comment which Cei makes on the hug of the Giant Herdsman's wife: 'Woman, had it been I thou didst squeeze in this wise, there were no need for another to love me ever.' And, as the latest translators of *Culhwch* have said:[1] 'The zest of this unknown story-teller still hits one like a bursting wave.'

There is a complete version in the late fourteenth-century manuscript, the Red Book of Hergest; an incomplete version in a manuscript at the National Library of Wales, known as the White Book of Rhydderch, was copied early in the same century.[2] Whether the Red Book text was copied from the White, or both were transcribed from the same exemplar is uncertain. But the Red Book scribe must have had access to the White Book. There are orthographical features which suggest an original recension earlier than 1100. The vocabulary is often archaic, and several glosses have been woven into the text. Thus *gleif* (Fr. *glaive*)—the only unmistakable Romance loan-word in the tale (as contrasted with three in the *Four Branches of the Mabinogi*)[3]—was incorporated in the text from the margin of a manuscript where it glossed an archaic *ennillec* (battle-axe); hence the confused reading in the White Book, 'gleif penntirec'.[4] Certain syntactical usages strengthen the case for a recension not later than 1100.

The main plot of *Culhwch* is that known to folklorists as the Giant's Daughter,[5] of which the most familiar example is the classical legend of Jason and Medea. In both the Greek and the Welsh versions the hero sets out to obtain one or more precious objects under great difficulties; in both he secures the help of men with supernatural powers; in both he woos and wins the daughter of the hostile personage who imposes the tasks. Though direct influence of the quest of the Golden Fleece on *Culhwch* is almost unthinkable, some sort of remote connexion cannot be ruled out.

Before the hero, Culhwch, sets out on his quest, however, the reader

---

[1] *Mabinogion*, trans. Jones and Jones, p. xxi.

[2] On the manuscripts and editions of them see ibid., pp. ix, xxxi. The White Book lacks the search for Mabon, the capture of Dillus, and the hunting of Twrch Trwyth.

[3] I. Williams, *Pedeir Keinc*, p. xxxiii.

[4] *BBCS*, xiii (1949), 75–77.

[5] G. L. Kittredge, *Study of Gawain and the Green Knight* (Cambridge, Mass., 1916), pp. 232–6. It is interesting to note that the combination of the Giant's Daughter theme with the motif of a 'destiny' sworn on the hero by a jealous stepmother is found not only in *Culhwch* but also in a folk-tale collected by Douglas Hyde in County Mayo, 'The Daughter of the King of the Glen of Loneliness', published in *An sgéaluidhe Gaedhealach* (London, 1901), pp. 340–59. For Irish analogues to Giant's Daughter see T. P. Cross, *Motif-Index of Early Irish Literature* (Bloomington, Ind., 1952), G530. 2; E765. 4. 1. 1; H335.

follows him through several preliminaries. First, according to Celtic conventions illustrated in the stories of Cuchulainn and Finn, the hero must be born and be given a name or nickname.[1] Thus we are given the names of his parents and grandparents, and are told how his mother, as her time approached, wandered away from the haunts of men and gave birth to the boy in a swine's burrow or pig-run; hence his name Cul-hwch, 'Burrow of Swine'. Long after his mother's death his stepmother places him under a 'destiny' (Irish *geis*) that his side shall never touch woman till he obtains Olwen, daughter of Ysbaddaden Chief Giant;[2] and he rides off to seek Arthur's help. There are clear Irish parallels to the description of Culhwch's steed, throwing up clods of earth with its hoofs;[3] to the admission of a craftsman to Arthur's court;[4] and to the speech of the gate-keeper, Glewlwyd Gafaelfawr, boasting of his journeys to the ends of the earth.[5] When Culhwch asks of Arthur the right to have his hair trimmed by the king, indicating a personal relationship between them, he is calling for a ceremony mentioned by Nennius in the ninth century, as Faral and others have shown.[6]

Arthur himself is presented in the story not only as 'the sovereign prince of this island' but also as the acknowledged ruler of far-flung dominions. Though there is a passing reference to Wales as his country and he retires to his court at Kelliwic in Cornwall to bathe himself and rest, he is able to assemble the warriors not only of Britain but also of France, Brittany, and Normandy for the invasion of Ireland; and in that country the saints beg for his protection and the inhabitants pay him food-dues. Among his prized possessions are a ship named Prydwen (mentioned in Chap. 2), a mantle, a sword Caledfwlch, a spear Rhongomyniad, a shield Wynebgwrthucher, and a dagger Carnwennan. Unlike the Arthur of many of the French romances he is no *roi fainéant* but takes an active part in perilous adventures.

Once recognized by Arthur as his cousin, Culhwch invokes the aid of the king and all the warriors and even the ladies of his court. The long list of names which follows is likewise paralleled in Irish saga,[7] but certainly nowhere else can one discover a more miscellaneous assortment. There are the helpful companions such as Clust son of Clustfeinad, who though buried seven fathoms underground could hear an ant fifty miles away stirring from its nest in the morning, and Ol son of Olwydd, who was able to track down the swine of his father which had been carried off seven years before he was

---

[1] T. P. Cross, C. H. Slover, *Ancient Irish Tales* (New York, 1936), pp. 142, 363.

[2] On this destiny see *Trans. of the Celtic Congress, 1921* (Swansea, 1923), p. 47.

[3] E. Windisch, *Das Keltische Brittannien bis zu Kaiser Arthur*, Abhandlungen der philologisch-historischen Klasse der K. Sächsischen Gesellschaft der Wissenschaften, Bd. XXIX, no. vi (1912), 158.

[4] Loth, *Mabinogion*, i. 252, n. 1; Cross and Slover, op. cit., p. 35.

[5] R. S. Loomis, *Arthurian Tradition*, p. 238; Cross and Slover, op. cit., p. 277.

[6] Faral, i. 107, n. 4; iii. 30; *Miscellany of Studies Presented to L. E. Kastner* (Cambridge, 1932), pp. 345-54.

[7] C. O'Rahilly, op. cit., p. 115.

born.[1] There is Sgilti Lightfoot, who skimmed along the tops of the trees, and in whom scholars have recognized the preternatural runner of the Irish Finn cycle, Cailte.[2] From the Ulster cycle comes the name Cnychwr mab Nes, through oral transmission of Conchobar mac Nesa, while Fercos mab Poch and Coruil Beruach represent misreadings of Fergus mac Róich and Conall Cernach.[3] Manawydan son of Llyr corresponds to the Irish sea-god Manannán mac Lir.[4] Loomis has urged that Llwch Llawwynnyawc, whose name is spelled in the Black Book poem (see p. 14 above) Lluch, and whose epithet probably means 'of the striking hand', is no other than the Irish god Lug, whose name is sometimes spelled Luch, and two of whose epithets were lámhfota, ' of the long hand', and lonnbémnech, 'of the fierce blows'.[5] In The Spoils of Annwfn, as already mentioned in Chap. 2, Arthur is accompanied on his raid on the island fortress of Annwfn by a warrior named Lluch Lleawc (though it is possible that these are simply two adjectives describing the sword),[6] while in Culhwch itself the corresponding personage who accompanies Arthur on a raid in Ireland is called Llenlleawc the Irishman. It is not unreasonable to accept both Llwch Llawwynnyawc and Llenlleawc the Irishman as representatives of the Irish Lug.[7]

This roll-call of Arthur's warriors, which also includes Taliesin the bard, Gildas the saint, and even Calchas the Trojan soothsayer, was evidently an *omnium gatherum* which could be added to indefinitely, as is suggested by the ten lines left blank in the White Book and partially filled in the Red Book list. Some of the names were transcribed from older forms; for instance, Teyrnon Twr Bliant is an archaic form of Teirnon Twryf Liant, which occurs in the first branch of the *Mabinogi, Pwyll.* The list is a haphazard compilation, a few names being repeated, while even the two whelps of the bitch Rhymhi have found their way into it.

The names of Cei and Bedwyr take first place in the list of Arthur's warriors, and it is they, the Sir Kay and Sir Bedivere of Malory, who actually accompany Culhwch when he finally sets out to seek his destined bride. Cei, however, is hardly recognizable as the disagreeable character of later romance; he displays, it must be admitted, a grudging hospitality when Culhwch seeks entrance to Arthur's hall, as Sir Kay does also on similar occasions; but his prowess is far from contemptible, and he possesses several remarkable properties (*cynheddfau*), among them the ability to grow to the height of the tallest tree and to provide heat for his comrades in cold weather.

---

[1] On helpful companions see Cross, *Motif-Index*, F601. 1, and *Trans. of the Celtic Congress, 1921*, pp. 48–51.   [2] C. O'Rahilly, op. cit., p. 115, n. 3.   [3] Ibid., p. 114.   [4] Ibid., p. 95, n. 2.
[5] ZCP, xii. 404; R. S. Loomis, *Wales*, pp. 161–3; in R, lxxix (1958), 57–61.
[6] On possible meanings of *lluch* and *lleawc* cf. I. Williams, *Canu Aneirin*, p. 196, and *Canu Llywarch Hen* (1935), pp. lxi, 242, and above p. 17.
[7] *Llenlleawc* might be explained as a misreading of *Lleulleawc*, with *lleu* a cognate of Irish *lugh* and *lleawc*, 'death dealing'; hence 'Lleu the death dealer'.

Culhwch and his little troop come upon a giant herdsman, are hospitably entertained by him and his monstrous wife, but are warned against proceeding farther. A meeting is arranged, however, with Olwen, and though she refuses to elope with Culhwch because of a pledge to her father, she counsels him to demand her of her father, the giant Ysbaddaden. This formidable figure resembles the one-eyed Balor of Irish tradition in that his eyelids have to be opened by his servants; Culhwch, having been thrice refused, hurls a poisoned spear through Ysbaddaden's one eye, much as Lug cast a slingstone which carried Balor's eye out through his head.[1] At last Ysbaddaden is ready to name the conditions on which he would consent to the union of his daughter with Culhwch, namely the performance of a series of difficult tasks (*anoetheu*). As W. J. Gruffydd pointed out,[2] these are all 'made necessary (1) in order to furnish the wedding feast, and (2) to enable Ysbaddaden to shave his head and comb his hair on the night of his daughter's wedding'.

Preparations for the wedding feast require that woodland be cleared and sown, that Amaethon son of Dôn, the great ploughman, be secured, that his brother Gofannon, the great smith, set the irons (the ploughshares?), and that three teams of oxen be found and yoked to the plough.[3] Flax must be grown for Olwen's wimple, honey procured for making bragget, and a self-playing harp also, to entertain the guests. Besides these, the first group of tasks includes the fetching of several vessels of plenty: a *cib* (cup) in which is the best of all drink, a *mwys* (platter or table) on which everyone would find the meat he wished for, a horn to pour out for the wedding guests, and a cauldron to boil the meat for them. Three of these vessels have their counterparts among the Thirteen Treasures of the Isle of Britain.[4] There is no account, however, of the completion of any of these tasks, except the procuring of the cauldron of Diwrnach the Irishman. Arthur sends messengers to demand it of the King of Ireland, and, being refused, sails in his ship Prydwen across the sea and makes for the house of Diwrnach. Bedwyr seizes the cauldron.[5] Llenlleawc brandishes the sword Caledfwlch and slays Diwrnach and all his host. Thus Arthur returns with the cauldron, filled with treasure, to South Wales. This is undoubtedly a euhemerized version of Arthur's expedition to Annwfn, as noted in Chap. 2.

The second group of tasks imposed by Ysbaddaden in order that he may

[1] C. O'Rahilly, op. cit., p. 118.

[2] *Y Cymmrodor*, xlii (1930), 134. This article on Mabon is of fundamental importance to the study of *Culhwch*, and is an illuminating example of Gruffydd's scholarship and intuitive methods.

[3] On Gofannon and Amaethon see W. J. Gruffydd, *Math vab Mathonwy* (Cardiff, 1928), pp. 145–8.

[4] Loomis, *Wales*, pp. 158–61; *Arthurian Tradition*, p. 387; H. Newstead, *Bran the Blessed* (1939), pp. 20, 86–120. Tudur Aled at the end of the fifteenth century mentions some of the Thirteen Treasures; T. Gwynn Jones, *Gwaith Tudur Aled*, i (1926), 23, vss. 95–100.

[5] On cauldrons and vats of plenty in Irish literature see *ZCP*, iii (1901), 39[9–11]; *RC*, xxv (1904), 20, 34; *Irische Texte*, iii. 516, 552; *Ériu*, iv. 30.

make a proper appearance at the wedding involves a series of dependent quests. To shave himself the giant must have the tusk of the boar Ysgithyrwyn, but only Odgar of Ireland can pluck it from the boar's head, and only Cadw of Pictland can keep it. To dress his beard he must have the blood of the Black Witch from the uplands of Hell, and the bottles of Gwyddolwyn the dwarf to keep the blood warm. To dress his hair he must have the comb and shears between the ears of Twrch Trwyth,[1] a king whom God had transformed into a swine; and the hunting of this boar could not be accomplished till a whelp, a leash, a collar, and a chain had been obtained, and several huntsmen, such as Mabon son of Modron and Gwyn son of Nudd, had been enlisted in the chase.

The procuring of the tusk of Ysgithyrwyn is rapidly narrated. There is an inconsistency, however, in that Cadw of Pictland, not Odgar, snatches it from the boar's head, and the author himself calls attention to another discrepancy: 'it was not the dogs which Ysbaddaden had named to Culhwch which killed the boar but Cafall, Arthur's own dog.' (No dogs had been named by the giant.) Still a third confusion arises when a superfluous razor turns up between the ears of the second boar, Twrch Trwyth. It is the tusk of Ysgithyrwyn, however, which seems to have performed the operation not only on Ysbaddaden's beard but also on his flesh and ears.

The chase of the Twrch Trwyth is a sort of duplication of the chase of Ysgithyrwyn, but is given in much greater detail, even including certain preliminary quests not even mentioned by Ysbaddaden. As noted in Chap. 1, the hunt of the boar Troit by Arthur's hound Cabal is mentioned in the *Mirabilia* appended to Nennius's *Historia Brittonum* early in the ninth century; and in a poem, probably of the seventh century, attached to the *Gododdin*, a warrior is compared to Twrch Trwyth (Trwyd).[2] The theme has, therefore, a long literary history. As we find it in *Culhwch*, Arthur, having accomplished the preliminary quests and assembled the warriors of Britain, France, Brittany, and Normandy, started the chase of the boar at Esgeir Oerfel in Ireland (probably Sescenn Uarbhéoil in Leinster).[3] After laying waste a whole province, the beast swam the channel to Porth Cleis near St. David's, followed a devious course through South Wales, and at last was forced into the sea in Cornwall. 'Never a one has known where it went.' But already at the crossing of the Severn Mabon had snatched the razor, and Cyledr the shears, from between its ears, and before it escaped the comb too had been won. The route of the chase across Wales is clearly traced, as Rhŷs has shown,[4] and it seems that the author arbitrarily localized certain

[1] For an explanation of these objects see J. Rhŷs, *Celtic Folklore, Welsh and Manx* (Oxford, 1901), ii. 519 f.

[2] I. Williams, *Canu Aneirin*, vs. 1340, and p. 363, n.; *Duanaire Finn*, pt. iii, Irish Texts Society, xliii (1953), 199 f.   [3] Kuno Meyer, in *THSC*, 1895–6, p. 73.

[4] *THSC*, 1894–5, pp. 1–34; J. Rhŷs, *Celtic Folklore*, ii. 509–37.

incidents at points along this route in order to explain the place-names, in the manner of the Irish *dinnshenchas*.

It is probable that the two boar hunts in which Arthur and his hound participated are local variants of the same original tradition.[1] Gruffydd has argued with great ingenuity that the stories of Mabon son of Modron and Eidoel son of Aer afford another case of duplication.[2] Both figures were apparently famous as prisoners and both had to be released, Mabon to hunt Twrch Trwyth, and Eidoel to discover the whereabouts of Mabon: and, if Gruffydd was right, the prison in each case was at Caer Loyw, Gloucester. It is generally agreed that Mabon is descended from the Romano-British Apollo Maponos, and his mother Modron from the Celtic goddess Mātrŏna[3]— strong evidence of the very archaic nature of certain elements in *Culhwch*.

Another mythological personage, already mentioned, is Gwyn. His father, Nudd, is recognized as the descendant of the British god Nodons,[4] and he himself is described in the sixteenth-century *Life of St. Collen* as King of Annwfn and the fairy folk *(tylwyth teg)*.[5] The author of *Culhwch* declares that God set in Gwyn the spirit of the devils of Annwfn.[6] He later tells how Gwyn's wife Creiddylad was stolen by Gwythyr, and how Arthur restored her to her father's house, and decreed that Gwyn and Gwythyr should fight for her every first of May till the Day of Judgement.[7]

The affinity of *Culhwch* with folk-tales has already been noted, and is illustrated further by three motifs woven into the fabric. To find Mabon, who had been stolen from his mother's side when he was three days old, Cei and Gwrhyr go in search of him. They ask in turn of an Ouzel, a Stag, an Owl, and an Eagle, each of whom has lived a preternatural length of time, but none can tell of Mabon's abode till they inquire of the Salmon of Llyn Llyw. This motif of the oldest animals is a close counterpart of an ancient Indian tale and is certainly cognate with, if not derived from, it.[8] The flax needed for the veil of Olwen is procured with the help of grateful ants, and this motif is found not only in India but all over Europe.[9] Even the detail of the lame ant occurs in a Slavonic version. The sword of Wrnach the Giant

[1] See Nitze in *ZRP*, lvi (1936), 416 f.; *Perlesvaus*, ed. Nitze and others, ii. 141–3; C. O'Rahilly, *Ireland and Wales*, pp. 120–2; Gruffydd in *Y Cymmrodor*, xlii. 137.

[2] *Y Cymmrodor*, xlii. 129.

[3] *Trans. Dumfriesshire and Galloway Nat. Hist. and Antiq. Soc.*, Series 3, xxxi (1954), 35–38, 43–57.   [4] Loth, *Mabinogion*, i. 314, n. 1; *RC*, xxxix (1922), 384; *RR*, xlv (1954), 12–14.

[5] Loth, op. cit. i. 314 n.; *Rhyddiaith Gymraeg*, i (Cardiff, 1954), pp. 36–41; Baring-Gould and Fisher, *Lives of the British Saints* (London, 1913), iv. 377.

[6] Loth, op. cit. i. 314 f. On Annwfn see Loomis, *Wales*, pp. 137–45.

[7] Loth, op. cit. i. 331 f.

[8] On this motif see E. Hull in *Folklore*, xliii (1932), 376–409; T. Jones in *National Library of Wales Journal*, vii (1951), 62–66; Wesselski in *Archiv. Orientální*, iv (1932), 1–22; *Trans. of the Celtic Congress, 1921*, pp. 52–56.

[9] A. H. Wratislaw, *Sixty Folktales from Exclusively Slavonic Sources* (1889), pp. 25–29; W. A. Clouston, *Popular Tales and Fictions* (1887), i. 223–48.

which Cei obtains is without much doubt related to the sword of light which is the object of quest in Irish and Scottish folk-tales, but there is not much correspondence in detail.[1]

Culhwch, then, in the words of Gruffydd, is 'a collection of folk-tales of diverse origins squeezed more or less skilfully into the framework of the Giant's Daughter theme'.[2] Many of the incidents had no original connexion with Arthur. Of the forty *anoetheu*, or difficult tasks, set by Ysbaddaden, twenty-one are carried out, though some of these are passed over perfunctorily. Arthur is engaged in the accomplishing of fourteen of the tasks.[3] It is with justice, therefore, that Ysbaddaden tells Culhwch to thank Arthur for securing Olwen as his bride, for what Arthur himself did not achieve his men achieved for him.

To the influences which bore upon *Culhwch* Tatlock would add Geoffrey of Monmouth's *Historia Regum Britanniae*, dated about 1136, basing his argument in general on the knowledge of the great world displayed by the references of Arthur's porter to India, Africa, Corsica, and Greece, and more specifically on Arthur's leading an army of Frenchmen, Bretons, and Normans into Ireland.[4] Tatlock also notes that 'fflergant brenhin llydaw' (King of Brittany) was identified by Loth with Alan Fergant, Duke of Brittany, who died in 1119.[5] But the speech in which the porter refers to the remote parts of the earth is plainly the echo of a similar formula employed by Curoi in *Bricriu's Feast*, as a comparison will show,[6] and this takes us back to the eighth century, and not forward into the twelfth. Though Arthur invades Ireland in the *Historia*,[7] there is not the slightest resemblance to the invasion in *Culhwch*. And there is nothing in the mention of Fergant or of Normandy and Brittany as lands subject to Arthur which need bring the date of composition of the Welsh romance down later than 1100.

A reasonable date for its final redaction (except for later accretions to the list of persons in Arthur's entourage) would be the second half of the eleventh century. In 1081 Gruffydd ap Cynan, who had been in exile in Dublin, crossed with a large force to Porth Cleis (near St. David's), where the Twrch Trwyth also came to land, and joining Rhys ap Tewdwr, King of South Wales, won the victory of Mynydd Carn, and in the same year Rhys con-

---

[1] On sword of light see T. F. O'Rahilly, *Early Irish History and Mythology* (1946), p. 69; *Perlesvaus*, ed. W. A. Nitze and others, ii (Chicago, 1937), 246–9. Wrnach the Giant is probably a name of Irish origin. *Ériu*, xvi (1952), 12. The name should probably be substituted for Awarnach in the Black Book poem described in the preceding chapter.   [2] *Y Cymmrodor*, xlii. 132.

[3] *Anoeth*, pl. *anoetheu*, 'wonder, marvel, something difficult to obtain'. Arthur and his men are named amoung the *anoetheu* by Ysbaddaden; two others, not named by him, are accomplished and are included in the total of twenty-one above.

[4] J. S. P. Tatlock, *Legendary History of Britain* (Berkeley and Los Angeles, 1950), pp. 195 f.

[5] Ibid., p. 195. Sir Ifor Williams has well remarked in *Pedeir Keinc*, p. xxx, that a possible reference to Fergant in *Manawydan* does not prove that it is later than 1100.

[6] See p. 33, n. 5.   [7] Faral, iii. 238.

cluded a peace with William the Conqueror, who visited St. David's. These were circumstances which might well have encouraged a Welsh *cyfarwydd* to give the tale of Culhwch the form which has been preserved to us.

Culhwch was read by Welsh poets in the centuries that followed.[1] Names of Arthur's warriors apparently derived from the tale occur in Cynddelw's elegy on Owain Gwynedd (1169). In the fourteenth and sixteenth centuries poets refer to Olwen as a paragon of beauty, and Lewis Glyn Gothi in the fifteenth alludes to the ravages of Twrch Trwyth.

Of course, the tale was not read abroad, but it is interesting to note that several elements in it found their way, though from other sources, into French and English romance. Like Culhwch, Perceval in Chrétien's poem sets out for Arthur's court, rides on horseback into the hall, asks a boon and receives it.[2] Likewise in both accounts Cei takes a churlish attitude toward the hero and is rebuked by Arthur. Twrch Trwyth, son of King Taredd, turns up in the First Continuation of *Perceval* as the boar Tortain, son of Heliares,[3] and he may possibly be detected in the disguise of Arthur's knight, Tor son of Ares or Thares.[4] Like Culhwch, Yvain meets a huge herdsman,[5] and Gawain in the *Carl of Carlisle* casts a spear at a giant in the giant's own hall and later marries his daughter.[6] Ysbaddaden, whose eyelids have to be propped up, has a counterpart in the *Merveilles de Rigomer*.[7] And, of course, the theme of a quest is a commonplace of French romance. Such are the curious links which join *Culhwch* to non-Celtic Arthurian fiction.

Rhonabwy's Dream (Breuddwyd Rhonabwy) is an early-thirteenth-century composition, preserved only in the Red Book of Hergest.[8] It is in many ways very different from *Culhwch*, as the following synopsis will show.

Madog son of Maredudd, ruler of Powys, sent Rhonabwy to hunt down his rebellious brother, who had gone raiding in England. Rhonabwy, with two companions, spent a night in a miserable lodging, whose squalor is described with satiric relish. There, sleeping on a yellow ox-hide, he dreamed that he was proceeding to a ford of the Severn when he was overtaken successively by two horsemen gorgeously arrayed. The first revealed himself as Iddawg,

---

[1] T. Stephens, *Literature of the Cymry* (London, 1876), pp. 121–3. Lady Guest's notes on *Kilhwch*, *sub* Olwen and Twrch Trwyth. *Duanaire Finn*, pt. iii, p. 200.

[2] *Percevalroman*, ed. Hilka (Halle, 1932), vss. 900–1032.

[3] G. Paris in *R*, xxviii (1899), 217; Lot, ibid., p. 578. For name-forms see W. Roach, *Continuations of the Old French Perceval* (Philadelphia, 1949–52), i. 169; iii. 163, vs. 2594, variant.

[4] *Histoire Littéraire de la France*, xxxi. 168. The form Thares is found in Brit. Mus. Royal 19 C xiii; Sommer, *Vulgate Version*, iii. 154, n. 2.   [5] Loomis, *Arthurian Tradition*, p. 286.

[6] Ed. R. W. Ackerman, *Univ. Michigan Contributions Mod. Phil*, no. 8 (1947), pp. 33 f., 42; ed. A. Kurvinen (Helsinki, 1951), pp. 93 f., 138–40, 156.

[7] S. Singer, *Germanisch-Romanisches Mittelalter* (Zürich, 1935), pp. 178 f.; *Merveilles de Rigomer*, ed. Foerster and Breuer (Dresden, 1908), i. vss. 3543 ff.

[8] As with *Culhwch*, the best translations are those of J. Loth and of G. and T. Jones. The text has been edited with introduction and notes in Welsh by M. Richards, *Breudwyt Ronabwy* (1948). See review by T. Jones in *Y Llenor*, xxvii (1948), 142–53.

nicknamed the Embroiler of Britain because he had brought on the battle of Camlann by distorting the peaceful messages which Arthur had sent to Medrawd (Modred). Accompanied by Iddawg, Rhonabwy found Arthur and Bedwin the bishop seated on an island in the river. Arthur asked Iddawg where he had found these 'little fellows', and smiled sadly that men like these should now have the keeping of Britain. Two bands, one accoutred in red, the other in black and white, arrived and camped near by. A rider spurred his horse through the ford, splashing Arthur and the bishop, and Elphin son of Gwyddno struck the animal on the muzzle. Caradawg Vreichvras (Stout-arm), son of Llyr, reminded Arthur that his men should be in the battle of Baddon by noon, fighting against Osla of the Big Knife, and the host set out. Rhonabwy, taken up by Iddawg on his horse, saw two troops coming to join Arthur, the first, clad in white, from Llychlyn under March son of Meir-chiawn, the other, clad in black, from Denmark under Edern son of Nudd. Having arrived below Caer Vaddon, Arthur dismounted. Cei rode into the middle of the army, both he and his steed clad in mail. Cadwr, earl of Corn-wall, presented Arthur's flaming sword to him; another servitor spread out his mantle of invisibility and placed a throne of gold on it. The king then engaged in a game of *gwyddbwyll* with Owain son of Urien, and, while they were playing, news was again and again brought to Owain that Arthur's men were attacking his ravens. No remonstrance on Owain's part moved Arthur to stop them. When at last the ravens had been killed or wounded, Owain bade his standard be raised, and the birds swooped on their foes and made havoc among them. Owain refused to call them off in spite of Arthur's appeals, and only when Arthur crushed all the golden pieces on the board did Owain order his banner to be lowered and peace was restored. Then ambassadors came from Osla to ask for a truce, and after consulting his advisers Arthur granted it. Bards sang a song in praise of Arthur and were rewarded with tribute from the Isles of Greece. Cei announced that Arthur would be that night in Cornwall, and the commotion awoke Rhonabwy, who had been sleeping three nights and days.

A colophon, probably added later, states that 'no one, neither bard nor *cyfarwydd* (story-teller), knows the *Dream* without a book because of the number of colours that were on the horses and all the different kinds of rare colours both on the arms and their equipments and on the precious mantles, and the magic stones'.

Rhonabwy's Dream is manifestly the work of a talented author. It has been described as 'an artist's piece, a succession of illuminated pages, deficient in movement and character, but a *tour-de-force* of close observation and description'.[1] The style is rich and rhetorical, and the dreamlike impression is admirably conveyed by the deliberate anachronisms, the fantastic happenings,

---

[1] *Mabinogion*, trans. Jones and Jones, p. xxvi.

and the rapidly shifting scenes. It is probable, as Thomas Parry suggests, 'that the story was never part of the traditional stock-in-trade of the story-tellers';[1] this would account for the explanatory nature of the colophon.

The geographical and historical background is indicated with precision. The setting is Powys, which comprised most of central Wales, extending to the north as far as Pulford near Chester, and eastward as far as the upper Severn. Madog son of Maredudd, whose brother was being sought by Rhonabwy, ruled over Powys from 1138 to 1160, and his death was followed by much discontent and strife until his grandson, Llywelyn the Great, took possession. It is likely, then, that *Rhonabwy's Dream* was composed by an author from Powys some time during the hundred years after Madog's death, and Richards has plausibly argued that the date lay between 1220 and 1225.[2]

The author set the main events of his narrative within the framework of a dream—a device which was certainly new in medieval Welsh literature. The fact that Rhonabwy dreams while lying on an ox-skin is probably related to an ancient Irish practice described by Keating,[3] in which hides of bulls were spread on wattles, and presumably the diviner went to sleep on the hide for the purpose of winning knowledge. It is the nature of dreams to disregard time and space; hence the battle of Camlann is referred to as having occurred before the battle of Badon.[4] Arthur is met by Rhonabwy on the borders of Powys, but, as in *Culhwch*, his home is in Cornwall.

The effect of unreality is intensified by the strange assortment of characters who appear in the *Dream*. Among Arthur's counsellors are numbered such figures as Nerth mab Kadarn (Strength son of Mighty), borrowed from *Culhwch*; Gilbert mab Katgyffro, who may represent Gilbert de Clare, Earl of Pembroke (d. 1147/8);[5] Caradawg Vreichvras;[6] March vab Meirchiawn, the husband of Essyllt, represented as leader of the men of Scandinavia;[7] Dyrstan mab Talluch, lover of Essyllt;[8] Edern mab Nudd, leader of the men of Denmark. Added to these counsellors are men from the Isles of Greece.

The influence of Geoffrey of Monmouth may be discerned. The presence of the hosts of Llychlyn and Denmark does not imply, as van Hamel thought,[9] that they had taken the place of the Saxons as traditional enemies

---

[1] *History of Welsh Literature* (1955), p. 82.

[2] Richards, op. cit., pp. xxxvii–xxxix.

[3] T. F. O'Rahilly, *Early Irish History and Mythology* (Dublin, 1946), p. 324; G. Keating, *History of Ireland*, ii (Dublin, 1908), ed. P. S. Dinneen, pp. 348–51.

[4] See Chap. 1 for information on dates.

[5] Zimmer in *ZFSL*, xiii (1891), pp. 20 f.; in *GGA* (1890), pp. 826 ff.; Richards, op. cit., p. 61.

[6] On Caradawg see Chap. 11; J. E. Lloyd, *History of Wales*, 3rd ed. (London, 1939), i. 90; Chrétien de Troyes, *Karrenritter*, ed. W. Foerster (Halle, 1899), pp. cxiii, cxxiv.

[7] On March (Marc) see Richards, op. cit., p. 47; J. J. Jones in *Aberystwyth Studies*, xii (1932), 21–33; and Chap. 12 below.

[8] 'Drystan m. Tallwch' is the normal Welsh form, though Tristan also occurs in medieval Welsh. See Bromwich in *THSC*, 1953, pp. 33–37, and Richards, op. cit., p. 60.

[9] *Arkiv för Nordisk Filologi*, l (1934), 237.

of the Britons, for they are on Arthur's side. Rather, their opportune appearance as his allies suggests the extensive dominion of the emperor Arthur. Likewise, Geoffrey's identification of Kaer Badum, the site of Arthur's great victory, with Bath (Bad) seems to be reflected in the march of Arthur's host to Gweith Vaddon (the battle of Badon) and his arrival below Caer Vaddon.[1] Geoffrey's description of Arthur's arming himself for the battle of Badon with Caliburnus may have suggested Arthur's taking his flaming sword after his arrival before Caer Vaddon;[2] and the prominent role which Geoffrey assigned to Cador 'dux Cornubie' in this campaign may be responsible for the role of Cadwr Earl of Cornwall as Arthur's armour-bearer and counsellor in the Welsh text.[3] The mention of Osla (or Ossa) in the same text as Arthur's prospective adversary may well represent the tradition in Nennius that Arthur's opponent was Octha son of Hengist.[4] It should be noted, at any rate, that the Dingestow version of Geoffrey's *Historia* gives Ossa as a cousin of Otca (Octa) mab Heingyst.[5]

Perhaps the most striking feature of *Rhonabwy's Dream* is the game of *gwyddbwyll* played by Arthur and Owain, concurrently with the conflict between Arthur's men and Owain's ravens. The game is played with gold pieces on a board of silver, and it takes place not far from Caer Vaddon. A. G. van Hamel drew attention to the basic similarity between this game in the Welsh tale and the 'game of the gods' in the Norse *Völuspá*, where also golden pieces are used.[6] 'The golden game is the magic through which the gods keep the world in order and prevent the intrusion of war.'[7] Arthur's game of *gwyddbwyll* and the 'divine game' in the *Völuspá* are parallel instances of the belief that the course of events may be directed by a game,[8] and Arthur 'could not maintain his title to perpetual victory but by crushing the enchanted chessmen'.

The struggle between Arthur's men and Owain's ravens has been given various interpretations. It has been suggested that the ravens represent the Viking armies;[9] again, that here is a form of the raven-fight which is found in early Irish literature.[10] A more acceptable explanation is that the episode embodies the tradition that Owain was the son of Urien by Modron daughter of Avallach. Modron has her counterpart in Morgain la Fée, daughter of Avallo (or Avalloc) and mother of Yvain by Urien (in the *Suite du Merlin*).

---

[1] Faral, iii. 98. Cf. also ibid., p. 232, 'versus pagum Badonis' with the Welsh 'hyt yg Caer Uadon', in H. Lewis, *Brut Dingestow* (1942), p. 147; and Faral, iii. 243, 'Urbgennius ex Badone' with the Welsh 'Vryen o Gaer Uadon', in Lewis, p. 158.

[2] Faral, iii. 233. On Arthur's sword see Loomis, *Arthurian Tradition*, pp. 491 f.

[3] Faral, iii. 234 f.   [4] Ibid. iii. 38.

[5] H. Lewis, *Brut Dingestow*, p. 122.

[6] *Arkiv för Nordisk Filologi*, l (1934), 218–42.

[7] Ibid., p. 227.   [8] Ibid., p. 240.

[9] Ibid., p. 237, and Richards, op. cit., p. xviii.

[10] *Arkiv*, l. 237 f.

In the *Didot Perceval*, a flock of large black birds swoop down upon Perceval during the combat at the ford with Urbain (probably a corrupt form of Urien) and try to tear out his eyes. Perceval kills one of them and it immediately turns into a beautiful woman; Urbain tells him that the birds were his mistress and her maidens. In Irish tradition, the fierce Morrígan, who may be said to pre-figure Morgain la Fée in many ways,[1] assumed the shape of a crow. If, therefore, the correspondence of Morrígan, Modron, and Morgain la Fée is established, then Owain's ravens in *Rhonabwy's Dream* can be recognized as the helpful forms of his mother Modron and her sisters (or companions).[2]

The author of *Rhonabwy's Dream* brought together two traditional themes which he then handled with considerable literary skill: first, the native British tradition of Arthur's struggle against the Saxons, with its climax in the battle of Badon; and second, the older tradition, common to the Irish and the Welsh, of the wife or mistress or mother, with her companions, bringing timely assistance in the shape of birds in the stress of conflict.

[1] L. A. Paton, *Fairy Mythology of Arthurian Romance* (Boston, 1903), pp. 148–56; Zenker in *ZFSL*, xlviii (1925–6), 82–92.

[2] Loomis, *Arthurian Tradition*, pp. 270 ff.; *Wales*, pp. 95–97. See below, pp. 49 f.

THE WELSH TRIADS

RACHEL BROMWICH

SOME of the most curious and significant evidence concerning the Welsh medieval traditions of Arthur and the figures associated with him is to be found in the short lists of three persons, objects, or events known as triads. This form has been popular as a literary device among the Celtic peoples since the early Middle Ages, if not longer. It was used commonly as a means of codifying moral aphorisms, general gnomic and antiquarian matter, and the technicalities of poetic composition and of the law. How ancient may be this addiction to the triple form must remain a matter of doubt; there are triads in the early poetry attributed to Aneirin and Taliesin; and one is tempted to connect the medieval predilection for the triad with the recurrent triple grouping of Celtic deities in Gaul and Ireland.[1]

It is the Welsh alone, however, who seem to have made a systematic use of triads as a means of putting the materials of heroic story into catalogue form; several manuscript collections are preserved, containing the names of traditional Welsh heroes of early times. Originally, no doubt, in Wales as in Ireland, the triads were drawn up in the bardic schools[2] as a mnemonic aid for students, who were required to show a proficient knowledge of the extensive body of oral lore inherited from the past. Thus it is clear that the Welsh historical and romantic triads are based on the debris of saga literature, the product of the professional story-tellers known as *cyfarwyddiaid* (sing. *cyfarwydd*), described in Chap. 2. So far as we can tell, these stories dealt both with mythological characters such as those which figure in the *Four Branches of the Mabinogi* and the early poems, and with semi-historical persons of the heroic age of the sixth and seventh centuries, many of them coming from the British kingdoms in north-west England and southern Scotland.

But it was only at the time when this oral literature was beginning to disintegrate, probably during the course of the eleventh and twelfth centuries, that the redactors of the triads set to work to classify and preserve it. They

---

[1] On triple divinities in Irish and Gaulish mythology see d'Arbois de Jubainville, *Irish Mythological Cycle*, trans. R. I. Best (Dublin, 1903), pp. 210 ff.; M. L. Sjoestedt, *Dieux et Héros des Celtes* (Paris, 1940), pp. 25 f., 36; G. Dottin, *Manuel pour Servir à l'Étude de l'Antiquité Celtique*, 2nd ed., pp. 329 f.

[2] G. J. Williams, *Gramadegau'r Penceirddiaid* (Cardiff, 1934), p. lxxxviii; J. Lloyd-Jones in *Proc. Brit. Acad.*, 1948, p. 29, n. 31.

were successful in so far as their activity gave an extended life to the names of the old heroes: we find the later medieval bards citing these as paragons of beauty and valour, when it is apparent that they knew nothing of the heroes in question except the triads which commemorate them.[1] In many instances the key-epithets used for classification in the triads consist of obscure and archaic words which were obsolete even in medieval Welsh; often, however, these words belong to the diction of bardic poetry.

The historical and romantic triads consist for the most part merely of three names linked by a descriptive epithet of this kind, without any other explanatory matter:

Tri ruduoavc enys prydein. Arthur. a run mab beli. A morgant mwynuavr.[2] (Three Red Ravagers of the Island of Britain: Arthur, and Run son of Beli, and Morgant the Wealthy.)

A few, however, are expanded to give some additional information about the stories to which they allude: such allusions are for the most part to stories which are lost, although, exceptionally, there is a reference to events narrated in the *mabinogi*:

Tri matkud ynys prydein. penn bendigeituran vab llyr a guduwyt yn y gvynuryn yn llundein. ae wyneb ar ffreinc. a hyt tra uu yn yr ansavd y dodet yno. ny doei ormes saesson byth yr ynys honn. Yr eil amatkud. Y dreigeu yn ninas emreis a gudyavd llud vab beli. Ar trydyd esgyrn gvertheuyr uendigeit. ym prif pyrth yr ynys honn. a hyt tra vydynt yn y kud hvnnv. ny doei ormes o saesson byth yr ynys honn. A llyna y tri anuat[dat]kud pan datkudywyt. A gvrtheyrn gvrtheneu a datkudyawd esgyrn gvertheuyr uendigeit yr serch gvreic. Sef oed honno ronnven baganes. Ac ef a datkudyavd y dreigeu. Ac arthur a datkudyavd penn bendigeituran or gvynn vrynn. Kan nyt oed dec gantav kadv yr ynys homm o gedernit neb. namyn or eidav e hun.[3]

(Three Fortunate Concealments of the Island of Britain. The Head of Brân the Blessed son of Llŷr, which was concealed in the White Hill in London, with its face towards France. And while it was in the position in which it had been put there, no Saxon oppression ever came to this Island. The second Fortunate Concealment: the Dragons which Lludd son of Beli concealed in Dinas Emreis. And the third, the Bones of Gwerthefyr the Blessed (Vortimer) in the chief ports of this Island; and while they were in that concealment, no Saxon oppression ever came to this Island. And they were the Three Unfortunate Disclosures when these were disclosed. Gwrtheyrn the Thin (Vortigern) disclosed the bones of Gwerthefyr the Blessed for the love of a woman; this was she, Ronnwen the pagan. And he disclosed the Dragons. And Arthur disclosed the Dragons. And Arthur disclosed the head of Brân the Blessed from the

---

[1] T. Gwynn Jones, 'Bardism and Romance', *THSC*, 1913–14, pp. 280 f., 302.

[2] *BBCS*, xii. 12, no. 20. *Ruduoavc*, 'Complete despoilers of the land' (cf. Irish *bongid*, 'reaps'); see I. Williams, *Cywyddau Dafydd ap Gwilym a'i Gyfoeswyr* (Cardiff, 1935), p. 214 (alluding to the later version of this triad in the Red Book of Hergest).

[3] J. Rhys and J. Gwenogvryn Evans, *Text of the Mabinogion from the Red Book of Hergest* (Oxford, 1887), p. 300; J. Loth, *Mabinogion* (Paris, 1913), ii. 239–41, no. 14.

White Hill, since he did not desire that this Island should be guarded by anyone's strength but his own.)

Although the triads have come down to us only in manuscripts of the thirteenth and later centuries, yet their contents bear marks of a high antiquity; and those in the oldest collections must be regarded as embodying much genuine early tradition, in however mutilated and fragmentary a manner. The thirteenth-century MS. Peniarth 16[1] contains the oldest collection of triads (except for a fragment of 'Triads of Horses' in the Black Book of Carmarthen).[2] The White Book of Rhydderch[3] (c. 1325) contains a fragment of a much fuller collection, and this same collection has been preserved in its entirety in the Red Book of Hergest (c. 1400).[4] Other collections appear in fifteenth- and sixteenth-century manuscripts,[5] some of which may nevertheless be derived from genuine early sources.[6] (A word of warning may here be given against the unreliable Third Series in the *Myvyrian Archaiology of Wales*,[7] since in this extensive collection the earlier triads have been unscrupulously manipulated by the eighteenth-century forger Iolo Morgannwg, with considerable additions of his own. There exists no manuscript authority for this version.) Throughout all these versions of the triads, the increasing popularity of Arthur and of the Arthurian material is apparent: Arthur is mentioned with much greater frequency in the Red Book collection than in the earlier one; an extended use has been made of the *llys arthur* (Arthur's court) formula as a convenient framework for assembling heroes from diverse and unrelated saga-cycles; and in two instances Arthur's name has even been superimposed as a fourth character on triads in which he was not originally included.[8]

[1] *BBCS*, xii. 12 ff. An incomplete copy of this version is found in Peniarth 45 (Hengwrt 536), from which it was printed and translated by W. F. Skene, *Four Ancient Books of Wales* (Edinburgh, 1868), ii. 456 ff.

[2] J. G. Evans, *Black Book of Carmarthen* (facsimile ed.), fol. 14[r], 14[v]; Loth, op. cit. ii. 227–9, nos. 1–4.   [3] *Y Cymmrodor*, vii, pp. 123–54.

[4] Rhys and Evans, *Text of the Mabinogion*, pp. 297 ff. This version forms Series II in the *Myvyrian Archaiology of Wales*, 2nd ed., pp. 395 ff. The Red Book text seems to be a copy of the White Book, though it is possible that both stem directly from a common exemplar.

[5] Of great importance are the two fifteenth-century manuscripts, Peniarth 47 and 50 (*Y Cwtta Cyfarwydd*), which derive from a source closer to Peniarth 16 than to the Red Book, but which in each instance contain a few triads not found elsewhere. With Peniarth 45 these manuscripts were transcribed by the seventeenth-century antiquary, Robert Vaughan of Hengwrt. Vaughan's transcript, recopied and 'edited' by the Morris brothers, formed the basis for the *Myvyrian* Series I, pp. 388 ff. (The writer of this chapter is preparing an edition of the Triads from these and other manuscripts.)

[6] e.g. *Tri gwyndorllwyth* (see below, p. 49, n. 5); *tri santeidd Linys* (p. 51, n. 3); *tri overddgat* (p. 47, n. 4).

[7] *Myvyrian Archaiology*, pp. 400–11; Loth, op. cit. ii. 294–325. Further work needs to be done on these triads; it is difficult to assess their value in view of our present ignorance of Iolo's sources and methods. Even if he used the seventeenth-century manuscripts to which he refers (but which have not yet come to light), it is hardly credible that he reproduced them faithfully.

[8] *Tri ruduoavc, Tri goruchel garcharavr*. Rhys and Evans, *Text of the Mabinogion*, pp. 300, 303,

Various early sources concur[1] in their evidence that already in eleventh-century Wales Arthur was in process of becoming the vortex to which were drawn the heroes of originally independent saga-cycles. Since the beginning of this movement can be assigned to so early a date, and the Welsh sources in which it appears are essentially independent, it seems certain that this cyclic growth of the Arthurian material was an indigenous development in Wales, and was not stimulated by external influences. Such influences, in fact, appear to be entirely absent from the earliest collection of triads in Peniarth 16, and yet the beginnings of the Arthurian cycle are already apparent here (nos. 1, 9, 26). In contrast, the Red Book collection shows the influence of Geoffrey of Monmouth, while in the later collections there figure characters from the Welsh versions of French Arthurian romances.

The 'Three Unfortunate Disclosures', quoted above, is in some ways the most valuable relic of native Arthurian tradition provided by the triads, since here, as in other early sources, Arthur appears in the primitive character of a defender of his country from dangers alike external and internal;[2] this was a natural offshoot from the remote historical memory of a great leader who championed the British cause against the Saxons.

Two triads in the Red Book refer to a single incident, Medrawt's raid on Arthur's court at Kelliwic and his violent treatment of Gwenhwyfar[3] (Guenevere), which is said to have been responsible for the battle of Camlann. Another triad (Loth no. 28) describes Arthur's threefold division of his troops with Medrawt (Modred) at this battle. It is possible that these allusions are based on a genuine tradition about the battle of Camlann and the events which preceded it,[4] and are not merely suggested by the *Brut* account,

306; Loth, op. cit. ii. 254 (no. 30), 238 (no. 11), 267 (no. 56, a better version of no. 11). In the last triad, 'the Three Supreme Prisoners', the circumstantial nature of the addition explaining Arthur's superiority to the other prisoners suggests that there really was a tale about Arthur's imprisonment.

[1] See the tenth- or eleventh-century poem in the Black Book of Carmarthen, no. xxxi, where Manawydan and Mabon figure among Arthur's followers; and to a less degree *The Spoils of Annwfn* in the Book of Taliesin, no. xxx (both discussed above in Chap. 2). See also the long list of characters at Arthur's court in *Culhwch*.

[2] See van Hamel in *Proc. Brit. Acad.*, 1934, pp. 27 f., and above, p. 46, n. 8. Further evidence is provided by *The Spoils of Annwfn, Culhwch*, and the twelfth-century *Life of St. Carannog* (or *Carantoc*) (Faral, ii. 240–2. W. J. Rees, *Lives of the Cambro-British Saints*, p. 99). Note also Arthur's words in *Rhonabwy's Dream*: 'I grieve that the defence of this Island should be entrusted to such weaklings, after the mighty men who once held it.' Loth, op. cit. i. 356.

[3] Loth, op. cit. ii. 246–8 (nos. 18, 19). Ifor Williams shows that in the first of these triads, *Teir gwith balvawt*, 'Three Fierce Handslaps', *Gwenhwyfach* should be emended to *Medrawt*; I. Williams, *Pedeir Keinc y Mabinogi* (Cardiff, 1930), p. xxvi. Cf. the following triad (Loth, no. 19), and the corresponding statement in the Red Book *Brut*: 'And he dragged Queen Gwenhwyfar from her throne and raped her, violating the divine law of marriage.' Rhys and Evans, *Texts of the Bruts from the Red Book of Hergest* (Oxford, 1890), p. 229.

[4] Cf. the triads *Tri Anyweir deulu*, 'Three Faithless Warbands' (Peniarth 16, no. 30; Loth, op. cit. ii. 264, no. 49), *Tri overgat*, 'Three Futile Battles' (Penarth 50; Loth, op. cit. ii. 283, no. 79). The reference in this last may merely be a repetition of the earlier triad (Loth, op. cit. ii. 246, no. 18). See also the references to the battle in *Rhonabwy's Dream* and the burlesque (?) triad of the 'Three

since the allusions in the triads do not correspond exactly with any extant narrative. But since the Red Book collection in more than one instance shows unmistakably the influence of the Welsh versions of Geoffrey of Monmouth,[1] these references are not beyond suspicion.

The triad of the *tri gwrdveichyat*, the 'Three Mighty Swineherds', proves that Drystan (Tristan) was already introduced into the Arthurian orbit in Wales at an early date:

Tri gwrdveichyat enys prydein. Drystan m. tallwch. A gedwis moch march m. meirchyawn hyt tra aeth y meichyat y erchi y essyllt dyvot yw gynnadyl. Ac Arthur yn keissyaw un hwch onadunt. Ae y dwyll ae y dreis. ac nys cavas. . . .[2]

(Three Mighty Swineherds of the Island of Britain: Drystan son of Tallwch, who guarded the swine of March son of Meirchyawn while the swineherd went to ask Essyllt to come to a meeting with him. And Arthur was trying to get one pig from among them, either by deceit or by force, but he did not get it. . . .)

The Red Book text of this triad adds that Arthur was accompanied by Cei and Bedwyr (Bedivere); these two usually appear as Arthur's inseparable companions in the earliest Welsh sources—they are undoubtedly the first of his knights.[3] In the case of Drystan mab Tallwch, however, we have an originally Pictish hero,[4] whose story has been freshly localized in a Brittonic-speaking milieu, probably in South Wales.[5]

There are a few other allusions to Drystan in the triads, but these consist of no more than the application of single epithets of a complimentary type, such as are conventionally applied by the bards to their patrons. He is thus

Men who escaped from Camlann' in *Culhwch* (Loth, op. cit. i. 259 f). The existence of such native traditions about Camlann may reasonably be inferred from the entry in the *Annales Cambriae*, anno 537. See above, Chap. 1.

[1] The triad *Trywyr gwarth*, 'Three Men of Dishonour' (Loth, op. cit. ii. 233, no. 10) is drawn straight from the *Brut*.

[2] Peniarth 16, no. 26 (Rhys and Evans, *Text of the Mabinogion*, p. 307; Loth, op. cit. ii. 270, no. 63). This triad was recognized as a genuine native tradition by Bédier in his edition of Thomas's *Tristan* (Paris, 1905), ii. 115. Arthur and his men are associated with the third of the three stories, the pursuit of the sow Henwen, only in the Red Book. The introduction of Arthur is doubtless due to the influence of the pursuit of the boar Twrch Trwyth (Nennius's Troit) in *Culhwch*.

[3] In the triads they are Bedwyr mab Bedrawc and Cei mab Kynyr Keinvarvawc (Peniarth 16, no. 21). Cei's patronymic appears also in *Culhwch*. Bedwyr and Cei are found as Arthur's companions in *Culhwch*, in the *Life of St. Cadoc*, in the Black Book poem mentioned above, p. 47, n. 1, and in Geoffrey's *Historia*.

[4] Shown first by Zimmer in *ZFSL*, xiii (1891), 67. See below, Chap. 12. Drystan is the correct form of this name in Welsh (< prim. Celt. Drŭstanos), but the spelling with the initial *T* also occurs in early Ml. Welsh, being influenced by the following *t*; see the early-twelfth-century Book of Llan-daff (ed. Rhys and Evans, p. 279), 'Avel mab Tristan'. Such an early *written* form must have given rise to the French Tristan, since *i* (later Welsh *y*) was pronounced quite differently in the two languages.

[5] See the writer's article in *THSC*, 1953, pp. 32–60, 'Some Remarks on the Celtic Sources of *Tristan*'.

included in the triads of the *tri galovyd* (enemy-subduers) and of the *tri thaleithyawc cat* (diademed battle-leaders).[1]

Two other heroes who appear independently in the triads, where they have not yet become associated with Arthur, are Owein ap Urien Rheged (Yvain) and Gwalchmei ap Gwyar (identified at some stage with Gauvain).[2] The first is a well-attested historical figure; both he and his father were heroes of the sixth-century wars against the Angles in north Britain and the subject of contemporary panegyrics by Taliesin.[3] Geoffrey of Monmouth may have been responsible for the subsequent association of Owein with Arthur, though his account shows that he knew that the two were not contemporaries.[4] It is significant that Owein is nowhere mentioned in *Culhwch*, since this suggests that the association with Arthur, absent from the triads, goes back no farther than Geoffrey. Owein appears in a triad, *Tri gwyndor-llwyth*, 'Three Fair Womb-Burdens', contained in two fifteenth-century manuscripts, Peniarth 47 and 50,[5] as the son of Urien by Modron daughter of Avallach. R. S. Loomis has pointed out[6] that the same genealogy can be constructed for Yvain on the basis of the *Suite du Merlin* (Huth *Merlin*), the interpolated *De Antiquitate* of William of Malmesbury, the *Vita Merlini*, and the *Gesta Regum Britanniae*, except that Morgain is substituted for Modron. A phonological connexion between these two names is not possible, but there is evidence that in the twelfth century the tradition of Modron influenced the conception of Morgain: for instance, in the Swiss *Lanzelet* the mother of Mabuz, presumably derived from Modron the mother of Mabon,

---

[1] Peniarth 16, nos. 19, 21 (Loth, op. cit. ii. 254, 260, nos. 29, 43). The above rendering of *gal(l)ovyd* is tentative and assumes that the word is composed of *gal(l)dovyd*; cf. *Red Book Mab.*, p. 160. 3. If so, Loth's translation, 'maîtres ès machines', is incorrect. In the second triad *taleith* is equivalent to the *cae* worn by the young heroes of the *Gododdin* (I. Williams, *Canu Aneirin*, p. 69) and seems to have been a mark of leadership.

[2] On the relationship between Gwalchmei and Gauvain see Loomis, *Arthurian Tradition*, pp. 146–8. The equation appears first in Welsh translations of Geoffrey's *Historia* and in the three Welsh romances, *Gereint*, *Owein*, and *Peredur*. See below, Chap. 16. A triad names Gwalchmei as one of the three 'Golden-Tongued Knights' (Loth, ii. 289, no. 93). On date cf. *THSC*, 1956, pp. 116–32.

[3] For these poems in the Book of Taliesin, see J. Morris-Jones in *Y Cymmrodor*, xxviii (1918).

[4] Geoffrey mentions Owein as Hiwenus or Iwenus in the *Historia*, bk. xi, ch. 1.

[5] Loth, op. cit. ii. 283, no. 80. We can take the existence of this triad in some form back at least to the late twelfth century on the evidence of an abbreviated version introduced as a gloss on the list of the daughters of Brychan Brycheiniog in Jesus College MS. 20, which was copied in the first part of the fourteenth century, though based largely on earlier material (ed. *Y Cymmrodor*, viii. 83). Here we find: 'Drynwin (*sic*) verch vrachan mam uryen. Er duduyl (=Eurdyl?) gwyndorliud. Owein m. uryen. A Morud verch uryen. Gwrgi a pheredur ac arthur penuchel. . . .' Unfortunately the name Modron is not here included, but the spelling of the triad in this corrupt version shows that it was copied from a manuscript earlier than 1200, in which *i* stood for *y*, *u* for *w*, *d* for *th*.

[6] *RR*, xxix (1938), 176 f.; *Spec*, xx (1945), 190. It may be noted that Aballac (Old Welsh for Afallach) appears in the Harleian genealogies, nos. I and X (Loth, ii. 329, 336), as the son of Beli Mawr, hence apparently an ancestor-deity of the family of Coel Hen (cf. genealogies VIII, X), the most famous members of which were Urien and Owein. Since in the triad Avallach is the father of Modron (a name corresponding to that of the Celtic goddess Mātrŏna), it seems possible that Modron was early regarded as having some special connexion with this family. See above, pp. 42 f.

corresponds as queen of the Isle of Maidens to Geoffrey's Morgen. It would seem also that Welsh tradition knew of a hero named Gwalchmei ap Gwyar, since the *Bruts*, which are translated from Geoffrey's *Historia*, insist on introducing him into Arthur's later campaigns in place of Geoffrey's Gualguanus, though previously they make him the son of Arthur's sister Anna and her husband Llew ap Kynvarch, the latter replacing Geoffrey's Lot of Lothian. Thus the Welsh versions seem to make Gualguanus into two characters. Gwalchmei ap Gwyar may, like Owein, have belonged to the northern Britons.[1]

The triad of the 'Three Fortunate Concealments' refers to the burial of Brân's head as a talisman to protect Britain from foreign invaders; just as, with similar significance, the bones of Vortimer were buried.[2] The *mabinogi* of *Branwen* quotes this triad as a conclusion to the story of Brân the Blessed, a character in whom a succession of scholars are agreed in finding the prototype of Bron, the Fisher King.[3] According to the *mabinogi*, Brân was the grandson of Beli Mawr, who appears in the early Welsh genealogies as the common ancestor-deity of the leading Welsh dynasties,[4] and the son of Llŷr, a sea-deity of whom little is known except that his name survived in bardic usage as a poetical term for the sea (Irish *ler*). *Brân*, 'raven', is a common epithet for a warrior, and it occurs as a proper name in Ireland as well as in Wales.[5] The portrayal of Brân in the story forcefully suggests a euhemerized deity. His size is such that no ordinary house will hold him, he crosses the sea to Ireland by wading, and carries his army on his back across the Shannon. He is the possessor of a magic cauldron of regeneration, and after his death his severed head is a marvellous talisman for the satisfaction of all human needs—and when buried, a defence to his country. Brân met his death by a wound in the foot from a poisoned spear: this suggests comparison with the

---

[1] Both Geoffrey and William of Malmesbury associate Gualguanus or Walwen with a northern milieu, and it is perhaps significant that Gawain was the most popular Arthurian hero in northern Middle English romances. See Chaps. 37, 38 below. Later Welsh tradition shows much uncertainty as to the parentage of Gwalchmei. A fourteenth-century text tries to reconcile the two traditions by making Gwyar the mother of Gwalchmei. *Y Cymmrodor*, xxiv (1913), 258. See also 'The Twenty-Four Knights', *THSC*, 1956, p. 126. Cp. the occurrences of the name in *Brut Dingestow*, ed. H. Lewis (Cardiff, 1942), pp. 152, 154, with those on pp. 171, 175, &c.

[2] For the burial of Vortimer see Nennius, *Historia Brittonum*, ch. 44. The Irish High-King Laoghaire was buried standing upright, fully armed, facing his enemies, the Leinstermen. *Lebor na Huidre*, ed. Best and Bergin (Dublin, 1929), p. 295. See also M. Dillon, *Cycles of the Kings* (London, 1946), p. 84; Loomis, *Arthurian Tradition*, p. 350, n. 29.

[3] See the list in Loomis, *Arthurian Tradition*, p. 386. Add J. Marx, *Légende Arthurienne et le Graal* (Paris, 1952), pp. 197–200; J. Frappier, *Perceval ou le Conte du Graal* (Paris), pp. 98 f.

[4] On Beli Mawr see the writer's article in *Studies in Early British History*, ed. N. K. Chadwick (Cambridge, 1953), p. 132.

[5] In the ninth-century saga, *The Voyage of Bran*, which shows slight but definite marks of contact with the Welsh tale. See Jarman, 'Mabinogi Branwen', *Llên Cymru*, iv. 131. Also in Breton documents of the ninth century. H. Newstead, *Bran the Blessed in Arthurian Romance* (New York, 1939), p. 37.

Fisher King's disabling wound through the thighs. Sir Ifor Williams has suggested[1] that the epithet *Bendigeit* for Brân may well replace an older epithet whose meaning had become obsolete. Since the many qualities of Brân's severed head appear to have been his most prominent feature in the underlying mythology,[2] I suggest that this original epithet was composed from *Pen* (head) with a following adjective. However this may be, the epithet *Bendigeit* became responsible for the growth of a legend to the effect that Brân introduced Christianity into Britain. Actually this tradition cannot be traced in any source earlier than the *Myvyrian* Third Series[3] and the equally dubious Iolo manuscripts,[4] where it seems to have been influenced by the identification made in both these sources, but not vouched for elsewhere, of Brân's son Caradoc (who figures in the triads and in the *mabinogi*) with the historical British leader Caratācus.[5] In view of the fundamental relationship between Brân and the Fisher King, however, it is, of course, conceivable that there was some authority for this story earlier than the *Myvyrian* text.

[1] I. Williams, *Pedeir Keinc y Mabinogi*, p. 222.

[2] Irish instances of severed heads presiding at feasts have been collected by N. K. Chadwick in *Scottish Gaelic Studies*, iv. 120 ff. A. H. Krappe in *EC*, iii. 27 f., compares the functions of the heads of Orpheus, Osiris, and Mimir.

[3] Nos. 18, 35; the latter trans. in Loth, ii. 308, no. 124. Loth does not translate *Myvyrian* no. 18, presumably because it is a rehandling of no. 42 in the First Series (Loth's no. 76). This is important since the reading of the Third Series caused an error in the text of the triad in the First Series, which is reproduced in Loth's translation. The triad in question, *Tri Santeidd Linys* or *Tair Gwelygordd Saint*, 'Three Saintly Stocks', occurs in several fifteenth- and sixteenth-century manuscripts. (For one cf. *RC*, l. 378). In all versions the families of Brychan and Cunedda are constant, but the third family, though given in nearly all versions as that of Caw of Prydein, has been replaced in Peniarth 50 by the line of Joseph of Arimathea. R. Vaughan copied the triad from this text (see p. 46, n. 5 above), but the *Myvyrian* editor, influenced by the Third Series and without any manuscript justification, substituted the line of Brân, and relegated Vaughan's reading to a footnote. The earlier form of the triad (the families of Caw, Cunedda, and Brychan) is alone justified by the Welsh *Bonedd y Saint*. On Caw see N. K. Chadwick in *Scottish Gaelic Studies*, vii (1953), 117–61.

[4] Published for the Welsh Manuscripts Society (1848), p. 100.

[5] I have not been able to trace this association beyond the *Iolo Manuscripts* (Llandovery, 1848), p. 185, and the *Myvyrian* Third Series, nos. 22, 34, 35. 55. Caratācus, betrayed by Cartismandua, was taken as a captive to Rome (Tacitus, *Annales*, xii. 33–37), and the *Myvyrian* triad no. 35 states that Brân brought back Christianity from Rome, where he had been in the capacity of hostage for his son (Loth, ii. 308, no. 124). Since this chapter was written, it has been pointed out by G. J. Williams, *Iolo Morgannwg*, i (Cardiff, 1956), p. 312, n. 114, that the identification of Caradoc vab Brân with Caratācus appears in Harleian MS. 4181, p. 37, written early in the eighteenth century by the Welsh antiquarian and herald Hugh Thomas; and that scholars had already associated Caratācus with the introduction of Christianity into Britain before this identification was made.

6

THE ORAL DIFFUSION OF THE
ARTHURIAN LEGEND

ROGER SHERMAN LOOMIS

THE preceding chapters have demonstrated the existence among the
Welsh of a flourishing body of tradition, both oral and written, of
which Arthur had become the central figure by 1100 at latest. We have
seen why it arose and how it drew not only on the legends about historic
persons but also on the mythic heritage of the Irish and British races. But
when we direct our attention to the vast literature which began to appear on
the European continent in the twelfth century and of which likewise Arthur
was the most conspicuous personage, we are faced with a puzzling, an amazing phenomenon.

Why this exaltation of an alien king and court by the most sophisticated
men of letters of Western Europe, men who, so far as one can tell, had not
the slightest incentive to popularize a figure of so remote a time and people?
How did poets who knew no Celtic language come into possession of a fund
of story, full of Welsh and Breton names, localized at Caerleon, Caerwent,
Cardigan, Tintagel, Edinburgh, and the city of Snowdon (Caer Seint near
Carnarvon), and embodying numerous Irish and Welsh motifs and story
patterns? The influence of Geoffrey of Monmouth and Wace affords no
explanation, for these authors supply only a small fraction of the Celtic elements in the early romances.[1] Surely this knowledge was not acquired by
continental poets through a visit to Great Britain. Only rarely can one feel
sure that a French author had seen the places he describes, as when the
author of *Fergus* shows an intimacy with southern Scotland. Knowledge of
Celtic tradition cannot be due, then, to travel in Celtic lands; it cannot be
due to the export of Celtic manuscripts since they would have been unread-
able outside of Brittany; it cannot be due to books in other languages written
by natives of Wales, for even the most influential of these books, Geoffrey of
Monmouth's works, made little impression on the verse romances. What,
then, could have been the transmitting agency?

The diffusion of the Matter of Britain is a subject of the greatest importance, for without some clear understanding of how it took place, much will
be incomprehensible or will be wrongly interpreted. Some recent writers have

[1] *R*, x (1881), 488; Bruce, i. 37 n.

ignored the problem, and even among those who recognize a considerable Celtic element in the Matter of Britain one finds either a certain vagueness or a marked divergence of opinion. The latter are divided into two principal camps, one battling to prove that the Celtic stories passed directly from the Welsh to the Anglo-Normans and through them to the French, the other contending that it was the bilingual Bretons who were mainly responsible for developing and transmitting to the Anglo-Normans and the French the tales which centred about their racial hero. Here we witness a most unusual spectacle in controversy, for the scholars who have most vigorously opposed the claims of the Bretons are their French compatriots, Ferdinand Lot, Joseph Loth, and Jean Marx, while among those who have conceded the claims of the Bretons have been two great Welsh literary historians, Thomas Stephens and W. J. Gruffydd.[1] The evidence, consisting of the testimony of contemporaries, name forms, and literary affinities, has been most formidably presented by the Germans, Zimmer and Brugger, and, for the Tristan legend, by Bédier.[2] In spite of some errors, they have made a case which establishes the preponderant share of the Bretons in popularizing the Arthurian legend in the courts and baronial halls of France and England during the twelfth century. On their work most of what follows is based.

First, let us observe that Wales was not the only Celtic territory which possessed a tradition about Arthur. Like the Welsh, the people of Cornwall were descended from the Britons, and though the Saxon victory of Dyrham in 577 and the conquest of Devon in the next century drove a wedge between the Cornish and their kinsmen of Wales, there can be no doubt that relations were maintained across the Bristol Channel. Several Welsh writers who mention Arthur's court at Kelliwic in Cornwall seem to be reflecting a local tradition; Caradoc of Lancarvan, telling (*c.* 1130) how Arthur set out to recover his queen from the possession of Melvas (Chrétien's Meleagant), represents him as gathering the forces of Cornwall and Devon to besiege Glastonbury.[3] A Frenchman, Herman of Laon, reports that nine canons of that city were shown in 1113 on their journey from Exeter in Devon to

---

[1] Lot in *R*, xxiv (1895), 497 ff.; xxviii (1899), 1 ff., 321 ff.; xxx (1901), 1 ff.; Loth in *RC*, xiii (1892), 475–503; J. Marx, *Légende Arthurienne et le Graal* (Paris, 1952), pp. 55–58; Thomas Stephens, *Literature of the Kymry*, 2nd ed. (London, 1876), pp. 399–405; Gruffydd in *Trans. Hon. Soc. Cymmrodorion*, 1912–13, p. 36. The controversy has been reviewed by K. Voretzsch, *Introduction to the Study of Old French Literature*, trans. F. Dumont (New York, 1931), pp. 309–19, and by Bruce, i. 59–70, who favours Breton transmission.

[2] Zimmer in *GGA* (1890), 788 ff.; in Hinneberg, *Kultur der Gegenwart*, Teil I, Abt. XI, i (Berlin, Leipzig, 1909), 11–15, 60–65; Kristian von Troyes, *Karrenritter*, ed. W. Foerster (Halle, 1899), pp. cxi–cxxiii; Brugger in *ZFSL*, xx¹ (1898), 79–162; xliv² (1922), 78–87; Thomas, *Tristan*, ed. Bédier (Paris, 1905), ii. 122–7. I have discussed the role of the Bretons in *MP*, xxxiii (1936), 225–38; *RR*, xxxii (1941), 7–11; in *Arthurian Tradition*, pp. 15–18, 21–23, 27–32.

[3] On Kelliwic cf. J. Loth, *Mabinogion*, 2nd ed. (Paris, 1913), ii, index des noms propres, and *Antiquity*, xix (1945), 156 f. For Melvas's abduction of Guennuvar cf. E. K. Chambers, *Arthur of Britain* (London, 1927), pp. 263 f.; R. S. Loomis, *Arthurian Tradition*, pp. 214–19, and below, p. 178.

Bodmin in Cornwall the chair and the oven 'of that King Arthur, famed in the fables of the *Britanni*'.[1] Herman also records a fracas between one of the canons' servants and a Cornishman, who declared that Arthur was still alive. Just so, he says, 'the Bretons quarrel with the French': 'Britones solent iurgari cum Francis pro rege Arturo.' Herman's careful distinction between *Britanni* and *Britones* makes it clear that the former were insular Britons, the people of Cornwall and Wales, and the latter were their cousins across the Channel, neighbours of the French. The 'fabulae Britannorum' which the canons heard on their tour may be represented in part by Geoffrey of Monmouth's account of Arthur's birth and passing, since he not only localizes these events in Cornwall but consistently uses Cornish place and personal names: Tintagol, Ridcaradoch, Dimilioc, Gorlois, Modredus.[2] Possibly, of course, he may have obtained these famous tales from Cornish reciters, and, if so, these would be the only clear evidence of their circulation outside Celtic territory. But Geoffrey may have heard them in Cornwall or read them in a book.

Herman's remarks about the Bretons are corroborated by the statement, wrongly ascribed to Alanus de Insulis, that anyone who proclaimed in Armorica that Arthur was dead like other men would be lucky to escape being crushed by the stones of his hearers.[3] And the more one studies the spread of Arthur's fame, the more it becomes clear that it was to these ardent Bretons that this prodigious phenomenon was due.

No early Breton literature concerned with Arthur has reached us, with the exception of two saints' lives in Latin. The *Life of Goeznovius*,[4] which mentions Arthur's victories, has been shown by Faral and Tatlock to be dependent on Geoffrey of Monmouth, in spite of the spurious dating in 1019.[5] The *Life of St. Efflam*[6] is surely independent of Geoffrey and may well go back to the twelfth century,[7] to which a very crude sculpture in the church at Perros can be assigned. It represents a figure with a crozier, presumably Efflam; a prostrate figure with a shield, possibly Arthur, exhausted by a battle with a dragon, the coils of which seems to be indicated by a pile of lumpish objects; a mysterious figure with exaggerated *membrum virile*.[8] Here, as with Welsh hagiographers, Arthur's prowess is contrasted with the miraculous power of the saint; but this attitude hardly proves that Arthur

[1] Chambers, op. cit., pp. 18, 184, 249; Zimmer in *ZFSL*, xiii (1891), 106–12; Tatlock in *Spec*, viii (1933), 454–65.

[2] *RR*, xxxii. 5; *R*, xxviii (1899), 342; xxx (1901), 11; J. Loth, *Contributions à l'Etude des Romans de la Table Ronde* (Paris, 1912), pp. 63 f.; *RC*, xxxvii (1917–19), 322 f.

[3] Chambers, op. cit., pp. 109 f., 265. On authorship see below, p. 62, n. 1.; p. 79, n. 1.

[4] Ibid., p. 242.

[5] Faral, i. 253–6; J. S. P. Tatlock, *Legendary History of Britain* (Berkeley, Calif., 1950), pp. 193 f.

[6] Tatlock, *Legendary History*, p. 193; *Annales de Bretagne*, vii (1892), 279–312.

[7] *Spec*, xiv (1939), 359, n. 2.

[8] R. S. and L. H. Loomis, *Arthurian Legends in Medieval Art* (New York, 1938), p. 31, fig. 3.

was not a hero for the laity,[1] and nothing is more significant for the problem of diffusion than the consistency with which the facts point to the Bretons as the most active propagandists for their racial hero.

The Norman Wace has a reference in his *Brut* (1155) to the Round Table, 'of which Bretons tell many stories'.[2] Thirty years earlier the Anglo-Norman chronicler, William of Malmesbury, had written in his *Historia Regum Anglorum*: 'He is that Arthur about whom the trifles of the Bretons (*nugae Britonum*) rave even today, a man worthy not to be dreamed about in false fables but proclaimed in veracious histories, for he long upheld his sinking fatherland and quickened the failing spirits of his countrymen to war.'[3] Giraldus Cambrensis, the ardent Welsh patriot, writing about 1216, likewise attributes to the 'fabulosi Britones' the story of Arthur's transportation by a certain imaginary goddess, named Morganis, to the island of Avalon (*Avalloniam*) for the healing of his wounds.[4]

The crucial word in both passages is *Britones*. When referring to Arthur's time the word, of course, meant the insular Britons, but by the twelfth century, as applied to contemporaries, it always meant the emigrants to Armorica and their descendants, the Bretons.[5] Thus in a thirteenth-century poem we have the *Britones* carefully distinguished from their kinsmen the *Cambrenses* (Welsh) and *Cornubienses* (Cornish).[6] We have seen above how clearly Herman of Laon differentiated the *Britones* from the *Britanni*, or insular Britons, and indicated that the former were neighbours of the French. We have the testimony of both Geoffrey of Monmouth and Giraldus that the word *Britones* was no longer applied to Welshmen.[7] Giraldus, moreover, in the passage cited above used the name-forms *Morganis* and *Avalloniam*, for which the Welsh equivalents were Modron and Avallach. The natural inference is that he had heard this tradition, not from his fellow-countrymen but from the Bretons. Thus the Norman Wace, the Anglo-Norman William of Malmesbury, and the Welshman Giraldus agree in attributing to the Bretons circulation of stories about Arthur, his Round Table, and his passing to Avalon.

Ferdinand Lot objected that it would be very odd if William of Malmesbury, living at no great distance from the Welsh border, should have the distant Bretons in mind when speaking of the *nugae Britonum* about Arthur.[8]

---

[1] *RR*, xxxii. 33 f.; *Scottish Gaelic Studies*, vii (1953), 137 f.

[2] See below, Chap. 9. Wace, *Brut*, ed. I. Arnold (Paris, 1938–40), ii, vss. 9747–60; Huet in *MA*, xxviii (1915), 234–49.

[3] Chambers, op. cit., p. 250; Faral, i. 244–50; Zimmer in *ZFSL*, xiii (1891), 86–88; Brugger in *ZFSL*, xx[1] (1898), 92 f.   [4] Chambers, op. cit., p. 272; Brugger, loc. cit., pp. 97–100.

[5] Ibid., pp. 79–162; *RR*, xxxii. 5, 7–9.

[6] T. Wright, *Political Songs of England* (London, 1839), p. 56. See also *Spec*, xv (1940), 414 f.: 'Britonum, Guallorum, Cornubiencium'.

[7] Faral, iii. 303; Giraldus Cambrensis, *Opera*, ed. Dimock (London, 1868), vi. 179.

[8] *R*, xxiv (1895), 499 f.

It is much more strange that a historian like Lot should have been unaware that England had attracted many Bretons after 1066.[1] Zimmer, as early as 1890, pointed out the significance of this fact, and was followed by Ahlström and Warnke.[2] Bédier in 1905 declared that after the battle of Hastings 'toute la civilisation normande se trouva brusquement transplantée telle quelle dans les châteaux d'Outre-Manche, et les jongleurs armoricains y suivirent leurs patrons: jongleurs armoricains, mais plus qu'à demi romanisés, mais vivant au service de seigneurs français, et contant pour leur plaire'.[3] Lot's objection has, therefore, no validity; William could easily have heard the fantastic tales of the Bretons not only in the hall of some transplanted Breton lord but also in Anglo-Norman households.

The testimony of William is in harmony with the facts; it is in accord with that of Wace and Giraldus Cambrensis; it is also supported by the internal evidence of the romances themselves, where we find a sprinkling of Breton names. Bédier discovered five of them in the Tristan romances; to which may be added Roald and Morholt.[4] Chrétien de Troyes's earliest extant romance assigns to the hero the Breton name Erec, and contains seven other names of the same origin—Brien, Gandeluz, Rinduran, Guerehes, Graillemer, Guigamor, Guivret.[5] Yvain is the Breton Ivan, recorded in the eleventh century and substituted for Welsh Owain,[6] and Lancelot has been recognized by Zimmer, Lot, and Bruce[7] as influenced by the name Lancelin, recorded in Brittany in the same century.

Further confirmation of Breton transmission of Arthurian matter to the French and Anglo-Normans is supplied by the marked resemblance between certain romances and the Breton lais. There is an intimate connexion between the episode of the testing horn in the *Livre de Caradoc* and Biket's *Lai du Cor*,[8] between Chrétien's *Yvain* and *Desiré*,[9] between the hunt of the white stag in the Second Continuation of Chrétien's *Perceval* and the same theme in *Tyolet*.[10]

[1] F. M. Stenton, *First Century of English Feudalism* (Oxford, 1932), pp. 24–28, especially p. 25: 'There is, in fact, hardly a county in which this Breton element is not found, and in some counties its influence was deep and permanent.' Lot's strange argument (*R*, xxiv. 498 f.) that because Henry of Huntingdon addressed Warinus Brito as a fellow countryman, Brito meant in this case 'Welshman' was easily refuted by Brugger in *ZFSL*, xx¹, 91. Men resident in England but of Breton extraction were commonly called Brito or 'le Bret'. Stenton, op. cit., p. 26, n. 1.

[2] *GGA*, 1890, pp. 788–91; A. Ahlström, *Studier in den Fornfransker Laislitteraturen* (Uppsala, 1892), pp. 28–34; Marie de France, *Lais*, ed. K. Warnke, 3rd ed. (1925), pp. xxv f.

[3] Thomas, *Tristan*, ed. Bédier, ii. 126 f.

[4] Ibid., pp. 122 f.; *R*, liii (1927), 96 f.

[5] Loomis, *Arthurian Tradition*, pp. 479–89.

[6] Ibid., p. 273.

[7] *ZFSL*, xiii¹ (1891), 43–58; xiv (1894), 180; *R*, xxv (1896), 12; Bruce, i. 193.

[8] O. Warnatsch, *Der Mantel* (Breslau, 1883), pp. 60–69; *Spec*, ix (1934), 38 f. See below, Chap. 11.

[9] Loomis, *Arthurian Tradition*, pp. 271 f., 304.

[10] Ibid., p. 69; J. L. Weston, *Legend of Sir Perceval* (London, 1906–9), i. 107–17; *Legend of Sir Lancelot du Lac* (London, 1901), pp. 30–39. See Chap. 11, below.

Again, there is a marked affinity between episodes in the romances and certain modern Breton folk-tales.[1] A variant of Béroul's story of King Mark's equine ears was told in Finistère in 1794; the falsehood about the black and white sails, which led to Tristan's death, was also the theme of tales current on the islands of Ouessant and Molène fifty years ago. The Provençal romance of *Jaufré*, the Italian *Pulzella Gaia*, and *Perlesvaus* contain incidents which bear so precise a likeness to Breton folk-tales of the nineteenth century that chance alone cannot be responsible.

To all this accumulation of evidence, external and internal, in favour of Breton transmission of Welsh and Cornish lore to the French-speaking world only one objection of consequence has been offered, namely, that the Bretons of the twelfth century did not possess the talent to make so momentous a contribution to culture. But how is such an estimate to be reconciled with the fact that two of the greatest geniuses of the period, Abelard and Adam of St. Victor, were Bretons? So, too, were Bernard of Chartres, 'the most abounding spring of letters in Gaul' in his day, his brother Thierry, Peter of Blois, and, in the opinion of some authorities, Geoffrey of Monmouth, who called himself 'Brito'.[2] Otto of Freising testified that Brittany produced in abundance clerics of genius, devoted to liberal arts.[3] It seems safe, therefore, to make the generalization that it was Bretons of a quite different species of talent, the *conteurs*, who successfully adapted their heritage of romantic tales to French taste and acquired such a reputation as entertainers that even in England they had little competition from the Welsh and Cornish.

Still, the possibility of exceptions is not ruled out, and it is an astonishing and misleading fact that the one reciter of Arthurian tales whose fame is attested from several sources was a Welshman, Bleheris.[4] He is mentioned by Giraldus Cambrensis as a 'fabulator famosus'; by Thomas, the author of *Tristan*, as one who knew the history of all the counts and all the kings of Britain; by the second continuator of *Perceval* as one who had been born and brought up in Wales and who had told a tale of Gauvain and a dwarf knight to the Count of Poitiers (either William VII or VIII), who liked it better than any other. The same person is cited in the *Elucidation*, prefixed

---

[1] *Annales de Bretagne*, lvi (1949), 203–27; *Comparative Literature*, ii (1950), 289–306. See below, Chap. 12.   [2] See below, p. 73, n. 1.   [3] Faral, ii. 381.

[4] On Bleheris see Weston in *R*, xxxiv (1905), 100–5; Brugger in *ZFSL*, xlvii (1924), 162–85; Van Dam in *Neo*, xv (1929), 30–34. Kellermann in *Colloques Internationaux du Centre National de la Recherche Scientifique*, iii, *Romans du Graal* (Paris, 1956), pp. 137–45, and H. Wrede, *Die Fortsetzer des Gralromans Chrestiens von Troyes* (Göttingen, 1952), pp. 176–83, have attacked the reliability of the testimony, particularly that concerning the visit of Bleheris to the Count of Poitiers, but Kellermann's argument has been answered at least in part by Hoepffner, Mme Lejeune, Roach, and Marx in *Colloques Internationaux*, iii. 145–8. I find nothing in the evidence to support Brugger's view that Bleheris committed his stories to parchment in the form of verse. Nor can I accept the identification of the *fabulator* with Bledri ap Cadivor, a South Welsh chief, put forward in *RC*, xxxii (1911), 5–17; xxxiii (1912), 180 ff.; *EC*, ii (1937), 219–45. Considering the social chasm between landed noble and wandering *conteur*, I cannot believe that Giraldus would have called Bledri ap Cadivor a 'fabulator'.

to *Perceval*, under the corrupt form Blihis, as an authority on the secrets of the Grail,[1] and under the disguise of the saintly name Blaise as an omniscient source for the early history of Arthur and Merlin.[2] These various independent testimonies to the reputation of Bleheris seem to prove that he was a story-teller of pre-eminent artistry and power. Certainly there was no more discriminating literary centre in Western Europe than that of the counts of Poitou in the time of the troubadour William VII and of his son William VIII, who died in 1137. Now, though Bleheris was a Welshman born and bred, he must have been fluent in French, and the internal evidence of such romances as profess, rightly or wrongly, to have been derived from his repertoire shows no closer relation to Welsh tradition than that of other romances in French, and in the Tristan and Grail poems one finds significantly Breton names.[3] Apparently his stories were not derived from his native inheritance but were polished and stirring versions of Breton tales, and there is no hint anywhere that any other Welshman crossed over into England or France to exploit his wares in a wider market. Despite the one exception of Bleheris, the evidence goes to show that the disseminators of the Matter of Britain outside Celtic territory in the eleventh and twelfth centuries were Bretons.

The records, moreover, agree in representing these early reciters not as amateurs but as professionals, and the stories themselves not as old wives' tales or tavern-haunters' yarns but as the stock-in-trade of a class of entertainers who appealed to the highest society. In this respect Bleheris at the court of Poitou was typical. Geoffrey of Monmouth ascribed to Merlin the prophecy that the deeds of Arthur would be *cibus narrantibus*, 'food to story-tellers', in the sense that telling Arthur's deeds of prowess would provide them with their bread and butter.[4] Wace reported that the story-tellers had so embellished their narratives that they had made everything seem to be fictitious (*fables*).[5] Chrétien referred to Erec as the hero of tales which those who wished to make a livelihood by telling stories, 'cil qui de conter vivre vuelent', were wont to mangle and spoil in the presence of kings and counts,[6] and he declared that his *Perceval* was the best tale ever told in a royal court.[7]

---

[1] *Elucidation*, ed. A. W. Thompson (New York, 1931), pp. 78–81, 86.

[2] *RR*, xxxiii (1942), 172 f.; *Prophecies de Merlin*, ed. L. A. Paton (New York, 1927), ii. 302; *MedAev*, xxv (1956), 184 f.

[3] See above, p. 56, n. 4. In the Grail texts we find Alain, Cavalon, Brianz.

[4] Faral, iii. 191. Tatlock in *Legendary History*, p. 201, assumed that 'cibus' meant 'narrative material', not 'livelihood', but a fourteenth-century gloss on the *Prophetiae* printed by Hammer in *Collection Latomus* (1949), ii. 113, explains that 'fabulatores cibos sibi quaerent de eo narrando'. See also a passage referring to the Emperor Henry III in 1045: 'infinitam multitudinem histrionum et joculatorum sine cibo et muneribus vacuam et merentem abire permisit.' Faral, *Jongleurs en France au Moyen Âge* (Paris, 1910), p. 274. Also *Annales Monastici*, Rolls Series, i. 485: 'histrionibus potest dari cibus, quia pauperes sunt.' See p. 111 below.

[5] Wace, *Brut*, ed. Arnold, ii, vss. 9795–8; Chambers, op. cit., p. 103.

[6] *Erec*, vss. 20–22.   [7] *Percevalroman*, ed. Hilka, vss. 61–65.

Most significant is a passage in the Second Continuation of that poem which expresses the haughty attitude of the literary man to these itinerant entertainers.

Now there are many vassals going from court to court telling tales, who distort the good stories, stretch them out, and add so many lies that the tales are entirely spoiled and thus throw discredit on the good books. Those who listen and hear do not know what good stories are worth, but they say, when these minstrels spend a night in their lodging and are made to tell a little of an adventure without rime, that they have heard the whole authentic history, which they will never hear in the course of their lives. Thus they are led to believe falsehood and are told spurious history and lies are spread.[1]

It is amusing to find the poet attacking the veracity of these wandering minstrels in view of the doubtful historicity of his own narrative. But he does give us a glimpse into their lives and he bears witness that (unlike the *jongleurs* who chanted the *chansons de geste* and unlike the Anglo-Saxon *scops* who used alliterative verse) these minstrels related the adventures of Arthur and his knights in prose. This fact would accord, as Zimmer has shown,[2] with the general practice of the Celts.

Without doubt the *conteurs* must have possessed histrionic talents or they would have had no audiences. The word *histriones*, in fact, is applied to them, both by the Scottish author of a *Life of St. Kentigern*, dated 1147–64, in speaking of Ewen the son of Urien,[3] and by Peter of Blois in a memorable passage: 'the *histriones* tell certain stories about Arthur, Gawain, and Tristan by which the hearts of the listeners are smitten with compassion and pricked even to tears'.[4] Another witness to the emotional effect of these tales is Ailred of Rievaulx in Yorkshire, who, writing his *Speculum Caritatis* in 1141–2, quotes a novice as confessing with shame that, though he could not squeeze out a tear at a pious reading or discourse, he had often in his former life wept over fables which were commonly composed about an unknown Arthur.[5]

The array of facts supplied by these scattered references furnishes a perfect explanation for the miraculous spread of the Arthurian legend throughout

---

[1] J. L. Weston, *Legend of Sir Perceval*, i. 265. Loomis, *Arthurian Tradition*, p. 22, n. 50. On the other hand, Arnold of Guines about 1200 retained in his household old and decrepit men to tell him stories from romance and history. Robert of Coutances, an old knight, was the authority on King Arthur, Walter of Écluse on Tristan, Isolt, and Merlin. *Mon. Germ. Hist. Script.* xxiv (Hannov er, 1879), 607. *SM*, nuova serie, ix (1936), 7.

[2] *GGA*, 1890, pp. 806–17. See Chap. 4 above.

[3] Loomis, in *Proceedings of the Soc. of Antiquaries of Scotland*, lxxxix. 11 f.

[4] Chambers, *Arthur of Britain*, p. 267; Migne, *Patrologia Latina*, ccviii. 1088. On *joculatores, histriones, mimi*, &c., cf. E. K. Chambers, *Medieval Stage* (Oxford, 1903), ii. 230–3; Faral, *Jongleurs en France*.

[5] Migne, op. cit. cxcv. 565; *RR*, xxxii. 10–14. Tatlock, op. cit., pp. 207–10, interprets the passage as referring merely to echoes of Geoffrey's *Historia*, but he does not explain why these should have had such a strong emotional effect, and he ignores, as always, the existence of professional *conteurs*.

Western Europe—a people passionately devoted to the memory of Arthur and believing him to be still alive, linked to the Welsh by blood and by continuing intercourse, but speaking a language which was current among the nobility from the Firth of Forth to the Jordan; a class of strolling minstrels who took advantage of this fact to make a livelihood by telling their tales, of which Arthur was the centre, with such verve that they were able to fascinate counts and kings who had not the slightest racial or political tie with the British hero.

The evidence thus far presented also shows that the *conteurs* were known to authors living in Scotland and Yorkshire, at Oxford and Malmesbury—regions where Breton and Norman lords were ready enough to hear the tales, not only because of their intrinsic interest but for local and historic reasons. Did not some of these magnates possess the very lands where Arthur had supposedly ruled and where strange adventures had taken place? But the casual references of the troubadours and Chrétien prove that the *conteurs* must have ranged far outside the Anglo-Norman sphere of influence, and it is an astonishing but demonstrable fact that they must have established a vogue in the Po valley about 1100. Rajna discovered in a document of 1114 an Artusius, brother of Count Ugo of Padua; another Artusius signed his name in 1122, and I discovered a third who was a benefactor of Modena Cathedral in 1125.[1] In 1136 and after, the name Walwanus appears with several variations in Paduan charters.[2] Artusius is the regular Italian Latinization of the name Arthur when the source is French,[3] and Walwanus is identical in form with the name of Gawain in one of the best manuscripts of Geoffrey's *Historia*. Evidently nobles were christening their sons by the names of the British king and his nephew before and shortly after 1100.[4]

It is also startling that the earliest appearance of Arthur and his knights in art is found on an archivolt over the north doorway of Modena Cathedral.[5] The art historians of Italy, Germany, England, and the United States are almost unanimous in dating this sculpture between 1099 and 1120.[6] The cathedral documents which reveal that the edifice was consecrated in 1106 and that some fine sculptures had already been completed, the costume and armour, and the name-forms incised above the figures are reconcilable with this date; the development of sculptural style in Lombardy proves it.[7] The scene represented is the deliverance of a woman, Winlogee, by Artus,

[1] *R*, xvii (1888), 355–61; *RR*, xxxii. 27–31. *Regesta Chartarum Italiae*, xvi (1931), 295.

[2] *R*, xvii. 171–5, 361–4.

[3] *RR*, xxxii. 28.

[4] Tatlock, op. cit., pp. 222–6, as usua lremains unconvinced.

[5] R. S. and L. H. Loomis, *Arthurian Legends in Medieval Art*, pp. 32–36, figs. 4–8.

[6] Quoted in *RR*, xxxii. 22 f., and R. S. Loomis, *Wales*, pp. 199 f. The arguments against an early date brought forward by Gerould in *Spec*, x (1935), 355–76, I refuted in *Spec*, xiii (1938), 221–31. Tatlock, op. cit., p. 214, dismisses the testimony of art historians as valueless.

[7] *RR*, xxxii. 24–26; R. S. Loomis, *Wales*, pp. 198–208.

PLATE 2

ARTHUR AND HIS KNIGHTS ATTACK A CASTLE

Archivolt, Modena Cathedral. c. 1106

Isdernus, Galvaginus, and Che from a moated fortress occupied by a trio of unpleasant characters, Burmaltus, Mardoc, and Carado. There is good reason to suppose that the incident is a variant of the rescue of Guenievre as described in *Durmart le Gallois*, and is related to the rescue of Gauvain from Carado of the Dolorous Tower in the *Vulgate Lancelot*, as Foerster and Mâle recognized.[1] The name Winlogee applied to Arthur's queen is a transitional form between Breton Winlowen and French Guinloie. It follows that the *conteur* who provided these names was a Breton. Possibly he came down into Italy with the Breton contingent to the First Crusade under their Duke.[2] They were at Bari during the winter of 1096–7, and the sculpture and architecture of Modena Cathedral, as Kingsley Porter showed,[3] were strongly influenced by work recently executed at Bari.

A mosaic pavement laid down in the cathedral of Otranto, near Bari, in 1165 still depicts 'Arturus Rex' bearing a sceptre and riding a goat.[4] No passage in literature assigns to the king so strange and so humble a mount. The only plausible explanation[5] is found in the fact that the immortal Arthur was identified in the twelfth century with various supernatural potentates, such as the ruler of a subterranean realm,[6] and that Walter Map about 1190 narrates a tale in which the king of a subterranean realm rode a large goat.

Gervase of Tilbury, who visited Sicily about 1190, reported that the British king had been seen, still alive, in the subterranean depths of Mount Etna.[7] Caesarius of Heisterbach gives a variant of the same story, and dates the event at the time of the conquest of the island by the Emperor Henry (*c.* 1194).[8] There is no hint in these Sicilian legends that they were imported by Bretons, but from 1072 to 1189 Sicily was ruled by a Norman dynasty, and Zimmer quoted a chronicler to the effect that spirited young Norman or Breton knights sought Italy for adventure at various times after 1017.[9] At the siege of Taormina in 1079 the life of Count Roger was saved by his nephew, 'natione Brito'.[10] At any rate, by the end of the twelfth century Arthur was at home in Sicily.

---

[1] *ZRP*, xxii (1898), 243; E. Mâle, *L'Art Religieux du Douzième Siècle* (Paris, 1922), p. 269; *RR*, xv (1924), 267–71.

[2] C. W. David, *Robert Curthose* (Cambridge, Mass., 1920), pp. 94, 221.

[3] A. K. Porter, *Romanesque Sculpture of the Pilgrimage Roads* (Boston, 1923), i. 67; *Burlington Magazine*, xliii (1923), 63; *Gazette des Beaux Arts*, per. 5, xviii (1928), 115, 121.

[4] R. S. and L. H. Loomis, *Arthurian Legends in Medieval Art*, p. 36, fig. 9; E. Bertaux, *L'Art dans l'Italie Méridionale* (Rome, 1904), i. 488–90; *SM*, ii (1906–7), 506.

[5] *MP*, xxxviii (1941), 300–2.   [6] See below, Chap. 7.

[7] *MP*, xxxviii. 298; Chambers, op. cit., pp. 221 f., 276 f. See below, Chap. 7.

[8] Chambers, op. cit., pp. 222, 277 f.

[9] *GGA*, 1890, p. 831. Guillaume de Jumièges, *Gesta Normannorum Ducum*, ed. J. Marx (Paris, Rouen, 1914), p. 187: 'agiles Normannorum seu Britonum tirones . . . Italiam diversis temporibus expetierunt.'

[10] Gaufredo Malaterra, *De Rebus Gestis Rogerii Calabriae et Siciliae Comitis*, ed. E. Pontieri, *Rerum It. Scriptores*, v, pt. 1, p. 66.

It is a matter of high significance that these early examples of Arthurian tradition in Italy—the sculpture at Modena, the mosaic at Otranto, the local legend of Etna—were not derived from any known literary source, and there is a strong presumption that they were transmitted orally by adventurous Bretons, seeking patronage wherever French was understood, as it was in northern Italy, Apulia, and Sicily, and creating as elsewhere a great sensation by their novel and fantastic fictions.

The most eloquent testimony to the permeation of Latin Christendom by the renown of the British hero is to be found in the work formerly attributed in error to Alanus de Insulis and now dated by De Lage 1167–74.[1] Commenting on the passage in Geoffrey of Monmouth's *Prophetiae Merlini*, 'In the mouth of peoples he [Arthur] will be celebrated', the author declared:

> Whither has not flying fame spread and familiarized the name of Arthur the Briton, even as far as the empire of Christendom extends? Who, I say, does not speak of Arthur the Briton, since he is almost better known to the peoples of Asia than to the *Britanni* [the Welsh and Cornish], as our palmers returning from the East inform us? The Eastern peoples speak of him, as do the Western, though separated by the width of the whole earth. . . . Rome, queen of cities, sings his deeds, nor are Arthur's wars unknown to her former rival Carthage. Antioch, Armenia, Palestine celebrate his acts.[2]

If one realizes how much of Asia Minor and Syria was at this time colonized by peoples of French blood or speech, one will not reject this affirmation as sheer balderdash. The writer was patently amazed by the phenomenon. That Geoffrey of Monmouth and Wace were being read in clerical and courtly circles throughout Christendom by 1175 may be readily acknowledged, but unless the evidence assembled in this chapter has been totally misleading, we may safely assign the major part in the spread of the Matter of Britain as far as the Latin states of the East to the activities of the Breton *conteurs*. Direct testimony is lacking; but when in instance after instance the signs point to oral rather than literary circulation, it is a logical inference that these same story-tellers accompanied or followed the Frankish hosts who conquered the lands of the eastern Mediterranean.

When we approach the question, how long did the reciters of such tales continue to be welcome in the courts of Europe? we find no definite answer. Béroul mentions them in his *Tristan*, vs. 1265; the author of *Perlesvaus* in l. 7277;[3] and that brings us well into the thirteenth century. A poem of the same century represents two *bourdeurs ribauds* boasting their knowledge of romances, which was badly muddled, for the first knew about 'the evil speech

---

[1] G. Raynaud de Lage, *Alain de Lille* (Montreal, Paris, 1951), pp. 13–15.

[2] T. Stephens, *Literature of the Kymry*, 2nd ed. (London, 1876), p. 405 n.; Alanus de Insulis, *Prophetia Anglicana* (Frankfort, 1603), pp. 22 f.

[3] *Perlesvaus*, ed. Nitze and others (Chicago, 1932), i.

of Gauvain and the good knight Queu [Kay], about Perceval le Blois and Pertenoble le Gallois'![1] The latest reference known to me is in the Provençal *Flamenca*, which possibly postdates 1272. During the wedding festivities of Flamenca at Bourbon, the *jongleurs* are described as reciting tales, among which the five Arthurian poems of Chrétien are recognizable, as well as other themes from the same cycle.[2] If this means that the *jongleurs* memorized Chrétien's lines and repeated them, the fact is significant. The old, less polished prose tales had gone out of fashion; the purely oral tradition had come to an end, and probably the Bretons had long since ceased to monopolize the exploitation of the Matter of Britain. Italian *cantastorie*, however, and English minstrels composed and sang *cantari* and verse romances from the fourteenth to the end of the fifteenth century, as we shall see on pp. 426, 482, 490, and 520.

Several characteristic features of oral recitation are to be detected in the Arthurian texts preserved to us. The wide variations in the handling of a given theme can sometimes be explained only as the result of a long preliterary development, when every reciter made his modifications. Certain proper names have been adapted to the speech-patterns of different peoples; thus the Welsh epithet *Gwallt-advwyn*, meaning 'Bright Hair', became successively Galvagin, Galvain, Gauvain, Gawain.[3] Nowhere are the earmarks of minstrel composition more plainly discernible than in the short form of the First Continuation of Chrétien's *Perceval*.[4] It is a collection of originally independent tales. It contains an appeal to the authority of Bleheris, who is identified in the Second Continuation as a *conteur*. There are frequent addresses to members of the audience as 'Signeur', and at one point they are asked to repeat a paternoster for the dead and to give the reciter a drink of wine before he proceeds. Thus internal evidence amply corroborates the external testimony to the oral diffusion of the Matter of Britain before, and even after, it came into favour with poets and prose romancers.

---

[1] E. Faral, *Mimes Français du XIII Siècle* (Paris, 1910), p. 96.

[2] *Flamenca*, ed. P. Meyer (Paris, 1901), vss. 661–90. See below, p. 398.

[3] See below, p. 475.

[4] See J. L. Weston, *Legend of Sir Perceval* (London, 1906–9), i. 233, 241–3, 246 f., 252, and *Continuations of the Old French Perceval*, ed. Roach iii (Philadelphia, 1952), especially pp. 423, 452.

7

THE LEGEND OF ARTHUR'S SURVIVAL

ROGER SHERMAN LOOMIS

I N the preceding chapter reference has been made to the belief in Arthur's survival which prevailed among the Cornish and Bretons as early as 1113.[1] We have at least two testimonies from the same century to the existence of this belief among the Welsh. In the *Verses on the Graves*, copied in the Black Book of Carmarthen about 1200, we read: 'A grave for March, a grave for Guythur, a grave for Gugaun of the Red Sword; concealed till Doomsday the grave of Arthur.'[2] If this translation is correct, it corresponds neatly to William of Malmesbury's statement (1125) that Arthur's grave was nowhere to be found, wherefore ancient ditties prophesied his return.[3] A continuator of Gaimar's *Estorie des Engles* (c. 1150) says that the Welsh of his time threatened the Normans that they would finally win back their land through Arthur and restore the name of Britain.[4]

But most of the allusions to this Messianic hope ascribe it to the Bretons. Henry of Huntingdon (1139) reported that they denied Arthur's death and expected his return.[5] There is the well-known passage in Wace's *Brut* (1155).[6] William of Newburgh (c. 1198) said that the Bretons were for the most part such brutes that they still expected Arthur to come again and would not hear of his death.[7] Peter of Blois (1160–75)[8] and Giraldus Cambrensis (c. 1216)[9] both compared the Bretons in this respect to the Jews who awaited their Messiah. The troubadours and the north Italians were familiar with these vain expectations.[10] Boncompagno da Signa (c. 1200) has a model letter

---

[1] The only comprehensive treatment of this subject known to me is the Columbia dissertation of Miss Mary Honora Scanlan, 'The Legend of Arthur's Survival', which has not been printed, but is available in microfilm. For references cf. *Mort Artu*, ed. J. D. Bruce (Halle, 1910), pp. 298–307; Bruce, *Evolution*, i. 74–82; Chambers, *Arthur of Britain* (London, 1927), especially pp. 104–12, 217–32; R. H. Fletcher, *Arthurian Material in the Chronicles* (Boston, 1906; reprinted Burt Franklin: New York, 1958), index, p. 289.

[2] This translation is based on supplying the word *braud* after *bid*. *Studies in Early British History*, ed. N. K. Chadwick (Cambridge, 1954), p. 112. Another translation is given above, p. 13.

[3] Chambers, op. cit., pp. 17, 250. Faral, i. 247 f.

[4] Chambers, op. cit., p. 109.   [5] Ibid., pp. 251 f.

[6] See p. 98 below. *R*, xxviii (1899), 573 n.   [7] Chambers, op. cit., pp. 275 f.

[8] Migne, *Pat. Lat.* ccvii. 112, 154.   [9] Chambers, op. cit., p. 272.

[10] See Chap. 29 below. E. G. Gardner, *Arthurian Legend in Italian Literature* (London, 1930), pp. 7–10.

from a lecturer to a student, sarcastically informing him that he will complete his academic course only when Arthur returns to Britain.[1]

During the next centuries we continue to get echoes of the tradition from English writers. The chronicle attributed to Robert of Gloucester (*c.* 1300) mentions the Cornish as sharing the hope with the Bretons.[2] Peter de Langtoft and his redactor, Robert Mannyng (1338), also mention it; the first author is noncommittal, the second calls it 'the Bretons' lie'.[3] In the *Fall of Princes* (1431–8) Lydgate ascribes to them the belief that Arthur 'shall resorte as lord and sovereyne Out of fayrye and regne in Breteyne'.[4] According to Malory (*c.* 1469), 'some men say in many parts of England that King Arthur is not dead, but had by the will of our Lord Jesu into another place; and men say that he shall come again, and he shall win the Holy Cross'.[5] Malory continues, with great caution: 'Yet I will not say that it shall be so, but rather I would say: here in this world he changed his life.' One of the most extraordinary stories which was in circulation, though after our period, was reported by Julian del Castillo in 1582.[6] According to common talk, King Arthur had been enchanted in England into the form of a crow, and some said that Philip II swore (evidently at the time of his marriage to Mary Tudor in 1554) that he would resign the kingdom if Arthur should return!

The vague belief in Arthur's survival took on certain specific forms. We have seen that Giraldus Cambrensis attributed to the 'fabulosi Britones' the story that the king had been borne to Avalon by Morgan; so also did Gervase of Tilbury.[7] Geoffrey of Monmouth in his *Vita Merlini* (*c.* 1150) and Guillaume de Rennes in *Gesta Regum Britanniae* (*c.* 1235) give elaborate and independent descriptions of this blissful isle, of its ever green vegetation, of its long-lived denizens, and of its mistress who was to heal Arthur's wounds.[8] According to the *Bataille Loquifer* (*c.* 1180), Renouart was transported through the air by Morgue and two sister fays to Avalon, and there he found Arthur, Gauvain, and Yvain in luxurious surroundings.[9]

At this point it seems fitting to consider the name Avalon and Morgain's connexion with the elysian isle.[10] In medieval Britain two interpretations of

---

[1] Ibid., p. 10.

[2] Robert of Gloucester, *Metrical Chronicle*, ed. W. A. Wright (London, 1887), i, vss. 4589–91.

[3] Langtoft, *Chronicle*, ed. T. Wright (London, 1866), i. 224; R. Manning of Brunne, *Story of England*, ed. F. J. Furnivall (London, 1887), ii, vss. 14290–306.

[4] Lydgate, *Fall of Princes*, stanzas 63–65. [5] Malory, bk. xxi, ch. 7.

[6] J. del Castillo, *Historia de los Reyes Godos* (Madrid, 1624), p. 365; C. B. Millican, *Spenser and the Table Round* (Cambridge, Mass., 1932), p. 36. On Arthur's survival as a crow cf. Chambers, op. cit., p. 229.

[7] Ibid., pp. 272, 276. On the meaning of *Britones* see p. 55 above.

[8] Chambers, op. cit., pp. 256 f. Faral, iii. 334 f.; L. A. Paton, *Fairy Mythology of Arthurian Romance* (Boston, 1903; reprinted Burt Franklin: New York, 1959), pp. 45 f. See pp. 92 f. below.

[9] Le Roux de Lincy, *Livre des Légendes* (Paris, 1836), pp. 248–56.

[10] On Avalon cf. Paton, op. cit., pp. 25–47, 250 f.; Lot in *R*, xxvii (1898), 529–73; *Perlesvaus*, ed. Nitze and others (Chicago, 1932–7), ii. 48–59; Chotzen in *EC*, iv (1948), 255–74.

the name were current. There were those, including Geoffrey of Monmouth, who connected the word with *aval*, meaning 'apple',[1] and the Welsh texts always refer to the island as 'ynys avallach'.[2] On the other hand, there was the alternative explanation that Avalloc or Avallo was a ruler of the island who dwelt there with his daughters,[3] including Morgan. Which of these two interpretations was the original?

The Irish had a word *ablach*, meaning 'rich in apple-trees', which they applied to the elysian isle of Manannan the sea-god,[4] and it is possible that similar Hesperian associations attached to the Welsh island paradise and were responsible for the interpretation of Avalon as the isle of apples. But Professor Thomas Jones informs me that *avallach* is not a common noun meaning 'orchard', but is a proper name which appears in the tenth-century Harleian genealogies as Aballac and Aballach. It is the same which occurs in a triad as Avallach and is assigned to the father of Modron, mother of Owein by Uryen.[5] As a common noun, then, *avallach* is a ghost word, and 'ynys avallach' originally and properly meant the 'island of Avallach'. But the Bretons apparently were not too certain about the meaning and gave Avallach a form approximating their own place-name Avaellon,[6] and in course of time the name of the famous Burgundian town and abbey Avallon had a decisive influence in standardizing the form and in creating the impression that Avalon was a place. The Bretons, too, substituted for the Welsh goddess Modron, daughter of Avallach and mother of Owein by Uryen, their own water fay Morgan, who thus became lady of the Isle of Avalon. The motif of a wounded hero borne away by his faery kinswomen to be healed was shown by Gertrude Schoepperle and Cross to occur in the Irish saga, *The Cattle-Raid of Fraech*,[7] and this or a cognate tradition was the source of the beautiful story of the passing of Arthur.

Why Avalon came to be identified with Glastonbury is a more difficult problem. It has often been assumed that Henry II, wishing to stifle the hope of Arthur's return, induced the monks to do some excavating in their cemetery, with the result that, after Henry's death, certain large bones were discovered, together with those of a woman; above was a leaden cross with an inscription, variously reported, identifying these remains as those of Arthur

---

[1] Chambers, op. cit., pp. 255, 266, 270; Faral, ii. 426, 439; iii. 334; Paton, op. cit., p. 76.

[2] *EC*, iv. 240, 260; *RC*, xxxiii (1912), 442; J. Loth, *Mabinogion*, 2nd ed. (Paris, 1913), ii. 237, 288; I. Williams, *Pedeir Keinc y Mabinogi* (Cardiff, 1930), p. 100.

[3] J. Armitage Robinson, *Somerset Historical Essays* (London, 1921), p. 12; Chambers, op. cit., pp. 266, 273; Faral, ii. 426, 442.

[4] *ZCP*, viii (1910), 194; *EC*, iv. 255-74.

[5] Loth, op. cit. ii. 284; *RR*, xxix (1938), 176 f.; *Spec*, xx (1945), 183-200. See p. 45 above.

[6] *ZFSL*, xiv (1892), 169.

[7] *Vassar Mediaeval Studies*, ed. C. F. Fiske (New Haven, 1923), pp. 3-25; *Manly Anniversary Studies* (Chicago, 1923), pp. 284-94.

and his queen.[1] As the story of the discovery is told by Giraldus in *De Principis Instructione* (1193–9), however, Henry told the brethren that he had learned of Arthur's burial-place from a 'historico cantore Britone', i.e. a Breton singer versed in history.[2] This may not be authentic, of course, but it does suggest that the idea of Glastonbury as Arthur's last resting-place did not originate with Henry but with some Breton who had abandoned the dream of Arthur's return. If so, we may guess why he identified Glastonbury with Avalon, for this could be proved according to the axiom that things equal to the same thing are equal to one another. About 1130[3] people of British stock called Glastonbury 'Ynis Gutrin', i.e. 'Glass Island', on the basis of a false etymology.[4] They must have already possessed a tradition about a Glass Island, for we learn from Welsh sources that it was (1) the abode of Melwas;[5] (2) a water-girdled Fortress of Glass (Caer Wydyr), where nine maidens dwelt.[6] Chrétien de Troyes knew something of the same tradition, for in *Erec*[7] he mentioned Maheloas, lord of the Isle of Glass, where there was never storm or winter's cold or excessive heat. The Isle of Glass, therefore, could be equated with an equally imaginary Hesperian Isle of Apples,[8] for Geoffrey of Monmouth described the latter as the abode of nine sisters, and the *Gesta Regum Britanniae* celebrated its winterless climate.[9] Anyone familiar with these traditions, therefore, could make the following series of equations: Glastonbury = Isle of Glass = Isle of Apples = the isle to which the wounded Arthur was conveyed. Possibly Giraldus was right, and the search for Arthur's body in the monastic cemetery, where other royal persons were known to have been buried, originated, not in the scheming of an Angevin king, or in the cupidity of the Glastonbury monks, but in the mistaken logic of a Breton minstrel. Of course, the consequences of the exhumation were such as to strengthen the Angevin state against the Welsh and to enrich the abbey.

Nevertheless, the discovery[10] did not put a quietus on the widespread belief that Arthur still lived on in a winterless isle. The author of *Floriant et Florete* (c. 1250) identified it with Sicily, for he informs us that the chief

---

[1] *Perlesvaus*, ed. Nitze and others, ii. 59–72; Nitze in *Spec*, ix (1934), 355–61; J. A. Robinson, *Two Glastonbury Legends* (Cambridge, 1926), pp. 8–17.

[2] Chambers, op. cit., p. 270; Faral, ii. 438 n., 439.

[3] On date see Tatlock in *Spec*, xiv (1939), 350–3.

[4] Chambers, op. cit., p. 264.   [5] *Spec*, xiii (1938), 39 f.

[6] *PMLA*, lvi (1941), 890 f., 907–9, 925 f.; Loomis, *Wales*, pp. 154–6, 165–7.

[7] Vss. 1946–51. Loomis, *Arthurian Tradition*, pp. 218–22.

[8] Chambers, op. cit., p. 123, says: 'It is only necessary to note that the Otherworld was also represented as an isle of glass, and that a poet's use of this conception for the realm of Melvas may perhaps have given a hint for the identification of Avallon with Glastonbury.' Cf. Lot in *R*, xxvii. 552 f.

[9] Chambers, op. cit., pp. 256 f.; Paton, op. cit., pp. 45 f.

[10] Faral argues plausibly (ii. 448–51) that it was the monastic authorities who were primarily responsible for the 'discovery'.

fortress of Morgain was Mongibel, that is, Etna, and that Arthur was destined to be brought there.[1] The waggish chronicler, Jean d'Outremeuse of Liége, seems to think of Avalon as in the Mediterranean, relating in *Ly Myreur des Histors*[2] (before 1400) how Ogier the Dane in the year 896 was shipwrecked on a rock nine days' sail from Cyprus, was rescued by angels, fought with a *capalus* (the Welsh Cath Palug)[3] and other monsters, and then with Arthur and Gawain. Morghe (Morgain) learned of Ogier's arrival in the isle of Avalon, conducted him to her palace, which was surrounded by pools and fruit-trees and adorned within with mural paintings, and placed on his finger a ring which restored his youth. There Ogier, forgetting the world, dwelt a long time with Arthur, Gawain, and many faery ladies.

Jean seems to have drawn on various sources, including a fourteenth-century poem about Ogier, which placed Avalon in the Far East, a little this side of the Earthly Paradise—a location evidently suggested by the elysian nature of both regions.[4] A Danish redactor of *Ogier* drew the natural inference that Avallon was India.[5] Its nearness to the Earthly Paradise is implied also by Guillem Torrella of Majorca, who in *La Faula*[6] (1360–70) told how he was transported by a whale 500 miles to the east, landed on an island, rode up to a palace decorated with paintings of Arthurian scenes (a recurring feature of Morgain's abode),[7] and discovered there the fay herself in the guise of a girl of sixteen, and a young man who, when asked if he were that Arthur whom the Bretons awaited, assented. His wound was healed by bathing in water from the Tigris River (which flowed from the Earthly Paradise) and his youth restored by annual visits of the Grail—a suggestion that as a wounded king he had been equated with the Maimed King of the Grail romances. An Eastern location for the land of Arthur and Morgain is also indicated in *Le Bastard de Bouillon* (c. 1350).[8] From the princes of Mecca Baudouin learned that beyond the Red Sea lay the land of faerie. With twelve barons he crossed over in a boat; they were welcomed by Arthur and his sister, and spent five years in a garden where a thousand fays disported themselves, losing all desire to return to their homes and wives.

The tradition of Arthur's sojourn in Sicily was blended by Gervase of

---

[1] *Floriant et Florete*, ed. H. F. Williams (Ann Arbor and London, 1947), vss. 566–9, 8200–250.

[2] Jean d'Outremeuse, *Myreur des Histors*, ed. S. Bormans (Brussels, 1877), iv. 47–58.

[3] See above, pp. 14 f.

[4] Paton, op. cit., p. 76.

[5] K. L. Rahbek, *Dansk og Norsk Nationalvaerk* (Copenhagen, 1828–30), i. 250.

[6] M. Mila y Fontanals, *Poetes Catalans* (Montpellier, 1876), pp. 9–21; W. Entwistle, *Arthurian Legend in the Literature of the Spanish Peninsula* (London, 1925), pp. 81–84, 186–9; *Canconer dels Comtes d'Urgell*, ed. D. G. Llabres (Societat Catalana de Bibliofils, 1906), pp. 131 ff. See Chap. 31 below.

[7] Loomis, *Arthurian Tradition*, pp. 93 f., 157; H. O. Sommer, *Vulgate Version of the Arthurian Romances*, v. 217 f.; vi. 238.

[8] *Bastars de Buillon*, ed. A. Scheler (Brussels, 1877), pp. 119–32.

Tilbury (*c.* 1211) with the belief that he dwelt in the cavernous depths of a mountain.[1] A groom of the Bishop of Catania, in pursuit of a runaway palfrey, entered the side of Mount Etna through a narrow path, emerged on a delightful plain, and discovered Arthur lying on a regal couch in a marvellous palace. Here the king had lain since the battle with Modred, his wounds annually breaking out afresh. The subterranean abode of Arthur was confused with Avalon by Étienne de Rouen in his *Draco Normannicus*[2] (*c.* 1169), in which he made a mock of the Breton hope. Arthur is said to have gone to the isle of Avalon to be healed and rendered immortal by his sister Morganis. He was made ruler of the lower hemisphere, and in an imaginary correspondence with Henry II he warns the Angevin against molesting the Bretons and announces that he has come, with a host of his antipodean subjects, to their rescue by way of India, Parthia, Arabia, and the Cyclades. In the nineteenth century several caves in Wales were reputed to be the dwelling-place of Arthur and his sleeping warriors, awaiting the day when they would come forth and recover their land.[3]

The legend of Arthur in the hollow mountain took other forms. The thirteenth-century *Wartburgkrieg* makes allusion to Arthur as dwelling 'in dem berge' with the Sibyl's child and with hundreds of knights whom he had brought from Britain; there they live in delight, supplied with food, drink, arms, and horses.[4] An English poem, *A Dispute between a Christian and a Jew* (*c.* 1375), describes a vision of Arthur and the knights of the Round Table in a magnificent manor, reached by a path under a hill.[5] Stories akin to the Welsh cave legends of Arthur and his sleeping men, awaiting their destined hour to sally forth, were reported in the last century from Richmond castle and Sewingshields in northern England, and quite recently from Alderley Edge, south of Manchester.[6] The country folk in the neighbourhood of Cadbury Castle, an earthwork in Somerset, firmly believed that Arthur lived on under the hill, and a party of antiquaries who visited this spot in the last century were approached by an old man with the question, 'Have you come

---

[1] Gervase of Tilbury, *Otia Imperialia*, ed. F. Liebrecht (Hannover, 1856), pp. 12 f. See on this legend and the similar one told by Caesarius of Heisterbach A. Graf, *Miti, Leggende, e Superstizioni del Medio Evo* (Turin, 1893), ii. 303–31; Krappe in *Mitteilungen der Schlesischen Gesellschaft für Volkskunde*, xxv (1935), 90–102.

[2] *Chronicles of the Reigns of Stephen, Henry II and Richard I*, ed. R. Howlett (1884–9), ii. 696–707. For discussion cf. Tatlock in *MP*, xxxi (1933), 1–18, 113–25; R. S. Loomis in *MP*, xxxviii (1941), 289–304.

[3] J. Rhŷs, *Celtic Folklore, Welsh and Manx* (Oxford, 1901), ii. 458–77; T. Gwynn Jones, *Welsh Folklore and Folk Custom* (London, 1930), pp. 87–89.

[4] *Wartburgkrieg*, ed. K. Simrock (Stuttgart, 1858), stanzas 83–87; P. S. Barto, *Tannhäuser and the Mountain of Venus* (New York, 1916), pp. 11 f., 116 f.

[5] *Minor Poems of the Vernon Manuscript*, ed. F. J. Furnivall, part ii (EETS 117), pp. 488–90.

[6] J. Hodgson, *History of Northumberland* (Newcastle, 1840), part 2, iii. 287; T. Parkinson, *Yorkshire Legends and Traditions* (London, 1889), ii. 169 f.; *Monthly Chronicle of North-Country Lore and Legend*, 1888, pp. 220–2; 1889, p. 41; 1891, p. 567; *Folklore*, lxix (1958), 15.

to take the king out?'[1] It surely makes one reflect on the fallibility of rational expectations that the belief in Arthur's survival was still flourishing at a place within sight of Glastonbury, where 700 years before his bones had been officially discovered and where his tomb had been displayed for centuries for all and sundry to behold.

Here at Cadbury there survived also the concept of Arthur as leader of the Wild Hunt, the phantom chase known to the peasantry throughout much of Europe; for an old track near the camp was called King Arthur's Lane, and on rough winter nights the king and his hounds were heard going along it.[2] In many parts of France likewise the phenomenon was called 'la Chasse Artu',[3] and this goes back to at least the twelfth century. Gervase of Tilbury and the *Didot Perceval* record the belief early in the thirteenth,[4] and about 1260 Étienne de Bourbon tells how on a moonlight night a woodcutter met near the Mont du Chat in Savoy a large hunting-party, who declared that they were of King Arthur's household and that his court was near by.[5] He followed them into a most noble palace, filled with knights and ladies, dancing and feasting. As directed, he lay down in a bed beside a beautiful lady, went to sleep, only to find himself the next morning ignominiously reposing on a bundle of faggots. This story combines three themes: 'la Chasse Artu', the voluptuous fay,[6] and the common folk-tale ending of the visit to the fairy palace.[7]

A related story is told about Peter des Roches, Bishop of Winchester, in the *Lanercost Chronicle* under the date 1216.[8] The worldly prelate was hunting when he saw with astonishment a splendid mansion. Servants invited him to dine with their master and ushered him into the presence of a king who confessed himself to be Arthur. In order that the bishop might convince sceptics that he had actually seen the ancient lord of Britain,[9] Arthur endowed him with the miraculous power of producing a butterfly whenever he wished by opening his closed fist.

We have a unique version of Arthur's survival alluded to by Godfrey of

---

[1] J. A. Robinson, *Two Glastonbury Legends*, p. 53; F. J. Snell, *King Arthur's Country* (London and New York, 1926), pp. 50–57.

[2] Snell, op. cit., pp. 52 f.

[3] F. Sébillot, *Folklore de France* (Paris, 1904), i. 167–9, 172, 177, 241.

[4] Gervase of Tilbury, op. cit., p. 12; *RR*, iii (1912), 191–3; xii (1921), 286–9; *Didot Perceval*, ed. W. Roach (Philadelphia, 1941), p. 277.

[5] Chambers, op. cit., p. 278; A. Lecoy de la Marche, *Anecdotes Historiques d'Étienne de Bourbon* (Paris, 1877), p. 321.

[6] Loomis, *Arthurian Tradition*, pp. 228–32.

[7] Rhŷs, *Celtic Folklore*, i. 100, 116.

[8] G. G. Coulton, *Life in the Middle Ages*, i. 52 f.; *Lanercost Chronicle*, ed. J. Stevenson (London, 1839), p. 23.

[9] On motif of evidential token cf. E. S. Hartland, *Science of Fairy Tales* (New York, n.d.), p. 148; T. P. Cross, C. N. Slover, *Ancient Irish Tales* (New York, 1936), p. 251; *Thomas of Erceldoune*, ed. J.A. H. Murray (London, 1875), pp. 18 f.

Viterbo, secretary to Frederick Barbarossa, about 1190.[1] Merlin prophesies that though the king will perish from wounds, he will not perish wholly but will be preserved in the depths of the sea and will reign for ever as before.

This array of diverse traditions about the survival of the British hero calls for three remarks. First, they embody an interesting variety of Celtic concepts of the Other World and its inhabitants. The concept of a sleeping deity surrounded by his attendants was attached by Plutarch to an island near Britain, where Cronus was imprisoned, with Briareus keeping guard over him as he slept; around him were many deities, his henchmen.[2] The concept, given us by Geoffrey of Monmouth, of an isle of nine enchantresses, endowed with gifts of prophecy and shape-shifting, who cured the ills of those who sought them, was attached by Pomponius Mela to Sein, an island off the coast of Brittany.[3] The island paradise is familiar to readers of the *Voyage of Bran*, the isle of amorous women, to readers of the *Voyage of Maelduin*.[4] The subterranean world of noble dwarfs was reported by Giraldus Cambrensis to have been visited by a boy of Swansea.[5] The Wild Huntsman was identified by the Welsh with Gwyn ap Nudd, a king of the Other World, whom we have already met in Chap. 4.[6]

Secondly, it must be obvious that the spread and elaboration of these beliefs in Arthur's survival were almost entirely oral. Not even by the exercise of extreme ingenuity and the multiplication of lost manuscripts can one trace them back to the *Prophetiae Merlini* and the *Draco Normannicus*.

Thirdly, there is a sort of corollary in the fact that these legends were largely ignored by the romancers who dealt with Arthur and his times, except for the references by Malory and the authors of the *Didot Perceval* and *Floriant*. Most literary men seem to have felt that they could not compromise their own credibility by taking such ridiculous notions seriously. Nevertheless, as we have seen, the legends cropped up in the most unexpected places, they resisted the attacks of scepticism, they outlasted the marble tomb of Arthur itself. It is an astounding phenomenon that belief in Arthur's survival was still living 1,300 years after his death.

[1] E. G. Gardner, *Arthurian Legend in Italian Literature*, p. 10.

[2] Plutarch, *De Defectu Oraculorum*, sec. 18; R. S. Loomis, *Celtic Myth and Arthurian Romance* (New York, 1927), p. 323.

[3] Mela, *De Situ Orbis*, bk. iii, ch. 6; L. A. Paton, *Fairy Mythology*, pp. 43 f. For a remarkable parallel in modern Irish folklore cf. Lady F. S. Wilde, *Ancient Legends, Mystic Charms, and Superstitions of Ireland* (London, 1888), p. 114.

[4] Cross and Slover, op. cit., pp. 589 f.; *RC*, x (1889), 62–71; H. D'Arbois de Jubainville, *Épopée Celtique en Irlande* (Paris, 1892), pp. 485–8.

[5] Giraldus, *Opera*, vi, ed. J. F. Dimock (London, 1868), 75 f.; *MP*, xxxviii (1941), 294 f.

[6] Rhŷs, *Celtic Folklore*, i. 216. On Wild Huntsman in Arthurian romance cf. below, pp. 535 f., and Loomis, *Arthurian Tradition*, index of subjects, *sub* Huntsman. On the Wild Hunt see Flasdieck in *Anglia*, lxi (1937), 225–340.

8

GEOFFREY OF MONMOUTH

JOHN J. PARRY AND ROBERT A. CALDWELL[1]

THE name of Geoffrey of Monmouth has already cropped up several times in the preceding chapters, and will inevitably crop up again and again in the rest of this book. It was he who, according to William of Newburgh (c. 1198), 'disguised under the honourable name of history, thanks to his Latinity, the fables about Arthur which he took from the ancient fictions of the Britons and increased out of his own head'. It was he who, according to the same ironic chronicler, made the little finger of Arthur thicker than the loins of Alexander the Great. Though many will question the extent of his influence on the Arthurian romances of England and the Continent, no one will question his enormous influence on the medieval prophetic tradition, or the fact that his account of early Britain was swallowed by most of the medieval chroniclers of Europe and was not generally discredited until late in the sixteenth century.

The Life

About Geoffrey's early life we know nothing.[2] The date 'about 1100' sometimes given for his birth is little more than a reasonable conjecture. He calls himself 'Galfridus Monemutensis',[3] but whether this indicates that he was born at Monmouth, with the neighbourhood of which he shows some familiarity in his writings, or that he later resided there is unknown. As a witness to documents he signed himself 'Galfridus Arturus', which means undoubtedly 'Geoffrey son of Arthur',[4] but nothing more is known of his

---

[1] Editor's note.—This chapter is in the main the work of the late Professor Parry, but owing to ill health he left it in a state with which, he frankly said, he was not satisfied. Accordingly, the editor has exercised his judgement to condense or clarify or expand Parry's text, and has had the valuable co-operation of Professor Caldwell in this task. They have scrupulously avoided attributing to Parry any opinions with which he would have disagreed, and have left standing the few statements to which they do not subscribe. Only the paragraphs dealing with the Variant Version of the *Historia Regum Britanniae* constitute an addition for which Parry is in no way responsible.

[2] The best biography is by J. E. Lloyd in *English Historical Review*, lvii (1942), 460–8. Others are in Faral, ii. 1–38; J. S. P. Tatlock, *Legendary History of Britain* (Berkeley and Los Angeles, 1950), chap. xx; Chambers, *Arthur of Britain* (London, 1927), chap. ii.

[3] *Historia*, I. i; VII. ii; XI. i. (For convenience the division into books and chapters employed by Commelius in his edition of 1587 is used, though it has little manuscript authority.) In the *Vita Merlini*, vs. 1526, occurs the form 'Gaufrido de Monumeta'.

[4] William of Newburgh's taunt in *Historia Regum Anglicarum*, Proemium, that Geoffrey was given this name because he had cloaked fables about Arthur with the honest name of history loses

parentage. Since both Geoffrey and Arthur were names rare in Wales but not uncommon in Brittany, some scholars,[1] as noted in Chap. 6, have suggested that he was of Breton descent and have tried to connect him with the priory founded at Monmouth by Wihenoc, a Breton, who became lord of the town in 1075. They also point out that Geoffrey's *Historia* is much more favourable to the Bretons than to the Welsh; but they forget that the Welsh were technically, and often actually, opposed to the party in power, whereas the Bretons were valued allies—a point which a man of Geoffrey's ambition could hardly overlook. It is well to observe, too, that his later *Vita Merlini* shows no lack of sympathy toward the Welsh.[2]

The earliest records of Geoffrey are connected with Oxford, not Monmouth.[3] He appears as one of the witnesses to the foundation charter of Osney Abbey, granted in 1129 or thereabouts, and during the next twenty-two years his name occurs as witness to six other documents connected with Oxford or its vicinity. Until Walter's death in the early part of 1151, he is associated in these with Walter, Archdeacon of Oxford, whom he mentions in the *Historia* as the source of his material; and in several also with Robert de Chesney, who later became Bishop of Lincoln. Walter was Provost of the secular College of St. George's at Oxford—a well-endowed house of five or six Augustinian canons, which in 1149 was transferred to Osney Abbey—and Robert was one of its canons. It is natural to infer that Geoffrey was connected with the same house and that, since he twice styled himself 'magister', he was engaged in teaching. Oxford was already a centre of instruction, though not yet a university. During the years 1129–1151 he wrote the works by which he is known.

The first to appear was the *Prophetiae Merlini* or *Libellus Merlini*, which, at the request of Alexander, Bishop of Lincoln, his ecclesiastical superior (Oxford being then in the diocese of Lincoln), Geoffrey laid aside the *Historia* to write. It was probably completed before 1 December 1135. His greatest effort, in which he incorporated the *Prophetiae*, was the *Historia Regum Britanniae*. Tatlock gives reasons for thinking that it was begun by 1130 or shortly after, but it seems from the dedications not to have been finished until after the death of King Henry I in December 1135. These dedications make it clear that Geoffrey was seeking for royal favour—for the time being without success. Probably his last work was a poem, the *Vita*

force when it is considered that Geoffrey was using the name before his account of Arthur became known. The Welsh form, Gruffydd ap Arthur, is not found before the end of the sixteenth century.

[1] Particularly Tatlock in *Legendary History*, pp. 396–402, 440, 443. On p. 439 Tatlock notes that Geoffrey calls himself a *Brito* (MS. Bib. Nat. latin 6233; see Faral, iii. 189, variants).

[2] The statement that Geoffrey was related to the Bishop and the Archdeacon of Llandaff rests on the *Gwentian Brut*, largely forged by Iolo Morgannwg (Edward Williams, 1746–1826). See W. Lewis Jones in *THSC*, 1898–9, p. 57. On Geoffrey's treatment of Llandaff see C. Brooke in *Studies in the Early British Church*, pp. 201–11.

[3] H. E. Salter in *English Historical Review*, xxxiv (1919), 382 ff.

Merlini, dedicated to his new bishop, Robert de Chesney, with the expressed hope that Robert would do more for him than had Alexander.

Bishop Alexander had been on the side of Matilda, but Robert, either directly or through his brother William, had influence with King Stephen, and early in 1151 Geoffrey somewhat prematurely witnessed a grant of land as 'Episcopus Sancti Asaphi'. Later in the same year he signed more correctly as witness to one of Robert's charters, 'Electus Sancti Asaphi'. The records at Canterbury show that on 11 February 1152 Archbishop Theobald ordained him to the priesthood, and on the twenty-first of the same month consecrated him Bishop of St. Asaph.[1] This unimportant bishopric had long been in abeyance until revived in 1143. It is most improbable that Geoffrey ever visited it, because of the revolt of the Welsh under Owain Gwynedd and Owain's victory at Coleshill in Flint in 1150, to which there may be allusion in the *Vita Merlini*. His one recorded episcopal act was the witnessing, last among the bishops, of the charter King Stephen issued at Westminster before Christmas in 1153 confirming the provisions of the Treaty of Winchester and preparing the way for Henry of Anjou to come to the throne the next year. Geoffrey's death, which took place some time in 1155,[2] is recorded only in the Welsh chronicles.

There is no indication that Geoffrey was an irreligious man, or that he was a bad ecclesiastic; but certainly his main interest was not in the cure of souls, and as an historian he had no devotion to historical truth. He was primarily a man of letters and no doubt entered the Church because it provided the only career open to a man of his abilities and interests. In the *Historia* he showed little concern for that institution or for religion, in his other writings none at all. The few churchmen he presents are not, with the possible exception of Dubricius, pre-eminent for their sanctity. In laymen he admires and praises the qualities exemplified by his Norman overlords: efficiency, even brutal and ruthless, the 'good security' for which the *Peterborough Chronicle* praises the Conqueror, foreign conquest, and liberality. There is little enough of Christian faith, charity, and good works.

But as a writer he wins high praise. Though the preferment we know him to have received came late and may have been less than he desired, he won from his contemporaries the reward which the dedications in the *Historia* and the *Vita Merlini* show to have been an impelling purpose of his writing, and he could have hoped for no greater literary success than that gained by the *Historia*. With more of talent than genius, he provided for the Britons, whom

---

[1] See Faral, ii. 37, and *R*, liii (1927), 41 f. There is ample evidence that the date 1151 is an error for 1152.

[2] All the Welsh manuscripts make Geoffrey Bishop of Llandaff, an error which must go back to their common Latin original. The Peniarth *Brut* gives the date of his death as 1154, but all the dates in this section are a year out. The statement in the Red Book *Brut* that Geoffrey died at Mass, *ar offeren*, is due to the scribe's misreading of *a rosser*, 'and Roger', written with long *s*.

he found without a history, one that was not seriously challenged for four centuries, established his greatest creation, Arthur, in history, contributed at least indirectly to the vogue of Arthurian romance, and left to later literature the stories of Sabrina, Ferrex and Porrex, and Lear. Well read, though not deeply learned, he pillaged other authors with unequalled audacity to fabricate what he certainly did not believe himself, and he did so with an unerring eye for what would prove acceptable. Vivid and concrete, practical and sophisticated, with a minimum of marvels and only a touch of grotesque humour, he mingled borrowed fact, which he twisted as he saw fit, with his own effective but purely imaginary detail to give an account that was plausible, if unverifiable, and convincing to most of his contemporaries because his characters behaved exactly as they did themselves. He wrote, as Tatlock says, 'very well indeed, competently, picturesquely and above all tersely . . . in the medieval manner, which did not pretend to be classical'.[1] The result was no more dishonest and far more brilliant than the creations of a multitude of hagiographers—which is perhaps the fairest judgement an age with different standards of literary and historical honesty can pass on his mendacities.

'Prophetiae Merlini'[2]

The title used by Geoffrey himself, *Prophetiae Merlini* (*Historia*, VII. ii), is in general adopted by later writers. He tells us that he had originally intended to deal with these prophecies after he had completed the *Historia*, but that when stories about Merlin began to circulate ('de Merlino divulgato rumore'), his associates—especially Alexander, Bishop of Lincoln—urged him to publish the prophecies first. This he did, dedicating the finished work to Bishop Alexander, as already noted.[3] That this was before the end of 1135 is probable, for Ordericus Vitalis in his *Historia Ecclesiastica* (xii. 47), writing after the death of Duke Robert of Normandy but while King Henry I was still alive—and therefore between 10 February 1134 and 1 December 1135—gives extensive selections from what he calls 'the Merlin pamphlet' ('de Merlini libello'); he does not mention Geoffrey by name, but the

---

[1] Tatlock, op. cit., p. 445.

[2] For the text of the *Prophetiae*, see editions of the *Historia*, bk. vii, and Faral, iii. 189–202. Early editions, without the *Historia*, are in Michel and Wright, *Vita Merlini* (Paris, 1837), and in San Marte (A. Schulz), *Sagen von Merlin* (Halle, 1853). The latter contains much valuable source material about Merlin, but also the forgeries of La Villemarqué. The *Prophetiae* are discussed as part of the *Historia* in the works cited below, p. 79, n. 10, and also by Rupert Taylor, *Political Prophecy in England* (New York, 1911), by Margaret E. Griffiths, *Early Vaticination in Welsh with English Parallels* (Cardiff, 1937), and by P. Zumthor, *Merlin le Prophète* (Lausanne, 1943).

[3] The fact that Geoffrey referred in his introduction to Alexander, who died in 1148, in the imperfect tense ('Non erat in clero', &c.) has been interpreted by Faral (ii. 11 n.), not as implying that the bishop was dead but as referring to the time in the past when Geoffrey received the commission from him.

reference is unmistakable.[1] Once the *Prophetiae* were finished, Geoffrey resumed work on the *Historia*, incorporating the prophecies, as well as the dedicatory letter and an account of the circumstances under which the work was composed.

Geoffrey tells us that he translated the prophecies from the Welsh,[2] and in a limited sense this was probably true. There is no evidence that at this time he had any command of that language, but he would have had little difficulty in learning the style and something of the substance of this material from those who did. William of Newburgh, no friendly critic, accepts Geoffrey's statement on this point, but says that he added much of his own.[3]

No one today doubts, of course, that much of the material in the *Prophetiae* is of Geoffrey's own invention. Some, too, is old material transmuted in the borrowing, like Nennius's tale of the marvellous boy Ambrosius,[4] whom Geoffrey identified with the prophet Merlin and to whom he attributed speeches of his own devising. But after allowance has been made for all inventions and transmutations, there seems to be a residue which is traditional. There are, as Tatlock points out, such ideas as the hope of a union of the Celts against the English and the proposal for the establishment of a bishopric at St. David's, which are at variance with sentiments which Geoffrey expresses elsewhere but are in accord with Welsh aspirations.[5] And the prediction of the coming of Cadwalader and Cynan to drive out the Saxon invaders, as well as the presentation of Myrddin as a prophet, is found in *Armes Prydein (The Omen of Britain)*, which is dated about 930.[6]

Further evidence of traditional sources comes from Giraldus Cambrensis, who in his *Itinerarium Cambriae* (II. viii) carefully distinguished two Merlins. The first, 'called Ambrosius, who prophesied in the time of King Vortigern', is, of course, the Merlin of Geoffrey's *Historia*, and the predictions which Giraldus ascribes to him are all to be found in that work. The other Merlin, Giraldus says, 'born in Scotland, was named Celidonius, from the Celidonian

---

[1] Tatlock, op. cit., p. 418, unlike other scholars, denies that there was more than one version of the *Prophetiae*. Admitting 'one advance copy, presumably for the bishop and his circle', he seems to imply that this copy was never reproduced, and it is quite clear that he believes the text to have been 'included in the *Historia* . . . with little or no change'. The seventeen or so manuscripts to which he refers (p. 418, n. 68) are meagre evidence for a sweeping conclusion. Cf. the wide divergence of the readings of the text noticed in *Spec*, xxiii (1948), 102–3.

[2] MS. Bib. Nat. latin 6233 makes Geoffrey assert that he translated from Welsh verse: 'quod in Britannico Merlinus dulciter et metrice cecinit.' Faral, ii. 24–26; iii. 189, variants.

[3] See Chambers, op. cit., pp. 274 ff.

[4] Faral, iii. 30 ff.

[5] This fact is used by Tatlock in support of his argument (*Legendary History*, pp. 409–16) that Geoffrey did not compose all the prophecies.

[6] When a scholar like Sir Ifor Williams, who has devoted his life to the study of the subject, says in his *Lectures on Early Welsh Poetry* (Dublin, 1944), p. 54: 'I think we can date *Armes Prydein* circa 930, without any hesitation whatsoever', we need not take too seriously the intuition of non-Celtists like Bruce, Faral, and Zumthor that Merlin is practically the creation of Geoffrey.

wood in which he prophesied, and Silvester, because, when engaged in martial conflict, he discovered in the air a terrible monster, and from that time grew mad, and taking shelter in a wood, lived a woodland life until his death.[1] This Merlin lived in the time of King Arthur, and is said to have prophesied more fully and explicitly than the other.' In the *Expugnatio Hibernica* (iii) Giraldus tells us further that the prophecies of Merlin Silvester have been preserved orally by many of the bards, in writing by only a few. He had sought for a long time for a manuscript of them and ultimately found one in a remote part of Lleyn in North Wales. He had translated these prophecies into Latin—after freeing them from the late matter with which modern bards had adulterated them—intending to publish the collection as a third part of the *Expugnatio*. Of this projected third part we have only the introduction, but Giraldus did, as he tells us, insert selections from the prophecies of both the Merlins in various places in the first two parts as the subject called for them.[2] Altogether he gives nineteen sentences, three of them twice, which he credits to Merlin Silvester. Not one of them is to be found in the work of Geoffrey; but eight of them are found in the *Prophecy of the Eagle*, which occurs in either Welsh or Latin in a number of manuscripts.[3] Native tradition is also found in a work attributed to John of Cornwall,[4] written between December 1154 and the early part of 1156, which covers much the same ground as Geoffrey and uses many of the same images, but does not seem to have been borrowed from the *Prophetiae*. It appears, rather, that both authors drew from a common source.

As Geoffrey presents his material it falls definitely into three parts, which follow one another without a break. In the first he deals with events which had already taken place—or were supposed to have taken place—at the time when he was writing, but which would still have been in the future in Merlin's day. Concerning these Merlin is able to be definite, although his presentation is cryptic. Portions of this part are, in both form and content, so like the vaticinations quoted by Giraldus and John of Cornwall, or those found in the *Prophecy of the Eagle*, as to make it certain that here Geoffrey mixed native traditions with matter of his own in order to give to the whole a semblance of veracity. The latest historical reference which can be identified

[1] That Giraldus is not drawing from Geoffrey is shown by the fact that this cause for Merlin's madness is not mentioned in any of the Welsh poems or in Geoffrey. It is given in the Scottish and Irish versions. See below, p. 90, nn. 4, 5; p. 91, n. 4.

[2] See under Merlin Ambrose and Merlin Silvester in the index to vol. v of the Rolls edition of Giraldus.

[3] *Brut y Brenhinedd*, ed. J. J. Parry (Cambridge, Mass., 1937), pp. 30–33. The Red Book text, a different version, is printed in *BBCS*, ix (1935), 112–15. Parry printed the Latin text on pp. 225 f. from MS. Cotton Faustina A viii, with variants from two other manuscripts.

[4] Printed by Carl Greith, *Spicilegium Vaticanum* (Frauenfeld, 1838), pp. 92–104; also, without introduction and notes, by Hersart de la Villemarqué in *Myrdhinn* (Paris, 1862), pp. 417–22. Discussed by Rupert Taylor, *Political Prophecy*, pp. 16–21.

with certainty is to the sinking of the White Ship in 1120: 'The Lion's Cubs [the children of Henry I] shall be transformed into fishes of the sea.' Some manuscripts also contain a reference to the death of King Henry I in 1135: 'Woe unto thee, Neustria, for the brain of the Lion shall be poured out upon thee', which must have been a late addition.

After establishing the reputation of Merlin as a prophet, Geoffrey goes on in the second, much longer, part to foretell events that were in the future for him as well as for Merlin. Some, like the coining of round halfpennies, had been discussed but not carried out when Geoffrey wrote.[1] Others, like the conquest of Ireland, might have been foreseen by anyone who followed the course of events; still other predictions are couched in such general terms that later commentators were able to make them apply to events as they happened. As this part progresses, the forecasts become more and more fantastic, until finally Geoffrey abandons any pretence of keeping in touch with reality. There are more disturbances of Nature, and in the animal symbolism asses, oxen, and goats are added to the dragons, wolves, and boars of the earlier part. Luxury and vice are castigated: 'Women shall become serpents in their gait, and all their steps be full of pride'; out of a worm 'shall issue forth seven lions disfigured by heads of goats. With the stench of their nostrils shall they corrupt women, and their own wives shall they cause to be as harlots.' There is something of an obsession, not very like Geoffrey, as Tatlock notes, with naked men and giants fighting and riding on monsters.

In the final part the symbolism is changed somewhat to produce an astro-logical nightmare, which Tatlock calls a 'Götterdammerung': 'Stilbon of Arcady shall change his shield, and the helmet of Mars shall call unto Venus. ... The Virgin shall forget her maiden shame, and climb up on the back of the Sagittary. ... In the twinkling of an eye shall the seas lift them up, and the dust of them of old again begin to live. With a baleful blast shall the winds do battle together, and the sound thereof shall be heard amongst the stars.' Tatlock follows Rydberg in finding the source of this material in Lucan's *Pharsalia* (i. 639–72), but the resemblance is not very close. Others have pointed out that the Bible had a considerable influence on the tone and style.

The *Prophetiae* are often found in manuscript by themselves,[2] as well as incorporated in the *Historia*. Some texts are provided with interlinear or marginal commentaries, a number of which have been printed by Hammer.[3] The most elaborate of all the commentaries is that which was formerly

---

[1] Tatlock, op. cit., p. 404.

[2] H. L. D. Ward, *Catalogue of the Romances in the Department of Manuscripts in the British Museum*, i (London, 1883), 292–303; Tatlock, op. cit., p. 418.

[3] *Spec*, x (1935), 3–30; xv (1940), 409–31; *Quarterly Bull. Polish Inst. of Arts and Sciences in America*, i (1943), 589–601; *Hommages à Joseph Bidez et à Franz Cumont* (Brussels, 1949), pp. 111–19; *Charisteria Thaddaeo Sinko ... Oblata* (Warsaw, 1951), pp. 81–89; Gerould in *Spec*, xxiii (1948), 102 f.

attributed in error to Alanus de Insulis, and which was written, as De Lage's evidence shows, between 1167 and 1174, and was printed at Frankfurt in 1603 and again in 1608.[1]

The *Prophetiae Merlini* were taken most seriously, even by the learned and worldly wise, in many nations.[2] The Welsh seized on them, as might be expected, and seem to have translated them separately from the *Historia*, even when both works are found together in one manuscript,[3] and there is evidence that more than one translation was made.[4] Wace omitted them in his version of the *Historia* because he did not know how to interpret them, but early translations into French were made and inserted into some of the Wace manuscripts, apparently in three different versions.[5] Abbot Suger, between 1138 and 1144, and Caesarius of Heisterbach (*c.* 1220) testified to their accuracy, and Jean Wauquelin translated them with the *Historia* in 1445.[6] The chronicler Salimbene tells us that the sayings of Merlin enjoyed an authority equal to that of the Sibyl, Michael Scott, and Isaiah in Italy,[7] where between 1272 and 1279 the pseudonymous Richard of Ireland produced the long French *Prophecies de Merlin*, combining adventures adapted from the *Vulgate Lancelot*, the *Prose Tristan*, and *Palamedes* with *ex post facto* and apocalyptic predictions.[8] Castile was plagued by pseudo-prophecies under the name of Merlin,[9] and the *Prophetiae* were translated in Holland and Iceland, as will be shown in Chaps. 34 and 35. There was scarcely a cranny of Christendom outside the Eastern Church which did not recognize Merlin as a great seer.

'Historia Regum Britanniae'

The title *Historia Regum Britanniae*[10] is that used, or at least implied, by Geoffrey in the first chapter of his most influential work, though in the Epistle dedicating the *Prophetiae Merlini* to Bishop Alexander (VII. ii) he

---

[1] See above, p. 62. Taylor in *Political Prophecy*, p. 88, dates the book 1174–9. Brial in *Hist. Lit. de la France*, xvi, 417, dates it on historical evidence 1167–83, and credits it to Alan, Prior of the Chapter of Canterbury in 1179, made Abbot of Tewkesbury in 1186 (whom he identifies with Alanus de Insulis). Alphandéry in *Enc. Brit.* (11th ed.), under 'Alain of Lille', accepts the attribution to Alan of Tewkesbury (but denies the identification with Alanus de Insulis).

[2] Taylor, *Political Prophecy*, pp. 134–42; P. Zumthor, *Merlin le Prophète* (Lausanne, 1943), pp. 49–114.

[3] *Brut y Brenhinedd*, ed. Parry, p. x.

[4] Ibid., p. xiv.

[5] Wace, *Roman de Brut*, ed. I. Arnold (1938–40), i, vss. 7539–40; pp. viii, x, xii.

[6] Taylor, *Political Prophecy*, pp. 138–40; Ward, *Catalogue of the Romances*, i. 251–53.

[7] G. G. Coulton, *From St. Francis to Dante* (London, 1908), pp. 213 f., 240, 245.

[8] *Prophecies de Merlin*, ed. Lucy A. Paton (New York, 1926). See below, pp. 352–4.

[9] W. J. Entwistle, *Arthurian Legend in the Literatures of the Spanish Peninsula* (London, 1925), p. 20; Gutierre Diez de Games, *Cronica de Don Pedro Nino*, ed. Laguno, pp. 29 f.

[10] The modern editions of the *Historia* are by A. Griscom (London, New York, 1929), who prints one manuscript and records the variants of two others in medieval spelling, and by E. Faral, iii. 63–303, who prints one manuscript with a minimum of correction from three others (the variants of which are recorded) in classical spelling. J. Hammer published a *Variant Version* (Cambridge, Mass., 1951), but unfortunately used as the basis of his text a manuscript in which the Variant Version was

implies that which he used in the *Vita Merlini* (vs. 1529), *Gesta Britonum*. The earliest reference we have to the *Historia* comes from January 1139, when Henry of Huntingdon stopped at the abbey of Bec in Normandy, and there, to his great surprise ('stupens inveni'), was shown by the monk Robert of Torigni a British history of which he had never heard—'the big book of Geoffrey Arthur'.[1] He sent a summary of this to his compatriot and friend Warinus, of Breton descent, and because this differs in certain respects from the text as we know it, some have thought that what Henry saw was an early version into which the *Prophetiae* had not yet been incorporated; others are convinced that a manuscript now at Leyden is the very one that Robert showed him. All that is certain is that the Leyden manuscript was in the library at Bec before 1154, and that no other has ever been found which agrees better with Henry's summary.

Attempts have been made to determine the early history of the work from the various forms of dedication in the different manuscripts.[2] There is no general agreement on the matter, but the following seems to be the most satisfactory interpretation. The work was completed very soon after the death of King Henry I on 1 December 1135. Henry had designated as his heir his daughter Matilda, now wife of Geoffrey Count of Anjou, whose son Henry was still an infant. Geoffrey of Monmouth showed his devotion to her cause by dedicating his book to her chief supporter, Robert Earl of Gloucester, whom he hailed as 'another Henry'. And for good measure, when Geoffrey inserted his *Prophetiae* into the *Historia*, he retained at the beginning of them his dedication to Bishop Alexander, a supporter of Matilda.

But the crown went to Stephen instead of to Matilda, and although Robert swore conditional allegiance to him, Geoffrey evidently felt the need of a more active display of loyalty. So he quickly wrote a new dedication, this time jointly to Robert and Waleran of Beaumont, Count of Meulan and later Earl of Worcester, who had been associated with Robert in the service of King Henry and was now enjoying Stephen's particular favour. Even this dedication was not enough for Geoffrey, and in one manuscript, the famous one at Bern, Robert is dropped to second place, replacing Waleran, and King Stephen is put at the head with the attributes formerly ascribed to Robert. The most likely date for such a double dedication is April 1136, when

---

conflated with the Vulgate. See pp. 86 f. below. The *Historia* has been discussed most fully by Faral in vol. ii of *Légende Arthurienne*; by Tatlock in *Legendary History of Britain*; by R. H. Fletcher in *Arthurian Material in the Chronicles* (Boston, 1906; Burt Franklin: New York, 1958); and most recently by W. F. Schirmer, *Die frühen Darstellungen des Arthurstoffes* (Köln, Opladen, 1958), pp. 7–40.

[1] Faral, ii. 18–23; Chambers, pp. 44–46, 251.

[2] Faral, ii. 10–28; *R*, liii (1927), 18 ff.; *Historia*, ed. Griscon, pp. 42–98; Brugger in *ZFSL*, lvii (1933), 270; Chambers, pp. 41–44; Tatlock, op. cit., pp. 436 f. Hammer has made it clear in *Bull. Polish Inst. of Arts and Sciences in America*, ii (1944), 501–64, and in *Variant Version*, pp. 4 ff., that the dedications can be relied on only for the external, not for the textual, history of the work.

Stephen and Robert met at Oxford, where Geoffrey was, but it may have been as much as two years later. In April 1138 Robert definitely broke with Stephen, and after that their names would hardly have been coupled. In still other manuscripts all dedication is omitted or appears in an abridged form. Robert died in 1147 and Alexander in 1148, and thereafter a dedication to either would have been pointless; Geoffrey was now looking to Stephen for preferment, and he secured it not long after.

In all forms of the dedication Geoffrey pretends that his book is merely a plain translation into Latin of 'a very old book in the British language'— 'britannici sermonis librum vetustissimum'—which Walter Archdeacon of Oxford (with whom we have seen Geoffrey was associated) has offered him and which contains the stories of all the kings of Britain from Brutus to Cadwalader, told in language of great beauty. At the close of the *Historia*, in relinquishing the story of the kings who had succeeded Cadwalader in Wales to Caradoc of Lancarvan, he adds the information that Walter had brought the book in the British language 'ex Britannia'. *Britannia* might be used at this time to designate the island of Britain, and also, as Geoffrey tells us, to refer to Brittany: 'Armoricum regnum quod nunc Britannia dicitur.' But the name was still used in a third sense to denote the British part of the island. Geoffrey, writing in England, could have meant by *ex Britannia* 'out of Wales', and this is the sense, surely, which he intended.[1]

Whether he had such a book as he describes is quite another matter, and the evidence is all against it. Geoffrey mentions also (xi. i) stories he had heard from Walter, and doubtless he did hear many tales told by Walter and others. But although we must assume that Geoffrey had access to insular tradition, perhaps to a good deal of it, we can only guess as to the form it took.[2] He found some in the Latin works of Gildas and Bede, whom he mentions, and of Nennius, whom he does not. He seems to have exploited without scruple a collection of Welsh pedigrees like that found in the Harley 3859 manuscript of Nennius. Those who consider it unbecoming for him to lie about his source may believe that he actually received from Walter just such a volume, though it does not, of course, fit his description. The works of contemporary historians, especially William of Malmesbury, furnished him with other material, both early and late.[3]

---

[1] This is Parry's conviction, *Spec*, xxix (1954), 290; A. W. Wade-Evans, *Welsh Christian Origins* (Oxford, 1934), pp. 40–45. R. S. Loomis and others are just as sure that Geoffrey meant Brittany, because he identified *Britannia* with 'Armoricum regnum', and because in the passage in which 'ex Britannia' occurs he referred to Wales, not as *Britannia* but as *Gualiis*. *Historia*, ed. Griscom, pp. 348, 536; Tatlock, *Legendary History*, pp. 422 f.

[2] The best accounts of the sources of the *Historia* are those of Fletcher, *Arthurian Material in the Chronicles*, pp. 49–115, and Tatlock, op. cit. The latter tends to discount unduly the influence of those contemporary traditions about Arthur referred to by Geoffrey himself. See Chap. 6. S. Piggott deals in *Antiquity*, xv (1941), 269–86, with the probable source for the pre-Roman king-list.

[3] Tatlock in *Spec*, xi (1936), 121–4. See also R. S. Loomis in *MP*, xxxviii (1941), 303 f.

The *Historia* as it stands, however, is Geoffrey's own creation. His starting-point is Nennius's story of Silvius and Brutus,[1] and a comparison of this as we find it in the extant manuscripts and the story as he retold it will show his method. In the Harley 3859 text Brutus, having accidentally killed Silvius, his father, is expelled by the Romans, goes to Greece but is driven out because Aeneas has killed Turnus, travels to Gaul where he founds the city of Tours, and finally comes to Britain, which with its people is named after him. Geoffrey has him find in Greece descendants of the Trojans, whom he leads in a successful rebellion against the king, Pandrasus, winning for his followers their freedom and for himself the king's daughter Innogen as wife. In the course of wanderings, obviously suggested by those of Aeneas, he receives Diana's prophecy that he and his people are to inhabit an island far to the west, adds to his company another group of Trojans under Corineus, the eponymous founder of Cornwall, fights successfully in Aquitaine against the Duke of Poitou and the kings and princes of Gaul, and finally arrives at Totnes in Britain.

From Nennius too he got a list of British cities, which he distributed judiciously throughout his narrative, and the hint for synchronizing events in Britain with those in other countries. The standard chronology in his day was that of St. Jerome's translation of Eusebius. This Geoffrey adopted, either directly or from some abridged version like Bede's or Prosper of Aquitaine's,[2] distributing throughout the first two books of his work references to contemporaneous events in other parts of the world to give it the appearance of truth and a sound chronology. Into this framework, at what seemed to him the proper places, he introduced names that would have been familiar to his readers: Partholon, Julius Caesar and Cassibellaunus, Claudius, Carausius, Vortigern, Hengist, Rowena, and others. That he confused the three Constantines and the three Helens, as others had done, miscalled Maximus 'Maximianus',[3] and mistook Bede's Caedwalla for the Cadwaladr of Welsh legend did not, even if he knew it, disturb him in the least. He embellished each story with details not given by the other historians, and so furnished additional proof that he had sources of information which they did not have.

It was the fashion in Geoffrey's day to explain place-names as derived from personal names, and he took full advantage of the opportunity thus given him, creating a person from the name of a place and telling a story to account for the latter. Brutus from Britannia came to him from Nennius, but Camber, Locrinus, Albanactus, Corineus, Ebraucus, Humber, Sabrina, and others were probably his own invention. Mixed with them were a good many genuine Welsh names which Geoffrey had taken from Gildas or from native

---

[1] Faral, iii. 6–9.   [2] Faral, ii. 113–15; *Spec*, iv (1929), 316–22.
[3] *Spec*, xiii (1938), 272 f.

genealogies like those in the Harley manuscript mentioned above. His explanation that Trinovantum was New Troy and that the native language (*Cymraeg*) was a dialectal form of 'crooked Greek' (*cam Roeg*) was plausible enough. Geoffrey was skilful too in building his stories about some material thing which could, if needed, have been exhibited to support his narration.[1] His story of Lear and the temple of two-faced Janus might have been corroborated by one of the coins of Cunobelinus which bore a Janus head. The fight between Corineus and Goemagog was perhaps suggested, and might have been verified, by the figures of two gigantic warriors cut in the turf on the side of Plymouth Hoe.[2] The story of Livius Gallus and his slaughtered legions must have been inspired by the finding of human skulls along the course of the Wallbrook, where a number have been found in recent years.[3]

Geoffrey's two chief contributions to the book are the stories of Merlin and Arthur. There were previous Welsh legends about Myrddin, as has been shown above in Chap. 3, but at this time Geoffrey seems to have known little about them. Apart from the form and something of the content of the prophecies, which have already been discussed, he perhaps got from oral tradition the remarkable account of the transference of the Giants' Dance from Ireland to Salisbury Plain, so fully treated by Laura Hibbard Loomis and Piggott.[4] But he took from Nennius the tale of Vortigern and his tower, the dragons in the drained pool, and the marvellous boy without a father— Nennius's Ambrosius, whom Geoffrey adopted by the simple expedient of saying that Merlin was also called Ambrosius. The rest of the Merlin story seems to have been the child of his own fertile brain.

Regarding the treatment of Arthur, much remains uncertain, but a few of the most plausible conjectures may be set down. As to Uther Pendragon, whom Geoffrey credits with the begetting of Arthur, opinion is divided as to whether there was a tradition about him or whether his name grew out of a misunderstanding of the Welsh *uthr*, 'terrible'.[5] For the story of Arthur's begetting there are many parallels.[6] Faral pointed to the classical myth of Jupiter and Alcmene.[7] Nutt preferred the Irish tale of *The Birth of Mongan*, while Gruffydd took the combined evidence of this tale and of the *mabinogi* of *Pwyll* to argue the existence of a Celtic tradition of a wonder child begotten by a god who visited the mother in the shape of a king, her husband.[8]

---

[1] Ibid. [2] *Devonian Year Book*, iii (1912), 109.

[3] *Historia*, ed. Griscom, pp. 211–15.

[4] L. H. Loomis in *PMLA*, xlv (1930), 400–15, and S. Piggott in *Antiquity*, xv (1941), 305–19. See, however, Tatlock, *Legendary History*, pp. 40–42.

[5] *Spec*, xiii. 276 f. See also Chap. 2 above, p. 14, n. 2.

[6] Tatlock, *Legendary History*, pp. 314–17. [7] Faral, ii. 252–5.

[8] K. Meyer and A. Nutt, *Voyage of Bran* (London, 1895–7), i. 44 f., 72 f.; ii. 10–25; Gruffydd in *THSC*, 1912–13, pp. 79–90. This hypothesis is introduced at the request of the editor. Tatlock, op. cit., pp. 58–61, thinks it probable that most of the four localities connected with the begetting of Arthur and his last battle (Tintagol, Dimilioc, Ridcaradoch, Camblanus) were linked

But if these stories came to Geoffrey in anything like the form in which we have them, he used his imagination freely upon them.

Nennius is the obvious source of Arthur's battles with the Saxons and of the natural marvels connected with *stagnum Lumonoi* (Loch Lomond) and Linliguan,[1] although the possibility that Geoffrey used other traditions cannot be excluded. At any rate, from Nennius's list of battle sites he took over three. The river Dubglas, which Nennius placed in the region of Linnuis, wherever that may be, Geoffrey placed south of York, perhaps under the impression that Linnuis was Lindsey (north Lincolnshire).[2] After interposing a siege of York and a battle at Lincoln, for which Nennius furnished no warrant, Geoffrey carried the war into Scotland and placed Arthur's next victory at the wood of Celidon, which he found in Nennius. The great historic battle of Mons Badonis, which is the climax of Nennius's list, Geoffrey arbitrarily located at Bath, and with characteristic ingenuity explained how the Saxons turned up at a place so far from their late defeat in the wood of Celidon by telling how they broke their promise to return to Germany, sailed round to Totnes, and advanced on Bath from the south.

The shield Pridwen, the sword Caliburnus, and the lance Ron which Arthur bore in the battle of Bath were derived more or less directly from Welsh sources, for in *Culhwch and Olwen* Arthur mentions his sword Caledfwlch and his spear Rhongomyniad, and both in *Culhwch* and the *Spoils of Annwfn* he voyages in a ship called Prydwen.[3] From Welsh tradition also Geoffrey took over the concept of Arthur as a king at whose court assembled the notable men of his time, for this concept had been anticipated in *Culhwch*. But, as always, he was not content merely to adopt without change the materials provided. He made of Arthur's court a glorification of the courts he knew. Instead of the fantastic warriors named and described in the Welsh tale, Geoffrey surrounded Arthur with nobles and barons assembled from many parts of Western Europe, and added others whose names he picked at random from old Welsh pedigrees.[4]

According to the *Historia*, Arthur's victories over the Saxons were followed by his subjugation of Scotland, Ireland, Norway, and Denmark, and one may guess that this career of conquest was inspired by even wilder flights of the Welsh imagination about the military exploits of Arthur, such as one

---

to him before Geoffrey wrote—a conclusion which would harmonize better with a Celtic than a classical origin. See p. 54 above.

[1] F. Lot, *Nennius et l'Historia Brittonum* (Paris, 1934), pp. 106 f., 194–6.

[2] See p. 4 above. Tatlock, op. cit., p. 22; *MP*, xliii (1945), 47 f.

[3] *Mabinogion*, trans. T. P. Ellis, J. Lloyd (Oxford, 1929), i. 179, 218; *PMLA*, lvi (1941), 889–91. Why Geoffrey transformed the ship Prydwen into a shield no one knows. On Caliburnus see Loomis, *Arthurian Tradition*, pp. 421–5.

[4] R. H. Fletcher, *Arthurian Material*, pp. 76 f.; Faral, ii. 275 f.

finds in the speech of Glewlwyd in *Culhwch*. But these triumphs only prepared the way for greater. Frollo, tribune of Gaul, felt the weight of Caliburnus and perished in single combat; thus all Gaul was added to Arthur's
dominions. The great climax, which Geoffrey carefully prepared, was the
humiliation of Lucius Hiberus, Emperor of Rome. The names of Lucius's
commanders and allies were sometimes drawn from the Moslem East, sometimes were combined from names Geoffrey had met in his classical reading,
particularly in Florus's *Epitomae* of Livy.[1] The account of the campaign
against Lucius corresponds point for point to the account in the *Suite du
Merlin* (*Huth Merlin*) of Arthur's war against King Loth.[2] Loomis thinks
that because there are no clear signs that the latter was imitating Geoffrey—
and of course Geoffrey could not have used the French text—both derive
from a common source which in turn went back to a hypothetical Welsh
story of Arthur's war with Llwch Llawwynnawc, alias Llenlleawc the
Irishman,[3] the name Llwch being latinized as Lucius and the 'Irishman'
being changed by accident or design from Hibernus to Hiberus (Spaniard).
But since Loomis offered no suggestion as to the precise form in which
Geoffrey met this story, we are thrown back on the statement that he used
Welsh traditions, though not in Welsh form, and that he elaborated them
with the aid of his imagination and his scholarship.

A hero as great as Arthur could not be conceived as falling except by
treachery, and so Geoffrey introduced Modred. It is possible that there was
a story about him, for the *Annales Cambriae*, we know, have the entry
'Battle of Camlann, in which Arthur and Medraut fell'.[4] There is no
indication whether the two were friends or enemies, but the triads[5] and
Rhonabwy's Dream[6] refer to the battle in terms which show no dependence
on Geoffrey's narrative.

For Geoffrey's contemporaries this story of Arthur seems to have been
the high point of the book, as it is for moderns, and Geoffrey clearly intended
it to be. Some of the interest in the Arthurian section was no doubt the result
of the tremendous vogue of current stories, but much is also the result of the
author's artistry. As Tatlock says: 'It is hard to think of a single medieval
work of any extent with such foresighted, indeed classical symmetry; it recalls the structure of good tragedy.' Here, as in the work as a whole, Geoffrey
employed a plain style with few deviations from classical Latin, though he
could be pompous and rhetorical, as in the dedications, when the occasion
seemed to demand ornament. The verses he introduced into Book I were
so good that John Milton, no mean Latinist himself, could hardly believe

---

[1] Tatlock, *Legendary History*, pp. 122–5; *Spec*, vi (1931), 206–20.
[2] *Merlin*, ed. J. Ulrich, G. Paris (Paris, 1886), i. 202–62.
[3] R. S. Loomis, *Arthurian Tradition*, pp. 188–91, 194.
[4] See Chap. 1 above. J. Loth, *Mabinogion* (Paris, 1913), ii. 372.
[5] Ibid. ii. 246. See Chap. 5 above.   [6] Loth, op. cit. i. 354. See Chap. 4 above.

that they were authentic: 'The Latin Verses are much better, then for the Age of *Geoffrey* ap-*Arthur*, unless perhaps *Joseph of Exeter*, the only smooth Poet of those times, befreinded him.'

Geoffrey's avowed purpose in composing his *magnum opus* was to provide the descendants of the Britons with a history of their race from the earliest times.[1] The French, the Normans, and the Saxons had theirs, but the Welsh and Bretons had only the meagre scraps provided by Nennius and the hostile narratives of the Anglo-Saxons and the Romans, before whom there was only a blank. Here was an opportunity which a man with Geoffrey's gifts—and lack of historical conscience—could hardly miss. If the account was not true, something like it was—or should have been.

The various dedications, it is obvious, were designed to gain the more personal end of securing the favour of patrons. The complimentary portrait of Eldol, Earl of Gloucester, was surely intended to please the living Earl Robert, and the pictures of good and highly capable queens were probably written to prepare the way for rule by Matilda, whom Henry I had first designated as his heir in 1127.[2]

Geoffrey seems also to have desired to help the English kings in their effort to assert their independence of the kings of France. As dukes of Normandy they were vassals of the French kings, who ruled as heirs of Charlemagne. But if Brutus, ravaging nearly all of Aquitaine and building Tours, had defeated the kings and peers of Gaul, if Belinus and Brennius had reduced 'the whole kingdom to submission', and if Arthur had again conquered France, all before Charlemagne's time, then the French kings should be subject to those of England. Another point brought out by the book was that all the king's subjects, no matter what their race—Geoffrey conveniently ignores the Anglo-Saxons—were kindred, for both Celts and French were descended from Trojan exiles. This would apply equally well to the subjects of Henry I or Matilda or Stephen, and when Henry II and Eleanor of Aquitaine came to the throne, its application was far broader than Geoffrey could have imagined when he first thought of the idea.

Recent discoveries concerning the text of the *Historia* raise some pretty problems, and it is barely possible that a fundamental revision of our opinions as to its authorship may be called for. It has now been established that besides the so-called Vulgate text, which is represented by almost all the extant manuscripts, there exists a Variant Version,[3] found in four manuscripts and

---

[1] Tatlock, op. cit., pp. 422–32.

[2] Ibid., pp. 46 f., 286–8.

[3] Geoffrey of Monmouth, *Historia Regum Britanniae, A Variant Version*, ed. J. Hammer (Cambridge, Mass., 1951), based on a manuscript which conflates the Vulgate with the Variant Version. There is also a group of some fifteen manuscripts which constitute a second variant version. Hammer collected materials for an edition of these, and they have been placed in the hands of Prof. Thomas Jones of University College, Aberystwyth, for publication.

published by Hammer, and that it was written in Geoffrey's lifetime since it was used (together with the Vulgate) by Wace before 1155.[1] The Variant gives the name 'Galfridus Arturus Monemutensis' only in the colophon.[2] There are no dedications, no reference to Walter of Oxford and the mysterious book in the Britannic language. It opens with a description of Britain based solely on Bede and lacks the additional details from Gildas and Nennius which are contained in the Vulgate. Passages from Orosius and Landolfus Sagax dealing with the Roman period are reproduced often verbatim, whereas they are rephrased by the author of the Vulgate. The Variant in many instances employs indirect discourse where the Vulgate prefers the more dramatic direct speech. The former, therefore, looks like an early draft put together from original sources, the latter like a deliberate revision.[3]

If, as the colophons of both versions declare, Geoffrey was the author of the Variant as well as the Vulgate, there is nothing here to disturb our conception of his character, learning, and literary talents. But Hammer, after decades of intensive study of the manuscripts, expressed the opinion that the differences between the two versions were such as to exclude the possibility of common authorship.[4] If this verdict is correct and if the Variant was the earlier and was not written by Geoffrey, then, of course, much of what has been said in the preceding pages about the Oxford canon must be transferred to the clever unknown who conceived the grandiose fraud, worked it out, palmed it off on Geoffrey, and left it to him to do the polishing and to reap the rewards. Hammer's judgement should be regarded with respect, but it is to be remembered that he arrived at it on the assumption that the Variant was a late and inferior recension of the Vulgate, and it was natural to conclude that so astute a man as Geoffrey would not have been at pains to remove from his finished work certain characteristic touches of his art and certain signs of his extensive reading. The problem deserves further study in all its facets. But until it has been demonstrated that Geoffrey was not the father of the work which has so long passed under his name, we may continue to give him the credit for his audacious and brilliant performance.

The history proved to be a great success, even if a serious chronicler like William of Newburgh denounced its patent falsehoods, and Giraldus Cambrensis, with more humour, showed that he recognized Geoffrey's fantastic narrative for what it was. According to Giraldus, in his *Itinerarium Cambriae* (I. v), there lived in the neighbourhood of Caerleon a certain Meilerius, a familiar of evil spirits, through whose aid he could predict the future, distinguish truth from falsehood, and, even though he was illiterate, pick out the

---

[1] Caldwell in *Spec*, xxxi (1956), 675–82. See next chapter.

[2] *Variant Version*, ed. Hammer, p. 264.

[3] The evidence was presented by Caldwell at the Fifth International Arthurian Congress, 1957. See *BBSIA*, no. 9, pp. 123 f.

[4] *Variant Version*, p. 17.

false passages in a book. 'It happened once, when he was being abused beyond measure by foul spirits, that the Gospel of John was placed on his breast; the spirits vanished completely, at once flying away like birds. When it was later removed and the *History of the Britons* by Geoffrey Arthur substituted for it, by way of experiment, they settled down again, not only on his entire body, but also on the book itself, for a longer time than they were accustomed to, in greater numbers, and more loathsomely.'[1] But Giraldus could also on occasion cite the *Historia*, and for the most part it was accepted as both authoritative history and interesting reading.

The number of manuscripts (about 200) that have come down to us is exceedingly large for a work of this period, and there are few medieval historians after 1150 who do not show extensive traces of Geoffrey's influence.[2] Even before his death Alfred of Beverley based his own history upon it, and Henry of Huntingdon, the early form of whose work Geoffrey had probably used, drew from it in the later recensions of his own *Historia Anglorum*. Prince Llywelyn ap Gruffydd justified his title to Wales by pointing out his lineal descent from Camber, to whom Brutus had given all the land west of the Severn. King Edward I, in his dispute with Pope Boniface VIII over the sovereignty of Scotland, cited, with the approval of his barons, Geoffrey's narrative as proof of his claim.[3] A monk of St. Albans, when he came to describe the wedding feast of this King Edward and Princess Margaret of France, copied almost verbatim Geoffrey's account of Arthur's Pentecostal feast.[4]

A number of versions were made in Latin, varying in length from the *Gesta Regum Britanniae* (c. 1235), usually credited to Guillaume de Rennes, down to brief summaries.[5] There were several translations of all or a part in French, the best known being that of Wace,[6] completed in 1155, from which were derived the English *Brut* of Layamon and by far the larger part of a later Middle English prose version, still unpublished.[7] The fourteenth-century verse chronicles of Robert of Gloucester, Thomas Bek of Castleford, and Robert Mannyng of Bourn translate Geoffrey (or Wace) for the earlier parts of their history; so did the prose *Brut of England*, which was so popular that more than 160 manuscripts of it are still extant.[8] There is a

[1] Chambers, op. cit., pp. 107 f., 268, 274.

[2] Fletcher, *Arthurian Material*; Hertha Brandenburg, *Galfrid von Monmouth und die frühmittelenglischen Chronisten* (Berlin, 1918); T. D. Kendrick, *British Antiquity* (London, 1950); Laura Keeler, *Geoffrey of Monmouth and the Late Latin Chroniclers* (Berkeley and Los Angeles, 1946).

[3] *Spec*, xxviii (1953), 121 f.   [4] Ibid. xxi (1946), 28–31; xxviii (1953), 120.

[5] Ibid. vi (1931), 114–23; Francisque Michel, *Gesta Regum Britanniae* (Cambrian Archaeological Association, 1862); *PQ*, xii (1933), 225–34; *MP*, xxxiv (1936), 119–32; *Latomus*, ii (1938), 131–51.

[6] See Chap. 9 below.

[7] On Layamon, see Chap. 10 below. For the prose version, *PMLA*, lxix (1954), 643–54.

[8] Friedrich Brie, *Geschichte und Quellen der mittelenglischen Prosachronik, The Brute of England oder The Chronicles of England* (Marburg, 1905).

large number of manuscripts in Welsh, the oldest, which is dated around the year 1300, being a copy of something earlier. Welsh scribes treated so freely the texts they were copying that it is difficult to determine the affiliations of these, but it seems probable that at least five separate Welsh translations were made.[1] Often in these manuscripts a Welsh version of the chronicle of Dares Phrygius is prefixed to the *History* (as the Latin text of Dares is sometimes prefixed to the *Historia*), and *The Chronicle of the Princes (Brut y Tywysogion)* follows it, the whole making a connected history of the Welsh people down to the scribe's own day. A free rendering into Old Norse under the title of *Breta sögur* was made some time before 1334. Geoffrey's influence extended as far as Poland, where Wincenty Kadlubek, who became Bishop of Cracow in 1208 and died in 1223, took him as a model for his *Chronica Polonorum*, and adapted some material from the *Historia* to his own use.[2]

In England the triumph of the Tudors brought about a revival of interest in Geoffrey's work. Though Ranulph Higden in his *Polychronicon* (*c.* 1327) expressed doubts about the reliability of the *Historia*[3] and Caxton reported in 1485 that 'divers men hold opinion that there was no such Arthur',[4] the Tudors had too strong a political stake in their Welsh ancestry to tolerate scepticism. When Richard III charged that Henry Tudor was an upstart with 'no manner of right, interest, title, or colour' in the kingship, Henry sent a commission into Wales which produced a report tracing his ancestry through the heroes of Geoffrey of Monmouth to Brutus.[5] Henry's son, born 19 September 1486, was christened Arthur and hailed as 'Arturus secundus'.[6]

The great controversy which raged during the next centuries over the credibility of the *Historia Regum Britanniae*, and the influence of the work on Spenser, Shakespeare, and Milton, lie beyond the scope of this book, and since these topics have been fully discussed by others[7] it is quite unnecessary to treat them here.

'Vita Merlini'

The title, *Vita Merlini*,[8] comes from the colophon, which is in a hand later than that of the text, in the earliest manuscript of the poem: 'Explicit

[1] *Historia*, ed. Griscom, pp. 585–99, plates x–xvi; *Brut Dingestow*, ed. Henry Lewis (Cardiff, 1942); *Brut y Brenhinedd*, ed. J. J. Parry, pp. ix ff.; *Spec*, v (1930), 424–31; *EC*, iv (1948), 221 ff.

[2] Hammer in *Bull. Polish Inst. of Arts and Sciences*, ii (1944), 538 ff.

[3] R. H. Fletcher, *Arthurian Material*, pp. 181 ff.; L. Keeler, op. cit., pp. 32 ff.

[4] Preface to Malory's *Morte d'Arthur*.

[5] Charles B. Millican, *Spenser and the Table Round* (Cambridge, Mass., 1932), pp. 16, 154.

[6] Ibid., pp. 17 f., 21.

[7] Ibid. Edwin Greenlaw, *Studies in Spenser's Historical Allegory* (Baltimore, 1932); Roberta F. Brinkley, *Arthurian Legend in the Seventeenth Century* (Baltimore, 1932); Ernest Jones, *Geoffrey of Monmouth, 1640–1800* (Berkeley and Los Angeles, 1944); T. D. Kendrick, *British Antiquity.*

[8] The two modern editions are those by Faral, iii. 306–52, and by Parry in *University of Illinois Studies in Language and Literature*, x, no. 3 (Urbana, Ill., 1925), the former edited to conform to classical usage, the latter following the manuscript. There are discussions by Parry, pp. 9–25, by

Vita Merlini Caledonii per Galfridum Monemutensem'. Whether this title is due to Geoffrey himself or to a later scribe, there is no reason to doubt— as some have done—that the work is Geoffrey's, or that the Bishop Robert of the dedication is Robert de Chesney,[1] who had been associated with Geoffrey at Oxford, and who early in 1149 became Bishop of Lincoln. The dedication must certainly be later than 19 December 1148,[2] when Robert was elected to this office, and since it is a plea for promotion, it must have been written before Geoffrey's own election to the bishopric of St. Asaph early in 1151. There is no external evidence to fix more closely the date of composition.

In this poem Geoffrey returned to the subject of his first literary effort, but he treated it very differently. When he wrote the *Prophetiae*, he seems to have had enough knowledge of the vaticinations attributed to Myrddin to be able to combine some of them with other material of his own invention so as to produce a convincing set of prophecies; but of Myrddin himself he knew almost nothing. In the *Historia*, into which he inserted the *Prophetiae*, he added other prophecies and other incidents to build up the character of Merlin (VIII. i, x–xii, xv, xix–xx). There is no indication that these had previously been connected with Myrddin, but in the years that followed Geoffrey learned something of the legends that clustered about the mage.

The interest in such stories, which Geoffrey mentions in the *Historia* (VII. i), was probably an outgrowth of the attempt of Earl David of Cumbria (who became King of Scotland in 1124) to find grounds for reviving the ancient bishopric of Glasgow. Soon after 1107 David assembled for this purpose a 'jury of inquisition', which included Norman ecclesiastics, knights, and barons, and 'the older and wiser of all Cumbria'.[3] Part of the evidence submitted to them consisted of an old life of St. Kentigern, the early bishop, which told of his dealings with a certain madman called Lailoken,[4] in whom the Welsh recognized their own Myrddin, also called Llallogan.[5] When the members of the jury returned to their homes, some, at least, must have remembered the stories they had heard, and talked about them. When Bishop

Faral, ii. 28–36, 341–85, by H. M. and N. K. Chadwick, *Growth of Literature*, i (Cambridge, 1932), 123–32, by Tatlock in *Spec*, xviii (1943), 265–87, and by Schirmer, op. cit., pp. 32–35. See also Chap. 3 above.

[1] See Parry's edition, pp. 9–15.

[2] Parry would date it about two years later because vss. 1498 ff. seem to refer to the battle of Coleshill in Flintshire, which was fought in 1150; *MP*, xxii (1925), 413–15. Faral and Tatlock reject this identification for what seem inadequate reasons.

[3] R. L. Graeme Ritchie, *Chrétien de Troyes and Scotland* (Oxford, 1952), p. 9.

[4] Apparently represented by the fragments printed by Ward in *R*, xxii (1893), 514 ff. See Faral, ii. 348–52.

[5] See Chap. 3 above; Parry in *PQ*, iv (1925), 193–207; K. H. Jackson in *Essays and Studies Presented to Professor Eoin MacNeill* (Dublin, 1940), pp. 535–50; Griffiths, *Early Vaticination*, pp. 67–137. For the opposite view see Faral, ii. 355–61.

Alexander asked him about these stories, Geoffrey could have known little. He was too young to have been present at the meetings; but a fair proportion of those who had attended were Augustinian canons, as we assume him to have been, and in time he was able to round out his knowledge.

Since there is no reason to believe that Geoffrey used as a direct source of his work any of the Welsh Myrddin poems treated in Chap. 3, we cannot determine the exact form in which the tradition came to him, but the poems probably give us an approximation of it. From it he got the names Silva Calidonis (Coed Calidon), Merlinus (Myrddin),[1] Thelgesinus (Taliesin, earlier Talgesin), Guennolous (Gwenddolau), Peredurus (Peredur), Rodarchus Largus (Rhydderch Hael), and perhaps Guendoloena (Chwimlean)[2]; Maeldinus is probably due to a misunderstanding of the Maelgwn of the Welsh poems rather than to the Irish *imram*,[3] and Barinthus, who comes ultimately from the Irish *Voyage of Saint Brendan*, had appeared in both French and Latin before Geoffrey wrote.

Welsh tradition accounts for the story of Merlin's madness induced by a battle,[4] which Geoffrey does not name, his life under the apple-trees in the forest with his sister, and his prophetic utterances. The Cadwaladr-Cynan prediction, it has already been noted, was in Welsh long before the time of Geoffrey. The prophecy of the 'triple death' is not recorded in Welsh until late, but it is found early in Irish and Scottish, and probably came to Geoffrey from a Celtic source although it is found in two Latin poems of the twelfth century.[5] Of the three motifs connected with Merlin's prophetic laughter— plucking a leaf, sign of her infidelity, from the queen's hair; buying of shoes to last for seven years; and the beggar sitting over a concealed treasure—the first two are found in the Irish *Death of Fergus Mac Leide*,[6] and the first is also found in the Scottish *Lailoken and Meldred*. The second and the third are found in the Babylonian *Talmud*, told in connexion with the demon Ashmedai,[7] and this may prove to be their ultimate source. The significant

[1] As Gaston Paris pointed out, Geoffrey probably changed Merdinus to Merlinus to avoid the unpleasant suggestion of the former name. *R*, xii (1883), 376. It may be noted that the name Merlinus occurs in a Pistoian document of 1128; E. G. Gardner, *Arthurian Legend in Italian Literature*, p. 3.

[2] On this name see Jarman in *BBCS*, xvi (1955), 71–76.

[3] Geoffrey could, however, have known some form of the *Voyage of Maelduin*. Faral, ii. 361–3.

[4] Giraldus Cambrensis mentions the portent in the air, which is not in Geoffrey or the Welsh poems, but is in the Scottish and Irish versions. See Chap. 3 above.

[5] See K. H. Jackson as cited on p. 90, n. 5, above. The triple death motif is found in the *Iolo Manuscripts*, which contain ancient material but so uncritically combined with modern that no reliance can be placed on them. For the Latin poems see Faral, ii. 266 f., and Migne, *Patrologia Latina*, clxxi, cols. 1445 f.

[6] *RES*, ii (1926), 230–2; T. P. Cross and C. H. Slover, *Ancient Irish Tales* (New York, 1936), pp. 480 f.

[7] I. Epstein, *Babylonian Talmud*, *Seder Nashim* (London, 1936), chap. vii, pp. 320, 324 f., 337. Oriental sources which have been cited for the incident are not convincing, nor is Zumthor's list of characters in the Bible who have laughed.

thing is that both the *Talmud* stories are told in the treatise on divorce, one section of which deals with the granting of a conditional divorce in case the husband stays away from his home for a specified length of time—exactly the circumstance under which Merlin gives his wife permission to marry again. Another section of the same treatise deals with the dumb man who desires a divorce. He is to be 'tested with three questions' to see if he is *compos mentis*; the situation is not the same as that in the poem, but it may have suggested it. Celtic tradition must have been the source from which Geoffrey got the first of these motifs; it may have been the immediate source from which he got the second and third, but there is no conclusive evidence that it was.

Of the prophecies uttered by Merlin much is simply a reworking of material in the *Prophetiae*. Ganieda's visions, on the other hand, are of a different kind, although still cryptic, and have been interpreted with some likelihood as referring to events in the war between Stephen and Matilda. Faral is doubtless right in seeing in the funeral laments (vss. 43–53, 692–727) the influence of medieval rhetoric, and in the pseudo-science the teachings of the School of Chartres, for which he lets William of Conches stand as an example. Both types could be paralleled also from Welsh literature,[1] but Geoffrey is more likely to have known the Latin forms. Four long interpolations follow so closely the medieval encyclopedia of Isidore of Seville as to leave no doubt that Geoffrey was merely versifying sections of that work. He also shows indebtedness to Ovid and to other classical writers, but in minor details rather than in major incidents.

The verse is good, by medieval standards, and in places rises to poetry. Among the most charming passages, and of most interest for Arthurian romance, is that in which Taliesin describes the Isle of Apples and tells how Arthur was conveyed there to be tended by Morgen (Morgain la Fée) and her eight sisters. 'The island of Apples, which men call the Fortunate Isle, is so named because it produces all things of itself. The fields there have no need of farmers to plough them, and Nature alone provides all cultivation. Grain and grapes are produced without tending, and apple trees grow in the woods from the close-clipped grass. The earth of its own accord brings forth not merely grass but all things in superabundance. . . . Thither after the battle of Camlan we took the wounded Arthur. . . . With the Prince we arrived there, and Morgen received us with becoming honour. In her own chamber she placed the King on a golden bed, with her own noble hand uncovered the wound, and gazed at it long. At last she said that health could return to him if he were to stay with her for a long time and wished to make

---

[1] The funeral laments from the elegies of the Gogynfeirdd, and the pseudo-science from the poems in the Book of Taliesin, which Parry assumes to represent the teaching of the Welsh schools. *Vita Merlini*, ed. Parry, p. 18.

use of her healing art. Rejoicing, therefore, we committed the King to her, and returning gave our sails to the favouring winds' (vss. 908–40). The description of the island, though derived in part, as Faral has shown,[1] from Solinus and Isidore, also reflects Celtic conceptions of the elysian isle of maidens.[2]

The *Vita Merlini* survives as a whole in only one manuscript and seems to have exercised no great influence on later literature. To be sure, it was responsible for the differentiation of Merlinus Celidonius or Silvester from Merlinus Ambrosius, as has already been noted.[3] Extracts from the *Vita* occur sporadically in chronicles. A few incidents were taken over into the French romances, but with much modification.[4] Tatlock's idea that the poem influenced all later descriptions of the Isle of Avalon and was mainly responsible for the convention which represented Yvain, Lancelot, and Tristan as driven mad and resorting to the forest as a result of their ladies' displeasure rests on general and unimpressive similarities.[5]

In conclusion, one may say of Geoffrey of Monmouth that he was a scholar with a very wide range of reading, a stylist of high competence in both prose and verse, a bold and imaginative writer of fiction in the guise of history. With such talents it needed no Merlin to prophesy that he would be read for generations to come. But even Merlin himself could hardly have foreseen that Geoffrey's work would affect the politics of Great Britain for five centuries, and that the greatest poets of England would drink from his fountain.

[1] Faral, ii. 301–4.

[2] See Chap. 7 above. On Morgen see R. S. Loomis, *Wales*, pp. 105–30. On the passing of Arthur see G. Schoepperle Loomis in *Vassar Medieval Studies*, ed. C. F. Fiske (New Haven, 1923), pp. 3–25; T. P. Cross in *Manly Anniversary Studies* (Chicago, 1923), pp. 284–94.

[3] The distinction was first made in a library catalogue shortly after the composition of the poem. *Spec*, xviii (1943), 272.

[4] Ibid., pp. 274 f.

[5] Ibid., pp. 275–7, 284–7. On Yvain's madness see A. C. L. Brown, *Iwain, Studies and Notes in Philology and Literature*, viii (1903), pp. 34–45; Loomis, *Arthurian Tradition*, pp. 296 f.

9

WACE

CHARLES FOULON

BETWEEN the date when Geoffrey of Monmouth's *Historia* burst upon the world and the period when Thomas composed his *Tristan* and Chrétien de Troyes his *Erec* there was an interval of about thirty years during which at least two adaptations of the *Historia* for Anglo-Norman and French readers were made.[1] One of them, now lost, was undertaken by Geffrei Gaimar at the request of Constance, wife of Ralph Fitz Gilbert, in the 1140's, and to it he added a history of England to the end of the reign of William Rufus, which has survived.[2] In all four manuscripts of the *Estorie des Engles*, Gaimar's version of the *Historia* has been replaced by that made by the Norman Wace and finished in 1155. The reason for this substitution, it is generally agreed, was the literary superiority of Wace's poem[3]—a superiority also indicated by the fact that it has survived in complete form in eighteen additional manuscripts.[4]

Indeed, the Norman poet was not unconscious of his talents and his artistic responsibilities. He admitted unblushingly that he sought to please the taste of wealthy patrons: 'I address myself to rich folk who possess revenues and silver, since for them books are made and good words are composed and well set forth.'[5] But, though he wrote for gain, he was an artist, and he reported, not without sardonic humour, that there were some who gave him nothing but who admitted that 'mult dit bien maistre Wace'.[6]

---

[1] These are the lost *Brut* of Gaimar and the Munich *Brut*, ed. K. Hoffmann, K. Vollmöller (Halle, 1877). The latter is a fragment which does not include Arthur. In addition there are five later French redactions of Geoffrey's *Historia* which have survived in fragmentary form, and a dubious reference in Bib. Nat. fr. 749 of the *Vulgate Merlin* to a Martin of Rochester who translated a *Brutus* from Latin into French. Tatlock has a good account of these fragments in *Legendary History*, pp. 456–62. Brugger in *ZFSL*, xxix, xxx, xliv, ascribes great importance to the lost work of Martin. See Bruce, index, *sub* Martin, and A. Bell in *MLR*, xxxiv (1939), 321–54.

[2] Perhaps the best accounts of Gaimar are in Tatlock, op. cit., pp. 451–56, and in *MedAev*, vii (1938), 184–98.

[3] G. Paris made the basic study of Wace in *R*, ix (1880), 592–7. More recent are those of R. H. Fletcher in *Arthurian Material in the Chronicles* (1906), 127–43; J. H. Philpot, *Maistre Wace* (London, 1925); I. Arnold in the introduction to his edition of Wace's *Brut* (Paris, 1938–40); W. F. Schirmer, *Die frühen Darstellungen des Arthurstoffes*, pp. 41–53; and Tatlock, op. cit., pp. 463–82. The early edition of Le Roux de Lincy (Rouen, 1836–8) gives variant readings of proper names, as Arnold does not.

[4] *Brut*, ed. Arnold, i. Introd., pp. viii–xii.

[5] *Roman de Rou*, ed. H. Andresen (Heilbronn, 1877–9), ii. 35.　　　　　　　　[6] Ibid.

What we know of his life is derived from his *Roman de Rou*, and it is confirmed by certain charters.[1] Born, probably about 1100, in the island of Jersey, he was taken as a child to Caen. There, he says, he began the study of letters, which he continued during a long residence in the Ile de France. On his return to Caen he began to write narratives in French (*romanz*), and among them we may include the *Vies de Sainte Marguerite et de St. Nicolas* and the *Conception de Notre Dame*.[2] There is no certainty, however, as to their date. Before the composition of his paraphrase of Geoffrey's *Historia*, the *Roman de Brut*, Wace had visited southern England, for Miss Houck pointed out in the poem a notable familiarity with that region, and observed that Robert of Caen and the two famous abbeys of that town owned lands in Dorset.[3] Perhaps it was also at this time that the poet made his famous and disappointing visit to the forest of Broceliande (Brecheliant) in the hope of seeing fays.[4] 'A fool I returned, a fool I went; a fool I went, a fool I returned!'

In the year of Geoffrey of Monmouth's death, 1155, Wace completed his version of the *Historia*, and Layamon tells us that a copy was presented to Eleanor, the new queen of England,[5] though the extant manuscripts preserve no sign of a dedication. The poem may well have brought Wace to the favourable attention of her husband, Henry II, for in 1160 we find him a clerk at Caen,[6] embarking, at the invitation of that king, on a chronicle of the dukes of Normandy, the *Roman de Rou*. In 1162 he was at Fécamp,[7] and about 1169 he received a canonry at Bayeux as a token of royal favour.[8] But this did not prevent Henry in 1174 from interrupting him in his poetic task, and assigning its completion to a certain Maistre Beneeit. Wace did not lay down his pen, however, without giving discreet expression to his wounded pride. 'The king formerly treated me well, gave me much, promised me even more, and if he had given me all that he promised, I would be better off.'[9] The rest is silence.

The chief source of the *Roman de Brut*, as already stated, was Geoffrey's *Historia*. That Wace knew and used the form edited by Griscom and Faral but also and mainly the Variant Version published by Hammer was

[1] *Brut*, ed. Arnold, i, pp. lxxiv–lxxix; *Jahrb. f. Rom. u. Eng. Lit.* i (1859), 1–43; *Rou*, ed. Andresen, ii. 243 f. Wace called himself 'clerc lisant' and 'maistre'. The former term is still subject to various interpretations (see especially E. A. Francis in *Mélanges Roques* [1953], ii. 81–92), but may well have signified 'secretary'. See Littré's examples, especially that from the *Roman de la Rose*. 'Maistre', like 'magister', often meant 'teacher'.

[2] *Vie de Sainte Marguerite*, ed. E. A. Francis, CFMA (1932); *Conception de Notre Dame*, ed. W. R. Ashford (Chicago, 1933); *Vie de Saint Nicholas*, ed. E. Ronsjö, *Études Romanes de Lund*, v (1942).

[3] M. Houck, *Sources of the Roman de Brut of Wace*, *Univ. Calif. Pub. in English*, v, no. 2 (Berkeley, 1941), 227 f., 282–7.

[4] *Rou*, ed. Andresen, ii. 283 f. See below, p. 100, n. 7.

[5] Layamon, *Brut*, ed. F. Madden (London, 1847), i. 3. See below, Chap. 10.

[6] *Rou*, ed. Andresen, i. 207, vs. 3.   [7] *R*, ix (1880), 597.

[8] *Rou*, ed. Andresen, ii, vss. 173 f.   [9] Ibid. ii. 481.

discovered by Robert Caldwell.[1] Between this source and its adaptation by Wace there is a great difference in length. To some 6,000 lines of Latin text in Faral's edition correspond nearly 15,000 French verses. Even if we take into account the shortness of the verses, even if we make allowance for the difference between a synthetic language and an analytical one, it must be conceded that Wace elaborated considerably. This expansion was due largely to the fact that one author posed as a sober historian, while the other felt free to exercise some of the privileges of a story-teller and poet, replacing dry, colourless narrative with descriptive scenes. Wace also felt free to add material from other sources.[2]

Before examining these amplifications, however, let us consider certain significant abridgements and omissions. Ivor Arnold, latest editor of the Brut, remarked that these are rare, but they bear witness to an art which avoids anything which might bore or shock the reader or cause him to smile in contempt. Wace abridges passages devoted to purely religious history; for example, the beginnings of the evangelization of Britain (vss. 5207–72, corresponding to the Historia, Bk. iv, ch. 19–Bk. v, ch. 7); and when speaking of Vortigern he does not mention the Pelagian heresy. He omits details concerning the martyrdom of St. Alban, particularly the way in which the saint sacrificed his life to save his confessor Amphibalus (vss. 5588–93, corresponding to Bk. v, ch. 5 in the Historia). Among the suppressions calculated to avoid the display of cruel or savage behaviour one may mention the omission of the tortures inflicted by Arthur on the conquered Picts and Scots.[3] Finally, Wace sometimes leaves out passages of exaggerated sentiment.[4]

Of far greater interest are the many additions made to Geoffrey's text. In the desire to be a trustworthy informant, Wace turned to certain sources for their historical value. The studies of Waldner, Miss Houck, and Arnold[5] have shown that he drew occasionally on the Bible for references to David, who 'arranged the psalter'; to Solomon, who founded the Temple 'as God had ordained'; to Ezechias, who lived at the time of the founding of Rome.[6] Many details cited by Miss Houck could have been borrowed from Goscelin's Vita Augustini.[7] It is fair to mention also Nennius's Historia Brittonum,

[1] BBSIA, no. 6 (1954), 109; Spec, xxxi (1956), 675–82.

[2] For comparisons between Wace and his sources see Brut, ed. Arnold, i, pp. lxxix–xci; R. H. Fletcher, Arthurian Material in the Chronicles, pp. 127–43; Tatlock, op. cit., pp. 468–75; M. Houck, op. cit.; M. Pelan, L'Influence du Brut de Wace sur les romanciers de son temps (Paris, 1931), pp. 147–66. All of these studies should be checked carefully against the Variant Version published by J. Hammer (Cambridge, Mass., 1951), since this and not the Vulgate was Wace's main source.

[3] Brut, ed. Arnold, ii, vss. 9407–526, corresponding to Historia, ix. 6. Wace composed a long speech for the Scots imploring Arthur's pity.

[4] Cf. Historia, i. 11, with Brut, vss. 611–16; and Historia, xii. 15, with Brut, vss. 14701 f. Wace also omits the list of bishops (Historia, ix. 15) and the genealogy of the kings of Brittany (xii. 6).

[5] Ulbrich in RF, xxvi (1909), 181–260; L. Waldner, Wace's Brut und seine Quellen (Karlsruhe, 1914); Houck, op. cit.; Brut, ed. Arnold, i, pp. lxxix–lxxxvi.

[6] Houck, op. cit., pp. 242–5.   [7] Ibid., pp. 261–82.

which may have suggested the appearance of Keredic as an interpreter at the meeting of Vortigern and Ronwen, though in Geoffrey's work he was a Saxon chief; the *Gesta Regum Anglorum* of William of Malmesbury, which probably inspired the story of Athelstan's illegitimate birth; and perhaps the Chanson de *Gormont et Isembart*.[1] The claim that Wace also introduced details from the *Aeneid* and the *Historia Romana* of Landolphus Sagax must be abandoned, since Robert Caldwell has discovered their origin in the variant version of Geoffrey's *Historia*.[2]

As has already been noticed, Wace also displayed personal knowledge of the geography of southern England. Even though he mistook Geoffrey's river named after Habren, namely, the Severn, for the Hampshire Avon, and called the latter Avren, he described correctly its meeting the sea at Christchurch.[3] He was bold enough to correct Geoffrey, who had represented the Saxons as fleeing after the battle of Bath to the isle of Thanet in Kent, and directed their flight much more plausibly to Teignmouth (Teignewic) in Devon.[4] His care for verisimilitude led him also to assign a full night to Arthur's ride from Barfleur (Barbeflue) to Mont St. Michel, instead of including in the same short space, as Geoffrey had done, Arthur's debarkation, his journey to the Mount, his fight with the giant, and his return.[5] He also seems to have drawn on observation for the statement that between Dinan and the coast the ruins of Kidalet were still visible.[6]

Some of Wace's additions have a special value for those interested in the history of Arthurian romance—references to story-tellers and their ways, a few names, comments on the Round Table and on Arthur's survival. Likewise significant is the passage in the *Roman de Rou* on the forest of Broceliande and its magic fountain, which were to furnish the setting for many adventures in Chrétien de Troyes's *Yvain*. Let us examine these much-discussed features which Wace did not derive from Geoffrey of Monmouth.

As to the tellers of Arthurian tales, let us first note that Wace's testimony is not to be taken lightly, for he made a practice of citing oral traditions. In the *Rou* he wrote of Richard of Normandy: 'I have heard it told by many who heard it from their ancestors.'[7] When he related the appearance of the comet in 1066, he invoked the reports of eye-witnesses.[8] Though he evidently kept his ears open, he reproached himself for not having heard and seen all that he ought.[9]

It is in this context that we should read the familiar verses in the *Brut*: 'During the long peace of which I speak—I know not whether you have heard of it—the wonders were demonstrated (*pruvées*) and the adventures

[1] Ibid., pp. 296–8.

[2] *Spec*, xxxi (1956), 676 f.

[3] *Brut*, ed. Arnold, i, vss. 1437–40.

[4] Ibid., ii, vs. 9376.

[5] Ibid., ii, vss. 11333–6.

[6] Ibid., ii, vss. 14225–8.

[7] *Rou*, ed. Andresen, ii, vss. 341 f.

[8] Ibid., vss. 6347 f.

[9] *Brut*, ed. Arnold, i, vss. 1531–6.

were found (*truvées*) which are so often related of Arthur that they have been turned into a fable.'[1] So, too, with the allusion to 'the Round Table, of which the Bretons tell many a tale'.[2] Again, referring to Avalon, Wace wrote that Arthur was still there. 'The Bretons still await him, as they say and hope.'[3] Finally, in the *Rou* he recalled the marvels of Broceliande, 'of which the Bretons go about telling tales'.[4]

All these utterances are the more precious because the poet was a practical man. He tried to verify the reported wonders of Broceliande on the spot. 'I went there to seek marvels; I saw the forest, I saw the land; I looked for marvels, but I did not find them.'[5] Nothing could be more cautious than his treatment of Arthur's survival. 'Maistre Wace, who wrote this book, does not wish to say more of his end than the prophet Merlin. Merlin said of Arthur—and he was right—that his death would be doubtful. The seer spoke truly. Always people have doubted and will doubt, I believe, whether he is alive or dead.'[6] A precursor of the modern historian, Wace applied critical standards. 'The tales of Arthur are not all lies nor all true. So much have the story-tellers (*cunteür*) told and so much have the makers of fables (*fableür*) fabled to embellish their stories that they have made everything seem a fable.'[7] This desire for accuracy, this scepticism, this common sense have been recognized by nearly all scholars. Even Tatlock applied to Wace the adjectives 'enquiring, critical, honest'.[8] Presumably, therefore, when the poet added anything besides rhetorical amplification to Geoffrey, he was not inventing but transmitting.

Let us then consider a few personages who do not figure in the *Historia Regum Britanniae* but do appear in the *Brut*. Guerguint, count of Hereford, is listed among the nobles who attended Arthur's coronation.[9] The origin of this name remains a mystery, though a Guerguesin, Duke of Hautbois, was a guest at Erec's wedding, according to Chrétien.[10] Teleusin is introduced by Wace as foretelling the birth of Christ.[11] Now Geoffrey in the *Vita Merlini* and Nennius tell us of a Thelgesinus or Taliesin, but both assign him to a period long after the beginning of our era and neither, of course, mentions such a prophecy. On the other hand, this seeming anachronism on Wace's part may well be traced to a Celtic source, since the Welsh believed that Taliesin had passed through many incarnations, had borne a banner before Alexander the Great, and had been an instructor to Eli and Enoc![12]

[1] *Brut*, ed. Arnold, ii, vss. 9787–92.   [2] Ibid., ii, vss. 9751 f.   [3] Ibid., ii, vss. 13279 f.
[4] *Rou*, ed. Andresen, ii, vss. 6395 f.   [5] Ibid., vss. 6415–18.
[6] *Brut*, ii, vss. 13282–90.   [7] Ibid., vss. 9793–8.
[8] Tatlock, *Legendary History*, p. 465; Paris in *R*, ix. 534, speaks of Wace's 'conscience'; Studer, in the *Study of Anglo-Norman*, of Wace's 'desire to impart trustworthy information'.
[9] *Brut*, ii, vs. 10259.   [10] *Erec*, vs. 1961.
[11] *Brut*, i, vss. 4855–69.
[12] C. Guest, *Mabinogion*, ed. A. Nutt (London, 1904), p. 307. Morris-Jones in *Y Cymmrodor*, xxviii (1918), 50 n., proposed that Wace received this prophecy through oral channels.

Geoffrey mentioned the kings of Orkney and Gotland as submitting themselves to Arthur in Iceland, and Wace added a third, Rummaret of Wenelande.[1] Some scholars have inferred from this geographical association that Wenelande must mean the land of the Wends along the Baltic coast.[2] But Layamon seems to have possessed additional knowledge about Rummaret since he gave his son a prominent role in breaking up a tumult in Arthur's hall, and it is odd that he changed the name of Wenelande to Winet or Winetlond, a form which recalls Guined, Nennius's name for North Wales.[3] We may suppose, though not too confidently, that Wace had a source for Rummaret and Winet in some obscure tradition.

His testimony concerning the circulation of tales about Arthur, as has been shown in Chap. 6, is corroborated by a series of witnesses antedating 1150.[4] In fact, the *Historia Regum Britanniae* itself opens with a sentence to the effect that the deeds of Arthur and many other kings of the Britons were pleasantly rehearsed from memory by word of mouth by many peoples; and Geoffrey would not have been the clever man we think him if he had commenced his book with a patent lie. Moreover, Arnold, recalling an article by Huet,[5] questions whether the lapse of less than twenty years from the publication of the *Historia* would be sufficient to produce a whole web of marvels and adventures relating to Arthur; and he adds that the events related in these legends seemed strange and incredible to Wace—a fact which renders it unlikely that they were based on Geoffrey's work.

Apparently one of the legendary marvels was the Round Table, of which Wace was the first to make mention in extant literature.[6] It was fashioned at Arthur's orders to prevent quarrels over precedence. 'At the table they sat on an equality and were served equally.' The poet added an important detail: 'all were seated within the circle (*assis meain*), and no one was placed outside (*de forain*)'.

Whence Wace derived this concept cannot be determined precisely, but he did credit the Bretons with many tales about it. Though one may readily

---

[1] *Brut*, ii, vs. 9710.

[2] Tatlock, op. cit., p. 473, n. 34; R. Blenner-Hassett, *Study of the Place-Names in Lawman's Brut* (Stanford, Cal., 1950), p. 67.

[3] Layamon, *Brut*, ed. Madden, ii. 534; Nennius, *Historia Brittonum*, ed. F. Lot, p. 179; Kittredge in *Studies and Notes in Philology and Literature*, vii (1900), 189.

[4] *RR*, xxxii (1941), 3–38; R. S. Loomis, *Wales*, pp. 179 ff. Tatlock's repeated assertion in *Legendary History*, pp. 201–11, 469–75, that it was Geoffrey's book which set imaginations going and produced a mass of stories is not based on facts; it is opposed by the facts. The stories existed before Geoffrey, as attested by Herman of Laon and William of Malmesbury, not to mention the Modena sculpture. Whenever the subjects of the tales are known, as in the case of the Round Table, the Modena sculpture, the Otranto mosaic, and the *contes* about Erec and Bron mentioned by Chrétien and Robert de Boron, not the slightest debt to Geoffrey can be proved.

[5] *MA*, xxviii (1915), 234–49; *Brut*, ed. Arnold, i, p. lxxxvi.

[6] *Brut*, ii, vss. 9747–60. On Round Table cf. Loomis, *Arthurian Tradition*, pp. 61–68; Tatlock, *Legendary History*, pp. 471–5.

concede the influence of a round table reputed to be that of the Last Supper and actually seen by pilgrims and Crusaders in the Holy Land,[1] or the influence of a circular seating arrangement adopted at the Council of Rheims in 1049,[2] may one not take Wace once more at his word and grant that, however modified, there was a Celtic tradition of Arthur and his board? This view of the problem, as Arthur Brown was the first to argue,[3] is supported by Layamon's passage about the fracas which led to the making of the Round Table by a Cornish carpenter—a passage to be discussed in the next chapter.[4] Even Bruce was convinced: 'This passage . . . must be accepted as undoubtedly derived ultimately from Celtic tradition.'[5]

Two other brief references mention the Round Table as a chivalric fellowship.[6] The second of these declares that among the doomed in Arthur's fatal battle near Camble were 'those of the Table Round, of whom such praise rang [literally 'was'] throughout the world'. Though the tense of the verb is imperfect, Wace was evidently cognizant of a contemporary renown which embraced not only Arthur but the knights who were worthy to sit at his festal board.

Besides these Arthurian additions to the *Brut*, there is the well-known excursus in the *Roman de Rou* on the forest of Broceliande,[7] the haunted woodland which was destined to serve as background for some of the most memorable scenes in the legends of Yvain and Merlin. Wace called the forest Brecheliant, described it as long and wide, said that the Bretons told tales about it, and that it was usual to see fays there 'if the Bretons tell us the truth'. He gave also an exact description of the fountain of Berenton and of the storms provoked by the sprinkling of water from the fountain on a block of stone near by. Here are clearly the elements of a local legend—a legend reported also by Giraldus Cambrensis and subsequent writers and presumably therefore genuine.[8] Though Wace in describing events and characters used the poet's privilege of rhetorical embellishment, he cannot be accused of

---

[1] L. H. Loomis in *MLN*, xliv (1929), 511–15.

[2] A. J. Denomy in *Mediaeval Studies*, xiv (1952), 143–9.

[3] *Studies and Notes in Philology and Literature*, vii (1900), 183 ff.

[4] There is remarkable similarity between Layamon's concept of the Round Table and the tent belonging to Arthur's sister, 'la fada del Gibel', which could be transported in a single cart and yet on the occasion of a banquet extended for half a league. *Jaufré*, ed. H. Breuer (Göttingen, 1925), vss. 10346–676. The Provençal poet derived this account of the tent from the French, who knew Morgain la Fée as the fay of Mongibel. Ibid., vs. 10654. See also Loomis, *Arthurian Tradition*, pp. 65 f.; Paton, *Fairy Mythology*, p. 250, n. 1; A. Graf, *Miti, Leggende e Superstizioni del Medio Evo* (Turin, 1893), ii. 308, 312.

[5] Bruce, i. 87. For an ultra-sceptical view see Hofer in *ZRP*, lxii (1942), 87–91; Delbouille in *R*, lxxiv (1953), 185–92.

[6] *Brut*, ed. Arnold, ii, vss. 10285, 13269 f.

[7] *Rou*, ii, vss. 6395–418. On the legends of the forest see F. Bellamy, *Forêt de Bréchéliant* (Rennes, 1896), and Foulon in *Yorkshire Celtic Studies*, v (1949–52), 12.

[8] Giraldus Cambrensis, *Opera*, v, ed. J. F. Dimock (London, 1867), pp. 89 f.; Zenker in *Beihefte zur ZRP*, lxx. 129–42; W. Foerster, *Kristian von Troyes, Wörterbuch*, pp. 99*–105*.

deliberate mis-statement of fact, and his witness regarding the Matter of Britain in that puzzling period between Geoffrey and Chrétien is both impeccable and important.

Apart from his omissions and additions, Wace modified the material of his source in other ways. He was no mere translator: he was a poet as well as a chronicler, and he wrote for a somewhat different public from Geoffrey's. His poem marks a stage between the comparative sobriety of his model and the charming extravagances of Arthurian romance. Though he excluded the fables of the Breton *conteurs* and did not exploit amorous sentiment as did his contemporaries, the authors of the *Enéas* and the *Roman de Troie*, he developed a vivacious style and sought pictorial effects which justify the encomia of the critics. Without attempting to go over thoroughly the ground which they have already covered we may note some of his characteristic traits.[1]

The chief general characteristic is a more direct appeal to the imagination of the reader or hearer. Though, as we have seen, he sometimes neglects or avoids opportunities offered by Geoffrey's text to exploit the emotional possibilities of a situation, he more frequently does the opposite, using direct discourse instead of summarizing a speech and, as in the case of Uther's feast for Gorlois, setting the stage and describing the physical reactions of the characters. He bursts into exclamations of sympathy or anger.

The most obvious feature of Wace's style is repetition of words and phrases. The effect at times is rather mechanical, but at others highly effective. Walwein's speech to the emperor Luces derives its force from the play on the phrase 'par bataille'.

> 'Ço te mande que rien n'i prenges
> E si tu sur lui la chalenges,
> Par bataille seit chalengee
> E par bataille deraisnee.
> Romain par bataille la pristrent
> E par bataille la cunquistrent
> E il l'a par bataille eüe
> E par bataille l'ad tenue;
> Par bataille reseit pruvé
> Kin deit aver la poesté. . . .'[2]

Wace uses antithesis with great skill.

> Les forz les fiebles craventer,
> Les vifs les muranz defuler.[3]

[1] On Wace's style see *Brut*, ed. Arnold, i, pp. xiv f., lxxxvi–xci; G. Biller, 'Style des Premiers Romans Français', *Göteborgs Högskolas Årsskrift*, xxii (1916), 188; J. Frappier, *Roman Breton des Origines à Chrétien de Troyes* (Paris, 1950), pp. 70–74; Malkiel-Jirmounsky in *Revue des Langues Romanes*, lxiii (1928), 261–96; Warren in *MP*, iii (1905–6), 179–209, 513–39; iv (1906–7), 655–75; R. H. Fletcher, *Arthurian Material in the Chronicles*, pp. 129–32.

[2] *Brut*, ii. vss. 11719–28. [3] Ibid., vss. 12571 f.

Again, in describing the plight of the gambler, he skilfully places the antithesis in the riming words.

> Tels i puet aseeir vestuz
> Ki al partir s'en lieve nuz.[1]

The poetic manuals laid great emphasis on the art of description, and
Arnold has said of Wace that 'one cannot find among the authors of his century a better craftsman' in that art. He was not to be tempted by the
apparently easy portrayal of womanly beauty, but he painted battle-scenes
with more colour and precision than his epic forerunners. He described the
brilliance of a feast or the joy of a crowd, evoking the very bustle of life.
Wace is the first French poet of the sea; in his childhood home of Jersey and
on his journeys he must have become familiar with ships and sailors. And he
gives us a good description of a storm and an elaborate picture of Arthur's
embarkation at Southampton, full of the technical terms of seamanship.[2]
Indeed, throughout his work he employs to advantage the resources of a
rich and accurate vocabulary.[3]

As for the influence of the *Brut*, the space at our disposal is limited, but
there is room for some brief notes. The poem was paraphrased and elaborated
by Layamon after Henry II's death, as will be shown in the next chapter, and
another redaction in English was made by Robert Mannyng of Bourn as the
first part of his chronicle.[4] The French authors of the *Vulgate Merlin*, the
Mort Artu, the *Didot Perceval*, and the *Livre d'Artus* also drew information
from Wace.[5] Margaret Pelan's study of the relation of the *Brut* to the early
romances makes it clear that Chrétien lighted his torch at the flame of Wace,
imitated the stylistic devices just described, borrowed a few names for use in
Erec and certain situations for use in *Cligès*, but that, beginning with *Lancelot*,
his indebtedness steadily waned.[6] Some critics have too lightly assumed that
every slight resemblance in matter or form which one can detect in a later
author is due to imitation. But set two medieval French poets to describe
independently the arming of a knight, a sumptuous feast, or a combat with a
giant, and it will be a miracle if there are no precise correspondences, even of
phrase. Thomas of Britain and Marie de France show signs of having read

---

[1] *Brut*, ii, vss. 10578 f.   [2] Ibid., vss. 11190–238.

[3] On Wace's vocabulary see H.-E. Keller, *Étude Descriptive du Vocabulaire de Wace* (Berlin, 1952);
B. Woledge in *MLR*, xlvi (1951), 16–30.

[4] Ed. F. J. Furnivall, Rolls Series, 1887. On Mannyng's version see A. W. Zetsche, *Über den I.
Theil der Bearbeitung des 'Roman de Brut' des Wace durch Robert Mannyng of Brunne* (Leipzig, 1887).
On the other chronicles see Fletcher, op. cit., *passim*, and F. Brie, *Geschichte und Quellen der mittel-
englischen Prosachronik, The Brute of England* (Marburg, 1915).

[5] For influence on the *Merlin* see article by Micha in *R*, lxxii (1951), 310–23; on the *Mort Artu*
see J. Frappier, *Étude sur la Mort le Roi Artu* (Paris, 1936), pp. 151–87; on the *Perceval* see *Didot-
Perceval*, ed. W. Roach (Philadelphia, 1941), pp. 103–9. See also chapters on these works.

[6] M. Pelan, *Influence du Brut de Wace*. See also Brugger's review of Annette Brown's book in
ZSFL, xliv[2] (1915), 13–100, and Chap. 15 below.

the *Brut*,[1] but of these the most clear and certain are confined to the historical framework—the story of Gormon in *Tristan* and Arthur's war with the Scots and Picts in *Lanval*. Wace kept a limited audience well into the fourteenth century, especially in England, as the manuscripts show, but by the fifteenth he was too archaic to hold them longer.

[1] E. Hoepffner in *Revue des Cours et Conférences*, July 1933, p. 600. Pelan, op. cit., pp. 72–97, 104–24, seems to attribute to Wace's influence a good many familiar names of Arthurian tradition and some descriptive details which were commonplaces.

LAYAMON'S *BRUT*

ROGER SHERMAN LOOMIS

'A PRIEST there was, living among the people, called Layamon. He was Leovenath's son; may God be gracious to him! He dwelt at Ernleye at a noble church on Severn bank near Radstone; goodly it seemed to him. There he read books. It came to his mind and his serious thought to relate the noble deeds of the English. . . . Layamon journeyed widely among the people and got those noble books which he took for his model. He took the English book which St. Bede made; he took another in Latin that St. Albin and the fair Augustine, who brought baptism hither, had made. A third book he took and laid in the midst which a French cleric made, named Wace, who well could write, and he gave it to the noble Alienor, who was the high King Henry's queen. . . . Layamon took quills in his fingers and set down on book-skin the truer words and condensed three books into one.'

This opening passage of the famous Middle English poem, generally known as the *Brut*,[1] tells us that its author was a parish priest at Arley Regis, Worcestershire, in the Severn valley. His use of 'was' in reference to Eleanor as queen of Henry II implies that Henry at least must have been dead, perhaps Eleanor also. If the latter alternative be accepted, the poem must have been written after 1204, but Tatlock assembled evidence which pointed rather to the reign of Henry's son, Richard I, 1189–99.[2] Tatlock also pointed out that, though the name of Layamon's father was Saxon, that of Layamon himself, meaning 'law man', was of Scandinavian origin and at this time was recorded only in the old Danelaw.[3] Probably, then, there was a Scandinavian

---

[1] The only complete edition is Layamon's *Brut*, ed. F. Madden (London, 1847), which gives the readings of both manuscripts and a fairly accurate translation. The manuscripts are the British Museum Caligula A ix (*c.* 1225) and Otto C xiii (*c.* 1250). The latter seems to show that the scribe knew the poem from memory. Prof. G. L. Brook is preparing a new edition for the *EETS*. The Arthurian portion is translated in *Arthurian Chronicles Represented by Wace and Layamon*, Everyman's Lib. The most important discussions are H. C. Wyld, 'Laȝamon as an English Poet', *RES*, vi (1930), 1–30; 'Studies in the Diction of Layamon's *Brut*', *Language*, ix (1933), 47–71, 171–91; x (1934), 149–201; F. L. Gillespy, 'Layamon's *Brut*: a Comparative Study in Narrative Art', *Univ. of California Pub. in Mod. Phil.* iii (1916), 361–510; R. H. Fletcher, *Arthurian Material in the Chronicles* (Boston, 1906; reprinted Burt Franklin: New York, 1958), pp. 125–66; J. S. P. Tatlock, *Legendary History of Britain*, pp. 472–531; D. Everett, *Essays on Middle English Literature* (Oxford, 1955), pp. 28–45; W. F. Schirmer, *Die frühen Darstellungen des Arthurstoffes*, pp. 54–82.

[2] Tatlock, op. cit., pp. 502–7. The linguistic features also favour a twelfth-century date. Cf. *Layamon's Brut*, ed. J. Hall (Oxford, 1924), p. vii.

[3] Tatlock, op. cit., pp. 511–14.

strain in the poet's family. But it is not necessary to accept Tatlock's theory, based on this fact and the poet's display of knowledge about Irish matters, that Layamon was born in Ireland of a Saxon father and a Scandinavian woman, and spent part of his youth there before he came to England and settled at Arley.[1] Surely an English priest with any curiosity would know of SS. Columkille (Columba), Brendan, and Bride, and would not have had to be born in Ireland to know that the natives when summoned to battle removed their breeches, for, after the Norman conquest of Ireland began in 1169, Irish fighting habits, especially one so bizarre, would have been common topics for conversation in England.

On one point Layamon's introduction is misleading; he made almost no use of Bede's *Ecclesiastical History of the English People*, either in King Alfred's translation or in the original Latin (which scholars agree is meant by the book of SS. Albin and Augustine).[2] He probably had every intention of doing so when he started, but since Wace's book went back to the beginnings of Britain, he had to rely at first on that, and finding it easier to stick to it than to conflate it with Bede, he forgot about his promise to the reader. Ironically enough, the poet who set out to celebrate the noble deeds of the English followed through to the end a book in which that race is held up to execration, for Layamon's poem is substantially a free paraphrase of Wace. Ironically, too, it uses the language, the poetic form, and the style of the people it disparages.

It is generally recognized that Layamon employed the verse form and the conventions, not of the great Anglo-Saxon masterpieces but of the popular poetry of the eleventh and twelfth centuries, the medium of the humbler minstrels who succeeded the courtly *scops* and learned clerics.[3] The basic verse form is still the alliterative line with four accents and a slight pause in the middle, but the alliteration is quite irregular, in many lines absent, and the lines are longer. Moreover, the hemistichs are often linked by assonance or rime, a feature which had already appeared in the Anglo-Saxon *Judith*. In all these respects Layamon's *Brut* shows a close likeness to the *Proverbs of Alfred*, written somewhat earlier.

The influence of Wace may be seen in the increasing use of rime as the poem proceeds, and in the effective employment of simile, a device very rare in Anglo-Saxon poetry. Wace has a few short comparisons, for example: 'As the proud lion, which has long been starved, kills rams, kills ewes, kills lambs, great and small, just so did the Britons';[4] 'They [a Roman troop] were without a commander, like a ship without a steersman, which the wind

---

[1] Ibid., pp. 515–30.

[2] Ibid., p. 487.

[3] Ibid., pp. 485–7, 497. Tatlock in *Manly Anniversary Studies in Language and Literature* (Chicago, 1923), pp. 3–11.

[4] Wace, *Roman de Brut*, ed. I. Arnold (Paris, 1938–40), vss. 8517–21.

drives wherever it wishes when there is no one who keeps it on its course.'[1] Layamon seems to have taken the hint from these passages (though, oddly enough, he does not paraphrase them), and from Merlin's prophecy that Uther's son will be 'like a boar fierce in battle', and he introduced many similes as consciously as did Homer. 'As a whirlwind does in the field when it raises the dust high from the earth, so Ridwathlan rushed on his foes.'[2] Again, we read that Arthur 'rushed like the fierce wolf, when he comes from the wood behung with snow, and thinks to bite such beasts as he pleases'.[3] When the Saxons were routed, 'some wandered as the wild crane does in the moor-fen when his flight is impaired and swift hawks pursue him and hounds meet him cruelly in the reeds. Then neither land nor water is good to him; hawks smite him, hounds bite him; then the royal fowl is doomed on his way.'[4] Again, when at Bath Arthur gazed on the mail-clad corpses of the Saxons lying in the river, Layamon put in his mouth this mocking shout: 'Yesterday was Baldulf boldest of all knights; now he stands on the hill and beholds the Avon, how steel fishes lie in the stream. . . . Their scales float like gold-painted shields; their fins float as if they were spears!'[5] This same battle of Bath inspired three other similes: the wild boar meeting the swine in the beech wood, hunters running the fox to earth and digging him out, and the goat defending himself with his horns against the wolf. Nothing seems to have stirred Layamon's imagination to these vivid flights except the triumphs of his ancestral foes.

Similes account only in very small part, however, for the fact that the English poet expanded Wace's 14,800 verses to 32,200 hemistichs. Though he omitted many trifling details and condensed the narrative of Arthur's embarkation for Normandy—one of Wace's purple passages—to six lines,[6] yet he more than made up for these cuts by his looser style and his inventions. Epic formulas, of which Tatlock counted more than 125, serve as padding.[7] On a voyage 'wind stod an willen' (the wind stood in the desired quarter); during a battle 'monie þer weoren faeie' (many there were doomed). Again and again Arthur is styled 'noblest of kings'. Some of these stereotyped phrases once had vigour but lose it through constant reiteration.

Far more important both in bulk and in significance are the many elaborations due simply to Layamon's feeling for the concrete and the dramatic, which has already been noted in his similes. Wace says merely that after Arthur had defeated Lucius he caused the body of the emperor to be taken and watched with great honour and sent it to Rome on a bier.[8] Layamon specifies that Arthur had a tent pitched in a broad field, had the body of

---

[1] Vss. 12061–4.   [2] Layamon, *Brut*, ed. Madden, iii. 102.
[3] Ibid. ii. 421.   [4] Ibid. ii. 422 f.   [5] Ibid. ii. 471 f.
[6] Wace, op. cit., vss. 11193–238; Layamon, iii, vss. 25537–48.
[7] Tatlock in *PMLA*, xxxviii (1923), 494–592.
[8] Wace, op. cit., vss. 12987–9.

Luces borne there and covered with gold-coloured palls and watched for three days while he had a long chest made, covered with gold. When the body had been placed in it, he sent it under the escort of three kings on a lofty bier to Rome.[1]

Most vital and original are the additions which describe behaviour, express feelings in speech, and even supply dramatic incidents. For instance, Wace tells the story of the poisoning of Uther by Saxon spies in general terms and uses no direct discourse.[2] Layamon is very specific, introduces six speeches, and sets the action at Winchester. He invents[3] the scene where the spies, dressed as almsmen, wait in the street for the king's dole. They hail a knight of the royal household, complain that they have been starving since the Saxons took their lands, and are now singing prayers for King Uther. The knight reports their complaint to Uther, and at his bidding they are admitted to his household. It is a fresh and realistic handling of an ironic situation.

Arthur's portentous dream which forecasts the treachery of Modred has been often noted as one of Layamon's best additions to Wace,[4] and though the idea was perhaps traditional, since we have variant versions of such a dream in texts which are not based on Layamon,[5] the handling seems very characteristic of his manner. Arthur dreamed that he was sitting astride the roof of a hall with Walwain before him. Modred came with a battle-axe and hewed the posts which upheld the building, and Wenhaver pulled down the roof so that Arthur fell and broke his right arm. Gripping his sword in his left hand, Arthur smote off Modred's head so that it rolled on the floor, and he hacked the queen to pieces.

This last detail illustrates one of Layamon's strangest and strongest idiosyncrasies, for this man of God was a barbarian at heart. He seems to belong in a milieu where the softening influences of woman-worship and courtesy were unknown. Whereas Wace attributes to Gawain the sentiment that 'for friendship (*amistié*) and for their mistresses knights perform deeds of chivalry',[6] the Saxon poet deletes the mistresses.[7] He seems to approve of Arthur's wholesale punishment of the kindred of those who quarrelled at his Yuletide feast: the males were to lose their heads, the females their noses.[8] The code which protects ambassadors from outrage had little sanctity for Layamon, for whereas Wace said merely that the Britons in anger would have insulted and

[1] Layamon, iii. 111 f.   [2] Wace, op. cit., vss. 8961–96.

[3] Layamon, ii. 400–7. I speak of this scene as an invention because Uther was not attached to the Arthurian legend until Geoffrey of Monmouth made him the father of Arthur. G. Schoepperle Loomis in *Vassar Mediaeval Studies*, ed. C. F. Fiske (New Haven, 1923), pp. 4 f. The statement that Uther appears in Nennius's text is, of course, a slip.

[4] Layamon, iii. 118–20.

[5] *Morte Arthure*, ed. E. Björkman (Heidelberg and New York, 1915), pp. 95–102; *Mort Artu*, ed. J. Frappier (Paris, 1936), pp. 199–201; Malory, bk. xxi, chap. 3; J. Frappier, *Étude sur la Mort le Roi Artu* (Paris, 1936), pp. 178–80.   [6] Wace, op. cit., vss. 10771 f.

[7] Layamon, ii. 627.   [8] Ibid. ii. 536.

rebuked the Roman embassy if Arthur had not interrupted,[1] Layamon has the Britons leap on the Romans, clutch them by the hair, and throw them to the ground before Arthur stops them.[2] Over and over again the priest of Arley repeats gleefully the curses which consigned the enemies of the Britons to hell. Even his humour has a grim flavour, for when Uther killed Pascent by driving a sword into his mouth, the poet remarks, 'such food was strange to him'.[3]

Though many critics have ignored this ferocious streak, Tatlock candidly called it Layamon's 'most intense and personal trait'.[4] He suggested that it was due to the poet's hypothetical Irish blood and contrasted it with what he termed 'the thoroughly Christian or at least restrained' character of Anglo-Saxon poetry. But even Tatlock had to admit that the *scop* in his battle-pieces exulted in slaughter; and the clerics who composed *Exodus* and *Judith* displayed a similar taste for blood. Racial distinctions are notoriously hazardous, and Layamon's brutality, ruthlessness, and hatred of the heathen, which Tatlock would derive from the Irish, may be matched abundantly in the *chansons de geste*.

Let us return to the subject of Layamon's additions and consider three which have provoked both curiosity and controversy. The first tells how, when Arthur was born, 'alven' (fays) took him and bestowed on him three gifts—strength, dominion, and long life.[5] Some readers have been struck by the Germanic word *alven* and have been reminded of the coming of the Norns at the birth of Helgi. But though the word is Germanic, the concept is widespread. The same story of the fays and their gifts is told of Arthur by the second continuator of *Perceval*, and of Floriant and Ogier the Dane by other French poets, who most significantly speak of Morgain la Fée as chief of the ladies and tell how, when the hero comes to die, she transports him to her island home.[6] Since three French poets knew this tradition and could not have got it from Layamon, evidently it was a French legend. If one wishes to trace it back to a Celtic source, one may find it surviving in Breton folk-lore.[7] Sébillot was told in 1880 that the fairies called Margots bestowed gifts on the new-born infants of noble houses and predicted what they would become.[8]

The second passage is the exquisite account of Arthur's departure.[9]

[1] Wace, op. cit., vss. 10717.   [2] Layamon, ii. 621 f.
[3] Ibid. ii. 334.   [4] Tatlock, *Legendary History*, p. 523.
[5] Layamon, ii. 384.
[6] C. Potvin, *Perceval le Gallois* (Mons, 1866–71), v. 123 f.; *Floriant et Florete*, ed. F. Michel (Edinburgh, 1873); ed. Harry F. Williams (Ann Arbor, 1947), vss. 549–70, 8177–217; Le Roux de Lincy, *Livre des Légendes* (Paris, 1836), pp. 178 f.; I. E. Rathborne, *Meaning of Spenser's Fairyland* (New York, 1937), pp. 186–9, 213 f.; L. A. Paton, *Fairy Mythology of Arthurian Romance* (Boston, 1903), p. 76.
[7] *Comparative Literature*, ii (1950), 297; *Annales de Bretagne*, lvi (1949), 214.
[8] P. Sébillot, *Traditions et Superstitions de la Haute Bretagne* (Paris, 1882), p. 110.
[9] Layamon, iii. 144 f.

Wounded in his last battle with a broad spear, he spoke to Constantine, his kinsman:

'I will fare to Avalun, to the fairest of all maidens, to Argante the queen, a fay most fair. She shall make my wounds all sound, make me all whole with healing potions. Then I will come again to my kingdom and dwell with the Britons with great joy.' Even with the words, there came from the sea a short boat gliding, driven by the waves, and two women therein wondrously clad. They took Arthur at once and bore him in haste and laid him down softly and moved away. . . . Bretons believe yet that he is alive and dwells in Avalun with the fairest of all fays.

The closest parallel is again furnished by a French text, the *Didot Perceval*,[1] which relates that Arthur, wounded by a lance, announced to Constantine that he would not die, but would be conveyed to Avalon to have his wounds tended by Morgain, his sister. The author adds a reference to the Wild Hunt and the Breton hope of Arthur's return. This story of Arthur's passing is, of course, closely related to that of the fays at his birth, and Giraldus makes it certain that it came from the Bretons since he credits it not to his countrymen, the *Wallenses*, but to the 'fabulosi Britones et eorum cantores'.[2]

The third passage concerns the fight over precedence at Arthur's Yuletide feast and the making of the Round Table by a Cornish carpenter.[3] Layamon paraphrased Wace's reference to the Bretons[4] and added the description of the fracas. He added also that the Table could seat 1,600 men and yet could be carried about wherever Arthur rode. Layamon, too, must have read of the Round Table in French, or listened to a tale told by a Breton *conteur*.

The evidence regarding these three passages is consistent and plain: their sources were not in the poet's own brain but in Breton stories, related in French, either orally or in manuscript. This is corroborated by the fact that the name which Layamon gives to one of Modred's sons, Melyon, matches the name Melehan which is given him in the Vulgate *Mort Artu*, and which is likewise applied to the hero of a Breton lai.[5] There is nothing to support the conjecture that Layamon picked up his Celtic matter from the Welsh,[6] nor has research revealed any manuscript of Wace's *Brut* which included these additions, as Immelmann and Bruce postulated.[7] It would appear that

[1] *Didot-Perceval*, ed. W. Roach (Philadelphia, 1941), p. 277; J. L. Weston, *Legend of Sir Perceval* ii (London, 1909), 111.

[2] E. K. Chambers, *Arthur of Britain* (London, 1927), p. 272.

[3] See p. 100 above.　　　　　　　　　　　　　　[4] Layamon, ii. 532–43.

[5] Brugger in *ZFSL*, xlix[1] (1926), 441, 466 ff.; Bruce in *MLN*, xxvi (1911), 68.

[6] Bruce in the article mentioned in the preceding note, and Tatlock, op. cit., pp. 492 f., dispose of the arguments for immediate Welsh sources put forth in *MP*, i (1903), 95–103, and in G. J. Visser, *La3amon, an Attempt at Vindication* (Assen, 1935).

[7] R. Immelmann, *Layamon, Versuch über seine Quellen* (Berlin, 1906); Bruce, i. 29–32. Tatlock in *Legendary History*, pp. 477–82, has adequately refuted the theory of an expanded version of Wace.

the tales were so familiar, so fascinating, and so widely believed that Layamon could hardly help including them.

Yet in spite of this demonstrated Breton influence and of a more questionable Irish or Scandinavian inheritance, Layamon is essentially, as Wyld maintained,[1] an English poet. To be sure, the claim that his sea-pieces carry on the tradition of the Anglo-Saxon *Seafarer*, or that Arthur's waking the giant of Mont St. Michel before attacking him shows a peculiarly English ideal of sportsmanship, cannot be accepted,[2] for only S. Ursula's voyage is described in more than landlubber commonplaces, and Huon of Bordeaux was as chivalrous as Arthur.[3] Nevertheless, anyone who has read much in the earliest English poetry will feel at home with Layamon, in spite of the looser lines, the presence of rime and assonance, and the rarity of kennings. The vocabulary is overwhelmingly Saxon; only 150 Romance words occur.[4] There is a wealth of synonyms for 'warrior', 'sea', 'go', &c. The nickers that haunt Grendel's mere in *Beowulf* bathe in Layamon's Loch Lomond.[5] There are *scops* in both poems, and there is *dream* (joy) in hall. Both poets, though Christian, accept the idea of an inexorable doom involved in the Saxon word *faege*, Middle English *feye*, Scottish *fey*. Though Layamon's use of the kenning is confined almost entirely to phrases descriptive of the Deity,[6] he achieves at one point such an agglomeration of these as to rival Caedmon's *Hymn*. Here is Caedmon:[7]

> Þa middangeard   moncynnes weard,
> Ece dryhten,   æfter teode
> Firum foldan,   frea ælmihtig.

While Caedmon managed to get three kennings into three lines, Layamon got five![8]

> Laverd drihten crist,   domes waldende,
> Midelarde mund,   monnen froure,
> Þurh þine aðmode wil,   walden ænglen . . .

Perhaps the most startling survivals of the old native tradition are certain details of Arthur's arming for the battle of Bath. Wace, following Geoffrey, had mentioned the sword Caliburne, the shield Pridwen, the spear Ron, and a hauberk without name.[9] Layamon says this byrnie was made by an elvish smith, calls it Wygar, and adds 'þe witeʒe wurhte', which may mean either

[1] *RES*, vi (1930), 1–30.

[2] R. M. Wilson, *Early Middle English Literature* (London, 1939), p. 210; W. H. Schofield, *English Literature from the Norman Conquest to Chaucer* (New York, London, 1906), p. 352.

[3] Gillespy, *Layamon's Brut*, p. 369.   [4] *MP*, iv (1907), 559–67.

[5] Layamon, ii. 489; *Beowulf*, vs. 1427.

[6] Gillespy, op. cit., pp. 479 f.

[7] E. V. K. Dobbie, *Manuscripts of Caedmon's Hymn and Bede's Death Song* (New York, 1937), p. 24; J. W. Bright, *Anglo-Saxon Reader*, 3rd ed. (New York, 1907), p. 10.

[8] Layamon, iii. 14.   [9] Wace, op. cit., vss. 9275–300.

'which a wizard wrought', or, 'which Witege wrought'.[1] Now Widia, as Kittredge observed, was in Germanic legend the son of the famous artificer Weland.[2] Arthur's helm, too, Layamon calls Goswhit, i.e. 'Goose-white'.[3] It cannot be wholly a coincidence that Beowulf's byrnie was wrought by Weland and that we read of his 'hwita helm'.[4]

Thus we find Layamon employing the traditions of his ancestors to glorify their most redoubtable foe. He even exults in the fulfilment of the forecasts which he had met presumably in some form of Geoffrey of Monmouth's *Prophetiae Merlini*[5] and had applied to Arthur: 'In ore populorum cele-brabitur, et actus eius cibus erit narrantibus.' 'Pectus eius cibus erit egentibus, et lingua eius sedabit sicientes.'[6] Twice Layamon paraphrases them. 'Of him shall gleemen sing gloriously; of his breast shall eat noble *scops*; of his blood shall men drink.'[7] 'Gleemen will make a table of that king's breast, and very many *scops* will sit at it and eat their fill ere they depart thence, and draw out wine-draughts from that king's tongue, and drink and revel day and night.'[8] Surely it was a happy prophecy, for Arthur has been the hero not only of Welsh bards and Breton *conteurs* but of some of the great poets of England, of whom Layamon himself was the first.[9]

---

[1] Layamon, ii. 463; *RES*, x (1934), 83 f.   [2] *MP*, i (1903), 99, n. 4.
[3] Layamon, ii. 464.   [4] *Beowulf*, vss. 455, 1448.
[5] The forecasts are not in Wace. Tatlock, op. cit., pp. 490 f.
[6] Geoffrey of Monmouth, *Historia*, ed. A. Griscom, pp. 385, 389; Faral, iii. 191, 195.
[7] Layamon, ii. 367.   [8] Ibid. ii. 544.
[9] I wish to thank Professor G. L. Brook for his kindness in reading this chapter and offering his comments.

THE BRETON LAIS[1]

ERNEST HOEPFFNER

IN Chapter 6 there was mention of certain 'Breton lais', short narrative poems in French which in their subject-matter sometimes display a marked resemblance to episodes found in the Arthurian romances.[2] There are other lais which, though offering no close parallel in incident to the romances, deal with Arthurian characters or are localized at Arthur's court. There are still others, the majority, which bear no relation to the longer works of fiction attached to the knights of the Table Round. These short poems known as Breton lais began to be composed in verse about the middle of the twelfth century and shared the widespread popularity of the Arthurian romances well into the fourteenth century, some of them being freely rendered into Norse, English, German, and Italian. Some lais have been preserved only in these foreign forms and some have been lost altogether, though their names have survived, such as *Merlin le Sauvage* and *Mabon*.[3]

The problem of the origin of the genre has not yet found a definitive solution, but some inferences may be drawn from the use of the word *lai* in what seem to be earlier senses, and from the fact, generally accepted by scholars, that it is related to the Irish word *laid*, meaning a 'song'.[4] Certain early uses of the term imply that it meant both a song and its musical accompaniment. The poet Thomas, in a charming scene, presents Isolt singing the lai of Guiron.[5] When Benoît de Ste-Maure compares the melodious cries of

---

[1] This chapter was revised by the editor and submitted to its author before his greatly to be lamented death. His corrections have been carried out, and all opinions expressed have received his approval: in fact, most of the material added by the editor—the general discussion of the type and the remarks on *Chèvrefeuil*—was summarized from Hoepffner's own book, *Les Lais de Marie de France* (Paris, 1955). Other editorial additions are the titles of two lost lais, the references to Tegau Eurvron and her mantle, the Breton place-names resembling Lanval, and much bibliographical material in the notes.

[2] On the Breton lais in general see Hoepffner's book cited in the previous note; K. Warnke, *Die Lais der Marie de France*, 3rd ed. (Halle, 1925), Einleitung; W. Hertz, *Spielmannsbuch*, 4th ed. (Stuttgart, Berlin, 1912); G. V. Smithers, in *MedAev*, xxii (1953), 61–92; A. Ahlström, *Studier i den Fornfranska Lais-Litteraturen* (Uppsala, 1892). On Breton origin of the lais see Brugger in *ZFSL*, xx (1898), 79–162; xlix (1927), 116–55, and on nomenclature ibid. 201–52, 381–484. For theory that Marie de France created the type see L. Foulet, *ZRP*, xxix (1905), 19–56, 293–322, and critique by Warnke, op. cit., pp. xlvi–lx, and by E. Levi in *Studj Romanzi*, xiv (1917), 113–246.   [3] For a thirteenth-century list of lais see *MLR*, xlv (1950), 40–45.

[4] On meaning of word *lai* see *ZRP*, xxxii (1908), 161–83; R. Bromwich in *MedAev*, xxvi (1957), 36–38.   [5] Ed. Bédier, vss. 833–42; ed. Wind, pp. 93 f.

the Amazons to the Breton lais, he is evidently thinking of vocal rather than instrumental compositions. On the other hand, Wace says that Baldulf was skilled in the art of harping 'lais and melodies (*notes*)', and that the *jongleurs* at the court of Arthur performed 'lais of vielles, lais of rotes, harps, and flutes'.[1] One can thus understand how Chrétien de Troyes in *Cligès* (vss. 4071 f.) could speak of two combatants who 'played lais on the helms' with their swords. Apparently the word *lai* first referred indifferently to the words of a song or the tune. Of such songs no example has survived, but one may conclude from the high admiration they evoked that the music was complicated and artistic.

What, then, is the relation between the extant narrative poems and the songs, also called Breton lais, which are forever lost? This is no easy question to answer. Marie de France stresses the titles of her lais. In *Eliduc* and *Chaitivel* she gives two titles; sometimes she gives the same title in two or three different languages. The fact that two of these alternative titles, *Laustic* and *Bisclavret*, are Breton, and a third, *Guildeluec ha Gualadun*, contains the Breton conjunction *ha* suggests that she had heard the Breton *jongleurs* announce their songs in this way. The song, then, would have been in the Breton tongue, and a tale would be told in French for the benefit of those who did not understand Breton, explaining the circumstances which were supposed to have inspired the song. The relation seems to have been like that between the Provençal *razo*, a short prose narrative prefixed to certain troubadour lyrics, and the lyrics themselves. Thus the term *lai* was extended from the original Breton composition, which embraced both music and words, to the oral narrative in French, the *cunte* or *reisun* (*Eliduc*, vss. 1–4), which preceded or followed it. The term was then further extended to a literary composition in verse, based on the oral tale. Only lais in this third sense were written down and have survived, and only those which have an Arthurian connexion are treated in this chapter.

The earliest surviving lai is probably the *Lai du Cor* of Robert Biket.[2] It is archaic in its verse form, being composed in six-syllable verses instead of the normal octosyllables; archaic also is the rather crude humour with which it treats the great King Arthur and his court. Indeed, Lucien Foulet and Bruce refused to accept the poem as a genuine lai because of its unromantic tone, and classed it as a *fabliau*.[3] But must a Breton lai necessarily be serious and sentimental? Must it treat Arthur's fellowship with high respect? There are other poems called lais which are even more grossly cynical,[4] and Chrétien himself is by no means consistently flattering in his portrayal of Arthur.

[1] Wace, *Brut*, ed. I. Arnold, ii, vss. 9103 f., 10548 f.
[2] Ed. F. Wulff (Lund, 1888), and H. Dörner (Strasbourg, 1907). For bibliography of the horn test see Loomis, *Arthurian Tradition*, p. 95, n. 55. See also T. P. Cross in *MP*, x (1913), 289–99.
[3] *ZRP*, xxix (1905), p. 55, n. 1; Bruce, i. 66, n. 61.
[4] *Lai du Lecheor, Lai d'Ignaure.*

The *Lai du Cor* has been dated in the third quarter of the twelfth century, but not by conclusive criteria. Of Biket we know nothing except that his language betrays the Anglo-Norman. He professes to have had the tale from an abbot (vss. 583 f.), and asserts that the magic horn was to be seen at Cirencester—statements which there is no more reason to doubt than that there was shown at St. Seurin at Bordeaux what professed to be the horn of Roland. Though Cirencester was then not more than twenty miles from the Welsh-speaking district beyond the Severn, it is significant that the personal names which Biket introduces are as remote from the corresponding Welsh forms as the names in any Continental French romance.

The hero of the *Lai du Cor* is a figure known to Chrétien de Troyes as Karadues Briebraz (Short-arm), to the Bretons as Karadoc Brech Bras (Armstrong), and to the Welsh as Caradawc Vreichvras.[1] The manuscript of the lai (Bodleian Lib., Digby 86) gives the name as Garadue. It also gives other well-known names: Arzurs, Artu, Gauuein, Gauwain, Iuuein, Iuwain, Giflet, Keerz, Lot, and Mangounz. Aguisiaus d'Escoce may have been borrowed from Chrétien's *Erec*. Kadoins, Kadoiners, Gohers, Glouien, Caratouns, and Galahal are of uncertain derivation,[2] and are not recognizably Welsh.[3] It seems clear that neither Biket nor his alleged informant derived his material directly from the lands across the Severn.

The general theme of the lai is found at different times and under different forms in the folk-lore of many peoples. In this poem it is a drinking-horn which is sent to Arthur's court at Caerleon by King Mangoun of Moraine[4] and which has the property of exposing the slightest infidelity of a wife. Arthur insists on the experiment and, when he tries to drink, is drenched with wine from top to toe. He would have killed the queen if his knights had not intervened. But he recovers his good humour when he finds that all who follow his example are similarly disillusioned by the magic horn, and he pardons her with a kiss. Finally Garadue passes the test triumphantly, and Arthur awards him the lordship of Cirencester.

Though stories of chastity tests are spread far and wide, and though the *Lai du Cor* was not derived directly from the Welsh, it may be significant that all medieval versions of the horn test are set in Arthur's banquet hall, and that the hero bears a name renowned in Wales and Brittany.

One cannot affirm that Biket knew Chrétien's *Erec*, but he must have known Wace.[5] The list of royal guests, the toast 'Wesseil' which Garadue

---

[1] Chrétien, *Erec*, ed. Foerster, vs. 1719. See above, Chap. 4, p. 41, n. 6.

[2] Some have undergone scribal distortion. Kadoiners should be Kadoins, and Keerz should be Kez. Gohers, which is coupled with *corns*, should be Gohors, riming with *cors*.

[3] The 'roi de Sinadoune' (vs. 415) is thus called from the Snowdon region in North Wales, not by its Welsh but its Anglo-Norman title. *Spec*, xxii (1947), 527; *Mélanges Hoepffner* (Paris, 1949), pp. 230–2.   [4] On Mangoun and his horn see Loomis, *Arthurian Tradition*, pp. 244–50.

[5] M. Pelan, *L'Influence du Brut de Wace* (Paris, 1931), pp. 131 f., is doubtful.

proposed to Arthur, the respectful treatment of Keerz (Kay), and certain stylistic features assure us of the fact. Though nearly contemporary with Chrétien's earliest work, the *Lai du Cor* belongs to an older world, and its importance lies largely in shedding light on the nature of Arthurian fiction before the influence of Chrétien was felt.

About fifty years after Biket had treated the theme of the chastity-testing horn it was again taken up by the anonymous author of the First Continuation of Chrétien's *Perceval* and introduced as the final episode in a sort of biography of Caradoc.[1] The principal characters are the same, the horn is again described as banded with gold and set with jewels, and other details suggest familiarity with the lai. But the differences are many. The town of Cirencester is not mentioned, nor are the sweet-sounding bells attached to the horn. The proper names assume a more familiar form: Caradoc's wife, nameless in the lai, is called Guignier; and even the horn is equipped with a name which varies from manuscript to manuscript but appears in two of them as Beneïz, Beneoiz.[2] Guenièvre, foreseeing that her infidelity will be revealed, prays God that the horn will spill its contents over her husband, and when this occurs Arthur interprets his humiliation as a miraculous answer to prayer rather than as proof of his wife's guilt—a clever bit of comedy which reminds one of Iseut's cynical use of the ambiguous oath in Béroul. The *Livre de Caradoc* thus provides an instructive example of how the material of a lai was modified to fit into a romance.

The comedy of the testing-horn underwent other developments. Biket had ascribed the making of the vessel to a malicious fay, and in the Prose *Tristan* it is Morgain la Fée who sends the horn to Arthur's court in order to expose the liaison of Lancelot and Guenièvre.[3] In a German farce of the fifteenth century it is again Morgain (though her name is not given) who wishes by the same means to humiliate her brother Arthur.[4] Two episodes in Heinrich von dem Türlin's *Krône* substitute for the horn a cup and a glove.[5] In several instances the talisman is a mantle which will fit perfectly a perfectly chaste woman but will shrink when worn by a woman of inferior virtue.[6] Since a mantle of precisely this kind is assigned in late Welsh texts to Tegau Eurvron, the wife of Caradawc Vreichvras, and since already in the thirteenth century she was renowned for her fidelity,[7] it is not improbable

---

[1] W. Roach, *Continuations of the Old French Perceval* (Philadelphia), i. 232–8, ii. 370–7, iii. 195–203. See below, pp. 212–14.   [2] Ibid. ii, vs. 12315.

[3] E. Löseth, *Roman en Prose de Tristan* (Paris, 1891), § 47.

[4] A. V. Keller, *Fastnachtspiele aus dem fünfzehnten Jahrhundert*, Nachlese (Stuttgart, 1858), pp. 183–215. See below, p. 559.

[5] Ed. G. H. F. Scholl (Stuttgart, 1852), vss. 918–3131, 22990–5543.

[6] On all versions of this theme see *Der Mantel*, ed. O. Warnatsch, *Germanistische Abhandlungen*, (Breslau, 1883), ii.

[7] Loomis, *Arthurian Tradition*, p. 98. That this Welsh tradition goes back to the thirteenth century is proved by the mention in the English poem, *Annot and Johon*, of Cradoc as carving the

that the motif originated in Wales and spread thence to Brittany, England, France, Switzerland, Germany, and Iceland.

The French version goes under the title of *Le Manteau Mautaillié* and may be regarded as a lai even though there is no manuscript authority for so describing it.[1] Several decades later than the *Lai du Cor*, it may have been influenced by that poem and has the same hero, Caradoc, and the same setting at Arthur's court. But by this time, surely, these features had become traditional, and the list of participants in the test is drawn not from Biket but from Chrétien's *Erec*. The author asserts that the mantle has been deposited in a Welsh abbey, that it has recently been discovered, and that it is again to be tried out on 'dames et demeiselles'. Plainly the author was writing with tongue in cheek, and if he hoped to be taken seriously he was probably disappointed.

If we turn back chronologically to the period about 1160 we meet a poet with a different spirit and far greater talent who composed at least twelve Breton lais in standard literary French with Norman colouring—the woman already referred to as Marie de France.[2] 'Marie ai nom, si sui de France', she declares in her *Ysopet*, a collection of Aesopic fables translated from English, and by this she presumably meant that her childhood home had been in France as distinct from the great duchies of Burgundy, Berry, Aquitaine, &c. She certainly had been well educated and moved in high society, dedicating her lais to a 'noble king', probably to be identified as Henry II, and her *Ysopet* to a 'cunte Willame', possibly William Longsword, natural son of Henry. The lais, which show the influence of Wace, would therefore have been composed between 1155 and 1189, the date of Henry's death. The *Ysopet* followed, and her last work, the *Espurgatoire St. Patrice*, was written after 1189. An identification of the poet with Marie, half-sister of King Henry, who became Abbess of Shaftesbury and died about 1216, would fit in with these dates and facts.[3] Another plausible theory would identify the 'noble king' with Henry II's son Henry, crowned in his father's lifetime, and the Count William with William Marshal, Earl of Pembroke.[4]

Living in England, the poet must have listened to the Breton singers and

roast at court and of Tegau as an example of truth. *Lyrics of the Thirteenth Century*, ed. Carleton Brown (Oxford, 1933), pp. 138, 226.   [1] Ed. F. A. Wulff in *R*, xiv (1885), 343–80.

[2] For editions of Marie's lais see Warnke, op. cit.; ed. A. Ewert (Oxford, 1944); ed. E. Hoepffner (Strasbourg, 1921); *Gugemar, Lanval, and a Fragment of Yonec*, ed. J. Harris (New York, 1930). For discussions see Brugger in *ZFSL*, xlix (1926), 116–55; E. Hoepffner, *Les Lais de Marie de France*; Hoepffner, 'La Géographie et l'Histoire dans les Lais de Marie de France', *R*, lvi (1930), 1–32; E. A. Francis, 'Marie de France et son Temps', *R*, lxxii (1951), 87–95; L. Spitzer, 'Marie de France — Dichterin der Problem-Märchen', *ZRP*, l (1930), 29–67; 'Prologue to the Lais of Marie de France and Mediaeval Poetics', *MP*, xli (1943), 96–102; M. de Riquer, 'La "Aventure", el "Lai" y el "Conte" en Maria de Francia', *Filologia Romanza*, ii (1955), 1–19.

[3] J. C. Fox in *English Historical Rev.* xxvi (1911), 317–26; but how could a daughter of Geoffrey of Anjou say that she was 'de France'?

[4] E. Levi in *Archivum Romanicum*, v (1921), 448–95.

conteurs who were then fascinating courtly circles with their strange musical compositions and their fabulous tales. She tells us frankly in her prologue to the lais that she had intended to employ her talents on translating some Latin narrative into French, but, finding the field occupied, she had decided to make a collection of lais, turn them into rime, and make poems of them. 'Rimez en ai e fait ditié.'

Though familiarity with Wace's *Brut* may account for the reference to the feast of St. Aaron at Carlion in *Yonec* (vss. 467 f.) and for the introduction of Hoël as King of Brittany in *Guigemar* (vss. 27–29),[1] this is not the only explanation possible, and in any case it does not bring these poems within the Arthurian cycle. The employment of certain supernatural motifs which appear later in Arthurian settings, such as the chase of the white hind in *Guigemar*[2] and the werewolf in *Bisclavret*,[3] does not make these poems Arthurian. Only two of Marie's lais can be so defined with any justice. To be sure, one of them, the *Lai du Chèvrefeuil*, may be excluded since Arthur is not named and there is no assurance that Marie linked Tristan, the hero, with Arthur's court; but since that association was firmly established by Béroul's time, not long after, and has continued down to our own day, *Le Chèvrefeuil* may be considered to lie within the scope of this chapter.[4]

Though containing only 118 verses, it was, judging by many references to it in later literature, one of Marie's most popular poems. She adopts the convention of ascribing to the hero the original musical composition: 'Tristram, ki bien saveit harper, En aveit fet un nuvel lai.' She gives us also the more reliable information that she had heard stories of the loves of Tristan and the queen from many persons and had also found them in writing. Indeed, she assumes on the part of her readers a complete familiarity with the romance, and the incident she relates is remotely similar to one told by the German, Eilhart von Oberge.[5] Tristan returns from exile in South Wales to Cornwall, and in order to inform the queen of his presence, he carves his name on a hazel rod and leaves it in the road along which she is to pass. She does indeed spy the token, stops her cavalcade, and on the pretext of resting leaves them to meet her lover. Though soon parted again from the queen, Tristan composed the lai in remembrance of the joy he had had in the meeting and in order to preserve the words he had written at the queen's direction.

[1] M. Pelan, op. cit., pp. 104–24.

[2] C. Pschmadt, *Sage von der Verfolgten Hinde* (Greifswald, 1911).   [3] *SNPL*, viii (1903), 162 ff.

[4] Much has been written about this lai, particularly about the message on the hazel rod. G. Schoepperle in *R*, xxxviii (1909), 196–218; L. Spitzer in *R*, lxix (1946), 80–90; G. Frank in *PMLA*, lxiii (1948), 405–11; A. G. Hatcher in *R*, lxxi (1950), 330–44; A.-M. Valero in *Boletín de la Real Acad. de Buenas Letras de Barcelona*, 1951–2, pp. 173–83; P. Le Gentil in *Mélanges H. Chamard* (Paris, 1951), pp. 17–27; J. Frappier in *Mélanges de Linguistique et de Littérature Romanes à la Mémoire d'István Frank* (Universität des Saarlandes, 1957).

[5] G. Schoepperle, *Tristan and Isolt* (London, Frankfurt, 1913), pp. 138–47.

What were these words?—a question much discussed by scholars. Marie tells us: Tristan has long waited the chance to see the queen, for he cannot live without her. It is with them as with the honeysuckle (*chèvrefeuil*) and the hazel-tree. When the vine has twined itself about the hazel trunk, they may endure together, but, separated, they die. 'Bele amie, si est de nus: Ne vus sanz mei, ne mei sanz vus.' In this couplet we have the essence of the whole Tristan legend. In its harmonious simplicity it reveals not only the art of Marie but also the profound feeling with which she entered into the sorrows and the joys of her characters. It has the poignancy of that other couplet, recorded by Gottfried von Strassburg: 'Iseut ma drue, Iseut m'amie, En vous ma mort, en vous ma vie.'

Lanval also is one of the most brilliant and moving of Marie's lais, and tells a dramatic story.[1] The titular hero, a king's son serving in Arthur's court, has fallen into disfavour and poverty. One day as he was lying, sad of heart, in a meadow, he was invited by two damsels to the tent of their mistress. She declared that she had left her land for his sake, granted him her love on condition that he would never reveal the secret, and even after his return to court supplied him mysteriously with wealth. Unfortunately Arthur's queen, unnamed, tried to seduce him, and in a reckless moment he boasted that even the handmaid of his mistress was lovelier and better bred than the queen. Thereupon she accused him to the king of improper advances, and Lanval was ordered to produce his faery mistress to prove that he had not slandered the queen. But since he had broken his promise of secrecy, the fay no longer visited him, and he was in despair. Summoned before the judges, Lanval confessed his inability to make good his rash words, but before decision was rendered against him two maidens, robed in cendal, rode in to ask hospitality for their lady. Presently two others arrived and created a sensation by their beauty. But Lanval had to admit that he did not know them. At last and in the nick of time his mistress arrived, riding a white palfrey, and all present, including the judges, agreed that Lanval was exonerated. As the fay rode away Lanval sprang onto the saddle behind her, and both departed to the isle of Avalun.

It would be unreasonable to dispute Marie's assertion that this story was told by the Bretons and that the Bretons called its hero Lanval.[2] Though as a man's name Lanval does not occur in historic records, two places called Lanvaux are to be found in Brittany and there was also a place called Lanvalay near Dinan. A Willelmus de Lanvaleio was seneschal of Rennes in Henry II's time.[3] Two other Breton lais, *Desiré*[4] and *Graelent*,[5] use the same

---

[1] Ed. J. Rychner (Geneva, Paris, 1958).   [2] Vss. 4, 660.

[3] *R*, lxxii (1951), 87–95.

[4] On plot of *Desiré* see Loomis, *Arthurian Tradition*, pp. 270–2, 302–5.

[5] *Graelent* remained closer to the original than *Lanval*, contrary to the claim of L. Foulet in *ZRP*, xxix (1905), 27.

plot, and the latter takes its title from an historic and also legendary figure, Gradlon, King of Cornouaille in the sixth century.[1] And though various elements in the plot, such as the faery mistress and her taboo and her bestowal of wealth on her favourite can be matched in the folk-lore of many peoples, it should not be overlooked that they are found in the medieval sagas of Ireland and in the modern folk-tales of Wales and Brittany.[2] The Potiphar's wife motif was also employed by the Irish.[3] And Giraldus Cambrensis himself testified that it was the 'fabulosi Britones et eorum cantores', not the Welsh, who told how Arthur had been borne away by a 'dea phantastica' named Morganis to the isle of Avalon.[4]

A comparison with the analogous lai of *Graelent* proves, however, that the Arthurian setting is not original. Can the queen who plays such a contemptible role in both lais be the Guenièvre of romance? Doubtless Guenièvre's reputation, as we have seen, was far from spotless, but this lying, vindictive female is someone else, and Marie recognized the fact by refusing to give her a name. Whether Marie was responsible for the localization of an originally independent *conte* at the court of Arthur, or merely accepted a connexion already made, one cannot say, but probably she added the reference in the opening lines to the raids of the Picts and Scots on the land of Logres, for this seems to be an echo of Wace.[5] It is highly probable, also, that the very faithful correspondence between the judicial procedure described in the lai and that employed in actual trials is due to the accurate knowledge and realistic feeling of Marie.[6] But her supreme achievement lies in her fine sense of the dramatic possibilities of her story, in the conduct of the passionate dialogue between the queen and Lanval, for example, or in the masterly use of suspense and climax in the arrival of the faery mistress. The poem is a triumph of sustained artistry.

There are two anonymous lais which, like *Lanval,* illustrate the tendency to bring non-Arthurian lais into the Arthurian orbit. Marie tells the story of the werewolf and his faithless wife in *Bisclavret* without mentioning a single name and without any historical setting. The author of *Melion* tells much the same story[7] but has fitted it with Arthurian names and an Arthurian background. Lucien Foulet and Bruce regard *Melion* as simply an adaptation of

[1] *ZFSL,* xii. 1–7. P. Sébillot, *Folklore de France* (1904–7), ii. 43–53.

[2] T. P. Cross in *MP,* xii (1915), 585–644; *Spec,* xx (1945), 189–96.

[3] *Spec,* xvi (1941), 50 f.; *RC,* xiii (1892), 368–97; T. P. Cross, *Motif-Index of Early Irish Literature* (Bloomington, 1952), p. 382.

[4] E. K. Chambers, *Arthur of Britain,* p. 272. On Avalon see ibid., pp. 266, 273; *EC,* iv (1948), 255–74; and Chap. 4 above.

[5] M. Pelan, op. cit., p. 106.

[6] E. A. Francis in *Studies Presented to Professor M. K. Pope* (Manchester, 1939), pp. 115–24.

[7] Ed. E. M. Grimes, *Lays of Desiré, Graelent and Melion* (New York, 1928), pp. 30–38, 102–22; W. Horak in *ZRP,* vi (1882), 94–106. On the general subject of werewolves see W. Hertz, *Der Werwolf* (Stuttgart, 1862) and S. Baring-Gould, *Book of Werewolves* (London, 1865).

Marie's poem,[1] but Kittredge in connexion with his elaborate study of *Arthur and Gorlagon* maintained that both lais had a common source.[2] However that may be, the author of *Melion* has taken as the name of his werewolf hero a name occurring in Chrétien's *Erec* and *Perceval* and other Arthurian romances.[3] He has introduced Gauvain, Yvain, and King Ydel (a variant form of Yder, invented to rime with *bel*). He has made considerable use of Wace,[4] identifying the nameless king of *Bisclavret* with Arthur, 'ki les terres conquerait et qui donna les riches dons', and referring specifically to his war with the Romans. As in Wace, there is an account of the devastation of Ireland, the slaughter of the cattle, the petition of the inhabitants to the king, and the succour which he brings them, though Wace attributes the calamity to Arthur's army while the lai attributes it to the band of wolves which Melion has gathered about him. The author of *Melion* thus built up a pseudo-Arthurian tale, more elaborate, more circumstantial than Marie's *Bisclavret*.

Tyolet is another anonymous lai originally independent of the Arthurian cycle;[5] its hero is never mentioned in any romance of the Round Table. But its author could not resist the attraction of the legend, and, as Lucien Foulet has shown,[6] clumsily combined two major plots in an Arthurian framework. The first part (vss. 37–320) is an imitation of Perceval's *enfances*, possibly based on Chrétien's poem, but possibly on a common source. Whichever view is taken, one recognizes the famous tale of the orphan boy brought up by his widowed mother in the woods, his chance meeting with a knight, his curiosity about the knight's arms, his departure from his mother, and his arrival at Arthur's court. However, if the author was following Chrétien's poem, he displayed his independence in several ways, particularly in the uncanny meeting of Tyolet with the 'chevalier beste'. For it was no ordinary knight who appeared to the youth as a presage of his destiny, but a stag, which, standing on the far bank of a deep river, suddenly was metamorphosed into a splendid warrior, fully armed. Such transformations are typical of the Breton lais, and this is a felicitous example.

The original lai of *Tyolet* probably began with the second part, since the hero is introduced (vss. 416–18) as if the reader had never heard of him before. The daughter of the king of Logres, like other heroines of romance, rides on a white palfrey into Arthur's court to find a champion to undertake a perilous adventure. This turns out to be the quest of the stag with the white

---

[1] *ZRP*, xxix (1905), 40 ff.; Bruce, ii. 185.

[2] See p. 117, n. 3, above.

[3] As Meliant de Lis (or del Lis) he appears in *Erec*, vs. 1698, and *Perceval*, vss. 4825 ff. On other examples of the name see *MLN*, xxvi (1911), 68, and *ZFSL*, xlix[1] (1926), 441, 466–70.

[4] M. Pelan, op. cit., pp. 127–31.

[5] Ed. by G. Paris in *R*, viii (1879), 40–50.

[6] *ZRP*, xxix. 48.

foot, an episode likewise found in the Second Continuation of Chrétien's *Perceval*, the *Didot Perceval*, *Peredur*, and the Dutch *Lancelot*.[1] When other knights have failed, Tyolet sets out and succeeds in cutting off the white stag's foot, but is attacked by lions and left half dead. The motif of the false claimant, well known from its employment in the Tristan legend and elsewhere, follows.[2] Gauvain searches for Tyolet, brings him back to court, the impostor is unmasked, and Tyolet wins the princess as his bride. Among the knights who kiss him on his return from his hazardous exploit are Gauvain, Uriain, Keu, Ewain, and Lodoer. The last name was recognized by Gaston Paris as a scribal corruption of Bedoer. Ewain (Yvain) is described here, as in the *Suite du Merlin* (*Huth Merlin*), as the son of the celebrated fay Morgain, and this seems to be based on tradition, for the corresponding Welsh hero, Owain, is likewise described as the son of the fay Modron.[3]

One cannot be dogmatic as to the precise sources from which the author of *Tyolet* derived his material, but Lucien Foulet has made it clear that he was familiar with Marie's *Lanval*.[4] Does he wish to describe the young princess of Logres on her arrival at Arthur's court? He has only to recall Lanval's mistress riding on her white palfrey, accompanied by a hound. Does he wish to emphasize his heroine's beauty? He compares her to Dido and Helen, just as Marie compared Lanval's lady to Venus, Dido, and Lavinia. He even reproduced three lines from *Lanval*, almost verbatim.

The Breton lais attached to the Arthurian cycle vary greatly in their artistic quality, but they include two of Marie's little masterpieces. The sources of the plots may lie sometimes in known surviving works, but not always. Wace frequently provided pseudo-historical detail. The most noteworthy conclusion to which the lais we have examined lead is that most of the tales which they tell had originally no association with Arthur and the court of Camelot. They illustrate the magnetic attraction of Arthur's name.

---

[1] G. Paris in *Hist. Lit. de la France*, xxx. 113–18; Loomis, *Arthurian Tradition*, p. 69, n. 10.

[2] *R*, viii. 41. On this motif in the Tristan legend see Chap. 12 below.

[3] Loomis, *Arthurian Tradition*, pp. 269 f.

[4] *ZRP*, xxix. 48 ff. Foulet's assertion (p. 51) that the prologue of *Tyolet* is merely 'un délayage de quelques indications données par ci par là par Marie' seems, however, mistaken. These knights who set out alone in quest of adventure and on their return have their feats recorded by clerks are not to be found in Marie's lais but in the romances.

THE ORIGIN AND GROWTH OF THE
TRISTAN LEGEND

HELAINE NEWSTEAD

W E have already noted in Chaps. 4 and 5 that a figure named Drystan appears in two Welsh texts of the thirteenth century, *Rhonabwy's Dream* and a triad in MS. Peniarth 16. The latter represents him in association with March, Essyllt, and Arthur, and we recognize, of course, the famous Tristan or Tristram of medieval romance. Even earlier, before 1160, he had been mentioned as an ideal lover by the troubadours Cercamon and Bernard de Ventadour in their lyrics.[1] Not many years later, as the preceding chapter has shown, Marie de France symbolized in her *Chèvrefeuil* the loves of Tristan and Isolt by the honeysuckle twined about the hazel; and from that time on, as the evidence not only of literature but also of art demonstrates,[2] few secular legends enjoyed such great renown throughout the Middle Ages as this tragic story.[3] When Tristan became attracted into the Arthurian orbit is not known, but it was surely before 1170. It is now generally agreed that an elaborate, fully developed narrative of his adventures from birth to death was already in existence in France by 1160.

Three poets of the twelfth century whose names we know wrote full-scale versions of Tristan's story. Most of the poem by Thomas, who wrote in French probably at the court of Henry II of England between 1155 and 1185,[4] is lost, but its contents can be safely reconstructed from its derivatives, particularly the unfinished masterpiece of Gottfried von Strassburg and the Norse *Tristrams Saga*.[5] The German, Eilhart von Oberge, about 1170, gave a faithful rendering of a lost French original.[6] Probably in the last decade of the century, a Norman poet, Béroul, composed a *Tristan* of which almost 4,500 lines are left.[7] Besides, we have the thirteenth-century Prose

[1] See Chap. 29 below. Delbouille has disputed this date in *Cultura Neolatina*, xvii (1957), 64–72.

[2] R. S. and L. H. Loomis, *Arthurian Legends in Medieval Art* (New York, 1938), pp. 42–69.

[3] For bibliography of Tristan up to 1939 see H. Küpper, *Bibliographie zur Tristansage, Deutsche Arbeiten der Universität Köln*, xvii (Jena, 1941), to be supplemented by Horrent's review in *RB* xxiii (1944), 357–63.

[4] Thomas, *Tristan*, ed. J. Bédier (Paris, 1902–5); *Fragments du Tristan de Thomas*, ed. B. H. Wind (Leiden, 1950).   [5] See Chaps. 14 and 35 below.

[6] Eilhart von Oberge, *Tristrant*, ed. F. Lichtenstein (Strasbourg, 1877). On date see Chap. 13.

[7] Most recent editions by A. Ewert (Oxford, 1939) and by E. Muret, rev. by L. M. Defourques, *CFMA* (1947). Latest discussion of author in *BBSIA*, 1957, pp. 134–6.

Tristan, which in addition to much late material contains a few episodes clearly derived from a source akin to the versions of Eilhart and Béroul,[1] as well as others reminiscent of Thomas.

It is noteworthy that the various forms of the Tristan legend, unlike the romances of the Grail, are fairly consistent. In spite of variations to be considered in the next chapter, the following synopsis may serve as the basis of our discussion of the legend's origin and growth.

A young noble or king named Rivalen came to Cornwall to take service with King Mark, fell in love with his sister Blancheflor, married her, and had by her a son Tristan. Blancheflor died the day the boy was born, and the orphan was brought up by a master. The accomplished youth arrived at King Mark's court incognito and won his uncle's favour. He slew in combat the Irish champion Morholt, who had demanded a tribute of Cornish youths. A fragment of Tristan's sword, lodged in Morholt's skull, was removed and preserved by the Irish princess Isolt, who vowed to find the slayer of her uncle and to avenge his death. Later, when Tristan was sent in search of a bride for King Mark, he reached Ireland and slew a dragon ravaging the land. As he lay unconscious, overcome by its poison, a false seneschal claimed the victory and the hand of the princess. But she discovered Tristan and tended his wounds. As he sat in a bath, she identified him as the slayer of Morholt by a breach in his sword matching the fragment she had kept. She spared his life only in order to save herself from the seneschal. After confounding the false claimant, Tristan won Isolt as his uncle's bride.

On the voyage to Cornwall a magic love potion intended for the bridal couple on their wedding night was given in error to Tristan and Isolt, who thenceforth were bound to each other by its spell. All duties and obligations were sacrificed to the demands of their consuming passion. The episodes deal in mounting suspense with the stratagems of the lovers to remain together and to escape the perils of detection. On the wedding night, Isolt, to conceal the loss of her virginity, persuaded her faithful attendant Brangain to take her place and then plotted to murder her to keep the secret, though afterwards she penitently cancelled the order. On another occasion, King Mark was induced by a spying dwarf to conceal himself in the branches of a tree beneath which the lovers had planned a rendezvous. His shadow revealed his presence to them, and they cleverly lulled his suspicions by a conversation suggesting their hostility to each other. The dwarf then plotted to trap the lovers by strewing flour on the floor of the royal chamber in the hope that Tristan's footprints would betray his visit to the queen's bed. Tristan outwitted the dwarf by leaping from his bed to Isolt's, but the effort broke open a wound that stained the queen's bed with blood. Since Mark was convinced of her guilt by the bloodstains, Isolt offered to swear publicly on red-hot iron

[1] See Chap. 26.

that she was faithful to her husband. She arranged for Tristan, disguised as a pilgrim, to meet her at the place appointed for the ordeal, and, stumbling apparently by accident into his arms, she was enabled to affirm the literal truth that no man save her husband and the pilgrim had ever embraced her. The red-hot iron left her unscathed, and Mark accepted this proof of her innocence.[1]

Eventually, however, the king banished the lovers, and they fled into the forest of Morois. One day when Mark was hunting he discovered them asleep with a naked sword between them. Reassured once more of their innocence, he recalled Isolt, but sent Tristan into permanent exile. In Brittany Tristan gained the friendship of the ruler's son Kaherdin. Though suffering from his separation, Tristan was persuaded to marry his friend's sister, Isolt of the White Hands, because she-bore the same name as his beloved. He remained faithful, nevertheless, to the Irish Isolt. One day, as his wife was riding with her brother and water happened to splash her leg, she remarked that Tristan had never been so bold with her. Accused by Kaherdin of neglecting her and so insulting her family, Tristan confessed that a more beautiful Isolt in Cornwall was his true love. To satisfy Kaherdin's demand for proof of this assertion, the friends travelled in disguise to Cornwall, where they spent the night with the queen and one of her maids. Kaherdin not only was convinced of the superior beauty of Isolt but he also fell in love with the maid. Although Isolt commanded her to lie with him, the clever maid outwitted her importunate lover by putting him to sleep with the aid of a magic pillow placed beneath his head.[2] Finally, after many other adventures following the return of the two friends to Brittany, Tristan was desperately wounded, and he sent for Isolt of Ireland to heal him. If she came with his messenger, the ship was to hoist white sails; if not, black sails. Isolt hastened to her lover, but his jealous wife falsely reported to him that the sails were black. He died in despair, and when Isolt found that she had arrived too late she died of grief beside him.

Abundant evidence for the Celtic origin of the legend has been assembled by Zimmer, Bédier, Deutschbein, Gertrude Schoepperle, and Rachel Bromwich, among others.[3] Their studies have revealed the contributions of Irish, Welsh, Cornish, and Breton tradition to the formation of the Tristan story

---

[1] This is the version of Thomas. According to Eilhart and Béroul, Mark decided to burn the lovers as adulterers after the discovery of the bloodstained bed. On his way to the stake, Tristan obtained permission from his guards to enter a chapel to pray; then he leaped from the window to the rocks below and escaped. When Isolt was brought to the stake, a company of lepers proposed as a more savage punishment that she be given to them to serve their lust. After the king had delivered her to the lepers, she was rescued by Tristan, and the lovers fled into the forest.

[2] For a discussion of this episode see *PMLA*, lxv (1950), 290–312.

[3] *ZFSL*, xiii[1] (1891), 65–72; Thomas, ed. Bédier, ii. 126 f.; *Beiblatt zur Anglia*, xv (1904), 16–21; G. Schoepperle, *Tristan and Isolt* (Frankfurt, London, 1913: reprinted Burt Franklin, New York, 1959); *THSC* (1953), pp. 32–60.

before it was transmitted to the French romancers, as Bédier in particular has maintained, by the Breton *conteurs*.[1] The composite legend reaching the romancers of the late twelfth century included not only Celtic tradition but elements from such heterogeneous sources as folk-tales, Arabic romance, and Oriental tales of trickery and deception.

The clue to the earliest stage of the Tristan legend is the name of the hero. It has long been acknowledged that Tristan owes his name to a certain Drust, son of Talorc, a king of the Picts, who reigned in northern Scotland about 780.[2] The names Drust and Talorc, and their derivatives Drostan and Talorcan, appear repeatedly as royal names in the chronicles of the Picts. The name Drust is thus distinctively Pictish.[3] As Bédier pointed out,[4] the connexion between the name of this historic king and the legendary Tristan is established by the Welsh sources. In the Welsh triads the name appears as Drystan or Trystan son of Tallwch—as close an equivalence in sound as one can expect to find in the transmission of proper names from one language to another. According to the Welsh triads, moreover, this Drystan son of Tallwch was the lover of Essyllt, the wife of his uncle March son of Meirchiawn.[5] Whether or not the triads were influenced by the French romances, the name Tallwch cannot be derived from that source, for the French texts assign entirely different names to the hero's father. Drystan son of Tallwch is the Welsh equivalent of Drust[an] son of Talorc; and since Tallwch is not a native Welsh name and since it occurs only as Drystan's patronymic, it is evident that Drystan son of Tallwch is the intermediate form between the Pictish Drust and the Tristan of the romances.[6]

---

[1] On the transmission see Thomas, ed. Bédier, ii. 103–33; R. S. Loomis, *Arthurian Tradition*, pp. 7–50; and Chap. 6 above.

[2] Zimmer in *ZFSL*, xiii[1], 65–72; Thomas, ed. Bédier, ii. 105–8; *R*, xxv (1896), 15; Bruce, i. 178 f.

[3] Alan O. Anderson, *Early Sources of Scottish History* (Edinburgh, 1922), i. cxiii–cxxviii; H. M. Chadwick, *Early Scotland* (Cambridge, 1949), pp. 1–49. The weaknesses in J. Loth's arguments (*Contributions à l'étude des romans de la Table Ronde* [Paris, 1912], pp. 72–90) for the Cornish origin and development of the Tristan legend have often been pointed out. Both Brugger (*MP*, xxii [1924], 159–91) and Smirnov (*R*, xliii [1914], 121–5) note that Loth does not distinguish carefully enough among the different and often contradictory versions of the Tristan romances when he identifies placenames with Cornish localities, sometimes attributing to Thomas a trait found only in Gottfried and drawing far-reaching conclusions from forms attested only in the Prose *Tristan*. The correspondences with Cornish place-names can be more plausibly explained as late localizations introduced by romancers familiar with the region. The inscription on the Castledôr stone, now read as DRUSTAUS HIC IACIT / CVNOMORI FILIUS (C. A. Ralegh Radford in *Journal of the Royal Institution of Cornwall*, N.S., i, Appendix, 1951), proves nothing about the Tristan legend. The identification of Mark with the Cunomorius of this inscription rests on particularly shaky evidence. R. Fawtier, *Vie de Saint Samson* (Paris, 1912), pp. 41 f., 64–68, and F. Lot, *Mélanges d'Histoire Bretonne* (Paris, 1907), pp. 450–3, 124–7, 253 f. Cf. H. Newstead in *RP*, xi (1958), 240–53. Finally, since Loth himself in a later article (*Comptes Rendus de l'Académie des Inscriptions et Belles-Lettres*, 1924, p. 128) admits the derivation of Tristan from the Pictish Drust and accepts the identification of Loenois with Lothian, little remains to support the hypothesis of Cornish origin.   [4] Thomas, ed. Bédier, ii. 106–8.

[5] Ibid.; J. Loth, *Mabinogion*, 2nd ed., ii. 284; R. Bromwich in *THSC*, 1953, pp. 33, 44–49. See above, p. 48.   [6] Bromwich, loc. cit., p. 35.

Fortunately the relationship is confirmed by more than the name. Although the Picts disappeared as a separate people after a crushing defeat in 843 and nothing remains of their language except a few dubious inscriptions, a precious fragment of the legend that developed around the royal name of Drust is preserved in the tenth-century recension of the Irish saga, *The Wooing of Emer*. In one episode Drust appears as a companion of the hero Cuchulainn. The episode, as Celtic scholars have proved, is an interpolation, and since Drust is the only one in the list of Cuchulainn's companions who does not figure elsewhere in the Ulster cycle and since he appears only in this story, he must have been the original hero, displaced when the episode was adapted to *The Wooing of Emer*.[1]

This episode relates that the hero, arriving with his companions at an island in the Hebrides, heard lamentation from the king's fort, learned that the king's daughter was to be delivered as tribute to three sea-robbers, and defeated each of them in single combat. The maiden bound his wound with a strip from her garment before he departed incognito. Later, when he joined the other guests in the fort, he heard them boast of the victory. But the princess, like Isolt, did not believe them. She had a bath prepared and ordered each guest to be brought before her in turn. When the hero came, she identified him.

The parallels with the Morholt episode and the later rescue of Isolt are striking. In both the Irish tale and the Tristan story the hero arrives in the stricken kingdom just when a human tribute is to be yielded; he hears the lamentation of the people and learns the cause. He defends the land alone and kills the enemy in single combat, but is himself wounded. There is also a recognition token: in the Irish story the strip from the maiden's garment corresponds in function to the fragment of Tristan's sword lodged in Morholt's skull. The true sequel of the Morholt episode, therefore, occurs when Tristan is identified as the slayer of Morholt. This later episode preserves two more elements present in the Irish tale: the false claimant and the recognition of the hero in a bath by a foreign princess. In the Tristan romances the rescue of the princess has been contaminated by a similar story of Breton provenance about her rescue from a dragon,[2] but the original connexion of the two episodes is demonstrated by the crucial importance of the recognition of Tristan as the slayer of Morholt.

The nucleus of the Tristan legend, then, was a tradition that Drust delivered a foreign land from a forced tribute and rescued the intended victim, a princess who later succeeded in identifying the hero in a bath and in thus

---

[1] Deutschbein in *Beiblatt zur Anglia*, xv (1904), 16–21; *Compert ConCulainn and Other Stories*, ed. A. G. van Hamel (Dublin, 1933), pp. 60–62; Zimmer in *ZDA*, xxxii (1888), 196–334; Meyer in *RC*, xi (1890), 433–8; E. S. Hartland, *Legend of Perseus* (London, 1896), iii. 50; Bromwich, loc. cit., pp. 38 f.

[2] Van Hamel in *RC*, xli (1924), 331–49.

confounding the false claimants to the victory. Since a version of this story was written down in the Irish *Wooing of Emer* in the tenth century, this part of the legend must have been in circulation as early as the ninth century.

The famous love story, however, springs from a different source. The triangular relationship of the principal characters was familiar in Wales, according to the evidence of the Welsh triads. Another Welsh tradition tells of the flight of Trystan and Essyllt to the forest and of March's pursuit of them.[1] Once again an Irish story illuminates the problem. The Welsh attached to Trystan and Essyllt one of the most celebrated plots in Irish legend—the *aithed* or elopement of Diarmaid and Grainne,[2] which existed in the ninth century. The Irish characters bear the same relation to each other as the principals in the Tristan legend. Diarmaid is the trusted nephew of the Irish chieftain Finn, and Grainne is Finn's young wife. A magic spell placed her under compulsion to love Diarmaid, but when he rejected her she imposed a spell that forced him to flee with her from Finn. Finn vengefully pursued them into the forest, hunting them like animals. But Diarmaid remained loyal. Each night he placed a cold stone between himself and Grainne, and left tokens behind to inform Finn of his chastity. One day, when some muddy water splashed Grainne's leg, she remarked to Diarmaid that the water was bolder than he. This taunt broke his resistance, and they became lovers. According to the evidence presented in Gertrude Schoepperle's study, such distinctive features of the Tristan legend as the magical compulsion that binds the lovers to each other, the flight to the forest, the separating sword (substituted for the stone), and the splashing water show that the plot has been strongly influenced by the Irish story of Diarmaid and Grainne.

It was the Welsh who adapted this Irish material to the originally independent saga of the Pictish hero. The Irish story pattern required the hero to elope with the wife of his uncle, to whom he was bound by special ties of loyalty and affection. It was probably the Welsh, too, who chose for this role a legendary monarch of Cornwall, King Mark. The initial linking of Tristan and Mark may have been suggested by a local legend about human tribute associated with Tintagel, the stronghold of King Mark.[3] Nothing more was needed to inspire a Welsh redactor to localize in Cornwall Tristan's early exploits as a deliverer.

King Mark was renowned in Wales as well as in Cornwall. The most

---

[1] *Trystan ac Esyllt*, ed. Ifor Williams in *BBCS*, v (1930), 115–29; ed., trans. T. P. Cross in *SP*, xvii (1920), 93 ff.; trans. Loomis, *Romance of Tristram and Ysolt*, pp. xiii ff. For comment see *R*, liii (1927), 92 ff.; I. Williams, *Lectures on Early Welsh Poetry* (Dublin, 1944), pp. 18–23; Bromwich, loc. cit., pp. 51–55.

[2] Schoepperle, op. cit. ii. 391–446; S. H. O'Grady's translation of the saga is reprinted in T. P. Cross, C. H. Slover, *Ancient Irish Tales* (New York, 1936), pp. 370–421.

[3] Loomis, *Arthurian Tradition*, pp. 320–6; Newstead in *RP*, xi. 244 f.

famous tradition about him—apart from his role in the love story—appears in an episode related by Béroul concerning a certain secret known only to the king's dwarf.[1] Questioned by the curious barons, the dwarf promised to confide the secret to a hawthorn bush. They could overhear it if they wished, and he would remain technically faithful to his trust. Accordingly, they listened as he announced to the bush the momentous news that King Mark had horse's ears. When the barons reported their knowledge to the king, he beheaded the dwarf.

This tale of the horse's ears was probably connected with King Mark at an early period, for in all Celtic languages his name means 'horse'. Onomastic stories of this kind are characteristic of Celtic narrative,[2] and variants of this particular tale are found in Ireland, Wales, and Brittany, usually attached to a person whose name means 'horse'. Although the story turns up in other areas as well, its popularity in Celtic lands is natural since Celtic tradition is especially rich in names with an equine meaning.[3] In Wales and Brittany the story of King March, who murdered his barbers to conceal his embarrassing secret, circulated as an independent folk-tale for more than 700 years. A Breton variant is the most likely source of Béroul's version.[4]

When the Tristan legend migrated to Brittany, the basic outline of the plot and the relations of the main personages were already established. The Bretons, however, made a number of important modifications. The name of Tristan's father was changed to Rivalen,[5] and an introductory romance was added about Tristan's parents, Rivalen of Brittany and Blancheflor, the sister of King Mark. This development may have been suggested by the fact that a certain lord of Vitré named Tristan, who ruled between 1030 and 1045, was the son of Rivalen.[6] It would have been flattering to his descendants to imagine that the great legendary hero was his namesake and perhaps his remote ancestor. If the Welsh patronymic Tallwch was replaced by Rivalen under these circumstances, it seems reasonable to assume that the insular legend reached Brittany in the early eleventh century.

The dragon episode is another Breton contribution. It is derived, as Van Hamel showed,[7] from a Breton folk-tale analogous to the story of human

[1] Béroul, *Tristan*, vss. 1306–50. Cf. Newstead in *RP*, xi. 246–53.

[2] Schoepperle, op. cit. ii. 269–72; W. J. Gruffydd, *Math Vab Mathonwy* (Cardiff, 1928), pp. 155, 335–9.

[3] T. F. O'Rahilly, *Early Irish History and Mythology* (Dublin, 1946), pp. 291–4.

[4] J. Rhys, *Celtic Folklore* (Oxford, 1901), i. 232–4; ii. 572–4; *RC*, xiii (1892), 485; *Revue des Traditions Populaires*, i (1886), 327 f.; vii (1892), 358 f.; *Aberystwyth Studies*, xii (1932), 21–33; *Annales de Bretagne*, lvi (1949), 204–6; *Comparative Literature*, ii (1950), 290 f.; and below, p. 139, n. 1.   [5] Loomis in *MLN*, xxxix (1924), 326 f.; *R*, liii (1927), 82 ff.

[6] Pierre le Baud, *Histoire de Bretagne* (Paris, 1638), pp. 7–9 (*Chronique de Vitré*); Borderie in *Revue de Bretagne et de Vendée*, xviii (1865), 436; A. Guillotin de Corson, *Grandes Seigneuries de Haute-Bretagne* (Rennes, 1898), ii. 392. For another explanation see Bromwich, loc. cit., pp. 56 f.

[7] *RC*, xli (1924), 331–49.

PLATE 3

RIVALIN AND BLANCHEFLOR
Munich, Staatsbib. germ. 51. c. 1300

tribute related of Drust. In this Breton folk-tale, as in the Tristan legend, the hero slays a dragon to whom the princess is to be sacrificed, and the false claimant, offering the head of the monster as a token of the victory, is exposed as an impostor when the hero produces the dragon's tongue. The Drust story lacks the motifs of the dragon combat and the severed tongue, which are characteristic of the Breton tale. The fusion of the two stories results in a double recognition of Tristan: he is identified as the slayer of Morholt by the matching sword fragment and also as the victor in the dragon combat by means of the monster's tongue. Both the Breton folk-tale and the story of Drust, of course, are cognate but independent versions of the ancient plot familiar in classical antiquity as Perseus's rescue of Andromeda.[1]

The localization in Brittany of the episodes after Tristan's banishment indicates that Breton influence was as potent in shaping the conclusion of the romance as it was in forming the introduction. The narrative theme of the Man with Two Wives in two of the Breton lais of Marie de France, *Eliduc* and *Fresne*, was familiar in Brittany and probably affected the story of Tristan's marriage to Isolt of the White Hands, although, as we shall presently see, it was not the only influence.[2] The motif of the black and the white sails seems also to be derived from Breton tradition. A folk-tale current in an island off the coast of Brittany relates how a princess arranged with her lover that if he returned successful from a certain journey, his ship was to hoist white sails; if not, black. As she languished gravely ill, a woman whom she sent to watch for the arrival of the vessel was instructed by the princess's hostile father to report falsely that the sails were black. On hearing this news the princess died.[3] Despite the obvious differences, the motif is handled as it is in the Tristan story. In both, the black and the white sails are used as a signal; a woman is sent to watch; and the false report inspired by hatred causes the death of the waiting lover.[4]

Not everything in the Tristan legend, however, is derived from Celtic

---

[1] Hartland, *Legend of Perseus*, iii; *Comparative Literature*, ii. 292. See below, p. 455.

[2] Schoepperle, op. cit. ii. 524–6; H. E. Matzke in *MP*, iv (1907), 471–9; v (1907–8), 211–39; L. A. Hibbard, *Medieval Romance in England* (2nd ed., New York, 1960), pp. 124, 298.

[3] *RC*, xxxvii (1917–19), 323; *Comparative Literature*, ii. 293 f.

[4] Can this modern Breton folk-tale be explained as a derivative of the medieval Tristan romance? Except for the motif of the sails, the two stories are so dissimilar in other respects that a connexion of this kind is highly improbable. Since the motif of the sails as a signal appears in other Celtic folk-tales that could not possibly have been affected by the Tristan legend (Schoepperle, op. cit. ii. 438), the Breton story can be most plausibly explained as a modern descendant of a tale from which the Breton *conteurs* of the twelfth century borrowed the motif for the tragic ending. Similarly, the Breton folk-tale of the dragon-slayer cannot be derived from the medieval Tristan romances. The Breton tale includes many important features, such as the helpful animals, which have no counterpart in the Tristan episode but which relate it closely to the standard formula of the folk-tale. Moreover, it lacks the recognition in the bath, a distinctive element in the Tristan story, and it is constructed as a single story rather than as two separate episodes. These facts support Van Hamel's conclusion that medieval versions of the dragon-slayer tale circulating in Brittany contributed to the Tristan legend.

tradition. Some episodes have a more exotic origin. The story of Isolt's attempt to murder Brangain, for example, is ultimately of Oriental derivation, although the earliest European version is preserved in an Irish text of the tenth century.[1] In this tale a princess betrothed to a noble youth accidentally suffocated her secret lover in an effort to conceal him during an inopportune visit from her father. She then killed a churl who helped her dispose of the corpse. After her marriage to her betrothed, she substituted her maidservant in the bridal bed. When the maid refused to yield her place, the princess set the bed afire and drowned the servant while she was drawing water to extinguish the flames. No one discovered these murders, but years later she repented and confessed them to her priest, who wickedly demanded her submission to his lust as the price of secrecy. When she refused, he revealed her sins to her husband. Though imprisoned in a hut by a cross-roads and left to die, she repented so ardently that her life was miraculously spared. Eventually she ascended to heaven, and the cross-roads became a shrine to the Virgin.

This Irish story is already partly christianized. Other versions in Latin and French, with some modifications, turn it into a *conte dévot* to illustrate the virtues of penitence and the unfailing mercy of the Virgin. In such a form it appears in collections used by the preaching friars and in anthologies of miracle legends. Since the Irish tale is already a little exemplum on the subject of penitence, it probably reached Ireland through some Latin source.

Whoever adapted this tale to the Tristan legend handled it freely. He borrowed certain elements to account for the first successful deception of King Mark and to show the astonishing devotion of Brangain to her mistress. One of the penitence versions of the tale, perhaps of Celtic provenance, must have been the source, to judge by Isolt's penitent conduct when she fears that her orders to murder Brangain have been carried out.

Another striking example of Oriental material in the Tristan legend is the equivocal oath by which Isolt escapes punishment in the ordeal of red-hot iron. This tale also has a remarkable history.[2] It originated in ancient India, in a Hindu ceremonial called the Act of Truth, a ritual based on the belief that a truthful statement has magical power. The Act of Truth is a formal statement of a fact—any fact—accompanied by a prayer or resolution that the purpose of the agent may be accomplished. In addition to stories illustrating this power of truth to turn back fire, to cause rain, to restore vision to the blind, other stories were told of Acts of Truth used by adulterous wives to

---

[1] Zenker in *RF*, xxix (1911), 332; *Book of Leinster*, ed. R. Atkinson (Dublin, 1880), pp. 279a–280a, l. 42; Mathews in *MLQ*, vi (1945), 187–91; Krappe in *Byzantion*, xvii (1944–5), 339–46; Schoepperle, op. cit. i. 206–10.

[2] Burlingame in *Journal of the Royal Asiatic Society*, 1917, pp. 429–67; M. Dillon in *MP*, xliv (1947), 137–40; Somadeva, *Ocean of Story*, trans. C. H. Tawney, ed. N. M. Penzer (London, 1924), i. 166 f.; ii. 31–33; iii. 179–83; Schoepperle, i. 223–6.

deceive their husbands. These appear in most of the great Sanskrit collections of tales. From India they spread east to China and west to Arabia, Persia, and Europe. The plot remains substantially the same, though some variants are more elaborate than others. A faithless wife accused by her husband offers to submit to a test of her innocence requiring a declaration of the truth. She secretly directs her lover to disguise himself as a repulsive character of low rank and to seize her when she arrives at her destination, usually a hallowed spot suitable for sacramental acts. When this happens as planned, she declares the literal truth and so escapes the penalty. The story was so popular that it is difficult to determine exactly how it reached the Tristan legend. In any case, it was a story easy to transpose from Orient to Occident; the original Hindu Act of Truth is replaced in the European versions by a Christian oath and an ordeal.

The episode of the tryst beneath the tree has also been influenced by two Oriental *fabliaux*, both immensely popular, especially in Arabic sources, and both well known in twelfth-century France. In the one, known as the Enchanted Tree,[1] an adulteress persuades her husband that a certain tree is enchanted; she tricks him into believing that her scandalous behaviour with her lover, which he observed from the branches of the tree, was only an optical illusion. This *fabliau* has contributed the unusual and distinctive feature of the observer hidden in a tree and his deception by the lovers beneath. The other *fabliau*, the Carpenter's Wife,[2] closely resembles the Tristan episode in structure. The suspicious husband, like Mark, pretends to go on a journey but actually conceals himself to spy upon his wife. When she discovers his presence by chance while she is entertaining her lover, she extricates herself by an impromptu discourse to her paramour that completely convinces the deluded husband of her innocence. The plot of the Carpenter's Wife in the setting of the Enchanted Tree accounts for the essential elements in the escape of Tristan and Isolt from detection during their interview beneath the tree that hides the spying king.[3]

Another Arabic source of a quite different sort, the famous romance of the poet Kais ibn Doreidsch (died 687) and Lobna, seems to have influenced the story of Tristan's marriage to Isolt of the White Hands.[4] We have already observed that the theme of the Man with Two Wives was known in Brittany. In such tales the second wife usually resembles the first either in appear-

---

[1] A. C. Lee, *The Decameron, Its Sources and Analogues* (London, 1909), pp. 236–44; W. F. Bryan, G. Dempster, *Sources and Analogues of Chaucer's Canterbury Tales* (Chicago, 1941), p. 341, n. 1; Bédier, *Fabliaux*, 4th ed. (Paris, 1925), pp. 260 f.

[2] J. Derenbourg in *Bibliothèque de l'École des Hautes Études*, lxii (1889), pp. xiii–xvii, 185–7; Somadeva, op. cit. v, appendix i; Schoepperle, op. cit. i. 213.

[3] See Newstead in *RP*, ix (1956), 269–84, for a study of the origin and development of this episode.

[4] S. Singer in *Abhandlungen der Preußischen Akad. der Wissenschaften*, 1918, phil.-hist. Kl., no. 18, pp. 8–10; J. van Dam in *Neo*, xv (1929–30), 97 f.

ance or in name, and the hero endures much mental anguish as a result of his double attachment. Otherwise, the Breton lais reveal no marked similarities to the Tristan legend. The Arabic romance, on the other hand, furnishes a more complete parallel. Like Tristan, Kais is forcibly separated from his true love, his wife Lobna; he meets another maiden with the same name; with the help of her brother he marries her; yet he neglects her, thinking only of his first love; the new wife's relatives are displeased; falling ill, he sends for the first Lobna; they are briefly reunited, but they die soon afterward. Somehow this romantic story was absorbed into the Tristan legend. Although the precise channel of transmission is uncertain, the parallel is too detailed and consistent to be the result of chance. In the process of adaptation, of course, all traces of Mohammedan life were expunged, such as the hero's pilgrimage to Mecca and the characteristic marriage customs. What remained was blended with the similar Breton theme of the Man with the Two Wives and the incident of the splashing water, inherited from the Irish story of Diarmaid and Grainne.

The Latin prose romance of Apollonius of Tyre was widely known,[1] and the adventures of the hero, as Laura Hibbard Loomis pointed out,[2] present a striking resemblance to two experiences of Tristan as related by Thomas. Apollonius was cast away on the shores of a foreign land, was directed to a city near by, won the attention of the king by his athletic skill, was entertained at the royal palace, played the lyre with unequalled charm, roused the love of the princess, and at her request became her tutor in music. Slightly adapted to medieval manners and divided into two episodes, this is Thomas's story of Tristan's arrival at the court of King Mark,[3] supplemented by his first arrival at the Irish court and his communicating his skill as a harper to the princess Isolt.

Thomas, it may be remembered, mentions one Breri as an authority on all the kings and all the counts that have been in Britain, and credits him with a version of the Tristan story. Eilhart introduced a certain Pleherin as a minor character. As has been pointed out in Chap. 6, there is cumulative evidence that a Welsh *fabulator* named Bleheris (Welsh Bleddri) flourished between 1100 and 1140, and recited his tales at the court of the count of Poitou, probably the troubadour, William VII, who died in 1127. This court, not far removed from the centres of Arabic culture in Spain and hospitable, as will be shown in Chap. 29, to the tales of the neighbouring Bretons, offered conditions favourable to the mingling of Oriental and Celtic

---

[1] Latin text, ed. A. Riese (Leipzig, 1893).

[2] L. A. Hibbard, *Mediaeval Romance in England*, p. 166, n. 4.

[3] There may be some influence also from the legend of Lothbroc, who came ashore on the coast of Norfolk, was brought before the king, won his favour, and was attached to the court as an expert fowler and huntsman. Matthew Paris, *Chronica Majora*, ed. H. S. Luard (London, 1872), i. 393. Date of text is 1195–1204. Ibid., p. xxxii.

story. If Bleheris introduced into the Tristan legend some of the *fabliau* themes, as well as the romantic idealism, of Arabic fiction, his version would have seemed sensational. This, however, can only be a subject for speculation. We cannot now discover to what degree and how directly the French romances of the twelfth century were indebted to Bleheris.

THE EARLY TRISTAN POEMS

FREDERICK WHITEHEAD

IN the last chapter the famous romance of Tristan and Isolt was summarized on the basis of three twelfth-century poems, those of Béroul,
Thomas, and Eilhart. These, together with a number of episodes in the
Prose *Tristan*, were regarded by Bédier as the 'primary' versions of the
legend. It is still doubtful, however, whether any traditional value should be
attributed to the Prose *Tristan* as a whole, and the question will be considered in Chap. 26. Therefore, in this chapter references to that romance
will be only incidental.

Authors and Dates

Béroul's fragment of 4,485 lines begins in the middle of the scene in which
Mark spies on the lovers from the tree and ends before Tristan's withdrawal
to Brittany.[1] Though for the most part the narrative corresponds to that of
Eilhart, the account of the forest life is fuller, and the concluding episodes,
the ambiguous oath and the murder of the barons Godoïne and Denoalen,
have no counterpart in the German poem. The treatment of the ambiguous
oath varies widely from that of Thomas. How Béroul ended his poem is a
matter of pure speculation.[2]

His name occurs in vss. 1268, 1790 in the nominative case as Berox. The
poem displays an unusual knowledge of Cornwall,[3] but it is doubtful how far
this is due to Béroul rather than his source. The text is in the Norman dialect,
though precise localization is difficult.[4] A *terminus a quo* of 1191 is generally

---

[1] For most recent editions of Béroul see Chap. 12, p. 121, n. 7. Some of the scholars who have
discussed the poem would limit Béroul's part to the first 2,754 or 3,027 lines, but Muret in his edition
of 1928, pp. vi–viii, granted the unity of authorship. Miss Pope's conjecture that after a certain point
the author began to show more and more independence of his original source is probably right.
MLR, viii (1913), 189–92. For dual authorship see Raynaud de Lage in *MA*, lxiv (1958), 249–70.

[2] Vss. 2707–22 and 2792–800 look forward to the final episode of the story and vss. 2696–706
to Kaherdin's visit to the Blanche Lande to see Isolt's beauty.

[3] On Cornish localizations see Chap. 12, p. 125, n. 3. Though some of Loth's identifications of
places in Cornwall in his *Contributions à l'Étude des Romans de la Table Ronde*, such as Maupas,
Constentin, and the forest of Morrois, have been disputed, there is a strong case for the equation of
Mark's capital, Lancien, which has a church dedicated to St. Samson, with Lantyan in the chapelry of
St. Sampson. See L. E. Elliott-Binns, *Medieval Cornwall* (London, 1955), p. 140. Béroul also knew
St. Michael's Mount in Cornwall (vs. 2733).

[4] M. K. Pope in *MLR*, viii (1913), 189–92, suggests Caen–Granville area. E. Muret in edition of
Béroul, *SATF* (1903), pp. lix–lxiii, suggests east Normandy.

accepted on the assumption that the 'mal dagres' (vs. 3849) is a corrupt reading of 'mal d'Acre' and refers to the epidemic which struck the Crusaders at the siege of Acre.[1] The high proportion of broken couplets points to a period after rather than before the beginning of Chrétien de Troyes's literary activity.[2]

Thomas's text[3] has survived in fragments from the latter part of his poem, totalling about 3,150 lines. The missing portions can be reconstructed more or less closely from the three somewhat free redactions, Gottfried von Strassburg's poem, the *Tristrams Saga*, and the Middle English *Sir Tristrem*.[4] The author names himself in vss. 2134, 3125. The language is 'standard Western French', with what may be a slight admixture of Anglo-Norman forms.[5] Thomas made Mark king of all England, disregarding the tradition which confined his rule to Cornwall, and eulogized the city of London. For historical matter he drew on Wace's *Brut* and imitated his style.[6] Various pieces of evidence suggest that his poem was greatly admired after his death by members of the royal Angevin house, and it is quite likely he wrote under the patronage of Henry II or a member of his family.[7]

The borrowings from Wace provide a sure *terminus a quo*, 1155. The *terminus ad quem* depends on the relationship the poem bears to Chrétien's *Cligès*. The story of Rivalen and Blancheflor in Thomas parallels the story of Cligès's parents too closely to permit any explanation but the influence of one work on the other; but which came first? Moreover, both authors introduce a triple pun on *lamer* in its three senses of love, the sea, and the freshness of the breeze, and critics have been sharply divided as to which of the two was the borrower.[8] One general consideration seems, however, to weight the scales in favour of Thomas as the earlier. His technique is based entirely on Wace and the romances of antiquity, and shows no trace of Chrétien's influence; the *Enéas* (*c.* 1150) in particular had a marked effect on the Rivalen–Blancheflor affair.[9] Chrétien's treatment of the love of Cligès's parents

[1] Muret, *SATF* edition, p. lxiv. Ambroise in *Estoire de la Guerre Sainte*, ed. G. Paris (Paris, 1897), vss. 4265–74, describes the malady. See, however, *Med. Aev.*, xxviii (1959), 167–71.

[2] Muret, ibid., p. xxv.   [3] For editions see Chap. 1², p. 121, n. 4.

[4] Bédier attempted a reconstruction in his edition of Thomas, vol. i. On these three redactions of Thomas see Chaps. 14, 35, and 37. A translation of Thomas's fragments, with missing portions supplied from the saga, was published by R. S. Loomis under the title *Romance of Tristram and Ysolt*, 3rd ed., 1951.

[5] Bédier, ii. 11–34; Wind, pp. 17–47.   [6] Bédier, ii. 99–101.

[7] R. S. Loomis in *MLR*, xvii (1922), 24–30; in *Burlington Magazine*, xli (1922), 54–64; R. S. and L. H. Loomis, *Arthurian Legends in Medieval Art*, p. 45.

[8] The corresponding passages are *Cligès*, vss. 545–63; Gottfried, vss. 11989–12014. Discussion of the pun was begun by G. Paris in *Journal des Savants*, 1902, pp. 354 f.; quoted by Bédier in edition of Thomas, ii. 53–55. For bibliography of controversy over the question of priority see Wind's edition, pp. 14 f.

[9] E. Langlois, *Chronologie des Romans de Thèbes, d'Enéas et de Troie, Bibl. de l'École des Chartes*, lxvi (1905), 114, n. 2. Singer in *ZRP*, xxxiii (1909), 729–33, proposed a possible connexion between the Rivalen–Blancheflor story and the story of Achilles and Polyxena in *Troie*.

displays a much more fluent and resourceful handling of rhetorical devices. That Thomas should have thrown over this developed technique and reverted to the stiffness of the earlier romances[1] is hard to believe.[2]

The only edition of the whole of Eilhart, that of Lichtenstein,[3] is based on three fifteenth-century manuscripts containing a text the metre of which has been modernized. The text so preserved seems fortunately to have undergone only slight changes of substance. Less than a thousand lines of the poem,[4] preserved in three fragmentary manuscripts of the late twelfth century, survive in a metrical and linguistic form close to the original. There is also a prose adaptation[5] first printed in 1483, and a Czech translation.[6]

An Eilhardus, son of Johannes de Obergen, appears as witness in a series of documents[7] beginning in 1189 and coming down at least to 1209. According to Lichtenstein,[8] this Eilhardus, a *ministerialis* of Henry the Lion, duke of Brunswick, is our poet. This identification has been disputed by Wagner,[9] who pointed out that the Eilhardus of the documents was connected not with Henry the Lion but with his son of the same name, and that the poem is written in the artificial literary language used in the Rhineland, where names from the Tristan legend first appear in German documents. Moreover, the Regensburg fragment of Eilhart's poem is found in a manuscript of about 1180, and the composition presumably goes back several years. Thus, though the identity of the two Eilharts is not excluded, it seems likely that the poet who wrote about 1170[10] belonged to an earlier generation than the *ministerialis* and that his home was on the Middle Rhine rather than in Brunswick.

The Archetype

Nineteenth-century scholars agreed in regarding the poems of Eilhart and Béroul as essentially a single version (*version commune* or *version des jongleurs*)

---

[1] The stylistic immaturity of the romances of antiquity compared with Chrétien's verse makes it hard to accept F. E. Guyer's thesis in *Romance in the Making* (New York, 1954), pp. 245–82, that Chrétien wrote earlier.

[2] For an attempt to date Thomas by the heraldry in the poem see G. L. Hamilton in *MLR*, xv (1920), 425–9; R. S. Loomis in *MLR*, xvii (1922), 24–28; L. M. Gay in *MLR*, xxiii (1928), 472–5. An excellent argument on political grounds for a date before 1173 has been presented by M. D. Legge in *BBSIA*, vi (1954), 95 f.

[3] Ed. F. Lichtenstein (Strasbourg, 1877).

[4] Ed. Kurt Wagner, *Tristrant, I: Die alten Bruchstücke* (Bonn, Leipzig, 1924).

[5] Ed. F. Pfaff, *Tristrant und Isolde* (Tübingen, 1881).

[6] Ed. W. Hanky (Prague, 1820). German trans. by J. Knieschek in *ZDA*, xxviii (1884), 261–358. For discussion of value of Czech text see G. Schoepperle, *Tristan and Isolt* (Frankfurt, London, 1913), ii. 476–518; J. Van Dam, *Zur Vorgeschichte des höfischen Epos* (Bonn, Leipzig), pp. 9, 40–57, 80 ff., and the literature there indicated.

[7] Wagner, op. cit., pp. *1–*5.   [8] Lichtenstein, op. cit., pp. xlviii f., cxviii.

[9] Wagner, op. cit., pp. *8–*20.

[10] Ibid., p. 21 (last years of the seventh decade); Van Dam, op. cit., pp. 121–8 (*terminus ad quem* 1174–6).

and in contrasting it with that of Thomas and his derivatives (*version cour-toise*). Bédier, having demonstrated that the three poems and the Prose *Tristan* were derived from a common source,[1] showed that Eilhart and Béroul reproduced this archetype with great fidelity,[2] whereas Thomas made considerable changes. This was also the opinion of Gertrude Schoepperle.[3] But Bédier believed[4] that Eilhart and Béroul had departed from the arche-type in limiting the effect of the potion to three or four years, and since this deviation could not have been made independently, he postulated an inter-mediate common source, which he called *y*.

The duration of the spell is bound up with the problem presented by Tristan's voluntarily abandoning Isolt and starting a new life in Brittany. According to Bédier,[5] the separation took place in the original as a result of a sudden awakening of the lovers' conscience, and the limitation of the potion in *y* was an attempt by this later redactor to explain something that his source had left unexplained. Thomas and the Prose *Tristan*[6] recast this account in order to avoid making the lovers' separation proceed from a sense of sin. But Bédier's hypothesis does not remove the fundamental incompatibility between the theme of the lovers' repentance and the idea that they are bound for ever by a spell whose chains they cannot break. A weakening of the potion seems the only way to give surface plausibility to a *motif* that is out of keeping with the fundamental assumptions of the story. It thus seems unnecessary to postulate an intermediate source *y*.

The archetype has been variously dated: Bédier put it not long after the Norman Conquest,[7] Gertrude Schoepperle after Chrétien de Troyes.[8] A date around 1150 or 1160 seems the most probable. Bédier treated the work as a story of love which, because it is unlawful, can only have a tragic end.[9] According to him, the plan is based on the theme of the lovers' sufferings, which grow in intensity as the story unfolds: from shame and remorse to

---

[1] Bédier, ii. 168–87; W. Golther in *Tristan und Isolde in den Dichtungen des Mittelalters und der neuen Zeit* (Leipzig, 1907), pp. 30–97, put forward a similar theory, deriving all extant versions from a lost Ur-Tristan. Likewise Miss Schoepperle, op. cit. i. 5–10, derived all versions except the Prose *Tristan* from an *estoire*, substantially represented by Eilhart's poem. In vol. ii, pp. 439 f., she ascribed the death of Tristan at the hands of Mark as related in the Prose *Tristan* to a source different from and perhaps earlier than the *estoire*. Most later scholars have accepted the existence of one main source for Béroul, Eilhart, and Thomas, though B. Panvini, *La Leggenda di Tristano e Isotta, Biblioteca dell' Archivum Romanicum*, xxxii (1951), proposes a much more complicated scheme of descent.

[2] This is clear from his reconstruction of the archetype, op. cit. ii. 194–306.

[3] Schoepperle, op. cit., p. 8.   [4] Bédier, ii. 236–9, 306–9.

[5] Ibid., pp. 88, 258.

[6] According to Thomas, Mark recalled the lovers from the forest when he had been convinced of their innocence by the separating sword, but was again disillusioned by finding them together in a garden, and Tristan escaped and left the country. According to the Prose *Tristan* (Bédier, ii. 362–4), Mark carried Isolt back to his castle by force, and Tristan, wounded, went off to Brittany to be healed by Isolt of the White Hands.   [7] Bédier, ii. 313.

[8] Schoepperle, op. cit. i. 182 f. This, of course, is impossible if Eilhart wrote about 1170.

[9] Bédier, ii. 175–8.

social degradation and then on to physical separation and the quarrel between them, with death as the final refuge. Later criticism[1] has insisted on the disparity between the two halves of the story; the second half, from the separation of the lovers onward, showing a courtly inspiration which is absent from the first. Yet it cannot be denied that the theme of the potion, i.e. the theme of love as inordinate desire, which is the source of tragic suffering, gives unity to the work, however disparate the elements it contains.

Eilhart and Béroul

Eilhart seems to have preserved more or less faithfully the substance of the archetypal narrative. He gives us, however, the bare facts of the story without much elaboration. Moreover, his work is not just a servile translation. He has probably omitted some episodes—for example, those of the ambiguous oath[2] and of the mysterious stranger who abducts Isolt[3]—and may have added others.[4] The narrative is in places drastically abridged, and it is usually passages of great psychological interest that suffer most.[5] That Eilhart is capable of freely remodelling the details of his narrative is shown by a comparison of all four versions in the tryst under the tree and the flour on the floor episodes.

In the former episode, Béroul and Thomas agree in making the lovers' behaviour extremely guileful. Isolt declares that she has always been faithful to him who had her maidenhood. Both lovers try to dissipate the suspicion that attaches to so compromising a meeting, asserting that Tristan has sought the interview only because he hopes that Isolt will work for a reconciliation between him and Mark or, if this fails, that she will provide him with means to leave the country. The same treatment is found in the version of the Prose *Tristan* (B.N. fr. 756–7)[6] which contains the episode. In Eilhart, however, Isolt displays hostility to the hero, refusing to help him because he has brought shame on her, and ending the interview by hoping that he will never make his peace with Mark. Since Isolt would obviously not consent to a compromising interview merely in order to overwhelm the hero with reproaches and to have the satisfaction of refusing his pleas for assistance, Eilhart's treatment is lacking in plausibility.

---

[1] Schoepperle, op. cit. ii. 448–54; F. Ranke, *Tristan und Isold* (Munich, 1925), pp. 8–39; A. Witte in *ZDA*, lxx (1933), 177–9. According to these writers the difference implies two separate stages in the growth of the story.

[2] Found in both Thomas and Béroul.

[3] Found in Thomas, the Prose *Tristan* (Bédier, ii. 346), and in the Berne *Folie Tristan* (the allusion to Gamarien, vss. 378–93), therefore presumably in Béroul.

[4] The visit of Tristan and Gurvenal to Cornwall, disguised as *jongleurs*, rouses suspicion since it breaks into the Kaherdin–Gargeolain story in an awkward way, and the names Haupt and Plot are obviously of Eilhart's invention.

[5] For example, the first visit to the hermit Ogrin and the marriage with Isolt of the White Hands.

[6] Bédier, ii. 347–53.

The real weakness of Eilhart's handling comes out in the subsequent scene, where Mark requires the queen to give an account of what happened between her and Tristan in the garden. The very form of the request should reveal to Isolt that Mark has learned of the interview. Nevertheless, she denies having seen Tristan and expresses the wish never to see him again. Mark is not disturbed by the lie, but merely says that he saw what happened in the garden and asks for Isolt's help in order to get Tristan back to court. Isolt still feigns anger, upon which Mark promises, if she will only persuade Tristan to stay, to allow them to see as much of each other as they wish. It is difficult to see the purpose of Isolt's lie, difficult also to understand Mark's attitude, seeing that he assumes that Isolt is at one and the same time an enemy of Tristan and on a footing of the closest intimacy with him. In Béroul, Mark asks Isolt if she has seen Tristan recently, and this gives her an opportunity to relate everything that passed between them.

Equally close agreement between Béroul and Thomas against Eilhart is found in the scene of the flour on the floor. In Eilhart the dwarf outlines his plot to sprinkle flour on the floor in order to have traces of Tristan's footprints when he goes to Isolt's bed, but at the same time seems to anticipate the situation that arises after its breakdown—Mark is to be roused when the lovers have come together and watchers are to be posted to prevent the hero's escape. In Béroul and Thomas the king is absent when Tristan goes to Isolt and so does not catch the lovers *in flagrante delicto*.

The substance of Béroul's narrative down to the return from the forest is found in Eilhart. Béroul's account of the forest life contains, however, four additional episodes—the slaying of the dwarf by Mark, the training of the dog Husdain to hunt silently, the death of the 'riche baron' at the hands of Governal, and the invention of the bow that never fails. As Eilhart's account of the forest life is abridged, all four may go back to the original poem. One —the training of Husdain—certainly does.[1]

Although the two versions have the same general subject-matter,[2] the details of the narrative are completely different. Where the evidence of the other versions is not available, we may suspect that Eilhart has altered his original, without necessarily assuming that Béroul's account is authentic. Take the treatment of the discovery of the lovers in the forest. While Béroul stresses Mark's grief and anger as he rides to avenge his wrongs, and then brings out

---

[1] It is mentioned in the Oxford *Folie Tristan* (vss. 873 f.) and in the Prose *Tristan* (Bédier, ii. 362). Eilhart seems to have known this feature since he described the escape of Husdain (vss. 4368–490) and later asserted that Tristan was the first man to train dogs (vss. 4541–5). The verbal similarity between Eilhart's vss. 4457–65 and Béroul's vss. 1694–6 suggests that Eilhart knew the 'riche baron' episode. On the possibly Celtic origin of the story of Mark's ears see Schoepperle, op. cit. ii. 269–71; Foulon in *Bulletin Philologique et Historique*, 1951–2; and above, p. 128.

[2] An important difference is that while in Béroul the spell of the potion is broken completely after three years (vss. 2133–46), in Eilhart it is weakened but not destroyed after four (vss. 2279–3000).

his revulsion of feeling when he spies the separating sword, the German poet makes nothing of this and seems to regard Mark's leaving the sword in the place of Tristan's as more important than the reasons that prompted the act. Eilhart's account, with its complete lack of psychological motivation, cannot be attributed to the original author. On the other hand, Béroul's motivation is excellent, but just as Eilhart's account is a simplification, so this may be an elaboration. Nevertheless, it is clear that a feature in Béroul cannot be condemned just because it is absent from Eilhart or appears there in a different form.

We should be better able to appreciate Béroul's originality if we were in a position to compare his style with that of his source. At once archaic and advanced, it has epic features, while at the same time the treatment of the octo-syllabic couplet is based on that of Chrétien de Troyes.[1] Whether Béroul has simply modernized the versification of an original the technique of which had affinities with that of the epic or whether the style is completely his own cannot be determined. The emotional vigour of Béroul's account are consequent upon the style that he has adopted. Mergell[2] contrasts the coarse realism, the inclination towards violence, and the harshness of tone that mark Béroul's version with Eilhart's more placid narrative methods. These characteristics may be bound up with Béroul's own method of presentation, but the tendency towards realism and violence already existed in his source, as is shown by the presence there of an episode such as that of the lepers[3] or that of the blades at the bed, with its strange mixture of chivalric elements and what Bédier calls 'une barbarie joyeuse et superbe'. At most, therefore, Béroul has developed the story along lines laid down by his predecessor; he has not reinterpreted it in a new way.

Béroul and Eilhart differ in their attitude towards the lovers' guilt, but what we have in Béroul is again not a reinterpretation but at most the development of an idea which was implicit in the original account. Eilhart, in the scene where Brangain is substituted for Isolt, attributes Tristan's treacherous action to the influence of 'der vil unsêlige trang' (the most unhallowed drink). Béroul, on the other hand, tries to vindicate the lovers' conduct in terms of feudal law. What matters is not whether Tristan and Isolt are guilty but whether they can be proved to be so by the standards of feudal justice. Tristan behaves correctly in submitting to the king, refrains from violence against the barons who demand punishment, and he has therefore the right to trial by battle. In refusing this right, Mark becomes in a sense the offender and hence God rescues Tristan by a miracle (the leap from the chapel).[4] When negotiating the return of Isolt to Mark Tristan likewise

---

[1] On Béroul's style see Muret's edition, *SATF* (1903), pp. xxv, lxvi.
[2] Mergell, *Tristan und Isolde* (Mainz, 1949), pp. 34 f.
[3] See Chap. 12, p. 124, n. 1.   [4] Ibid.

PLATE 4

MARK FINDS THE LOVERS IN THE FOREST

Bib. Nat., fr. 2186. *c.* 1260

insists that their innocence can be proved by a judicial battle. This interpretation arises too naturally out of the events of the story to be dismissed as foreign to the original poet's intentions.[1]

The episodes in Béroul that follow the separation of the lovers offer special problems. The ambiguous oath episode occurs in Thomas in a different form, but there it fits awkwardly into its context,[2] since it presupposes a situation in which the lovers are either permanently or temporarily separated. In Béroul, it seems to come at the right place—before Tristan has left Cornwall but after he has given Isolt back to Mark. It may therefore have occurred in the original at this point.[3] The noteworthy feature of the episode is its inordinate length. It branches out into a number of sub-episodes and contains an extraordinary wealth of detail, more appropriate to an episodic poem than to a chapter in a long romance. It contains farcical incidents[4] but also chivalric scenes, treated in a broadly popular style.[5] The following episode, which relates the death of the two barons, Denoalen and Godoïne, at the hands of Tristan, is introduced somewhat abruptly into the story, very much as if it were an independent *conte*. Nevertheless, it carries on the theme of vengeance over Tristan's enemies which is so prominent a feature of the first part. The absence of this episode from the archetype and the fact that the ambiguous oath episode is so much out of scale indicates a change in Béroul's original plan, if not a change of author.[6]

Thomas

The original story, which we have called the archetype, fell into the hands of Thomas, a refined and courtly poet, whose rhetorical style was modelled on that of Wace and the romances of antiquity. He recast this material quite freely in order to bring it into accord with his own aims and tastes. His residence in England presumably led to his encomium of London;[7] his court connexions may have led him to attribute to Tristan the royal arms; for less clear reasons he rejected all connexion with Arthur and made Mark king not only of Cornwall but of all England.

Certain changes were made in the interest of rationality, and the somewhat fantastic notion of sending Tristan in search of a princess whose strand

---

[1] In a very fine study, 'La Légende de Tristan vue par Béroul et Thomas', *RP*, vii (1953), 111–29, Le Gentil takes the view that Béroul's treatment is independent of the archetype.

[2] Bédier, ii. 260.

[3] Bédier suspected (ii. 265) that the ambiguous oath episode was not in the *estoire*, but was a parasitic growth attached to it.

[4] The behaviour of Tristan at the Mal Pas (vss. 3697–878).

[5] The threats of Arthur's knights against the three barons and the jousts in which Tristan is disguised as the Noir de la Montaigne.

[6] Muret in his edition of Béroul for the *SATF*, pp. i–xiv, suggested that the second half of the poem (vss. 2765–4485) was due to a continuator, but abandoned this view in his 1928 edition, pp. vi–viii. See above, p. 134, n. 1.   [7] Bédier, i. 397 f.; Wind, pp. 163 f.

of golden hair had been dropped by two swallows was abandoned in favour of a purposeful voyage to fetch the beautiful Isolt as a bride for Mark.[1] Some of the savagery of the old story was eliminated by expunging the scene in which Mark delivered Isolt over to a group of lepers to satisfy their lust. Indeed, the character of Mark is softened and made more sympathetic. Though later he turns his faithless wife and her paramour out of doors, he permits them to depart unmolested to the forest, and when convinced of their innocence by the separating sword he promptly has them brought back to court.

Isolt, too, is no longer quite the crude, hardened, and conscienceless heroine of the older story. To be sure, she still is willing to have Brangain murdered and she is still capable of brazening out the trial by red-hot iron on the basis of an equivocal oath; but with Tristan at least she is less cruel. According to Eilhart,[2] when she heard a false report that Tristan, fleeing, had failed to stop when asked to do so in Isolt's name, she ordered him to be beaten and laughed at his humiliation. But after months had passed she repented, wore a hair shirt, and begged his forgiveness. Her barbarous glee at her lover's suffering Thomas will not tolerate, and he remodels the incident completely.[3] Tristan is not even accused of an offence against love; Isolt imposes no violent punishment on him; when, much later, she dons a shirt of mail, she does so not out of remorse for any wrong she has done her lover but out of a desire to share his unmerited suffering. Of similar import is the poignant episode concerned with the dog Petit Cru, which Tristan sent to his lady in order that the tinkling of its bell should make her forget the woes of separation. According to Gottfried and presumably Thomas, when the queen realized the magic potency of the bell she tore it off rather than enjoy content while her lover grieved.

Thomas's primary theme is the exaltation of love. True love proceeds from 'desir', the longing of the heart, and from 'raison', not from 'voleir', the lusts of the flesh.[4] It is this conception which explains the transformation of Kaherdin's somewhat ignoble love-affairs; the light-hearted adventure with Camille becomes a serious passion for Brangain, and the story of his intrigue with Gargeolain is completely dropped. Most significant of all is Thomas's refusal to believe that the power of the potion really waned. So there is no repentant visit of the lovers to a hermit, as in Eilhart and Béroul. The marriage to Isolt of the White Hands is handled as a problem in fidelity. Tristan in a long and finely realistic soliloquy debates the issue,[5] and tries to justify his union with a new Isolt by the suspicion that the queen has forgotten him and is finding consolation in the embraces of Mark. But he

---

[1] Schoepperle, op. cit. i. 86 f. On Thomas's realistic psychology see Le Gentil in *RP*, vii. 121 f.
[2] Schoepperle, op. cit., pp. 47–49.
[3] Bédier, i. 341–60, 374.
[4] Ibid. i. 286 f.; Wind, p. 87.
[5] Bédier, i. 261–70.

wonders whether this is possible; can an 'Ovre ki est contre amur' be a sub-stitute for true love? On the wedding night he finds the answer; he cannot bring himself to consummate his union with the young bride and upbraids himself for his folly and treachery.

One of the most significant of Thomas's innovations is the creation of the 'Salle aux Images', the subterranean vaulted chamber in which Tristan visited and caressed the image of his lady.[1] Possibly he took a hint from Wace's brief story of a 'celier desoz terre' which Locrin had made and where he visited his mistress Estrild, though it is also possible that both writers drew ultimately on a story of Essyllt.[2] Thomas, at any rate, gives quite an elaborate description of this hidden shrine, wrought by the most skilled craftsmen and goldsmiths of Brittany. Here Tristan set up an image of his love, the fairest in the world, crowned, sceptred, and wearing on her finger the ring, the pledge of faith. As in contemporary images of saints, Isolt was represented trampling on her persecutor. As in certain statues of the Virgin, a cavity filled with perfume sent out sweet odours from her mouth. A medieval Pygmalion, Tristan lavished his caresses on his unresponsive mistress, and poured out his woes. In this whole episode the cult of human love audaciously assumes the trappings and the forms of the cult of the saints and even of the Queen of Heaven.

To be sure, Thomas was not consistently successful in idealizing and refining the old legend. Many of the incidents still reveal their source in *fabliaux*. In abandoning the notion of the abatement of the philtre's power and the voluntary separation of the lovers, Thomas invented a quite im-probable episode in which Mark, discovering the pair sleeping together in a garden, goes to fetch his barons as witnesses, whereupon Tristan wakes, bids farewell to Isolt, and leaves the country for good. Nevertheless, Bédier went too far in asserting that Thomas was a careless narrator and that his alterations had no other result than to enervate and sentimentalize the story.[3] The task which he attempted, to fit together the old plot and his new conception, called for more drastic procedures than he could or would adopt. The archetype depicted a world where crude violence and low subterfuge prevailed, and where love at its highest was a criminal infatuation and at its lowest an over-mastering lust. One may sympathize, therefore, with a poet who sought to rise, not always successfully, into a better world. Without Thomas's pre-paratory effort Gottfried von Strassburg would not have written his master-piece of sublimated love—one of the supreme works of the Middle Ages.[4]

---

[1] Ibid., pp. 306–13.
[2] Wace, *Brut*, ed. I. Arnold, i, vss. 1381–96; *MP*, xxxviii (1941), 303 f.
[3] Bédier, ii. 318.
[4] See Chap. 14, Gottfried von Strassburg.

The Minor Poems

Besides the biographical narratives of Béroul, Eilhart, and Thomas there remain to us from the twelfth and thirteenth centuries five episodic poems, of which one, *Le Chèvrefeuil*, has already been treated in an earlier chapter. Two others, of 572 and 898 lines respectively, are known as the Berne *Folie Tristan* and the Oxford *Folie Tristan*.[1] Both develop a situation, already found in Eilhart and presumably contained in a lost portion of Béroul, in which Tristan makes a hazardous visit to Mark's court disguised as a court fool, obtains access to Isolt and convinces her, by allusions to their common experiences, of his identity. Both poems handle with humour, vivacity, and poignant feeling the dramatic possibilities of the theme. The author of the Berne *Folie* was a Norman, somewhat lax in his rimes and limited in his vocabulary, and all his allusions seem to have been based on Béroul. The Oxford *Folie*, composed in Anglo-Norman, follows in its allusions exactly the sequence of events in Thomas. In fact, both poems have proved helpful in determining the contents of the lost portions of Béroul and Thomas. Opinions differ as to the relation between the two *Folies*, some critics suggesting a common source; but Hoepffner maintains that the Berne version inspired the author of the Oxford *Folie* to attempt a longer and better-organized treatment.[2]

Two other poets were attracted by the possibilities of the visit in disguise. Gerbert de Montreuil inserted in his continuation of Chrétien de Troyes's *Perceval* an episode in which Tristan assumes the role of a minstrel,[3] and an unknown German poet wrote *Tristan als Mönch*.[4] Finally we may mention the *Donnei des Amants* (*A Dispute between Lovers*),[5] in which the moral that there can be no love without courage is illustrated by telling how Isolt, on hearing her lover's imitation of bird-songs in a garden below, braves the dangers which surround her and joins him.

[1] Bédier, ii. 282–96, 372–9. *Deux Poèmes de la Folie Tristan*, ed. Bédier, *SATF* (1907); *Folie Tristan de Berne*, ed. Hoepffner (Paris, 1934); *Folie Tristan d'Oxford*, ed. Hoepffner (Paris, 1938).

[2] *Folie Tristan de Berne*, pp. 7–13.

[3] *R*, xxxv (1906), 497–530; Gerbert de Montreuil, *Continuation de Perceval*, ed. Mary Williams, *CFMA* (1922), i, vss. 3309–4832; G. Schoepperle, op. cit. i. 239 f.

[4] Ed. H. Paul in *Sitzungsberichte der Münchener Akad. der Wissenschaften*, 1895, pp. 317 ff.; Schoepperle, op. cit. i. 234–8.

[5] Ed. G. Paris in *R*, xxv. 508 ff.; Schoepperle, op. cit. ii. 288–90. On a mysterious La Chievre or Li Kievres who composed a lost poem about Tristan and about whom various guesses have been offered see the references in J. Kelemina, *Geschichte der Tristansage* (Vienna, 1923), p. 29, n. 2, and Bédier, ii. 308, n. 2.

14

GOTTFRIED VON STRASSBURG

W. T. H. JACKSON

GOTTFRIED VON STRASSBURG's *Tristan und Isolt*[1] begins with an acrostic. The solution of the acrostic produces a name, whose significance for the author and his poem we are unable to determine, and a few additional letters whose meaning is equally dark.[2] This tantalizing alternation of solutions with new problems is characteristic of the whole poem. As a key is found to one puzzle, another difficulty presents itself. Perhaps nowhere in Arthurian literature, not even in Wolfram von Eschenbach's *Parzival*, is it harder to rediscover the religious and moral principles which determine the author's treatment of his characters.

In one respect at least there is no problem. Gottfried himself declares that the immediate source of his poem is Thomas of Britain.[3] Unfortunately the extant portions of the poems overlap for only a few lines, so that a full and exact comparison of the incidents and the treatment is hardly possible. We are compelled to have recourse to the Norse version of Brother Robert, which was closely modelled on Thomas's poem. It is clear from this that Gottfried also must have followed his Anglo-Norman predecessor in the

---

[1] The best editions are those of F. Ranke (Berlin, 1930), which is followed in the quotations in this chapter; K. Marold, *Teutonia*, vi (Leipzig, 1912); and A. Bechstein, 5th ed. (Leipzig, 1930). The selection, with introduction and notes, by A. Closs (Oxford, 1947) is also useful. The following are the most important general studies of Gottfried's work: G. Ehrismann, *Geschichte der deutschen Literatur bis zum Ausgang des Mittelalters* (Munich, 1927), 2, ii. 297–332; H. de Boor, 'Die Grundauffassung von Gottfrieds Tristan', *Deutsche Vierteljahrsschrift für Literaturwissenschaft und Geistesgeschichte*, xviii (1940), 262–306; J. Schwietering, *Die deutsche Dichtung des Mittelalters* (Potsdam, 1941), pp. 183–94; G. Weber, *Gottfrieds von Strassburg Tristan und die Krise des hochmittelalterlichen Weltbildes um 1200* (Stuttgart, 1953). It contains a valuable survey of previous research; E. Nickel, *Studien zum Liebesproblem bei Gottfried von Strassburg, Königsberger deutsche Forschungen*, i (1927); H. de Boor and Richard Newald, *Geschichte der deutschen Literatur* (Munich, 1953), ii. 127–45; M. Bindschedler, 'Der heutige Stand der Forschung über Gottfried von Strassburg', *Deutschunterricht*, 1953, no. 2, pp. 90–94. The best translation (into modern German) is that by W. Hertz. J. L. Weston's translation into English is much condensed.

[2] An interesting theory of the relation between the letters in the names 'Tristan' and 'Isolde' and the construction of the poem is advanced by F. Maurer in *Leid* (Bern, 1951), pp. 211 ff. The general thesis of the book in regard to *Tristan* seems to lead to purely negative conclusions. The earlier work of Schotte (*Beiträge zur Geschichte der deutschen Sprache und Literatur*, lxv [1942], 280–302) raises interesting questions about the symmetry of the poem as indicated by the initials of the names. Such interpretations must, however, remain conjectural.

[3] Gottfried refers to Thomas in vss. 149 ff. Vss. 18199–313 and 19424–552 of Gottfried's poem correspond to vss. 1–52 and 53–142 in Bédier's edition of Thomas (Paris, 1902). For a comparison see S. Singer in *Tieche Festschrift* (Bern, 1947).

narration of events, and that he owes little or nothing to Eilhart.[1] To Thomas are to be attributed, as the preceding chapter has shown, the refinement of the tone, the shedding of much coarseness and cruelty, the details of the courtly setting, and the paramount interest in character rather than incident. Thomas alone, says Gottfried, has told the tale aright.[2] If this interest in character takes a completely different form in Gottfried, this is due to his different view of man's place in society and in the universe. Such additions and changes as he made are all to be attributed to this difference in attitude.

A very detailed study of the relationship between the two poems was made by Piquet in 1905.[3] He makes clear throughout his work the difficulty of knowing exactly how great is the correspondence in detail between Gottfried's poem and what Thomas himself wrote. Brother Robert often suppresses character description and motivation in those parts of the poem where it is possible to make comparison between his version and the original and there is no reason to believe that he did not follow the same procedure in the earlier parts. It is quite clear, however, that the prologue must in great part be an original creation of Gottfried himself. In it he indicates the extent of his indebtedness to Thomas and expounds his views on the purpose of the poem.

An examination of the variations in detail within the narrative shows that Gottfried departs from his model for two principal reasons: either he wishes to motivate action more clearly and 'naturally' or he desires to base an action on different standards of conduct. As an example of the first we may mention the changed reason for Tristan's addressing in their own language the merchants who kidnapped him. Brother Robert has Tristan act as an interpreter for these merchants, a situation which appeared unnatural to Gottfried. He obviously thought it unlikely that merchants would be unable to speak the language of their customers and has Tristan use their language only to issue the challenge to a chess game. His use of their own language at this point called their attention to him much more sharply than it would have done had he been merely an interpreter. The same 'naturalness' is sought in Gottfried's account of Morold's attempt at reconciliation, which is not found at all in Thomas's version.

More significant than these changes are those which belong to the second category. Isolt's frank admiration of Tristan in the scene immediately preceding her discovery of the notch in the blade foreshadows her later conduct,

---

[1] A study of the relationship is to be found in : J. Gombert, *Eilhard von Oberg und Gottfried von Straßburg* (Amsterdam, 1927), and H. Stolte, *Eilhard und Gottfried, Studien über Motivreim und Aufbaustil* (Halle, 1941).

[2] *Tristan*, vss. 131 ff.

[3] F. Piquet, *L'Originalité de Gottfried de Strasbourg, Travaux et Mémoires des Facultés de l'Université de Lille*, N.S., no. 5 (1905).

her inability to strike him down when he is at her mercy and her anguish of unfulfilled love. The most striking example of a change to more fitting conduct is Brangaene's hurling overboard of the remains of the love-potion. To Gottfried it was unthinkable that Mark should drink the rest of the liquid, as he does in the Thomas version, and thus make it possible for a comparison to be made between his love for Isolt and that of Tristan.

It is in the description of the lovers' life in the wilderness that Gottfried departs most markedly from his original. Numerous points of detail are altered—Gottfried insists, for example, that the lovers could live together without material food—but the whole conception of the *Minnegrotte* and its allegorical interpretation is so entirely Gottfried's invention that it must be treated separately.

Gottfried's poem is incomplete. It breaks off at the beginning of the love episode between Tristan and Isolt of the White Hands and thus deprives us of the opportunity to compare Gottfried's handling of the tragic conclusion with that of Thomas, but there is no reason to think that there would have been any major difference in incident. As always with Gottfried, incident is less important than motivation, action less important than feeling. It is in this regard that Thomas and Gottfried stand far apart. For Thomas is interested in his main characters as human beings moving in a society motivated by normal human passions and controlled by a code essentially secular, whatever originally Christian elements it may contain. Gottfried, as will appear, sees in their love a reflection in human terms of the bond between the mystic and his God.

Some knowledge of Gottfried's life would give us much help in interpreting his work, but this knowledge we do not possess. The scattered references to Gottfried by other authors[1] tell nothing except that he lived in Strasbourg, and the appellation 'Meister', given to him in the manuscripts, shows that he was not of noble birth. His own references to the death of Reinmar der Alte,[2] and to Walther von der Vogelweide[3] and Wolfram von Eschenbach[4] indicate that he must have been writing in the first two decades of the thirteenth century. We do not even know whether death was responsible for the incomplete state of his poem or whether the difficulty of resolving the questions he had raised caused him to postpone too long his attempt at their solution.[5]

Of one thing there can be no doubt. Gottfried had enjoyed the best education his generation could afford and he was deeply versed in literature and theology. The references to philosophical and theological concepts are too

---

[1] Particularly Konrad von Würzburg and Rudolf von Ems.
[2] *Tristan*, vss. 4779 ff.
[3] Ibid. vss. 4800 ff.
[4] Ibid. vss. 4665 ff.
[5] Mergell, in *Tristan und Isolde* (Mainz, 1949), argues, unconvincingly, that the work is complete.

numerous to be accidental and the whole work is essentially that of a person theologically trained.[1]

It is customary to refer to Gottfried's *Tristan und Isolt* as a courtly epic. This is true only in so far as the milieu in which the story is set is courtly and the material of the story belongs to the Arthurian cycle. In order to discover the type of audience for which Gottfried was writing, we must turn to the information he himself provides in the prologue.

> Ich han mir eine unmüezekeit
> der werlt ze liebe vür geleit
> und edelen herzen zeiner hage,
> den herzen, den ich herze trage,
> der werlde, in die min herze siht.
> ine meine ir aller werlde niht,
> als die, von der ich hoere sagen,
> diu keine swaere enmüge getragen. . . .
>
> .   .   .   .   .
>
> ir leben und minez zweient sich.
> ein ander werlt die meine ich,
> diu samet in eime herzen treit
> ir süeze sur, ir liebez leit,
> ir herzeliep, ir senede not,
> ir liebez leben, ir leiden tot,
> ir lieben tot, ir leidez leben.[2]

(I have taken on a task for the pleasure of the world and the delight of lofty spirits, that is, for the spirits whom I love and the world into which my heart looks. I do not mean the everyday world, of which I have heard it said that it can bear no grief. . . . This world and mine stand far apart. It is another world that I mean, which bears in one heart at the same time bitter-sweetness and the misery of love, its heart's love and its yearning misery, its life of love, its death of misery, its death in love, its life in sorrow.)

There he makes the unequivocal statement that he is writing for 'edele herzen'. These 'lofty spirits'—for so, I think, should the words be translated —are clearly not to be identified with the general court audience or even with the lovers for whom Thomas says that he writes. They are the persons capable of comprehending the Tristan experience, those who can share Gottfried's knowledge, who have suffered and can understand; for such people the love experience is mystically conceived and mystically expressed. It is thus inept and unfruitful to apply to Gottfried's poem any real or imagined canon of 'courtly ethics'. The external features of life at court are, indeed, depicted as might be expected. Stress is laid on the intellectual aspects

---

[1] Weber, *Tristan*, gives many examples, especially in chaps. iii and iv. See also U. Stökle, *Die theologischen Ausdrücke und Wendungen im Tristan Gottfrieds von Strassburg* (Tübingen, 1915). On Gottfried's classical learning see W. Hoffa in *ZDA*, lii. 339 ff.

[2] *Tristan*, vss. 45 ff. See Fourquet in *Bull. de la Faculté des Lettres de Strasbourg*, xxxi (1953), 251–9.

of the knightly education which Tristan receives, on his skill in the arts and in the ceremonies of the chase; relatively little attention is given to his physical prowess.

> 'Tristan, ich horte dich doch e
> britunsch singen und galois,
> guot latine und franzois:
> kanstu die sprache?' 'herre, ja,
> billiche wol.'
>
> .   .   .   .   .
>
> 'hora!' sprach diser, 'hora!' sprach der
> 'elliu diu werlt diu hoere her:
> ein vierzehenjaerec kint
> kan al die liste, die nu sint!'[1]

('Tristan, I heard you singing in the languages of Brittany and Wales, in good Latin and French: do you know the languages?' 'Yes, my lord, fairly well.' . . .'Listen,' said this man, 'listen,' said that. 'Let everyone hear how a fourteen-year-old child knows all the arts there are.')

It is his musical skill which is the direct cause of his coming into a closer relationship with Isolt. But these remain the externals. Of an ethical code such as is found in Chrétien and Hartmann von Aue there is little trace. When features of that code are introduced into the poem, when minor characters are motivated by them, it is only so that they may be discredited or shown to be ineffective in determining the conduct of the lovers.

The realization by the lovers that their love is not that of the court or even a simple, uncomplicated physical attraction comes slowly. All around them they see the externals of courtly existence. Their confidante, Brangaene, assumes after her first shock that their love is to take the normal course of an attachment between a handsome and personable young knight and the young wife of an old husband. She attempts to use the tricks and deceits customary in such cases, and the lovers, themselves unsure of their position, at first agree with her and acquiesce in her schemes. These methods never have more than a superficial success. The misery caused by their attempts at subterfuge spoils all pleasure and poisons their existence. Despair overwhelms them, as Tristan laments to Brangaene:

> Si clagete ime und er clagt ir:
> 'a reine' sprach er, 'saget mir,
> welch rat gewirdet dirre not?
> wie gewirbe ich und diu arme Isot,
> daz wir sus niht verderben?
> ine weiz, wie wir gewerben,
> daz wir behalten unser leben.'
> 'Waz rates mac ich iu gegeben?'

---

[1] Ibid. vss. 3609 ff. The quotation begins at v. 3690.

sprach aber diu getriuwe
'daz ez got iemer riuwe,
daz wir ie wurden geborn!
wir haben elliu driu verlorn
unser vröude und unser ere:
wirn komen niemer mere
an unser vriheit als e.'[1]

(She lamented to him and he to her. 'O lady,' he said, 'tell me, what counsel can meet our need? What can we do, I and the wretched Isolt, to escape destruction? I do not know how we may preserve our life!' 'What counsel can I give you?' replied the faithful maid. 'May God regret that ever we were born! We three have lost our joy and our honour. Never again can we be free as once we were.'

The inadequacy of the normal courtly view of life is made plain throughout the poem. In spite of his training, Tristan is never in spiritual accord with the life of the court. Although capable of knightly achievements which are far above those of his companions, he has little interest in them. His battle against Morold of Ireland is undertaken entirely from a sense of duty to King Mark, and his parting words to Mark show calm resignation but no joy at the prospect of combat.[2] The fight with Morold is a bitter business, fought out with little regard for knightly convention, and it ends in death for one and misery for the other. As so often happens in the poem, the generality of society exults and applauds the victory, but the principal character is merely haunted by a sense of foreboding and a feeling of inadequacy. Tristan's followers are overjoyed; Tristan himself has received a wound, as yet only physical, which can be healed only by Isolt. Its cure will lead to further pain, even less curable than the wound.

Indicative of Gottfried's attitude to worldly chivalry is his refusal to describe the most important ritual in the life of a knight, the *swertleite* or induction into knighthood. For this is a categorical refusal and not an omission, nor is the excuse valid that Gottfried was a bourgeois and ignorant of the ritual. He is refusing to place Tristan among the company of those initiated into courtly service, for this would have implied that his life was to be governed in future by its conditions.

The contrast between Tristan and all his contemporaries grows sharper as the poem progresses. Tristan himself feels the weight of it, of the inability to find understanding anywhere. Mark is unable to conceive of love in anything but sensual terms. He seeks always for proof of physical contact and his own yearnings for Isolt are entirely those of the flesh. 'To him one was as another, he found gold or brass in either. They performed their services for him in their turn, so that he never noticed anything.'[3] That the two lovers are indissolubly bound is beyond his comprehension.

---

[1] *Tristan*, vss. 14391 ff.   [2] Ibid. vss. 6757 ff.   [3] Ibid. vss. 12669 ff.

Tristan too makes one attempt to prove that he can break free. He determines to put the inevitability of his love to one last test. Separated from Isolt,
he marries Isolt of the White Hands, hoping to find in her a relief from the
pain of separation. The experiment is a total failure. All his yearning for
Isolt the Fair returns when he is brought face to face with the problem of
proving his love to his new bride. Again the opposition to courtly love becomes clear, for the contrast between the love for the two Isolts is emphasized
in a score of antitheses and contrasts.

> 'a de benie, wie bin ich
> von disem namen verirret!
> er irret unde wirret
> die warheit und daz lougen
> miner sinne und miner ougen.
> er birt mir wunderliche not:
> mir lachet unde spilt Isot
> in minen oren alle vrist
> und enweiz iedoch, wa Isot ist:
> min ouge, daz Isote siht,
> daz selbe ensiht Isote niht:
> mirst Isot verre und ist mir bi:
> ich vürhte, ich aber gisotet si
> zem anderen male.'[1]

('Alas, how this name [Isolt] confounds me! It misleads and confuses truth and falsehood, both of heart and eye. Strange is the misery it brings me. Isolt laughs and plays
always in my ear and yet I know not where Isolt is. My eye, that sees Isolt, sees her
not; Isolt is near me and yet far. I fear I may be ensnared by Isolt for a second time.')

His broken faith—broken only in his mind, for there is no physical infidelity—proves ultimately his undoing in Thomas's version of the story, and
there is no reason to suppose that Gottfried would have changed the ending.
Physical death comes because of the conflict with accepted morality.

The deep attraction of the two lovers, their almost mystic union, should
not be allowed to give the impression that their characters are identical. Isolt
is more determined, more ruthless, more passionate than Tristan—and her
love is more firmly based. The realization of the true nature of their love
comes to her earlier than it does to Tristan and she hands herself over to fate.
Her effort to preserve the outward forms by the sacrifice of Brangaene and
later by the attempted murder shows her before she has achieved the sense
of spiritual independence which she demonstrates at the trial by ordeal and
in depriving herself of the beautiful music of Petitcriu.[2] She is the vital force
which draws Tristan on. She is the power of *Minne* in its loftiest sense, and
physical separation does not lessen her unity with him.

---

[1] Ibid. vss. 18994 ff.   [2] See above, p. 142.

'ir sit mir verre oder bi,
son sol doch in dem herzen min
niht lebenes noch niht lebendes sin
wan Tristan, min lip und min leben.
herre, ich han iu nu lange ergeben
beidiu leben unde lip;

.   .   .   .   .

unser beider leben daz leitet ir.
nu gat her und küsset mich:
Tristan und Isot, ir und ich,
wir zwei sin iemer beide
ein dinc ane underscheide.'[1]

('Whether you are with me or far away, there shall be nothing alive or dead in my
heart but Tristan, my life and being. Lord, I gave you long ago both my life and myself. . . . You now guide both our lives yourself. Now come and kiss me. Tristan and
Isolt, you and I, we are ever one thing indivisible.')

Tristan himself learns only slowly what is really involved.

It is natural that readers who believe that *Tristan* is a courtly poem
should seek an explanation for Tristan's 'unknightly' conduct, for his flouting
of the basic loyalty due to Mark not only as his king but also as his uncle and
virtual father.[2] It is clear that any consideration of his conduct must begin
with a clarification of the compulsion under which both the lovers act, for
there can be no question of free will here, of a loose and cynical disregard
for all feelings of honour in the determination to satisfy sensual desires. The
lovers act under compulsion and this compulsion is symbolized by the
Minnetrank.

Tristan do er der minne enpfant,
er gedahte sa zehant
der triuwen unde der eren
und wolte dannen keren:
'nein' dahter allez wider sich
'la stan, Tristan, versinne dich,
niemer genim es keine war.'
so wolte et ie daz herze dar;
wider sinem willen crieget er,
er gerte wider siner ger:
er wolte dar und wolte dan.
der gevangene man

---

[1] *Tristan*, vss. 18294–9, 18350 ff.
[2] All the critics deal with this point. The clash between courtly honour and the power of love is
regarded by many, notably Ehrismann, and, in a modified form, Maurer, as the core of the poem. For
the 'courtly system', see G. Ehrismann, 'Die Grundlagen des ritterlichen Tugendsystems', *ZDA*
lvi (1919), 137–216.

> versuohtez in dem stricke
> ofte unde dicke
> und was des lange staete.[1]

(As Tristan felt himself in love, he thought at once of faith and honour and wished to turn back to them. 'No', he thought to himself, 'abandon it, Tristan, come to your senses. Let no one know it.' Thus did the heart want it; he battled against his will, desired against his passions. He wished to be here, he wished to be there. Captive as he was, he struggled in the noose hard and long, and for long he held out.)

In the earliest versions of the story the *Minnetrank* had doubtless been a true magic potion. The more sophisticated versions reject this, and in Thomas it is little more than a symbol of the overwhelming power of love. In Gottfried's poem it is more than this. In drinking the love potion, the lovers drink not simply of inextinguishable love for each other but of death itself. The cup contains a cure for the physical pain of unsatisfied love; it drugs the senses into an oblivion which conceals for a time the deadly consequences of such love. But in doing so it hands them over to the tyranny of the senses, and this tyranny is so powerful that it brushes from its path all considerations of honour and loyalty.[2] It forces Tristan to abandon his loyalty to Mark; it forces Isolt to plot the murder of her faithful companion Brangaene; it forces both to commit one act of dishonour after another against the person of the king. So strong is it, indeed, that the ultimate sin is committed in its name, when the oath before God is reduced to a mockery by a crude piece of deception which observes the letter of the oath but ignores its spirit.

The truth lies deeper. That sensuality held the lovers in its grip cannot be denied. But equally it was not the core and inner being of that love, a fact which emerges most clearly when the lovers are separated and their love remains. It is rather the inadequate reflection of the bond which unites them and which is mystical in character. The high point of their love does not come with its consummation, where sensuality triumphs, nor at any of the subsequent incidents in hall or garden, where their pleasures are furtive and guilty, but rather in the *Minnegrotte*. Here their love leaves intrigue behind and rises to sublimity. As far as is possible on earth, the sensual aspect is subordinated to the spiritual, the physical delight to the mystical realization.

> si sahen beide ein ander an,
> da generten si sich van;
> der wuocher, den daz ouge bar,
> daz was ir zweier lipnar;
> sin azen niht dar inne
> wan muot unde minne.[3]

---

[1] *Tristan*, vss. 11741 ff.; for Isolt, see vss. 11789 ff.

[2] Weber, *Tristan*, gives a full and well-documented account in the chapter entitled 'Dämon' (i. 133 ff.).   [3] *Tristan*, vss. 16815 ff.

(They looked at one another and on that they lived. That which grew in the eyes of each was food. There they had no food but that of the spirit and of love.)

The elaborate allegory of the grotto is Gottfried's own invention. It is, as Ranke has shown,[1] a temple of love with the structure of the church clearly depicted in it. Within this temple there is ground hallowed to the cause of *Minne*, and in its centre is the crystalline bed. This is the shrine for the *edele herzen*, the holy place to which they alone could penetrate. Only those who have achieved complete sacrifice to Christian love can enjoy its delights. Gottfried himself could reach the bed but not enter it, for his surrender had been incomplete and his sacrifice was not accepted. The grotto is a place of miracles, not merely a hiding place. For here the lovers' misery changes to delight, they are fed magically by their love and need no other food.

The only light which reaches them comes through the windows of *güete* (loving kindness), *diemüete* (humility), *zuht* (propriety), and *êre* (reputation). These are the virtues which illuminate their life in the grotto, but the cave itself is of beauty unfathomable and immeasurable, impossible of access and barred to all but those who love completely. There can be no doubt that in describing the grotto Gottfried is drawing deliberate comparisons between the love of Tristan and Isolt and Christian mysticism and eucharistic communion.[2] The ecstasy of the Christian soul yearning for the heavenly Bridegroom and losing completely its individual entity is translated into terms of earthly passion. The lovers experience this ecstasy while still on earth, although such ecstasy can only be short lived while it is unable to free itself from the demon of sensual passion.[3] The love of Tristan and Isolt is a mystic love in human terms. Its purer aspects were subjected through drinking the potion to the devil of sensual passion. Only by death can their love be freed from this snare and the 'love-death' means that the lovers can be reunited in mystic love, freed from all grossness and carnal attraction. Tristan unknowingly proclaims this on hearing for the first time that he has drunk the potion.

> 'nu waltes got!' sprach Tristan
> 'ez waere tot oder leben:
> ez hat mir sanfte vergeben.
> ine weiz, wie jener werden sol:
> dirre tot der tuot mir wol.

---

[1] F. Ranke, *Die Allegorie der Minnegrotte in Gottfrieds Tristan, Schriften der Königsberger Gelehrten Gesellschaft*, geisteswissenschaftliche Klasse, ii, no. 2 (1925).

[2] Weber, *Tristan*, i. 69 ff.; J. Schwietering, *Der Tristan Gottfrieds von Strassburg und die Bernhardsche Mystik*, Abhandlungen der Preußischen Akademie der Wissenschaften, phil.-hist. Klasse, 1943, no. 5. The views expressed in this chapter are deeply indebted to Schwietering's ideas as expressed here and in *Deutsche Dichtung des Mittelalters*.

[3] The existence of the lovers is portrayed as an idyll. See especially vss. 17139 ff. The resemblance to Paradise is obvious.

> solte diu wunnecliche Isot
> iemer alsus sin min tot,
> so wolte ich gerne werben
> umb ein eweclichez sterben.'[1]

('Now may God determine', said Tristan, 'whether it be life or death: it has brought me sweetness. I know not, how *that* will be: *this* death pleases me well. If the lovely Isolt is always thus to be my death, then I would gladly ask for death eternal.')

This use of unchristian mysticism has exposed Gottfried to charges of heresy and contempt of the Church. It is unlikely that he was consciously flouting religion. Rather he was using its terms to describe what seemed to him to be the most exalted of human experiences and in doing so he used the only possible terms, those of Christian mysticism. To Gottfried, as to St. Bernard, love is the dominating power of the universe, but to Gottfried it is not the yearning for the divine in heaven but for the divinity of another human soul.

Gottfried's language reflects the parallelism with Christianity.[2] The desire for analogy and antithesis gives rise to a series of closely interwoven reiterations and contradictions which force upon the reader the unbreakable bond between the lovers and yet defy accurate analysis. The essentially recondite nature of all mystical language combines in Gottfried with a delight in word patterns which often seem to be prolonged merely for the pleasure the poet found in weaving them. If any aspect of the poem is open to criticism it is this, for Gottfried's purpose can be obscured and even lost in these verbal images. Yet deliberate mystification must be admitted as part of his purpose.

It is difficult to speculate on the ending which Gottfried intended to give to his poem. That it would have differed essentially in details from the work of Thomas of Britain is unlikely. Much more important is the question of how Gottfried would have treated the return of Tristan, Isolt's quarrel with Brangaene, and the death scene. There must surely have been an increasing awareness on the part of the lovers that they could live no longer in pretence. The quarrel with Brangaene might well indicate the end of even an outward acquiescence in the conventions of the court. As the cloak of pretence is removed, the awareness of inevitable doom, a doom foreshadowed by the lovers and Brangaene, when the cup was drunk, must have grown upon them, an awareness at once terrifying and infinitely reassuring. The cry 'diz tranc ist euwer beider tot' (This drink means death to you both), uttered in despair after the potion was drunk, takes on a new meaning—release and reunion.

Many later poets mention Gottfried with admiration but no one dared

---

[1] *Tristan*, vss. 12494 ff.

[2] There are many studies of the details of Gottfried's style. See in particular: A. Dijksterhuis, *Thomas und Gottfried, ihre konstruktiven Sprachformen* (Amsterdam, 1930).

to continue his style of writing. Two later poets, Ulrich von Türheim and Heinrich von Freiberg, continued his *Tristan*, or at least claimed to do so.[1] That they completely failed to understand it is clear from the spirit of their versions. They adhered closely to the purely narrative style of Eilhart, making the love of Tristan and Isolt a love adventure in the courtly tradition, a tale of successful intrigue ending in death. These authors did not belong to the circle of the initiated for whom Gottfried wrote, and they were unable to appreciate either the emotional turmoil of the lovers or the spiritual forces which caused them to act as they did. To them Gottfried was a magic name and to continue his poem was to be illuminated by reflected glory. But they had no conception of his true stature.

Gottfried's *Tristan* is one of the greatest achievements of medieval literature. In his delineation of human love, the poet embraces all contemporary knowledge and refines it for his purposes. For him the dominance of *Minne* in the world is a sublime and noble thing. It can be debased by sensual passion and misunderstood by lesser spirits, but in its purest form it exalts to the skies. Such a love is that of Gottfried's Tristan and Isolt.

---

[1] Ulrich von Türheim's continuation may be found, ed. E. K. Busse, in *Palästra*, cxxi (Berlin, 1913). Heinrich von Freiberg, *Tristan und Isolde, Liebesroman des 13. Jahrhunderts*, ed. A. Berg (Reichenberg, 1935). See on these authors W. Stammler, *Deutsche Literatur des Mittelalters, Verfasserlexikon* (Berlin, Leipzig, 1933–55), iv. 603–7; ii. 261–5.

15

CHRÉTIEN DE TROYES

JEAN FRAPPIER

CHRÉTIEN DE TROYES is one of the great names in French literature and certainly one of the most eminent in Arthurian literature.[1] Though he has been called the father or the inventor of the romances of the Table Round, the title is liable to misinterpretation and leaves the precise nature of his originality obscure. He no more created the genre than Corneille and Racine created out of nothing classical French tragedy, but he raised the Matter of Britain, still new and uncertain, to a high eminence and made it something hitherto unknown.

In Chrétien's work several currents flowed together. When he began to write about 1160, the literature of North France had taken a new turn, corresponding to the change in sentiment among the nobility, to the exaltation of the lady, and the refinement of manners known as *courtoisie*. The octosyllabic couplet had begun to replace the epic *laisse*. Authors were becoming more conscious of their art. A kind of 'humanism', characterized not only by a return to classical subjects and models but also by a desire for personal fame, was represented by the romances of antiquity, *Alexandre*, *Thèbes*, *Enéas*, and *Troie*. Did not the troubadours of the South offer examples of amatory expression more stimulating than the manuals of poetics? Were not imaginations stirred by the sensational discoveries of Geoffrey of Monmouth, by the Tristan legend, already shaped into a powerful romance of tragic love, and by the tales and lais of the Breton *jongleurs*?

All these influences played on Chrétien in the years of his apprenticeship, and all left their mark on his work. Though his trial efforts were almost certainly Ovidian, he turned to the Matter of Britain in his mature years, allured by its novelty and beauty. He gave to it an alloy of his own, reduced it to harmony, and fashioned a world in which fantasy was wedded to reason. His originality consisted in setting the clear spirit of Champagne and of France to the classic task of endowing old materials with a more exquisite savour, a clearer meaning, and broader human values.

---

1 The following are general works on Chrétien: W. Foerster, *Kristian von Troyes, Wörterbuch zu seinen sämtlichen Werken* (Halle, 1914); Gustave Cohen, *Un Grand romancier d'amour et d'aventure au XIIᵉ Siècle*, 2nd ed. (1948); M. Borodine, *La Femme et l'amour au XIIᵉ siècle d'après les poèmes de Chrétien de Troyes* (Paris, 1909); Reto R. Bezzola, *Le Sens de l'aventure et de l'amour (Chrétien de Troyes)* (Paris, 1947); A. Pauphilet, *Le Legs du moyen âge* (Melun, 1950), chaps. v, vi; Stefan Hofer, *Chrétien de Troyes, Leben und Werke* (Graz-Köln, 1954); J. Frappier, *Chrétien de Troyes, l'homme*

The Man, His Life and Work

All that we know of Chrétien's life we learn from his works. The dedication of *Lancelot*, or the *Chevalier de la Charrette*, shows that the poem was composed for Marie de Champagne, daughter of Louis VII of France and Eleanor of Aquitaine. Since Marie became Countess of Champagne by her marriage with Count Henri in 1164, *Lancelot* was written after that year. A second date is furnished by the prologue of *Perceval*, or the *Conte du Graal*, which was dedicated to Philippe of Alsace, who became Count of Flanders in 1168. This incomplete work was begun, therefore, before the death of Philippe at Acre, 1 June 1191, or rather before his departure in September 1190.

Though the poet's statement that his name was 'Crestiens de Troies' does not necessarily mean that he was born at Troyes, it can hardly be doubted that he spent many years there, for his language, though close to pure *Francien*, preserves dialectal traits of Champagne. Does his dedication to Philippe of Flanders mean that late in life he accompanied his patron to his seat at Bruges? It is a possible but not a necessary inference, for Philippe often visited Troyes, and in 1182 he proposed marriage, though unsuccessfully, to the Countess Marie, widowed the year before. Paris's conjecture that Chrétien was a herald is without foundation.[1] He has been identified with Christianus, canon of St. Loup, mentioned in a document of 1173.[2] But this was not a rare name, and much of his work shows a secular spirit. Nevertheless, he must have been a cleric in the sense that he studied the trivium at least, perhaps in the flourishing schools of Troyes.[3] Thus without taking priestly orders he could have acquired his knowledge of Latin literature and of poetic theory.

Gaston Paris thought that he must have crossed the Channel because of his singularly full and accurate knowledge of places in south-eastern England,[4] and Hofer believes that he knew Nantes,[5] but the evidence is not conclusive. Chrétien could have learned much of the great world at the court of Champagne or in the town of Troyes, where the two great fairs brought merchants, *jongleurs*, and story-tellers from every corner of Christen-

et l'œuvre (Paris, 1957). On classical influence see F. E. Guyer, 'Influence of Ovid on Chrestien de Troyes', *RR*, xi (1291), 97–134, 216–47. On Celtic and other sources see R. S. Loomis, *Arthurian Tradition and Chrétien de Troyes* (New York, 1949). On style see G. Biller, *Étude sur le style des premiers romans français en vers* (Göteborg, 1918); A. Hilka, *Die direkte Rede als stilistisches Kunstmittel in den Romanen von Kristian von Troyes* (Halle, 1903). On manuscript transmission see A. Micha, *La Tradition manuscrite des romans de Chrétien de Troyes* (Paris, 1939).

[1] *Mélanges de littérature française du moyen âge* (Paris, 1910), i. 251 f.
[2] Vigneras in *MP*, xxxii (1934–5), 341 f.
[3] Wolfram speaks of 'meister Cristjân von Troys'—a title given to clerks, but not necessarily to priests. Geoffrey of Monmouth was styled *magister* years before he took priestly orders.
[4] Paris, *Mélanges*, i. 260.
[5] *ZRP*, xlviii (1928), 131–3.

dom. Unless new documents come to light, there is little chance that we shall know more of our poet's biography.

As for his works, Chrétien listed at the beginning of *Cligès* the poems already composed: *Erec, Les Comandemanz Ovide, L'Art d'Amors, Li Mors de l'Espaule, Li Rois Marc et Iseut la Blonde, La Muance de la Hupe, l'Aronde et le Rossignol*. Of these the second and third were presumably translations of Ovid's *Remedia Amoris* and *Ars Amandi*, and the *Mors de l'Espaule (The Shoulder-Bite)*, a version of the story of Pelops. All three are lost. The *Muance*, usually called *Philomena*, also based on Ovid, was incorporated in the late-thirteenth-century *Ovide Moralisé* and thus has survived.[1] On the nature of the lost poem on Marc and Iseut hypotheses have multiplied, but it was probably a short episodic poem, and there is no reason to suppose that it was the archetype from which the extant versions were derived. Hofer has urged that *Erec* preceded the *Ovidiana*,[2] but, though this is possible, it is hard to conceive of *Erec* as the work of a beginner. It is therefore most likely that Chrétien fulfilled his apprenticeship in translating Ovid before he yielded to the charm of Arthurian tales.

After *Cligès* there followed three works which he signed with his name and genius, *Lancelot* or *Le Chevalier de la Charrette*, *Yvain* or *Le Chevalier au Lion*, and *Perceval* or *Le Conte du Graal*. He left *Lancelot* to Godefroy de Lagny to complete, and died before finishing *Perceval*. If we add two songs of uncertain date, one in the manner of Bernard de Ventadour, we have listed all the authentic works of Chrétien.[3]

There is the debated attribution of *Guillaume d'Angleterre*, an adaptation of the St. Eustace legend. Though the name Chrétien appears in the first line as that of the author, I confess that I cannot recognize in the poem the turn of mind and the style of the author of *Lancelot, Yvain*, and *Perceval*.

The difficult problem of Chrétien's chronology has been studied most recently and carefully by Hofer and Fourrier.[4] Certain reflections of contemporary events and personages seem to put the date of *Erec* at 1170, of *Cligès* about 1176. Between 1177 and 1179 or 1181 Chrétien probably worked alternately on *Yvain* and *Lancelot*, and after 4 May 1181 he began *Perceval*. Thus Foerster's datings have been moved forward considerably.

Among the qualities displayed by our author the most significant is the learning without which he could not have won favour in chivalric and courtly circles. It appears in his borrowing of themes and images from classical poets, especially Ovid, in his practice of principles of composition taught in the schools, in his fondness for dialectic and subtle reasoning. He possessed

---

[1] On *Philomena* see edition by C. de Boer (Paris, 1909); F. Zaman, *L'Attribution de 'Philomena' à Chrétien de Troyes* (Amsterdam, 1928); Hoepffner in *R*, lvii (1931), 13–74.

[2] *ZFSL*, lx (1936–7), 335–43, 441–3.

[3] Foerster, *Wörterbuch* (1914), pp. 205–9*.

[4] See above, n. 2, and *BBSIA*, ii (1950), 69–88.

also something of the mental attitude of a humanistic scholar. At the beginning of *Erec* (vss. 23–26) he asserted his faith in the value of his work and his assurance of long-lasting fame. And in the prologue to *Cligès* (vss. 24–44) he celebrated the alliance of learning and chivalry and their glorious migration from Greece to Rome and from Rome to France.

Though the theme of the *translatio studii* was a commonplace with a long past, there is no mistaking the pride in Chrétien's tone. Moreover, the union of learning with military prowess was a living ideal of the time. It was symbolized in *Erec* (vss. 6736–93) by the allegorical figures representing the arts of the quadrivium which were embroidered on the coronation robes of the hero. It was incarnated in the person of Chrétien's protector, Henri I of Champagne.

Admiration for pagan antiquity did not, of course, exclude a familiarity with the Scriptures. Though Chrétien's romances revolved about situations and problems in secular life, and consequently it is not surprising that he drew little on the Bible, nevertheless one may discover its influence in the adaptation of sacred comparisons and images to a profane context. Indeed, in the prologue to *Perceval* (vss. 47–50) Chrétien translated with moving simplicity a verse of St. John, which by mistake he attributed to St. Paul.

Symbolism, as already noted, is not absent from his work, but it is possible greatly to exaggerate the poet's use of it.[1] Certainly the principle, based on the interpretation of the Scriptures, of attaching spiritual meanings to tangible objects and historic or fictitious events was deeply planted in the medieval mind, and *gloser la lettre* was the duty of scholars and poets. But though this habit is perceptible here and there in Chrétien's romances, in certain subtleties and in correspondences between concrete details and the conduct of persons, it was restricted by a strong feeling for psychological realities and normal motivation. He was neither a Dante nor the author of the *Queste del Saint Graal*.

To the *chansons de geste*, to Wace, and to the romances of antiquity Chrétien owed something in the way of names, motifs, and technical features, but his main debt lay elsewhere. The troubadours were the source of his conceptions of *l'amour courtois* and provided him with a higher notion of stylistic refinement. Even more powerful was the impact of the *Tristan*, which was not limited to the composition of the poem on Marc and Iseut. In *Erec*, in one of his lyrics, and above all in *Cligès*, he reveals a will to oppose and a will to surpass the famous love-story. Even in *Lancelot* and *Yvain* the influence is felt, and only in *Perceval* is he released from this obsession.

As a professional writer, Chrétien was eager for success, liberal in praise of his patrons, and scornful of the cruder efforts of the *conteurs*. Far more

---

[1] Bezzola's work cited in n. 1, p. 157, is rich in delicate analyses, but exaggerates the symbolic element, particularly in *Erec*. See Misrahi's critique in *RP*, iv (1951), 348–61.

important was his awareness of critical concepts. He may have been the first to use the word *roman* to designate a distinct genre; in any case he observed its laws. The words *matière*, *conjointure*, and *sen*[1] are terms of literary aesthetic which will be defined and discussed later. He knew that it was not enough to add adventure to adventure, as did the *jongleurs*, but that he must organize his materials. Though he felt and exploited the spell of the fantastic, he recognized the classic qualities of balance and reason. He speaks in *Lancelot* of 'sa peine et son entencion', in other words 'hard work and careful attention'. Though he learned and adopted some of the artificial precepts of the *artes poeticae*, he quickly acquired a personal style, both polished and at the same time natural, modelled on the rhythms of actual speech. The octosyllabic lines move without monotony, the phrases are euphonious, the words fitted to their task, sometimes clear and precise, sometimes delicately tinted.

More than any of his contemporaries, except perhaps Thomas of Britain, Chrétien exemplified the striving for lucidity. He sought to illuminate the mysteries of the heart and the conscience. He treated of love, sometimes with a tincture of comedy, sometimes with tragic emphasis. He liked to knot and unknot situations humanly significant. He defined and sought to solve the problems of conscience posed by the conflicting claims of love, morality, and knightly honour.

Without contradicting the moral doctrines of the Church, he taught (except in *Perceval*) a somewhat distinct code of worldly ethics. He did not reject the joys of this transitory life, but he conceded nothing to baseness, demanded of his heroes greatness of soul, and exalted the virtue of sacrifice. What he condemned was futile excess and lack of balance. Though as a psychologist he was interested in the amorous obsession of Lancelot, the madness of Yvain, and the love-trance of Perceval on seeing the blood-drops on the snow, his knightly ideal combined clarity of vision and a strong will. He preferred those characters who make themselves, who develop power and self-knowledge through trials. Though at the dictate of the Countess Marie he idealized an adulterous and extravagant passion, his own standards of moderation and reason led him to depict the marriage of true love as the ideal union; Enide is at the same time the wife, the mistress, and the lady of Erec. On the other hand, Chrétien was repelled by the Tristan legend, which exalted a love uncontrolled and heedless of honour.

Chrétien and the Matter of Britain

The generally recognized influence of the *Tristan* on Chrétien brings up the much larger question of the influence of the so-called Matter of Britain, that body of stories localized for the most part in Great or Little Britain and

[1] The most important work on Chrétien's theory of the romance is still that of Nitze in *R*, xliv (1915–17), 14–36.

dealing with adventures in the far-off days of King Arthur. Did such stories exist before Chrétien? Much of the evidence on this crucial question has already been surveyed in previous chapters and need not be rehearsed. Let me, however, treat the problem briefly as it relates to Chrétien.

It has sometimes been asserted that Chrétien's preoccupation with Arthurian story is fully accounted for by the vogue established by Geoffrey of Monmouth and Wace. Now it is plain that several passages and some names in Chrétien's romances betray this influence,[1] but it seems equally plain that the *Historia Regum Britanniae*, though too romantic to be acceptable as history, was not romantic enough to inspire the mysterious adventures and the sentimental affairs in which Chrétien deals. Nor is it reasonable to believe that he created this poetic world. Though he undoubtedly enriched, polished, and rationalized it and peopled it with more fully developed characters, he could not have invented this faery mythology, this supernatural machinery, so different from that of Ovid, so significantly akin to that of Marie de France and the Breton lais.[2] In fact, he never pretended to be the inventor of his narratives, and referred regularly to a *conte*, an *estoire*, or a *livre*.

Certain passages in *Erec* are significant for their bearing on the issue. In vss. 13–22 the poet clearly implies that, as Rita Lejeune has remarked,[3] there existed a *conte d'Erec*, that it was recited before an audience of kings and counts, and that it had become corrupted in the process by professional story-tellers. Another important indication of the development which the Matter of Britain had already attained is the list of knights of the Round Table which Chrétien gives at the point where Enide enters the royal hall, perhaps as a sort of *aide-mémoire* from which he might draw names at a future time.[4] Whence came these names, these personages? Geoffrey and Wace might have supplied Gauvain, Yvain, Bedoier, Keu, Yder, and Count Cadorcaniois, but these authors never mentioned Erec, Lancelot, Gornemant, and many others present that day at Arthur's court. A second passage giving the names of the counts and kings invited to the nuptials of Erec and Enide provokes the same question.[5] Did Chrétien invent them? Some, to be sure, may well have been coined in a playful spirit, but a considerable number are certainly of Celtic derivation.[6] Note particularly three figures named

---

[1] M. Pelan, *L'Influence du Brut de Wace sur les romanciers français de son temps* (Paris, 1931).

[2] The principal works to consult on the much debated subject of Celtic sources are Loomis's work cited in n. 1, p. 157, and Jean Marx, *La Légende Arthurienne et le Graal* (Paris, 1952); also reviews of these books and Loomis's *Wales and the Arthurian Legend* (Cardiff, 1956).

[3] *MA*, liv (1948), 278.

[4] *Erec*, ed. Foerster, vss. 1682–750; ed. Roques, vss. 1671–706. After the eleventh name the variant readings are numerous.

[5] Ed. Foerster, vss. 1932–2014; ed. Roques, vss. 1882–962.

[6] To cite only one example, the name Caradoc Briebras (Short-Arm) is the result of mistranslating the Breton Karadoc Brech Bras, meaning 'Arm-Strong'. See Chap. 11 above.

together: Maheloas, lord of the Isle of Glass (*Isle de Voirre*); Graillemer de Fine Posterne (Finistère), identifiable with Graalant Muer, hero of a lai resembling Marie de France's *Lanval*; Guingamor, lord of the Isle of Avalon and paramour of Morgain la Fée. Here is a group of traditional persons, united by their common association with the blissful island paradise of Celtic myth. It is pushing doubts of Celtic origin too far to suppose that this grouping is accidental and that Chrétien was unaware of the traditions attached to these three persons. It seems more reasonable to credit him with a knowledge of their stories and with a perception of their basic resemblance.

In the difficult quest for Celtic origins the most systematic and detailed effort is that of R. S. Loomis in his fundamental work, *Arthurian Tradition and Chrétien de Troyes*. He employs the comparative method, as is legitimate under the circumstances, and recognizes the characteristic features of a traditional literature.[1] Though unable to support all his conclusions with decisive proof, and failing at times to distinguish sharply between hypothesis and fact, he has succeeded in placing the episodes and personages of Chrétien in such a framework that any other theory but that of Celtic origin seems improbable. We cannot for lack of space explore the background of Welsh and Irish myth and hero-tale which Loomis traced, and our main purpose will be to set in relief the creative work of the poet; but a brief summary of Loomis's conclusions may be permitted.

Erec reflects Welsh legends concerned with the fays Modron and Rhiannon, with Mabon, son of Modron, with the dwarf king Beli and his brother Brân. *Lancelot*, as Gaston Paris long since observed, is based on a Nature myth. *Yvain*, in the first part, combines several versions of the testing of the warriors of Ulster by Curoi with the Breton traditions of Berenton, while in the second part there are traces of the *Sick-bed of Cuchulainn*, blended with traditions of Modron as a water-nymph. *Perceval* represents a highly complex amalgam of many Irish and Welsh elements. The direct sources of these four poems seem to have been four tales in French prose,[2] elaborations of material furnished by Breton *conteurs*. The Welsh romances of *Gereint* and *Owein* are not derived from *Erec* and *Yvain* but from common sources, the works of a single man and therefore probably coupled together in manuscript.[3] Clearly distinguished from the four poems named is *Cligès*, an original composition in the sense that the plot was of Chrétien's invention, that its atmosphere and its geography conform to the realistic tendencies of Chrétien's own mind, and that the clearly defined intention to correct and to surpass the *Tristan* legend was a personal one. If this be granted, *Cligès*, which contains some

---

[1] For a classification of these phenomena see Loomis, pp. 38–58.

[2] Loomis bases his contention (pp. 10, 11, 22) in part on Chrétien's use of the word *rimoiier* (*Perceval*, vs. 63), which he interprets as 'to turn into rime'; though this sense is possible, it is not certain, for *rimoiier* can mean merely 'to write in verse'.   [3] See Chap. 16.

obvious borrowing from Wace and the Tristan legend, but nothing suggesting a Celtic basis, is the most truly representative of Chrétien as man and artist. It was entirely his own work.

Loomis did not maintain that in the four other romances Chrétien followed his models slavishly, but he did ascribe the greater coherence and the more adequate motivation of *Erec* and *Yvain*, as contrasted with *Lancelot* and *Perceval*, to the merits of the two sources of the former poems, which Chrétien chose himself; while, on the other hand, Loomis attributed the looser structure and the more fantastic matter of *Lancelot* and of *Perceval* to the cruder narratives on which they were based and which were chosen for him by his patrons. Though this distinction is not without a basis, I do not believe that such awkwardness and incoherence as one finds in the two latter poems was due to Chrétien's failure to recognize and eliminate the defects of his sources. In both *Lancelot* and *Perceval* an attentive analysis reveals a fine gradation from one episode to another and a careful structure.

Far from being mastered by the Matter of Britain, Chrétien treated it with a light and skilful hand, often retaining its inconsequences and extravagances deliberately in order to pique the curiosity of his readers by an enigma or to startle them with a surprise, at times also seasoning the tale with ironic humour. Poet and artist, he was not insensible to the charm of this mythology in ruins, a world of marvels more attractive than moralizing symbolism or the legends of classical antiquity. But his taste for the reasonable and the realistic led him to dilute these myths and to introduce the actuality of his own time. Thus like a virtuoso he played on two strings: the fantastic and remote, the natural and near. And by presenting his heroes and heroines in this legendary perspective he lent them a superhuman stature, comparable to that of figures over the portal of a cathedral.

Chrétien, in short, conferred on the Matter of Britain a new worth. It probably seemed to him more fluid, more supple than the material supplied by the authors of Greece and Rome, more suited to illustrate the ideas which he sought to convey. In a sense, perhaps, he was the Ovid of a disintegrating Celtic mythology.

'Erec'[1]

In the opening lines of his first romance Chrétien boasts of having extracted from a certain 'conte d'aventure', telling of Erec son of Lac, 'une

---

[1] Editions: by W. Foerster, with variant readings, not altogether reliable (Halle, 1890); later small editions 1896, 1909, 1934; by M. Roques on basis of MS. Bib. Nat. fr. 794, *CFMA* (Paris, 1952). From the numerous studies of *Erec*, besides the general works cited in n. 1, p. 158, let me cite a few: Lot, 'L'Episode des larmes d'Enide', *R*, xxviii (1899), 1–48, 341–7; Lot, 'Les Noces d'Erec et d'Enide', *R*, xlvi (1920), 42–45; Nitze, 'The Romance of Erec Son of Lac', *MP*, x (1912–13), 445–89; Nitze, 'Erec's Treatment of Enide', *RR*, x (1919), 26–37; Sheldon, 'Why does Chrétien's

mout bele conjointure' (a well-organized narrative),[1] whereas those who earn their livelihood by reciting, spoil and mangle it.

The first part of this story, called by Chrétien 'li premerains vers',[2] prettily linking two motifs, the chase of the White Hart and the jousts for the Sparrow-hawk, tells how Erec, a king's son and a brilliant knight of the Round Table, takes revenge on Yder son of Nut for a grave offence done to Queen Guenièvre and himself; how Erec falls in love with and affiances himself to Enide, the daughter of a mere vavasour, and takes her to Arthur's court, where she is admired by everyone. This prelude has the unity of a lai and is in itself a fair 'conjointure'.

The action now takes a new start. After a magnificent wedding and a month of rejoicing, the young couple repair to Erec's own land to enjoy their honeymoon. But conjugal felicity makes Erec forget arms and chivalry. His companions blame Enide for his unknightly conduct, and the rumour reaches Enide. One morning, as she watches her sleeping husband, she weeps and accuses herself. Erec, waking, overhears her self-reproach and forces her to reveal the reports circulating about him. He decides to recommence a life of perilous adventure. There would be nothing mysterious about this if he did not order Enide to ride before him, clad in her fairest robe, and not to speak to him without permission. Not merely is his honour impugned, but a secret doubt leads him to test her loyalty. Enide meekly obeys, and the two ride forth. In the encounters which follow with robber knights, with a dwarf king, and other formidable antagonists, Erec's exploits are equalled by Enide's proofs of devotion. Thus reassured as to his own prowess and his wife's fidelity, Erec addresses her:

> 'Ma dolce suer,
> Bien vos ai de tot essaiee.
> Or ne soiez plus esmaiee,
> C'or vos aim plus qu'ainz mes ne fis,
> Et je resui certains et fis
> Que vos m'amez parfitemant.
> Or voel estre d'or en avant
> Ausi con j'estoie devant,
> Tot a vostre comandemant;
> Et se vos rien m'avez mesdit,
> Je le vos pardoing tot et quit
> Del forfet et de la parole.' . . .
> Par nuit s'an vont grant aleüre,

Erec treat Enide so harshly?', *RR*, v (1914), 115–26; Hoepffner, ' "Matière et Sens" dans le Roman d'Erec et Enide', *AR*, xviii (1934), 433–50; Hofer, 'Alexanderroman: *Erec* und die späteren Werke Kristians', *ZRP*, lx (1940), 245–61; Hofer, 'Erecstudien', *ZRP*, lxii (1942), 19–32; Nitze, 'Erec and the Joy of the Court', *Spec*, xxix (1954), 691–701.

[1] On the meaning of *conjointure* see Nitze in *MLN*, lxix (1954), 180 f.

[2] Ed. Foerster, vs. 1844; ed. Roques, vs. 1796. See n. 3, p. 167, below.

Et ce lor fet grant soatume
Que la nuit luisoit cler la lune.[1]

('Sweet sister mine, fully have I tested you. Be no more dismayed, for now I love
you more than ever I did, and I am certain and sure that you love me perfectly. From
henceforth I desire to be as I was before, wholly at your command. If you have spoken
any ill of me, I pardon you in full for the wrong and the speech.' . . . Thus through the
night they hasten on, and it gave them great bliss that the moon shone brightly that
night.)

The romance would seem to be finished, but another and supreme adventure, known by the curious name of 'la Joie de la Cort' (the Joy of the Court),
remains. This episode, added to the conclusion, comprises 1,592 lines, almost
the equivalent of the 'premier vers'. A guest of King Evrain in the island
castle named Brandigan, Erec proceeds to a beautiful garden surrounded by
a wall of air. He sees a row of heads, impaled on stakes, and a single stake
from which a horn is suspended. Proceeding farther, Erec comes upon a fair
lady lying on a silver couch beneath a sycamore. A very tall knight named
Mabonagrain, lover of the lady, assails Erec, a fierce combat ensues, but
when noon has passed Mabonagrain yields. He tells his history and instructs
Erec to blow the horn. When this has done, Mabonagrain is released
from captivity in the garden, and great joy comes to Evrain and all his people;
hence the adventure is called 'the Joy of the Court'. The lady of the garden
alone is grieved at the ending of the spell, but is consoled by Enide, who turns
out to be her cousin.

Thus having reached the summit of glory, Erec returns with his wife and
the dwarf king Guivret to Arthur's court. On the death of his father, King
Lac, he goes with the entire court to Nantes,[2] and there on Christmas Day
Erec and Enide are crowned with great splendour.

It has sometimes been questioned whether there is in *Erec* a real *conjointure*, but surely there is order and progression. Chrétien did not share the
ideas of a Boileau or a Racine on unity; he did not adopt a plan of linear
simplicity but rather a more secret and subtle architecture; he appreciated
the value of the surprising and the fanciful. But he marked the stages in the
development of *Erec* and organized it as a triptych.

The first act, 'le premier vers', is a unit but it prepares us for the second
act by its characterization of the hero and heroine. Erec is courteous,
generous, but proud, a little secretive and quick to take offence, reluctant
to owe anything to anyone, prompt to decide, resolute in carrying out the

---

[1] Ed. Foerster, 4920–38; ed. Roques, vss. 4882–900.
[2] The choice of Nantes may have been suggested by the fact that Henry II presided at the investiture of his son Geoffrey as Duke of Brittany at that city on 25 Dec. 1169. Fourrier in *BBSIA*, ii
(1950), 70–74.

decision at any hazard,[1] moved by a deep but imperious love for his beautiful bride. Enide, lovely in soul as in body, is active in household duties, modest in manner, with little experience of life, filled with love, gratitude, and an almost superstitious awe for the son of a king who chose her from her humble station. Yet Chrétien, though noting the poverty of Enide and her father, carefully avoids the implication that her marriage is a *mésalliance*.[2] Beauty and virtue render Enide a worthy bride for a prince. There is a springlike freshness in this romantic idyll which forms the 'premier vers'.[3]

The happiness of the honeymoon extends briefly into the second part of the poem, but is broken by an emotional crisis which is only resolved at its close. The sequence of episodes which fills the interval owes something to the *roman à tiroirs*, but displays a conscious art in variety and gradation. The psychological continuity is not broken, and the tender reconciliation of husband and wife in the moonlight is another phase of the *conjointure*.

It would have been natural to close at this point, but the poet opens the third leaf of his triptych[4] with still another chivalric exploit, differentiated, however, from those which precede. The 'Joie de la Cort' is an adventure entered upon without any compulsion, without any motivation except a sort of knightly dilettantism. It has broader consequences, however, bringing joy to a king and his people. It is distinguished by that eerie atmosphere which is the peculiar contribution of the Matter of Britain and which confers on the successful hero a more than mortal stature, a superiority even to the supernatural. The episode has been considered an *hors d'œuvre*, but, paradoxically speaking, its very superfluity may be considered its justification.[5] It is followed by a magnificent and appropriate conclusion, the coronation at Nantes, arranged by Arthur himself and attended by nobles from all over the Angevin world. It is perhaps this third part which is most original, since, if the Welsh *Gereint* is a cognate story,[6] the common source furnished little to Chrétien but a very inferior analogue to the 'Joie de la Cort', and not even a hint of the coronation.

Psychologically and structurally, then, *Erec* is a fine and intelligent work. If Chrétien put it together from the disjointed narratives of the *conteurs*, he performed a minor miracle. Though it is probable that the skeleton of events

---

[1] Though, for lack of arms, Erec does not immediately assail the insolent Yder, he does not hesitate to promise the queen to avenge her shame.

[2] Ed. Foerster, vss. 1504–16; ed. Roques, vss. 1484–96.

[3] I adopt the ingenious interpretation of Hoepffner in *AR*, xviii (1934), 433 f. The 'premier vers' corresponds to the introductory stanza of a lyric, which often celebrated the revival of Nature and contrasted with the melancholy mood of the stanzas which followed. Note that the action of Erec begins on 'un jor de Pasque, au tans novel' (vs. 27).

[4] In *Erec* Chrétien employed with supreme art the pattern of a triptych which recurs in *Yvain*.

[5] A detailed study of the structure of *Erec* would take account of the parallelism between certain scenes or motifs—for example, the tears of Enide and those of her cousin, the mistress of Mabonagrain.   [6] See the next chapter.

was not original with him, it is certain that it consists of elements from a variety of sources. Some are of Celtic provenance. The chase of a white animal, usually sent by a fay to lure a mortal to her, is a theme which recurs in the Breton lais of *Guigemar, Graelent,* and *Guingamor,* as well as in the *mabinogi* of *Manawydan.* Chrétien has transformed this bit of faery lore into courtly custom, a pretext for giving a kiss to the fairest of maidens.[1] But the casual way in which he announces the presence of the White Hart in the forest shows that the creature was not unknown to his readers, that he was following a beaten path.

The Celtic origin is more clearly perceptible in 'la Joie de la Cort'. Thanks to the labours of Philipot, Helaine Newstead, and R. S. Loomis[2] it is possible to detect here a confusion of two themes, originally quite distinct: the visit to the castle of Brân and the liberation of Mabon from captivity.[3] From Brân King Evrain derives the attributes of a hospitable host in an isle of plenty. The horn in Evrain's garden, though it is represented as a wind instrument, may have been Brân's horn of plenty, a metamorphosis partly due, as Loomis points out, to the double uses of a horn. This would explain Chrétien's curious words about the joy which Erec felt after blowing the horn.

> Bien fu de joie Erec peüz
> Et bien serviz a son creant.[4]

(Well was Erec fed with joy and well served to his heart's desire.)

Loomis also thinks that it would explain the cryptic expression 'la Joie de la Cort', through the substitution of *cort* (court) for *cor* (horn).[5] The part of Mabonagrain in the same episode, his imprisonment,[6] his release, and the fact that no one outside the land knew his name, corresponds to that of Mabon in *Culhwch;* other characteristics suggest that he was descended ultimately from the Gallo-Roman Apollo Maponos. A mythical ancestry might also explain the incongruous mixture of noble and savage attributes in his nature. Celtic tradition will also account for a number of other features in *Erec:* Guivret, the dwarf king;[7] his sisters; Guingalet, Gauvain's horse; the heads mounted on stakes. Even in the role of Enide traces of faery ancestry may be detected, but they have been almost effaced.

---

[1] In *Gereint* there is no mention of a kiss, but Enid is presented the day after her wedding with the head of the hart.

[2] *R,* xxv (1896), 258–94. H. Newstead, *Bran the Blessed in Arthurian Romance* (New York, 1939), pp. 106–20. R. S. Loomis, *Arthurian Tradition,* pp. 168–84.

[3] The name Brân may be recognized in Brandigan, the castle of King Eurain, and the name Mabon in Mabonagrain.

[4] Ed. Foerster, vss. 6190 f.; ed. Roques, vss. 6138 f.

[5] See, however, the criticism of J. Marx, op. cit., pp. 106 f.

[6] The wall of air which encloses the garden recalls the imprisonment of Merlin by Niniane. Sommer, *Vulgate Version of the Arthurian Romances,* ii. 461.

[7] On dwarfs see Vernon J. Harward, Jr., *The Dwarfs of Arthurian Romance and Celtic Tradition* (Lieden, 1958).

Wace's *Brut* supplied a few names and probably influenced the descriptions of Erec's marriage and coronation.[1] It is much less probable that Chadwalein's being wakened from sleep by the tears of his nephew was imitated by Chrétien in the waking of Erec by the lament of Enide.[2] It is possible that Cador's short speech on the dangers of idleness[3] may have helped Chrétien to realize the possibilities of this theme (though not to invent it).[4] But the sum total of borrowings from Wace is very small. Equally small is the debt to the romances of antiquity, though they, particularly *Enéas*, set the example for rich descriptions of dress and other luxuries.[5] Some classical scholarship is implied in Chrétien's reference to Macrobius and the figures representing the quadrivium embroidered on Erec's robe.[6] But of Ovid's influence there is no vestige.[7]

Several reasons lead one to conclude that Chrétien found the main outlines and much of the detail of *Erec* in one principal source. When in his opening lines he speaks of a *conte d'aventure* which the *jongleurs* are wont to 'depecier et corrompre', he implies that the *conte* possessed some coherence. If he speaks of extracting a 'mout bele conjointure' from the *conte*, he implies that he took much of his material from it. It is, of course, well known that the Welsh tale of *Gereint* corresponds in plot to *Erec*, and the most plausible theory, recently and strongly supported by R. S. Loomis,[8] is that this correspondence is due to a common source. The problem will be more fully discussed in the next chapter. Though both the Welsh and the French authors used a common French source, a 'conte d'aventure', the former failed to link up and harmonize the episodes, failed to introduce the tripartite division, and failed to develop as deftly the psychology of his characters. What Chrétien, on the other hand, did seems best defined by Roques: 'from a "conte d'aventures", that is, a series of unrelated incidents in which the characters are involved without adequate motivation, he produced a fine "conjointure"; to be explicit, a coherent, organized whole, an "action", let us say, which the

[1] Pelan, *L'Influence de Wace*, pp. 21–40.

[2] Ibid., pp. 36–38.

[3] Wace, *Brut*, ed. Arnold, ii, vss. 10733–64.

[4] M. Wilmotte, *Origines du Roman en France* (Paris, 1940), p. 204, n. 1; Nitze in *MP*, xxxvi (1939), 309, and *BBSIA*, v (1953), 77.

[5] The story of Aeneas is briefly summarized in the description of the arsons of Enide's saddle. Ed. Foerster, vss. 5337–46; ed. Roques, vss. 5289–98. Lavinia is mentioned ed. Foerster, vs. 5891; ed. Roques, vs. 5841.

[6] Hofer in *ZRP*, xlviii (1928), 130 f. Delbouille in *Mélanges de linguistique et de littérature romanes offerts à M. Roques*, iv (Paris, 1952), 89–98, noted possible borrowings from *Floire et Blancheflor*.

[7] Guyer in *RR*, xii. 97, 127, 232. It is possible, however, to make a comparison between vss. 4656 f. (ed. Foerster), 4618 f. (ed. Roques), where Enide apostrophizes Death, and vss. 754–57 of the *Piramus et Tisbe*, an imitation of Ovid.

[8] *Arthurian Tradition*, pp. 32–36, and *Mélanges Hoepffner*, pp. 227–30. The objective argument drawn from the different names assigned to the father of Enide in *Gereint* and *Erec* serves to confirm the other deductions as to a common source.

characters create or at least direct or bend, and which takes on from this fact a significance and the value of an example.'[1]

It is necessary to defend Chrétien against the not infrequent charge, that of inconsistency and confusion in motivating Erec's conduct towards his wife when he learns from her the aspersions on his hardihood. But there is no fundamental obscurity in the emotional reactions of the two characters to this crisis. Rather the discord which separates them arises from the logic of their personalities. Modest, fearful, Enide exaggerates her part in her husband's disgrace. He, on the other hand, is deeply wounded in his pride and knightly honour, all the more because he recognizes the truth of the criticism,[2] and he avenges himself by adopting a course of cold, imperious, laconic severity. He doubts her love, not as in *Gereint* because he suspects her of infidelity, but because he infers from her own words that she has succumbed to the influence of others and shares their feelings. In a way more natural in the Middle Ages than today he resolves to assert his right as a husband and to test her.[3] Paradoxically, his harshness is proof of the depth of his love for her. If he had merely wished to punish her, would he have commended her to his father's watchful care in case she should be widowed on the perilous journey? If he had wished to humiliate her, would he have ordered her to wear her best robe?[4] By her docility and even by her disobedience when danger threatens her husband, Enide convinces him of her perfect loyalty and devotion, and she herself emerges from her trial reassured of his courage and prowess.

Chrétien shows himself in this poem not only as a master of psychology and dramatic situation but also as a moralist. A knight, especially one destined for kingship, must not allow his armour to rust, even when he has the excuse of a honeymoon. A wife may be also the mistress of her husband and the inspirer of his valour, but she must lay aside all egotism and know how to efface or even sacrifice herself for his good. Chrétien teaches an equilibrium between romantic love and social duty. The ideal marriage of Erec and Enide provides a contrast to the all-absorbing and anti-social relation of Mabonagrain to his mistress, as well as to the fatal spell which binds Tristan to Iseut. Chrétien does not set forth these lessons as precise formulas, but he enlists the imagination of the reader and sets it to work.

In this poem, as well as throughout the rest of his work, we recognize the hand of a stylist, one who combines smoothness and polish with something of the raciness, the verve of a popular reciter of tales. He changes tone as the narrative moves from the dramatic to the sentimental to the humorous. His descriptions, to be sure, do not altogether escape the formalism of the schools,

---

[1] Roques in edition of *Erec*, Introduction, vi.
[2] Ed. Foerster, vss. 2576 f.; ed. Roques, vss. 2572 f.
[3] Nitze in *RR*, x (1919), 26–37.
[4] In *Gereint*, on the other hand, the hero ordered his wife to wear her worst robe.

but they evoke the varied aspects of a sumptuous civilization. The verse is supple and expressive. His was no idle boast that the history of Erec and Enide would last as long as Christendom.

'Cligès'[1]

Cligès, plausibly dated by Fourrier in 1176,[2] differs notably in content and spirit from *Erec*. It is the most studied, the most intellectual, and in some ways the most amusing of Chrétien's romances.

For once he discarded in large measure the typical extravagances of the Matter of Britain, its outlandish customs, impossible adventures, and mysterious geography. He retained only such features as were close to reality—for example, participation in a tournament in arms of various colours. He substituted for the vague, poetic realm of Logres a geography which included not only a real Constantinople and a real Germany but also a south-eastern England so accurately described that every movement can easily be traced on a modern map. He even reflected real events which interested the courts of Byzantium, Germany, France, and Champagne.

Even more striking is the new concentration on the analysis of emotion, the casuistry of love. The characters study themselves and define their inward conflicts. They struggle, yield, suffer, hope, debate. The soliloquies and dialogues display finesse, even though they may seem to modern taste tedious and artificial. It is evident that Chrétien was imitating and seeking to surpass the treatment of psychology by the lyric poets, Ovid, Benoît de Sainte-Maure, and probably Thomas of Britain, the author of *Tristan*. The critical references to Iseut in *Erec* may have been inspired by some early form of the legend. But it was the version of Thomas, composed probably between 1170 and 1175, which seems to have provoked Chrétien to attempt a reply.[3] Some critics have seen in *Cligès* an anti-*Tristan*; others a hyper-*Tristan*. It is in fact both, for it aims both to criticize Thomas's poem and to improve

---

[1] Editions : by W. Foerster with variant readings (Halle, 1884); later smaller editions 1901, 1910, 1921. A new edition has appeared by A. Micha, author of *Prolégomènes à une édition de Cligès* (Paris, 1939). Besides general studies cited in n. 1, p. 157, *Cligès* has been treated in the following : G. Paris, *Mélanges de littérature française du moyen âge*, pp. 229–327; Van Hamel, 'Cligès et Tristan', *R*, xxxiii (1904), 465–89; H. Hauvette, *La 'Morte Vivante'* (Paris, 1933), pp. 100–8; L. Maranini, 'I Motivi psicologici di un anti-Tristano nel *Cligès*', *Annali della R. Scuola Normale Superiore di Pisa*, ser. ii, vol. xii (1943); Micha, '*Enéas et Cligès*', *Mélanges Hoepffner* (Paris, 1949), 237–43; J. Frappier, *Cligès, Les Cours de Sorbonne* (Paris, 1951); Micha, 'Tristan et Cligès', *Neo.* xxxvi (1952), 1–10; F. Lyons, 'La Fausse Mort dans le *Cligès*', *Mélanges M. Roques*, i (1950), 167–77.

[2] *BBSIA*, ii (1950), 74–81.

[3] On relation of *Cligès* to Thomas's *Tristan* see Chap. 13 above. Hoepffner argued in *R*, lv (1929), 1–16, for the priority of *Cligès*, but did not bring conviction. Micha (loc. cit.), though yielding priority to Thomas, maintained that Chrétien conceived *Cligès* on the basis of a complete Tristan poem of his own, to which he referred as 'Del roi Marc et d'Iseut la blonde', but there is little support for this view.

on it. It would be more exact to consider it a neo-*Tristan*, a new version of the legend.

Following his model, Chrétien preluded the amorous history of his hero Cligès with that of his father, which occupies about a third of the poem. Alexandre, elder son of the Emperor of Constantinople, sailed to Britain, to the court of Arthur, attracted by his great renown, and there fell in love with Gauvain's sister, Soredamors, and she with him, but neither dared reveal the secret to the other. Count Angres of Guinesores (Windsor) rebelled against Arthur, and thus gave an opportunity to Alexandre to distinguish himself in arms, to capture both the count and his castle. Guenièvre detected the symptoms of his passion, encouraged him to speak out, and brought about a love match. From this union Cligès was born.

On the death of Alexandre Cligès would have been the rightful heir to the throne of Constantinople, but his uncle Alis cheated him of his rights and in violation of a pledge sought to wed the daughter of the Emperor of Germany, Fénice. Cligès was present at the nuptials at Cologne, and was smitten with love for the bride, and she with love for him. She was determined never to follow the example of Iseut.[1] Thanks to a magic philtre prepared by her duenna, Thessala, she was able to delude Alis into thinking that he possessed her when he clasped only the air. On the return journey to Greece Alis's party was attacked by the Duke of Saxony, and Cligès not only rescued Fénice from his clutches but also defeated him in single combat. Like his father, Cligès decided to seek fame at Arthur's court, and on bidding adieu to Fénice declared that he was 'tout à elle' (vs. 4327), leaving her in a torment of doubt. Were the words a polite formula, or an avowal of love? Arrived in England, Cligès took part on four successive days in a tournament near Oxford, disguised each day in arms of a different colour, and proved himself a better man than Lancelot and Perceval. After his return to Greece, he confessed his love to the empress, and she disclosed that she shared his passion and that she was still a maid. He proposed an elopement to Britain, but she refused to imitate Tristan and Iseut and involve herself and her lover in scandal. Rather she would feign death and be entombed, so that Cligès could steal her away by night. The plan was carried out; Thessala gave her mistress a potion which produced for a day and a night all the appearance of death; and from the tomb Cligès rescued her and they lived secretly together for many months, first in a tower with modern plumbing, then in a garden. Here they were discovered, lying under a spreading grafted tree, locked in each other's arms. They managed to escape the vengeance of the emperor through Thessala's magic arts; they reached King Arthur's court, and there received the news of Alis's death from mortification. Returning to Greece, they were married and crowned.

---

[1] Vss. 3161 f.

De s'amie a feite sa fame
Mes il l'apele amie et dame,
Que por ce ne pert ele mie,
Que il ne l'aint come s'amie,
Et ele lui tot autresi,
Con l'an doit feire son ami.
Et chascun jor lor amors crut.[1]

(His mistress he has made his wife, but he calls her mistress and lady, and she loses nothing by it, for he loves her as his mistress, and she loves him too as a woman ought to love her lover. Every day their love grew stronger.)

Of the various elements assembled in this complex plot the kernel is the theme of Feigned Death, which Shakespeare used in *Romeo and Juliet*. Derived from the Orient, it was best known in the West as an incident in the history of Solomon's wife.[2] The particular version which Chrétien used and which he claimed to have found in the cathedral library of Beauvais must have resembled closely a thirteenth-century romance called the *Marques de Rome*. In it he would have discovered a nephew of the Greek emperor named Cligès, and he would have been struck by the similarity in situation to the triangular affair in *Tristan*. Chrétien doubtless found the model for the treason of Count Angres in Wace's account of the treason of Mordret,[3] and the suggestion for the marriage of a Greek emperor to a German princess in the efforts which Frederick Barbarossa made between 1170 and 1174 to cement a matrimonial and political alliance with the Greek emperor, Manuel Comnenus.[4] Even the splendour and renown of Arthur reflect the contemporary magnificence of the Angevin empire under Henry II.

Other influences affected not so much the plot as the treatment of love. To Ovid, already so familiar to his translator, may be traced the description of the surprises of the heart, the allegorical imagery of the tyrant-god, his arrows, his flame, and his stratagems, and the enumeration of the physical symptoms of nascent passion. From the author of *Enéas*, himself a disciple of Ovid, Chrétien learned to use the monologue as a means of psychological analysis, and Lavine set the example for Fénice of refusing to belong to two men.[5] Chrétien carried the play of metaphors even farther in the direction of preciosity, perhaps under the influence of Provençal lyric, and profited from the advances made by Benoît de Sainte-Maure.[6]

As has already been noted, the influence of *Tristan* was most profound.

---

[1] Vss. 6753–9.
[2] See Lyons, loc. cit. Chrétien alludes to this tale of Solomon in vss. 5876–8.
[3] *Brut*, ed. Arnold, ii, vss. 13010–274.
[4] See p. 171, n. 2.
[5] *Enéas*, ed. Salverda de Grave, *CFMA*, vss. 8301–4.
[6] The expression 'fine amor', absent from *Enéas*, appears in the *Roman de Troie* and Thomas's *Tristan*; and though it is not used by Chrétien, we do find 'fins amanz' in *Cligès*, vs. 3861, and 'fin amant' in *Lancelot*, vs. 3980.

Both poems begin with the sentimental history of the hero's father and mother; both treat sympathetically the love of the hero for his uncle's wife. Both stress the fateful effects of potions; both describe secret meetings in a subterranean retreat, elaborately decorated; both depict a blissful interlude in an arboreal setting, suddenly interrupted by the discovery of the lovers lying together. From Thomas apparently came the play on the words *l'amer* and *la mer*,[1] and certain little dissertations on the nature of love, somewhat artificial but interesting as efforts to develop a psychological vocabulary.[2] In his deep concern with the complexities of emotion and in the delicacy of his analysis Chrétien was laying the foundations of French classical tradition, even when he was delighting in mere preciosities.

But though he borrowed from Thomas material and techniques, he could not accept the *sen*, the doctrine of *amour courtois*, particularly as exemplified in the conduct of Iseut.[3] In revolt he created the contrasting figure of Fénice, who, menaced by the same destiny as Iseut, refuses to submit to fate and preserves her liberty of choice, declaring:

'Ja ne porroie acorder
A la vie qu'Iseuz mena.
Amors an li trop vilena,
Car ses cors fu a deus rantiers
Et ses cuers fu a l'un antiers. . . .
Ja voir mes cors n'iert garceniers,
Ja n'i avra deus parceniers.
Qui a le cuer, si et le cors,
Toz les autres an met dehors.'[4]

('Never could I agree to live the life that Iseut lived; love was debased in her, for her body was at the disposal of two, and her heart was wholly for one. . . . Never shall my body be a common thing; never will there be two partners in it. Let him who has the heart have the body and exclude all others.')

This spiritual daughter of Chrétien is a new type, ready to forsake the luxuries of the imperial court,[5] daring to face the terrors of entombment in order to live with the man she loves,[6] but at the same time rejecting with horror the adulterous compromise accepted in *amour courtois*. She is a perfectionist, and she has the wit and the will to realize her ideal of a love free from constraint and from the taint of *partage*.

Chrétien's solution of the problem raised by the romance of Tristan and Iseut could be realized only in a poetic universe. Given the enormous compulsive powers possessed by the family and the Church, there was in most cases, when Chrétien wrote, no possibility of free choice. But let us give him

---

[1] Vss. 545–63.
[2] In vss. 2820–54 Chrétien compares the union of two wills to two voices singing in unison.
[3] Vss. 3145–9, 5251 f.
[4] Vss. 3150–64.
[5] Vss. 5346–60.
[6] See Maranini, loc. cit.

credit for pointing out the ignominy inherent in a certain form of *amour courtois* and for imagining a happier way, a way which his Erec and Enide, his Alexandre and Soredamors were lucky enough to find.

At the same time we must realize that he missed the human and tragic truth of *Tristan*. His modification of the story is an exercise in virtuosity. It is comparable to the grafted tree which formed a shelter for Cligès and Fénice, with its branches trained downward by a skilled gardener to form a screen. It contrasts significantly with the 'bel arbre' in the wilderness, springing and spreading in natural luxuriance, which according to the poems of Thomas and Gottfried sheltered Tristan and Iseut under its vast shade.

'*Lancelot*' or '*Le Chevalier de la Charrette*'[1]

So far as we know, Chrétien chose the subjects of *Erec* and *Cligès* in complete freedom, but in the prologue of *Lancelot* he stated explicitly that he obeyed the command of the Countess of Champagne, and that she alone was responsible for the *matière* and the *sen*;[2] that is, the 'subject-matter' and the 'controlling purpose'. He seems to be adroitly excusing himself for both, in the form of a compliment to his patroness. It is odd, too, that he entrusted the composition of the last thousand lines to Godefroi de Lagny.[3] It is the current opinion that Chrétien followed the countess's instructions with reluctance; after all, the *Lancelot* is a sort of palinode, a recantation of *Cligès*.

Though this interpretation has much in its favour, one should not imagine that the task imposed on the poet produced a great struggle of conscience, even though it involved the glorification of adultery and the degradation of Arthur to the level of a coward and a poltroon. When the task was abandoned, the essential purpose was already accomplished. Chrétien declared that he had devoted his *peine* and his *entencion*, his intellectual and artistic ability, to the performance of his commission. It is likely that the difficulties involved and a concern for his reputation served as stimulants. How could he render credible a hero who was a paragon of physical prowess and energy, and at the same time a lover ecstatically submissive to a tyrannical divinity? How

---

[1] Ed. by W. Foerster as *Der Karrenritter (Lancelot) und Das Wilhelmsleben* (Halle, 1899), with a long introduction on the origins of the Matter of Britain. Very inaccurate text; see H. K. Stone in *R*, lxiii (1937), 398–401. Ed. M. Roques, *CFMA*, 1958. Other special studies are: G. Paris in *R*, x (1881), 465–96; xii (1883), 459–534; T. P. Cross and W. A. Nitze, *Lancelot and Guenevere* (Chicago, 1930); K. G. T. Webster, *Guinevere: A Study of Her Abductions* (Milton, Mass., 1951); Micha, 'Sur les sources de la *Charrette*', *R*, lxxi (1950), 345–58; Adler, 'Note on the Composition of Chrétien's *Charrette*', *MLR*, xlv (1950), 33–39; L. Maranini, '"Queste" e Amore Cortese nel "Chevalier de la Charrette"', *Rivista di Letterature Moderne*, 1951, pp. 204–23; Jonin, 'Le Vasselage de Lancelot dans le *Conte de la Charrette*', *MA* (1952), 281–98; E. Southward, 'Unity of Chrétien's *Lancelot*', *Mélanges Roques*, ii (1953), 281–90.

[2] On the meaning of these terms see Nitze in *MP*, xiv (1916–17), 14 ff.

[3] Godefroi says explicitly in vss. 7120–34 that he carried out his task in full accord with Chrétien.

transfer from lyric to narrative form the love concepts of the troubadours? How harmonize the ideal of a hero who is a free agent and dominates his fate with the ideal of a hero who is a slave to his mistress?

Whatever his motives, it seems clear that Chrétien did his best to unify and ennoble the materials provided, even though one may suspect that he permitted himself occasional ironies and exaggerations at the expense of his hero and heroine. In the main, however, he put aside his personal feelings and achieved a brilliant success in creating the character of Lancelot, for centuries a rival in popular favour to Tristan. The narrative may thus be briefly summarized.

On Ascension Day a stranger knight appears at Camaalot, boasts that he holds many of Arthur's subjects captive, and dares Arthur to send the queen under escort out to a neighbouring wood, there to be the prize of a combat. Keu obtains the custody of the queen, but is vanquished and both are taken away as prisoners. Setting out in pursuit of the abductor, Gauvain overtakes Lancelot, who is incognito, lends him a spare horse, but soon after finds the horse dead as a result of a fight, and Lancelot himself walking behind a cart, such as was used to convey malefactors to execution. Lancelot, faced with a choice between love and reason, hesitates while he takes two steps before love conquers and he mounts the cart. Gauvain rides beside the cart, and both knights arrive at a castle where a damsel gives them welcome. That night Lancelot passes successfully the test of the perilous bed and flaming lance. The next morning he witnesses from a window a procession passing below, recognizes the queen escorted by her captor, and falls into a love trance. But, equipped with a new horse, he sets out with Gauvain in pursuit. A damsel informs them that the abductor is Meleagant, son of Baudemagus, king of the land of Goirre. Lancelot, parting from Gauvain, is lost in dreams of Guenièvre, and, deaf to the challenge of a knight, is hurled from his saddle into a ford. He recovers himself and forces his opponent to beg for mercy. At another castle this perfect lover resists the temptations of the flesh offered by a seductive hostess. Journeying on, he beholds a comb left beside a spring, and on learning that the golden tresses caught in it are those of his mistress, he adores them with religious fervour. The adventure of the cemetery, where he raises the heavy stone lid of a tomb destined for himself, reveals his messianic role, and designates him as the liberator of the captives in the land whence no one escapes. After meeting some of these captives and overcoming sundry adversaries, Lancelot arrives before a sword-bridge which separates him from the castle of Meleagant. The description of his crossing is superb, epic in its revelation of prowess, lyric in its exaltation of love, realistic in material detail and in the record of subconscious states. The father of Meleagant, Baudemagus, welcomes Lancelot and urges him to wait till he has recovered from the wounds he has suffered on the bridge, but Lancelot insists on settling the issue with Meleagant the next morning. In his weakened state he is getting the worst of the combat till a damsel calls his attention to the queen watching from a window. The sight of her renews his strength and he presses Meleagant so hard that Baudemagus is obliged to intercede with Guenièvre for his son's life. Meleagant, enraged, will not concede his defeat, and Lancelot consents to meet him again in combat for the queen at Arthur's court one year after Meleagant has issued a challenge. Unexpectedly she treats her deliverer with coldness and scorn, and only relents and reproaches herself bitterly when she hears a false report of his death. He in turn hears a rumour of her death, and at once tries to commit suicide by hanging himself from his saddle-bow. But he is prevented by his companions, and when brought into the presence of the queen, he finds a very different reception. She explains that his fault had been to hesitate before mounting the cart, forgives him, and invites him to a rendezvous at a window that night. He breaks the bars that separate them, kneels before her as if she were a saint, and enjoys her favours to the full. In the morning Meleagant finds her bed stained with the blood of Lancelot, who has cut his fingers on the bars, but he charges her with misconduct with the wounded Keu. Lancelot, of course, offers to defend her against this accusation, once more fights Meleagant, and once more spares his life only at the intercession of Baudemagus and the queen. He sets out to rescue Gauvain but is ambushed and imprisoned, and in the meanwhile Gauvain is rescued from drowning at the water-bridge and has the honour of escorting Guenièvre back to Logres. Lancelot's jaileress is enamoured of him, and allows him to take part in a tourney which Guenièvre attends. At first, incognito, he eclipses all the other jousters, but at the queen's behest, conveyed by a damsel, he plays the coward, and again at her behest carries off the honours of the contest. Imprisoned again, Lancelot is freed by Meleagant's sister, and arrives just in time at Arthur's court to defend the queen against Meleagant, and this final combat ends with the death of the villain at the hands of the Knight of the Cart.

The poem may be divided into two contrasting parts. The first part, extending to the passage of the sword-bridge, has been severely criticized as incoherent and even absurd; the second part, on the other hand, is more logically constructed about the dramatic relations between Lancelot and Guenièvre. It is generally admitted that an ancient myth of Celtic origin forms the basis for the story.[1] The variant forms in Irish and Welsh present the following pattern. A mysterious stranger claims as his own a married woman, and either by force or by obtaining a rash promise from her husband he takes her away to his supernatural realm. The husband pursues the abductor, triumphs over obstacles, enters the strange land, and wins back his wife. Guenièvre had already been assigned the role of heroine of this tale in

---

[1] See Cross and Nitze, op. cit.

Arthurian tradition before Chrétien's time, for such seems to be the theme represented on the bas-relief at Modena cathedral,[1] and even if this iconographic testimony be rejected, there is the *Vita Gildae* by Caradoc of Lancarvan, dated by Brooke before 1136.[2] Here one reads[3] that Melvas, king of the Summer Country (*aestiva regio*), carried off Guënnuvar, the wife of Arthur, to his home at Glastonbury, which Caradoc interprets as the Town of Glass (*Vitrea Civitas*). Arthur, after a year's search, discovered her whereabouts, besieged the place, and through the intervention of the abbot of Glastonbury received back his queen without combat. This is evidently a monastic adaptation of a Welsh myth, which reached Chrétien also in another form represented by the lines describing Maheloas in *Erec* as lord of the 'Isle de Voirre', where no thunder is heard, no lightning strikes, and it is never too hot or wintry.[4] The name Melvas, or rather Maelwas, is a compound of the Welsh nouns *mael* and *gwas*, and means 'Prince-Youth', and despite corruption is recognizable as the original form of Meleagant.[5]

Lancelot du Lac also is no newcomer. In *Erec* he is ranked third in the list of knights of the Round Table, and reappears in *Cligès* at the tourney near Oxford. His name implies the existence of a legend about his childhood under the care of a water-fay. The *Lanzelet* of Ulrich von Zatzikhoven not only preserves a version of this legend but also reveals, by its loose construction and its total ignorance of any guilty relationship between the hero and Arthur's queen, that it drew on other traditions about Lancelot than those used by Chrétien.[6] One cannot reject the hypothesis that Lancelot had become the lover of Guenièvre before Chrétien so represented him, but this development accords so well with the *sen* of the poem that it seems likely to have been suggested by Marie de Champagne or to have been invented by the poet himself. In recognizing, therefore, the traditional elements in *Lancelot*, let us avoid the mistake of concluding that Chrétien merely followed an established pattern and did not feel free to add new features, such, for example, as his imitation of the *Tristan* in the episode of the bloodstained bed.[7]

---

[1] R. S. and L. H. Loomis, *Arthurian Legends in Medieval Art*, pp. 32–34. On date see Loomis, *Wales*, pp. 198–208.

[2] C. Brooke in *Studies in the Early British Church* (Cambridge, 1958), p. 230.

[3] E. K. Chambers, *Arthur of Britain*, pp. 263 f. *Cymmrodorion Record Series*, ii (London, 1901), 410.

[4] Ed. Foerster, vss. 1945–51; ed. Roques, vss. 1895–901.

[5] For more detailed consideration of these matters see Cross and Nitze, op. cit., pp. 20–62, 65–66; Loomis, *Arthurian Tradition*, pp. 187–266; Webster, op. cit., pp. 22–58. Micha's attempt in *R*, lxxi. 345–58, to disprove the mythical origin of *Lancelot* neglects essential matters. The sword-bridge, to be sure, may well derive in part from the Visions and the Purgatory of St. Patrick, but to derive the whole romance from a 'production hagiographique' on the basis of one feature seems a curious aberration.

[6] See Chap. 33 below, and *R*, lxxix (1958), 57–62.

[7] This imitation, which is not without *gaucherie*, was visibly based on Thomas's version.

But if one compares his characterization of Lancelot with Ulrich's *Lanzelet*, it is evident that his most original achievement lay in the domain of psychology. A figure somewhat loosely compounded of conventional, though not Puritan, virtues has been transformed into a well-defined, clearly individualized character, in which courtesy and chivalry are touched with ecstasy. His dominant trait—absorption in the thought of the queen—is symbolized in such acts as swooning before the comb and the hairs of his lady; it is carried to such extremes of heroism as the crossing of the sword-bridge, and even to the verge of caricature in the episode of the ford. Don Quixote is already present in Lancelot. Though it is true that he is a type, an ideal lover as conceived by the *précieuses* of the court of Champagne, he is also in some measure drawn from life. One has the impression that his reveries and trances had their counterparts in the actual experiences of religious mystics in Chrétien's own time. The poet has modelled the ecstasies of the lover on those of the contemplative. But he has also conceived of his hero as a man of practical sense and effective action. In the intervals between trances Lancelot consults with men of prudence, debates with himself, keeps cool in the face of the gravest dangers. By a sort of inversion his most rational act is to use the magic ring given him by his faery foster-mother, not to work a spell but to undo a spell and to recall him to reality.[1] Even if Chrétien undertook the poem reluctantly, he was seduced by the possibilities of the theme.

Guenièvre, too, is more than a type of the domineering female, 'la belle dame sans merci'. One must admit her cruel coquetry, her pleasure in submitting the most valiant of knights to the most humiliating trials. But even when she commanded Lancelot to fight his worst at the tournament of Noauz, it was not with the intent to render him contemptible or to depreciate the chivalric ideal.[2] She would be a traitor to herself if she ceased to be the inspirer of prowess. Has she not herself been subjected to the extreme degradation of being turned over to the custody of Keu and being made captive by Meleagant? And was she not, after all, faithful in love? Her feeling for Lancelot, revealed early in the poem, passes through stages indicated with more subtlety than emotion, yet not without a tragic tone. Chrétien painted in Guenièvre not only a haughty and wilful mistress but also a despairing woman who judged herself guilty of grievous wrong to her lover.[3]

Some of the sentiments expressed in the poem to the effect that 'he who

---

[1] An excellent example of Chrétien's resistance to the marvellous in vss. 2347–67, 3138–43.

[2] It seems to me that Jonin in his article cited in n. 1, p. 175, has misinterpreted the poem. I do not believe that Guenivère ever sought to depreciate the chivalric ideal in the person of Lancelot or that the latter in the eyes of the poet was really degraded by mounting the cart.

[3] A less rapid analysis of the characters would bring out the variety exemplified by the secondary personages—Gauvain, a model of chivalry and courtesy without Lancelot's sublime extravagance; Keu, the comic lover; Meleagant, violent, proud, and perfidious; Baudemaguz, the soul of generosity and honour.

loves is very obedient', and that 'love and courtesy consist in doing what one can for one's mistress', correspond to certain *regulae* in the *De Amore* of Andreas Capellanus and seem to reflect the spirit which reigned at the court of Marie de Champagne, rather than the personal views of the author. Chrétien was too wise a moralist not to comprehend the dangers involved in a doctrine of total submission of will and conscience to the whims of a lady. Rather he insinuated a doctrine of equality when in vss. 5893–5 he declared that the queen rejoiced, knowing that she belonged to Lancelot as he belonged to her.

Even more completely than in *Cligès* Chrétien preached love as a virtue with claims which overrode the claims of social law. Though not without an *arrière-pensée*, he set forth a religion of woman-worship which went far beyond the more or less sacrilegious gestures of devotion paid to the queen as to a 'cors saint'; it penetrated into the depths of the heart. Like a Christian before God, Lancelot lived in dread of sinning and suffered in patience every affliction. But this religion of love had also its graces in the ecstasies of contemplation and in the power to pass serenely through every trial.[1] Thus conceived and elaborated by Chrétien, more or less in spite of himself, the cult established itself in the imaginations of the laity even more firmly. And long the fascination lasted of the magnificent but unrecognized knight, lost in his rapturous dream, of the hero on whom the adventure of the tomb conferred the aspect of a Messiah.[2]

'Yvain' or *'Le Chevalier au Lion'*[3]

As already noted, Chrétien probably had undertaken *Yvain* before commencing *Lancelot*, and perhaps the two romances occupied his attention simultaneously between 1177 and 1181. Fourrier has produced arguments for this chronology,[4] and it is curious that Gauvain, who is prominent in the

---

[1] Vss. 3126–9, 3739.

[2] If Chrétien did not complete his poem, the reason in my opinion is not that he belatedly developed moral scruples but rather that he was prevented by some unknown circumstance or that he realized that the conclusion was rather banal.

[3] Editions: with variant readings by W. Foerster as *Der Löwenritter* (Halle, 1887); small editions 1891, 1902, 1906, 1912, 1913, 1926; by T. B. W. Reid (Manchester, 1942, 1948); by R. W. Linker (Chapel Hill, N.C., 1940). Special studies are: E. Philipot, 'Roman du Chevalier au Lion de Chrétien de Troyes', *Annales de Bretagne*, 1892–3, pp. 33–83, 321–45, 455–79; A. C. L. Brown, *Iwain*, *SNPL*, viii (1903), 1–147; Brown, 'The Knight of the Lion', *PMLA*, xx (1904), 673–706; Brown, 'Chrétien's *Yvain*', *MP*, ix (1911–12), 109–28; R. S. Loomis, 'Calogrenanz and Crestien's Originality', *MLN*, xliii (1928), 215–23; Zenker, *Ivainstudien*, *Beihefte zur ZRP*, lxx (Halle, 1921); Chotzen, 'Le Lion d'Owein et Ses Prototypes Celtiques', *Neo*, xviii (1933), 51–58, 131–6; Brugger, 'Yvain and His Lion', *MP*, xxxviii (1941), 267–87; Brodeur, 'The Grateful Lion', *PMLA*, xxxix (1924), 485–524; Adler, 'Sovereignty in Chrétien's *Yvain*', *PMLA*, lxii (1947), 281–305; L. Maranini, 'Cavalleria, Amore Conjugale e Amore Cortese nel *Chevalier au Lion*', in *Saggi di Umanismo Cristiano* (1949), no. 2, pp. 22 ff.; Nitze, 'Yvain and the Myth of the Fountain', *Spec*, xxx (1955), 170–9; J. Frappier, *Yvain, Les Cours de Sorbonne* (Paris, 1952).

[4] *BBSIA*, ii (1950), 81–88.

first part of *Yvain* and again in the *dénouement*, is thus left free for a time to take part in the pursuit of Meleagant and the rescue of Guenièvre, as described in *Lancelot*.

It is clear that *Yvain* represents a return to the narrative type of *Erec*. There is no attempt, as in *Cligès*, to amalgamate the Matter of Britain with contemporary history, or to replace the misty lands of romance with a realistic European geography, or to improve on the art and morality of *Tristan*. There is no attempt, as in *Lancelot*, to illustrate and glorify the uncongenial doctrines of *amour courtois* at the behest of a patron. Rather, as with *Erec*, Chrétien seems to have selected the story himself, and treats once more the conflict between the obligations of chivalry and of marriage. In fact, there is a striking parallelism in the structure of the two poems. Both narratives fall into three parts: both tell how the hero wins a beautiful and worthy bride; both tell how their wedded happiness is seemingly lost for ever; both conclude with a complete reconciliation after a period of trial. There are, to be sure, differences; *Yvain* contains a larger element of the supernatural and also introduces scenes of comedy and an occasional note of satire. At times Chrétien anticipates the art of Boiardo and Ariosto. *Yvain* is a tragicomedy of adventure and love, in which fantasy and reality, tenderness and irony are deftly blended in an admirable plot.

The poem opens with a scene at Arthur's court of Carduel (Carlisle). A knight named Calogrenant tells how, seven years before, he had been hospitably entertained by a vavasour and his fair daughter in the forest of Broceliande, had then met a monstrous churl, watching a herd of bulls, who had directed him to a spring, and there, after producing a violent storm by pouring water on a block of emerald, he had been attacked and unhorsed by a knight, and thus been obliged to return ignominiously on foot. Stirred by this narrative, Yvain sets out, is the guest of the vavasour, meets the herdsman, and in combat with the knight of the spring wounds him fatally. Pursuing him to his castle, Yvain is trapped in the gateway between two portcullises, but is saved from his enemies by the damsel Lunete out of gratitude for a service he had rendered her at the court of King Arthur. Rendered invisible by a ring which she gives him, Yvain witnesses the funeral procession of his late antagonist and the grief of his widow, Laudine, and falls violently in love with her. Lunete favours his cause and manages to bring her mistress round to marrying the slayer of her husband, since he alone is now capable of defending the spring. Soon after the wedding, Arthur and his knights arrive to attempt the adventure, Yvain in his new capacity hurls Keu from his saddle, then discloses his identity, and welcomes the party at his castle. All is joy and gaiety till Gauvain persuades Yvain to return with him to Arthur's court to maintain his reputation for prowess. Laudine reluctantly consents, but warns her husband that if he does not return within a year her love will turn to hate. Yvain allows the year to slip by, absorbed in feats of arms, and when a messenger from Laudine denounces him as a traitor and a liar, he is so desolated with shame and grief that he goes stark mad and resorts to the forest. Recognized by a damsel, he is cured by an ointment supplied by her mistress, and saves his benefactress from the attack of a hostile count. He rescues a lion from a fiery serpent, and the grateful beast does homage to him, and becomes his companion and protector. The 'Knight of the Lion' delivers Gauvain's niece from the giant Harpin and arrives in the nick of time to save Lunete, condemned to the stake as a traitress, from the flames. At the castle of 'Pesme Aventure' (Evil Adventure) he overcomes two sons of a devil in a judicial combat and liberates their victims, 300 maidens forced to work at weaving. He defends the younger daughter of the lord of 'la Noire Espine' (the Black Thorn) against the champion of her elder sister, who turns out to be Gauvain. When, after exchanging terrible blows, the antagonists discover their identity, each wishes to concede the victory to the other, but Arthur intervenes and settles the dispute of the rival sisters. Lunete tricks her mistress into promising that she will do her utmost to reconcile the Knight of the Lion with his lady, and though Laudine is in a fury when she discovers that the knight is her husband, she relents when Yvain begs her forgiveness, and all ends happily.

The author has arranged a fine gradation of adventures. After Yvain's first great exploit at the spring, there follows a year of purposeless and selfish tourneying and then a period of disgrace and madness. But from this nadir of his fortunes Yvain rises through a series of generous and selfless acts in the service of the weak and oppressed till he has performed his penance and by his supreme testing in the combat with Gauvain has demonstrated his prowess and magnanimity. A sort of unity, or rather duality, of place is maintained by centring the principal events at Arthur's court and at the spring. The neat organization of the poem may best be appreciated by comparing it with the Welsh text, *Owein* or *The Lady of the Fountain*.[1] The two narratives run parallel in their general lines up to the deliverance of Lunete from the pyre; then the Welsh author adds that Owein and Luned 'went to the dominions of the Lady of the Fountain; when he came away, he brought the lady with him to Arthur's court, and she was his wife as long as she lived'.[2] He tacks on an episode corresponding to Chrétien's 'Pesme Aventure' but does not attempt to attach it to the main plot. It is extremely improbable that Chrétien furnished the model for the Welsh *Owein*; rather both authors followed a common source, a 'conte d'aventure'. Chrétien would seem, therefore, to have fitted the 'Pesme Aventure' into the framework of his story and turned a dry and irrelevant narrative into a lively and dramatic scene.

[1] See pp. 198 f. below.   [2] J. Loth, *Mabinogion* (Paris, 1913), ii. 43.

The 'conte d'aventure' which furnished material for *Yvain* contained elements of faery lore from more than one body of tradition. In the theme of the marvellous fountain and its defender one may find traces of sympathetic magic and of sacred marriages—practices noted among many peoples; but the setting in the forest of Broceliande and the figure of the monstrous herdsman argue in favour of Celtic provenience.[1] So too does the love of the hero for a lady who was at an earlier stage a fountain fay and who had as her confidante and intermediary a second fay.[2] On the other hand, the motif of the grateful lion undoubtedly derives through a series of stages from the famous anecdote of Androcles.[3]

Into this fabulous framework Chrétien introduced many details from the real life of his own day—costume, furniture, arms, combats. Of these the most remarkable is the complaint of the poor operatives in the weaving shop run by the two devils. The precise figures in which their earnings and the profits of their masters are given must reflect a contemporary reality.[4]

It was contemporary reality and contemporary custom which made it possible for Chrétien to render plausible and even commendable the marriage of Laudine to her husband's slayer three days after her husband's death. Too much has been said about the widow of Ephesus; there is nothing except a very broad resemblance to suggest that she was the model for Laudine. On the other hand, Chrétien probably took hints from a passage in *Enéas* on Dido[5] and even more probably from the conduct of Jocasta in *Thèbes*.[6] But for a twelfth-century audience the sudden remarriage of a great heiress needed no explanation and hardly a justification. From the feudal point of view the fountain had to be defended as if it were a frontier, and Laudine, unmarried, invited attack. Common sense and duty urged her to wed, and the sooner the better.

Nevertheless, the poet was keenly aware that, if he was to keep the sympathy of his readers for his heroine, she must not exchange one husband for another without a struggle, without ample reason. First, she learns that the fountain is to be menaced by Arthur and his knights. Secondly, her vassals are all cowards. Thirdly, the suitor is the son of Urien—a fine match! Fourthly, there is Lunete, the confidante of Laudine and the advocate of Yvain, bound by ties of gratitude to plead his cause. Laudine's decision, then, is fully motivated by external circumstances. Equally realistic and even more natural are the emotions of curiosity and of physical attraction which lead

---

[1] R. S. Loomis, *Arthurian Tradition*, pp. 273–93.

[2] Ibid., pp. 293–308. See p. 198 below.   [3] *PMLA*, xxxix. 485–524.

[4] In my opinion Chrétien reflects the 'gynaeceum' of a feudal castle rather than a city workshop. See my *Yvain, Cours de Sorbonne*, pp. 60–63.   [5] *Enéas*, vss. 1600–10.

[6] *Thèbes*, vss. 223 ff. The episode of Yvain's first return to the fountain borrows features from *Piramus et Tisbé*—the apparent death, the attempt at suicide, dialogue conducted through a crack in the wall.

her in the same direction. She acts out a pretty comedy when she treats her wooer with *hauteur* even after she has decided on marriage, and again when she consults her vassals, even though sure of their assent. The other principal characters are well drawn: clever, guileful, yet essentially loyal Lunete; Yvain, impulsive, brave, magnanimous, direct. But Chrétien can be reproached with one serious improbability in his characterization. Is it credible that a really devoted husband could be tempted to leave his bride after a week or two of honeymoon and stay away for over a year, forgetting the day when he was to return to her?

As in his earlier romances, Chrétien was not content to tell a story for its own sake merely, and in *Yvain* he offered a lesson in wisdom and nobility. When his hero forgot the time fixed for his return, he sinned against Laudine and against love. Chrétien thought, like Laudine, that Yvain was required to expiate his fault, but he deemed also that her righteous anger should not last for ever. So the guilt of the lover was atoned for by the feats of the knight. Laudine had the right to condemn Yvain; it was her duty to pardon the Knight of the Lion.

The peculiar quality of *Yvain* is one of plenitude and harmony, a harmony composed of various voices and different tonalities. Chrétien was not unaware of polyphonic song which was making notable progress in his day and which he himself described in vss. 465–9.

> Et trestuit li oisel chantoient
> Si que bien s'entracordoient.
> Mes divers chans chantoit chascuns;
> Qu'onques ce que chantoit li uns
> A l'autre chanter c'i oï.

(All the birds sang so that they were in complete harmony, but each one sang a different note; for never did I hear one sing the same tune as another.)

Likewise, in the romance the individual voice, even the dissonances, are organized into a superior harmony.

'Perceval' or 'Le Conte du Graal'[1]

Chrétien's last romance ends abruptly at vs. 9234. As already noted, it was written at the behest of Philippe of Alsace, who died in June 1191 on the

---

[1] Editions: by C. Potvin, *Perceval le Gallois* (Mons, 1866–71), ii, iii; by G. Baist (Freiburg, 1911); by Hilka (Halle, 1932). Special studies are: W. Kellermann, *Aufbaustil und Weltbild Chrestiens von Troyes im Percevalroman, Beihefte zur ZRP*, lxxxviii (Halle, 1936); A. Pauphilet, *Le Legs du moyen âge*, pp. 169–83; J. Marx, *La Légende Arthurienne et le Graal* (Paris, 1952); W. A. Nitze, 'Perceval and the Holy Grail', *Univ. of Calif. Publ. in Mod. Phil.* xxviii (Berkeley, Los Angeles, 1949), 281–332; Micha, 'Le *Perceval* de Chrétien de Troyes', in *Lumière du Graal* (Paris, 1951), pp. 122–31; J. Frappier, *Perceval ou le Conte du Graal, Cours de Sorbonne* (Paris, 1953). See also contributions of Hofer, Imbs, Frappier, Delbouille, Nitze, and Loomis in *Les Romans du Graal dans la littérature des XIIᵉ et XIIIᵉ siècles* (Paris, 1956). On the origin of the Grail legends see Chap. 21 below. For

Third Crusade. The poet was surely telling the truth in asserting that he had received from his patron a *livre* which contained the story of the Grail.

> Donc avra bien sauve sa peine
> Crestiens qui antant et peine
> A rimoier le meillor conte,
> Par le comandement le conte,
> Qui soit contez an cort real;
> Ce est li contes del graal,
> Don li cuens li baille le livre.[1]

(Then Chrétien will not have wasted his effort, who strives and toils to turn into rime, at the command of the Count, the best tale that may be told in a royal court; it is the story of the Grail, of which the Count gives him the book.)

What, precisely, did the book contain? The answers to this question tend to be influenced by theories concerning the origin of the Grail legend. Some have surmised that the book was written in Latin and described a ritual about a Christian relic; others have maintained—in my opinion with greater probability—that it was a 'conte d'aventure', filled with Celtic marvels. Was the story of Perceval already linked to the legend of the Grail? In *Erec* Perceval le Gallois is listed among Arthur's knights and he reappears in *Cligès*, but without any hint of a peculiar destiny. The Middle English *Sir Perceval* has not a word of the Grail or the Fisher King. It is impossible to say whether the *livre* combined the *enfances* of Perceval with the Grail theme, or the poet took the initiative.

The praise which Chrétien bestows on his Maecenas, however grandiloquent, reaches a higher level than mere flattery. It is made up mainly of paraphrases from the gospels; it contrasts the ostentatious largess of Alexander the Great with 'charity' in the strictly religious sense of the word. Indeed, there is a correspondence between this prelude and the ascent of Perceval from ignorance and coldness of heart to comprehension of his duties and the discovery of the divine.

Let me give a brief sketch of this long, though incomplete, poem. Perceval's mother, robbed by death of her husband and two older sons, brings up her youngest in a remote forest of Wales, ignorant of chivalry and its perils.[2] But one spring morning the youth meets five knights, and his innate destiny is revealed to him. Returning to his mother, he announces his decision to go to Carduel, where Arthur dwells, 'the king who makes knights'. She

---

nomenclature see Nitze and Williams in *Univ. of Calif. Pub. in Mod. Phil.*, xxxviii (1955), 265–98, and Loomis *Arthurian Tradition*, pp. 477–92.

[1] Bruce, i. 220, n. 1.

[2] The *enfances* of Perceval may be compared with the Irish sagas of the youth of Cuchulainn and Finn. See Loomis, *Arthurian Tradition*, pp. 335–9; Nitze, *Perceval and the Holy Grail*, pp. 312 f.; Zimmer in *GGA*, 1890, p. 519; Pace in *PMLA*, xxxii (1917), 598–604; A. C. L. Brown in *MP*, xviii (1920), 211–21.

consents with reluctance, makes him a clumsy suit 'à la mode de Galles', gives him hasty advice about his behaviour with damsels, about seeking the companionship of gentlemen (*prodomes*), and about entering churches to pray. As he departs, he sees her fall in a swoon, but he whips his horse and gallops away.

Mistaking a splendid tent for a church, he enters and with boyish exuberance kisses a damsel lying within. After his departure, her lover returns and, convinced of her infidelity, forces her to ride forth in sad array. Meanwhile Perceval makes a heroi-comic entrance at Arthur's court, riding in on horseback, is insulted by Keu but is greeted by a damsel as the best knight of the world.[1] Leaving the hall, he kills with a javelin the Red Knight who had insulted King Arthur and Guenièvre, and with the help of a squire strips him of his arms and armour. In the castle of the friendly Gornemant de Gohort he learns how to manage horse and arms and receives the order of knighthood. Gornemant, moreover, gives him wise counsel and warns him against too many words, for loquacity is a sin. Perceval now seeks to return to his mother, but finds himself at the castle of the beautiful Blancheflor, the niece of Gornemant. She welcomes him and visits his bed by night, clad only in a shift and a mantle, to implore his help against the enemies who besiege her castle. He reassures her, draws her under the covers beside him, and they spend the night together, mouth to mouth. In the next two days he vanquishes her enemies and sends them as prisoners to Arthur. Though he continues to enjoy her embraces, and promises to return, he leaves her, being haunted by the image of his swooning mother.

He comes to a river, inquires of a mysterious fisherman in a boat where he may find harbourage, and is directed to his castle near by. There he finds in the hall his host, already arrived before him and lying on a couch. He receives a sword which is destined for him. Then he witnesses the procession of the bleeding lance, candelabra, the golden vessel called a *graal*,[2] and the carving platter. Chrétien is here at particular pains to emphasize effects of light and colour—light from torches and fire-place and candelabra, eclipsed by the splendour of the *graal* and its jewels; colour of precious metals, of red blood and white lance. The bearer of the *graal* is clearly visualized, holding the vessel between her two hands.[3] Though fascinated by this cortège as it passes repeatedly before him, Perceval is mindful of Gornemant's injunction and fails to ask whom one serves with the *graal*. When he wakes in

---

[1] The arrival of Perceval at Arthur's court recalls the description of the arrival of Culhwch at the same court. Loth, op. cit. i. 251–8, 285 f.

[2] On etymology and meaning of word *graal* see Nitze in *MP*, xiii (1916), 681–4, and *American Journal of Philology*, lxvi (1945), 279 ff.; R. S. Loomis in *PMLA*, lxxi (1956), 845 f.; Roques, *Le Graal de Chrétien et la Demoiselle au Graal* (Geneva, Lille, 1955), pp. 1–7; Marx, *Légende Arthurienne et le Graal*, pp. 241–3.

[3] On the cortège of the Grail see Frappier in *Lumière du Graal*, ed. R. Nelli (Paris, 1951), pp. 175–221. On the phrase 'trestot descovert' see *BBSIA*, vi (1954), 75–78.

the hall the next morning, he finds the castle deserted and rides away in bewilderment.

In a wood near by he meets a female cousin, who, learning of his adventure of the night before, violently upbraids him for his silence, for if he had asked concerning the *graal*, his infirm host, the Fisher King, would have been healed. She tells him also of his mother's death and declares that his silence was the consequence of his sin in leaving her. Perceval next meets the damsel of the tent, mounted on a wretched nag and followed by her jealous lover, and forces him in combat to admit her innocence. After a fall of snow he sees the blood of a wild goose against the white background, and falls into a reverie on the fresh colour of his love Blancheflor.[1] Sagremor and Keu in turn interrupt him and are knocked out of their saddles, the latter breaking his arm. But Gauvain, the model knight, employing courtesy, succeeds in bringing the love-smitten youth to Arthur's camp, where because of the report of his deeds he is deemed worthy to sit at the Round Table.

One day after the court has returned to Carlion, a damsel of fantastic ugliness rides in on a mule and pours out curses on Perceval for his silence at the Grail castle. The disastrous consequences for the Fisher King and his land are irremediable. She then announces other high adventures, and these are at once undertaken by Gauvain and other knights. But Perceval vows that he will repair his error and will not sleep two nights in the same spot till he has learned who is served with the *graal* and why the lance bleeds. To the crucial nature of this episode I will recur later.

Suddenly a knight, Guingambresil, enters, accuses Gauvain of killing his father, the King of Cavalon, and challenges him to a combat forty days later. Gauvain sets out to answer this accusation and *en route* comes to Tintagel, and there in the course of a tourney displays his prowess at the request of the Maid with the Little Sleeves, the younger daughter of Tiebaut de Tintagel. It is a piquant situation to find the great champion and the veteran lover risking his honour by his delay, all for the sake of an innocent girl. As he approaches the castle of Cavalon he meets the new king out hunting, who recommends him to the hospitality of his sister. This takes the agreeable form of an ardent wooing, but is interrupted by an attack by the townsfolk, who have recognized the alleged murderer of their former king. When things are looking critical, Guingambresil arrives and arranges to postpone the duel for a year, while in the meantime Gauvain is to seek and bring back the bleeding lance.

Perceval wanders in search of the Grail castle, surmounting all perils, dispatching sixty knights as prisoners to Arthur, but, unmindful of God, he

---

[1] On the Celtic origin of this episode see Loomis, *Arthurian Tradition*, pp. 414 f.; Nitze, *Perceval and the Holy Grail*, p. 311. See, however, de Riquer in *Revista de Filología Española*, xxxix (1955), 186–219.

has not once entered a church. On a Good Friday he comes to a hermit, who on hearing his confession explains that his tongue had been tied at the Grail castle because he had left his mother in a swoon. Perceval learns, moreover, that the Fisher King is his cousin, that the Fisher King's father has been an invalid for fifteen years, and that he is of so pure a spirit that a single mass wafer brought to him in the *graal* suffices to keep him alive. The hermit himself is Perceval's uncle, gives his nephew pious counsels, and for penance prescribes that he eat sparingly till Easter Day.

The remainder of the poem is concerned with the adventures of Gauvain in a world where fragments of reality mingle with magic and sheer fantasy. He heals the ungrateful Greoreas of his wound; humbly endures the insults of L'Orguelleuse de Logres (the Proud Lady of Logres)—the earliest appearance of the *Damoisele Maudisante*; arrives at a Castle of Ladies; there passes successfully the test of the Perilous Bed; learns that his reward is to remain in this gynaeceum; nevertheless, obtains leave to depart and vanquishes the knight who guards the water-crossings of Galvoie (Galloway); finds on the other side of a perilous ford a falconer, Guiromelant, who informs him that among the residents of the Castle of Ladies are Gauvain's grandmother, Igerne, his mother, and his sister—all, it seems, unrecognized by Gauvain himself. Guiromelant reveals, moreover, that he is in love with Gauvain's sister, Clarissant, though he has never seen her, but he is hostile to Gauvain, arranges a duel with him at the perilous ford a week later, in the presence of the lords and ladies representing both sides. With the dispatch of Gauvain's messenger to Orcanie to procure the attendance of King Arthur the narrative abruptly ends.

The poem thus briefly sketched bristles with problems. First, how is one to account for the fact that a poet who had limited his previous romances consistently to 7,200 lines or less carried *Perceval* to 9,234 lines and was evidently far from bringing to a suitable conclusion the supreme adventure of the Grail? This is less understandable since at vs. 4,747 he abandoned his hero (except for 300 lines concerned with the visit to the hermit) and devoted himself to the fortunes of Gauvain, which are utterly unrelated to the central theme. This duality of interest has seemed to certain critics so gross a flaw in composition that they have refused to believe in Chrétien's responsibility. Becker reduced his authentic work to the first 3,427 lines (up to the departure from the Grail castle);[1] Hofer, more generously, concedes to him all the adventures of Perceval but assigns those of Gauvain to a maladroit continuator.[2] Hoepffner believes that two independent poems were unscrupulously stitched together after Chrétien's death.[3]

---

[1] *ZRP*, lv (1935), 385 ff.   [2] S. Hofer, *Chrétien de Troyes, Leben und Werke*, pp. 210–14.
[3] *R*, lxv (1939), 412. De Riquer takes much the same position in *Filología Romanza*, iv (1957), 119–47, but see my reply in *MA*, lxiv (1958), 67–102.

None the less, there are reasons for thinking that it was the poet's own intention to give Gauvain a minor but still important part. In *Lancelot* Chrétien had done precisely that, maintaining a sort of parallelism between the roles of Gauvain and the hero. In *Perceval* he sends Gauvain on a sort of secondary quest for the Bleeding Lance, paralleling the hero's quest for the Grail. Moreover, is there not a significant contrast between the nature of the experiences which come respectively to Gauvain and Perceval? Gauvain indeed possesses the merits of honour, tact, and elegance, but this varnish scarcely hides a basic frivolity, a preoccupation with earthly glories and an incurable weakness for casual amours. Is there not a muffled irony in the treatment of a model knight who allows himself to be deflected from his rendezvous with Guingambresil by the bright eyes of the Maid of the Little Sleeves, and who after swearing to seek the Bleeding Lance forgets all about it? It may therefore be argued that Gauvain's adventures are not irrelevant to Chrétien's purpose, that he is deliberately presented as a counterpoint to Perceval.

If this interpretation of Gauvain's character is accepted, it becomes easier to understand the author's conception of Perceval. In the first part of the romance the uncouth manners and laughable blunders of the youth brought up in the Welsh forest contrast with the refined courtesy and *savoir vivre* of Arthur's nephew. But through precept and example Perceval acquires the mundane graces and virtues until in the scene where he falls into a love-trance at sight of the blood drops on the snow and responds with courtesy to Gauvain's courteous invitation to Arthur's court the two knights appear to stand on the same level of excellence. Perceval, however, rises to a higher sphere. When the Loathly Damsel announces before the assembled knights of the Round Table a number of glorious enterprises to be undertaken, Gauvain characteristically chooses the liberation of the Maid of Montesclaire, and Perceval too might have redeemed his reputation by some romantic exploit. But Chrétien emphasizes the contrast between the two in the single line: 'Et Percevaus redit tot el.' (Perceval speaks quite otherwise.) Though the Damsel has just told him that he is doomed never to succeed, never to restore the Fisher King to health, he refuses to be dominated by Fate and undertakes in remorse and humility to repair the disaster which he had unwittingly wrought. He has reached a higher moral plane than Gauvain. He has yet, however, to learn the spiritual significance of his failure and the way to success. Now Chrétien gives two explanations of his silence at the Grail castle: according to the first, it was due to an excessive docility, a too strict obedience to Gornemant's warning against loquacity; but according to the hermit, Perceval's silence was due to his heartless desertion of his mother as she swooned at her castle gate. Though these two explanations are different, it is possible to regard them as valid, each on its plane. To lack judgement is a practical, a worldly flaw. To lack compassion and love is a spiritual, a religious flaw. As, through the teaching of the hermit, Perceval becomes conscious of this fault and learns the remedy for it through repentance, the sacraments, and submission to God's will, he reaches a third plane of which Gauvain never dreams. We may suppose that if Chrétien had completed his poem, his hero would have returned to the Grail castle, made wise by experience, and would have healed the Fisher King.

Thus interpreted, the growth of Perceval falls into three stages. The first is an apprenticeship in the accomplishments and virtues of chivalry but remains incomplete through an error of judgement in failing to ask the fateful question. The second is a moral drama and it reaches its climax when Perceval asserts his liberty of choice, and, though the Loathly Damsel has predicted failure, sets out to undo the wrong he has done. The third is a spiritual experience, represented by a slowly dawning conscience in relation to his mother's suffering and death, a glimmering awareness of divine mysteries roused by the vision of the Grail, and a full illumination and purification appropriately timed at the Paschal season.

It cannot be denied that many obscurities and many seeming irrationalities remain, and have sometimes been ascribed to sheer carelessness or to the weariness of age. But is it not likely that Chrétien realized that much of the charm of his recital lay in tantalizing concealments and partial mysteries? Was it not wiser to hint at probable or possible meanings, rather than to supply a postil for every incident, as did some later authors of Grail romances? If this is so, as I am inclined to believe, his refusal to make everything clear, especially in connexion with the Fisher King, his father, the Grail maiden, her office, and the question test, was deliberate. He allowed the paganism of a very old myth to remain but created around it an atmosphere of Christian spirituality.

As to what the old myth was and whence it came, the most diverse opinions have been held. It is the most knotty problem of all. A survey of these opinions and an attempt to answer the problem will be found in Chap. 21.

Chrétien's Influence

Though Chrétien was not, strictly speaking, the head of a school, he exercised a wide and lasting influence which only a long and minute study could fully define. He was recognized by his contemporaries and immediate successors as a master of language and style, as one who, according to Huon de Méri, spread abroad 'le bel françois tout à plain'. He transformed a genre still new, and all the romancers of the end of the twelfth century owed him something. If they too often ignored his art of *conjointure*, they drew from their model numerous motifs. Even those who like Jean Renart had no taste for the Matter of Britain reveal his influence, and, as will be shown in Chap. 28, the Arthurian poets of the thirteenth century followed in his footsteps. Even in the fifteenth and sixteenth century prose modernizations of his *Erec* and *Perceval* were made. Though the grandiose prose romances beginning with the Vulgate cycle introduced new aesthetic principles, expanded enormously the corpus of material, and recast the history of the Grail, the debt to the Champenois master is still patent, particularly in the Prose *Lancelot*. For the penetration of his influence beyond the limits of the *langue d'oïl* it is only necessary to consult the chapters in this book concerned with Hartmann von Aue, Wolfram von Eschenbach, and the Dutch, Scandinavian, Provençal, and English romances. It was Chrétien who first gave prestige to the Matter of Britain as it was fecundated by the French genius.

16

GEREINT, OWEIN, AND PEREDUR

IDRIS LLEWELYN FOSTER

IT was pointed out in Chap. 4 that five of the tales in Lady Guest's collection, entitled *The Mabinogion*, assigned to Arthur a considerable place, and that two of these showed almost no trace of continental or Anglo-Norman influence. It is quite a different matter with the remaining three—*Gereint*, *Owein* (Lady Guest's title, *The Lady of the Fountain*, translates *Chwedyl Iarlles y Ffynnawn*), and *Peredur*. These have long been the subject of a controversy, inaccurately called by German scholars 'die Mabinogion-frage'—inaccurately because the tales are not, strictly speaking, *mabinogion*. The history of this controversy up to 1922 was reviewed by J. D. Bruce,[1] who came to the conclusion that the Welsh tales were 'undoubtedly derived from the extant romances of Chrétien',[2] namely, *Erec*, *Yvain*, and *Perceval*. While the opposite contention that Chrétien's poems were derived from the corresponding Welsh versions has now no advocates, the problem of the relationship has yet to be definitively resolved. It has been stated by Loomis as follows:[3] 'Was Chrétien the sole source of the corresponding portions of the Welsh tales? Was Chrétien only one of the sources of the Welsh tales? Was there a common source for each of the three pairs of romances?'

It is not proposed here to attempt a final anwer to these questions, but rather to consider some of the findings of recent scholarship, for there may never be complete agreement regarding the relation of Chrétien's poems to the three Welsh tales. Synopses of the Welsh tales are omitted since the corresponding French narratives, already summarized in Chap. 15, give a general idea of the plots, and since the translation by Gwyn Jones and Thomas Jones in Everyman's Library makes for easy reference. Additional details will be supplied in the course of the discussion. References to the Welsh texts are to the edition of the tales in the Red Book of Hergest (RM) by J. Rhŷs and J. G. Evans (Oxford, 1887) and to the edition of the White Book Mabinogion (WM) by J. G. Evans (Pwllheli, 1907).[4]

---

[1] Bruce, ii. 59–74. A useful survey of the early stages of the controversy by J. Loth may be found in *RC*, xiii (1892), 475–503.

[2] Bruce, i. 46.

[3] *Arthurian Tradition*, p. 33.

[4] The RM references are to pages, the WM references to columns.

'*Gereint*'

The agreement between *Gereint*[1] and *Erec*, both in general design and in many details, was recognized by Lady Guest, and an elaborate comparison was made by K. Othmer in *Das Verhältnis von Christian's von Troyes 'Erec et Enide' zu dem Mabinogion [sic] des roten Buches von Hergest 'Geraint ab Erbin'* (Bonn, 1889). Nevertheless, the many points of dissimilarity between them have been adduced by several scholars as arguments that they are derived from a common source, which may be called X. The 'most cogent' of these arguments have been summarily set forth by R. S. Loomis.[2] First, there is Windisch's observation[3]—which applies also to the other tales—that there is no coincidence of Romance loan-words in the Welsh text and the text of *Erec*. Windisch held that these loan-words were taken from Anglo-Norman and not from continental forms. Secondly, the name of 'Gereint vab Erbin' has been substituted for 'Erec li fiz Lac'. Lot showed that Chrétien's form was probably a modification of the regular Breton name Guerec;[4] and if this is so, then the Welsh substitution may well have been suggested by Guerec rather than Erec. Thirdly, the name of Enid's father in *Gereint* is Ynywl (variants Nywl, Ynwl), and it occurs frequently without any corresponding form in *Erec*. On the other hand, *Erec* supplies a name for him toward the end (vs. 6896), the manuscripts reading Liconaus, Licoranz, Leconuials. Loomis pointed out that the last form must be a scribal corruption of 'li cons uials', 'the old earl', and it is fair to conclude that 'the French source of *Erec* and *Gereint* contained a young count and an old count'.[5] The redactor of *Gereint* read *uials* as *niuls* and transformed it into a proper name, 'y Nywl iarll', while Chrétien, also coming across the two counts in his source, called the younger simply 'li cuens' and the other 'li vavassors' until he decided to give him a name, and then, misunderstanding 'li cons uials', he wrote 'liconuials ot non ses pere'.

Loomis put forward other arguments whose value may be assessed at a somewhat lower rate. In *Gereint*, after the White Hart has been killed its head is cut off and given to Enid as a tribute to her beauty,[6] whereas Chrétien says nothing of the head, and the tribute which Enide receives is a kiss from Arthur. This suggests that Chrétien was modifying a repulsive feature in X.

[1] Complete texts of *Gereint* in White Book (Peniarth MS. 4, National Library of Wales; early fourteenth century) and in Red Book (Jesus College, Oxford, MS. CXI; date 1375–1425). There are parts of *Gereint* in Peniarth MS. 6, one written about 1275, and two others about 1285. See for details Historical MSS. Commission, *Report on Manuscripts in the Welsh Language* (London, 1898–1910), i. 305 f., 316; ii. 1–30; R. M. Jones in *BBCS*, xv (1953), 109–16. The best translations are those of Loth and G. and T. Jones. See Chap. 4, n. 1, p. 31.

[2] *Arthurian Tradition*, pp. 34–36.

[3] E. Windisch, *Das keltische Brittannien bis zu Kaiser Arthur* (Leipzig, 1912), p. 240.

[4] *R*, xxv (1896), 588. See also Loth, *RC*, xiii (1892), 483 f.

[5] *Arthurian Tradition*, p. 35.

[6] Jones translation, pp. 245 f.

Again, though the two romances concur in describing the heroine as wearing an old ragged dress in her father's home and on her ride to Arthur's court,[1] later, when her husband's anger is aroused, in the Welsh version Enid is told to put on her worst dress (WM 417),[2] but in the French Erec bids Enide put on her loveliest robe (vss. 2580 f.). Loomis plausibly argues that again Chrétien made a deliberate change, and that, disliking the repetition, he ineptly altered Erec's instructions as found in X. Loomis believes that *Gereint*, on the other hand, 'has preserved the original tradition in representing Enid, the victim of her husband's offended pride and jealous suspicion, as wearing not her best but her worst gown'.[3]

As already noted in Chap. 15, the motive behind the harsh treatment of Enide has been the subject of much debate,[4] and here too some scholars hold that the Welsh narrative gives an explanation which is the original and the more satisfactory one. In the White Book, col. 417, we read:[5]

Another thought distressed him, that it was not out of care for him that she had spoken those words, but because she was meditating love for another man in his stead and desired dalliance apart from him.

Now some critics have regarded this motivation of Gereint's behaviour as a crude and unnecessary gloss. Bruce, for instance, argued that for a twelfth-century audience 'Erec's conduct towards Enide called for little explanation', and that 'nothing could be more illogical than the conception of jealousy as the cause of the hero's conduct'.[6] On the contrary, if we accept the ingenious theory of Sparnaay[7] that the story shows a partial fusion of two separate motifs, namely, the ride of a hero who is determined to exhibit his prowess to a doubting lady (as in the Fair Unknown romances and Malory's Book of Gareth) and the ride of a knight whose purpose is to humiliate a wife or mistress suspected of infidelity (as in the episode of the Proud Knight of the Glade in Chrétien's *Perceval*), then the account in *Gereint* is far from being 'a crass blunder'. But, whatever one's opinion may be as to the dramatic propriety of jealousy as the motive for Gereint's harshness and his compelling Enid to wear her shabbiest dress, it seems clear from the French analogues that this was a traditional situation and that the Welsh author did not invent it. And if so, then one must suspect Chrétien of suppressing the motive for easily understandable reasons, and of substituting, for less understandable reasons, the fairest robe for the poorest.

The situation is reversed, however, when it comes to the geography of the two romances, for in this respect Chrétien seems to have clung to his source,[8]

---

[1] Jones translation, pp. 235, 240.   [2] Ibid., p. 251.
[3] *Arthurian Tradition*, p. 105.   [4] Ibid., p. 121, n. 8, and above, p. 170.
[5] Jones translation, p. 251.   [6] Bruce, ii. 61.
[7] H. Sparnaay, *Hartmann von Aue, Studien zu einer Biographie* (Halle, 1933), i. 78–101.
[8] On Gereint see Loth, *Mabinogion*, 2nd ed. ii. 121, n. 1; R. Bromwich in *Studies in Early British History*, ed. N. K. Chadwick (Cambridge, 1953), p. 53; Windisch, op. cit., pp. 175 f

whereas the Welsh author, having adopted for his hero the historic Cornish figure, Gereint ab Erbin,[1] made him the heir and later the king of Cornwall, and being unable to identify the place-names in his source,[2] arbitrarily set Arthur's court at Caerleon, the stag hunt in the Forest of Dean, and the sparrow-hawk contest at Cardiff—indications that he himself lived between the Severn and the Taff.

One of the most striking differences between *Gereint* and *Erec* is the absence from the Welsh text of a multitude of names, even those which have a Welsh flavour. The roll-call of the knights of the Round Table and the invitation list to Erec's wedding are missing. So too are Galoain, Guingalet, Eurain, Mabonagrain, Cadoc de Tabriol,[3] and the participants in the tourney below Danebroc. In fact, instead of a full account of the tourney we have only a few lines about Gereint's devotion to such sports and the fame he acquired (WM 409).[4] Morgain la Fée, whose marvellous plaster heals the wounds of Erec, twice appears in *Gereint* as Morgan Tud, Arthur's male physician[5]—a metamorphosis which suggests that the fay was unknown to the Welsh author under that name.[6] Similarly, though he knows the friendly dwarf Guivret, he is unfamiliar with the name, for he remarks (WM 433) that the Cymry call him 'the Little King' but the French call him 'Gwiffret Petit'.[7] Count Galoain figures as 'yr jarll dwnn' (WM 431), which may mean 'the dark red earl'.

The author of *Gereint* seems to have made up for the omission of many names which are found in *Erec* by picking a few which are found in *Culhwch*:[8] Glewlwyd Gavaelvawr, Goreu, Penpinghon, Llaesgymyn, Drem vab Dremhidydd, Clust vab Clustveinydd, Gweir Gwrhyt Vawr, Gwrei Gwalstawd Ieithoedd, and Gildas vab Caw.[9] Odyar Franc, steward of Arthur's court, seems to derive from Odgar,[10] whose steward owned the cauldron required for Culhwch's wedding feast. Cadyrieith and Cradawc vab Llyr come out of *Rhonabwy's Dream*. Amhar son of Arthur is surely the Amr of Nennius's *Mirabilia*.[11]

Perhaps the most remarkable difference between *Erec* and *Gereint* lies in the respective treatments of the adventure which in the Welsh text takes place within a 'hedge of mist' (WM 446–51) and in the French text (vss. 5367–6410) is referred to by the mystifying title of 'la Joie de la Cort', 'the Joy of the Court'. On the assumption that both versions derive from the same

---

[1] See note 8 on p. 194.   [2] Loomis, *Arthurian Tradition*, pp. 70–76.

[3] Ibid., pp. 480–7.   [4] Jones translation, p. 246.   [5] Ibid., pp. 244, 266.

[6] See Loth in *RC*, xiii (1892), 496 f.; Lot in *R*, xxviii (1899), 322 ff.; Loomis, *Wales*, p. 155, n. 126.

[7] Jones translation, p. 261. On Guivret see Loomis, *Arthurian Tradition*, pp. 139–44, 485.

[8] WM, 385 f., 411.

[9] On Gildas see N. K. Chadwick in *Scottish Gaelic Studies*, vii (1953), 115–83.

[10] Loth, *Mabinogion*, 2nd ed. ii. 122, suggests that Odyar is from French Oger (pronounced Odger).

[11] See Chap. 1.

source, one concludes that the Welsh redactor took over little of the weird machinery and romantic plot which Chrétien employed in his tale of Mabonagrain and his mistress. Nitze described the episode as a 'footless addition' to the Welsh tale.[1] Philipot's statements are, however, more to the point.[2] 'Comparison of the episode of the Hedge of Mist with that of the Joy of the Court does not prove, in our opinion, that it goes back to another source, differing from the French poem. . . . Rather, the mabinogi [sic] adds to the text of *Erec*, which it abridges so clumsily, new obscurities. . . . At the end of the episode the function of the horn is indicated with greater precision than in *Erec*.' For that matter, the Hedge of Mist (*kae nywl*) has more in common with Celtic stories of magic mists than with Chrétien's garden surrounded by a wall of air (vss. 5739 f.). Rachel Bromwich has made the ingenious suggestion that the French title of the adventure, 'la Joie de la Cort', represents a misunderstanding of 'le Jeu del Cor'; for *jeu* would correspond to the Welsh word *gware*, 'game', by which the adventure is repeatedly designated, and it is the blast of a horn which dispels the enchanted mist.[3] But one should not overlook the fact that in the *Elucidation*, prefixed to Chrétien's *Perceval*, there is much emphasis on the joy which attends the finding of the Fisher King's court, and this would seem to corroborate the association of joy, rather than a game, with the court of the hospitable king.[4]

Owein

The Welsh counterpart of *Yvain* is for convenience' sake usually entitled *Owein*, though the final sentence of the Red Book text reads: 'And this tale is called the Tale of the Lady of the Fountain (*Chwedyl Iarlles y Ffynnawn*).'[5] A detailed comparison of the narrative sequences in *Owein* and *Yvain* is given by Greiner in *ZCP*, xii (1918), 5–184, and an analysis of the structure by Loomis in *Arthurian Tradition*, p. 308.

A. C. L. Brown published an important article bearing on the problem of the relationship between the two tales.[6] According to Chrétien, Yvain, galloping after Esclados through a gateway, is trapped between two portcullises, the portcullis behind him cutting off the haunches of his horse. As the narrative proceeds, we discover that this narrow passage has become a chamber, richly painted and equipped with seats and a bed—a completely unrealistic description of a castle gateway. Now *Owein* tells a consistent,

[1] *MP*, xi (1914), 472. For Nitze's more recent opinion see *Spec.*, xxix (1954), 691–701.

[2] *R*, xxv (1896), 293 f.

[3] See forthcoming *Medieval Welsh Texts*, ed. by R. Bromwich and I. Ll. Foster, vol. i.

[4] Loomis, *Arthurian Tradition*, pp. 172 f.

[5] The earliest complete text of *Owein* is in the Red Book, only fragments being found in the White Book. The opening of the story occurs in the early fourteenth-century manuscript, Jesus College XX, and has been published by R. M. Jones in *BBCS*, xv (1953), 114–16, who suggests that the scribe had no competent knowledge of Welsh. There are also later manuscripts. Ibid., pp. 109–16.

[6] *RR*, iii (1912), 143–72.

rational story (RM 172–4):[1] the hero escapes from the trap with the aid of a ring of invisibility, and is led by Luned into a gorgeous chamber, equipped with a couch. Despite Smirnov's assertion[2] that the inconsistencies in Chrétien are only apparent and that it is *Owein* which has misunderstood the original account, it is hard to avoid Brown's conclusion that 'Chrétien was here very carelessly transposing and rearranging a description that he did not understand'.[3] Or perhaps there was a disarrangement in the leaves of the manuscript he was following.

There are differences also in the earlier part of the narrative. Thus, when Cynon vab Clydno,[4] whom the Welsh redactor has substituted for Calogrenant, arrives at the castle of the 'Yellow Man', he is waited upon by twenty-four maidens more beautiful than Gwenhwyvar (RM 164).[5] In *Yvain*, on the other hand, Calogrenant is delightfully entertained by a single fair maiden (vss. 225–55). There is some evidence that in referring repeatedly to the yellow-haired, yellow-garbed host as the 'Yellow Man' the Welsh author preserved a feature in his source which was ultimately derived from the account of the visit of the Ulster heroes to the house of Buide mac mBain, 'Yellow son of White', as given in a version of the Beheading Test in *Bricriu's Feast*.[6] Since Chrétien does not mention this colour, his *Yvain* could hardly have been the source of this detail.

The Giant Herdsman as he appears in *Owein* seems to be akin to the herdsman Custennin in *Culhwch*,[7] for both are encountered sitting on a mound, surrounded by animals, and both warn the hero against proceeding with his enterprise. Moreover, the herdsman in *Owein* is called *coydwr*, 'wood-man',[8] holds a big club, and has only one eye and one foot, and in these respects bears a strong resemblance to a herdsman, *bachlach*, in the Irish saga of the *Destruction of Da Derga's Hostel*, who is called *Fer Cailli*, 'Man of the Wood', who carries an iron pole, and has only one eye and one foot.[9] Except for the club, Chrétien's herdsman does not retain these Celtic features. T. F. O Rahilly has suggested[10] that, since the herdsman in *Owein* is referred to as 'the black man (*y gŵr du*)', he may be identical with 'the black oppressor (*y du traws*)', who appears later in the same story, promising Owein to establish a hospice for weak and strong.[11] In that case, he may have a forerunner or

---

[1] Jones translation, pp. 164 f.   [2] *RC*, xxiv (1913), 37.

[3] *RR*, iii. 148.

[4] Cynon son of Clydno is one of the traditional north British heroes of the late sixth century. Ifor Williams, *Canu Aneirin* (Cardiff, 1938), p. 175; Loth, op. cit. ii. 2, n. 1. On relation of names Cynon and Calogrenant see R. M. Jones in *BBCS*, xv. 122 f., and Loomis, *Arthurian Tradition*, p. 275, n. 5.   [5] Jones translation, p. 157.

[6] Loomis, *Arthurian Tradition*, pp. 278–80.   [7] Jones translation, pp. 108, 158.

[8] Jones, following the Red Book reading 'wtwart' (from ME. *wode-warde*), translates (p. 158), 'keeper'.

[9] Loomis, *Arthurian Tradition*, p. 287.   [10] *Ériu.* xvi (1952), 7–20.

[11] Jones translation, p. 182. See also *RC*, xxv (1903), 18 ff.

a counterpart in the herdsman Buchet in the Irish saga, *Esnada Tige Buchet*, who returned to Leinster to reopen his house for hospitality.

As we have seen, the alternative title of the Welsh tale is 'the story of the Lady of the Fountain'; likewise, the text itself bears witness that the heroine was called 'The Lady of the Fountain'.[1] In *Yvain*, though Laudine does not bear the title, she refers in vs. 2034 to 'ma fontaine'. Analogies between the plot of *Yvain* and *Owein* on the one hand and that of the lai of *Desiré* on the other,[2] show that originally the heroine was actually a fountain fay. It can hardly be a coincidence, therefore, that the lai places the fountain itself in the land of Calatir, now the district of Calder in Lothian, while Chrétien gives the lady of the fountain the name Laudine and makes her the daughter of Duke Laudonez, an easily recognizable medieval form of Lothian.[3]

There is another widowed countess in *Owein* besides the heroine, and she, too, seems to have been in origin a water fay, for she appears first walking beside a lake with her handmaids, is skilled in the healing art, and bestows on the hero the best horse in the world[4]—all features frequently associated with the fays of the Matter of Britain. In *Yvain* she enjoys the title of 'la dame de Noiroison' and she possesses an ointment, the gift of 'Morgue la sage', that is, Morgain la Fée.[5] Now Morgain was not only famed for her healing powers, but she was also a water nymph and capable of turning into a bird. In the Didot *Perceval* a fay from Avalon appears turned into a black bird, a *noir oisel*.[6] Is it too venturesome to propose that this fact has something to do with the title of the 'dame de Noiroison'? If that be so, there is a connexion with the strange scene in *Rhonabwy's Dream*, where Owein's ravens are first attacked and slaughtered by Arthur's men, and then at the signal turn on their enemies and destroy them. It was pointed out in Chap. 4 that the ravens were probably Owein's mother Modron and her sisters and attendants. This, too, is the explanation of the reference at the end of *Owein* to 'the Flight of Ravens' and to the victory which they always brought to Owein wherever he went.[7]

The Welsh and French versions differ in their telling of the Grateful Lion story. It is known that in its main features this reproduces a French chivalric version close to those given by Jaufré de Vigeois and Alexander Nequam.[8] The Welsh romance gives two details which are found in Nequam but not

---

[1] Jones translation, p. 167.
[2] Ahlström in *Mélanges de Philologie Romane Dédiés à Carl Wahlund* (Mâcon, 1896), pp. 297–9; A. C. L. Brown in *SNPL*, viii (1903), 128 f., 140 f.
[3] Loomis, *Arthurian Tradition*, pp. 272, 301–5.
[4] Jones translation, pp. 174–6.
[5] Loomis, *Arthurian Tradition*, pp. 310 f.
[6] *Didot-Perceval*, ed. W. Roach, pp. 200–2.
[7] Jones translation, p. 182; *Breudwyt Ronabwy*, ed. M. Richards (Cardiff, 1948), pp. xvi–xviii; Loth, op. cit. ii. 45 n., 197.
[8] *PMLA*, xxxix (1924), 485–524. See also Chotzen in *Neo*, xviii (1932), 131–6.

in *Yvain*: the lion was discovered in a cleft in a rock, and after its rescue it sported about Owein like a greyhound. Brodeur concluded from these correspondences that *Owein* was not dependent on Chrétien's version of the episode.

The same inference may be drawn from a remarkable transposition which Chrétien seems to have effected and which constitutes one of the major differences between the two versions. Both represent Arthur and his knights arriving at the storm-making spring and narrate an encounter between Yvain (Owein) and Keu (Cei). The Welsh author, however, follows this with a second encounter in which Cei is again worsted, then with a series of triumphs by Owein over the rest of Arthur's retinue except Gwalchmai, and finally with a ferocious duel between Gwalchmai and Owein which ends happily with recognition.[1] Of this sequence Chrétien has nothing, but he does have a very similar combat between Yvain and Gauvain near the end of the poem, where it serves as a supreme demonstration of his hero's prowess. He introduces, moreover, a theme of rival sisters, seeking champions, in order to bring about the incognito combat between the two knights. Now if this duel between Yvain and Gauvain had been placed at the end in his source, it is not easy to understand why the Welsh redactor moved it back. But, if it was placed early in the story, it is easy to perceive why Chrétien deliberately reserved it as an appropriate climax to the career of his hero.

As with *Gereint*, *Owein* contains features which are peculiarly Welsh and which are in all likelihood the author's own additions.[2] Arthur's court is located not at Carduel but at Caerleon on Usk. Glewlwyd Gavaelvawr is there 'with the rank of porter to receive guests and far-comers'. Arthur is called an emperor and is seated 'on a couch of fresh rushes, with a coverlet of yellow-red brocaded silk under him'. Cei performs certain humble duties which would hardly be demanded of the seneschal of a great French or English court; he goes to the kitchen and the mead-cellar to fetch chops and a goblet of mead. In spite of the imperial rank conferred on Arthur, his household is depicted as that of a Welsh chief.

'Peredur'

The relationship between *Peredur* and Chrétien's *Perceval* offers a more complicated problem than that of the other two pairs of tales. For one thing, there are considerable differences between the four medieval manuscripts which contain the whole or part of *Peredur*.[3] For another, the Welsh tale

---

[1] Jones translation, pp. 172 f.   [2] Ibid., p. 155.

[3] The most complete text of *Peredur* is that of the White Book; the Red Book lacks certain parts. MSS. Peniarth 7 and Peniarth 14 (1325 50) represent fragments of a shorter version. These fragments are printed in J. G. Evans, *White Book Mabinogion*, pp. 286–312, and are translated in

introduces many episodes to which there are no counterparts in Chrétien's text or in the continuations. Furthermore, there are correspondences between the Welsh and other versions of the Perceval story in German, English, and Italian.[1]

Thurneysen, in an examination of Mary Williams's book on *Peredur*,[2] made the following structural analysis of the tale.

I. (*a*) From beginning to close of incident of the blood drops on the snow, when Peredur is found by Arthur's knights (WM 117–145. 8; Jones translation, 182–202).

   (*b*) The account of Peredur's love for Angharad Law Eurawc and his reconciliation with her (WM 145. 9–152. 2; Jones translation, 203–7).

II.   The section extending from WM 152. 3 to 165. 26 (Jones translation, 207–17). This includes the accounts of the Black Oppressor (*y gŵr du*), the court of the Sons of the King of Suffering, the killing of the *Addanc*, Edlym Red-Sword, the countess's court, the Dolorous Mound, the slaying of the Worm or Dragon, the hospitable miller and the empress of great Constantinople,[3] with whom Peredur 'ruled fourteen years, as the story tells'.

III.   The rest of the story, beginning with the visit of the Loathly Damsel to Arthur's court.

The oldest manuscript of *Peredur*, the thirteenth-century Peniarth 7, contains sections I and II only.[4] According to Thurneysen, I (*a*) is a free adaptation of corresponding material in Chrétien, 'mit (geringer) Beimischung einheimisch-kymrischen Sagenmaterials'. Sections I (*b*) and II are the inventions of Welsh story-tellers, independent of each other, but influenced by I (*a*), in which Peredur first appears in Welsh literature 'als fahrender Ritter'. Section III represents a later addition or supplement, following Chrétien as far as the Welsh redactor had material at hand, but also making use of another non-Welsh source, and supplying a conclusion of his own devising, though connected with material in I (*a*).

Mühlhausen, in a very detailed study,[5] accepts Thurneysen's analysis, and says that sections I (*b*) and II can be put aside without affecting the essentials of the story. On I (*a*) he remarks that the divergences from the French *Perceval* do not seem to have been caused by an independent handling of a

T. P. Ellis and J. Lloyd, *Mabinogion* (Oxford, 1929), ii. 138–86. See further *Report on Welsh Manuscripts*, i. 317–19, 325–34; M. R. Williams, *Essai sur la Composition du Roman Gallois de Peredur* (Paris, 1909), pp. 1–3, 18–40; L. Weisgerber in *ZCP*, xv (1925), 66–186.

[1] M. R. Williams, op. cit., pp. 50 f., 81–95; C. Strucks, *Der junge Parzival* (Borna-Leipzig, 1910); R. Zenker in *RF*, xl (1927), 251–329.

[2] *ZCP*, viii (1912), 185–9.

[3] On the relationship between this episode and the Dame de Malehot story in the Vulgate *Lancelot* and the Ade episode in *Lanzelet* see Loomis, *Arthurian Tradition*, p. 257, n. 13.

[4] Ellis and Lloyd, op. cit., pp. 148–86.

[5] *ZRP*, xliv (1924), 465–543.

common source but rather by innovations, often clumsy, on the part of the Welsh adapter. He does not agree that what Mary Williams calls the 'idée fondamentale du récit' (namely 'une vengeance')[1] is worked out at all in I (*a*); he maintains rather that the vengeance motif first appears towards the end of section III. This last section is indeed intended as a supplement to I (*a*), but it does not harmonize neatly with it. At the beginning of III the Loathly Damsel equates the Lame King with the host in whose castle Peredur had seen the bleeding spear, not with the lame host who had offered to instruct him in the ways of chivalry. The Damsel mentioned only one youth bearing the spear, whereas there had been two. She also described only one stream of blood as running from the tip of the spear to the hand-grip, instead of three which ran down to the floor. She strangely omitted all mention of the head on the platter. Of these four discrepancies between section III and section I (*a*) Mühlhausen maintained that the second and third showed that the author of III was well acquainted with the whole of Chrétien's poem because they correspond to Chrétien's version of the Grail scene and not to the speech he put in the mouth of the Loathly Damsel. Here it may be remarked that when, at the end of section III, the yellow-haired youth explains to Peredur that he was the 'black maiden' (the Loathly Damsel) who came to Arthur's court, he also says that it was he who 'came with the head all bloody on the platter'. The same identification of the Loathly Damsel with the Grail Bearer appears in *Perlesvaus*.[2]

Mühlhausen's conclusion is that, apart from additions of little interest or importance, sections I (*a*) and III depend entirely on Chrétien. Both he and Mary Williams suggest that there is evidence for assuming that some sort of 'draft manuscript' lies behind the Welsh version. Thus the latter thinks that Peniarth 7 is the work of a copyist who had only the notes of a fuller manuscript, while Mühlhausen, in his effort to explain the seemingly chaotic state of *Peredur* and its departure from the French pattern at so many places, would derive all the Welsh manuscripts from a common exemplar, which consisted of excerpts from the French poem or which supplied an outline of it. The Welsh authors then, according to this hypothesis, set to work to clothe this skeleton, and provided two sets of clothing. It is clear, however, that much more detailed study of the manuscript affiliations is necessary before a final judgement can be reached about Mühlhausen's theory, which has, in fact, been vigorously challenged by Zenker and Weisgerber.[3]

Bruce recognized five main differences between the Welsh and the French versions.[4] (i) The much abbreviated account of Gwalchmei's (Gauvain's) adventures. (ii) The omission of much material about chivalric life. (iii) The absence of the Grail 'as such'. (iv) The introduction of motifs from native

[1] M. R. Williams, op. cit., pp. 44–50.   [2] Loomis, *Arthurian Tradition*, p. 377, n. 6.
[3] *RF*, xl (1927), 251–329, 483–93.   [4] Bruce, i. 346.

Welsh folk-tales, of which the principal are the episodes dealing with the Witches of Caerloyw[1] and the killing of the *Addanc* (which Bruce calls a 'serpent'). (v) The substitution of the name Peredur for Perceval. Presumably, then, Bruce did not attach much importance to other differences; for example, the confusion of the two uncles of Peredur, curiously corresponding to the confusion of Gornemant with the Fisher King in Gerbert's continuation of *Perceval*;[2] the displacement of the Blancheflor incident in *Peredur* (Bruce attempts, not very convincingly, to explain this as the result of 'some disarrangement of leaves in the French manuscript which the Welshman had before him');[3] the Welsh author's creation of two proud knights of the glade;[4] the small but significant difference in the episode of the blood drops on the snow;[5] the identification of the Loathly Damsel with the Grail Bearer.[6]

Bruce's third main difference has to do with the extraordinary contrast which Peredur's visit to the castle of his second uncle presents to Chrétien's account of Perceval's visit to the castle of the Fisher King, in spite of certain common features which indicate a basic correspondence. According to the Welsh version,[7] after Peredur had been welcomed by his grey-haired uncle and his retinue and had passed successfully the sword test, he beheld two youths bearing 'a spear of exceeding great size, and three streams of blood along it, running from the socket to the floor'. Everyone set up a crying and a lamentation at the sight. Presently, 'lo, two maidens coming in and a great platter between them, and a man's head on the platter, and blood in profusion around the head' (WM 130). Many years later Peredur (section III)[8] learns the story of the spear and the platter: a yellow-haired youth tells him that it was he who bore the platter with the head on it; the head was that of Peredur's cousin, killed by the witches of Caerloyw, and Peredur was destined to avenge the murder.

Bruce tried to explain this variation from Chrétien's poem as a stupid blunder,[9] contending that the Welsh author 'could make nothing out of the mysterious Grail' in the French poem and so 'substituted the motif of vengeance which he found in Manessier's continuation'. This explanation is not altogether convincing, for Manessier does not mention a severed head. There are, on the other hand, several striking parallels between this scene and other texts. *Perlesvaus* presents us with a damsel who brings to the hero the head of his male cousin in an ivory vessel and informs him of his duty to take

[1] For Irish analogue see J. Rhŷs in *Anthropological Essays Presented to E. B. Tylor* (Oxford, 1907), pp. 285–93; M. R. Williams, op. cit., pp. 117–19; Windisch, op. cit., pp. 137 f. On the tradition attached to Caerloyw see Loomis, *Arthurian Tradition*, pp. 89, n. 21, 177, 219, 455 f.; Loomis, *Wales*, p. 111, n. 24; and above, p. 15.

[2] Loomis, *Arthurian Tradition*, pp. 336 f., 360, 361, n. 7.

[3] Bruce, i. 345. [4] Loomis, *Arthurian Tradition*, p. 395.

[5] Ibid., pp. 414 f. [6] Ibid., p. 377.

[7] Jones translation, pp. 191 f. [8] Ibid., pp. 226 f.

[9] Bruce, i. 346.

revenge.[1] Mary Williams called attention to two other remarkable parallels.[2] Wolfram von Eschenbach, like the author of *Peredur*, mentions the lamentation which greets the entrance of the youth with the bleeding spear.[3] Pierre Bercheur in his *Reductorium Morale* briefly recounts how when Galvagnus (Gauvain) beheld in a mysterious palace a table spread with viands, suddenly the head of a dead man appeared on a platter (*in lance*), and a giant was lying on a litter near the fire. Unless these three correspondences between our Welsh text on the one hand and *Perlesvaus*, *Parzival*, and the *Reductorium* on the other are due to mere chance, the only reasonable inference is that they are due to the common use of floating traditions.

Mary Williams suggested that the tradition of the severed head in a dish was developed from the legend of the feasting of Brân's retinue in the presence of his head in a royal hall, as described in *Branwen*.[4] Loomis and Helaine Newstead have also argued for a connexion between these severed heads on dishes, seen in mysterious halls, and a collection of more than a hundred boars' heads on grails (*graaus*), seen by Gauvain in the castle of Bran de Lis.[5] They suggested that the surprising conversion of human heads into those of boars was due to a confusion of *sanglanter*, 'to bleed', and *sangler*, 'boar'—a suggestion rendered plausible by similarities between Galvagnus's situation in the palace of the severed head and Gauvain's situation in the castle of Bran de Lis.

If these hypotheses are accepted, then it would seem that *Peredur* gives a very confused version of the scene in the Grail castle. The vessel borne by the maidens is called a *dyscyl*, the semantic equivalent of *graal*.[6] In most versions of the legend, this vessel is emphatically a miraculous feeding vessel, corresponding, as has been observed,[7] in form and function to the *Dysgl* of Rhydderch, listed among the Thirteen Treasures of the Isle of Britain: 'whatever food one wished thereon was instantly obtained.'[8] It is this property which the Grail displays in the continuations of Chrétien's *Perceval*, in Wolfram's *Parzival*, in the Vulgate cycle, and elsewhere.[9] How is it that in *Peredur* nothing is said of its traditional function, but instead it serves as a receptacle for the head of a murdered man?[10] The preceding paragraphs

---

[1] *Perlesvaus*, ed. W. A. Nitze and others (Chicago, 1932–7), i, ll. 8678–710.

[2] M. R. Williams, op. cit., pp. 47 f., 91 f.

[3] Zenker in *RF*, xl. 292–4. See below, p. 292.

[4] M. R. Williams, op. cit., p. 47; Jones translation, p. 39.

[5] *RC*, xlvii (1930), 39–62; H. Newstead, *Bran the Blessed in Arthurian Romance* (New York, 1939), pp. 76–85.

[6] *ZCP*, viii (1910), 187; Windisch, op. cit., p. 195.

[7] T. Gwynn Jones in *Aberystwyth Studies*, viii (1926), 85; Büsching in *Jahrbücher der Literatur*, v (1819), pp. 42 f.

[8] *RF*, xlv. 70; Newstead, op. cit., p. 68.

[9] It is highly significant that this property of the Grail—feeding a large company with whatever food they desire—does not appear in Chrétien, and must therefore be derived from some traditional source.　　　　　　　　　　　　　　[10] Newstead, op. cit., pp. 80 f.

have shown that there was an independent tradition of a severed head on a dish or *graal*, set on a table in a perilous castle, possibly identical with the head of Perlesvaus's cousin brought to Perlesvaus in a vessel by a damsel to incite him to revenge. Apparently, the author of *Peredur*, who was capable of confusing Gornemant with the Fisher King, confused the two dishes and substituted for the feeding Grail the *dyscyl* with the bleeding head, and thus added one more to the mysteries of the Grail legend. At any rate, this complicated theory provides a better explanation of all the pertinent facts than the suggestion made by Bruce.

It is obvious that the author of *Peredur* identified his hero with an historic Peredur, son of Eliffer of North Britain, about whom stories must have been in circulation, for he declares in his opening sentences that Peredur's father held the earldom of the North.[1] It is perhaps the same Peredur who is mentioned in the Black Book of Carmarthen (*c.* 1200) as the father of Mor and who bears the epithet *penwetic*. J. G. Evans translated this as 'chief physician', supposing that it referred to Perceval as the healer of the Maimed King.[2] A more plausible suggestion is that it refers to his home. Penweddig is a commote in north Cardigan, and in the *Parochialia* of Edward Lhuyd, the antiquary, we find a note: 'Predyr Peiswyrdh Ld. of higher Cardigan had a place or Pallace, call'd Kayro, vizt. Lhŷs Predyr ynghayro (the court of Peredur in Kayro).' As R. J. Thomas has observed, Aberceiro was the centre of the commote of Penweddig.[3]

What, then, of the immediate origin of these three tales? That they are not translations in the usual sense of the word becomes abundantly clear on close examination. Comparison with Chrétien shows that sometimes the French and sometimes the Welsh author has preserved more accurately the matter of the common source. It is particularly noticeable that the nomenclature and the geography of that source are reproduced by Chrétien much more fully and accurately than by the Welshman, who suppresses and substitutes with great freedom. Comparison of the two versions shows furthermore that the Welsh redaction must have been made from memory, not from a perusal of the French text, for there are far too many traditional features in Chrétien's poems, derived presumably from his source, which are omitted or changed for no intelligible reason except failing recollection. Indeed, the Welsh tales in their handling of motifs and incidents, in their structure and style, in their vocabulary and syntax are something quite other than translations from a written French source. Rather, *Gereint*, *Owein*, and *Peredur* are

---

[1] On Peredur in early Welsh literature see A. O. H. Jarman, *Ymddiddan Myrddin a Thaliesin* (Cardiff, 1951), pp. 12 ff.; H. Zimmer in *GGA*, 1890, pp. 818 ff.; Windisch, op. cit., p. 171.

[2] *White Book Mabinogion*, p. xvi; M. R. Williams, op. cit., p. 47. Mühlhausen wrongly tried to explain the word as a metathesized from of *pen-defic* (*sic*), 'lord'; *ZCP*, xxii (1941), 67.

[3] *Enwau Afonydd a Nentydd Cymru* (Cardiff, 1938), i. 222.

adaptations of three French romances which provided Chrétien also with his material—adaptations which included the addition of fresh native ingredients to the blend of French and Celtic narrative.

One of these native ingredients is the style. Much comment on the relative merits of the Welsh and French texts is of doubtful value, being based too often on English or French translations from the Welsh versions. A feature which has been generally overlooked is the employment of *Araith,* that is, Rhetoric, which Melville Richards has pointed out.[1] *Rhonabwy's Dream* is often quoted as the classic Welsh example of rhetorical richness, but on scrutiny both *Gereint* and *Peredur* are seen to be richer and more intricate, while *Owein* is more restrained. Though it is dangerous to argue from the amount of rhetoric in a given work as to its relative date, Richard's chronological arrangement of the works mentioned may have a tentative value: (i) *Owein,* (ii) *Peredur,* (iii) *Gereint,* (iv) *Rhonabwy's Dream.*

More solid are the arguments from the age of manuscripts and from orthographical and linguistic features. The oldest manuscript containing any portion of the three Welsh romances is Peniarth 6, pt. iv, in which a fragment of *Gereint* was copied about 1275. The complex relationships between the various manuscripts are not yet determined with certainty,[2] but it may safely be said that there is good orthographical and linguistic evidence for an exemplar dated about 1200. As to the locality where the tales were written down for the first time, it would be unwise at present to offer more than a suggestion. The manuscript history of *Owein* points toward Glamorgan and south-east Wales,[3] and it is not improbable that *Gereint* and *Peredur* are also to be traced to that region.

[1] *Breudwyt Ronabwy,* ed. M. Richards, pp. xix–xxiv.
[2] *BBCS,* xv. 109–16.
[3] G. J. Williams, *Traddodiad Llenyddol Morgannwg* (Cardiff, 1948), pp. 164, 176.

ADDITIONS TO CHRÉTIEN'S *PERCEVAL*—
PROLOGUES AND CONTINUATIONS

ALBERT WILDER THOMPSON

CHRÉTIEN DE TROYES was prevented by death from completing his *Perceval*—or as he named it, the *Conte del Graal*. This information is given by one of his continuators in a passage generally considered to be truthful.[1] It is not surprising that other men undertook to complete the story. Of the fifteen extant Old French manuscripts of Chrétien's *Perceval*, only four stop at the end of the work of the original author. In many manuscripts the *Perceval* attains tens of thousands of lines. In the past there has been a great deal of discussion as to how to delimit the parts of this great corpus. There is now general agreement, on the basis of evidence in the manuscript tradition, that the limits of the work of Chrétien are those indicated by Alfons Hilka in his edition.[2] Furthermore, there is at last general agreement on the limits of the additions to Chrétien's work. The most difficult decision concerned the first two continuations. At one time, these two were considered to be one and were ascribed to Wauchier de Denain, whose name (with variations in form) is found in the Second Continuation. When it was realized that the so-called work of Wauchier was in reality two separate compositions, the first came to be called the Pseudo-Wauchier or the anonymous continuation. Now it is generally agreed that Wauchier de Denain should not be considered the author of the Second Continuation either. He was a pious writer of saints' lives, referred to as an authority rather than as an author of the *Perceval*.[3] We shall refer to these first two continuations, both now considered anonymous, merely as the First and the Second Continuation.

The additions to Chrétien's *Perceval* are six in number. Two of these pieces are referred to as prologues because they precede Chrétien's work in the manuscripts; they are the *Elucidation* and the *Bliocadran*. The other four follow Chrétien's work and are properly called continuations; in addition to the two anonymous continuations, there are two of which the author's

---

[1] Gerbert de Montreuil, ed. Mary Williams, *CFMA*, i, vss. 6984–7.

[2] *Der Percevalroman von Christian von Troyes* (Halle, 1932).

[3] Maurice Wilmotte, *Le Poème du Gral et ses Auteurs* (Paris, 1930); F. Lot, *R*, lvii (1931), 123 ff.; Hilmar Wrede, *Die Fortsetzer des Gralromans Chrestiens von Troyes* (Göttingen, 1952), pp. 138–45.

names are known: Manessier and Gerbert. No one manuscript contains all the additions. The two so-called prologues are sparsely represented; the *Elucidation* survives in only one manuscript and the *Bliocadran* in only two. The continuations have fared better; there are eleven manuscripts each for the First and Second Continuations, seven for Manessier's work, but only two for that of Gerbert.[1] In addition to the Old French manuscripts, there is a prose version of the *Perceval* printed in 1530 which contains the two prologues and all the continuations except that of Gerbert. The *Parzifal* of Wisse and Colin[2] in fourteenth-century German verse is an expansion of the *Parzival* of Wolfram von Eschenbach; it includes one of the prologues (the *Elucidation*) and all the continuations except that of Gerbert.

Up to the present, scholars interested in using these documents to study the development of the Grail legend have been hampered by the lack of adequate editions. The pioneer edition of Charles Potvin[3] was based on only one manuscript and has been difficult to obtain. Hilka published the two prologues in the appendix of his edition of Chrétien's *Perceval*,[4] and one of them has been separately edited.[5] Hilka promised that his edition of Chrétien would soon be followed by the continuations, but he died without achieving his purpose. His materials have recently been found,[6] but they are not ready for publication. Meanwhile, at long last, an edition by William Roach has begun to appear.[7] It will eventually include all the continuations except that of Gerbert, which has been partly published by Mary Williams.[8]

Let us examine these six additions to Chrétien's *Perceval* one at a time.

The Elucidation

This prologue of 484 lines is pedestrian in style, confused in motivation, and has been garbled in transmission. It is ironical that the name *Elucidation*[9]

---

[1] A. Micha, *La Tradition manuscrite des romans de Chrétien de Troyes* (Paris, 1939); see also the introduction to Hilka's edition of Chrétien's *Perceval* and to Roach's edition of the *Continuations*.

[2] Ed. Karl Schorbach (*Elsässische Litteraturdenkmäler*, v, Strassburg, 1888).

[3] *Perceval le Gallois* (Mons, 1866–71). Vols. ii–vi give the whole corpus of the *Conte del Graal* as contained in the manuscript of Mons; this manuscript includes the two prologues and three of the continuations. The remaining continuation—that of Gerbert—is given by Potvin in the form of a synopsis and long extracts.

[4] Hilka's text of the *Bliocadran* is a composite of the two extant manuscripts; his text of the *Elucidation* is a reprint of Potvin's inaccurate text.

[5] A. W. Thompson, *The Elucidation, a Prologue to the Conte del Graal* (New York, 1931).

[6] *BBSIA*, iii (1951), 107.

[7] *The Continuations of the Old French 'Perceval' of Chrétien de Troyes* (Philadelphia: vol. i, 1949; vol. ii, 1950; vol. iii, pt. 1, 1952). The volumes which have appeared contain the First Continuation in its three redactions. Future volumes will contain the Second and Third Continuations, glossaries, and a critical study. See Roach in *Romans du Graal* (Paris, 1956), pp. 107–18.

[8] Gerbert de Montreuil, *La Continuation de Perceval*, *CFMA*, tome i (1922), tome ii (1925). A third volume is needed to complete the work.

[9] This name by which modern scholars have come to designate the work is found only in the prose

has come to be attached to this far from lucid composition. To make matters worse, there are interpolations. The most interesting of these is a sort of rimed table of contents[1] of a Grail poem in seven branches—a compilation that has not come down to us, although the names of some of the branches resemble episodes in preserved works.

Since the *Elucidation* serves as a prologue to the *Perceval*, it is only natural that it contains allusions to the work to which it is prefixed. These mention episodes of the poem of Chrétien and at least his first two continuators. The verbal resemblances to passages in the First Continuation are especially striking. The only clue to the date of composition of the *Elucidation* is the fact that its author knew the first two continuations. As authority a 'maistre Blihis' is cited; this is doubtless the Bleheris or Bledhericus mentioned in several works of the period as a well-known storyteller.[2]

The most original part of the *Elucidation* is the tale of the maidens who lived in wells and who served food and drink to wayfarers. Finally a wicked King Amangon and his followers deflowered the maidens and carried off their golden cups, whereupon the land became desolate and the court of the Rich Fisher could no longer be found. The connexion of these maidens with the Arthurian knights and the Grail is not clear in the *Elucidation*; the reader gains the impression that the author was crudely trying to unite the story with the Grail material in order to force it to serve as an introduction to the *Perceval*. Many parallels have been pointed out to stories dealing with robberies from fairyland, fountain fairies, and magic wells influencing vegetation. We may feel sure that we are dealing with an authentic bit of Celtic folk-lore.[3] The cups stolen from the maidens can be compared with Arthur's stolen cup in Chrétien's *Perceval*, perhaps with the Grail itself.[4] The connexion of the well-maidens with fertility of the land has often been commented upon in its possible relation to the ever-present motif of the blight on the land in the Grail stories.[5] The evil King Amangon has been

---

version of 1530, where the title *Elucidation* includes not only this prologue but also a truncated version of the *Bliocadran*.

[1] Cf. the rimed table of contents in MS. fr. 794 of the Bibliothèque Nationale, printed by Roques, *R*, lxxiii (1952), 184–5.

[2] See Chap. 6 above and Thompson, op. cit., pp. 79–81; Wrede, op. cit., pp. 176–83.

[3] Thompson, op. cit., pp. 37–55; Helaine Newstead, *Bran the Blessed in Arthurian Romance* (New York, 1939), *passim*; R. S. Loomis, *Arthurian Tradition*, *passim*. The editor has kindly called my attention to a story from Glamorganshire which bears an especially striking resemblance to this episode: Marie Trevelyan, *Folk-lore and Folk-stories of Wales* (London, 1909), pp. 19 f. Water-ogres carried off girls and imprisoned them in springs. So long as certain wicked men lived by robbery and murder and neglected the fields, the Shee Well near Ogmore Mills remained dry and there were no fish, but when they promised to reform, the water flowed again and the people rejoiced.

[4] W. A. Nitze, *Perceval and the Holy Grail* (1949), pp. 315 f.

[5] According to an ingenious theory, the references here to the court of the Rich Fisher are due to a misunderstanding; originally it was a horn (*li cors, le cor*) of plenty which was sought—the horn of

compared with a bewildering number of personages—not only in French romances but also in Celtic stories—who are similar in name or function or both.[1]

A surprising amount of ink has been spilled over this confused and confusing prologue. Any conclusion in regard to it is hazardous. The only really distinctive thing in it is the folk-tale of the maidens. The exact connexion of this Celtic tale with the Grail is not clear, but at least its presence in this prologue to a Grail romance shows that someone at an early date in the development of the legend thought that it did have a connexion. Probably that fact is one more item of proof that the Grail was not Christian in origin.

The 'Bliocadran'

The *Bliocadran* is a composition of 800 verses. It bears no name in the manuscripts, but it has become customary to refer to it by the name it assigns to Perceval's father. Usually it has been called the *Bliocadran Prologue*. However, it does not serve as a prologue, as the *Elucidation* does, but rather purports to be the beginning of the action of the *Perceval* itself. It is therefore preferable to drop the word *prologue* from its name. There is evidence that the correct form of the name is *Bliocadron*,[2] but the form consecrated by usage will be kept in this chapter.

Scholars have often made disdainful remarks about the literary quality of this composition. To be sure, it lacks the sparkle of Chrétien's verse. On the other hand, it is a straightforward narration, coherent and well motivated. Human emotions are sympathetically described, and feudal customs are well portrayed. It is more realistic than most medieval romances and bears no overt traces of folk-lore. In most respects the *Bliocadran* is an excellent beginning to Chrétien's poem. The name of Perceval is not mentioned, even when he is baptized (vss. 253–8); Chrétien likewise withholds the name until Perceval's interview with his cousin (vs. 3575). His mother calls him 'fair son' (vss. 750, 766), as she does repeatedly in Chrétien's poem. The forest has the same name: la Gaste Forest (vss. 76, 531, 674). The

---

Brân, who was prototype of the Rich Fisher, and the joy which the finding of the court would bring is comparable to the episode in Chrétien's *Erec* called 'Joie de la Cort' (Newstead, op. cit., pp. 81 ff., 113 ff.; Loomis, op. cit., chap. xxv).

[1] For example, the name has been related to the first component of *Mabonagrain* in Chrétien's *Erec*, the second component of *Baudemagus* in Chrétien's *Lancelot*, &c., and all of them with Manawydan, brother of Brân the Blessed in Welsh tradition: Newstead, op. cit., *passim*; Loomis, op. cit., chaps. xxv, xl. A. C. L. Brown, *Origin of the Grail Legend* (1943), chaps. xiii, xiv, tries to connect *Amangon* with Irish *Amargen*; the resemblance in form is striking, but his attempt to equate this episode of the *Elucidation* with *Loch Erne* is unconvincing; cf. *California Folklore Quarterly*, iii (1944), 68–70.

[2] The one time the name occurs in rime, it is with *maison*, and there is no instance of confusion of -*an* and -*on* in rimes in the rest of the *Bliocadran*. The form of the name varies in both manuscripts; the one used by Potvin usually has -*an*(s); the other and better manuscript usually has -*on*. The prose has only *Bliocadras*. See A. W. Thompson, 'Text of the *Bliocadran*', *RP*, ix (1955), 205–9.

Bliocadran ends with the boy in his teens, old enough to hunt with *gavelos* (vss. 728, 781)—weapons conspicuous in Chrétien's account—but still naïve ('qui mout avoit de sens petit', vs. 747) as in Chrétien ('Et cil qui petit fu senez', vs. 281). His mother warns him that if he sees men covered with iron, he should flee because they will be devils (vss. 754–67). This prepares for the episode in Chrétien's portion where the lad meets Arthurian knights and remembers such a maternal warning (vss. 114–18).

It is only in regard to Perceval's family that the *Bliocadran* is in contradiction to Chrétien's poem. We are told that Bliocadran had had eleven brothers, all of whom were killed in wars and tourneys. Bliocadran himself was killed in a tournament a few days before his son's birth. Perceval was the only child of his parents. The bereaved mother withdrew with her infant son to the Waste Forest soon after her husband's death. She was accompanied by a faithful *maire* and his wife and their twelve children, and also by servants. In Chrétien's poem the family history as told to Perceval by his mother (vss. 408–88) is entirely different. His father (who is never named) was wounded and fell into poverty and had himself transported in a litter to a manor he owned in the Waste Forest. Perceval had had two elder brothers, both of whom became knights and were killed. The father died of grief after the death of his two sons.

If this one passage in Chrétien's poem did not exist, there would be no contradictions.[1] The author of the *Bliocadran* was evidently a redactor who intended to omit that passage, or else he had a manuscript that lacked it. Except for that passage—not essential for the rest of Chrétien's romance—the *Bliocadran* is an excellent introduction. It motivates strongly the desire of the widow to keep her child from knowledge of knighthood; her husband and his eleven brothers had all been killed in wars and tourneys.

The name Bliocadran itself needs to be considered to see what light it might throw on the origin of the work. The name is not found elsewhere. Chrétien de Troyes leaves Perceval's father nameless; Gerbert de Montreuil's continuation calls him Gales li Caus; *Perlesvaus* and the *Didot Perceval* call him Alain le Gros; some of the later romances call him Pellinor; the *Parzival* of Wolfram von Eschenbach uses the name Gahmuret; and in the Welsh *Peredur* the hero's father is Efrawc, Earl of the North. A good deal of evidence has been gathered together to show that Brân was the prototype of Perceval's father,[2] but that does not explain the name. There is no agreement as to its origin.[3] It looks Celtic—but an author arbitrarily

---

[1] Before there was an edition based on all manuscripts, it was even suggested that this passage was an interpolation. R. H. Griffith, *Sir Perceval of Galles* (Chicago, 1911), p. 25 n. Hilka's edition now shows that all manuscripts contain this passage.

[2] Helaine Newstead, 'Perceval's Father and Welsh Tradition', *RR*, xxxvi (1945), 3–31; Loomis, op. cit., chap. lx. See below, pp. 291 f.

[3] For theories of Celtic origin of the name, see Bruce, ii. 90 n., and the elaborate theory of

choosing a name would choose one which sounded Welsh because of the emphasis on the Welsh background of Perceval. A somewhat similar name, Blancand(r)in, occurs in the *Chanson de Roland* and in two other *chansons de geste*; the first part of the name Bliocadran might have been influenced by the name Bliobliheris found in the *Elucidation,* in Chrétien's *Erec,* and in a number of other romances.[1] There is a *roman d'aventure* of the thirteenth century called *Blancandrin et Orgueilleuse d'amour,*[2] in which the hero, Blancandrin, has adventures similar to those of Perceval—without the Grail.

It has often been observed that the *Bliocadran* in its account of the hero's parentage and childhood corresponds in detail to other forms of the Perceval story. When the *Bliocadran* is closer than Chrétien's version to these other romances, that fact is often taken as testimony to the existence of a pre-Chrétien form of the story, perhaps indeed the book Chrétien mentions as his source. The most frequently cited are the *Parzival* of Wolfram von Eschenbach, the Welsh *Peredur,* and the English *Sir Perceval of Galles.*[3] This is not the place to consider the question of the origins of the Perceval story. It should, however, be pointed out that the three stories mentioned are all later than Chrétien de Troyes and derived at least partly from him (although some might dispute this assertion in regard to *Peredur* and *Sir Perceval*). The manuscript of Chrétien which was their source may have contained the *Bliocadran,* which might very well have been considered a genuine part of the poem. We have already seen that the *Bliocadran* was in the manuscript of the *Perceval* used by Wisse and Colin in their expansion of Wolfram's *Parzival.*

The childhood experiences of Perceval have been compared with the boyish exploits of the Irish heroes Finn and Cuchulainn,[4] but it is not clear that the *Bliocadran* can be said with certainty to derive anything not found in Chrétien from such Celtic traditions. The *Bliocadran* has never been studied for its own sake, but always incidentally, tangentially. In the present state of

E. Brugger, 'Bliocadran, the Father of Perceval', in *Medieval Studies in Memory of G. Schoepperle Loomis* (1927), 147–74.

[1] *Elucidation,* ed. Thompson, pp. 52–53.

[2] Ed. H. Michelant (Paris, 1867).

[3] The bibliography is very voluminous. Among works particularly important in regard to the *Bliocadran* are: Carsten Strucks, *Der junge Parzival in Wolframs von Eschenbach Parzival, Crestiens von Troyes Conte del Gral, im englischen Syr Percyvelle und italienischen Carduino* (Borna-Leipzig, 1910); R. Zenker, 'Zu Perceval-Peredur', *Germanisch-romanische Monatsschrift,* xi (1923), 240–54; M. Wilmotte, *Le Poème du Gral; le Parzival de Wolfram d'Eschenbach et ses sources françaises* (Paris, 1933); Mary Aloysia Rachbauer, *Wolfram von Eschenbach;* a study of the relation of the content of Books III–VI and IX of the *Parzival* to the Crestien manuscripts (Catholic University of America Studies in German, iv, 1934); J. Fourquet, *Wolfram d'Eschenbach et le Conte del Graal* (Paris, 1938); F. W. Panzer, *Gahmuret: Quellenstudien zu Wolframs Parzival* (Heidelberg, 1940), pp. 52–56. See below, pp. 225, 291 f.

[4] Loomis, op. cit., chaps. lviii, lix; Nitze, *Perceval and the Holy Grail,* pp. 312 ff.; Jean Marx, *La Légende arthurienne et le Graal* (Paris, 1952), chap. iii.

our knowledge it would be rash to conclude that its author had access to other versions of the original story. It may well prove to be, as some have thought,[1] simply an invention of its author to give a more adequate introduction to Chrétien's poem, with no knowledge of Perceval except what he found there.

The First Continuation

The First Continuation, formerly known as the Pseudo-Wauchier, has often been admired as one of the finest of the Grail stories. It is a lively series of adventures usually told in a sprightly style. Roach[2] distinguishes six principal sections, which are briefly as follows: (1) a duel between Gauvain and Guiromelant and the marriage of the latter to Clarissant, Gauvain's sister; (2) Arthur's siege of the castle of Brun de Branlant, and Gauvain's adventure with a damsel in a tent, leading to Gauvain's killing of her father and a brother and to the prospect of a duel with another brother, Bran de Lis; (3) adventures of Caradoc, hero of the *Lai du Cor*; these include a beheading challenge, an enchanted serpent which fastens itself to Caradoc's arm, and a chastity test with a drinking horn;[3] (4) an expedition of Arthur's knights to rescue Girflet from the Chastel Orguelleus, involving a duel of Gauvain with Bran de Lis on the way,[4] and Gauvain's defeat of the Riche Soudoier; (5) Gauvain's visit to the Grail castle; (6) adventures of Gauvain's brother, Guerrehés, involving a swan-drawn boat.[5]

The First Continuation has sometimes been called the Gawain Continuation and with good reason.[6] Four of the six sections, it will be noted, deal with Gauvain, and another, with his brother. Only the section dealing with Caradoc stands apart in subject matter—it embodies several folk motifs— and in the fact that neither Gauvain nor Perceval is involved. This series of adventures evidently existed once as a separate story; it is often called the *Livre de Caradoc*.

Chrétien clearly intended Perceval to be his chief character and yet included two series of Gauvain adventures in his poem, and it breaks off in the midst of them. The duel with which the First Continuation begins is merely the conclusion of an adventure left dangling at the end of Chrétien's unfinished poem. The reader is not surprised to read that Arthur's knights must rescue Girflet son of Do from the Chastel Orguelleus, because Girflet had

[1] Bruce, ii. 90; Panzer, op. cit., pp. 52–56; Fourquet, op. cit., chap. iv.

[2] *Continuations*, i, pp. xlvi–lxii. On the continuations see Roach in *Romans du Graal*, pp. 107–18.

[3] On beheading challenge see Chap. 39 below; on serpent episode see Bruce, i. 89–91; on testing horn see Chap. 11 above.

[4] Newstead, op. cit., pp. 70–85; R. E. Bennett in *Spec*, xvi (1941), 34–43. See below, p. 500.

[5] For story of Guerrehés see R. E. Bennett in *Spec*, xvi (1941), 43–50. For bibliography of Swan-Knight legend see L. A. Hibbard, *Medieval Romance in England* (1924), pp. 239–52.

[6] On the role of Gauvain in the First Continuation see Frappier in *RP*, xi (1958), 331–44.

set out for that castle in Chrétien's poem.[1] Chrétien obviously intended Perceval to be the successful Grail quester. None the less he had Gauvain vow to seek the bleeding lance[2] so that even the latter's visit to the Grail castle was motivated by the original author. In many ways, the first continuator does seem to have carried out the intentions of his predecessor. But some indications of the original author are not fulfilled, and there are some contradictions.

The episode of the Grail castle is in startling contrast to Chrétien's account.[3] The Grail castle is now reached by a long causeway running out into the sea. There is no procession. The Grail has become an automatically moving food-producing vessel. The lance no longer bleeds upon the hand of a bearer, but stands in a rack and drips blood into a vessel, and is identified with the lance which pierced the side of the crucified Christ. There is a corpse on a bier and a sword broken in two which needs to be joined by the quester.

We have been discussing the First Continuation in general terms as if it were the same in all manuscripts. This is far from the truth. Even Potvin realized that it exists in a long and a short version. In fact, the manuscripts differ so widely that Roach has found it necessary to print three separate redactions which he calls respectively the mixed, the long, and the short. The length of the First Continuation ranges from about 9,500 verses to about 19,600 according to the redaction. And yet the story told is always essentially the same; the six sections enumerated above are present in all redactions and in the same order. Some additional incidents are found only in the long redaction—or, in some cases, in the long and the mixed. There are several, for example, between the first and second sections as outlined above. These include Gauvain's rescue of the damsel at Montesclaire and his obtaining of the Sword of Strange Hangings in accordance with his intention as told by Chrétien,[4] the sequel to the Guingambresil episode in Chrétien, and even an additional visit of Gauvain to the Grail castle.

Which of the redactions of the First Continuation is the original? Hugo Waitz[5] thought the short redaction was the earlier, but Jessie L. Weston[6] and Hilka[7] held the opposite view. The most recent study of the question, that of Hilmar Wrede,[8] presents evidence for the priority of the shorter redaction. Although Wrede used the materials Hilka had prepared for his projected edition of the continuations, he differs with the views of his distinguished predecessor on this point. The habit of the copyists and redactors of medieval romantic literature was to lengthen rather than to shorten. It is ordinarily to be expected that a shorter version is an earlier one.

---

[1] Ibid. vss. 4721–3.   [2] Ibid. vss. 6196–8.
[3] See below, pp. 283 f.   [4] *Percevalroman*, vss. 4701–20.
[5] *Die Fortsetzungen von Chrestiens Perceval le Gallois nach den Pariser Handschriften* (Strassburg, 1890).   [6] *Legend of Sir Perceval*, i (1906), 46–56.
[7] *Percevalroman*, p. xi.   [8] Op. cit., pp. 50–82.

It has sometimes been thought that the *Livre de Caradoc* is an interpolation, but there is no manuscript authority for that view. Ferdinand Lot thought that the remainder was the work of two successive authors.[1] The edition of Roach should make it possible to reach a final decision on such matters in the near future.

The Second Continuation

The first continuator brought the story to no conclusion; his successor, after writing 13,000 lines, had no better success. Perceval, who had scarcely been mentioned by the first continuator, now becomes the chief character again as in Chrétien. The Second Continuation is sometimes called the Perceval Continuation in contrast to the preceding Gawain Continuation. The style is now less sprightly, the adventures continue to be varied and even more worldly. Again there are signs of a longer and shorter redaction, but the differences between them are now much less marked.

Perceval turns aside from his journey to the Fisher King's castle to another castle where he plays on a magic chessboard; a beautiful maiden appears, bids him bring her the head of a white stag, and lends him her hound for the purpose. The loss of the hound gets him involved in a long series of adventures involving among others the Fair Unknown and the Handsome Coward[2]—characters found in other Arthurian stories. Other striking episodes concern a knight in a tomb, a child in a tree, and a mysterious lighted tree.[3] There are no adventures of Gauvain except in so far as he searches for Perceval. The second continuator shows a good knowledge of Chrétien's work and some familiarity also with the work of the first continuator.

The work of the second continuator ends with Perceval at the Grail castle. There is a procession—as had been the case in Chrétien, but not in the First Continuation; this time it includes Grail, bleeding lance, and broken sword. There is no corpse. Earlier it had been explained that the Grail contains Christ's blood.[4] Perceval joins the pieces of the sword, but a seam still shows, so that his Grail visit is only partially successful.

Manessier

Chrétien and two successors had not brought the story to a satisfactory

---

[1] *R*, lvii (1931), 117–36.

[2] Brugger, 'Der schöne Feigling in der arthurischen Literatur', *ZRP*, li–lvii (1941–51). Brugger considers the Handsome Coward and the Fair Unknown to be different versions of the same theme. On magic chessboard see B. Weinberg, *PMLA*, l (1935), 25–35.

[3] On the lighted tree see Brugger, *Illuminated Tree in Two Arthurian Romances* (New York, 1929); R. S. Loomis in *Annales de Bretagne*, lvi (1949), 215–17, and *Comparative Literature*, ii (1950), 298 f. On the child in the tree see E. S. Greenfield in *Traditio*, x (1954), 323–71.

[4] Ed. Potvin, vss. 28072–6.

conclusion. This was finally achieved by Manessier after he had added ten thousand more lines.[1] Nothing is known about the author except his name and the fact that he wrote at the behest of Countess Jeanne of Flanders (1206–44), grandniece of Philippe, Count of Flanders, for whom Chrétien wrote the original *Perceval*.

Perceval is the central figure again, but there are also episodes dealing with Gauvain and other knights. Manessier borrowed motifs from all three of his predecessors and also from the *Queste del Saint Graal*. In addition to the usual succoured damsels and single combats, there are encounters of Perceval with Satan in different guises.

This time Perceval has to carry out a mission of vengeance in order to heal the Fisher King. There is a procession of Grail, lance, and *tailleor*. Once again the Grail magically provides food instead of being a blood relic. At last Perceval is crowned as successor to his uncle the Fisher King; and when Perceval dies, Grail, lance, and *tailleor* are carried up to heaven.

Gerbert

Even though Manessier brought the story to a conclusion, another continuator remains to be mentioned. In two manuscripts there is a vast composition of 17,000 lines appearing as an interpolation between the Second Continuation and that of Manessier. Its author, who seems not to have known the work of Manessier, probably wrote a completion to the *Perceval* independently of him. The form in which we have it would therefore be due to a redactor who altered it at the end so that it would lead into Manessier's portion. The author of this continuation calls himself Gerbert. He is taken to be identical with Gerbert de Montreuil, author of the *Roman de la Violette*.[2] His contribution to the *Perceval* was composed probably between 1226 and 1230.[3]

There are more didactic episodes in the work of Gerbert than in other parts of the *Perceval*. The author appears to have known the *Queste del Saint Graal* and *Perlesvaus*.[4] Perhaps he was a monk. He borrowed motifs from all his predecessors. The composition ends as it began, in the midst of a visit of Perceval to the Grail castle.

---

[1] Cf. R. H. Ivy, Jr., *Manuscript Relations of Manessier's Continuation of the Old French Perceval* (Univ. of Penn. Pub. in Rom. Lang. and Lit., Philadelphia, 1951).

[2] Ed. D. L. Buffum, *SATF* (Paris, 1928); cf. C. François, *Étude sur le style de la continuation du 'Perceval' par Gerbert et du 'Roman de la Violette' par Gerbert de Montreuil* (Bibliothèque de la Faculté de philosophie et lettres de l'Université de Liège, l, Paris, 1932).

[3] Amida Stanton, *Gerbert de Montreuil as a Writer of Grail Romances* (Chicago dissertation, 1942 —unpublished except that chap. iv dealing with the date was lithoprinted).

[4] A. Hilka, 'Die geistliche Tendenz und das Motiv vom geprellten Teufel in Gerberts Gralfortsetzung', *ZRP*, liii (1933), 330 ff.; Nitze, 'The Beste Glatissant in Arthurian Romance', *ZRP*, lvi (1936), 409–18.

Conclusion

A new day is about to dawn in research on the *Perceval*, when at last the whole vast compilation will be accessible. Roach's edition is appearing at an encouraging rate. His critical comment is reserved for a final volume, so that he has not yet expressed an opinion on important issues. When the Roach edition is at last complete, and when Mary Williams likewise finishes her text of Gerbert and gives her critical commentary, previously expressed theories can be tested in the light of complete knowledge of the texts. Until that day comes, conclusions on many subjects can be only tentative.

A debate has been raging for decades on an important question: Do the prologues and continuations give an indication of the sources of Chrétien de Troyes? Did some of these authors utilize other versions of the Perceval-Grail story? Did they perhaps know the book given him by Count Philippe? This is in reality only part of the complex question of the relation of all the later Grail romances to Chrétien de Troyes.

For those who would see in the continuations the possibility of studying Chrétien's sources, the description of the Grail castle in the First Continuation, for instance, may be closer to the original story than the account given by Chrétien himself. This method has been used in some thoughtful recent books,[1] but is somewhat discredited by the rash use made of it by some earlier scholars.[2] The opposite attitude is that all later Grail stories derive from Chrétien. When they differ from his account, it is because of misunderstanding or because they are making arbitrary changes on their own initiative.[3] Neither attitude should be assumed too uncompromisingly. Chrétien mentioned a book as a source, and others might have known the same book. The contemporaries of Chrétien had access to a great deal of Celtic lore—as shown by the Celtic motifs in the various continuations—and some of it might have concerned the prototypes of Grail and lance. The patient labours of many scholars have made it increasingly likely that the basis of the Grail story, as of the Arthurian matter in general, is predominantly Celtic. On the other hand, hidden sources must not be postulated when extant documents suffice as an explanation; allowance must always be made for the originality of the medieval author of romance; the chronology of the works in question must not be completely forgotten.

On the question of the dates of the continuations, it seems best—pending the publication of Roach's final volume—to accept the conclusions of

---

[1] Loomis, *Arthurian Tradition*; Newstead, *Bran the Blessed*; Jean Marx, *La Légende arthurienne et le Graal* (Paris, 1952).

[2] Jessie L. Weston, *Legend of Sir Perceval* (London, 1906, 1909), and *Quest of the Holy Grail* (London, 1913); A. C. L. Brown, *Origin of the Grail Legend* (Cambridge, Mass., 1943); &c.

[3] A. Pauphilet, *Le Legs du Moyen Âge* (Paris, 1950), chap. vi; Wrede, op. cit., part ii, chap. v, 'Die Entwicklung der Gralsage'. This was the attitude of Bruce.

Wrede's well-documented recent dissertation. These are as follows: the first two continuations in their shorter and earlier redaction were written before 1200—soon after Chrétien and without knowledge of other Grail romances. There is an interval before the other two continuators composed their separate conclusions to the corpus. Manessier's work falls between 1214 and 1227 and Gerbert's after 1225—at a time when Robert de Boron's poem, the *Didot Perceval*, *Perlesvaus*, the *Queste del Saint Graal*, and the *Estoire del Saint Graal* were already in existence. It was only after Manessier had written his part that the longer redaction of the first two continuations came into being.

The *Perceval* with its various accretions attains a length of 60,000 or 70,000 lines. A number of authors and redactors contributed to it over a period of several decades. In general it can be said that as we pass from Chrétien through the two anonymous continuators to Manessier and Gerbert there is a decrease in literary quality with each new author. The compilation is sometimes tedious or absurd, often inconsistent, and yet contains passages of great beauty and at times of great power—all in all, an impressive monument of medieval literature.

18

WOLFRAM'S *PARZIVAL*

OTTO SPRINGER

LITTLE is known about the life of the great German poet who dealt with the Grail, Wolfram von Eschenbach.[1] No official records ever mention his name; hence, whatever we know about him is deduced from the direct or indirect evidence of his works or is based on a critical sifting of the popular tradition which grew up about him soon after his death. Although not a member of the high nobility, he took pride in being a knight, and would rather win his lady's love with lance and shield than with his song alone.

The question, once hotly debated, as to which of the various towns called Eschenbach may plume itself on being the birthplace of the poet has long been settled in favour of Wolframs-Eschenbach, an idyllic rural town a few miles south-east of Ansbach in northern Bavaria. Strongest evidence is the number of little towns and villages located in its vicinity which are mentioned in Wolfram's works. Typical examples of such names are Trühendingen (P. 184, 24 f.), whose sizzling stewpans could never be heard in famine-ridden Pel-

[1] Bibliographies of Wolfram literature have been published by G. Bötticher (1880), F. Panzer (1897), and by G. Ehrismann in his *Geschichte der deutschen Literatur im Mittelalter*, ii. 2, 1 (1927, reprint 1954) *passim*. For excellent reviews of recent scholarship see H. Rupp, *Der Deutschunterricht* (1953), pp. 82–90; Mergell in *Euphorion*, xlvii (1953), 431–51; Eggers in *Wirkendes Wort*, iv (1953–4), 274–90; H. Kuhn in *DVLG*, xxx (1956), 161–200. For general treatments see Ehrismann, loc. cit., pp. 212–97; F. Vogt, *Geschichte der mittelhochdeutschen Literatur*, 3rd ed. (1922), i. 257–315; J. Schwietering, *Die deutsche Dichtung des Mittelalters* (1941), pp. 160–83; H. Schneider, *Heldendichtung, Geistlichendichtung, Ritterdichtung*, 2nd ed. (1943), pp. 293–312; Kuhn in *Annalen der deutschen Literatur*, ed. H. O. Burger (1952), pp. 144–51; Hartl in *Die deutsche Literatur des Mittelalters*; *Verfasserlexikon* (1953), iv, 1058–91; H. de Boor, *Die höfische Literatur* (1953), pp. 90–127; Halbach in *Deutsche Philologie im Aufriß*, ed. W. Stammler, ii (1954), 596–617. The best editions of Wolfram's works are those of A. Leitzmann (Halle, 1947–50), from which quotations are taken; K. Lachmann, 7th ed. (Berlin, 1952), i (only *Lieder, Parzival*, and *Titurel*); E. Martin (Halle, 1900–3; only *Parzival* and *Titurel*; valuable commentary in vol. ii); K. Bartsch, 4th ed., rev. by M. Marti (Leipzig, 1927–9). There is a complete translation of *Parzival* into English by J. L. Weston (London, 1894), and translations of the major parts by M. F. Richey (Oxford, 1935) and E. H. Zeydel (Chapel Hill, 1951). Translations into modern German are those of W. Hertz (Stuttgart, 1898, with valuable notes); W. Stapel, 4th ed. (Munich, 1950); F. Knorr and R. Fink (Jena, 1943). There are French translations by M. Wilmotte (Paris, 1933); E. Tonnelat (Paris, 1934). Valuable monographs are: A. Schreiber, *Neue Bausteine zu einer Lebensgeschichte Wolframs von Eschenbach* (Frankfurt, 1922); G. Weber, *Wolfram von Eschenbach, seine dichterische und geistesgeschichtliche Bedeutung* (Frankfurt, 1928); B. Mergell, *Wolfram von Eschenbach und seine französischen Quellen*, ii (Münster, 1943); W. J. Schröder, *Der Ritter zwischen Gott und Welt* (Weimar, 1952); Weber, *Parzival. Ringen und Vollendung* (Oberursel, 1948); M. F. Richey, *Studies of Wolfram von Eschenbach* (Edinburgh, 1957). For a fine analysis of Parzival's spiritual growth see W. T. H. Jackson in *Germanic Rev.*, xxxiii (1958), 118–24.

rapeire; Nördeling (Wh. 295, 16), Regensburg (P. 377, 30); whereas the repeatedly mentioned Speht(e)shart (P. 216, 12; Wh. 96, 16; 377, 25) may refer to the well-known mountain range between Frankfurt and Würzburg, the Spessart, or to a small wood of the same name west of Eschenbach.[1]

The name of Wildenberg, on the other hand, which Wolfram compares with the castle of the Grail (P. 230, 13), has remained controversial to the present day. Scholars have suspected that the German poet's Munsalvaesche, i.e. *mons silvaticus*, is nothing but Wolfram's own playful translation of the German name. Although probably no one will ever be able to prove it, whoever has seen the picturesque ruins of Wildenberg rise above the wooded heights of the lonesome Odenwald will indeed be tempted to see in it the castle which gave Wolfram shelter while he composed the Grail episode of his *Parzival*. Its grand late Romanesque architecture may have suggested to him some of the features not found in the Old French description of the castle of the Holy Grail.[2]

While we remain sceptical as to the identification of Wildenberg, there can be no doubt that, like Heinrich von Veldeke, Walther von der Vogelweide, and others, Wolfram, too, stayed for a while at the literary centre of greatest renown during his lifetime, at the court of Landgrave Hermann von Thüringen (1155–1217) in Eisenach. He praises this patron of the arts (P. 297, 16–30), whose generosity attracted people of all sorts, 'boese unde guot', as he quotes Walther addressing the motley gathering of talent at the court. Slyly, Wolfram wonders whether the good landgrave was not more in need than King Arthur of as intrepid and intimidating a seneschal as Keie (P. 297, 16–30).

Contemporary and personal allusions of this kind are characteristic of the German poet's style. So we learn that Wolfram was not blessed with an excess of worldly goods. In his home, he jokes wryly, even the mice have difficulty in finding enough to eat (P. 184, 29 ff.). That he nevertheless enjoyed a very happy family life, we may infer here and there by reading between the lines. That he travelled extensively and was particularly well acquainted with parts of Steiermark, we gather from the detailed topography of Trevrizent's journey (P. 496, 1 ff.) and other passages.

However, we are less inclined to take him seriously when he prides himself on being illiterate, 'ich enkan deheinen buochstap' (P. 115, 27), and 'swaz an den buochen stêt geschriben, des bin ich künstelôs beliben' (Wh. 2, 19 f.). The meticulous planning of the structure of his *Parzival*, the mass of

[1] Schreiber, op. cit., pp. 81–88; Ehrismann, op. cit., pp. 214 f.; J. B. Kurz, *Wolfram von Eschenbach; ein Buch vom größten Dichter des deutschen Mittelalters* (Ansbach, 1930), pp. 5–12. See also 'Wolfram Map' in F. Panzer, *Bibliographie zu Wolfram von Eschenbach*, appendix.

[2] S. Singer in *Sitzungsberichte d. Wiener Akad.*, phil.-hist. Kl., clxxx. 4 (1916), pp. 89 f.; Schreiber, op. cit., pp. 36–58; Kurz, op. cit., pp. 20–23; P. A. Albert, *Die 'Gralburg' Wildenberg im Odenwald und die historische Kritik* (Buchen, 1949).

scientific lore which he parades before and imposes on the reader, as in the passage devoted to a description of precious stones (P. 791, 1–30) and that of the kings defeated by Feirefiz (P. 770, 1–30), each section being exactly thirty lines in length—all this, in addition to his wide knowledge of medieval literature, can hardly be ascribed to an illiterate artist. With his ironical boasting he merely protests against the manner in which some of his fellow artists—we may think of Hartmann von Aue—seem to make their own book-learning a measure of poetic achievement.[1]

References to contemporary poets and works of poetry, whether explicit or not, give us at the same time very definite clues concerning the date when *Parzival* was composed. In Book III (143, 21 ff.) Wolfram mentions Hartmann's *Erek*, which was written between 1190 and 1195; Books V (253, 10 ff.) and IX (436, 5 ff.) allude to Lunete's frivolous counsel in *Iwein*, Hartmann's last work. Wirnt von Gravenberg, who by 1204 had completed the first two-thirds of his *Wigalois*, begins from vs. 6343 on to follow Wolfram as his master.[2] These dates are very strikingly confirmed by a few specific historical events referred to in Wolfram's *Parzival*. Toward the end of Book VII (379, 18 f.) the poet speaks of the trampled-down vineyards of Erfurt—no doubt the result of the siege in 1203 of Erfurt by Wolfram's patron, Landgrave Hermann von Thüringen. Book XI contains a statement about the *former* wealth of the Greek emperor (563, 8 ff.) and is therefore believed to have been written after the fall of Constantinople in April 1204. On the other hand, we know that Wolfram's other two works, *Willehalm* and *Titurel*, fall between 1212 and 1220. Hence the date of his *Parzival* may safely be placed between 1200 and 1212.[3]

As already indicated, the *Parzival* did not at once become known in its entirety to the poet's contemporaries. The inference drawn from Wirnt's *Wigalois* that Books I to VI were first made public as a separate unit is confirmed by the sixty verses between Books VI and VII not found

---

[1] Ehrismann, op, cit., p. 218 and notes 2–4; Kurz, op. cit., pp. 193–203. For recent discussions of Wolfram's literacy see E. H. Zeydel in *Euphorion*, xlviii (1954), 210–15; H. Adolf in *Deutsche Literaturzeitung*, lxxvi (1955), 741 f; W. T. H. Jackson in *Germanic Reveiw* xxxiii (1958), 118 f.

[2] For Wolfram's relationship to Eilhart's *Tristrant* see Eggers in *Beiträge*, lxxii (1950), 39–51, and Ehrismann, op. cit., p. 221 and n. 2. To Veldeke's *Eneide*, see F. Panzer, *Gahmuret* (Heidelberg, 1940), pp. 13 f., 20, 34, 49, 71 f., and Ehrismann, p. 219, n. 1. To Hartmann's *Erek*, see Wesle in *Beiträge*, lxxii (1950), 1–15; Ehrismann, p. 220, n. 1; Singer, loc. cit., pp. 56–61. To *Gregorius* see p. 229, n. 3 below. To *Iwein* see H. Schneider in *Sitzungsberichte d. Bayer. Akad.*, phil.-hist Kl., 1944–6, pp. 32–46. To Walther von der Vogelweide see Rompelmann in *Neo*, xxvii (1942), 185–205; xxxiv (1950), 15–20; and Ehrismann, op. cit., p. 221, n. 5. Concerning the controversial relation to *Nibelungenlied* see Ehrismann, p. 222 and n. 1.

[3] The most important discussion of chronology is by L. Wolff in *ZDA*, lxi (1924), 181–92, with the following conclusions: V. 227, 9 written shortly after 1200; VI. 297, 16 in 1201–2; VII. 379, 18 in the autumn of 1203 or in 1204–5; VIII. 403, 26 after 25 May, 1204; XI. 563, 8 after April 1204. See also Vogt, op. cit., pp. 259 f.; Schreiber, op. cit., pp. 59–71; Ehrismann, op. cit., pp. 216 f., 232 and n. 1: E. Cucuel, *Die Eingangsbücher des Parzival und das Gesamtwerk* (Frankfurt, 1927), pp. 5–7; Kurz, op. cit., pp. 90 f.

in most manuscripts. In them the author expresses the hope of continuing at some later date, depending on the encouragement which he expects from his unnamed lady love. Moreover, while the first six books tell of Parzival up to the time when, cursed by Cundrie, he leaves King Arthur's court together with Gawan, who has been challenged to show his knightly prowess anew, Books VII and VIII are almost exclusively devoted to Gawan's adventures. Book IX returns to Parzival and the dispute with his hermit-uncle Trevrizent, Books X to XIII again concentrate on Gawan, Book XIV culminates in the meeting of Gawan and Parzival, Book XV in that of Parzival and his half-brother Feirefiz. Book XVI concludes with Parzival's second journey to Munsalvaesche and his enthronement as King of the Holy Grail. No doubt Wolfram's poem is on the whole the story of Perceval as told by Chrétien in his *Perceval*. But there is nothing in Chrétien's unfinished work which corresponds to the two introductory Books as well as to the last three and a half Books, to certain features which Wolfram ascribes to the Grail, and to large parts of Book IX of his *Parzival*.

What has the poet himself to say, however, concerning the source of his work? As was customary with medieval authors, at the very end of the poem, and only there, Wolfram mentions Chrétien by name:

> Ob von Troies meister Kristjân   dô in verworhte Amfortas.
> disem mære hât unreht getân,   von Provenze in tiuschiu lant
> daz mac wol zürnen Kîot.   diu rehten mære uns sint gesant
> der uns diu rehten mære entbôt,   und dirre âventiure endes zil.
> endehaft giht der Provenzâl,   niht mêr dâ von nû sprechen wil
> wie Herzeloiden kint den grâl   ich Wolfram von Eschenbach,
> erwarp, als im daz gordent was,   wan als dort der meister sprach.[1]

(If master Chrétien of Troyes has not done justice to this, Kyot has every right to be angry, he who has presented us with the authentic tale. In conclusion the Provençal relates how Herzeloide's son, as he was destined, acquired the Grail when it was forfeited by Anfortas. From Provence the authentic tale has been transmitted to us into Germany, with all its happenings to the very end. No more do I wish to say about it now, I, Wolfram von Eschenbach, than what my master there reported.)

No doubt, the German poet knew that Chrétien had written a poem on the same subject. However, he appears to be critical of Chrétien's version— he prefers 'Kyot from Provence'. This Kyot is invoked in five other passages, three times in a very brief and casual manner, as in VIII. 431, 2, 'ich sage iu als Kîot las', XV. 776, 10, 'ob Kîot die wârheit sprach', and XVI. 805, 10, 'ob der Provenzâl die wârheit las'. Two other passages, however, go into almost bewildering detail:

---

[1] *Parzival*, 827, 1–14.

der was geheizen Liddamus.   Kîôt ist ein Provenzâl,
Kîôt in selbe nennet sus.   der dise âventiur von Parzivâl
Kîôt laschantiure hiez,   heidensch geschriben sach.
den sîn kunst des niht erliez, swaz er en franzois dâ von gesprach,
er ensünge und spræche sô,   bin ich niht der witze laz,
des noch genuoge werdent vrô.   daz sage ich tiuschen vürbaz.[1]

(He was named Liddamus. Kyot himself calls him thus. Kyot's own epithet was *laschantiure,* he who by his art was so inspired that he would sing and tell only in such a way as to bring joy to many people. Kyot is a Provençal who saw this story of Parzival written in the heathen tongue. Whatever he told of it in French that I shall tell in German, unless I am devoid of wit.)

The most elaborate passage, 453, 5–455, 12, describes the supposed source of Kyot, the work of a half-Jew called Flegetanis on the history of the Grail, which Kyot found, cast aside in the city of Toledo in Spain. This Flegetanis, whose father was a pagan, is alleged to have been a great astronomer who had read the name of the Grail in the stars. According to Flegetanis a host of angels had left the Grail on earth where only the chaste of the Christian faith might guard it. Without any knowledge of necromancy Kyot was able to decipher the strange characters in which this heathen (i.e. Arabic) book was written and to understand its contents, thanks to his Christian baptism. He then began to search in Latin books for a people that might be suitable to take care of the Grail. He read chronicles of various countries, of Britain, France, and Ireland, and he found at last (455, 12) in a chronicle of Anschouwe—doubtless Anjou in France—the story of Mazadan and how the Grail descended in succession to Titurel, to his son Frimutel, and to Frimutel's son, Anfortas, who was Parzival's maternal uncle and keeper of the Grail at the time that Parzival visited the Grail castle.[2]

It is easy to see that Wolfram's statements about Kyot[3] are not without contradictions within themselves. Kyot hails from Provence but writes in French; his name reflects a French *Guiot,* which again is 'franzois' because it would be *Guizot* in Provençal. The suggestion that Wolfram's Provenz and Provenzâl refer to the name of the city, Provins, is not plausible; moreover, Wolfram does know the name of that city and refers to it in his *Willehalm* (437, 11); the form there is Provîs, while Provenz and Provenzâl in the same poem designate the whole surrounding district. Furthermore, while

---

[1] *Parzival,* 416, 19–30.   [2] Bruce, i. 316 f.

[3] For scholars before 1923 favouring Kyot as Wolfram's principal source see Ehrismann, op. cit., p. 235 n. Of these Singer presented the strongest case. For those who reject Kyot entirely see ibid., p. 236, n. 1; also Schwietering, op. cit., pp. 160 f.; Walshe in *MLR,* xliii (1948), 514–19; Wesle, loc. cit. Kyot is accepted as Wolfram's secondary source by Weber, *Wolfram von Eschenbach,* esp. pp. 52 f., 128 f., 132, 141–50, 308–15; Schreiber in *ZRP,* xlviii (1928), 1–52; Schneider, *Heldendichtung,* pp. 301–4, 562, and *Parzival-Studien* (Munich, 1947), *passim.* Scholte has come out for a modified Kyot-thesis in *Neo,* xxxiii (1949), 23–26, and so has Zeydel in *Neo,* xxxiv (1950), 11–18; xxxvi (1952), 21–32; xxxvii (1953), 25–35; *MLN,* lxvii (1952), 377–81.

Kyot is labelled a *chanteur*, that is, a singer and lyrical poet, Wolfram credits him with a long narrative poem. Little is gained by Singer's interpretation of *laschantiure* as (*l'*)*enchanteur*—why should Kyot be called a magician?

And then the fantastic tales about the source of this source! It had been recorded, originally, in Arabic by Flegetanis, a name which has nothing to do with the Grail tradition, whether it reflects Arabic *Felek thani*, the title of a treatise on *sphaera altera*, or, as others have thought, a distorted form of Phlegethon, the river in Hades. There are, furthermore, the curious ancestry of this half-Jew, the equally strange combination of historical interests and poetic talent in Kyot, his hunting around in chronicles of all sorts, and finally, the forced association of the Grail tradition with the Angevin dynasty. No wonder that few have ever taken the story of Kyot's source very seriously. It sounds too much like dozens of imaginary source citations in medieval works.

On the other hand, inconsistent as it may seem, Kyot himself as the immediate source of Wolfram's *Parzival* has been neither so readily nor so generally discounted. He was eagerly identified with the French poet Guiot de Provins, who in the early part of the thirteenth century composed a satirical poem entitled *La Bible* and wrote some lyrical verse in addition. Since *La Bible* itself could not possibly represent Wolfram's source, Guiot was credited with another large work, which concerned the Grail and which is now lost without a trace, although, if we give credence to Wolfram, it was an outstanding work, complete and more authentic than Chrétien's *Perceval*. In style, to judge by his *Bible*, Guiot was pedestrian, obvious, and satirical rather than fanciful, obscure, and humorous, as we should expect him to be if these well-known features of Wolfram's style were actually inspired by Guiot. Further, Guiot in *La Bible* shows an unmistakable dislike for the Templars, whom Wolfram admires.

In the light of these and similar considerations, a growing number of scholars have abandoned Kyot as *the* major source—a source which was supposedly complete and thus not only provided Wolfram with raw material for whatever his *Parzival* has in excess of Chrétien, but also, as Singer suggested, imposed on him most of the features of his style. Instead, with the pendulum swinging to the other extreme, there are many who insist on Chrétien's *Perceval* as Wolfram's one and only source. Whatever differed in content, form, and underlying ideas was Wolfram's own, was due to his creative genius. This view seemed to be sanctioned by philological evidence as the comparison of Wolfram's Middle High German text with the Old French version of Chrétien became more readily accessible through the publication of Chrétien's poem by Hilka in 1932. The unavoidably sporadic checks made by Rochat, Küpp, Lichtenstein, Heller, Paetzel, and others, were now continued more systematically in the minute investigations of

Rachbauer, Fourquet, and, especially, Bodo Mergell.[1] One thing clearly emerged from these studies, namely that for long stretches of Books III through XIII Wolfram's *Parzival* shows similarities to Chrétien's work which are understandable only if Chrétien was Wolfram's source. These similarities simply leave no room for any *main* source other than Chrétien.

On the other hand, Wolfram's *Parzival* is no word-for-word translation from the French, comparable, let us say, to Wisse and Colin's translation of parts of the *Continuations*. Indeed, there are differences in content as well as in form and in general perspectives. Many of these differences, especially in the last two categories, are very convincingly attributed to Wolfram, because, as Mergell demonstrated, Wolfram's *Willehalm* shows the same differences in form and in leading ideas as compared with the Old French original. Moreover, for *Willehalm*, we are not plagued by the spectre of Kyot: we know that the French *chanson de geste*, *La Bataille d'Aliscans*, is Wolfram's source, and that wherever the German poem differs it is the German poet who has recast the older French epic. Incidentally, Wolfram's citation of Chrétien as the source of *Willehalm* (125, 20 ff.) is not likely to enhance our faith in any similar protestations. As we compare *Parzival* with Chrétien's *Perceval*, we shall have occasion, again and again, to point out features which we believe show Wolfram at work.

Still, there remains a residue of discrepancies between the two works which we find difficult to attribute to Wolfram's creative imagination. There is the Gahmuret prelude of Books I and II, there are the last three and a half Books, there is much additional lore about the Grail, and there are throughout Wolfram's poem certain details which coincide with traditions reflected in other sources to such a degree that we hesitate to accept them as Wolfram's original invention. In fact, modern Wolfram scholarship seems to be more and more persuaded of Wolfram's inclination to draw on a motley array of sources which he, with a certain impish delight, weaves into the texture of his poem, covering them with the general denomination 'Kyot', in accord with the medieval practice of appealing to literary predecessors.

A very illuminating case in point is the Gahmuret prelude of Books I and II.[2] It used to be ascribed to Kyot by people like Singer, while others praised

---

[1] There have been many comparisons of *Parzival* with Chrétien's *Perceval*. See especially Ehrismann, op. cit., pp. 237–46 (a convenient summary); Weber, *Wolfram von Eschenbach*, i. 1–152; M. Paetzel, *Wolfram von Eschenbach und Crestien von Troyes* (Berlin, 1931); M. A. Rachbauer, *Wolfram von Eschenbach, A Study of the Relation of the Content of Bks. III–VI and IX of the Parzival* (Washington, 1934); J. Fourquet, *Wolfram d'Eschenbach et le Conte del Graal* (Paris, 1938); Mergell, op. cit.; Weigand in *PMLA*, liii (1938), 917–50; Richey in *MLR*, xlvii (1952), 350–61; Mergell in *Anzeiger für deutsches Altertum*, lviii (1939), 121–5; W. Kellermann, *Aufbaustil und Weltbild Chrestiens von Troyes im Percevalroman* (*Beihefte zur ZRP*, lxxxviii, 1936); and below, pp. 290–3.

[2] M. F. Richey, *Gahmuret Anschevin* (Oxford, 1923); E. Cucuel, op. cit.; F. Panzer, *Gahmuret*; Mergell, op. cit., pp. 313–33; Hatto in *ZDA*, lxxxiv (1953), 232–40.

or condemned it as Wolfram's own work of fancy. In 1940, however, F. Panzer in elaboration of some older suggestions presented a very plausible case for Wolfram's use of several sources, such as the Old French *Ipomedon* by Hue de Rotelande for the Belakane-Feirefiz chapter, and the story of Joufrois for Book II, Gahmuret and Herzeloide. Moreover, Panzer is convinced that Wolfram took some of his inspiration from the events of the day, and thus in the figure of Gahmuret erected a poetic monument to the most glamorous knight and crusader of his time, a member of the house of Anjou, Richard the Lion-heart. Others have argued that the glorification of the Anjou dynasty, too, could not have originated with the German poet but must be derived from a medieval French source.[1] Many of the details, however, such as the siege of Zazamanc or Gahmuret's conquest of Belakane, according to Panzer and others, are recastings by Wolfram of events of Book IV, in this case of the siege of Pelrapeire and of Parzival's winning the love and the hand of Condwiramurs.[2]

Of course, there also is the so-called *Bliocadran* prologue, extant in L and P of the manuscripts of Chrétien's *Perceval*, which likewise tries to furnish a more detailed account of the unhappy fate of Perceval's kin and to explain thus the mother's concern and her decision to rear the boy in the solitude of the forest.[3] Again opinion is divided whether Wolfram knew and used this particular prologue. Panzer[4] believes that he did if the *Bliocadran* prologue can be dated as early as the last decade of the twelfth century. More plausible are the arguments advanced by R. S. Loomis[5] for his assumption that the *Bliocadran* prologue and the corresponding part of Wolfram's *Vorgeschichte* had a common source.

The Gahmuret episode in Wolfram's *Parzival* is preceded by the much-debated introduction (1, 1–4, 26), the major part of which deals with his literary antipode, Gottfried von Strassburg. Only the first few lines, the so-called *Vorspruch* (1, 1–14), sound the principal theme of the entire work: man beset by doubt (*zwîvel*), that is, 'unbelief, defection from God'. The result of doubt is a situation in which man partakes of both heaven and hell, *staete* and *unstaete*, or, as the poet metaphorically puts it, white and black in

---

[1] W. Snelleman, *Das Haus Anjou und der Orient in Wolframs Parzival* (Nijkerk, 1941); see critique by Schwietering in *ZDA*, lxxxi (1944), 51 f.; Bruce, i. 321 f.; W. Golther, *Parzival und der Gral in der Dichtung des Mittelalters und der Neuzeit* (Stuttgart, 1925), pp. 141 f., 159, 181 f.; Weber, *Wolfram von Eschenbach*, pp. 53, 142 f.; M. Wilmotte, *Le Poème du Graal* (Paris, 1933), p. 19; Panzer, *Gahmuret*, pp. 59–70; Mergell, op. cit., pp. 146 f., 170 f.

[2] Panzer, *Gahmuret*, pp. 8, 78 n.; Ehrismann, op. cit., p. 244, notes 1–4.

[3] Included in Hilka's edition of Chrétien's *Perceval*, pp. 498–501. See Chap. 17 above. For opinions about the possible influence on Wolfram see Bruce, ii. 85–90; Schwietering in *ZDA*, lxi (1924), 71–73; Ehrismann, op. cit., p. 244, n. 1; Brugger in *Medieval Studies in Memory of G. Schoepperle Loomis* (Paris, 1927), p. 152, and in *ZFSL*, liii (1930), 437; Lot in *R*, lvii (1931), 135; Panzer, *Gahmuret*, pp. 53–56; Fourquet, op. cit., pp. 105–16; and pp. 291 f. below.

[4] *Gahmuret*, pp. 55 f.

[5] *Arthurian Tradition*, pp. 347 ff.

magpie wise. Yet, for an individual like Parzival, whose very nature is *triuwe*, 'consistent loving devotion', as pointed out in vss. 4, 9–26, Wolfram asserts that this *zwîvel* may be the very experience to bring his personality to full bloom and maturity. How fast or how slowly he matures matters little. Indeed, he may well be 'trâclîche wîs', 'slowly wise', as Wolfram here at the very outset characterizes his hero's gradual inner growth in a singularly pregnant phrase.[1]

From the beginning of the Third Book of *Parzival* to the middle of Book XIII we are able to compare the narrative almost step by step with Chrétien's text. There are, nevertheless, a great many discrepancies in detail, in motivation and characterization, which will be briefly discussed in the following analysis in order to bring into focus what has happened to Arthurian tradition in Wolfram's hands.

The French poem opens with the young hero's encounter with the Arthurian knights, and only, in retrospect do we get occasional glimpses into Perceval's life in the solitude of the forest (vss. 69–99). Wolfram, on the other hand, in three times as many lines (117, 7–120, 10) gradually unfolds the idyl of Parzival's *Waldleben* before our eyes. And, what is more important, he develops at the very outset some of the most characteristic and fateful traits in the growing youth—the unconscious longing for adventure which swells his breast, his dissolving in tears of compassion, and his pleading for the little birds, culminating in young Parzival's question: 'ouwê, muoter, waz ist got?'[2] ('Alas, mother, what is God?').

The fact that there is nothing corresponding to all this in Chrétien, while the Middle English *Sir Perceval of Galles*[3] has these lines: 'He was fosterde in the felle, He dranke water of þe welle, And ȝitt was he wyghte', and the Welsh *Peredur*[4] shows certain resemblances, has caused some speculation as to whether or not Wolfram here, as supposedly elsewhere, followed sources other than Chrétien. While Jessie Weston, Strucks, and R. S. Loomis favour the possibility that Wolfram, *Sir Perceval*, and *Peredur* derived these

---

[1] On the Prologue see K. Lachmann, *Kleinere Schriften* (Berlin, 1876), i. 480–518; Ehrismann in *ZDA*, xlix (1908), pp. 413–21; H. Adolf in *Neo*, xxii (1937), 116–20, 171–85, and in *JEGP*, xlix (1950), 285–303; and articles of Schröder and Hempel in *ZDA*, lxxxiii (1951–2), 130–43, 162–80.

[2] Vogt, op. cit., p. 284; Golther, op. cit., pp. 118–34; Ehrismann, op. cit., p. 238; Mergell, op. cit., pp. 13–20; Loomis, *Arthurian Tradition*, pp. 355–40; Richey in *MLR*, xlvii (1952), 354.

[3] Ed. Campion and Holthausen (Heidelberg, 1913), vss. 6–8. On *Sir Perceval* see Chap. 37 below. On its relation to *Parzival* see C. Strucks, *Der junge Parzival* (Borna-Leipzig, 1910), pp. 8–57; Ehrismann, op. cit., p. 234, and notes 1, 2; Golther, op. cit., pp. 118 ff.; Weber, *Wolfram von Eschenbach*, pp. 94–104.

[4] On *Peredur* see Chap. 16 above. On relationship to Chrétien and Wolfram see Mühlhausen in *ZRP*, xliv (1924), 465–543, and replies of Zenker and Weisgerber in *RF*, xl (1927), 251–329, 483–93; Ehrismann, op. cit., pp. 137, 235; Golther, op. cit., pp. 109 ff.; Weber, *Wolfram von Eschenbach*, pp. 90–94; M. R. Williams, *Essai sur la composition du roman gallois de Peredur* (Paris, 1909), pp. 81–95; and Loomis, *Arthurian Tradition*, pp. 344 f., 354.

points of agreement from a common source, others, like Mergell and Mühlhausen, are sceptical. I agree with the latter, as far as the *Waldleben* is concerned; the similarity is too vague.

As for young Parzival's question, 'ouwê, muoter, waz ist got?', that has been so superbly motivated by Wolfram through the device of Herzeloide's casual reference to the Almighty, who is Lord also over the little birds, that without any doubt this dramatic climax, foreshadowing future fateful events, was created by Wolfram and no one else. Why should we continue to hunt for dubious parallels and unknown sources to which to credit all artistic talent and invention that we find in a work such as *Parzival*? Why not rather credit such talent and invention to the poets well known to us? If we analyse our medieval romances, and in this particular case Wolfram's *Parzival*, from the point of view of their total structure, we become aware that almost the same question as that addressed to his mother is asked by Parzival after he has been cursed by Cundrie and is about to leave Arthur's court—again motivated through a casual reference to God, this time by Gawan:

> 'dâ gebe dir *got* gelücke zuo
> und helfe ouch mir, daz ich getuo
> dir noch den dienst, als ich kan gern.
> des müeze mich sîn kraft gewern.'
> der Wâleis sprach: 'wê, waz ist *got*?'[1]

('May God grant you success in this and help me, too, that I may be able to serve you as I desire. May God's might grant me this.' Parzival said: 'Alas, what is God?')

In this passage, too, the idea is altogether Wolfram's own since neither Chrétien nor any of the other sources referred to have any counterpart.

The detailed analysis of this particular motif enables us to continue our comparison of Chrétien's and Wolfram's poems with a better understanding of the liberties which the German poet was capable of taking with his French source.

On the whole, in treating the events which follow, Wolfram deviates little from Chrétien's account. He has shortened considerably the story of Parzival's encounter with the four knights (Chrétien has five), whose leader Karnahkarnanz is addressed as *got*, *helferîcher got*, and *ritter got* by the young boy. The German poet gives a much less colourful picture of the external pride and glory of the representatives of King Arthur's world, and he omits all religious ceremonies.[2] Also the remainder of his sojourn at his mother's home is described much more briefly by Wolfram, and the character of young Parzival appears in a somewhat milder light. He is not the callous youngster

---

[1] *Parzival*, 331, 27–332, 1.
[2] Lichtenstein in *Beiträge*, xxii (1897), 10 ff.; Bruce, i. 340 n.; Ehrismann, op. cit., pp. 238 f.; Mergell, op. cit., pp. 20–25.

who treats his mother rudely and rides away even though he sees her swoon and fall to the ground. Wolfram's Parzival does not realize his mother's anguish, which breaks her heart as soon as she loses sight of her one and only child. This is an important difference, for Perceval, according to Chrétien, later fails to ask the question because of this moral failing.[1] Wolfram's story of the young fool's encounter with the damsel of the tent, though less colourful and grotesque, follows Chrétien rather closely,[2] except for a long boastful speech by Orilus de Lalander (Chrétien mentions the name of Orguelleus de la Lande only much later, vs. 3817). This quite obviously is borrowed from Hartmann's *Erek*[3] and *Iwein*, or their French originals.[4]

Much more significant is Wolfram's transformation of Chrétien's anonymous *pucele* or *dameisele*. While Perceval meets her only once after the first and unfortunate visit to the Grail castle (vss. 3454–90), Wolfram's Parzival sees his cousin Sigune, as she is called, on four different occasions, each time at a crucial point of his inner struggle.[5] In contrast to Chrétien, Wolfram has placed the first meeting of Parzival and Sigune at a point in the narrative preceding his visit to Gurnemanz and to the castle of the Grail, most probably in order to reveal his hero's true name and genealogical descent, and also Parzival's inherited moral characteristic of *triuwe*, that is, loving devotion.[6] As Parzival rides on toward King Arthur's court, he finds shelter with a gruff fisherman, an episode which was suggested by Chrétien's *charbonier* (vs. 859 f.) but was remodelled by Wolfram in accordance with a very similar character in Hartmann's *Gregorius*. The literary precursor here is clear since the contemporary German poet is mentioned and comes in for some rather caustic remarks.[7]

Like Chrétien's Perceval, Wolfram's hero before arriving at Arthur's court meets the 'Red Knight' (*li vermaux chevaliers*), who is called Ither von Gaheviez—no doubt in accordance with Hartmann's *Iher Gaheries* (*Erek*, vs. 1658).[8] Parzival's unchivalrous slaying of Ither, whom he mistakes

---

[1] Ehrismann, op. cit., p. 239; Mergell, op. cit., pp. 35 f., 216 ff.; Richey in *MLR*, xlvii. 353.

[2] Pschmadt in *ZDA*, lv (1914), 63–75; Ehrismann, op. cit., p. 239, n. 3; Mergell, op. cit., pp. 36–48; Hatto in *MLR*, xlii (1947), 244.   [3] See below, p. 434.

[4] Singer in *Sitzungsberichte d. Wiener Akad.*, phil.-hist. Kl., clxxx. 4 (1916), 75 f.; Ehrismann, op. cit., p. 240; Mergell, op. cit., p. 42.

[5] Lichtenstein, loc. cit., pp. 15, 36–38; Bruce, i. 333, n. 35; Golther, op. cit., pp. 158 ff.; Ehrismann, op. cit., p. 240; Rachbauer, op. cit., pp. 75, 153–7; Mergell, op. cit., pp. 141–8.

[6] *Parzival*, 138, 9–142, 1. Concerning the name Perceval or Parzival see Bartsch in *ZRP*, ii (1878), 309; Hertz's translation, n. 59; Ehrismann, p. 246; Mergell, op. cit., pp. 145 f.; Loomis, *Arthurian Tradition*, pp. 341–6.

[7] *Parzival*, 143, 21–144, 4. On the gruff fisherman see Singer, loc. cit., pp. 71 f.; Schröder in *ZDA*, liii (1916), 398–400; Vogt, op. cit., p. 283; Ehrismann, op. cit., p. 241; Mergell, op. cit., pp. 48 ff.; Richey in *MLR*, xlvii (1952), 355.

[8] On Red Knight see Küpp in *ZDP*, xvii (1885), 16 ff.; Lichtenstein, loc. cit., pp. 16 ff.; Hertz's translation (1898), p. 494; Singer, loc. cit., pp. 74 f.; Scholte in *Neo*, v (1920), 115–21; Golther, op. cit., p. 151; Richey in *MLR*, xxvi (1931), 315–29; Strucks, op. cit., pp. 43–46, 61, 65; Loomis, *Arthurian Tradition*, pp. 356 f.; Kellermann, op. cit., p. 11; Mergell, op. cit., p. 49, n. 72.

for Lehelin (i.e. Llewelyn), is a serious matter which according to Wolfram he will regret on some future occasion (161, 7 f.).[1]

The education in the ways of chivalry which the young hero receives from the wise old man, Gurnemanz (Old French Gornemant), is essentially the same in Chrétien and in Wolfram. Only the sequence of the various fields of instruction differs: Wolfram does not place the use of weapons first but, quite significantly, religious and ethical teachings, then initiation into the art of handling sword and spear, and last but not least, an introduction to the code of courtly love.[2] And to this Wolfram adds what has no counterpart in Chrétien's work, the family idyl of the budding knight's gentle affection for Liaze, handsome daughter and only surviving child of his kindly host. Also, while Chrétien refers only in passing to the death of a brother of Gornemant, Wolfram has his Gurnemanz survive the death of three sons whose names and fates he culled from the story of Erek. Incidentally, the figure of Liaze, too, whose name remains unexplained, has its counterpart and probable model in one of Hartmann's characters, namely Enite, who in *Erek* wins the hero's love (vss. 314 ff.)—Enite, too, and her impoverished father are seated at the dinner table with their guest, like Liaze and Gurnemanz. Even the picturesque sparrow-hawk which perches on the host's hand as the guest arrives figures in both passages.[3]

Wolfram's narrative of the siege of Pelrapeire and of Parzival's meeting with, liberation of, and marriage to the mistress of the city in Book IV differs from Chrétien only in two major respects.[4] Here, more than anywhere else, in describing the beleaguered town and its starving inhabitants, the German poet indulges in humorous allusions and digressions of a very personal sort: here we have the reference to the Trühendingen stewpans which no one would hear sizzle in Pelrapeire (184, 24 f.); the mockery directed at the poverty of his own home, where even the mice must steal their food (184, 27–185, 8); the teasing of his feudal lord, the Count of Wertheim, who would hate to be a soldier in that town (184, 4 f.). The other significant deviation from Chrétien is Wolfram's version of Parzival's attitude to the mistress of Pelrapeire. Chrétien's Perceval has an *affaire d'amour* with Blancheflor of Belrepeire, though there seems little doubt that it stopped short of carnal union. Wolfram, on the other hand, portrays his Parzival as naively ignorant at first.[5] Even after their official wedding they both remain

---

[1] On traces of an older tradition and the vengeance quest see Bruce, i. 333, n. 34; Ehrismann, op. cit., p. 234, n. 2; Richey in *MLR*, xlvii. 356; and especially Loomis, *Arthurian Tradition*, pp. 394–415.

[2] Lichtenstein, loc. cit., pp. 21 ff.; Golther, op. cit., pp. 153 f.; Ehrismann, op. cit., p. 241; Keferstein, *Parzivals ethischer Weg* (Weimar, 1937), pp. 35–42; Mergell, op. cit., pp. 56–64.

[3] Mergell, op. cit., pp. 64–66; Loomis, *Arthurian Tradition*, pp. 360–3.

[4] On Pelrapeire see Ehrismann, op. cit., p. 241; Mergell, op. cit., pp. 70–82; Richey in *MLR*, xlvii. 357.

[5] Chrétien's description of the conduct of Perceval and Blancheflor leaves room for different

innocent for two nights (193, 2–14). Only on the third night does Parzival remember his mother's advice and Gurnemanz's teaching (202, 21–203, 1). Then he and Condwiramurs, as she is called by Wolfram, are at last united in love (203, 2–10), firmly resolved to be forever husband and wife.

Then follows Parzival's first visit to the castle of the Grail (Book V). On the whole Wolfram's narrative runs parallel to that of Chrétien except for the curious 'jester episode', which recently has been explained as reflecting the unnerving horror of those who witnessed the bloody lance being thrust into Anfortas's wound to relieve the pain—a prelude to the subsequent events which leave the young hero still more bewildered.[1] Before the procession begins, a page enters with a lance from the end of which blood is dripping into his sleeve. This particular passage, not found in Chrétien, but in *Peredur*, has been noted as evidence for Wolfram's employment of another traditional source.[2]

From here on Wolfram concentrates on the mysteries of the Grail which he describes in the well-known lines:

> zwei mezzer snîdende als ein grât   erden wunsches überwal.
> brâhten si durch wunder   Repanse de Schoi si hiez,
> ûf zwei tweheln al besunder. . .   die sich der Grâl tragen liez.
> ûf einem grüenen achmardî   der Grâl was von solcher art:
> truoc si den wunsch von pardîs   wol muoste ir kiusche sîn bewart,
> bêde wurzeln unde rîs.   die sîn ze rehte solde pflegen:
> daz was ein dinc, daz hiez der Grâl,   die muoste valsches sich bewegen.[3]

(They brought two knives cutting like fishbone, miraculous to see, on two towels separately. . . . On precious green silk she bore the most precious thing of Paradise, which was both root and shoot in one. That was an object called the Grail, the superabundance of everything one may desire on earth. She who was allowed to bear the Grail was called Repanse de Schoie. The Grail was of such a kind that she who was to tend it properly must have preserved her chastity, and to her all falsity had to be foreign.)

As far as this passage is concerned, the German poet does not give a clear concept of what the Grail was like. In Chrétien's parallel passage the word *graal* is used as a common noun designating a vessel, while with Wolfram the proper name *Grâl* singles out the most precious thing this side of Paradise.[4]

---

interpretations, but the fact that she is referred to as a *pucele* several times afterwards should be decisive. See Loomis, *Arthurian Tradition*, p. 363, n. 1; Newstead in *RP*, vii (1954), 171–5; and the lucid, common-sense interpretation by Wesle in *Beiträge*, lxxxii (1950), 15–27.

[1] Weigand in *PMLA*, lxvii (1952), 485–510; Singer, loc. cit., pp. 90 f.; Golther, op. cit., p. 155; Mergell, op. cit., p. 119 and n. 11.

[2] Ehrismann, op. cit., p. 253 and n. 2.

[3] *Parzival*, 234, 18–20; 235, 20–30.

[4] On the word *Grâl* as a proper name see Mergell, op. cit., p. 130, n. 28 (opposing Singer, loc. cit., p. 85). See also Golther, op. cit., p. 157; *Perceval*, ed. Hilka, pp. 680 ff.; Kellermann, op. cit., pp. 218 f.; and p. 233, n. 4, below.

It may be carried only by a chaste maiden;[1] it provides the entire Grail community with whatever food they wish (238, 8–239, 7), again a feature unknown to Chrétien but mentioned in Manessier, the *Estoire del Saint Graal*, and the *Queste*, thus suggesting that Wolfram had access to another traditional source.[2] At the close of the meal it is carried out past a beautiful old man, Titurel, father of Frimutel and grandfather of the Fisher King.[3] The two sharp silver knives, which for the time being remain without any function whatever, have long been explained as due to Wolfram's misunderstanding of 'tailleor d'arjant' in Chrétien's text (vs. 3231).[4]

Parzival who eagerly watches the miraculous spectacle refrains from asking the fateful question because of *zuht*, i.e. because of the courtly education which Gurnemanz had instilled in him:

wol gemarcte Parzivâl   er dâhte: 'mir riet Gurnemanz
die rîcheit und daz wunder grôz: mit grôzen triuwen âne schranz,
durch zuht in vrâgens doch verdrôz.   ich solde vil gevrâgen niht.'[5]

(Parzival eagerly observed the lavish and miraculous proceedings. However, for reasons of courtly etiquette he refrained from asking any questions. He thought: 'Gurnemanz, in great unfailing loyalty, advised me not to ask too many questions.')

Even Anfortas's presentation of the precious sword to Parzival, which, as R. S. Loomis has suggested, may be a 'blurred reminiscence of the more common account in which the hero is presented with the fragments of a sword and is asked to unite them', fails to have the intended effect of prodding the young hero into asking the question.[6] Early on the following day Parzival leaves the castle; nothing stirs but a page who lowers the drawbridge and shouts words of angry disappointment after him (247, 26–30).

As he rides away from the Grail castle, he meets his cousin Sigune, according to Wolfram's version, for the second time.[7] When she learns that Parzival has seen the Grail but has failed to ask the question, she shifts, unconsciously, as it were, from the familiar *du* to the distant *ir*. It is as if the

[1] Loomis, *Arthurian Tradition*, pp. 374, 376–9, 396 f., 416.
[2] On *Tischleindeckdich* motif see Ehrismann, op. cit., p. 252; Weber, *Wolfram von Eschenbach*, pp. 84 ff.; Mergell, op. cit., p. 134 and n. 35; and Chap. 21 below.
[3] On the Grail dynasty and the feeding of Titurel see Weber, *Wolfram von Eschenbach*, pp. 131, 144 ff.; Kellermann, op. cit., pp. 216 ff.; Mergell, op. cit., p. 134, n. 33, p. 175.
[4] On 'tailleor d'argent' see Heinzel in *Denkschriften der kaiserlichen Akad. der Wissenschaften zu Wien*, xl (1891), p. 40; Hertz's translation (1898), n. 177; Singer, loc. cit., pp. 88 f. (against misunderstanding of *tailleor*); Bruce, i. 328 and n. 28; Ehrismann, op. cit., pp. 242 f.; Brugger in *ZFSL*, liii (1930), 451 n.; *Perceval*, ed. Hilka, p. 683; Rachbauer, op. cit., pp. 147 ff.; Mergell, op. cit., p. 128 and n. 25 (assumes deliberate modification by Wolfram).
[5] *Parzival*, 239, 8–13.
[6] Loomis, *Arthurian Tradition*, pp. 407 f. and notes.
[7] For Parzival's second meeting with Sigune, see Mergell, op. cit., pp. 148–54; Hatto in *MLR*, xlii (1947), 244–6; and specially Schwietering in *ZDA*, lvii (1920), 140–3.

bonds of kinship had been severed, and Parzival is sent away with curses that anticipate his subsequent condemnation by Cundrie before the assembled knights of King Arthur's court (314, 23–318, 30).[1] Yet, in significant contrast to the French poem, where Perceval is berated because he missed the opportunity to ask whom the Grail served and the cause of the bleeding lance, Wolfram's Parzival is cursed because he displayed such utter lack of compassion for the suffering King of the Grail (255, 17 and 316, 3).[2]

However, before Parzival appears at King Arthur's court, he falls into a daze at the sight of three drops of blood in the snow which remind him of the colours of Condwiramurs's complexion.[3] Only after fierce combat, first with Segramors, then with Keie—in this connexion Wolfram puts in a good word for the true worth of the ill-tempered seneschal (296, 16–297, 29)[4]— is he finally persuaded by his friend Gawan to accompany him to King Arthur.

It is Gawan who, having been challenged on the same occasion by Kingrimursel (Chrétien's Guingambresil),[5] sympathizes with the young hero in his hour of utter humiliation and despair and wishes him God's blessing for the future. With the instinct of the true artist Wolfram turns Gawan's casual mention of God into the spark which touches off Parzival's defiance of the Almighty:

> Der Wâleis sprach: 'Wê, waz ist got?   ich was im dienstes undertân,
> wære der gewaldec, solhen spot   sît ich genâden mich versan:
> hete er uns beiden niht gegeben,   nu wil ich im dienest widersagen:
> kunde got mit kreften leben.   hât er haz, den wil ich tragen.'[6]

(The Welshman said: 'Alas, what is God? Were He almighty, He would never have exposed you and me to such disgrace, could He rule with power. I have devoted myself to His service because I was hopeful of His grace. Now I will forswear His service: if He hates me, that hatred I will bear.')

Parzival's sceptical outburst in bitter disillusionment, 'Alas, what is God?', as we have seen, calls to mind the child's innocent wonderment, 'Alas, mother, what is God?' (119, 17). Thus, again and again (121, 2; 122, 21 f.; 228, 21 ff.; 259, 15 ff.; 332, 1–8) and especially in the Ninth Book (461, 9: 'ouch trage ich hazzes vil gein gote') Wolfram underlines Parzival's relationship to God, while there is nothing comparable here or elsewhere in Chrétien, who only in retrospect makes Perceval admit his neglect of church services.

[1] Mergell, op. cit., p. 96 and n. 46.

[2] Ehrismann in ZDA, xlix (1908), especially pp. 442 ff.; Brugger in ZFSL, xliv (1917), 166; Bruce, i. 337 f.; Weber, Wolfram von Eschenbach, pp. 101, 129 f.; Mergell, op. cit., p. 154; Loomis, Arthurian Tradition, p. 389 and n. 76.

[3] Mergell, op. cit., pp. 88 ff.; Zenker in RF, xl (1927), 314–22, 414 f.; M. de Riquer in Revista de Filologia Española, xxxix (1955), 186–219.

[4] J. L. Weston, Legend of Sir Perceval, i (1906), 300; Singer, loc. cit., pp. 98 f.; Rachbauer, op. cit., pp. 201 f.; Mergell, op. cit., pp. 91–93.

[5] Mergell, op. cit., pp. 97–110.   [6] Parzival, 332, 1–8.

In other words, Chrétien's Perceval is drifting away, unconsciously and passively, from the life of a good Christian, whereas Wolfram's Parzival is a rebel against God—to be sure, not in the modern sense of denying the existence of God but rather of doubting His power and good will. Wolfram portrays for his medieval audience man's situation as between God and the devil, heaven and hell, good and evil—man, as Wolfram puts it, beset by *zwîvel*, that leitmotif which runs through his *Parzival* as well as through his *Willehalm*.

This is particularly true of the Ninth Book,[1] to which we shall now proceed immediately, postponing the discussion of the Gawan adventures as told in Books VII, VIII, and X–XIII. The Ninth Book, usually entitled 'Trevrizent', is the very core of Wolfram's work; with its 2,100 lines (433, 1–502, 30) it has grown to almost seven times the length of the corresponding section in Chrétien (vss. 6217–513). Unlike Chrétien's hero, Parzival on the way to his hermit uncle meets, for the third time, Sigune, who forgives him and hopefully speaks to him of finding the Grail and God's forgiveness.[2]

When the young knight arrives at Trevrizent's lonely abode in the wood, he admits at the outset that he is 'a man of sin'.[3] He is amazed to learn that he has passed four years and a half in despondent knight-errantry, years during which he visited no church and in hatred of his Creator thought that he could force the hand of God, his feudal lord, through acts of knightly valour. However, it has been of no avail (461, 1–26). This anthropomorphic concept of God gives Trevrizent occasion to instruct his visitor on the Fall of Man and on his redemption through God's *triuwe*, a word which from its feudal meaning of 'loyalty' is extended by Trevrizent to designate the Christian concept of the 'love and grace' of God (461, 27–467, 10).

When Parzival now confides that his heart is heavy because of the Grail —without admitting as yet his failure to ask the question—and because of his longing for Condwiramurs, his wife, Trevrizent reveals to him the mysteries of the Grail.[4] The Grail is a stone, its name is *lapis exillis*.[5] Much has been

---

[1] For discussions of Bk. IX see Ehrismann in *ZDA*, xlix (1909), 422–49; Keferstein, op. cit., pp. 70–87; Mergell, op. cit., pp. 155–245; H. Meyer, Jr., in *Neo*, xxxi (1947), 18–27; Henzen in *Erbe der Vergangenheit, Festgabe für K. Helm* (Tübingen, 1951), pp. 189–217.

[2] On the third meeting with Sigune see Ehrismann in *ZDA*, xlix. 423 f.; Mergell, op. cit., pp. 153–8; Henzen, loc. cit., pp. 198 f.   [3] *Parzival*, 456, 29 f.

[4] On Wolfram's concept of the Grail see Hertz's translation (1898), pp. 415–35; Vogt, op. cit., pp. 265–71; Golther, op. cit., pp. 199–215; Ehrismann, op. cit., pp. 246–50; Weber, *Wolfram von Eschenbach*, pp. 53–150; Wilmotte in *Bull. de la Classe des Lettres de l'Acad. Roy. de Belgique*, 5e série, xix (1933), 247–64; K. Burdach, *Der Gral* (Stuttgart, 1938), pp. 503–60; Ranke in *Trivium*, iv (1946), 20–30, and review of Burdach in *Anzeiger für deutsches Altertum*, lxiv (1948), 20–24; Hatto in *MLR*, xliii (1948), 216–22; Mergell in *Germanisch-romanische Monatsschrift*, N.F., i (1951), 143 ff., and *Euphorion*, xlvii (1953), 431–51.

[5] On 'lapis exillis' see Ehrismann in *ZDA*, lxv (1928), 63; Weber, *Wolfram von Eschenbach*, pp. 58 ff.; Ranke, loc. cit., pp. 24–26; W. Wolf in *Studien zur deutschen Philologie des Mittelalters*, F.

written about the meaning and the origin of this name, which, as the variant forms of the manuscripts indicate, *iaspis*, *lapis* and *erillis*, *exilis*, *exillix*, *exilix*, bewildered the medieval scribes no less than modern commentators. If we add to these readings the emendations proposed in more recent years, such as *lapis herilis*, *berillis*, *textilis*, *lapis ex celis*, *lapis electrix* or *elixir*, we can understand the present trend of assuming that several functions and hence several names have merged in this miraculous stone. However, the most satisfactory explanation seems to be the one first offered by Ehrismann and then elaborated by Ranke and Krogmann, namely that Wolfram's concept of the Grail was partly shaped by a passage in the well-known *Iter Alexandri Magni ad Paradisum*, which describes a stone (*lapis*) sent to the great conqueror from the Earthly Paradise. Though the size of the stone is that of a human eye and it is referred to as a 'substantia exilis', 'a small or worthless object', its weight turns out to be many times that of gold, but when covered with dust it weighs nothing at all. When the significance of this *lapis exilis* is explained to Alexander, he is cured of ambition and pride. Ranke believes that Wolfram took the stone as a symbol of humility, deliberately substituted it for Chrétien's *graal*, and perhaps recalled its origin when he twice referred to the Grail and its miraculous power as the 'wunsch von pardîs' (235, 21; 470, 14).

That Wolfram knew the *Iter* is rendered probable not only by his use of the Latin words, but also by his reference (481, 19–26) to the sweet taste of the herbs which floated down the rivers of Paradise, including Fison, for Alexander saw drying on the banks of that river 'folia maxima . . . per amnis decursum effluentia', which when powdered yielded a wonderful taste. Ranke's interpretation of the stone, moreover, would accord with the emphasis which Wolfram placed on humility. He described Herzeloide as 'ein stam der diemüete', 'a stem of humility' (128, 28). Gurnemanz charged her son Parzival to practise that virtue: 'vlîzet iuch diemüete!' (170, 28). This is the leit-motif also of Trevrizent's teaching: 'ir müestet aldâ vor hôchvart mit senftem willen sîn bewart', 'you must with a meek will guard against pride' (472, 13 f.); and again 'diemüet die hôchvart überstreit', 'humility vanquishes pride' (473, 4). The suffering king himself resolves to turn from pride to humility: 'des grâles krône is alsô guot, die hât mir hôchvart verlorn, nû hân ich diemuot mir erkorn' (819, 18–20). When Parzival is at last hailed as the newly chosen king of the Grail, Trevrizent sums up his counsel in the words, 'kêrt an diemuot iuwern sin', 'now direct your mind to humility' (798, 30).

Panzer z. 80. Geburtstag (Heidelberg, 1950), pp. 73–95; Krogmann in *ZDA*, lxxxv (1954), 35–38; R. Hartmann in *Volume of Oriental Studies Presented to E. G. Browne*, ed. Arnold and Nicholson (Cambridge, 1922), pp. 179–85; M. M. Lascelles in *MedAev*, v (1936), 36–45; *La Prise de Defur and Le Voyage d'Alexandre au Paradis Terrestre*, ed. Peckham and La Du (Princeton, 1935), pp. xxxii–lii.

As Trevrizent proceeds with his discourse on the Grail, its associations with the East accumulate. He reveals that on this stone the phoenix alights, is burned to ashes, and is revived (469, 8–13), and though this statement conflicts with the accepted tradition, we may remember that according to the *Historia de Proeliis* (A.D. 950) Alexander in the course of his explorations in the remote East beheld the phoenix sitting on the Dry Tree. Trevrizent's description of the guardians of the Grail as a military order, vowed to chastity and called Templeisen,[1] also carries our minds to the great strongholds of the Knights Templars in the Near East.

Even when Wolfram preserves certain reminiscences of Chrétien's account of the Grail and its guardian, he adds and modifies. The Fisher King has been given a name, Anfortas, perhaps a distorted form of *infirmitas*, suggested by his malady.[2] The miraculous Host, which was described to Perceval on Good Friday as contained in the Grail and as sustaining the Fisher King's father alone, is described to Parzival as a sacramental wafer, brought by a dove on Good Friday, laid on the stone, and endowing it with the power to feed the whole brotherhood of the Grail. Wolfram also displays, in reporting Trevrizent's discourse, a marked desire to tie together by the bond of kinship figures whom Chrétien fails to connect in that way. One is surprised to learn that Anfortas is the brother not only of Trevrizent and Herzeloide (as in Chrétien), but also of Repanse de Schoie, the Grail Bearer; and that the 'Red Knight', Ither von Gaheviez, is Parzival's cousin.

So when Parzival discloses that he is the son of Gahmuret and has killed Ither, his uncle declares that he is guilty of 'slaying his own life'. Shocked and grieved, the hermit goes on to charge him with another sin of which the young knight was not aware, the death of his mother. As yet there is no mention of the hero's most fateful sin, his failure to show compassion for his suffering uncle at the Grail castle. With keen dramatic sense Wolfram postpones the climax of this dialogue. So the first phase of the interview closes with Trevrizent's telling of a knight who has visited the Grail castle but has not in pity asked: 'Sir, what is the cause of your suffering?' Still, even though Parzival cannot but recognize himself in this knight, he refuses to break down. Only after the humble meal which he shares with his hermit uncle does he bring himself to the crucial confession:

'der ûf Munsalvæsche reit   daz bin ich unsælic barn:
unt der den rehten kumber sach,   sus hân ich, hêrre, missevarn.'[3]
unt der deheine vrâge sprach,

---

[1] On *templeisen* see E. Martin's ed., ii, pp. xl, 345; Singer, loc. cit., pp. 93 ff.; Bruce, i. 335 and n. 40; Ehrismann, op. cit., p. 254; Mergell, op. cit., p. 210 and n. 125.

[2] On Anfortas see Bruce, i. 317 and n. 9; Nitze in *RP*, vi (1952), 14–22; Loomis in *RR*, xlv (1954), 12–15; Brugger in *RP*, ix (1956), 285–97; H. Newstead, *Bran the Blessed in Arthurian Romance* (New York, 1939), chaps. ii, v, xii.

[3] *Parzival*, 488, 16–20.

('He who rode to Munsalvaesche and saw the true grief there and failed to ask any question whatever, that am I, unfortunate man. Thus, Sir, have I sinned.')

As throughout his poem, so in the conclusion of the Trevrizent episode, Wolfram again places much less emphasis than Chrétien upon priestly exhortation and ecclesiastic rites. Instead, he has the hermit sum up the three great sins of Parzival, the killing of Ither, his mother's death, and his failure to ask the compassionate question. And Parzival, instead of going through the regular observances during the three days from Good Friday to Easter, remains fully two weeks in spiritual communion with Trevrizent until he, a layman, absolves him of his sins.

The deliberate expansion, the artistic structure, and the penetrating exposition of the underlying problems make the Trevrizent episode by far the most significant phase of Wolfram's *Parzival* and one of the highlights of Arthurian and medieval literature as a whole. However, before the fulfilment of Parzival's fate is reached, we must briefly follow the other strand of the story, the Gawan theme,[1] which occupies Books VII and VIII and most of Books X through XIII. These sections correspond to Chrétien's version, vss. 4797–6216 and 6514–9234, more closely than any other, except for one thing, namely Wolfram's obvious and artistic endeavour, in spite of the temporary emphasis on Gawan, never to lose sight of Parzival altogether. After all, he is and remains, as Wolfram puts it at the very outset of this digression, 'des mæres herre' (338, 7).

In Book VII[2] Gawan sets out to meet and to defeat Kingrimursel (Guingambresil). As always, Wolfram provides names for most of the anonymous figures of the French poem, such as Poidiconjunz, Astor de Lanverunz, and the notorious abductor Meljacanz (from Hartmann's *Iwein*, vs. 5680) already mentioned 125, 16, in addition to Obie's and Obilot's father, whose French name, Tiebaut, was misread as Lyppaut.[3]

Much more significant, however, for Wolfram's modification of the Gawan episodes is the difference between Gawan and Parzival with regard to *zwîvel*. Whereas Parzival's *zwîvel*, as indicated above, is essentially on the religious plane, Gawan's *zwîvel*, as he advances against the castle of Bearosche (349, 28 ff.; 350, 30 f.), is a human conflict of mere worldly, courtly obligations—in this particular instance it is his choice between participation in the

---

[1] On Gawan's role in *Parzival* see Küpp in *ZDP*, xvii (1885), 31–60; Ehrismann in *ZDA*, xlix (1909), 457 f.; Heller in *JEGP*, xxiv (1925), 463–503; Golther, op. cit., pp. 183–90; M. Paetzel, *Wolfram von Eschenbach und Chrétien von Troyes, Parzival, Buch 7–13 und seine Quelle* (Berlin, 1931); Kellermann, op. cit., pp. 19 ff., 27 ff., 86, 146 ff.; Keferstein, op. cit., pp. 88–95, and in *Germanisch-romanische Monatsschrift*, xxv (1937), 256–74; Mergell, op. cit., pp. 246–312.

[2] Singer, loc. cit., pp. 102–4; Golther, op. cit., pp. 168–71; Paetzel, op. cit., pp. 7–22; Stapel, 'Die kleine Obilot', *Deutsches Volkstum*, xviii (1936), 108–14; Mergell, op. cit., pp. 249–64.

[3] On proper names in *Parzival* see Ehrismann, op. cit., p. 245 and n. 4; Fourquet in *Mélanges offerts à E. Hoepffner* (Paris, 1949), pp. 245–60.

battle of Bearosche and saving himself for the promised struggle with Kingrimursel. Once Gawan has decided in favour of fighting at Bearosche, the love of little Obilot becomes the central theme, beginning with her first glimpse of Gawan from the distant castle and ending with the charming *tête-à-tête* between the gallant knight and his childlike love (369, 1–370, 7). It is a consciously playful parody of courtly *minne*, all the more impressive as Wolfram in the same breath (370, 8–30, esp. 18 ff.) contrasts Gawan's notion of *minne* with Parzival's ideal of *triuwe* toward women as the supreme force in a life without God.

However, in his effort to give Parzival a share even in the books devoted to Gawan, Wolfram reintroduces his hero. Once the fighting before Bearosche has got under way, suddenly, at the critical moment, an unknown knight clothed all in red—Parzival—enters the fighting and tips the scales in favour of those attacking Bearosche (383, 23 ff.). Thus not Gawan alone, as in Chrétien's version, but both Gawan and Parzival are the heroes of the day (388, 6 ff.). To end the fighting, Parzival asks his captives to free Meljanz or to seek the Grail on his behalf (388, 11 ff.). In fact, the two motives which for four years and a half have driven Parzival on—the quest of the Grail and the longing for his wife Condwiramurs—are echoing significantly at the end of the first Gawan Book.

In his Eighth Book[1] Wolfram brings Gawan to the capital of the land of Ascalun. On the way there, he meets the king of the land, Vergulaht,[2] and is sent to his sister Antikonîe (404, 23). No doubt Wolfram derived the latter name from that of Antigone in the *Roman de Thèbes*. There are similar classical reminiscences in this book, such as *Enêas*, *Kartâgô* (399, 12), *frouwe Tŷdôn* (399, 14), all of them probably from Veldeke's *Eneit*, and there are, in addition, the much-debated allusions to the native German heroes, especially those of the *Nibelungenlied*, such as Wolfhart, Rûmolt, Gunther, and others (420, 22 ff.).[3]

Moreover, in contrast to her French counterpart, Wolfram's Antikonîe in addition to physical beauty possesses most of the courtly virtues (403, 26 ff. and 404, 22 ff.), and for a time at least remains bashful and demure (405, 26 f.), until she can no longer resist the bold advances of Gawan. In both the French and the German poem Gawan and Antikonîe are caught in amorous embrace, but in the former the lady takes the initiative, in the latter Gawan. Again, the ensuing fierce battle in which Gawan fights off the townsmen with the huge chessboard differs in some detail from Chrétien's account. What is more significant is the discrepancy between Chrétien and Wolfram

[1] Singer, loc. cit., pp. 104–8; Golther, op. cit., pp. 171 f.; Paetzel, op. cit., pp. 22–34; Mergell, op. cit., pp. 264–73.   [2] On this name see *PMLA*, xlviii (1933), 1025–7.

[3] On Antikonîe see Singer, loc. cit., pp. 104 f. On names taken from German heroic poetry see H. de Boor in *ZDA*, lxi (1924), 1–11. For other references see Ehrismann, op. cit., p. 245, n. 4.

concerning the motivation of Gawan's search for the lance or for the Grail respectively. While at the end of his Cavalon episode Chrétien has Gauvain urged by the 'sage vavassor' to find the bleeding lance and thus to free the land of Logres from the age-old threat of doom, Wolfram ignores this motif completely. Instead, his idea of never losing sight of the main hero has caused Wolfram to assign to Vergulaht the role of a connecting link: Vergulaht at one time had been commissioned by Parzival to find the Grail or, failing that, to see his wife Condwiramurs; he now, upon Liddamus's advice,[1] transfers this mission to Gawan, who is thus made to compete with Parzival in his quest of the Holy Grail.

In fact, as the Gawan story continues after Book IX, both Gawan and Vergulaht appear on the Grail quest (503, 21–24).[2] Thus Gawan in Book X[3] comes to Orgeluse of Logrois (506, 25; cf. Chrétien's Orguelleuse de Logres, vss. 8638 f.),[4] the haughty lady who, in contrast to Obilot and Antikonîe, will teach him that courtly love may be consummated only if tested by daring adventure and persevering courtship (cf. especially 509, 23–511, 30). However, again, Wolfram is not content with reproducing the traditional traits of this strange female. He intimates at the outset that there are reasons for Orgeluse's annoying behaviour (516, 3 ff.). At the same time he hints at the affair between Orgeluse and Anfortas which ended with his unholy wound— one of the many cross-references through which Wolfram very skilfully connects Gawan's fortunes with the main theme of his work (519, 10–30). Again, Chrétien's nameless and ugly squire appears as Cundrie's congenial brother and is called Malcrêâtiure in Wolfram's poem.[5]

As Gawan and the ferryman, whom Wolfram has christened Plippalinôt,[6] approach Schastel Marveil (Book XI),[7] they meet at the gate a vendor of precious foreign merchandise. No doubt this merchant in the German poem takes the place of Chrétien's mysterious figure, the *eschacier* with the silver leg. According to Loomis's ingenious surmise he owes this artificial member to nothing but a confusion of *eschacier* with *eschaquier* and *eschac*, the latter meaning 'chessboard' and 'chessman' respectively.[8] It certainly does credit to Wolfram's good sense that he simply ignored this nonsensical passage,

---

[1] On Liddamus see Singer, loc. cit., pp. 105 f., and in *Abh. d. Preuss. Akad.*, phil.-hist. Kl. (1918), fasc. 13, pp. 7 f.

[2] For Gawan's quest of the Grail see Weber, *Wolfram von Eschenbach*, p. 39; Paetzel, op. cit., p. 32; Kellermann, op. cit., pp. 211 f.; Burdach, *Der Gral*, pp. 443 ff.; Mergell, op. cit., pp. 270–3.

[3] Küpp in *ZDP*, xvii. 46–49; Singer, loc. cit., pp. 108–15; Heller in *JEGP*, xxiv. 475–85; Paetzel, op. cit., pp. 52–76. Mergell, op. cit., pp. 274–83.

[4] On name Orgeluse see Schröder in *ZDA*, lxx (1933), 234 f.

[5] Mergell, op. cit., p. 277 and n. 27.

[6] The name probably derived from Inpripalnôt, Hartmann's *Erek*, vs. 1686.

[7] On *Lît Marveile* see Mergell, op. cit., pp. 283–8; Loomis, *Arthurian Tradition*, pp. 442–7.

[8] Loomis, *Arthurian Tradition*, p. 446. Singer (p. 115), Weber (p. 42), and Hilka (ed. of *Perceval*, p. xxxvii) find the man with the silver leg difficult to explain.

replacing it by the invention of the merchant whose fabulous wares, incidentally, gave the poet another chance of a cross-reference to Feirefiz and thus to the Parzival theme of his story.

Then follows the crucial test of Gawan's fearlessness, *Lît Marveile* (561, 22), the Magic Bed, Chrétien's 'Lit de la Mervoille' (vs. 7805). As all the horrors of the world seem arrayed against him, Gawan places his life in God's hands:

er lac, und liez es walten   der wîse herzehafte man,
den der *helfe* hât behalten,   swâ dem kumber wirt bekant,
und den der *helfe* nie verdrôz,   der rüefet an die hôhsten hant:
swer in sînem kumber grôz   wan diu treit *helfe* rîche
helfe an in versuochen kan.   und *hilft* im *helfecliche*.[1]

(He lay there, and let Him take care who has always been able and who has never been loath to help those who in their great distress appealed to Him for help. The wise, courageous man, wherever he experiences distress, calls upon the hand of the Almighty: for He is capable of true help and helps him helpfully.)

It has been pointed out[2] that this passage with its deliberate recurrence of *helfe, helfen, helfeclîche* was intended by Wolfram as a counterpart to the corresponding climax in Parzival's life—here Gawan, the courtier, in the extreme peril of adventure—there Parzival, *der zwîvelaere*, driven to the depth of human despair in his struggle between God and the world:

er sprach: 'waz ob got *helfe* pfliget,   sîner *helfe* sîn sô wert
diu mînem trûren ane gesiget?   und rehtiu manlîchiu wer,
wart aber er ie ritter holt,   daz sîn *helfe* mich vor sorgen ner,
gediende ie ritter sînen solt,   ist hiute sîn *helflîcher* tac,
oder mac schilt unde swert   so *helfe* er, ob er *helfen* mac.'[3]

(He said: 'What if God is able to give help such as will overcome my grief? If He was ever well-disposed toward a knight, if a knight ever earned his due, or, if shield and sword and true manly fighting are worthy of His help, so that His help may save me from trouble,—and if today is His day of helpfulness, let Him help me, if He is able to help.')

After Gawan has successfully fought his way through all the hazards of the Magic Castle, Orgeluse begins to show her affection, so that the two for the first time ride side by side to the Dangerous Ford, where Gawan will submit to the final and most dangerous adventure of all (Book XII).[4] Incidentally, while Chrétien calls the Magic Castle 'Roche de Sanguin',

---

[1] *Parzival*, 568, 1–10.
[2] Vogt, op. cit., p. 308; Ehrismann, op. cit., p. 238; Henzen, loc. cit., p. 201.
[3] *Parzival*, 451, 13–22.
[4] Küpp, loc. cit., pp. 51–57; Singer, loc. cit., pp. 115 f.; Heller, loc. cit., pp. 489–95; Paetzel, op. cit., pp. 88–105; Mergell, op. cit., pp. 288–300.

probably, as Loomis suggests, a distortion of the old name of the Severn, Wolfram offers a form much closer to the original, namely 'Rosche Sab(b)îns' (610, 26). We have met *Sabîns* earlier as the name of the river which Gawan has to cross before reaching Gramoflanz (604, 1)—indeed, a very strong argument in favour of Wolfram's using here another source, besides Chrétien, which preserved an older tradition.[1]

At last, the long-tried hero is found worthy of Orgeluse's love. The latter now reveals to him the cause of her aloofness, at the same time (and in contrast to Chrétien's version) connecting her own destiny with that of Anfortas and of Parzival (616, 11–617, 10; 618, 19–619, 14). It was Anfortas whose unhappy fate she caused, and it was Parzival who scorned her love and her land because Condwiramurs and the Grail were uppermost in his mind. Thus Orgeluse, who appears as the highest prize in Gawan's courtly career, is rejected by Parzival because of his marital loyalty (*triuwe*) to Condwiramurs and his preoccupation with the Grail.

This is the point, about one-third through Wolfram's Book XIII[2] (644, 20), where Chrétien's *Perceval* breaks off (vs. 9234), to be followed in the majority of the manuscripts, as we know, by three continuations, and in two manuscripts by a fourth, that of Gerbert. Yet, as has been pointed out repeatedly, the verbal resemblances of the French and the German texts continue further, ending with the reconciliation of Gawan and Gramoflanz, that is, almost to the end of Wolfram's Book XIV (731, 30), which corresponds to vs. 1193 of the First Continuation.[3] However, much of the content of Book XIII—the revealing of the mysteries of the Magic Castle and of Clinschor, the reception of the inhabitants of the castle by King Arthur and the recognizing of the relatives long thought dead—represents a very picturesque expansion of the sober French summary, for which Wolfram must have drawn rather freely on all kinds of medieval sources. Altogether his own, no doubt, is the final episode of this Book in which Gawan encounters a knight by the river *Sabîns*—Wolfram knows he need not mention his name although he assures us in the concluding line (678, 30) that with him 'the narrative has returned to the hero proper'.

In Book XIV[4] Gawan and Parzival engage in fierce combat until Gramoflanz happens to come by and some of his retainers, full of apprehension, mention Gawan's name. At once, Parzival casts away his sword, horrified by the thought that he has almost killed his own kin. He makes himself known to Gawan (688, 21 ff.) and then, instead, fights with Gramoflanz until through

---

[1] On Sab(b)îns see Loomis, *Arthurian Tradition*, pp. 451, 454; Martin's ed., ii. 429; Hilka's ed. of *Perceval*, p. 745, n. on vs. 6602; p. 767, n. on vs. 8816.

[2] Küpp, loc. cit., pp. 57–59; Singer, loc. cit., pp. 116–18; Mergell, op. cit., pp. 301–7.

[3] J. L. Weston, op. cit. i. 210–12; Heller, loc. cit., pp. 495–500; Fourquet, op. cit., pp. 130 ff.; H. Wrede, *Die Fortsetzer des Gralromans Chrestiens von Troyes* (Göttingen, 1952), pp. 183–98.

[4] Ibid.; Mergell, op. cit., pp. 308–12.

his sister Itonje's (i.e. Clarissant's) and King Arthur's intercession the two are reconciled and four weddings are celebrated (instead of one in the French text). However, no matter how much human interest and poetic life of its own it has, the Gawan story appears to serve, after all, as the grand contrasting foil to the fortunes of the main hero, Parzival. He has been gradually emerging from his remote and solitary existence. Yet, as he witnesses the joy of the knightly company in King Arthur's entourage, he realizes that his unfulfilled pledge to find the Grail and his yearning for Condwiramurs allow him as yet no share in love and happiness (732, 19–22 and 733, 16–20).

With Books XV and XVI[1] Wolfram's narrative returns to the leading theme and to the principal figures of his courtly-religious romance. Just as Gawan, Parzival's foil in the courtly sphere, eventually faces him in a fierce, though ultimately undecided combat, so does his foil on the religious plane, Feirefiz, at last engage him in a fight which makes all other fighting seem like 'child's play' (734, 18 f.). And again the battle ends on an indecisive note: Parzival's sword, which he has taken from his own dead kinsman Ither, breaks in pieces, symbolically ending the hero's uncourtly *tumpheit* (immaturity), whereupon the heathen Feirefiz, Parzival's half-brother, throws his own sword away and is the first to reveal his identity. God's grace, which is with Parzival, now that he has confessed to Trevrizent, has spared him the sin of fratricide. Again, a feast is celebrated at Arthur's court, this time in honour of Feirefiz, and again Cundrie appears, this time to kneel before Parzival, the king-elect of the Grail:

'Wol dich des hôhen teiles,   daz epitâfjum ist gelesen:
du krône menschen heiles!   dû solt des grâles herre wesen.'[2]

('Blessed be thy destination, thou crown of human salvation! The inscription has been read: Thou shalt be lord of the Grail.')

With conscious art the German poet now gathers up the many strands of his work. Condwiramurs, whose love, in addition to the quest of the Grail, had been Parzival's guiding star through four and a half dark years, had been named in the Grail inscription together with Parzival and their son Loherangrin.[3] Anfortas, whose sins and suffering, whose life and death epitomize the fate of the Grail community, will be healed through the redeeming question, as Cundrie explicitly declares. Thus the German poet discards not only the ancient motif that the Grail castle must be found by mere chance but also the traditional notion that the redeeming question must arise unconsciously in the visitor. The two motifs have been replaced, as it

---

[1] Golther, op. cit., pp. 144 f., 190 ff.; Keferstein, op. cit., pp. 96–103; Mergell, op. cit., pp. 333–50; Wesle in *Beiträge*, lxxii (1950), 1–15.

[2] *Parzival*, 781, 13–16.

[3] On Loherangrin see Martin's ed., ii. 534; Singer, loc. cit., pp. 121 f.; Golther, op. cit., pp. 191, 245–54; Ehrismann, op. cit., p. 255; Mergell, op. cit., pp. 348 f. and n. 30.

were, by the more meaningful and Christian idea that Parzival has matured
from an anthropomorphic and feudalistic concept of God, whose hand might
be forced through services rendered, to a transcendental and Christian concept according to which sinful man lives by God's grace. Accordingly, in
Wolfram's last Book Parzival accepts the kingdom of the Grail humbly, as
an act of God's grace:

al weinde Parzivâl dô sprach: op die gotes güete an mir gesige,
'saget mir, wâ der grâl hie lige.   des wirt wol innen disiu schar.'[1]

(Parzival wept as he said: 'Tell me where the Grail is to be found here. This company
will indeed perceive whether God's grace prevails in me.')

As soon as Parzival has been chosen King of the Grail he finds his wife
Condwiramurs at the very spot where the three blood drops in the snow had
once kept him spellbound (796, 29–797, 15 and 799, 14–804, 7)—a scene
gay with humour and personal intimacy, thus contrasting with the awesome
grandeur of the festivities in the Grail castle. He also meets Trevrizent
again (797, 16–799, 13) and, for the fourth time, Sigune, now lying dead
upon the body of Schionatulander (804, 8–805, 2).[2]

At the final celebration in the castle of the Holy Grail Feirefiz becomes a
Christian and marries the bearer of the Grail, Repanse de Schoie; their son,
Prester John, later preaches Christianity in the Eastern world.[3] Thus Occi-
dent and Orient are united under the sway of the two half-brothers Parzival
and Feirefiz, just as God's grace and the love of men are reconciled in
Parzival, 'des mæres herre'.

This analysis of Wolfram's poem has been necessary not only because his
main source is incomplete and other sources are problematic or lost, but also
because the differences between his *Parzival* and the sources which he used
are more significant than in the case of any other medieval German work.

One of the poet's favourite ideas, at times almost an obsession, of which
there is hardly a trace to be found in Chrétien or elsewhere, is the importance
which he attaches to family relationships.[4] Nearly all of the characters of his
work, most of them anonymous figures in Chrétien's poem, are somehow
linked by family ties, after they have been given individual and often tongue-
twisting names, borrowed from all sorts of medieval works. So it happens that
Gurnemanz's daughter Liaze, whom her father would like to see married

---

[1] *Parzival*, 795, 20–23.
[2] On Parzival's fourth meeting with Sigune see Ehrismann, op. cit., p. 241; Mergell, op. cit.,
p. 345.
[3] On Prester John see Zarncke in *Abh. d. phil.-hist. Kl. d. Sächs. Gesellschaft d. Wiss.* vii (1879),
827–1030; viii (1883), 1–186; Hagen in *Quellen und Forschungen*, lxxxv (1900), 4–32.
[4] On family relationships see Panzer, *Gahmuret*, pp. 78 f.; Schwietering, op. cit., pp. 164 ff.;
Fink in *Zts. f. Deutschkunde*, lvii (1943), 12–25; Mergell, op. cit., pp. 32–35, 108–10, 150–7, 166–
72, 219 f., 320 f.; Henzen, loc. cit., pp. 194 f. (warns against exaggeration of *Sippenidee*).

to Parzival, is the young hero's great-aunt! And so Wolfram again and again suggests through similar epithets and phrases that certain family traits are bound to come out in members of the same clan. Most suggestive is this leitmotif technique when the unconscious longing that 'swells' young Parzival's breast, as he listens to the singing of the birds (118, 17 and 26 f.), echoes the youthful yearning of his own father, Gahmuret (35, 27–30). Even more significant is the characterization of Gahmuret and his two sons as 'pure of heart' and 'bold' (*kiusche* and *vrech* or *vrävel*), a leitmotif which runs through the entire poem and recurs hundreds of lines apart (5, 22 f.; 437, 12; 734, 25; 737, 21 ff.).

Another feature which distinguishes Wolfram from his sources as well as from most of his contemporaries is his treatment of the relationship between men and women.[1] Courtly love, *minne*, which needs no legalization through marriage, has been relegated to Parzival's courtly counterpart, Gawan. It is Gawan who like a host of other Arthurian knights liberates and woos and makes love to ladies fair and fickle, thus proving ever anew his courtly prowess and personal chivalry. In deliberate contrast to this kind of courtly love, Parzival's affection centres in the one and only woman whom he allows to enter his life, Condwiramurs. It is a relationship whose ethical foundation is loyalty (*triuwe*) and whose crowning events are marriage and family. Only such a high ideal of the relationship between the sexes could take its place alongside the Grail as a source of strength and inspiration and as the ultimate goal of all the earthly striving of Wolfram's hero. Only because Condwiramurs was held in such high esteem by Parzival and loved by him with such unfailing loyalty could her name be shown in the Grail inscription, together with his own and that of their son Loherangrin.

Most important, however, in Wolfram's *Parzival* is man's relationship to God.[2] There can be no question that the German poet made the reconciliation of courtly teachings and Christian faith the all-important issue of his *Parzival*. This is apparent from the ignorant child's wonderment 'ouwê, muoter, waz ist got?' (119, 17) to the despairing knight's angry protest (332, 1–8); from his humble confession, as inimitable in its simplicity as it is disarming in its candour (456, 29 f.), through Trevrizent's mild-spoken lesson about God and His attitude to man, to the triumphant concluding lines

---

[1] On relations between men and women see Keferstein in *Festschrift für A. Leitzmann* (Jena, 1927), pp. 15–32; K. Boestfleisch, *Studien zum Minnegedanken bei Wolfram von Eschenbach* (Königsberg, 1930); Mergell, op. cit., pp. 32, 63, 76 f., 196, 326, 330; Wesle in *Beiträge*, lxxii. 15–27.

[2] On man's relation to God see G. Weber, *Der Gottesbegriff des Parzival* (Frankfurt, 1935); B. Mockenhaupt, *Die Frömmigkeit im Parzival Wolframs von Eschenbach* (Bonn, 1942); Schwietering, *Parzivals Schuld. Zur Religiosität Wolframs in ihrer Beziehung zur Mystik* (Frankfurt, 1944; first pub. in *ZDA*, lxxxi. 44 ff.); Maurer in *DVLG*, xxiv (1950), 304–50; von Simson in *Deutsche Beiträge zur geistigen Überlieferung*, ii (1953), 25–45; Bayerschmidt in *GR*, xxix (1954), 214–23; P. Wapnewski, *Wolframs Parzival. Studien zur Religiosität und Form* (Heidelberg, 1955). See p. 227, n. 1; p. 233, n. 1 above.

which sum up Parzival's achievement as well as the poet's own thoughts about man's relationship to God and the world:

Swes leben sich sô verendet,	und er doch der werlde hulde
daz got niht wirt gepfendet	behalten kan mit werdekeit,
der sêle durch es lîbes schulde,	daz ist ein nütziu arbeit.[1]

(He whose life so ends that his soul is not alienated from God because of carnal guilt and who nevertheless can retain the good will of the world with dignity, he has achieved a useful work.)

The synthesis of a dignified courtly life in this world and a firm Christian belief in a transcendental God is according to Wolfram symbolized by the Grail, for whose possession man strives in vain if his striving is not sanctioned by God's will. The question arises: is human endeavour of any avail at all? In the earlier parts of the poem we are told that the Grail castle cannot be sought or found intentionally (250, 26–30). Yet toward the end Parzival undauntedly seeks and finds the castle. He also asks the redeeming question by no means unwittingly or spontaneously but after an explicit exhortation and announcement by Cundrie herself (781, 27–30). This obvious contradiction has been explained in various ways, most recently and indeed very ingeniously in the light of the shifting theological and philosophical views of the time.[2] The theory is that the traditional motif of the castle which no man can find intentionally allowed itself, on the higher plane of Parzival's quest of the Holy Grail, to be interpreted in terms of St. Augustine's doctrine of predestination: only he whom God has chosen will find his way to the castle, ask the question, redeem Anfortas, and succeed him as King of the Grail. However, toward the end of the twelfth and at the beginning of the thirteenth century, that is, while Wolfram was meditating his *Parzival*, the doctrine of predestination gave way to the idea that man himself had to contribute his humble effort to bring about the act of God's grace—an idea which a few decades after Wolfram's lifetime was first codified by Albertus Magnus, to be systematized later by Thomas Aquinas. There is indeed no reason why a medieval poet as deeply concerned with religious problems and as well-versed in theological lore as Wolfram should not have been aware of the most significant intellectual reorientation of his day.

Wolfram's unique and novel concept of the ideal knight finally emerges as Parzival is proclaimed king of the Grail community,[3] where the courtly code is identical with a life in God, and courtly misconduct with sinning against the Holy Ghost. King Arthur's Round Table, on the other hand, as well as

---

[1] *Parzival*, 827, 19–24.

[2] Weber, *Der Gottesbegriff*, and *Parzival, Ringen und Vollendung*. See review by Schwietering, in *Anzeiger für deutsches Altertum*, lxiv (1948), 14–20.

[3] W. Mielke, *Die Charakterentwicklung Parzivals* (Gartz, 1904); Misch in *DVLG*, v (1926–7), 213–315; Ehrismann, op. cit., pp. 261–3.

its most active and most illustrious exponent, Gawan, represent merely the courtly world at its best.

Gahmuret, too, represents a certain phase of chivalry, though different from Gawan's as well as Parzival's. To Gahmuret adventure is not an exciting pastime or sport for the purpose of demonstrating one's skill in the use of arms. To him adventure means fighting for one's life and, at the same time, fighting against the infidels for the glory of the Christian God. So love for Gahmuret is not gallantry and erotic play but the conquest of some world-renowned, preferably Oriental beauty, on whom he will beget children either in or out of wedlock, until his thirst for more adventure and war rushes him into new campaigns. And these campaigns, no matter how far they may take the soldier-knight, are always fought in a realistic world, not, like the adventures of the Arthurian knights, in the imaginary world of enchanted castles and magic springs.[1]

The pagan world in Wolfram's poem is represented by Belakane and her son Feirefiz. Like Gahmuret, Feirefiz is ever eager for the fighting of battles and the possession of beautiful women. And like Parzival, Feirefiz has the pure heart (*kiusche*) of the Gahmuret tribe. He even excels his half-brother in magnanimity as he casts away his own sword after Parzival's has broken in two.[2]

His feminine counterpart is Belakane, 'diu swarze mœrinne', with whom his father Gahmuret fell in love in spite of her colour and in spite of her faith. Like Feirefiz, the figure of Belakane serves to symbolize Wolfram's attitude toward the non-Christian world. Her personal virtues, her *kiusche* ('purity of heart') in particular, make her equal to any Christian, just as Feirefiz has human qualities which predestine him to share with Parzival the Christian reign over mankind—a motif which was to form the main theme of Wolfram's subsequent work, *Willehalm*.[3]

Herzeloide, Parzival's mother, on the other hand, is Anfortas's sister and thus by birth a member of the Grail family. She makes an ideal wife for Gahmuret because she combines her womanly affection with an understanding of her husband's prowess and soldierly sense of duty. Only when he is killed in the prime of life, does she turn her back on the courtly world to rear young Parzival in the solitude of the forest, far from the temptations and dangers of the knightly life. When her intentions fail and Parzival leaves her for King Arthur's court, it is consistent with Herzeloide's character that

---

[1] On Gahmuret see Ehrismann, op. cit., p. 262, n. 1; Schwietering in *ZDA*, lxiv (1927), 139–42; Panzer, *Gahmuret*; Loomis, *Arthurian Tradition*, pp. 347–55.

[2] Feirefiz from Old Fr. *vair fiz*. See Vogt, op. cit., p. 273; Bruce, i. 314, n. 2; Panzer, *Gahmuret*, pp. 16–20; Mergell, op. cit., pp. 232–6.

[3] On Belakane see Schwietering in *ZDA*, lxi (1924), 65 ff.; H. Naumann in *Ehrismann-Festschrift* (Berlin, Leipzig, 1925), pp. 90 f.; Panzer, *Gahmuret*, pp. 3–16; Mergell, op. cit., pp. 323–6; Newstead in *RR*, xxxvi (1945), 10–20.

young Parzival's parting shatters her entire being, which is the essence of *triuwe*, motherly devotion.[1]

What fate had withheld from Herzeloide, namely lasting happiness by the side of a loving and celebrated spouse and a life enriched by a thriving family, all that was granted to Parzival's wife, Condwiramurs, in full measure. The chaste maiden, who according to Wolfram takes every precaution not to have her nocturnal visit to Parzival misunderstood, blooms forth into a devoted wife and mother. She, trustingly and with understanding, awaits her husband's return, and in the end, together with him and her son Loherangrin, ascends the throne in the kingdom of the Holy Grail. Indeed, both Herzeloide and Condwiramurs have been portrayed by Wolfram with intense personal sympathy, by the same Wolfram who elsewhere expresses himself sarcastically, at times bitterly, not only about certain court ladies who failed to appreciate. his gallant attention, but also about the conventionalized type of courtly *minne* in general.[2]

The most beautiful creation, however, of Wolfram's poetic genius, and the most appealing feminine character of his work is Parzival's hapless cousin, Sigune, whom the hero encounters on four occasions. The first time he finds her in 'tearless grief', holding the body of Schionatulander lovingly in her lap. Then, after his visit to the Grail castle, he encounters her again, now like a saintly dryad resting in a tree and still holding the body of beloved Schionatulander in her arms. The third time, before he meets Trevrizent, he sees Sigune as a recluse immured in her cell. She now devotes her entire life to the love of God, which has become one with her love of Schionatulander—divine and profane love have merged for her in mystical fervour. At the very end of Wolfram's poem, Parzival and Trevrizent together come once more, late in the evening, upon the lonely recluse, only to find her at the end of her earthly pilgrimage. Sigune is buried next to Schionatulander, for whom she has cherished a maidenly love all her life.[3]

The deliberate evolution of the character of the main persons and the development of the underlying ideas are the most significant achievements of Wolfram's work, if we compare it with earlier medieval narratives and romances. In other words, the experiences of the hero no longer take their own more or less accidental course but represent successive phases of the hero's inner metamorphosis. What may be said of poetry is paralleled in the plastic arts of this period. As Schwietering once put it, speaking of the new trend

---

[1] On Herzeloide see Singer, loc. cit., pp. 32, 73; Bruce, i. 314, n. 2; Panzer, *Gahmuret*, pp. 20–45; Mergell, op. cit., pp. 112 f., and n. 2; Adolf in *PMLA*, lxii (1947), 310; Loomis, *Arthurian Tradition*, pp. 193, 348; Newstead in *RR*, xxxvi. 25, 28, 30.

[2] On Condwiramurs see Singer, loc. cit., pp. 81 f.; Weber, *Wolfram von Eschenbach*, pp. 97, 135; especially Wesle in *Beiträge*, lxxii (1950), 15–27; also p. 229, n. 5, p. 243, n. 1 above.

[3] On Sigune see p. 228, n. 6, p. 231, n. 7, p. 233, n. 2, p. 242, n. 2 above. On name see Singer, loc. cit., pp. 72 f.; Adolf in *JEGP*, xlix (1950), 296.

in the art of the time, the garment of a sculpture now no longer has its own independent life but reflects most expressively the form and rhythm of the body which it covers.[1]

Thus also the external structure of *Parzival*, with its total of 24,810 lines, is a masterpiece of poetic composition.[2] The deliberate organization of this mass of material shows even in the smallest subdivisions of thirty lines each. That they go back to the original is evident from the fact that they are uniformly the same in the majority of our *Parzival* manuscripts; what means more, for long stretches these sections also in content form well-rounded entities.[3]

The division of the whole work into sixteen 'Books' may be also traced to Wolfram himself, as suggested by the concurrence of our manuscripts in this regard and especially by the initial and final lines of most of these books which clearly indicate the beginning and the end of the chapter.[4] Moreover, we have been shown of late that Wolfram, like other medieval poets and in spite of his supposed illiteracy, has indulged in an almost mathematical symmetry as to the number of lines and sections allotted to the major parts of his work. If we discount the first 108 sections of 30 lines each which constitute the Gahmuret prelude, we are left with 324 sections (109–432) before and 324 sections (503–826) after the Ninth Book, which itself numbers exactly 70 sections.[5] This amazing balance would seem to confirm the common suspicion that Books I and II were a late addition,[6] and, what is infinitely more important, it proves that the Ninth Book, 'Parzival and Trevrizent', represents the very core of the poem.

This book, then, in which the inner struggle of the hero reaches its climax, is preceded and followed by Gawan's adventures, which, as has often been observed, are seen in deliberate contrast to Parzival's, as illustrated by analogues like Grail castle and Schastel Marveil, Cundrie and Malcreatiure, Condwiramurs and Orgeluse. Similarly Wolfram has Parzival paralleled and contrasted with several other figures which played only an episodic role in Chrétien's work. Thus, as already stated, the hero's path is again and again crossed by Sigune, from his first entry into the world to the very threshold

---

[1] *Anzeiger f. deutsches Altertum*, lxiv (1948), 144.

[2] Ehrismann, op. cit., p. 228 and n. 1 (bibliography). The most recent structural analysis by W. J. Schröder in *Beiträge*, lxxiv (1952), 160–92, 409–53, was critically reviewed by Mergell in *GRM*, N.S., iii (1953), 99 f.

[3] Ehrismann, op. cit., p. 228 n.; L. Wolff in *ZDA*, lxi (1924), 181 ff.; Ranke in *Anzeiger f. deutsches Altertum*, xlv (1926), 9 ff.

[4] Ehrismann, op. cit., p. 228 n.; E. Karg-Gasterstädt, *Zur Entstehungsgeschichte des Parzival* (Halle, 1925).

[5] Eggers in *Euphorion*, xlvii (1953), 260–70.

[6] L. Grimm, *Wolfram von Eschenbach und die Zeitgenossen* (Leipzig, 1897); Schreiber, op. cit.; Karg-Gasterstädt, op. cit.; Schwietering, 'Die Bedeutung des Zimiers bei Wolfram', *Germania*, *Sievers-Festschrift* (Halle, 1925), pp. 554–82; Cucuel, op. cit.; Hatto in *ZDA*, lxxxiv (1953), 232–40.

of his final success (Books III, V, IX, and XVI). His half-brother Feirefiz appears not only in Book I, when he is born, and in Books XV and XVI, when he is reunited with Parzival, but also in Books VI and X. Similarly, Herzeloide, in addition to her significant role in the beginning (Books II and III) and her repeated mention at the end (Books XV and XVI), is also referred to in Books VI and IX because of certain character traits which Parzival has inherited from her and because through her he is related to the Grail family. So is his father Gahmuret and his *art*, the Anschevin legacy, hardly ever lost sight of (except in Books IV and X–XI). Most deliberately, of course, the Grail, for which Parzival searches and longs ever since he has been in its presence (Book V), is kept also in the reader's mind through significant allusions in nearly every subsequent Book—twice, we remember, in striking conjunction with Condwiramurs, Parzival's wife (Books VI and XI). This art of composition must be Wolfram's own, since we find it not only in *Parzival* but also in his later work *Willehalm.*

A poet as original as Wolfram in content, the development of character, and composition is not likely to have been a slavish imitator in matters of style.[1] Hence, if various features of Wolfram's manner of writing have been shown to occur elsewhere, especially in the so-called *trovar clus* of contemporary French poetry, this fact merely confirms what we have always known: first of all, the homogeneity of many aspects of European culture in medieval times, and furthermore the possibility of the same or similar expressions arising independently for the same basic or general concepts. Ironically enough, the far-fetched and obscure metaphors, though relatively infrequent and by no means the most characteristic feature of Wolfram's style, have, on the one hand, given rise to the theory of the poet's complete surrender to the foreign model of 'Asianism', while on the other they have been claimed as the most genuinely Germanic elements of his style. In fact, the epithets which the German poet quite ostentatiously favours for Gahmuret and his sons, such as 'der minnen geltes lôn', i.e. Gahmuret (23, 7), 'ein waltswende', i.e. Feirefiz (57, 23), 'ein smit mit swerten', i.e. Parzival (112, 28), suggest the atmosphere of the native heroic epics, some of them come very close to the kennings of Old Germanic and Old Norse convention.[2]

Much more typical of Wolfram's style is his obvious predilection for extremes, for a crass realism or sober rationalization on the one hand, and uncontrolled fancy and vague suggestiveness on the other. It is this incongruity that has caused some modern critics to look for foreign models or parallels

---

[1] For older bibliography on Wolfram's style, see Ehrismann, op. cit., pp. 264–70. More recent analyses are Weber, *Wolfram von Eschenbach*, pp. 153–307; Mergell op. cit., *passim*; Wehrli in *Deutschunterricht*, vi (1954), 17–40. On Wolfram's humour see K. Kant, *Scherz und Humor in Wolframs von Eschenbach Dichtungen* (Heilbronn, 1878).

[2] Weber, *Wolfram von Eschenbach*, pp. 252–85; Springer in *JEGP*, l (1950), 218–42 (on 'ein smit mit swerten').

and to describe his style with so elastic a label as 'baroque'. And it was no doubt this same incongruity that fascinated or bewildered, misled or irritated his contemporaries and immediate successors.

Nobody attacked Wolfram more viciously, and specifically from the stylistic point of view, than the author of *Tristan* in his famous critical review of the poets of his day (*Tristan*, vss. 4636–88).[1] To Gottfried von Strassburg, lover and master of harmonious form, of a crystal-clear mode of expression, of even-tempered rhythm and exquisite rime, Wolfram was the artistic antipode, whose *Parzival*, Gottfried raged, was written in uncourtly, far-fetched, obscure language, so that commentators were needed to understand what he wanted to say.[2] Moreover Wolfram was a 'vindære wilder mære, der mære wildenære',[3] a poet of wild imagination who deviated from well-established authorities and even invented, as the spirit moved him, whole characters and episodes without a source.

In contrast to this furiously hostile contemporary, almost all later narrative poets admired the author of *Parzival*; many tried to imitate, some to outdo him in his own poetic manner. Most telling is the case of Wirnt von Gravenberg, already referred to, who in his *Wigalois* followed Hartmann's literary example, until the first six books of *Parzival* fell into his hands, whereupon he decided to emulate Wolfram (beginning about vs. 6343).[4] Many others imitated him slavishly, adopted literally many of his words and phrases, or even lifted entire passages from his work, such as Berthold von Holle, Rudolf von Ems, Der Pleier, Reinbot von Dürne, Reinfrid von Braunschweig, and, at the end of the thirteenth century, Albrecht von Scharfenberg both in his *Seifrid de Ardemont*, and even more so, in his *Jüngere Titurel*.[5] Half a century later, two Alsatians, Claus Wisse and Philipp Colin (1331–6), expanded Wolfram's work by a huge interpolation of 36,426 lines between Books XIV and XV, most of which was a verbatim translation of the French *Elucidation* and the so-called Continuations, except that of Gerbert.[6]

This popularity of Wolfram's *Parzival* is confirmed by the survival of over seventy more or less complete manuscripts, the largest number for any work of medieval German literature.[7]

---

[1] For bibliography of Wolfram-Gottfried relations see Ehrismann, op. cit., pp. 220 f., n. 5. See also K. K. Klein in *Ammann-Festgabe* (Innsbruck, 1953), pp. 75–94, and in *ZDA*, lxxxv (1954), 150–62.

[2] See Gottfried's *Tristan*, ed. Ranke, vss. 4638, 4684–6, 7954.　　　[3] Ibid., vss. 4665 f.

[4] Ehrismann, op. cit., p. 223, notes 3, 4; *Wigalois*, ed. J. M. N. Kapteyn (Bonn, 1926), i. 267.

[5] Ehrismann, op. cit., pp. 222–5, and notes.

[6] Ed. K. Schorbach (Strasbourg, 1888). See Ehrismann, op. cit., Schlussband, pp. 471 f.; Roach, op. cit. i, p. xxxiii.

[7] For list of manuscripts see Ehrismann, op. cit., pp. 225 f., and the editions by E. Martin, i, pp. i–xxxiv, and Lachmann, 7th ed. For comparison of *Parzival* with manuscripts of Chrétien's *Perceval* see Fourquet, op. cit.

At the end of the fifteenth century Ulrich Füetrer used 'Wolforam's' poem to incorporate the story of Parzival in his gigantic compilation *Buch der Abenteuer* (c. 1490).[1] It is quite possible that Füetrer, who was a friend and contemporary of Püterich von Reichartshausen, the belated admirer of chivalry and ruthless collector of courtly poetry, became acquainted with *Parzival*, as with so many other medieval works, through Püterich's unique library. It was Püterich who, as he recalls in his *Ehrenbrief* (1462), vss. 127–30, on his 'antiquarian' travels visited the grave of Wolfram in the little town of Eschenbach.[2] As late as 1608 the Nuremberg patrician Kress still saw the grave,[3] at a time when the proud exponent of courtly life and medieval thought had long been relegated to the homely fame of being one of the Meistersinger and the author of the so-called *Titurel*-stanza. Another century and a half were to pass until by the middle of the eighteenth century Bodmer, and early in the nineteenth century both the German romanticists and the first students of Old German literature, brought Wolfram to life again as the author of the greatest medieval German epic.[4]

---

[1] Excellent introduction by F. Panzer to the edition of Füetrer's *Merlin* and *Seifrid de Ardemont*, *Bibl. d. Lit. Vereins zu Stuttgart*, ccxxvii (1902), pp. vii–xxiii. Biographical sketch by Ring in U. Thieme, F. Becker, *Allgemeines Lexikon der bildenden Künste*, xii (Leipzig, 1916), 574 f.; J. Boyd, *Ulrich Füetrer's Parzival; Material and Sources* (Oxford, 1936).

[2] Von Karajan in *ZDA*, vi (1848), 31–59, and facsimile edition by Behrend and Wolkan (Leipzig, 1920).

[3] Frommann in *Anzeiger für Kunde der deutschen Vorzeit*, N.F., viii (1861), cols. 355–9. Helm in *Beiträge*, xxxv (1909), 323–9.

[4] J. Götz, *Die Entwicklung des Wolframbildes von Bodmer bis zum Tode Lachmanns* (Endingen, 1940); R. Lowet, *Wolfram von Eschenbachs Parzival im Wandel der Zeiten* (Munich, 1955).—I am indebted for much helpful criticism to Prof. Helen Adolf and Dr. Richard Clark.

THE WORK OF ROBERT DE BORON
AND THE *DIDOT PERCEVAL*

PIERRE LE GENTIL

A STARTLING and most important development in the literary history of the Grail is represented by the work of a poet endowed with bold-ness and piety but with mediocre talent, Robert de Boron.[1] The one source of information about him is MS. fr. 20047 in the Bibliothèque Nationale. It preserves our sole copy of a poem of 3,514 verses, known generally as *Joseph d'Arimathie*.[2] This poem is followed without a break by 502 verses, presumably by the same author, which after introducing the story of Merlin are interrupted in the middle of a speech.

The *Joseph*, after a prologue dealing with the Fall of Man and leading up to the Passion, tells how the *veissel* in which Christ made His sacrament at the Last Supper (vss. 395 f.) was first given by a Jew to Pilate, and then by Pilate to Joseph of Arimathea, who used it at the deposition from the Cross to catch the last drops of the Messiah's blood. Joseph, victim of the Jews' hatred, is imprisoned, but the risen Saviour visits him, bearing the precious vessel, and entrusts it to him, with the information that only three men, in-cluding himself, will have it in their care. Long after, the emperor Vespasian, having been cured of leprosy by Veronica, arrives in Jerusalem to avenge Christ's death, and releases Joseph, who has been miraculously kept alive without food or drink. We are now abruptly introduced to a new cast of characters, Joseph's sister Enygeus and her husband Hebron or Bron. With these two and other followers of the Christ, Joseph leaves Judea and for a long time dwells in foreign lands. Some of the company are guilty of lechery, and all suffer consequently from starvation. In order to detect the guilty and in obedience to the Holy Spirit, Joseph sets up, in memory of the Last Supper, the table and the service of the Grail. On this table he places the vessel and

---

[1] Besides the bibliographical references provided by R. Bossuat, *Manuel Bibliographique* (1951) and U. T. Holmes, *Critical Bibliography*, i (1952), one should consult Bruce, i. 230–45; ii. 114–35; Nitze in *Spec*, xxviii (1953), 279–96; Hoepffner in R. Nelli, *Lumière du Graal* (Paris, 1951), 139–51; A. Pauphilet, *Legs du Moyen Âge* (Paris, 1950), pp. 184–9; R. Brummer, *Die erzählende Prosadichtung in den romanischen Literaturen des XIII Jahrhunderts* (Berlin, 1948), i, chap. ii; P. A. Becker in *ZRP*, lv (1935), 260–9; Frappier in *R*, lxxv (1954), 165–210; Micha in *R*, lxxv. 317–52.

[2] The most recent and best edition is that of Nitze, entitled *Roman de l'Estoire dou Graal, CFMA* (1927).

opposite to it a fish specially caught by Bron. Only those who believe in the
Trinity and live cleanly are summoned to sit at the table, and there they
have all that their hearts desire. 'Car nus le Graal ne verra, Ce croi je, qu'il
ne li agree' (vss. 2660 f.). (For no one will see the Grail, I believe, that it does
not delight him.) Thus, mistakenly, the word *graal* is derived from the verb
agreer. The sinners, however, feel no pleasure. One of them, Moyses,
attempts to sit in the vacant seat reserved for the unborn son of Bron, and is
swallowed up by the earth. The voice of God declares that the seat will not
be filled till Bron's grandson (note the contradiction) shall fill it. Time passes
and twelve sons are born to Bron and Enygeus. Eleven of them marry,
but the twelfth, Alain, is to remain celibate, to take charge of his brothers,
and to lead them to the farthest west, preaching Christ. Nevertheless
(another contradiction), Alain is to have a male heir, who will be a keeper
of the holy vessel (vss. 3091–3). A certain Petrus is also to betake himself
to the west to the 'vaus d'Avaron' (the vales of Avaron), and there await
the coming of Alain's son. Bron, who is to be called the Rich Fisher because of the fish which he caught for the Grail table, is to receive the holy
vessel from Joseph and to proceed likewise to the west and await the coming
of his grandson, to whom the vessel will be delivered. Thus the meaning of
the blessed Trinity will be fulfilled. First Alain, then Petrus, then Bron depart, Bron taking the Grail and everything with him, while Joseph remains
behind.

The poem thus briefly summarized contains several references to the
author and his plans, but they are more fitted to rouse curiosity than to satisfy
it. As for Robert's name, vs. 3155 prefixes the title *meistres*; vs. 3461 the
title *messires*; the former reads *Bouron*, the latter *Beron*. It is thought, rightly
it seems, that *messires* is preferable to *meistres*, and if so, Robert would have
been a knight rather than a cleric.[1] Then there are the oft-quoted verses of
the epilogue:

> A ce tens que je la [l'estoire dou Graal] retreis
> O mon seigneur Gautier en peis,
> Qui de Mont Belyal estoit,
> Unques retreite esté n'avoit.

(At the time that I related [the history of the Grail] with my lord Gautier in peace,
who was of Mont Belyal, it had never been related.)

One is led to believe that Robert, being connected with a lord of Montbéliard—how else should one interpret 'Mont Belyal'?—was a native of
Boron, a village about eleven miles distant from Montbéliard.[2] We know

---

[1] Nitze in *Spec*, xxviii. 280; L. Foulet in *R*, lxxi (1950), 22.

[2] Nitze in *MP*, xl (1942), 113–16, and in *Spec*, xxviii. 280 f. The connexion of Robert de Boron
with Burgundy is confirmed by his dialect, which, according to Nitze, is Francien-Picard with Bur-

that a certain Gautier de Montbéliard set out in 1202 for Italy, took part in the Fourth Crusade, and died in the Holy Land in 1212. How, then, can one account for the mention of the 'vaus d'Avaron' (vss. 3123, 3221), apparently a reference to the flat marshlands surrounding Glastonbury?[1] What does 'related with my lord Gautier' signify? Does 'at peace' apply to a period before the Crusade or after the death of Gautier, or is it a mere rime tag?[2] Does 'retreis' refer to a reading of the manuscript of the *Joseph*, and, if so, was this an earlier redaction than the one we possess? Naturally various opinions have been set forth as to Robert's home and the date of his poem. One point seems settled: he originated in eastern Burgundy and dwelt at or near Montbéliard—a view supported by his language, though it does not exclude the possibility of contacts with south-western Britain.[3] As for date, if the past tense of the verb *estoit* in vs. 3491 means that Gautier was dead, then the epilogue to the *Joseph* was written after 1212, but this is no necessary conclusion. If the verb refers to the period before Gautier's departure, then the epilogue would be written after 1202. If the 'vaus d'Avaron' refer to Glastonbury, as most probably they do, we have a fairly secure *terminus a quo* in 1191, the year when Arthur's grave was discovered and Glastonbury was equated with Avalon.[4]

Robert's allusions to his sources and his literary projects are equally tantalizing. He refers in vss. 932–6 to his possession of the great book, written by the great clerks, which contains the 'grant secré . . . qu'en numme le Graal'—a strange formula because of the unusual sense it gives to the word *graal*.[5] Moreover, as we have seen, Robert asserts in his epilogue that the story of the Grail had never been told before he told it himself. Are these two passages contradictory? In vss. 3456–8, we are informed that many tales were told, 'meintes paroles contées', about the good Fisher, that is Hebron or Bron. Furthermore, Chrétien de Troyes had already described Perceval's

gundian traits. The Anglo-Norman Robert de Burun, on the other hand, belonged to a family of that name, of which two members were mentioned in Domesday Book and several members were christened Robert. C. H. Pearson, 'On the Early Byrons and Robert de Burun', in *Seynt Graal or the Sank Ryal*, ed. F. J. Furnivall, Roxburghe Club, ii, pp. xiii–xix.

[1] On Avalon-Glastonbury tradition see J. Armitage Robinson, *Two Glastonbury Legends* (Cambridge, 1926); Bruce, i. 198–200, 262–8; Faral, ii. 451–60; F. Lot, *Étude sur le Lancelot en Prose* (Paris, 1918), pp. 126–32, 204–14; *Perlesvaus*, ed. Nitze and others (Chicago, 1932–7), ii. 47–72; J. Marx in *MA*, lix (1953), 69–86; and Chap. 7 above and Chap. 21 below.

[2] Is 'o' to be translated 'with', 'in the company of', and does 'en peis' imply that Gautier had not yet left for the Crusade or that he was dead? See Nitze in *Spec*, xxviii. 280.

[3] F. Michel and Suchier sought to identify the poet with a certain Robert de Burun, mentioned in an Essex charter, granting land in Hertfordshire to a monastery in Picardy. This view is accepted by Marx, loc. cit., and in his *Légende Arthurienne et le Graal* (Paris, 1952), pp. 308 f., 391, but is questioned by Nitze in *Spec*, xxviii. 282 f., by Hoepffner in *Les Romans du Graal* (Strasbourg, 1956), p. 94, and denied by R. S. Loomis in *Spec*, xxvii (1952), 410, and in Chap. 21 below. On the poet's language see Nitze in *Spec*, xxviii. 280 f.

[4] *Perlesvaus*, ed. Nitze, ii. 59–70.

[5] Nitze in *Spec*, xxviii. 283; Hoepffner in Nelli, *Lumière du Graal*, p. 145.

meeting with the Fisher King and the Grail procession in the castle. How does one reconcile these statements?

What is certain is that Robert, having finished the *Joseph*, did not think his work complete. According to vss. 3463–80, he had not yet related Alain's adventures; he had not followed Petrus to Avaron nor Moyses into the pit; he had not accompanied on his travels the Rich Fisher, the custodian of the Grail. 'But', continues Robert, 'if God grants me life and health, I will assemble these parts if I can find them in a book (se en livre les puis trouver)'. He concludes thus (vss. 3501–7).

> Ausi cumme d'une partie
> Leisse, que je ne retrei mie,
> Ausi couvenra il conter
> La quinte, et les quatre oublier,
> Tant que je puisse revenir
> Au retreire plus par loisir.

(Just as I leave out a part which I do not tell, so I must relate the fifth part and forget the four, until I can return to telling them more at leisure.)

This characteristically obscure passage seems to mean that the poet is postponing the sequel to the story begun in the *Joseph* for lack of information. He intends later to take up Alain, Petrus, Moyses, and Bron, but for the time being he is introducing a fifth tale, presumably the *Merlin*, which immediately follows.[1]

The *Joseph*, as we have seen, contains a number of contradictions and obscurities which leap to the eye. Are they due to carelessness or to the diversity of Robert's sources? To read a few pages of the poem is enough to convince one that its style is crude and inartistic. But mediocre artistry does not necessarily entail lack of logic, nor does it explain, for example, why, within the space of a few lines, the third keeper of the Grail ceases to be Alain and becomes Alain's son, though Alain has been represented as vowed to celibacy.[2]

Are the sources, then, responsible for the strange disharmony? Some of them are known. Everything concerned with the destruction of Jerusalem and the imprisonment of Joseph comes either from the *Gesta Pilati*, which forms a large part of the apocryphal *Evangelium Nicodemi*, or from the *Vindicta Salvatoris* and the *Cura Sanitatis Tiberii*, or from an early version of Titus and Vespasian; while the symbolism of the mass derives from Honorius Augustodunensis.[3] But these works, even supplemented by the

---

[1] Nitze in *MP*, xli (1943), 1–5; in *Spec*, xxviii. 287.

[2] On these contradictions see Hoepffner in Nelli, *Lumière du Graal*, pp. 143 f.; Nitze in *Spec*, xxviii. 286; Micha in *R*, lxxv (1954), 240–3; Marx in *MA*, lix. 73, 77.

[3] *Roman de l'Estoire dou Graal*, ed. Nitze, pp. ix–xii; Becker in *ZRP*, lv (1935), 262 ff.; Gryling in *Mod. Lang. Journal*, xxxviii (1954), 15–17.

new cult of the Holy Blood,[1] do not explain everything. In particular they do not explain why Robert extended the role of Joseph and laid such stress on the vessel of the Last Supper, the Grail, and why, above all, he forecast the arrival of the Grail and its keeper in the West, presumably in Britain. Was it his purpose to combine elements from the gospels and the apocrypha with suggestions furnished by Chrétien's *Perceval* in order to provide a prologue to the latter work? But can one be sure that Robert was acquainted with Chrétien's poem?[2] The similarities and the differences between the two works are equally remarkable. In both a vessel called the Grail is the centre of interest; in both a keeper of the Grail is known as the Rich Fisher or the Fisher King; in both the Grail provides sustenance either to a company seated at a table, or to a single holy invalid; in both the Grail is conceived as a sacred vessel, preserved or destined to be preserved in Britain. But for Robert the vessel is filled with the Holy Blood and represents the chalice of the sacrament, whereas Chrétien makes it the receptacle of the sacred Host, and implies that it was large enough to contain a salmon. Furthermore, Robert does not mention Chrétien's lance, gives a quite different explanation for the title of the Fisher,[3] makes no allusion to the Arthurian world, and offers no hint that the third keeper of the Grail is to be a knight of the Round Table called Perceval.[4] If, indeed, Robert knew Chrétien's poem, he must have found it unsatisfactory and felt obliged to make drastic changes.

But what could have given him the idea of linking the evangelization of Britain with the transfer of the Grail to the West? How did he know of the identification of the 'vaus d'Avaron' with Glastonbury? Where did he find the name Bron or Hebron attached to the Rich Fisher, Joseph's brother-in-law? If one grants the possibility that Robert de Boron could have been in contact with Glastonbury, what might he have learned there late in the twelfth or early in the thirteenth century? Certainly traditions about the settlement of a Christian community there as early as apostolic times, and certainly the notion that Glastonbury was Avalon. But it is far from certain,

---

[1] On cult of the Sacred Blood see Bruce, i. 287; Marx, *Légende Arthurienne*, pp. 244, 300 f.

[2] Hoepffner discusses this question in *Les Romans du Graal* (Strasbourg, 1956), pp. 93–105, and most critics agree with him that Robert knew Chrétien's poem (ibid., pp. 105 f.). But see Nitze in *Spec*, xxviii. 288; Marx in *MA*, lix. 79. Loomis admits as a possibility that Robert used Chrétien but only if he composed a *Perceval* continuation of his *Merlin* and only in that part. *RR*, xxxii (1942), 173 f.

[3] In Chrétien the king is wounded and fishes to amuse himself, but in Boron he owes his title to the fish he caught and laid on the Grail table. For Robert's etymology *graal < agreer*, see Nitze in *Spec*, xxviii. 285; typically medieval, it calls for no further comment. On Moyses as representative of the Old Law see Nitze, ibid., p. 286. It is unnecessary to point out that Robert connected the fish with the *ichthus*, symbol of Christ and the eucharist. L. H. Loomis in *Art Studies*, v (1927), 71–78. Bruce, i. 261.

[4] Among the features common to Chrétien and Robert should be noted the use of the word *descovert* applied to the Grail. For recent discussions of the word see Frappier in *R*, lxxi (1950), 243; lxxiii (1952), 82–93; in *BBSIA*, 1950, pp. 88–93; Nitze in *Spec*, xxviii. 284, n. 10.

in fact, it is a matter of vigorous controversy, whether the monks of Glastonbury had at this time even heard of the Grail or of any evangelistic mission
sent out by Joseph of Arimathea.[1] Are we any better informed about Bron,
alias Hebron?[2] Robert seems to have had the book of Numbers in mind, for
Hebron, a son of Kohath, was one of those named as serving the Ark of the
Covenant. But it is probable that Robert employed the alternative form Bron
because he had some confused and indirect acquaintance with the Welsh
legends of Brân the Blessed, renowned for his hospitality and his wounded
foot, legends to which in their French form he alludes as the 'meintes paroles'
told about the good Fisher.

The effort to combine such heterogeneous materials as the biblical and
apocryphal elements, the Glastonbury claims, and the strange tales about
Bron would account in large measure for the imperfections of Robert's
narrative. And one should not exclude the possibility that the great book
containing the secret of the Grail, to which he appealed as the source of his
knowledge, actually existed, that in it he found assembled the miscellaneous
ingredients of his poem, and that his worst blunders were due, not entirely
to his own incoherent thinking, but to the obscurities of that alleged source,
passages which lent themselves to inconsistent interpretations. The fact that
the new work, the *Merlin*, is noticeably free from such self-contradictions
might be regarded as favouring this view. If we take him at his word, we
must envisage him as baffled by the abrupt termination of his source and
obliged therefore to turn to another subject until he should find a sequel to
the stories of Bron, Alain, Petrus, and Moyses.

The new subject he found in the stories of Merlin, which could be used
as a bridge from Eastern lands and apostolic times over to the Britain of King
Arthur's days, when presumably the marvels of the Grail would reach their
culmination. As has been said, Robert's *Merlin* survives only as a fragment,[3]
but there is general agreement that a prose redaction of the complete poem
was made which has come down to us in two slightly different forms, as a
part of the Vulgate cycle and as an introduction to the *Suite du Merlin*.[4] There
is no reason to doubt that the poem represented the fifth part which Robert
announced at the end of the *Joseph*, for the links are clear. It begins with a
prologue which matches the prologue to the earlier work. While the *Joseph*

---

[1] See Chap. 21 below.

[2] *Roman de l'Estoire dou Graal*, ed. Nitze, p. xii; Nitze in *Spec*, xxviii. 286 f., in *Medieval Studies
in Memory of G. Schoepperle Loomis* (New York, Paris, 1927), pp. 135–45; H. Newstead, *Bran the
Blessed in Arthurian Romance* (New York, 1939), pp. 29–46. For Enygeus, the name of Bron's wife,
see Imbs in *BBSIA*, 1954, pp. 67–73.

[3] Included in Nitze's edition of Robert's *Roman de l'Estoire dou Graal*. See the chapter on Robert
in P. Zumthor, *Merlin le Prophète* (Lausanne, 1943), and Brummer, *Die erzählende Prosadichtung*,
pp. 52 ff.

[4] The prose version found in the Huth and Cambridge manuscripts is closer to Robert's poem than
the Vulgate redaction. See Brugger in *RF*, xxvi (1906), 1–166.

begins with expounding God's scheme to thwart the Fiend through the gift of His Son, the *Merlin* begins with a similar exposition of the infernal plot to undo the work of the Messiah. Moreover, the two poems were connected by Merlin's retelling the history of Joseph and by his causing King Uther to establish a third table on the model of the table of the Last Supper and the table of the Grail.[1] Thus the continuity between the two works is maintained. Since the contents of Robert's *Merlin* are most fully preserved in the prose redactions, his treatment of the theme will be reserved for discussion in Chap. 23.

Two very corrupt versions of the prose *Joseph* and the prose *Merlin*, found in MS. Bib. Nat., nouv. acq. fr. 4166, and in MS. 3.39 at the Estense Library, Modena,[2] are followed by a third prose romance, known as the *Didot Perceval*, so called after a former owner of the first manuscript.[3] The two texts of the *Didot Perceval*, which will be designated respectively by the letters E and D, vary considerably from each other and must be regarded as defective renderings of a common original.[4] They tell, however, in spite of divergences, substantially the same story, which was intended as a sequel to the *Joseph* and the *Merlin*, for we meet again Bron and his son Alain, there is reference to Moyses, Merlin plays his familiar role,[5] and the adventures of the Siege Perilous and the Grail are brought to an end. But of Petrus we learn nothing, and there are astonishing discrepancies between the two earlier romances and the Perceval continuation. There follows also an unanticipated *Mort Artu*, corresponding roughly to Geoffrey of Monmouth's narrative of the end of Arthur's reign. Let me summarize.

Very abruptly we are introduced to Alain and a new character, his son Perceval. According to E, Alain often expressed his intent to take the youth to Arthur's court; according to D, the Holy Ghost informed Alain that his father Bron was dwelling in the isles of Ireland; that Perceval was destined to find him and to heal him of his infirmity; but that first the youth must go to Arthur's court. According to both texts, when Alain dies, Perceval goes to the court, and after acquitting himself brilliantly in a tournament to win the favour of Gauvain's sister, he rashly takes his seat in the Siege Perilous

---

[1] Nitze in *Spec*, xxviii. 289.

[2] Roach has published the Modena text of the Prose *Joseph* in *RP*, ix (1956), 313–42.

[3] The authoritative edition is *The Didot Perceval according to the Manuscripts of Modena and Paris*, ed. W. Roach (Philadelphia, 1941). For reviews of this book see R. S. Loomis, *RR*, xxxiii (1942), pp. 168–74; A. Henry, *R*, 1948, pp. 85, 256 f.; J. Frank, *MA*, 1948, pp. 170–6; H. F. Williams, *MP*, 1948–9, pp. 252–8. Brugger's treatment of the *Didot Perceval* in *ZFSL*, liii (1930), 389–459, whose conclusions are adopted by Roach, is still of prime importance.

[4] *Didot Perceval*, ed. Roach, pp. 2–11, especially p. 9. Since the texts of the Prose *Joseph* and *Merlin* in the two manuscripts are among the most defective and abridged, the *Perceval* in the same manuscripts is all the more suspect.

[5] Merlin's appearance after Arthur's coronation, which is found only in D and E, should be regarded as the conclusion of the *Merlin*. See Brugger in *ZFSL*, liii. 389 ff., Nitze in *Spec*, xxviii. 289, and Roach's edition, pp. 11–15 and appendix A.

at the Round Table. Beneath him the stone splits with a roar, great darkness issues from the earth, and a voice proclaims that, because of Perceval's temerity, Bron will not be healed of his malady, nor the stone joined together, nor the enchantments of Britain removed till a knight who has surpassed all others in prowess, shall ask what the Grail is and 'cui on en sert' (whom one serves with it). Perceval swears never to stay two nights under one roof till he has found the house of Bron, the Fisher King. He triumphs over Orguelleus de la Lande; he enters the Castle of the Chessboard, and for love of its lady undertakes to procure the head of the White Stag. After fighting the Black Knight of the Tomb, he visits in turn his sister and his uncle, the Hermit, both of whom tell him that he is destined to find his grandfather and receive from him the Grail. And we have a number of assorted adventures: the meeting with the Ugly Damsel and her escort, 'li Biaus Mauvais' (the Handsome Coward); the combat at the ford with Urbain and his flock of black birds; the vision of the children playing in the tree; Merlin's appearance as a shadow, prophesying Perceval's arrival at his destination. Riding on, Perceval sees the Fisher King in his boat, and entering his fortress witnesses the passing and return of a procession consisting of a richly robed damsel bearing two dishes (*tailleors*), a youth carrying a bleeding lance, and a second youth holding aloft Joseph's vessel. But Perceval remains silent for fear of displeasing his host. The next morning he wakes to find the castle deserted, and, riding forth, is reproached by a weeping damsel. He brings to a successful conclusion the adventure of the White Stag, spurns the temptings of the Lady of the Chessboard, and wanders for seven years in desperation, forgetting God. At last he finds his uncle, the Hermit, confesses and does penance. There follows a long description of a tournament before he comes once more to the Grail castle and asks the disenchanting question. The Fisher King is healed and at the bidding of the Holy Ghost instructs his grandson in the secrets of the Grail and entrusts the vessel to him, only to die on the third day. The split in the Siege Perilous closes; Merlin announces to Arthur the fulfilment of the Grail quest and the end of the enchantments of Britain, and dictates an account of these events to Blaise.

There follows the *Mort Artu* section. The King, being reminded of a prophecy of Merlin's, undertakes and achieves the conquest of Gaul. He returns in triumph, only to be faced by the demand of the Roman envoys for tribute. The rest is well known: the second victory on the continent, Mordred's treason, the wounding of Arthur, and his departure to Avalon to be healed by his sister Morghain. There is a reference to Arthur's survival as a huntsman and to the Bretons' belief in his return.[1] Merlin, after recounting all these sad matters to Blaise, takes leave of him and Perceval, retires to a

---

[1] See Chap. 7 above.

dwelling called by the puzzling name, 'l'esplumoir Merlin', and has never been seen since.

The problem of the authorship and composition of the *Didot Perceval* is far from simple, and has taxed the critical powers of many learned men. Brugger and Roach have proposed an attractive and elaborate theory,[1] which may be sketched as follows: Since the texts concerned with Perceval and the *Mort Artu* found in MSS. D and E are preceded by the prose *Joseph* and the prose *Merlin*, and are linked to them by references backward and forward, they must have had the same origin. Peculiarities of diction common to all four works support this conclusion.[2] The *Didot Perceval* would then belong to a homogeneous *ensemble*, entirely conceived and executed by Robert de Boron in the form of a tetralogy, containing as well as the *Joseph* and *Merlin*, a *Perceval* and a *Mort Artu*, also in verse. Like the two preceding sections, the *Perceval* and the *Mort Artu* were turned into prose, but the E and D texts offer but a remote likeness to the initial form. Whereas the *Joseph* and *Merlin* were taken over intact except for certain omissions and minor changes, the *Perceval*, on the other hand, was subjected to considerable inter-polation and recasting. Hoffmann drew up a long list of borrowings made by the *Didot Perceval* from Chrétien and the so-called Wauchier (Second) Continuation.[3] Brugger and Roach assert that Robert cannot be held respon-sible for these borrowings; very probably he did not know Chrétien's work, and even less probably the Wauchier Continuation; in any case he could not have failed to note the violent disharmonies between them and what he had already written in the *Joseph* and *Merlin*. Only a clumsy and irresponsible *remanieur* could have thought of introducing into Robert's *Perceval*, com-posed in conformity with his earlier work, these foreign, discordant elements which upset the balance of the tetralogy. Therefore we must postulate an archetype p, representing a faithful prose redaction of Robert's work, which was succeeded by *rifacimento* z, from which in turn the version D, shortened and carelessly copied, was directly derived; while E, more careful and rela-tively free, was linked to z through an intermediary w, which sought to reduce some of z's inconsistencies. This, then, is the solution proposed by Brugger and Roach to the difficulties raised by the *Didot Perceval*.

As to the problem of date, these authors argue that since the original p or the redaction z was used by Manessier in his Continuation and doubtless by Raoul de Houdenc in *Meraugis de Portlesguez*, Robert's tetralogy must have been rendered into prose between 1190 and 1212, probably in 1202; in other words very soon after the completion of the verse *Joseph*, dated about 1200.[4]

---

[1] See above, p. 257, n. 3. [2] *ZFSL*, liii. 402 ff.
[3] W. Hoffmann, *Die Quellen des Didot Perceval* (Halle, 1905).
[4] *Didot Perceval*, ed. Roach, pp. 125–30.

It remains to reconstruct the probable contents of the archetype, stripped of all the clumsy patchings it has suffered, bearing in mind, too, the amputations of which it may also have been the victim. Brugger and Roach have not failed to apply their learning and ingenuity to this task, but the bulky chapter which the editor of the *Didot Perceval* devotes to 'the composition and sources' of the work is enough to reveal the dangers involved. It appears that ten at least of the sixteen episodes forming the *Perceval* proper must be eliminated from the hypothetical archetype, since they come undeniably from Chrétien and the Second Continuation.[1] Under such conditions, as certain critics have stressed,[2] the archetype dwindles to such an extent that it is hard to see what sequel it could have provided for the Siege Perilous test, and in what form it could have presented the final success of the hero. Inevitably the question arises: is it certain that the archetype existed? This, of course, is to challenge the whole hypothesis put forward by Brugger and Roach. Must one then, with R. S. Loomis,[3] make Robert himself responsible for all the faults of the *Didot Perceval*, as well as those of the *Joseph*? One could then economize a *remanieur* by identifying p and z in the stemma proposed above. But is it not simpler to follow Gröber, Heinzel, Bruce, and others[4] in thinking that the author of the *Joseph* and *Merlin* did not supplement these poems with a *Perceval*? Why should not the *Didot Perceval* represent, though in corrupt form, the work of a continuator, who had the bold notion of combining the tradition created by Robert with that created by Chrétien but was ill fitted to cope with the formidable difficulties of his task? All that can be said at present is that the arguments of Brugger and Roach are not so conclusive as to eliminate these other possibilities.[5]

In any case, it must be admitted that the tetralogy consisting of the *Joseph*, the *Merlin*, the *Perceval*, and the *Mort Artu* is loose in construction. The *Joseph* makes no reference to Merlin or Perceval, nor does the *Merlin* mention Perceval, in spite of the fact that Robert seems anxious to maintain continuity and to forecast the future. In the *Merlin* the Grail theme is almost forgotten, and in the *Perceval* it is worked out in a fashion which accords ill with the *Joseph*. The *Mort Artu*, except for the activities of Merlin, seems a postscript. It is tempting to join Pauphilet in regarding the tetralogy as a unit only in the sense that the parts are preserved together in manuscripts D and E.

Confining our attention to the *Didot Perceval*, let us examine the sources. There are, of course, certain features carried over from the preceding works:

[1] A more detailed account of Roach's theory cannot be given here, since too brief a summary might not represent it adequately.

[2] H. Tiemann in *RF*, lxiii (1951), 306–28; Nitze in *Spec*, xxviii. 293.

[3] *RR*, xxxii. 169 f.

[4] Roach in his edition, pp. 119–25, provides a full account of the views of these scholars.

[5] This is also the opinion of Nitze in *MP*, xli (1943), 1–5, and in *Spec*, xxviii. 293. Many will regard Micha's argument in favour of a continuator(*R*, lxxv [1954], 334–52) as decisive.

the reappearance of Bron and Alain, the announcements of the divine voice, the Siege Perilous, the Grail and its mysteries, Merlin and his amanuensis Blaise. There are also the many chivalric and romantic adventures required as a result of the identification of the son of Alain with Perceval and borrowed from Chrétien and his Second Continuator—adventures which are ill suited to the destined keeper of the Holy Vessel, the successor of Joseph of Arimathea and Bron. There are also some traditional themes of Celtic origin, such as the roaring stone, which Marx has traced back to the Irish Lia Fail,[1] and the combat at the ford, in which R. S. Loomis has detected several reminiscences of the *Mabinogion*.[2] In the *Mort Artu* the general resemblance to Geoffrey's *Historia* is easily recognizable, though the immediate source was probably Wace's *Brut* or a lost redaction by an enigmatic Martin of Roecestre or Gloucestre or Rouen.[3] The mysterious *esplumoir* to which Merlin retired must be connected with the verb *esplumer*, meaning 'to pluck out feathers'; an *esplumoir*, then, would be a cage in which birds were kept during the moulting season. Why was the wizard confined in such a cage, and is there any connexion with the familiar theme of his entombment by the perfidious fay? These are unsolved mysteries.[4]

But rather than try to discover of what the *Didot Perceval* was made, should one not try to discover how it was made?[5] Have not scholars, absorbed in the task of distinguishing the elements in the composition, failed to do justice to the composition itself? For, however well or ill the *Didot Perceval* is linked to the *Joseph* and the *Merlin*, it possesses a recognizable structure. Three scenes, the fateful occupation of the Siege Perilous and the two visits to the Grail castle, constitute the main pattern. The first proclaims for Perceval his ultimate destiny; the second marks his progress but also reveals his unripeness to fulfil that destiny; the third crowns his triumph, at last fully merited. To be sure, there is a certain vagueness as to what his merits are and as to the benefits which his achievement of the Grail quest will bring. Otherwise, his exploits are not as haphazard and inconsequential as at first sight they seem to be. On one occasion Perceval redresses an evil custom; on another, though he involved himself in an intrigue with the mistress of the Chessboard Castle, he disentangles himself by pleading his commitment to the Grail quest; he learns from the Handsome Coward and his lady not to trust appearances. It is true that the significance of these episodes is not clarified

---

[1] Marx, *Légende Arthurienne*, pp. 96, 121; R. S. Loomis, *Wales*, pp. 26 f.

[2] *Wales*, pp. 91–104. On the children in the tree, the magic chessboard, and the Handsome Coward see above, p. 214, n. 2, n. 3.

[3] *Didot Perceval*, ed. Roach, pp. 103–10; Nitze in *Spec*, xxviii. 293. The suggestion goes back to Brugger in *ZFSL*, xxix¹ (1905), 60, n. 8; liii (1930), 419, n. 31. See above, p. 94, n. 1.

[4] On *esplumoir* see especially Nitze in *Spec*, xviii (1943), 69–79; R. S. Loomis in *BBSIA*, 1957, pp. 79–83; Brugger's articles on the *Enserrement Merlin* in *ZFSL*, xxix–xxxv.

[5] Pauphilet has been almost alone in this attempt. *Mélanges d'Histoire du Moyen Âge offerts à M. F. Lot* (Paris, 1925), pp. 603–18.

as are similar episodes in the Vulgate *Queste del Saint Graal*, and there are long passages which have no bearing whatsoever on Perceval's chivalric or moral progress. Still, there is in the fortunes of Perceval a noble design, and, without going so far as Pauphilet in claiming that the *Mort Artu* with its blood and tears provides a timely return to the human and realistic plane,[1] it is possible to justify its incorporation in the cycle.

To sum up: Robert de Boron, by reinforcing the eucharistic meaning of the Grail and by transferring the precious relic of the Last Supper to Britain, brought the legend to a new height, whether he did so of his own initiative or was guided by an unknown source. The *Didot Perceval*, whether or not it completes a cycle conceived and realized by Robert himself, does round out, however imperfectly, certain anticipations of the *Joseph* and the *Merlin*, and effects a synthesis of the romantic type of adventure found in Chrétien's poem with the ascetic and sacramental tendencies established by Robert. It also provides the first example of French prose,[2] not entirely successful, to be sure, but full of promise, for even obscurity and incoherence may sharpen the curiosity of readers and stimulate in other authors the ambition to excel. Indeed, though the exact chronology of French literature at the beginning of the thirteenth century is by no means fixed,[3] there is good reason to believe that, without Robert de Boron and without the *Didot Perceval*, the Prose *Lancelot* might not have taken shape at all, or at least would have been something quite different.

---

[1] Ibid., p. 616. See on this point Roach's edition, pp. 123–5. I also consider over-ambitious the religious-allegorical interpretation of the 'Boron cycle' proposed by Zumthor in his *Merlin*, pp. 117–32. See rather Frappier, 'Le Graal et la Chevalerie', *R*, lxxv (1954), 165–210.

[2] Brummer, *Die erzählende Prosadichtung*, pp. 35 ff. Ingenious rather than searching; see Tiemann's criticism in *RF*, lxiii (1951), 306–28.

[3] I have said little of dates in this chapter since I do not think that any can be fixed with certainty In general I regret the tendency of many scholars to place texts of this period as early as possible. See Frappier in *RP*, viii (1954–5), 27–33.

PERLESVAUS

WILLIAM ALBERT NITZE

IT has been well said that the French prose romance of the Grail, *Perlesvaus*, is the Cinderella of Arthurian literature, so slow has it been in winning recognition. For many years scholars regarded it as a late and unoriginal composition, written in the second quarter of the thirteenth century as the last of a series of works dealing with the Grail. This view, first advanced by Birch-Hirschfeld in *Die Sage vom Gral* (1877), has had a long line of adherents, including Nutt, Bruce, Lot, and in part Heinzel. Indeed, Bruce went so far as to reproach the author of *Perlesvaus* for his 'want of judgement' and 'the low level on which his imagination moves'.[1] Almost the only voice raised against this adverse opinion was that of Gaston Paris. Though he did not take occasion to set forth his own ideas in detail, his *Littérature Française au Moyen Âge* places the romance earlier than the *Queste del Saint Graal*, in the composition of which he thought it had a share. With these matters I shall deal presently. Suffice it to say here that the purpose of this chapter is to justify the view that *Perlesvaus* belongs among the earlier Grail romances in prose and that it is by no means a secondary or unimaginative piece of writing, while its historical connexions give it additional interest.

Let us first consider the manuscripts in which it has survived. In 1866 Potvin[2] edited the work from a manuscript (11145) in the Bibliothèque Royale at Brussels.[3] He was not a careful editor, the list of errors is long, and the manuscript is a poor one, but it has an interesting colophon, containing the following assertions:

1. The original from which the story was taken came from a holy house of religion in the Island of Avalon, where King Arthur and Queen Guenevere lie buried.

2. The author promises at some later time to add a continuation in which Brian des Illes will lend his aid to Claudas, Lancelot's enemy, while Lancelot in turn will be helped by a knight of his lineage, Galobrus of the Red Glade.

---

[1] Bruce, ii. 19.

[2] *Perceval le Gallois ou le Conte du Graal*, i (Mons, 1866). Based on the inferior text of MS. Br., this has been translated twice: once into German by Gerhard Gietmann, *Ein Gralbuch* (Freiburg, 1889), and into English by Sebastian Evans, *The High History of the Holy Graal* (London; also Temple Classics and Everyman's Library).

[3] Potvin also lists variants from the fragmentary MS. at Bern.

3. The claim is made that the Lord of Cambrein translated the text from the Latin for the Lord Jean de Nesle. It had been translated once before but that version is so old that one can scarcely make out the letters.

One need not admit that a Latin original of the romance once existed before agreeing that the colophon contains valuable information. In the first place, assertion 1 is found also in MS. O in the Bodleian Library, and, as we shall see, refers definitely to Glastonbury. Assertion 2 cannot refer to the Vulgate cycle because Galobrus does not appear in that work. Finally, assertion 3 mentions Jean de Nesle II, and harmonizes with the fact that the eight manuscripts of *Perlesvaus* fall into two distinct families, one of which must have antedated the other.

It is from MS. O, Hatton 82 at the Bodleian Library, that Thomas Jenkins and I, together with collaborators, edited in 1932–7 the romance as *Le Haut Livre du Graal, Perlesvaus*.[1] This text is written in the *koiné* of north-eastern France and is complete and fairly accurate. It represents the first redaction, and stands close in substance to MS. C and to W, a Welsh redaction.[2] It has an Anglo-Norman superscription, 'Le liuer Sire Brian fitz alayn', designating the owner, Brian Fitzalan, Lord of Bedale, who took part in the Welsh campaign of 1282, and whom Edward I made one of the guardians of Scotland during the vacancy of the throne.

With these facts before us, we can now take up the plot of the romance. The author divides his story into eleven 'branches'. Briefly summarized, it goes as follows:

Branch I. Josephes (i.e. Flavius Josephus, author of the alleged Latin original) begins his story of the chaste knight with an invocation to the Trinity, 'three persons in one substance, and that substance is God'. A full discussion of the eucharistic tradition to which the author is referring will be found in Roach's article in *ZRP*, lix (1939), 10–56. The story then proceeds to say that the Grail had been previously found but that evil had befallen Great Britain because Perceval had failed to ask the Grail question—an evident reference to Chrétien's *Perceval*. King Arthur himself is one of the chief sufferers; he has lost his desire to practice largess and win honour, and his knights are leaving court. On Ascension Day, at Cardueil, Guenevere prevails upon him to redeem himself by visiting St. Austin's chapel in Wales; the journey thither is fraught with peril, but by the grace of God it can be achieved. At first an invisible barrier prevents the king from entering the

---

[1] *Modern Philology Monographs*, University of Chicago, reviewed by Brugger, *ZRP*, lix (1939), 554–76, and by R. S. Loomis, *RR*, xxxix (1938), 175–80. After we completed our edition a leaf of a lost manuscript (F) was discovered at the Library of Congress; now published by Roach in *Spec*, xiii (1938), 216–20. On matters of style see also Spitzer's review, *MLN*, liii (1938), 604–8, and note that Brugger, loc. cit., p. 578, adheres to his view that the romance was once part of a cyclic redaction.

[2] *Selections from the Hengwrt MSS.*, i, *Y Seint Greal*, ed. Robert Williams (London, 1876). Pp. 437–720 contain a literal translation of the Welsh text into English.

chapel. When he succeeds in entering, the celebrant of the mass—a hermit who had known Uther, Arthur's father—exhorts Arthur to mend his ways by actively supporting the New (Christian) Law, which had been impeded because Perceval had failed to ask about the Grail and Lance: 'de coi ce servoit, ne cui on en servoit.' The cure of Arthur is now achieved. On his way back to court he meets a damsel who is seeking Perceval and who tells him the story of Perceval's ancestry and youth.

It is clear from this summary that the author plans to lift Arthurian romance out of the sphere of worldly aims and desires to interpret it in the spirit of religion. The knight who craves glory shall fight for his faith and shall convert the heathen. The quest of the Grail will be a successful war waged for the Church; and the holy vessel itself will stand for a spiritual goal which many will seek but only the perfect (chaste) knight will attain. Moreover, from a political point of view, Arthur's chapel ride foreshadows the union of the temporal with the spiritual order—an inference which the author apparently wished his readers to make. The New Law or Testament is everywhere placed in opposition to the Old Law, which includes not only the Jews but the heathen in general. Hence we shall see that, after Perceval's conquest of the Grail castle, Arthur beholds two suns in the sky, one in the east, the other in the west. This union of the temporal power with the Church is crowned by Arthur's later pilgrimage to the Grail castle (Branch IX). How strikingly the symbolism of the New and Old Testaments is reflected in the romance is shown in a study by Carman.[1]

The ensuing branches relate the separate Grail-quests of Gauvain, Lancelot, and Perceval. But, distinct as these are, they are skilfully interwoven and show the author's sense of structure.

Branches II–VI deal with the adventures of Gauvain. He meets the Damsels of the Cart, messengers of Fate; gives the Coward Knight a lesson in valour; wins the sword that beheaded John the Baptist, without which he cannot enter the Grail country; and finally reaches the languishing Fisher King. But, seeing the Grail and Lance pass before him, he fails to ask the question because three drops of blood that fall from the Lance so arrest his attention that he forgets the object of his quest. As he departs on the morrow, a voice shouts to him that the King of Castle Mortal, having renounced the New Law, is attacking the Fisher King.

Lancelot, who now assumes the quest, is the traditional *courtois* character, attractive to women but devoted to Guenevere. He has an adventure at the Waste City, where his head is placed in 'jeopardy' with the understanding that he will return a year later to submit to a return blow—obviously the motif found also in *Gawain and the Green Knight*.[2] In Branch VIII he

---

[1] *PMLA*, lxi (1946), 42–83. See also M. Schlauch in *Spec*, xiv (1939), 448–64, where the allegory of Church and Synagogue is brought out.　　　　　　　　[2] See below, p. 532.

arrives at the Grail castle, but as he takes his seat at the 'ivory table' the Grail fails to appear. His only hope is to find Perceval, who is staying with his uncle, King Pelles, and urge him to undertake the quest. When Pelles upbraids him for his attachment to Guenevere, Lancelot extols the virtues she inspires: 'sens et cortoisie et valor . . . ausi doivent fere tuit li chevalier' (l. 3866). Nowhere else in the romance are the ideals of knighthood better expressed.

Branch VII is an interlude bringing Perceval on the scene. Leaving his uncle, he has various clashes with Red Knights, and in Branch VIII visits a hermitage where he finds the body of Arthur's son, Loholt, whom Keu has treacherously slain. Longing for his mother, 'la Veve Dame', he reaches her home and takes vengeance on her enemy, the Lord of the Fens, in a frightful manner which his reference to the Bible (cf. Num. xxxv. 16–17) hardly justifies. Then the Damsels of the Cart arrive and urge him to destroy the Old Law by delivering the Grail castle from the King of Castle Mortal.

Branch IX deals primarily with Perceval's retaking of the castle and the reappearance of the Grail together with the Lance and Sword. The King of Castle Mortal kills himself. But, the Fisher King having died, no Grail procession takes place and the expected question is never asked.

Perceval's conquest is followed by Arthur's own pilgrimage to the Grail, to which Branch X is devoted. Before he can depart, a damsel brings the head of his dead son, Loholt, to court, and news comes that Keu has joined Brian des Illes in a revolt against Arthur. The well-known Three Days' Tournament is interjected to furnish another example of Gauvain's chivalry, and it is learned that Guenevere, overcome by Loholt's death, has succumbed to grief. When Arthur finally beholds the Grail during the consecration of the Mass, it appears in five shapes or *muances*, the last of which is that of a chalice. Thus he is instructed in the ceremonial use of the chalice and of the bell, neither of which objects had been employed before in the Arthurian kingdom.

At this point the narrative splits into two threads: the one concerns Perceval, the other treats a political intrigue against Lancelot (and Arthur) in which Brian, Keu, and Claudas are involved. The second, however, contains an incident of historical importance. After their departure from the Grail, Arthur and Gauvain go to Avalon to mourn at Guenevere's tomb. Not to be outdone in his devotion to Guenevere, Lancelot decides to seek Avalon himself. This leads our author to describe the place in terms that leave no doubt that by 'Avalon' he meant Glastonbury. Thus, assertion 1 of the colophon is supported by internal evidence of the text.

Branch XI restores Lancelot to Arthur's favour in the war against Brian and ends the story with Perceval's voyage to the island Castle of the Four

Horns and his retirement from the world. This island is a Celtic Other-world[1]—much Christianized—akin to the Welsh Annwfn or *Caer Pedryvan* 'Four-Cornered Fortress', also called *Caer Wydyr*, 'Fortress of Glass'. There Perceval is welcomed by thirty-three monks clad in white and is led to a 'glass cask', in which there is an armed but silent knight. In him Carman (p. 59) sees an analogue to Elijah, Enoch, or John the Evangelist, who, according to tradition, escaped death. Pelles's son, Joseus, remains at the Grail castle until he too dies; thereupon it falls into ruins. Those who visit the place fail to return, except two 'Welsh knights', who lead saintly lives ever afterward.

It requires no penetration to see that among the French sources of *Perlesvaus* are Chrétien's *Perceval* (as well as the First and Second Continuations) and his *Lancelot*. To Robert's *Joseph* it owes references to Joseph of Arimathea and Nicodemus as well as the figure of Alain le Gros, father of Perceval. Two names have a special Welsh imprint. Loholt is doubtless Welsh Llacheu. Rare in French romance, it recurs in the Vulgate and is found as Lout in *Lanzelet*. Pelles, Corn.-Eng. 'peller' ('wizard' or 'wise man'), is probably Welsh *Pwyll*, well known from the *Mabinogion*.[2] But the substance of the romance—the quests of Gauvain, Lancelot, and Perceval—is developed out of Chrétien's *Perceval* and its continuations.

This brings us to the role played by Glastonbury in the twelfth century. Throughout the century Glastonbury Abbey[3] was a centre of literary activity and religious propaganda. Situated close to the Bristol Channel, it drew on Wales and Ireland to enrich its culture and give to it an imprint in which French and Celtic strains are blended. Henry II fostered its claims, and when in 1184 a destructive fire wrecked the Abbey, he ordered its rebuilding on a splendid scale. Henry died in 1189, but by 1186 the Lady Chapel had been reconstructed, with a leaden roof and a narthex to connect it with the unfinished monastery buildings. Then in 1191 occurred the event that throws light on our text and makes it significant. The Glastonbury monks,

---

[1] On the source here see R. S. Loomis in *PMLA*, lvi (1941), 887 ff., and his *Arthurian Tradition*, p. 362. As Loomis's article, p. 935, shows, the *tonel de voirre* containing the silent knight has an important analogue in Nennius's *turris vitrea*, to which may be added the island on which Cronus sleeps, according to Plutarch, *De Defectu Oraculorum*, xviii; cf. *Perceval and the Holy Grail* (*Univ. Calif. Pub. Mod. Phil.* xxviii, 1949), p. 318.

[2] On the derivation of *Pelles* see our edition, ii. 192. Pelles, known (l. 38) as 'Rois de la Basse Gent', was connected by Loomis, in *PMLA*, lvi. 917–24, and in *Arthurian Tradition*, p. 142, with Bilis, 'rois d'Antipodes', in Chrétien's *Erec*, vs. 1994. But Loomis would derive the name from Welsh Beli and identifies the character with the pigmy monarch described by Giraldus Cambrensis. See our remarks (loc. cit.) on the possibility that Pwyll, Beli or Bilis, and Pelles were originally the same person. Cf. Pelliz, Pellit 'le devin', in Wace's *Brut*, ed. Arnold, vss. 14156 and 14188.

[3] The Glastonbury question is discussed fully in vol. ii, ch. ii, of our edition; see also above, pp. 66 f.; *Spec*, ix (1934), 355–61, and J. Armitage Robinson, *Two Glastonbury Legends* (Cambridge, 1926). C. H. Slover in *Spec*, x (1935), 147–60, gives the evidence on Glastonbury as a cultural and intellectual centre. On Glastonbury and the Grail legend see the preceding and the next chapter.

in digging around the Abbey, exhumed two bodies which they fraudulently stated were those of Arthur and Guenevere.

The effect of the exhumation can be imagined. It flattered the pride of Henry's successors to discover in Arthur an ancestor of their dynasty, and it shattered the belief of the Celts in Arthur's return from Avalon. If the Bretons and Welsh still cherished the hope that Arthur would lead them to victory, the tomb in the Lady Chapel was witness to the futility of such an idea. Arthur buried at Glastonbury was better propaganda, dynastic as well as religious, than Geoffrey of Monmouth's Arthur carried to a legendary Avalon 'to be healed of his wounds'. As late as 1485 Caxton, in the prologue to his edition of Malory's work, defended the historicity of Arthur with the words: 'First ye may see his sepulture in the monasterye of Glastyngburye.'

As for the date of *Perlesvaus*, such evidence as we possess points to the period between 1191 and 1212. 1191 is fixed by the exhumation, and 1212 is the appropriate time for the dedication to Jean de Nesle mentioned in the colophon of the second redaction. Jean II, lord of Nesle and castellan of Bruges, succeeded his father, Jean I, some time before 1202, and played a prominent but independent role in the Fourth Crusade. On his return from the Orient (1206) he became a French partisan in the struggle between Flanders and France. And by 1212 he began to give up his Flemish connexions, so that in 1225 he entered upon the sale of the castellany of Bruges. Unfortunately we know nothing about the Lord of Cambr(e)in, the dedicator and presumably author of the second redaction. But Cambrin then belonged to Flanders, and the relationship between him and Jean II was doubtless close. In short, no reason exists for not placing the second redaction between 1212 and 1225 and thus setting 1191–1212 as the date of the original—provided always *Perlesvaus* preceded, as Gaston Paris thought, the *Queste del Saint Graal*.

In dealing with the latter problem, let us first note the influence of our romance on two other works, the *Chevalier aux Deux Epées* and the *Fouke Fitz Warin*. In the former work Gauvain is opposed by Brian des Illes, mentioned above as Arthur's enemy, and at verse 2604 there is reference to 'Perceval, le fil Alain le gros, des Vaus de Kamelot'—an obvious borrowing from our work. On the other hand, the *Fouke Fitz Warin*, written in Shropshire, puts into verse the incident about Arthur's squire (Cahus) in Branch I of our romance. But neither of these works, written respectively about 1235 and 1256, throws light on the date of *Perlesvaus*. Hence we are confronted with the question: did *Perlesvaus* antedate the *Queste* and influence its composition?

The affirmative to this question has been well presented by Carman.[1]

---

[1] *The Relationship of the Perlesvaus and the Queste del Saint Graal. Bulletin of the University of Kansas, Humanistic Studies,* v, no. 4, July 1936. See pp. 323 ff. for Carman's treatment of the

A comparison of the characters and episodes of the two romances shows that in every instance where they offer parallels *Perlesvaus* is the simpler and less sophisticated of the two. In the *Queste* Pelles is not the Hermit Uncle but a problematic character whom contemporary readers took to be the Fisher King. He is the uncle (or grandfather) of Galaad, the immaculate knight, son of the sinful Lancelot. To Galaad alone of all Arthurian knights the Grail appears *apertement* or 'face-to-face' according to 1 Cor. xiii. 12. The holy vessel or *escuele* is now an essential part of the Mass, not merely a concomitant of it. Finally, Perceval, Gauvain, Lancelot, Bohort, have adventures connected with the Grail, but there is no climactic rise similar to the three Grail-quests in *Perlesvaus*. In view of these and other differences, it would be strange if our author, having the *Queste* in front of him, had reverted to the earlier tradition and replaced Galaad by Perceval.

But the decisive fact is that, while the setting of our romance is still Benedictine, the *Queste* is a Cistercian document, embodying in its religious practices and rules the life at Cîteaux in the thirteenth century. As Gilson said so well,[1]

L'idéal dont l'œuvre s'inspire et l'idée profonde qu'elle exprime ne sauraient être la connaissance de Dieu par l'intelligence, mais la vie de Dieu dans l'âme par la charité, qui est la grâce.... Que la *Queste* soit ... une œuvre abstraite et systématique, nous le reconnaissons si complètement qu'à peine oserions-nous promettre d'y découvrir dix lignes de suite écrites pour le simple plaisir de conter.

With such a work *Perlesvaus* offers the sharpest of contrasts. Let us see what these are.

The doctrine proclaimed at Cîteaux was pacific. Although bent on uprooting heresy, the Cistercians took pains to avoid war. This becomes evident from the distinction the *Queste* makes between Gauvain and Galaad in their treatment of miscreant knights; the former kills some of the knights, the latter 'les conquist sanz ocirre'. In *Perlesvaus* Arthur and his knights establish the New Law at the point of the sword; the Grail hero wreaks barbaric vengeance on his enemies; and in accord with this spirit is the custom (going back to the Celts) of carrying about the heads of slain enemies, and the system of tribal retribution so prominent in Branch VI.

Again, the monastic life portrayed in the *Queste* is primarily coenobitic. Galaad is reared by white monks, whose rule and organization are conventual. On the other hand, in *Perlesvaus* the religious life is eremitic. Even at Avalon Lancelot is received by three 'hermits', and at the close of the romance the

---

episodes. But Frappier in Nelli, *Lumière du Graal* (Paris, 1951), pp. 215 ff., still holds that *Perlesvaus* belongs to the same period (1225–30) as the *Queste*, and thus he would leave the question of priority in doubt. Frappier does not mention Carman, whose dissertation was probably inaccessible to him.

[1] *Les Idées et les Lettres* (Paris, 1932), pp. 11 f. See also A. Pauphilet, ed., *Queste del Saint Graal*, *CFMA* (1923), p. x.

sacred relics pass to the care of 'hermits', who then begin to build churches and houses of religion.

Lastly, the surrender of the ego to the mystery of 'grace'—glorified in the Grail—which makes the *Queste* so impressive, is foreign to the belligerent tone of *Perlesvaus*. In both romances Lancelot is reproved for his attachment to Guenevere, but only in *Perlesvaus* does he assert the wish that he may never have 'volenté de guerpir s'amor', 'the will to forsake his love'. And this individualistic trend is exemplified elsewhere, by the political function of Arthur and the worldly wisdom and courtesy of Gauvain.

Consequently, *Perlesvaus* is the earlier work and preceded and influenced the *Queste*, as Carman maintains.

We need a good book on the development of literary technique in Arthurian romance. For that we may have to wait until all the texts are available in critical editions. Meantime, an admirable guide to the subject is Vinaver's Introduction to his edition of Malory's book.[1] He remarks that 'just as in a tapestry each thread alternates with an endless variety of others, so in the early prose romances of the Arthurian group numerous seemingly independent episodes or "motifs" are interwoven in a manner which makes it possible for each episode to be set aside at any moment and resumed later'. This process is well illustrated by *Perlesvaus*. But, as Vinaver observes, it was Chrétien de Troyes who served as model for the type of fiction with which we are concerned. The prologue to *Erec* sets forth the method employed in the monastic schools whereby the *matière* of a story is expounded in order to bring out the *sens* or 'meaning' the author had in mind. Of course, the exegesis of the Bible underlies the technique employed. Added to this is the term *conjointure*—derived from Horace's *Ars Poetica*—which Chrétien uses to designate not only the interweaving of the episodes but also the unifying theme of his plot:

> Ex noto fictum carmen sequar . . .
>
> .   .   .   .
>
> . . . tantum series juncturaque pollet (vss. 240 ff.)[2]

Our author, who lacked Chrétien's poetic genius, nevertheless has literary qualities which give his work distinction. He has a sense of structure and a pronounced feeling for style. The structure of the romance—as outlined in the three quests—is enhanced by two devices. The first of these is conflation. An excellent example of this device occurs in Branch VI, where the Magic Chessboard—an incident taken from the Second Continuation of

---

[1] *Works of Sir Thomas Malory* (Oxford, 1947), i, pp. xlviii–lii. See p. vi on the title, *Morte Darthur*, imposed by Caxton.

[2] For a discussion of *sens* and *matière*, with special reference to the *Liber Sapientiae*, chaps. vii and viii, see *R*, xliv (1915), 14–36. Cf. Godefroy, vol. ii, on *conjointure*. The theme in *Erec* is the hero's uxoriousness; in the *Perceval*, Perceval's education.

Chrétien—is put at the end of the Grail episode, when Gauvain is left alone in the hall. By locating the incident at the Grail castle the author not only makes his story compact but adds 'another marvellous element to the *merveilleux chrétien* of the castle itself'—as Weinberg has said.[1] Another instance of the device is the Magic Fountain (Branch VI) of which the three cups symbolize the Trinity and the doctrine of the Real Presence. Such merging of incongruous matter may strike the modern reader as inartistic. Yet a medieval student may have been impressed; he would have seen in it a proper allegorization of a pagan background, and he could have justified the author with a reference to Geoffrey of Vinsauf:

> Sic se contraria miscent,
> Sed pacem spondent hostesque morantur amici.[2]

The second device employed is linking. This gives the work an elaborate system of cross-reference. Yet it integrates the plot by constant emphasis on a leading motif. A striking example is the theme of the Waste Land, running through the story like a silver thread. Developed out of Perceval's failure to ask the question, it links together all the misfortunes (*meschaances*) of Great Britain: Arthur's languor, the desuetude of the Round Table, the Fisher King's illness, and even his death. The same motif appears in Gauvain's visit to the Poor Knight, whose land is described as 'seche et povre et sofraiteuse de toz biens' (l. 2529) and his castle as 'molt agasti'. The author reiterates the word *gaste*, and the city where Lancelot undergoes the 'beheading' test (Branch VI) is known as the *Gaste Cité*. When one considers that all of these passages precede the conquest of the Grail, he sees how effectively the author contrasted the Waste Land with the country of the Grail, 'avironé de granz eues et plentëureuses de toz biens' (l. 2268). Out of his sources he has preserved the fertility ideal so prominent in many Grail works.[3] In this way, the narrative, whatever its imperfections, has been woven into a connected and unified whole.

---

[1] *PMLA*, l (1935), 25 ff.

[2] *Poetria Nova*, ed. E. Faral, *Arts Poètiques du XIIe et du XIIIe Siecle* (Paris, 1924), p. 223.

[3] The theme of T. S. Eliot's *Waste Land* (1922) is taken from Jessie L. Weston, *From Ritual to Romance* (Cambridge, 1920). The ritual theory, which I believe would explain the succession of challengers at the *Gaste Cité*, was brilliantly defended by Loomis in *Celtic Myth* (New York, 1927), pp. 263–70, but is now rejected in *Arthurian Tradition*, p. ix, as an explanation of the scene in the Grail castle, though still accepted in *JEGP*, xlii (1943), 170–81, as an explanation of the seasonal combat and Waste Land features of the *Gaste Cité*. See my comment in *Perlesvaus*, ii. 281–3, and *RP*, vi (1952), 16–18. On Lancelot as an annual king see Mary Williams in *Folklore*, xlviii (1937), 263–6. Loomis has treated in *Arthurian Tradition* various motifs: the bridges of the Grail castle (pp. 225 f.); the King of Castle Mortal (pp. 246 f.); Cahus's fatal dream (p. 274); the Damsel of the Cart (pp. 299, 377); the youthful-seeming knights of the Grail castle (p. 386); the various Red Knights (pp. 396–405); the damsel with the head of a knight (pp. 395 f.); the valleys of Camaalot (pp. 480 f.). I have treated the same motifs in *Perlesvaus*, ii. 261 f., 193 f., 227–9, 266, 221–4, 213 f., 196–8.

But the trait that gives the work distinction is its rich and variegated style. As a writer of effective prose, the author is probably unsurpassed in Old French. His style seems almost modern when compared with that of historical writers like Villehardouin or Joinville.[1] An outstanding feature is cadence; the use of the 'well-rounded period', inherited from Cicero and indicative of the schoolman's training that the author underwent. His tone is direct and elevating, as befits the exalted purpose he has in mind. Note the following period, enhanced by the use of chiasmus:

> Cez trois persones, sont une sustance,
> e cele sustance si est Dex,
> e de Dieu si muet li hauz contes du Graal (l. 9)

—unmatched for its concision and depth; and contrast it with the swift phrasing of:

Messire Gavains s'en torne, e la damoisele a pié li escrie: 'Sire, Sire! vos n'estes pas si apensez com ge cuidé.' (l. 860).

Could Gauvain's besetting trait of self-absorption be more clearly stated than it is here? Or take the falling rhythm of

> Iglais ot non sa mere,
> li Rois Peschierres fu ses oncles,
> e li Rois de la Basse Gent, qui fu nomez Pelles,
> e li Rois du Chastel Mortel; (l. 37)

and compare it with the rising accent on the adjectives in

> E esgarde li rois devant soi,
> e voit un vallet grant e fort e bel e juene. (l. 107).

Isolated lines, like that in which Lancelot extols the knightly virtues (*sens et cortoisie et valor*), read as verse, which may have led Gaston Paris to think that the work is a translation from a version in rime.

Another stylistic feature is the use of indirect speech to portray attitude or mood; for instance the passage (l. 1360) where the comic figure of the Coward Knight interrupts the reverie of Gauvain:

'Par foi, fet Messire Gavains a soi meïsme, vos ne sanblez pas home que on doie mal fere.' Et se ne fust la pesance qu'il avoit il eüst molt volentiers ris de sa contenance.

But it is in direct speech that the author is at his best. Dialogue is meant to be authentic, and the use of it, especially in longer conversations, has the imprint of veracity. A good example is the following (l. 2784):

'Dame, fait Lanceloz, granz merciz, mes je ne puis demorer en un chastel que une nuit devant que j'aie esté la ou je doi aler. — Ou avez vos la voie enprise? fait

---

[1] Alfred Foulet in *MLN*, xlvii (1933), 346f.

ele.—Dame, fait il, au Chastel des A(r)mes.—Je sé bien le chastel, fet la dame. Li rois a non Messios, et gist en langeur par .ii. chevaliers qui ont esté eu chastel, qui ne firent la bone demande. Et avez vos volenté d'aler i? fait la dame.—Oïl, fet il.'

Thus *Perlesvaus* is literally 'li hauz livres du Graal' in more respects than one. Written as a sequel to Chrétien's *Perceval*, it carries out the proselytizing aim announced in Branch I. Inferior to Chrétien's romances in psychology and characterization and to the *Queste* in idealism and mood, it excels in firmness of outline and solidity of form. But the greatest merits of *Perlesvaus* lie in its style. Its diction alone—fluent, varied, and picturesque—makes it one of the most distinguished prose works which France produced in the Middle Ages.

Judging from the number of surviving manuscripts, the vogue of *Perlesvaus* was not great, but it furnished the introduction (from Branch I) to two manuscripts of the Vulgate cycle, and in 1516 and 1523 Galiot du Pré printed the *Estoire del Saint Graal*, *Perlesvaus*, and the *Queste* in a black-letter edition, with the avowed purpose of edifying and uplifting the reader.[1] Moreover, we have seen that our romance was translated into Welsh, and seems to have been highly regarded there. In the early part of the fifteenth century the Abbot of Valle Crucis, near Llangollen, sent the bard Guto'r Glyn all the way to Glamorgan to borrow 'the goodly Greal, the book of the blood, the book of heroes, where they fell in the court of Arthur; a book still in the Briton's hand,—the race of Horsa could not read this; the kingly book, which should the venerable chief obtain, he would be content to live without other food'.[2] This book was presumably the Welsh *Perlesvaus*, which opens with the words: 'This history treats of the very precious vessel which is called the Greal, in which was received the blood of our Creator, Jesus Christ.'

---

[1] See A. B. Swanson, *Study of the 1516 and 1523 Editions of the Perlesvaus*, University of Chicago Libraries (private edition), 1934. It is the redactor who is responsible for the appeal to the reader. A number of copies of both editions were sold between 1784 and 1836, though Dunlop, *History of Fiction*, 3rd ed. (London, 1845), p. 74, states that 'the *Sangreal* [i.e. *Perlesvaus*] is the scarcest romance of the Round Table'.

[2] *Perlesvaus*, i. 8–10; T. Stephens, *Literature of the Kymry*, 2nd ed. (London, 1876), pp. 424–6.

THE ORIGIN OF THE GRAIL LEGENDS

ROGER SHERMAN LOOMIS

EVERY reader of the preceding chapters, every student of the Grail romances, cannot help being struck most forcefully by the astonishing disharmony, the consistent inconsistency, of those strange narratives.[1] This is one of several reasons why the subject of the Grail so piques the curiosity of modern men of letters and so exercises the ingenuity of scholars as to the origin and the meaning of this particular branch, of the Arthurian legend. It is this same diversity which is doubtless responsible for the utterly different solutions that have been offered for the mystery. The cradle of the tradition has been sought among the mountains of Persia, in the Pyrenean fastnesses of Catharist heretics, in the orthodox sanctuaries of Constantinople.[2] On the other hand, there are—or were—scholars who maintain that the story of the vessel and its quest sprang, a complete novelty, from the fertile brain of Chrétien de Troyes.[3]

It is indeed proper to speak of the legends, rather than the legend, of the Grail. Except for translations and other close adaptations, the authors of the Grail texts seem to delight in contradicting each other on the most important points—the number of kings in the Grail castle, their names, their physical state, the cause and exact nature of the 'Waste Land', the name of the successful hero, the very form and attributes of the Grail itself. If Chrétien's poem was the chief inspiring force behind these works, his successors, and most conspicuously his first continuator, flouted his authority in the boldest fashion, often for no discoverable reason. This state of affairs strongly sug-

[1] No complete bibliography of the origins of the Grail exists. The footnotes to Bruce's chapters on the Grail cover most of the significant speculations on the subject up to 1922, but Bruce overlooked, as most scholars had done, the derivation of the Grail from the *Dysgl* of Rhydderch, made by Büsching as far back as 1819 in *Jahrbücher der Literatur* (Wien), v, 42 f. Writings later than Bruce are listed in J. J. Parry's bibliographies and in the annual bulletins of the Société Internationale Arthurienne. In my not completely disinterested judgement, the soundest discussions of the problem are in H. Newstead's *Bran the Blessed in Arthurian Romance* (New York, 1939), and chaps. lxvii–lxix, lxxi, lxxv of my *Arthurian Tradition and Chrétien de Troyes*. Four somewhat recent works by eminent scholars which defend the Celtic hypothesis are W. A. Nitze's 'Perceval and the Holy Grail', *Univ. of Calif. Pub. in Mod. Phil.*, xxviii, no. 5 (1949), 306–25; J. Marx's *La Légende arthurienne et le Graal* (Paris, 1952); J. Frappier's *Chrétien de Troyes, Perceval ou le Conte du Graal* (Les Cours de Sorbonne, 1953); M. Dillon's 'Les sources irlandaises des romans arthuriens', *Lettres Romanes*, ix (1955), 143–59.

[2] O. Rahn, *Kreuzzug gegen den Graal* (Freiburg-in-Breisgau, 1933), trans. R. Pitrou as *Le Croisade contre le Graal* (Paris, 1933); K. Burdach, *Der Graal* (Stuttgart, 1938).

[3] W. Foerster, *Kristian von Troyes, Wörterbuch* (Halle, 1914), pp. 155*–8*; Bruce, i. 246–51.

gests that Chrétien did not invent his story, and that later romancers, even when they knew and drew upon his poem, drew also on an amorphous mass of traditional material.

In attempting to determine what that material was, no text is more important than Chrétien's; no hypothesis can be regarded as sound which does not account first of all for his treatment, and secondly for the later and divergent treatments. Let me sketch his story so far as it concerns the Grail.[1]

The youth Perceval, brought up by his mother near the base of Snowdon in total ignorance of the ways of chivalry, received his first lesson in the management of horse and arms and in courtly manners from a hospitable vavasour, Gornemant, who warned him not to speak too much, for this was a sin. A few days later he came on two men fishing from a boat on a river, and one of them invited him to his castle for the night. On his arrival Perceval found his host arrived before him, lying richly clad on a couch. While they were conversing, a squire entered the hall from a chamber, bearing a lance from the tip of which a drop of blood flowed; he was followed by two squires bearing candelabra, then by a fair damsel holding between her two hands a *graal* of gold, studded with precious gems and shedding a brilliant light. A second damsel bore through the hall a silver *tailleor*, or carving platter, and all these mysterious figures passed on to another chamber. Perceval was consumed with curiosity, but, remembering Gornemant's advice, he kept silent. A sumptuous banquet followed, and with each course the same procession passed through the hall, but still the youth failed to ask what person was served with the *graal*. At last the lord of the castle was carried out, and Perceval's couch was made up in the hall, where he slept till dawn. On waking he found the castle deserted, and departed without finding anyone of whom he might inquire whither the *graal* was taken and why the lance bled. In a wood near by he met a damsel sitting with the body of a headless knight in her arms. Perceval told of his strange experience of the previous evening and was informed that the fisherman was a king who had been wounded through both thighs with a javelin in battle. The damsel added that she was Perceval's cousin and reproached him bitterly for his silence, for if he had asked about the *graal* the infirm king would have been cured; now calamity awaited Perceval and others. Some time afterwards, when Perceval was welcomed to Arthur's court at Caerleon, a malformed, hideous damsel entered and cursed him for failing to ask concerning the bleeding lance and the *graal*; as a result ladies would be widowed, lands wasted, and knights slain. Perceval vowed that he would seek until he learned who was served with the vessel and why the lance bled. Five years later he came to the cell of a hermit, who turned out to be his uncle, and who, after learning of his adventure at the Fisher King's castle, revealed that it was the Fisher King's father who had lain in the chamber whither the damsel had borne the *graal*. It was not a pike, a lamprey, or a salmon he had received, but he sustained his life with a single mass-wafer (*oiste*) which was brought him in the *graal*. Thus he had lived for fifteen years without quitting his chamber.

[1] Kristian von Troyes, *Percevalroman*, ed. Hilka (Halle, 1932), vss. 1312–1698, 2974–3592, 4603–83, 6217–513.

This is all that we learn from Chrétien about the Grail. Some notable commentators have been impressed by the irrationality of the narrative; for example, Albert Pauphilet expressed himself as follows:[1]

The old maimed king, who would have been cured by a magic question, was not, apparently, the only lord of the marvellous castle, nor the only invalid. For the other invalid, his unseen father, since he had not left his chamber for fifteen years, must have been even more of a cripple than the Fisher King. Would he also have been healed by Perceval's question? But there is never a hint of this. And how can all this be reconciled with the story which Chrétien himself has told? The old man is kept alive by a single mass wafer which is brought to him in the *graal*: nevertheless, with each new course the *graal* has reappeared and passed into his chamber. Why these repeated servings of 'une seule oiste'? Moreover, a mass wafer ought not to have been placed in any but a liturgical vessel: behold, then, the *graal* transformed by sleight of hand into a ciborium or a chalice, and this singular procession transformed into the beginning of a Christian liturgy. But then, what do these unusual accessories mean, this lance, and above all the absence of a priest? It is a young damsel, beautifully garbed, who holds the *graal*, 'tant sainte chose'. In reality, these interpretations are artificial and do not harmonize at all with the beginning of the poem. They imply that a transformation has been wrought which has completely altered the original theme.

Other scholars have emphasized even more strongly the grotesque employment of the *graal* as a receptacle for the Host. Practically all the etymological and testimonial evidence on the meaning of the word *graal* indicates that it was a wide, capacious dish; according to the definition of Helinandus, written about forty years later, 'scutella lata et aliquantulum profunda'.[2] The first continuator of Chrétien's poem presents us with the spectacle of a hundred boars' heads on grails,[3] and Chrétien himself clearly expected his readers to envisage a vessel commonly used to contain a salmon or a lamprey or a pike;[4] otherwise his remark that the *graal* did not contain one of these large

---

[1] Pauphilet, *Legs du moyen âge* (Melun, 1950), p. 183. See, too, H. Adolf in *MLQ*, viii (1947), 8.

[2] Migne, *Patrologia Latina*, ccxii, col. 814; *PMLA*, lxxi (1956), 845 f.; Nitze in *MP*, xiii (1916), 681–4. On date of Helinandus, 1211–23, cf. J. N. Carman, *Relationship of the Perlesvaus and the Queste del Saint Graal* (Lawrence, Kan., 1936), pp. 12 f. In *Le Graal de Chrétien et la Demoiselle au Graal, Société de Publications Romanes et Françaises* (Genève, Lille, 1955), Roques refers to Helinandus's definition and to the lines about the boars' heads on grails. He arbitrarily identifies as grails the large dishes with feet depicted in the *Hortus Deliciarum*, and even more arbitrarily equates these with sacramental chalices, though he admits on p. 18 that the equation is not exact. He fails to explain in accordance with this theory the freakish elements in Chrétien's story, such as those set forth by Pauphilet above. See Frappier, *Chrétien de Troyes* (Paris, 1957), pp. 193–7, and Marx in *MA*, lxiii (1957), 469–80.

[3] *Continuations of the Perceval*, ed. Roach, i (Philadelphia, 1949), vss. 9649 f.; ii (1950), vss. 13431 f. Lucien Foulet defines *graal* as 'un plat peu profond mais assez large pour contenir une hure de sanglier'. Ibid. iii, pt. 2 (1955), p. 139. In the *Estoire del Saint Graal* and the *Queste* the word *escuele* is used as the equivalent of *graal*, and the vessel is identified with the dish from which Christ partook of 'l'aignel le jor de paskes avoec ses disciples'. Sommer, i. 13, ll. 24, 27; vi. 190, ll. 32 f.

[4] R. Lejeune in *SM*, xvii (1951), 8; Frappier in *R*, lxxiii (1952), 87–89.

piscatory prizes would be fatuous. Would any sane person explain that a certain tureen did not contain soup but a *brioche* if tureens were normally used for *brioches*? Chrétien was eminently sane and he must have realized the oddity of placing a mass wafer, perhaps 15 centimetres in diameter,[1] in a vessel at least 60 or 70 centimetres in length.

Moreover, there is the question, 'whom does one serve with the *graal*?' Why should it have such momentous consequences, not for the Fisher King's father, to whom it refers, but for the Fisher King himself? Why, looked at from the point of view of common sense and ordinary morality, should Perceval's failure to satisfy his curiosity by asking this question be regarded as a monstrous sin, especially when his silence was motivated by respect for the instructions of Gornemant, to whom he owed the honour of knighthood and who had told him that loquacity was a sin?[2] If Perceval had been at fault in bridling his tongue and maintaining silence, he had done so in total ignorance of the consequences and in the belief that it was wise to take the advice of the old and experienced. If he had asked the question, he would have set up his own judgement as superior to that of Gornemant. Yet that is what Chrétien, through the hermit's mouth, declares that he should have done. It is an odd moral for a medieval tale that the worst thing a young man could do was to follow the counsel of a noble and experienced mentor. To be sure, the hermit explains that this sin was the consequence of Perceval's leaving his mother in a swoon. But the causal nexus between the abandonment of his mother and his silence in the presence of the Grail is certainly not clear and was probably invented by Chrétien or his predecessor, feeling that the silence alone could not be considered under the circumstances to justify such harsh denunciation and punishment.

Efforts have been made, to be sure, to account for some of these absurdities.[3] Rose Peebles tried to excuse Chrétien's placing the sacramental vessel in the hands of a woman by reference to certain laxities, recorded or implied, which involved the handling of the Host by laymen or women.[4] Far from proving the acceptability of this practice to Chrétien's readers, the documents prove quite the opposite, for in the sixth century it was condemned as an 'inaudita superstitio', and a long line of conciliar decrees and episcopal edicts cited by Micha shows that it was regarded as an abuse down to the thirteenth century.[5] The ecclesiastics who composed the *Didot Perceval*, the *Queste del Saint*

---

[1] The diameter of the twelfth-century Warwick ciborium in the Victoria and Albert Museum is 20 cm.

[2] Kristian von Troyes, *Percevalroman*, vss. 1632–6, 1653 f.

[3] *PMLA*, lxx (1955), 223–43; lxxi (1956), 840–52.

[4] R. J. Peebles, *Legend of Longinus in Ecclesiastical Tradition and in English Literature* (Baltimore, 1911), pp. 209–13; *PMLA*, lxxi (1956), 846, n. 25.

[5] *Colloques internationaux du Centre National de la Recherche Scientifique*, iii, *Romans du Graal* (Paris, 1956), p. 246.

Graal, and the *Estoire del Saint Graal* carefully substituted for the beautiful maiden a youth or a priest. Chrétien's account of the Grail violates not only common sense but the most solemn sacramental usage.

Then there is the lance. In what conceivable way did it minister to the life or health of the Fisher King's father? If not, why did it accompany the Grail to his chamber? Burdach first, and several others since,[1] have tried to adjust it to the theory of Christian ritual by pointing to the presence of a knife, symbolizing the lance of Longinus, in a sacramental procession described in the 'Mass of Chrysostom', a work of the seventh or eighth century. This procession, as it passed through the church, consisted of lictors bearing candelabra; deacons bearing the bishop's pallium, ceremonial fans, and censers; a priest with a chalice; a deacon with a *diskos* (apparently, in the Greek rite, a round, deep dish) containing the Host; other priests carrying the aforementioned knife, a sponge, a gospel book, and relics. As the procession passed, all the people knelt.[2]

The view that Chrétien was influenced, more or less directly, by some description of this Byzantine ritual derives its plausibility, of course, from the presence of candelabra, a vessel containing the Host, and a knife representing the spear of Longinus, which correspond to objects in the Grail procession. But that the poet was conscious of any such borrowing is hard to believe. Why are no clerics involved? Why did Chrétien predict that the lance was destined to destroy the realm of Logres? Why did 'all those who were there present' (vs. 3196) and who witnessed the repeated passage of the procession through the hall, fail to show any sign of reverence? As Marx and Frappier have clearly and forcefully shown,[3] any theory, however attractive, which presents so many difficulties must be discarded. Accordingly the hypothesis that Chrétien invented the Grail story and conceived it as harmonious with Christian ethics and ritual practice, though widely held, is far from satisfactory.

Another theory, which Jessie Weston expounded in two of her books and in an article in the *Encyclopædia Britannica*,[4] has received much attention. As briefly stated by her, the legends of the Grail are

the confused record of a form of worship, semi-Christian, semi-Pagan, at one time practiced in these islands, the central object of which was initiation into the sources of life, physical and spiritual. This, and this alone, will account for the diverse forms assumed by the Grail, the symbol of that source. Thus it may be the dish from which

[1] *Archiv*, cviii (1902), 131; Peebles, op. cit., p. 208; Bruce, i. 257–9; Burdach, op. cit.; Nitze in *Univ. of Calif. Pub. in Mod. Phil.*, xxviii. 308–10. Cf., however, Nitze in *MP*, xxxvii (1940), 316–19; M. Lot-Borodine in *R*, lvii (1931), 181–4.

[2] Burdach, op. cit., p. 140.

[3] Marx, op. cit., pp. 225–7, 236–40, 261–9; Frappier, *Chrétien de Troyes, Perceval*, pp. 84–92.

[4] J. L. Weston, *Quest of the Holy Grail* (London, 1913); *From Ritual to Romance* (Cambridge, 1920); *Enc. Brit.*, 14th ed., x. 602 f.

the worshippers partook of the communal feast; it may be the cup in juxtaposition with the lance, symbols of male and female energies, source of physical life, and well-known phallic emblems. It may be the 'Holy Grail', source of spiritual life, the form of which is not defined, and which is wrought of no material substance.

Miss Weston seems to have believed that this cult was widely diffused throughout Western Christendom and that Wolfram von Eschenbach and the author of *Peredur* made changes in Chrétien's version dictated by their familiarity with these esoteric teachings.

In spite of the ingenuity and learning with which Jessie Weston argued her case, few, if any, scholars accept it. The gap in time between the Adonis cult and the Naassene document on the one hand and the Grail texts on the other is too wide. The rites described offer little resemblance to any ceremonial observed in the Grail castle. And if such pagan beliefs and practices had survived into the Middle Ages, they would have been denounced as one of the prominent heresies.

There is, however, one element in the Weston hypothesis which deserves serious attention. The suggestion that Chrétien's description of the Fisher King as wounded 'parmi les hanches ambedeus', 'through the two thighs', was a euphemism for emasculation[1] seems to be confirmed by Wolfram, who says explicitly that the king had been wounded in the genitals.[2] In *Sone de Nausay*, a romance of the latter half of the thirteenth century which betrays familiarity with archaic Grail traditions, the Fisher King is identified with Joseph of Arimathea,[3] and it is said that when he was wounded by God 'in the reins and below' as a punishment for his marriage with a heathen princess, the land of Lorgres (England) fell under an enchantment.[4] 'Neither peas nor wheat was sown there, no child was born to man, nor maiden had husband, nor tree bore leaf, nor meadow turned green; neither beast nor bird had young so long as the king was maimed.' Chrétien's last continuator, Gerbert de Montreuil, also makes it clear that the hero's asking the fateful question which was to heal the Fisher King of his malady, also restored his realm.[5] The romances themselves, therefore, amply support the Weston thesis that in the traditions of the Maimed King and the Waste Land is embodied a heathenish belief that the reproductive forces of Nature were affected by, even depended on, the sexual potency of the ruler.

While these facts prove the existence of a substratum of Nature myth

---

[1] *From Ritual to Romance*, p. 12.

[2] *Parzival*, 479, 8–12.

[3] *Sone von Nausay*, ed. M. Goldschmidt (Tübingen, 1899), vs. 4823.

[4] Ibid., vss. 4775 f., 4846–53. Cf. Loth, *Mabinogion*, i. 234.

[5] Gerbert de Montreuil, *Continuation de Perceval*, ed. Mary Williams, i (Paris, 1922), pp. 2, 11–17. On Waste Land cf. Loomis, *Arthurian Tradition*, pp. 389–91; *Elucidation*, ed. A. W. Thompson (New York, 1931), pp. 86–89, 98; Nitze in *MP*, xliii (1945), 58–61.

(not ritual), they also tend to strengthen the theory of Celtic origin, the last of the three most prominent theories on the subject.[1] They form a small part of the evidence which demonstrates that the legends of the Grail are a conglomerate of materials paralleled in the literature and lore of Ireland, Wales, and Brittany. As for the sympathetic relation between king and kingdom, we have a Breton example in Walter Map's *De Nugis Curialium* (*c.* 1181).[2] In the parish where Alan, King of Brittany, was castrated, it came about that 'no animals even today can bring forth young, but, when ripe for bearing, they go outside of the parish to deliver the offspring'. This is plainly a somewhat rationalized form of the superstition that the sterilization of the ruler extended itself to all forms of life in his realm, and here it is recorded as a Breton legend.

If, discarding the theories of Christian and of ritual origin, we accept as a working hypothesis the assumption that we are dealing with a medley of old Celtic themes, sometimes crudely, sometimes ingeniously and beautifully adapted to the ideas and manners of medieval France, we do not have to proceed far for corroboration. What could be more likely, since the Grail stories form an integral part of the Arthurian legend, and no one can deny that Arthur's legend first sprang up in Wales? Indeed, Welsh literature provides the counterparts of the Fisher King, his wound, the Waste Land, and the Grail itself.

Though Chrétien leaves the Fisher King nameless, the *Didot Perceval* calls him Bron,[3] and it is hardly a mere coincidence that in the *mabinogi* of *Branwen*, composed in the eleventh century, we find a king of Britain, Brân son of Llŷr, who, like the Fisher King, was wounded in battle by a spear.[4] As with the Fisher King, the wounding of Brân was followed by the wasting of Britain.[5] A Welsh list of the Thirteen Treasures of Britain, which survives in a number of late manuscripts, includes the Platter (*Dysgl*) of Rhydderch; 'whatever food one wished thereon was instantly obtained'.[6] Likewise, according to Manessier's continuation of *Perceval*, after the Grail had passed, 'then all the tables were provided with delectable viands and so

---

[1] Besides Nitze, Marx, and Frappier, whose principal works on the subject have been cited in n. 1, p. 274, the outstanding defenders of the Celtic origin of the Grail legend have been Rhŷs, A. C. L. Brown, and Nutt. In my opinion, Rhŷs's *Studies in the Arthurian Legend* (Oxford, 1891), and Brown's *Origin of the Grail Legend* (Cambridge, Mass., 1943), in spite of their learning, were vitiated by vague analogies and improbable reconstructions. On the other hand, Nutt's *Studies on the Legend of the Holy Grail* (London, 1888) correctly analysed the confused material as a combination of an unspelling quest and a feud quest, and recognized its derivation in part from stories of Finn and Brân the Blessed. The chief defect lay in arguing too much from modern Celtic folk-tales.

[2] Distinctio IV, chap. 15; trans. Tupper and Ogle (London, 1924), p. 242.

[3] *Didot Perceval*, ed. W. Roach (Philadelphia, 1941), pp. 150, 180, &c.

[4] Christian von Troyes, *Percevalroman*, vss. 3509–13; Loth, *Mabinogion*, 2nd ed. (Paris, 1913), i. 144. For a fine study of Brân see P. MacCana, *Branwen Daughter of Llyr* (Cardiff, 1958).

[5] R. S. Loomis, *Arthurian Tradition*, p. 391.

[6] *RF*, xlv (1931), 70; *PMLA*, lvi (1941), 911–13.

nobly filled that no man could name a food which he could not find there'.[1] In the *Estoire del Saint Graal* we read that the vessel brought to the holy in life 'all the good viands which heart of man could conceive'.[2] The *Queste del Saint Graal* says that as the vessel passed before the tables, 'they were instantly filled at each seat with such food as each desired'.[3] Thus in function the Welsh platter corresponds to the Grail; it also corresponds in form. For the Grail was not a chalice or a ciborium,[4] but, as contemporary evidence, including that of Chrétien himself, shows, was a 'scutella lata et aliquantulum profunda', 'a wide and somewhat deep platter', whilst the meaning of *dysgl* was indicated by Giraldus Cambrensis when he stated that his compatriots ate from 'scutellis latis et amplis', 'wide and capacious platters'.[5] Thus as to function and form the Grail had its exact counterpart in the *Dysgl* of Rhydderch. That this magic vessel had originally belonged to the euhemerized god, Brân son of Llŷr (Irish *ler*, the sea),[6] rather than to Rhydderch, a historic king of Strathclyde in the sixth century, seems at the very least a probable conclusion, for how, otherwise, did it become the possession of Bron in French romance?

Brân's brother, Manawydan, had a stepson Pryderi, who was therefore a nephew of Brân.[7] Perceval, according to several texts, was a nephew of the Fisher King. Pryderi brought on the desolation of Dyfed (south-western Wales) by sitting on a perilous mound after a banquet;[8] likewise Perceval, according to the *Didot Perceval*, brought on the calamitous enchantments of Britain by sitting in the Siege Perilous before a banquet.[9] This was accompanied by a cry (*brait*); a cry (*diaspat*), according to *Lludd and Llevelys*, brought a desolating enchantment on Britain.[10] For other significant connexions between the Grail tradition and Welsh literature, one should turn to Helaine Newstead's *Bran the Blessed in Arthurian Romance*, and my *Wales and the Arthurian Legend*, pp. 53–60.

Welsh literature, most scholars agree, absorbed a great deal of mythic and heroic lore from Ireland during the Dark Ages,[11] and one should not

---

[1] C. Potvin, *Perceval le Gallois* (Mons, 1866–71), vi. 151.

[2] H. O. Sommer, *Vulgate Version of the Arthurian Romances* (Washington, 1908–16), i. 250.

[3] Ibid. vi. 13; *Queste del Saint Graal*, ed. A. Pauphilet (Paris, 1949), p. 15.

[4] The word *graal* was not common and was frequently misunderstood. Robert made the error (*Joseph*, vss. 907–9) of identifying the Grail with a chalice. Some illustrators of manuscripts made the same error; others depicted a ciborium. On the etymology and correct meaning of *graal*, see above, p. 276, nn. 2, 3.

[5] Giraldus Cambrensis, *Opera*, ed. Dimock, vi (London, 1868), 183.

[6] H. Newstead, *Bran the Blessed*, pp. 17–22.

[7] *Mabinogion*, trans. G. and T. Jones, pp. 41 f.; Loth, op. cit. i. 153.

[8] *Mabinogion*, trans. G. and T. Jones, pp. 42 f.; Loth, op. cit. i. 154 f.; Loomis, *Wales*, pp. 36, 172 f.

[9] *Didot-Perceval*, pp. 149–51.

[10] J. Gwenogvryn Evans, *White Book Mabinogion* (Pwllheli, 1907), p. 97; Loth, op. cit. i. 234.

[11] *Transactions of the Fourth Celtic Congress* (Swansea, 1923), pp. 39–56; C. O'Rahilly, *Wales and*

therefore be surprised to discover in Irish sagas many of the motifs and patterns which passed through Wales and so into the Matter of Britain. This
is particularly true of the Grail romances, portions of which are strikingly
foreshadowed in the literature of Ireland. There is an essential similarity
between the French stories of visits to the Grail castle and a group of sagas
which narrate the visit of a mortal to the palace of a god or goddess, and
sometimes the likeness extends to precise detail. The sagas in question have
been collected and summarized by Myles Dillon under the title of 'Adventures'—a translation of the Irish word *echtrai* (sing. *echtra*).[1]

One of them, *The Prophetic Ecstasy of the Phantom (Baile in Scail)*, was
composed before 1056.[2] After some preliminaries, we read that a phantom
horseman approached King Conn and invited him to his dwelling. On his
arrival at the palace, Conn saw a crowned damsel seated on a crystal chair,
and the phantom on his throne, who revealed himself as Lug. The damsel
was the Sovranty of Ireland, Lug's wife,[3] and she served Conn with enormous portions of meat. When she served the ale in her golden cup, she repeatedly asked: 'To whom shall this cup be given?' and Lug gave the names
of the princes who would succeed to the throne of Tara. When the list was
finished, the phantom and his house disappeared, but the cup and other
vessels remained with Conn. This narrative, though it presents marked differences from Perceval's adventure at the Grail castle, also offers impressive
parallels: a supernatural figure who invites the hero to his abode, arrives
before him, and acts as host; the lavish provision of meat and drink; the damsel with a golden vessel; the question, 'Who shall be served with this vessel?'
which cannot but raise echoes of the question Perceval was expected to ask;
the vanishing of the host.

If there is still a doubt whether this pattern in some form influenced
remotely Chrétien's narrative, it may be pointed out that Lug's wife, the
Sovranty of Erin, not only corresponds to the Grail Bearer in her function
as provider of food in an Otherworld dwelling, but also in assuming a hideous
appearance, as the Grail Bearer does in *Perlesvaus* and *Peredur*.[4] Further-

Ireland (London, 1924); Gruffydd in *THSC*, 1912–13, pp. 14–29; P. Hinneberg, *Kultur der Gegenwart*, Teil I, Abt. XI, i (Berlin, 1909), p. 118; P. MacCana, op. cit.

[1] M. Dillon, *Early Irish Literature* (Chicago, 1948), pp. 101–23.

[2] For summary and references cf. ibid., pp. 107–9; J. Marx, op. cit., pp. 117 f., 275 f.; Dillon in
Lettres Romanes, ix (1955), 145 f. See also *Eriu*, xiv (1943), 14–21; H. M. and N. K. Chadwick,
Growth of Literature (Cambridge, 1932), i. 462 f.; *EC*, vii (1955), 77–86.

[3] W. J. Gruffydd, *Math Vab Mathonwy* (Cardiff, 1928), pp. 109 f.; J. Rhŷs, *Lectures on the Origin
and Growth of Religion as Illustrated by Celtic Heathendom*, 2nd ed. (London, 1892), pp. 414–16.
Irish text in *ZCP*, iii (1901), 244: 'a banas rigi', 'his [Lug's] wedding of the kingship'. It is not a
serious objection that other texts give conflicting names to Lug's wives. *Medieval Studies in Memory
of G. Schoepperle Loomis* (New York, 1927), pp. 400, 406.

[4] R. S. Loomis, *Arthurian Tradition*, pp. 377, 415 f.; *Celtic Myth*, pp. 296–9; *Perlesvaus*, ed.
Nitze and others (Chicago, 1932–7), i, ll. 600 f., 647–52, 1404–11; Loth, op. cit. ii. 65, 103 f.,
118 f.

more, the spear of Lug, which afterwards came into the hands of Celtchar and was known as the Luin of Celtchar, is described in one text as dripping blood when raised aloft, and in another as held before a cauldron of blood.[1] Chrétien describes the lance as bleeding, and his first continuator describes it as fixed upright and bleeding into a silver vessel.[2] It would seem, therefore, that though modified to incorporate the Welsh traditions of Brân and his fateful wound, the *Prophetic Ecstasy of the Phantom* furnished the basic outline for Chrétien's story of Perceval at the Grail castle.

It has already been noted that Chrétien's successors give strangely different versions of this theme, and it is of the highest significance that one account corresponds even more strikingly to an Irish *echtra*. In the First Continuation of *Perceval* Gauvain is the partially successful hero of the quest and his adventure may be summarized as follows:[3]

Gauvain rode down to the seashore and followed a causeway, which was lashed by the waves and winds. Coming to a great hall, he was welcomed and led to a fire, but suddenly the folk vanished. A procession of clerics entered, chanted the vigil for the dead about a body (*cors*), and departed.[4] Then servants came in and prepared a banquet. A tall king entered; Gauvain washed, and both sat down. The rich *graal* moved about and served them with seven courses of food, though no hand held it.[5] Again the hall was emptied, and Gauvain now observed the bleeding lance fixed upright over a silver vessel (as has already been mentioned). When the king had returned, both he and his guest adjourned to a chamber. Gauvain inquired about the lance and the body. While the king was explaining these things, Gauvain fell asleep and woke at last to find himself lying on a cliff above the sea. As he rode away, he found the land, hitherto known as the Waste Kingdom, partly restored to fertility because he had asked the momentous question about the lance. 'The waters flowed again through their channels and all the woods were turned to verdure.'

A similar story is found in the *Adventures of Art Son of Conn*.[6]

The same King Conn who figures in the *Prophetic Ecstasy* married an evil woman, so that there was no grain or milk in Ireland. Setting out to remedy this, he embarked in a coracle and for six weeks was tossed about on stormy seas. He landed on an island and approached a palace very like that of the sea-god Manannan as described in the *Adventures of Cormac* (Conn's grandson).[7] Conn entered and saw the niece of Manan-

---

[1] Loomis, *Arthurian Tradition*, pp. 379–82; *PMLA*, xxv (1910), 14–24; R. Thurneysen, *Irische Helden- und Königsagen* (Halle, 1921), pp. 574, 648.

[2] *Continuations of Old French Perceval*, ed. Roach, i. 362; ii. 519 f.; iii. 468–71.

[3] Ibid. i. 356–69; ii. 514–32; iii. 456–97. Trans. J. L. Weston, *Sir Gawain at the Grail Castle* (London, 1903), pp. 16–29. See *R*, lxxix (1958), 63–67.

[4] In *RF*, xlv. 87–91, I tried to show that this body was due to a misunderstanding of the horn (*cors*) of Brân. Cf. also Newstead, op. cit., pp. 86–93.

[5] On Grail as self-moving vessel cf. *RF*, xlv. 74 f., 82; *Queste del Saint Graal*, ed. Pauphilet, p. 15; *Elucidation*, ed. A. W. Thompson, pp. 60 f., 95.

[6] *Eriu*, iii (1907), 155–7; T. P. Cross, C. N. Slover, *Ancient Irish Tales* (New York, 1936), pp. 493–5.

[7] Ibid., pp. 504 f.

nan, her husband, and their son. His feet were washed by unseen agency. He was led to the fire. Food-laden boards rose up automatically before him, and a drinking-horn appeared, though he did not know who brought it.

From this point on, the saga has no concern for us except that we learn that the cause of the dearth in Ireland was eventually removed, and may presume that fertility was restored. If one asks oneself why the first continuator departed so far from Chrétien's account of the Grail adventure, is there any answer half so adequate as the ultimate influence of an early form of this Irish saga? For here is the mission to restore the fertility of the land, the stormy journey over the sea, the arrival at an Otherworld dwelling, the hospitable reception, the provision of food by invisible agents, and the restoration of fertility. Though Conn in this saga does not wake to find the palace and his host vanished, as did Gauvain, that is just what happened in another *echtra*, *The Adventures of Cormac in the Land of Promise*.[1] Though differing often in motivation and in detail, these Irish sagas recounting the visits of heroes to the homes of the gods provided the basic patterns for the visits to the Grail castle, just as the *Boyhood Deeds of Finn* furnished the outlines for the *enfances* of Perceval.[2] Even the theme of the disenchantment of the land by the asking of a certain question finds its unique analogue in a folk-tale collected in County Mayo about 115 years ago.[3]

Thus the origin of the Grail romances lies very clearly in the fund of Irish and Welsh stories exploited by the Breton *conteurs*, and we need no longer wonder at their diversity and irrationality. But there is still reason to wonder why those particular legends out of all the Arthurian cycle were so persistently given a Christian colouring.

A theory which counts among its adherents some eminent names would attribute the sanctification of the Grail legends to the influence of Glastonbury Abbey and the Plantagenet kings.[4] Though this view conjures up fascinating images of poets plotting with abbots and monarchs, and seems to have the analogy of the *chansons de geste* in its favour, it fades away in the

---

[1] Ibid., p. 507. The motif of waking in the open after a night in an Otherworld castle is found in other Arthurian texts: Heinrich von dem Türlin, *Crone*, ed. G. H. F. Scholl, vss. 14881–91; Gerbert de Montreuil, *Continuation de Perceval*, ed. M. Williams, i. 5; *Continuations of Old French Perceval*, ed. Roach, ii. 115 f.; C. Potvin, *Perceval le Gallois*, iii. 372; iv. 6 f., 226 f.; Renaud de Beaujeu, *Bel Inconnu*, ed. G. P. Williams (Paris, 1929), p. 165; *Tristan en Prose*, ed. E. Löseth (Paris, 1890), sec. 290a; *Studies and Notes in Philology and Literature*, iv (1895), 142 f.; *RC*, lix (1933), 561; *RF*, xlv (1931), 72, 74, 76, 82.

[2] Nutt in *Folklore Record*, iv (1881), 7–21; Pace in *PMLA*, xxxii (1917), 598–604; A. C. L. Brown in *MP*, xviii (1920), 211–21; Nitze in *Univ. of Calif. Pub. in Mod. Phil.* xxviii. 312–14; Loomis, *Arthurian Tradition*, pp. 337 f.

[3] Ibid., pp. 382 f.; Caesar Otway, *Sketches in Erris and Tyrawley* (Dublin, 1841), pp. 39–41. Cf. also ibid., pp. 80, 104 f.

[4] A. Nutt, *Legends of the Holy Grail* (London, 1902), pp. 40–49, 66; J. Marx, *Légende arthurienne*, pp. 302–15; *MA*, lix (1953), 69–86; Viscardi, in *Cultura Neolatina*, ii (1942), 87–103. For refutation see Bruce, i. 262–7.

light of the Glastonbury documents themselves. A cautious study of these by Joseph Armitage Robinson, Dean of Wells and Fellow of the British Academy, brought out the following facts.[1] About 1000 an anonymous biographer of St. Dunstan stated that the first preachers of Christ in Britain found at Glastonbury a church built by no skill of man and consecrated to the Virgin. About 1140 William of Malmesbury, who had examined the documents of Glastonbury Abbey, suggested the possibility that these disciples of Christ had been sent over from Gaul by St. Philip. Then we have a forged charter of St. Patrick,[2] dated by Robinson about 1220, and interpolated in William's *De Antiquitate Glastoniensis Ecclesiae*. This shows that William's suggestion had hardened into a claim that twelve disciples, sent over by St. Philip and St. James, built the old church at Glastonbury. It is clear that any story of the conversion of Britain promoted by the abbey would have at least mentioned St. Philip, but the romances of the Grail know nothing of him. Gradually, however, the monastic authorities made concessions to the novel claims made by the French romancers. Some time before 1247 the last reviser of William's *De Antiquitate* added that the leader of Philip's mission was Joseph of Arimathea.[3] But it was not till 1367 that the legend was taken seriously enough to warrant the report that Joseph's body had been found in the hallowed precincts,[4] and not till the end of the century that John of Glastonbury gave official sanction to the account of Joseph's history as given in the *Estoire del Saint Graal*. But he made certain changes; most significant were the total omission of the Grail and the substitution of two cruets filled with the blood and the sweat of the Saviour.[5]

Let it be admitted that Robert de Boron's *Joseph*, echoes very faintly the early claim that the first preachers of Christ had visited Glastonbury. As we learned in Chap. 19, Robert forecasts that Petrus, one of the disciples of Joseph, is destined to go to the 'vaus d'Avaron' in the Occident, and that Bron, custodian of the Grail, is also to proceed independently to the Occident.[6] Though nothing is said of their eventual meeting, both are to await the coming of Alain's son, and one may suspect that the Grail Keeper was destined to reach the 'vaus d'Avaron', that is, Glastonbury, which, as

---

[1] J. Armitage Robinson, *Two Glastonbury Legends* (Cambridge, 1926), pp. 28–50, especially pp. 35–37. Another great medievalist, M. R. James, in his *Abbeys* (London, 1925), pp. 19 f., supports Robinson's judgement that the introduction of Joseph of Arimathea into Glastonbury tradition was a late borrowing from French romances. Other treatments of the interpolations in William of Malmesbury's *De Antiquitate* are Newell's in *PMLA*, xviii (1903), 459 ff.; Baist's in *ZRP*, xix (1895), 326–45; Faral's in *Légende arthurienne*, ii. 421–60, and in *Revue Historique*, clx (1929), 1–49.

[2] J. Armitage Robinson, *Somerset Historical Essays* (London, 1921), pp. 13–17.

[3] Robinson, *Two Glastonbury Legends*, p. 36.

[4] Ibid., p. 64.

[5] Ibid., pp. 29–40.

[6] Robert de Boron, *Roman de l'Estoire dou Graal*, ed. W. A. Nitze (Paris, 1927), vss. 3120–34, 3215–22, 3343–54. On these passages see Nitze in *Spec*, xxviii (1953), 281 f.; Loomis in *RR*, xxviii (1942), 171 f.

was shown in Chap. 7, was publicly recognized in 1191 as the isle of Avalon and which was surrounded by marshlands. Therefore, it is probable that Robert's references to the 'vaus d'Avaron 'were based ultimately on some early version of the Glastonbury claim. But his elaborate story of Joseph, Bron, Petrus, and the Grail does not reflect Glastonbury tradition of the late twelfth or early thirteenth century, but rather contradicts it. It is therefore incredible that Robert de Boron composed his poem at the instigation of the abbey authorities. Nor is there any cogent reason for adopting Suchier's guess[1] that the poet, who took his name from the village of Boron in Burgundy and wrote for Gautier de Montbéliard, was identical with a Robert de Burun, who held lands in Essex in 1186 and who, so far as anyone knows, was not connected with Burgundy on the one hand or with Glastonbury on the other.[2]

Another continental romance, *Perlesvaus*, outlined and discussed in the preceding chapter, has sometimes been thought to support the view that the Somerset abbey was responsible for the Christianization of the Grail legend. Nitze has demonstrated that its author had some knowledge of the site of the abbey and of its traditions.[3] But his dialect[4] and certain inaccuracies in his description[5] seem to prove that he was not a monk of the house, and he has not a word of St. Philip's mission. One has only to read *Perlesvaus* and then the Charter of St. Patrick to realize that they emanate from quite different sources. Though without much doubt Nitze is right in claiming that the French romance is indebted to Robert's *Joseph* for certain details,[6] there is, significantly, no reference to Petrus's arrival at the 'vaus d'Avaron', no effort to connect the evangelization of Britain with Glastonbury, such as Robert seems to forecast. It is as vain to ascribe *Perlesvaus* to a propagandist effort by the monks of the Somerset house as to make the same claim for the *Joseph*.

If any further proof is needed that the Christianization of the legend was a continental development, it is only necessary to emphasize the fact that not a single Anglo-Norman Grail romance has survived; that although Henry II was reputed to have had a hand in the discovery of the tomb of Arthur,[7] there is no reliable evidence that he or his successors took any interest in the Grail till Edward III and Richard II are recorded as owning one or two manuscripts on the subject.[8] The Glastonbury monks were capable of

[1] *ZRP*, xvi (1892), 269–74.   [2] See above, pp. 252 f.

[3] On Glastonbury and *Perlesvaus* see above, Chap. 20; Nitze in *SP*, xv (1918), 7–13; *MP*, xvii (1919), 153–65.   [4] *Perlesvaus*, ed. Nitze and others, ii. 19 f.

[5] Ibid., ii. 46 f.; F. Lot, *Étude sur le Lancelot en Prose* (Paris, 1918), p. 449.

[6] *Perlesvaus*, ii. 121–4.   [7] See Chap. 7 above.

[8] *Trans. of Bibliographical Soc.*, ser. 2, xiii. 145. So far as I am aware, no scholar now takes seriously the statement in the *Queste* (ed. Pauphilet, p. 280) that Walter Map translated the book from Latin into French for the love of King Henry. See *Queste*, p. iii; Bruce, i. 368–71; Lot, op. cit., pp. 128 f.

brazenly forging documents to advance their claims to sanctity or to territory, but they were not responsible for the French romances which purported to tell how a holy vessel appeared in Arthur's time and how it had reached Britain.

Thus we return to the original problem. How can one explain the creation of pious legends which shed such lustre on a land to which the creators owed, so far as one can tell, no allegiance secular or religious? Why is there not more harmony between them? Why was Joseph of Arimathea (not Philip) chosen as the first guardian of the Grail and later as the first missionary to Britain?

I venture to put forward again[1] a theory which, though not at first glance as plausible as the theory of monastic propaganda, stands up far better when examined in the light of the texts themselves. It is based on the observed phenomenon that some of the most irrational, freakish features in the Matter of Britain, as well as in medieval literature generally, find a wholly rational explanation in misreading and misunderstanding, and nowhere was misinterpretation more likely to occur than in handling the phantasmagoric stories of the Grail and its quest. I have pointed out in my work on Chrétien some obvious examples,[2] and in the case of the Grail legend it has long been recognized that Wolfram mistranslated Chrétien's *tailleor* (carving platter) as *messer* (knife),[3] and the unfamiliarity of the word *graal* led to the substitution of *sang real* for *saint graal*.[4] No procedure could be more reasonable than to seek the cause of the sanctification of the Grail legends in a series of misunderstandings.

It has been noted above that the Grail as a self-moving vessel in an Otherworld palace corresponds to a drinking horn served by invisible agency, described in an Irish *echtra*; and another Irish text mentions similar self-moving horns in the house of the Sovranty of Ireland, the bride of Lug.[5] Evidently magic horns were to be expected along with other vessels in the homes of the Irish gods.[6] Let us now turn to the Welsh list which has already furnished the prototype of the Grail; there we find also the horn of Brân: 'the drink and the food that one asked for, one received in it when one desired'.[7] Its distinctive attribute was therefore the same as that of the Welsh

---

[1] *RF*, xlv. 66–94; *Spec*, viii. 430 f.; Loomis, *Arthurian Tradition*, pp. 171–5, 387–93; *Colloques internationaux du Centre National de la Recherche Scientifique*, iii, *Les Romans du Graal* (Paris, 1956), pp. 233–47.

[2] Loomis, *Arthurian Tradition*, pp. 49 f., 145, 219, 275, 445–7, 458 f., 488.

[3] Bruce, i. 328.

[4] Malory, *Works*, ed. Vinaver (Oxford, 1947), i, p. cxv. See *Oxford English Dictionary sub* Sangrail and Sang royal.

[5] W. Stokes, E. Windisch, *Irische Texte*, iii (Leipzig, 1891), 322 f.

[6] *RF*, xlv. 71–77.

[7] Ibid., p. 71; Newstead, op. cit., p. 20. 'Bran galed or Gogledd' is a figure derived directly from some Welsh redaction of Geoffrey of Monmouth's *Historia*. See Griscom's edition, p. 276, where

dysgl of plenty: 'whatever food one wished thereon was instantly obtained'.
Here the horn is in the possession of Brân, the prototype of Bron, the Fisher
King. We know that the word *dysgl*, when translated into French as *graal*,
led to misunderstandings. What about the Welsh word *corn* when translated
in the nominative as *cors*? *Cors* could have at least five meanings: horn, corner, court, course, body; few words in Old French were more ambiguous,
and the meaning had to be guessed from the context. Though we have in the
Anglo-Norman *Lai du Cor* and in the *Livre de Caradoc* magic drinking
horns,[1] Schultz says in connexion with medieval table service that 'only seldom do I find any mention of the drinking horn'.[2] Since this rarity would
tend to eliminate the first meaning, and since corner, court, and course would
not fit the context, one meaning alone remained, body. This, in the sense of
the Corpus Christi, the sacramental wafer, though it offered difficulties, was
plausible enough, since there were legends about the miraculous nutritive
powers of the Host.[3] Caesarius of Heisterbach, for example, tells (Book IX,
chap. 47) how a woman lived on the Body of Christ alone. Here, then, is a
possible explanation of the *graal* and the *oiste*, which sustained the life of the
Fisher King's father, in Chrétien's poem. The two Welsh vessels of plenty,
the platter and the drinking horn, have been converted as a result of the
ambiguity of *cors* into the Grail and the Body of Christ.

Another instance of the same confusion is found in the *Estoire del Saint
Graal* and the *Queste*, to be treated in the next chapter, and this time the
evidence is stronger. The castle of the Grail, we are told, was called Corbenic,
which meant in Chaldean 'saintisme vaissel', 'most holy vessel'.[4] Since *c* and
t were constantly mistaken for each other, and since the Dutch *Lancelot*
gives the name of the castle as Cambenoyt, and a manuscript of Manessier
as Corlenot,[5] we may well suspect that the original form was Corbenoit; in
other words, the castle of the Blessed Horn. The author of the source understood the words and provided the correct interpretation as 'saintisme vaissel',
but the author of the *Queste* took the words 'cors benoiz' as he found them
in his source to mean the sacred Host, which Henry of Lancaster likewise

Gogledd translates *Northumbria*. But, in spite of many differences, this Brân must be Geoffrey's remodelling of Brân the Blessed, since Geoffrey retained the latter's character for hospitality and the
feud with Beli which we find in the *mabinogi*, transferred to the next generation. Ibid., pp. 276,
283 f.; Loth, *Mabinogion* (1913), i. 119–32, 146 f.; Newstead, op. cit., pp. 163–7, and in *RR*, xxxvi
(1945), 3–26.

[1] See Chap. 11 above.

[2] A. Schultz, *Das höfische Leben zur Zeit der Minnesinger*, 2nd ed. (Leipzig, 1889), i. 382.

[3] P. Browe, *Die eucharistischen Wunder des Mittelalters* (Breslau, 1938), pp. 49 f.; *PMLA*, lxxi
(1956), 852, n. 44. A modern case is that of Theresa Neumann. Bergen Evans, *Spoor of Spooks* (New
York, 1954), p. 97. Chrétien perhaps knew of a case in the neighbouring diocese of Sens, recorded
by Guillaume de Nangis under the year 1180.

[4] Newstead, op. cit., pp. 89 f.; Sommer, op. cit. i. 289.

[5] J. L. Weston, *Legend of Sir Lancelot du Lac* (London, 1901), p. 159; Potvin, *Perceval le Gallois*,
vi. 150, n. 2.

called the 'tresbenoit corps en forme de payne'.[1] Thus we have the sublime
scene in the castle of Corbenic when Christ Himself fed the twelve knights
with the consecrated wafer in the Grail.[2]

Still another author who shows the influence of the same basic error is the
unknown who composed *Sone de Nausay*.[3] Though he knew and in part
followed the *Estoire del Saint Graal*, he had independent sources, for he not
only preserved, as we have seen, the most primitive account of the Waste Land
but also described the Grail as in the possession of a monastic community, dwelling in an island castle called Galoche (evidently a corruption of the French
feminine adjective *galesche*, 'Welsh'), which had been founded by Joseph of
Arimathea, but he even identified Joseph with the Fisher King.[4] Why this
extraordinary equation? Can any reason more plausible be offered than the
inference that since the Fisher King was the possessor of a most holy *cors*, he
must be that Joseph who was the custodian of the most holy *cors* of all?

Now this original inference that the *cors* possessed by the Fisher King was
the physical body of Christ, though it sufficed to identify him with Joseph,
could not be consistently maintained, since the *cors* was now in the keeping
of the monks of Galoche. The sacred body in this context had to be that of
the Fisher King himself. We read of Galoche: 'Ce castiel fonda Li sains
cors, dont vous vees la Le saint vassiel u se repose.'[5] 'This castle was founded
by the holy body whose holy vessel you see there where it lies.' The abbot
exhibited to Sone the Grail, the head of Longinus's spear, and the reliquary
containing the body of Joseph.[6] We learn that the abbot was supplied with
(or by) holy bodies, and he had served them right well, God first and the
relics (*sains*) afterwards. This sounds very much like a muddled account of
the food-providing function of the *cors* of the Fisher King, originally the
horn of Brân. And the picture of the monks feasting in their island castle
of Galoche in the presence of the holy *cors* of the Fisher King[7] recalls the
prolonged sojourn of the followers of Brân in a royal hall on the Welsh isle
of Gwales,[8] and since they were provided 'without stint', we may presume
that they enjoyed the service of Brân's magic horn.

Thus we see that three of the queerest, most puzzling features of the
sanctified Grail legend—the use of a dish, large enough to hold a salmon, as
the receptacle for the Corpus Christi; the setting of a eucharistic feast, not in
a church but in the hall of a castle named Corbenic or Cambenoyt; the

---

[1] Henry of Lancaster, *Livre de Seyntz Medicines*, ed. J. Arnould (Oxford, 1940), p. 11.
[2] Sommer, op. cit. vi. 190; *Queste*, ed. Pauphilet, pp. 269–71.
[3] On the Arthurian element in *Sone* see J. D. Bruce in *Hesperia*, Ergänzungsreihe ii, pp. xxxiv f.;
Loomis, *Arthurian Tradition*, pp. 174, 221, 243, 362, 391; Loomis, *Wales*, pp. 53–60, 174–6;
Weston in *R*, xliii (1914), 403–20; Newstead in *RR*, xxxvi (1945), 10–12.
[4] *Sone von Nausay*, ed. M. Goldschmidt, vs. 4823.
[5] Ibid. vss. 4557–9.   [6] Ibid. vss. 4885–930.
[7] Ibid. vss. 4931–46; cf. vss. 4401–8.
[8] Loth, op. cit. i. 145–9; *Mabinogion*, trans. G. and T. Jones, pp. 37–39.

identification of Joseph of Arimathea with the Fisher King—can be most satisfactorily explained by the confusion of *cors*, 'horn', with *cors*, 'body', by the substitution of the body of Christ, either in a literal or a sacramental sense, for a horn of plenty.

These were not the only transmogrifications which the horn of Brân underwent. Sometimes it was mistaken for a court, sometimes owing to the confusion of *c* and *t* it became a *tors*, 'bull', as I have shown elsewhere,[1] but it still remained the source of wealth. But the eucharistic suggestions of the word *cors* and the cult of saintly bodies were the most potent forces which led one continental author after another to struggle with the problem of Christianizing this originally heathenish material. The more mysterious and intractable it appeared, the more it fascinated, and one cannot but be amazed at the ingenuity and the fertility of imagination which these authors brought to their task. The more one realizes the nature of the task, the more the wonder grows as one studies Wolfram's *Parzival*, the *Estoire del Saint Graal*, and the *Queste*. But one need no longer remain in sheer bewilderment as to whence these great stories came and as to the motives which led to their transformation into works of high spiritual significance.

The question of the traditional origin of the story of Perceval and the Grail involves the question, already touched on in Chap. 18, whether Wolfram had a secondary source besides Chrétien. For some investigators, having rightly decided that Wolfram's account of Kyot is incredible, have concluded not only that there was no Kyot but also that there was no source for the Grail legend but Chrétien's poem, no antecedent tradition, no Celtic origin.

But it is hardly logical to conclude that, because Wolfram indulged in much characteristic mystification about his sources, he could have had only one, namely Chrétien. Chaucer invoked a certain Lollius as the sole authority for his romance of Troilus. It has long been suspected and has recently been demonstrated that Lollius as an authority on the Trojan war is fictitious;[2] and that Chaucer derived his material almost entirely from Boccaccio. But no scholar has been so bold as to argue that because Lollius was a phantom Boccaccio never existed. It is equally illogical to argue that because Kyot may well be a phantom, Wolfram had no access to other traditions about Perceval and the Grail than what he learned from Chrétien. It is also unreasonable to charge those who have tried to prove that Wolfram drew upon more than one version of the legend with denying his poetic powers.

In Chap. 18 certain differences between Chrétien and Wolfram have already been noted which point to at least one secondary influence. As a

---

[1] Loomis, *Wales*, pp. 43–50; *Arthurian Tradition*, pp. 171–5; Newstead, *Bran the Blessed*, pp. 95–106.

[2] R. A. Pratt in *MLN*, lv (1950), 183–7.

matter of fact, a considerable number of variations and additions in the German poem are paralleled in other romances of the Arthurian cycle, particularly in those concerned with Perceval or the Grail, which Wolfram could hardly have read and which could not possibly have been derived from him. There are too many to be regarded as accidental. They can be explained only as offshoots from some more or less remote traditional material in French. To be sure, some of the analogies adduced by Wechssler and Singer are not close enough to carry conviction;[1] but others remain which are not easily disposed of, and which have been supplemented by other analogies noted by Heinzel, Zenker, Strucks, Mary Williams, and Jessie Weston.[2] Without attempting a complete list of these deviations of Wolfram from Chrétien's narrative which seem to have traditional warrant, let me cite some of the more significant features which Wolfram shares not with Chrétien but with other romances.

There is the striking series of correspondences between the Gahmuret prologue of *Parzival* and the so-called *Bliocadran* prologue of *Perceval*, which has already been mentioned in Chap. 18. The list of resemblances has been drawn up by Jessie Weston and Sister M. A. Rachbauer and need not be repeated,[3] especially since Fourquet has recognized their existence,[4] and some critics have frankly admitted that Wolfram was indebted to the *Bliocadran* prologue. Fourquet, however, properly recognized the vast differences which exist between the two prologues and which make direct dependence of one upon the other unlikely. He therefore postulated a common source in the form of a short introduction to Chrétien's poem which would be responsible for the similarities, and argued that the differences would be accounted for by independent development. Plausible though this hypothesis may be, I fail to see that it has any advantage over the claim that Wolfram used at least one other form of the Perceval legend besides Chrétien's; indeed, it fails to account for certain curious parallels between Gahmuret's story and that of the Welsh Brân,[5] including the fact that both were kings connected with North Wales, Gahmuret through marriage to the Queen of Norgals, Brân through holding court at Harlech, Aberffraw, and Caer Seint. It is significant that, according to Chrétien, Perceval's mother, after her husband's death, brought up her child near the mountain

---

[1] E. Wechssler in *Philologische Studien, Festgabe für E. Sievers* (Halle, 1896), pp. 237–51; S. Singer, *Wolfram und der Gral. Neue Parzival-Studien* (Bern, 1939).

[2] R. Heinzel, 'Über Wolframs von Eschenbach Parzival', *Sitzungsberichte der kais. Akad. der Wissenschaften zu Wien*, cxxx (1893); Zenker in *RF*, xl (1927), 251–329; C. Strucks, *Der junge Parzival* (Borna-Leipzig, 1910); M. R. Williams, *Essai sur la composition du roman Gallois de Peredur* (Paris, 1909), pp. 81–95; J. L. Weston, *Legend of Sir Perceval* (London, 1906), i, *passim*.

[3] Weston, op. cit. i. 71 f.; M. A. Rachbauer, *Study of the Relation of the Contents of Books III–VI and IX of the Parzival to the Chrestien Manuscripts* (Washington 1934), pp. 6–12.

[4] J. Fourquet, *Wolfram d'Eschenbach et le Conte del Graal* (Paris, 1938), pp. 113–15.

[5] R. S. Loomis, *Arthurian Tradition*, p. 350; H. Newstead in *RR*, xxxvi. 3–31.

passes of Esnaudone (Snowdon),[1] and according to the *Bliocadran* prologue she retired to a castle on the sea of Wales called Caflé, which can hardly be other than Caer Leu, now known as Dinlle, on the coast near Carnarvon.[2] Thus all four preludes to the story of Perceval lead us to North Wales, but in such different ways that it seems impossible to regard Chrétien as the source of the other three.

Moreover, Strucks has drawn up a list of the parallels between *Parzival* and the English *Sir Perceval*.[3] Both *Parzival* and *Perlesvaus* mention specifically two lords who persecuted the hero's mother and invaded his patrimony.[4] There are several points on which both *Parzival* and *Peredur* deviate from the French *Perceval*: namely the substitution of a lake for the river where the Fisher King is first descried; the change in the relationship of the Fisher King to the hero, from cousin to uncle; the outbreak of lamentation which greets the entrance of the bleeding spear.[5] Are all these fairly specific correspondences between Wolfram and the Perceval romances which he could not have read due to mere chance?

Most significant are the divergences from Chrétien which are concerned with the Grail and the Grail castle. It is possible, of course, that Wolfram converted the vessel into a stone because he, like others, did not understand the word *graal* and erroneously interpreted Chrétien's mention of the 'pierres précieuses' which adorned the vessel as the object itself. But other remarkable features cannot be so accounted for. Chrétien made it perfectly clear that the vessel served only the Fisher King's father and no one else, yet Wolfram wrote that 'each man found ready in front of the Grail whatever he held his hand out for, warm dishes or cold, fresh or old, flesh of wild or tame. . . . If a man held out his cup, it was filled with whatever beverage he might name.'[6] Now this property, unknown to Chrétien, is repeatedly ascribed to the Grail by authors whom Wolfram could hardly have read and who could certainly not read him. The First Continuation of Chrétien's poem, we remember, represents the Grail as a vessel moved by unseen agency, filling the cups of the knights with wine and dispensing course after course.[7] Likewise,

---

[1] *Mélanges offerts à E. Hoepffner* (Paris, 1949), pp. 230–2.

[2] Ulrich von Zatzikhoven, *Lanzelet*, trans. K. G. T. Webster (New York, 1951), pp. 186 f.

[3] Strucks, op. cit., pp. 28–38.

[4] *Parzival*, 128, 3–128, 12; 140, 26–141, 10; *Perlesvaus*, ed. Nitze, i, ll. 1065–78, 3201–9.

[5] M. R. Williams, op. cit., pp. 90–92; Zenker in *RF*, xl. 286–92. In *Peredur* the Fisher host is the hero's uncle. *Mabinogion*, trans. G. and T. Jones, pp. 190 f.; *Parzival*, bk. ix.

[6] *Parzival*, 238, 8–239, 7. Trans. M. F. Richey, *Story of Parzival* (Oxford, 1935), p. 83. See Hertz's translation, 5th ed., n. 102.

[7] See p. 283, n. 3 above. Fourquet, op. cit., pp. 158–66, maintains that Wolfram knew the First Continuation, including Gauvain's Grail visit. Chronologically this is possible, but I find it hard to understand how one who took his sources as seriously as Wolfram did (ibid., pp. 98 f.), and who in spite of his originality left the prints of those works so plainly, could have worked so differently with the First Continuation, transferring from it to his own poem little besides the bounty provided by the Grail. Fourquet is supported, though corrected, by Wrede, *Fortsetzer des Gralromans*, pp. 186–98.

as we have already observed, in Manessier's continuation and in the Vulgate cycle the vessel performs this same function. In this respect it resembles not Chrétien's *graal* but the *Dysgl* of Rhydderch.

Again, Wolfram is explicit in stating that 'whosoever beholds that stone [the Grail] shall keep the freshness of life's prime. If one gazed upon that stone for two hundred years, no other sign of age but grey hairs would appear.'[1] Now this same virtue is assigned to the Grail in *Perlesvaus*.[2] Gauvain meets a hermit who declares that, though he is over sixty years old, he appears to be only forty because of his service in the Grail chapel; and later Gauvain joins twelve knights feasting in the Grail castle, who are over a hundred years old but look no older than forty.

Lastly, Parzival is informed by his cousin Sigûne that whoever seeks the Grail castle with care and striving cannot find it.[3] This motif turns up also in *Perlesvaus*, where the hermit tells Gauvain that no one can teach him the way to the Fisher King's dwelling unless the will of God leads him;[4] and in the Prose *Tristan* likewise we read that the castle of Corbenyc was placed under a spell so that no knight who sought it would reach it unless guided by luck.[5]

Thus a survey of the correspondences between *Parzival* and certain other Perceval and Grail romances can afford little satisfaction to those who would see the starting-point of these stories in Chrétien's poem. Surely some parallels are due to chance, but the remainder force us to conclude that Wolfram had access to at least one French source which provided him with bits of information known also to the continuators of Chrétien and the authors of *Peredur*, *Perlesvaus*, and *Sir Perceval*. One need not, of course, suppose that all had obtained copies of the same text; the very possibility is hard to conceive. But just as the extraordinary diversity of these romances on the same general theme must be explained in large measure by pre-literary ramifications in the days when the *conteurs* first fascinated courtly audiences by their recitals, so also the extraordinary interlinking of the same romances by the introduction of the same motifs and details by authors who could not have had the same literary models can best be explained by the existence of a common stock of tradition, still partly oral in the days when Wolfram and the authors of *Perlesvaus*, *Peredur*, and the French source of *Sir Perceval* were writing.[6] Though Wolfram obscured the Celtic origins of this tradition, particularly by his predilection for Oriental and mystical lore as a device to

---

[1] *Parzival*, 469, 18–469, 27. Trans. Richey, *Story of Parzival*, p. 136.
[2] *Perlesvaus*, ed. Nitze, i, ll. 897–900, 942–7, 2414–17.
[3] *Parzival*, 250, 25–250, 30. See Hertz's trans., 5th ed., n. 109, and p. 244 above.
[4] *Perlesvaus*, ll. 947–9.
[5] MS. Bib. Nat. fr. 101, f. 312 v. '. . . nulz chevaliers estranges qui le queist nel trouvast saventure ne lui amenast.'
[6] See Chap. 6 above.

heighten the exotic and mysterious tone of his poem, the Celtic patterns are traceable not only in the scenes adapted from Chrétien, but also in the first two books; Gahmuret's connexion with Wales is not limited to his wedding the Queen of Norgals, and the power of the Grail to supply whatever food one desires may legitimately be derived from the Welsh vessel of plenty.

Let me sum up in a few words the probable development of the Grail legends. Their ultimate sources lay in Irish sagas, recounting the visits of mortal heroes to the palaces of pagan gods, where they were feasted sumptuously from vessels of plenty. Combined with other narrative patterns, these sagas passed on to the Welsh and left their traces in the *Mabinogion*; the original characters were replaced, the gods were euhemerized, and their dwellings localized. The deliverance of a Waste Land through the healing of its wounded king became a principal theme; a platter and a drinking horn became the principal sources of supply. This confused material,[1] transmitted orally through the Bretons to the French and Anglo-Normans, roused enormous curiosity, partly because of its obscurities. The men of letters who inherited the legends of the Grail from the *conteurs* exercised their ingenuity to straighten out the inconsistencies and solve the mysteries; and once they had found a false clue in the words 'cors beneiz', the process of Christianization proceeded rapidly. Before Chrétien's time, the platter had acquired eucharistic attributes, and soon after, if not earlier, the Maimed King was either identified or otherwise linked with Joseph of Arimathea, custodian of the Holy Body. Though the Church never gave official sanction to the fantastic stories, pious authors discovered in them moral and mystic truths and claimed angelic or even divine authority. As we shall see in the next chapter, French clerics, following Robert de Boron, enormously elaborated the account of Joseph and the conversion of Britain, explained the presence of the vessel in the castle of Corbenic, and provided the standard version of the Quest. The conversion legend was gradually adopted by Glastonbury, and at the great Church councils of the fifteenth century the English delegates claimed precedence over the French and Spanish on the basis of Joseph's mission.

---

[1] The confusion has been worse confounded by the interweaving of two other Celtic traditions into the Grail fabric. The obligation to avenge a kinsman's death, which is the main theme of *Sir Perceval* and intrudes itself into the Grail quest (First Continuation of *Perceval*, Manessier, *Peredur*, *Perlesvaus*), derives from the famous saga of Finn mac Cumaill. King Pelles, who in the Vulgate cycle takes over from the Maimed King the lordship of the Grail castle, derives from the Welsh King Beli, who except in size seems to have resembled his brother Brân and gave his name to a faery castle in Cornwall; whereas Pelles' daughter goes back to Beli's granddaughter, Modron, prototype also of Morgain la Fée; thus, through her affinity to Morgain, her healing power, her jealousy of Guenièvre, and her dwelling with her maidens on the winterless Isle of Joy are accounted for. See on the vengeance motif Loomis, *Arthurian Tradition*, pp. 394–414; on Pelles and his daughter ibid., pp. 142–5, 205–14, 430–3; V. J. Harward, *The Dwarfs of Arthurian Romance and Celtic Tradition* (Leiden, 1958), index *sub* Pelles.

THE VULGATE CYCLE

JEAN FRAPPIER

THE most widely read and the most influential group of Arthurian prose romances is called by modern scholars the Vulgate cycle. With the addition of another romance, the so-called *Livre d'Artus*, which is preserved in only one manuscript, it was published by H. O. Sommer in seven quarto volumes.[1] This cycle consists of five romances: (1) the *Estoire del Saint Graal*; (2) a prose version of Robert's *Merlin*, with a lengthy sequel; (3) the *Lancelot*, occupying volumes III to V of Sommer's edition; (4) the *Queste del Saint Graal*; (5) the *Mort Artu*. Of these five romances the first two are generally regarded by scholars as later additions, not contemplated in the original scheme, and one of these, the Vulgate *Merlin*, is reserved for treatment in the next chapter. The remaining three I shall refer to as the Prose *Lancelot*, since Lancelot is a prominent figure throughout. This trilogy—the *Lancelot* proper, the *Queste del Saint Graal*, and the *Mort Artu* —is our first concern.

Dated probably between 1215 and 1230, it belongs to a period when Arthurian romance, still profiting from the impulse given by Chrétien, was taking new directions. Already the tendency to turn verse narratives into prose and to combine them in groups had manifested itself in the combination of the prose versions of Robert's *Joseph* and *Merlin* with the *Didot Perceval*. Already, too, the process of Christianizing the Grail legend had gone far, and had brought new mysteries and a new spirit into the world of chivalry. These tendencies which found their crude expression in the combination just cited attained a high degree of artistic fulfilment in the Prose *Lancelot*. Even *Perlesvaus*, whether it is dated before or after the Prose *Lancelot*, and though it possesses fine qualities of imagination and style, is inferior in organization and clarity of purpose.

Compared with either the *Didot Perceval* or *Perlesvaus*, the Prose *Lancelot* impresses one by its consistency and solidity. A system of forecasts and con-

[1] Vol. i, *Estoire del Saint Graal* (1909); ii, *Estoire de Merlin* (1908); iii (1910), iv (1911), v (1912), *Lancelot del Lac*; vi, *Queste del Saint Graal, Mort Artu* (1913); vii, *Livre d'Artus* (1913). An Index of Names and Places was added in 1916. Except for the *Livre d'Artus* (see Chap. 25 below) Sommer followed the Brit. Mus. MSS. Additional 10292–4, with variant readings from other manuscripts. It is in no sense a critical text. On the manuscripts of the Vulgate cycle see Sommer, op. cit. i, pp. xxiii–xxxii; F. Lot, *Étude sur le Lancelot en prose* (Paris, 1918, 1954), pp. 1, 2; as well as the editions of the *Queste* and the *Mort Artu* cited on p. 302, n. 1 and p. 307, n. 4 below.

cordances binds the mass of adventures together. Even in the first sentences we learn that Lancelot was called Galaad in baptism. Later the displacement of Lancelot as the greatest knight of the world and the messianic role of his son Galaad are predicted. With the begetting of Galaad by Lancelot on the daughter of the Grail King the mystic part of the cycle is indissolubly linked to the profane. At the beginning of the *Queste* portents multiply to indicate the arrival of the messianic hero and the beginning of new and high adventures. Besides the bond of prophecy and fulfilment there is the bond of lineage to hold together the past, the present, and the future. Galaad, through his father Lancelot, is descended from David and Joseph of Arimathea, and through his mother from the holy kings of the Grail.

The *Lancelot* proper looks forward not only to the *Queste* but also to the *Mort Artu*. Imprisoned by Morgain la Fée, Lancelot paints on the walls of his chamber the story of his amour with Guenièvre, and it is these paintings which in the *Mort Artu* are destined to reveal the secret to Arthur.[1] Likewise, visions and other prognostics throw into the future a lurid light, betokening the treachery of Mordret and the downfall of the Round Table. Thus the stately arch of prophecy which springs from the *Lancelot* is closed in the *Queste* and the *Mort Artu*.[2]

The 'Lancelot' Proper

Though Lancelot did not appear with Gauvain and Keu in the *Historia Regum Britanniae*, he was destined to outshine them in the later history of Arthurian literature. Whatever his remote origins,[3] the most primitive feature of his biography was his childhood in the palace of a fay, who stole him from his mother and reared him on an island of the sea or at the bottom of a lake. By the middle of the twelfth century he seems to have become the hero of a legend; this was made about 1180 into an Anglo-Norman romance, which in turn was translated by the Swiss priest, Ulrich von Zatzikhoven, into Middle High German about 1195.[4] Before that, Chrétien in *Erec* had ranked him third among the knights of the Round Table, and mentioned him with honour in *Cligès*,[5] but not till the poem which is usually called by his name was Lancelot promoted to the role of hero and made the lover of the queen. Here he appeared as the perfect example of fidelity and ardour,

---

[1] Sommer, op. cit. v. 216–18; vi. 238–41. See above, Chap. 7, p. 68, n. 7, and R. S. and L. H. Loomis, *Arthurian Legends in Medieval Art* (New York, 1938), pp. 16 f., 24 f., fig. 297.

[2] There are notable examples of symmetry indicated by Micha in *ZRP*, lxvi. 369–71. At the end of the *Queste* a hand, representing God the Father, descends from heaven and takes away the Grail and the lance (Pauphilet's edition, p. 279). Likewise at the end of the *Mort Artu*, a hand rises from the lake, seizes Escalibor, and disappears with it under the waters (Frappier's 1936 edition, p. 224). Was this symmetry due to the author of the *Mort Artu* or to the architect of the trilogy? I cannot decide.

[3] Ulrich von Zatzikhoven, *Lanzelet*, trans. and ed. K. G. T. Webster, R. S. Loomis (New York, 1951), pp. 12–18.   [4] See below, Chap. 33.

[5] *Erec*, vs. 1694; *Cligès*, vss. 4765, 4787, 4789, 4798.

a more refined and submissive Tristan.[1] With the publication of the Prose *Lancelot*, in which strands drawn from the sources of *Lanzelet* and from Chrétien's poem are happily combined, he acquired fresh glory.

The first part of the trilogy, the *Lancelot* proper,[2] is three times as long as the *Queste* and the *Mort Artu* combined. In a work of such length one expects an unevenness, an occasional slackening of inspiration. Especially in Sommer's volumes IV and V of the Vulgate corpus is the reader impressed by the banality and the irrelevance of many of the episodes. More than one critic has been led to believe in a multiplicity of authors, and indeed there may well have been interpolations which only a critical edition may reveal. But in spite of its meanderings the *Lancelot* proper is far from planless and in the next few pages I will endeavour to trace the evolution of the principal character and to bring out the continuity of the work as well as the changes of manner and spirit. For this purpose I adopt F. Lot's division of the work into two parts: (1) from the birth of the hero to the preparation for the *Queste*; (2) the preparation for the *Queste*.

1. From the Birth of the Hero to the Preparation for the *Queste*.[3] In spite of his descent from King David, Lancelot appears at the beginning of the romance as the child of calamity. While he is still in his cradle, his father, Ban of Benoic (a region vaguely placed in western France), is vanquished by Claudas, King of the Terre Deserte (identified with Berry), and dies. The infant is snatched away under the eyes of his mother by the Dame du Lac and is brought up in her palace, together with his cousins, Lionel and Bohort, who have precociously avenged their own father's death by killing Claudas's son. At the age of eighteen Lancelot is conducted by his foster-mother to Arthur's court and at her request is knighted.

In general outline these *enfances* parallel those of Lanzelet in the Swiss poem. Ban de Benoic corresponds to Pant von Genewis;[4] the abduction of his son and his training by a water fay in ignorance of his parentage are likewise matched. But there are marked changes from the traditional pattern which seem to be dictated by a purpose.[5] Ban has become wise and pious, in contrast to Pant. The Dame du Lac, who takes the place of a queen of a sea-girt isle, acts not in her own interests but for the good of her charge. A tendency to rationalize and humanize mythical elements may be discerned in the author's statement that the lake which concealed her abode was a mere

---

[1] M. Lot-Borodine in *Medieval Studies in Memory of G. Schoepperle Loomis* (Paris, New York, 1927), pp. 21–47.

[2] Besides the edition of the *Lancelot* proper by Sommer, op. cit., vols. iii–v, the students of Wechssler began the publication of a critical edition in *Marburger Beiträge zur romanischen Philologie* (1911-16). A critical edition, based on MS. Bib. Nat. fr. 768, has been undertaken by Elspeth Kennedy.

[3] Sommer, op. cit. iii; iv. 3–301, l. 10.

[4] *Lanzelet*, trans. and ed. Webster and Loomis, p. 157; Lot, *Étude*, p. 147, n. 8.

[5] Lot, *Étude*, pp. 167–9; E. Kennedy, 'Social and Political Ideas in the French Prose *Lancelot*', *MedAev*, xxvi (1957), 90–106.

illusion.[1] Though sorceries, allegorical dreams, and other marvels abound, the author is too 'scientific' to believe in fays. Highly realistic is the portrait of Claudas, and the revolt of his barons against him is told with an intensity of feeling which suggests that it had a contemporary reference.[2]

The author's serious purpose comes out clearly in the long discourse which the Dame du Lac delivers to her foster-son before she introduces him to the great world.[3] The origins of knighthood, the symbolic significance of the knight's weapons and his horse, the obligations which rest on him, are set forth. Though devoted to the pursuit of arms, he must subordinate worldly pride and egotism to the protection of the weak and, with repeated emphasis, to the defence of Holy Church. Here the ideal of chivalry, though still essentially worldly, is harmonized with Christian morality and placed at the service of religion.

A quite different intent may be suspected in two unusual circumstances which attend the knighting of the young hero. The Dame du Lac arranges with the king beforehand that during the ceremony Lancelot shall not wear arms given him by the king but those which she herself has provided.[4] Moreover, the king by an odd lapse of memory forgets to gird the new-made knight with a sword, and this significant office of supplying a sword falls to the queen.[5] The attentive reader is presumably given to understand that Lancelot's obligation to Arthur is thus curtailed and complicated with another loyalty—to Arthur's wife. A charming page describes his first meeting with the queen in the palace hall;[6] he dazed with love, almost paralysed with timidity yet stealing side-glances at her beauty; she curious about the young prodigy and touched by his grace and bashfulness, praying that God would make him a 'preudomme'.

The hero has not waited to embark on the career of strenuous adventure prescribed by the Dame du Lac. Fantastic vows, combats, enchantments, incognitos succeed each other and lead up to Lancelot's conquest of the Douloureuse Garde and the discovery of his name inscribed on the lid of a tomb where his body will ultimately lie. But not till he has removed the enchantments of the castle does he change its name to the Joyeuse Garde.

At this point the author begins to use systematically the narrative technique to which Lot applied the term *entrelacement* (interlacing).[7] Every episode is interrupted by another, which in turn is broken off in order to con-

---

[1] Lot, *Étude*, pp. 272 f.; Sommer, op. cit. iii. 19, ll. 18–24; 22, ll. 17–22; iv. 305, ll. 4–7.

[2] On Claudas see Lot, *Étude*, pp. 158, 356–8; Kennedy, loc. cit., pp. 91–96. It is possible that both legend and historic reality contributed to the creation of this person.

[3] Sommer, op. cit. iii. 112–17. See Frappier, 'L'"Institution" de Lancelot dans le *Lancelot en Prose*', in *Mélanges de philologie romane et de littérature médiévale offerts à E. Hoepffner* (Paris, 1949), pp. 269–78; Kennedy, loc. cit., pp. 100–6.

[4] Sommer, op. cit. iii. 122.   [5] Ibid., p. 137.

[6] Ibid., pp. 196 f.   [7] Lot, *Étude*, pp. 17–28.

PLATE 5

LANCELOT LEARNS ARCHERY
Bodleian Library, Ashmole 828. c. 1325

tinue the earlier narrative. Thus the adventures are knit together, and are even fitted into a careful time-scheme of days and hours.[1] This principle of interlacing was practised by Boiardo and with great virtuosity by Ariosto; it received unexpected praise in 1555 from the pen of Jacques Peletier du Mans.[2] Bruce overlooked this firmness of texture when he wrote that the *Lancelot* was 'unquestionably one of the most rambling productions of European literature'.[3]

There is no better proof of the control which the author exercised over his material than the 382 quarto pages which are devoted in Sommer's edition[4] to the story of Galehaut, perhaps better known as Dante's Galeotto and Malory's Galahault the Haut Prince.[5] A character delineated with a fine subtlety, he plays a role which is closely interwoven with the destinies of Lancelot and the queen; indeed without a Galeotto there would have been no guilty intrigue, with all its fateful consequences. As lord of the Lointaines Isles he invades Logres, but, smitten with admiration for the warlike exploits of Lancelot, he yields to his persuasions and pays homage to Arthur. An absorbing devotion to the young hero quickly leads to the discovery of his secret, the passion and the hope aroused in him by the queen's conventional but equivocal farewell, 'Adieu, biaus dous amis'.[6] Galehaut arranges an interview between Guenièvre and her lover, which, thanks to Dante, has become a part of universal literature.[7] It was when reading this passage that Paolo was moved to kiss, all trembling, the mouth of Francesca. 'Galeotto fu il libro e chi lo scrisse.' It is only after a long interval of separation, during which Lancelot's passion has been deepened by absence, that the lovers are brought together again in Scotland, and on the very night when Arthur, faithless to his marriage vows, lies with the enchantress Camille, the queen receives Lancelot into her chamber and their love is consummated.[8] One may detect again an effort on the author's part to excuse their disloyalty to Arthur, an effort which is repeated in the long episode where Arthur is infatuated with the false Guenièvre and proclaims the true Guenièvre an impostor.

The hypertrophied friendship of Galehaut for Lancelot brings in the course of time an element of sorrow into their relations. Galehaut becomes jealous of Guenièvre's power over his friend.[9] Symbolic nightmares, interpreted by wise clerks, warn him that he has less than four years to live. He enters the twilight of his life with a proud melancholy, which caused Lot to describe him as 'a sort of medieval Hamlet'.[10]

---

[1] Ibid., pp. 29–62.

[2] *L'Art poétique*, second livre, ch. viii (Paris, 1930), p. 201, ll. 2–7.

[3] Bruce, i. 410.   [4] Sommer, op. cit. iii. 201–iv. 156.

[5] For different explanations of the name Galehaut or Galehot see Lot, *Étude*, p. 168; Bruce, i. 405, n. 77; Loomis, *Arthurian Tradition*, pp. 255–8.   [6] Sommer, op. cit. iii. 131.

[7] *Inferno*, v, vss. 127–38.   [8] Sommer, op. cit. iii. 410 f.

[9] Ibid., p. 427, ll. 12 f.   [10] Lot, *Étude*, p. 66.

The Galehaut section is followed by an elaborate recasting of Chrétien's *Lancelot*. The author discarded the passages of psychological analysis as if he felt that he had already worked the sentimental possibilities of his theme enough. More realistic than Chrétien, he rationalized the bizarre elements, dissipated some of the mysteries, and even removed from the famous cart every ignominious association.[1]

Predictions that Lancelot's primacy as the best knight of the world is drawing to an end, already found in the Galehaut section, accumulate. When he is unable to approach the tomb of Symeu because of the flames, a voice announces that his failure is due to his lechery, and that a knight of his kindred, spotless in life, will succeed in freeing Symeu and achieve the high quest of the Grail.[2] The revelation comes as a shock, and though Lancelot's triumphs in the land of Gorre restore his confidence for a time, his character seems to undergo a change. He loses something of his ardour and magnanimity and no longer shows mercy to defeated adversaries.[3] His cousin Bohort comes to the fore as an embodiment of valour, modesty, and high spirits. He too, however, loses his virginity, being induced by magic to lie with King Brangoire's daughter, and thus is reckoned the least worthy of the three knights who achieve the high quest of the Grail.[4]

Bohort's affair with Brangoire's daughter, as R. S. Loomis has shown,[5] follows a traditional pattern, and the vows pronounced by the twelve knights who distinguished themselves at Brangoire's tourney are obviously related to the gabs of the paladins in the *Pèlerinage de Charlemagne*.[6] In fact, many of the incidents which have given the *Lancelot* proper its reputation for prolixity and incoherence have their counterparts not only in the Swiss *Lanzelet* but also in Chrétien's *Perceval* and its continuations, in the *Didot Perceval*, and in *Le Bel Inconnu* and *Méraugis de Portlesguez*.[7] Some of these parallels may be due to borrowing by the author of the *Lancelot*, but others, such as those shared with *Lanzelet*, must be derived from old tradition.[8] In spite of the profusion of these secondary and unessential episodes the main structure remains firm.

2. The Preparation for the *Queste*.[9] In this division of the *Lancelot* proper the reader again seems to be lost in a maze of tourneys, strange encounters,

[1] On episode of the cart in the Prose *Lancelot*, see M. Lot-Borodine in Lot, *Étude*, pp. 383–417; Frappier, *Étude sur la Mort le Roi Artu* (Paris, 1936), pp. 87–94; Gweneth Hutchings, *Conte de la Charrette en Prose* (Paris, 1938), pp. ix–lix.

[2] Sommer, op. cit. iv. 175–7.   [3] Ibid., pp. 281–92.

[4] Ibid. iv. 262–70.   [5] *Arthurian Tradition*, pp. 241–6, 254.

[6] *University of Michigan Publications, Lang. and Lit.* viii (1932), 29–35, 44–47.

[7] See Loomis, *Arthurian Tradition*, Index, p. 500, *sub* Vulgate Lancelot; K. G. T. Webster, *Guinevere* (Milton, Mass., 1951), pp. 12 f.; J. Marx, *Légende arthurienne* (Paris, 1952), Index, p. 401, *sub* Lancelot en Prose.

[8] Märtens in *Romanische Studien*, v (1880), 687–700.

[9] Sommer, op. cit. iv. 301–62; v.

perilous forests, enchanted caroles,[1] and so forth. Still it is easy to disengage certain crucial events. The begetting of Galaad is the hinge on which the whole book turns. Lancelot, under the influence of a potion administered by the duenna Brisane with the connivance of the Grail King Pelles, engenders on the king's daughter the future hero of the quest under the impression that he is lying with Guenièvre.[2] It must be granted that this momentous situation is handled awkwardly, placing King Pelles in a very unfortunate light and suggesting a burlesque on the conception of another and greater Messiah. Nevertheless, there may have been a traditional pattern as in the case of Bohort and King Brangoire's daughter, and the author may have lacked the courage and the initiative to discard it.

Already in an earlier scene Pelles had played host to Gauvain at his castle, and his daughter had borne in the Grail, here described as a chalice; but Gauvain suffered a series of humiliations, receiving no food from the vessel, being wounded by a flaming lance as he lay on the Adventurous Bed, and being driven away at last in a cart of shame.[3] Bohort later had a similar experience, but in spite of his sufferings, his visit did not end in humiliation and he was initiated into some of the mysteries of the Grail.[4] Lancelot on his visit to the castle saw the chalice and its miraculous provision of food, but enjoyed no such privilege as Bohort.[5] It is evident that the author is foreshadowing in these experiences at the Grail castle the future success or failure of these same knights in the Grail quest.

Other forecasts relate to the *Mort Artu*—veiled references to the discovery of the adultery, to the war between Arthur and Lancelot, to the treachery of Mordret and the final catastrophe.[6] Though easily understood by the reader, they are too partial and vague to be recognized by the victims. Lancelot refuses to believe that his sin will bring on him the condemnation of God, and, unrepentant, he blames his misfortunes on chance.[7] The queen, however, becomes aware of the reason for his failure and realizes her responsibility. In one of the finest scenes of the Prose *Lancelot* she gives utterance to her anguish: 'It would be better for me that I had never been born.'[8]

Indeed for Guenièvre love becomes a torment. When she has no news of her lover, she fears his death, is ready to kill herself, and pines away.[9] She has a prevision of Lancelot's second union with King Pelles's daughter.[10] Unaware that this, like the first, is brought about by deception, she drives

---

[1] On caroles see Lot in *R*, xxiv (1895), 325 ff.; Philipot in *R*, xxv (1896), 267, 269; J. Rhŷs, *Celtic Folklore* (Oxford, 1901), i. 85; E. S. Hartland, *Science of Fairy Tales*, pp. 162–5; Krappe in *ZFSL*, lvii (1933), 156–62.   [2] Sommer, op. cit. v. 107–12.

[3] Ibid. iv. 341–9; Loomis, *Arthurian Tradition*, pp. 204–12.

[4] Sommer, op. cit. v. 294–303.   [5] Ibid., pp. 107 f.

[6] Ibid., pp. 192; iv. 321, ll. 7–9; 348 f.; 359, ll. 20–30.

[7] Ibid. v. 94, ll. 8–19.   [8] Ibid., p. 193, ll. 15–17.

[9] Ibid. iv. 319 f.; v. 59–63.   [10] Ibid., pp. 63 f.

him away, and for the third time he goes mad, and remains so until, coming by accident to Corbenic, he is healed by the Grail. To make Lancelot succumb to the wiles of Brisane a second time and to lose his wits a third time is an artistic blunder. Economy was not one of the virtues of the author of these scenes. Moreover, a 'double esprit', to use Lot's phrase, a shifting attitude, is characteristic of the *Lancelot* proper and becomes more conspicuous as the advent of Galaad draws near. At first it would seem that love of woman, even when it involved adultery, deceit, and disloyalty, was the source of all good; the author's sympathy seems to be wholly with the lovers and their go-between Galehaut. This attitude gives way more and more to the doctrine that adulterous love is sin and the cause of calamity, but until we reach the *Queste* there is ambiguity. Some critics have seen in this contradiction signs of dual authorship of the *Lancelot* proper, but the strands of courtly and religious idealism are too tightly interwoven to permit such an explanation. Perhaps this gradual annunciation, which in the form of a romance led from an Old Testament to a New Evangel of chivalry, implied fluctuations, but it proceeded none the less from a majestic conception, and if one is willing to follow the author as he pursues his way towards his end, one will find on each page that he is in the company of one of the masters of French prose.

'La Queste del Saint Graal'[1]

On the day of Pentecost, 454 years after the Lord's Passion, Galaad, already knighted by his father at a nunnery where his grandfather had left him some years before, is conducted to Arthur's court by an aged man in a white robe. The new knight in vermilion arms passes the test of the Siege Perilous and of the sword in the stone, thus proving that he is the long-awaited deliverer and the supreme hero of the quest. When the knights are assembled in the great hall, behold, announced by a clap of thunder and an intense light, the Grail floats in, covered by white samite, and without visible support circulates before the tables, serving each one with such food as he desires. The vessel vanishes. The knights of the Round Table swear to go in quest of it.

Though they depart together, they soon separate, and their individual adventures correspond to their merits. The greater number, including such illustrious personages as Lionel, Hector, and Gauvain, are blind to the significance of the enterprise, meet with obstacles and humiliations, and eventually return to court. Lancelot takes warning from his misfortunes and, instructed

---

[1] Besides the Sommer edition, the *Queste* has been edited by F. J. Furnivall (London, Roxburghe Club, 1864), and in a critical ed. by Pauphilet, *CFMA* (1923, 1949). For general discussions see A. Pauphilet, *Études sur la Queste del Saint Graal* (Paris, 1921); R. Heinzel, *Über die französischen Gralromane, Denkschriften der kaiserlichen Akad. der Wissenschaften zu Wien*, phil.-hist. Cl. xl, Abh. 3; M. Lot-Borodine, *Trois essais sur le roman de Lancelot du Lac et la Quête du Saint Graal* (Paris, 1919).

PLATE 6

GALAAD RECEIVES A KEY TO THE CASTLE OF MAIDENS
From Ivory Casket, Victoria and Albert Museum. *c.* 1320

GALAAD AT CORBENIC
Yale University Library (formerly Phillipps 130). *c.* 1290

by a hermit, confesses his guilt, and enters upon a life of penitence. Conse-quently, though denied the supreme vision, he is able to reach the Grail castle and to enjoy an ecstatic trance before returning to the mundane life. Galaad, Perceval, and Bohort are the elect. Galaad moves in the loftiest regions of the spirit as in his native air. Perceval and Bohort, less pure, are hampered in their mystic ascent by uncertainties and temptations, but are united with Galaad in the supreme experience.

One day the three are joined by Perceval's sister on a marvellous ship, which we learn presently had been built by Solomon to carry a message 2,000 years later to the virgin knight, the last of his lineage. Three spindles are fixed to the head of a bed, and a sword which had belonged to David lies on it. The maiden replaces the hempen girdle attached to the sword with one which she had woven of gold threads and her own hair, and hangs the sword at Galaad's side. Some days later she gives her blood for the healing of a leper-woman, dies, and her body, placed in a boat, is committed to the waves.

Later the three elect are welcomed at the castle of Corbenic by King Pelles and are joined by nine other knights. In a scene of great solemnity, the Maimed King is borne into the palace on a couch; Bishop Josephé, son of Joseph of Arimathea, descends from heaven and sits before the silver table on which the Grail is placed; angels bring in the bleeding lance and set it beside the vessel. When Josephé is performing the sacrament of the mass, the wafer takes the semblance of a child. From the Grail the crucified Christ issues and administers the sacrament to the twelve. Galaad takes the lance and, anoint-ing the Maimed King with the blood, heals him. A still higher revelation is destined for the three in the land of Sarras, whither they are wafted in Solo-mon's ship and where they find the body of Perceval's sister in the boat and bury it. There Galaad enters into his kingdom, and having seen openly (*apertement*) the ultimate mystery within the holy vessel he dies in ecstasy. A hand removes Grail and lance to heaven, and no one since then has seen them. When a year later Perceval passes away, Bohort alone returns to Camaalot to report his experiences.

The *Queste del Saint Graal* differs in certain remarkable ways from the *Lancelot*. The principle of *entrelacement* is relaxed to permit longer stretches of continuous narrative, and the chronology is loose rather than strict.[1] On the other hand, there is no longer any ambiguity regarding moral and spiritual values. The work is pivoted on the doctrine of asceticism; its centre is a mystic vision of man and the world.

The narrative materials are of diverse origins.[2] There are such common-

---

[1] Pauphilet, *Études*, pp. 163–9; Imbs in *Mélanges E. Hoepffner*, pp. 279–93.

[2] On literary sources of the *Queste* see Lot, *Étude*, pp. 191–3; Bruce, i. 419 f. On survivals of Celtic tradition see Loomis, *Arthurian Tradition*, especially pp. 173–5, 235 f., 388–91, 410–13, 431 f., 452–7; M. Speyer in *RR*, xxviii (1937), 195 ff.

places of romance as tourneys and quests; there is a perilous seat and a castle of maidens. Some of the more fantastic themes, as Pauphilet asserted, are 'the deformed expression of ancient pagan beliefs'.[1] There are adumbrations of great scenes in the New Testament. The first appearance of the Grail in the hall at Camaalot is full of reminiscences of the first Pentecost.[2] King Mordrain's address to Galaad echoes the 'Nunc dimittis' of Simeon.[3] The Siege Perilous and the sword in the stone designate the new Messiah; a tourney between white knights and black allegorizes the conflict between the forces of good and evil. The strange voyages of the Breton *contes* are converted into journeys of the soul, and their significance is interpreted by visions.

The most intricate and ingenious of these manipulations of traditional material is the symbolic treatment of Solomon's ship.[4] It is founded on the traditional comparison of the Church with a ship: 'Ecclesia est navis.' With this have been combined the memory of self-propelled vessels described in Breton lai or Arthurian romance and the strange legend of the wood from which the cross was made. Solomon, builder of the temple, the Church of the Old Law, is the builder of the ship. Eve took with her from Paradise a branch of the Tree of Knowledge and planted it; originally white, it turned green when she lost her virginity, and turned red when Cain committed the first murder. From this tree at various times were cut the three spindles which Solomon placed in the ship in the form of a cross.[5] His wife, who in Oriental story supplanted the harem of Scripture and was represented as the incarnation of feminine guile, becomes in the *Queste* the mouthpiece of heavenly wisdom under the Old Covenant and instructs her husband in the preparation of the ship. The sword, according to the epistle to the Ephesians, is the Word of God, the Scriptures. The hempen girdle[6] attached to it indicates the inferior inspiration of the Old Testament; the new girdle, made of a virgin's hair and worn by the messianic figure of Galaad, is of course the New Testament. Perceval's sister, who had played an insignificant part in earlier Perceval romances, is transfigured and her mystic union with Galaad imparts an idyllic grace to the austerity of the celestial chivalry.[7] Such an elaborate symbolism is of course in accord with the intellectual habits of all Christendom, but it displays a freshness and a poetry which are rare.

Pauphilet, to whom we owe a beautiful exposition of this symbolism, also shows how the principal characters 'represent different types of humanity,

---

[1] Pauphilet, *Études*, p. 193.   [2] *Queste*, ed. Pauphilet, pp. 15 f.

[3] Ibid., pp. 262 f.; Pauphilet, *Études*, p. 143.

[4] Pauphilet, *Études*, pp. 144–54.

[5] The wood of the Cross was used only for the spindles, not the ship. Pauphilet on p. 8 of his *Études* erred on this point.

[6] For the meaning of the word *renges*, here translated 'girdle' and by Malory as 'hangings', see M. D. Legge in *R*, lxxvii (1956), 88–90.

[7] Perceval's sister sacrificed her hair, the thing she held most dear (*Queste*, p. 227), on hearing of the knighting of Galaad, and he became *her* knight (p. 228).

judged from the religious point of view and ranged in order from impiety to sainthood'.[1] At the bottom of the ladder we find two of the illustrious knights of the *Lancelot* proper. Lionel is seized with a murderous fury and is ready to kill even his own brother.[2] Gauvain, the friend and lover of ladies, is treated with some respect but not without irony. First of all the knights to undertake the quest, he does so without conforming his life to the high emprise. Fourteen years he has gone without confession. He, too, is guilty of manslaughter, and accidentally slays Yvain. Hence his quest is barren and he is wounded by Galaad as a divine punishment.

Of the elect Bohort stands lowest, for he has sinned, though involuntarily, with King Brangoire's daughter. This he compensates for by his humility and the mortification of his flesh. The Devil tempts him in subtle ways through brotherly love, pity, and lust, but triumphing over them all he is granted heavenly visions.[3] A warm devotion to his kinsmen relieves the sternness of his asceticism.[4] Perceval, a virgin knight, retains something of the ingenuousness of Chrétien's hero. Incapable of conceiving evil, he fails to recognize it in others. From the beginning he does not understand the meaning of the adventure, but he is ready to sacrifice the worldly honour which is precious to him, overcomes the temptations of despair and lust, and deserves at last to hear a voice proclaiming: 'Perceval, tu as vaincu.'[5]

The perfection of Galaad seems unreal; a saint untroubled by temptation, a foreordained Saviour, he proceeds in the certitude of his mission, and, to use a prophetic expression in the *Lancelot* proper, 'all adventures draw back and make way for him'. His very name puts him above ordinary humanity, for it is derived from the Vulgate Bible, corresponding to Gilead in the King James translation, and is one of the mystic appellations of Christ.[6] But Pauphilet went too far in calling him 'un être de raison'—a figment of the mere reason.[7] He exercises upon some readers at least that attraction which in the *Queste* he exercised on his companions, and the scenes with his father,[8] so tender, so free of priggishness, are among the most appealing in the Prose *Lancelot*. A highly stylized but not a desiccated character, Galaad is the culmination of the effort to fuse chivalry with religion.

In the portrayal of Lancelot, the author of the *Queste* was confronted with a problem. As the ideal of worldly chivalry and romantic passion, Lancelot must be condemned, but as the father of the messianic Galaad he must be treated with sympathy. The contradiction is solved by making him a sincerely repentant sinner. The course of his development is traced through a series of crises—the shock of discovering that he is no longer invincible, the loss

---

[1] *Queste*, ed. Pauphilet, p. x.
[2] Ibid., pp. 189–93.
[3] Ibid., pp. 167 f., 170 f., 179 f., 184–7.
[4] Ibid., pp. 2, 9.
[5] Ibid., p. 115.
[6] Pauphilet, *Études*, pp. 135–8.
[7] Ibid, p. 141.
[8] *Queste*, pp. 250–2.

of joy, the inward struggle leading up to his confession and penitence. Questioned by a hermit, he declares in poignant words his plight:[1] 'Sire, I am in mortal sin because of my lady, whom I have loved all my life, and she is Queen Guenièvre, the wife of King Arthur. It is she who has given me gold, silver, and rich gifts, which I have at times given to poor knights. It is she who has placed me in great splendour and in the high estate where I am. It is she for whose love I have done great deeds of prowess of which all the world speaks. It is she who has brought me from poverty to riches and from misery to all earthly joys. But I know well that for this sin with her Our Lord is so severely wroth with me as He showed me last night.' There is, to be sure, a certain precipitancy in the promptness with which, after this tribute, he renounces the queen and breaks the old enchantment. But in the main the emotional and spiritual stages through which Lancelot passes, the relapses and the new resolutions,[2] until he receives his reward in the incomplete vision at Corbenic, are traced with a sensitive and fine observation.

The teachings of the *Queste* and the rule of life prescribed for those who seek the Holy Grail are suffused with the monastic spirit. When a hermit expounds the hierarchy of the virtues,[3] he places highest virginity and below it in descending order humility, patience, justice, and last, strangely enough, charity. Unchastity is the root of all evil; wives and mistresses may not accompany the knights on their quest. Pauphilet was the first to demonstrate in detail that the book was of specifically Cistercian origin.[4] Holy men wear a white garb, the distinctive colour of the Cistercian habit. The very first sentence describes the tables set up in Arthur's hall on the vigil of Pentecost at the hour of nones after service, in exact accordance with the programme for the day observed at Cîteaux. Gilson has revealed correspondences between the mystical doctrines of the romance with the doctrines of St. Bernard of Clairvaux.[5] Central to both are the problems of grace and of transubstantiation. The Grail itself is a symbol of grace[6] and is at the same time represented as the dish (*escuele*) from which Christ ate the lamb at the Last Supper and a vessel containing the host.[7] It appeared for the first time on the day of Pentecost when the assembled knights had been 'illumined by the grace of the Holy Spirit'.[8] After they had been miraculously fed by the vessel, they thanked Our Lord for having filled them with 'the grace of the Holy Vessel'.[9] Several passages expound the indispensable role of grace and the part of human freedom in

[1] *Queste*, p. 66.
[2] Ibid., pp. 140–5, 253.
[3] Ibid., pp. 123–5.
[4] Pauphilet, *Études*, pp. 53–83.
[5] E. Gilson, 'La Mystique de la Grace dans la Queste del Saint Graal', *R*, li (1925), 321–37. M. Lot-Borodine in *Lumière du Graal*, ed. R. Nelli (Paris, 1951), pp. 151–74, tries to harmonize the theses of Pauphilet and Gilson by deriving the theology of the *Queste* from Guillaume de Saint-Thierry, a friend but not a disciple of St. Bernard.
[6] E. Gilson, *Les Idées et les lettres* (Paris, 1932), pp. 62–64.
[7] *Queste*, p. 270.
[8] Ibid., p. 15.
[9] Ibid.

salvation.[1] At no point do these ideas clash with the conceptions of Augustine and Bernard.

The full significance of the Grail as representing divine grace communicated through the eucharist is revealed in the vision accorded to the elect at Corbenic. Here, in a scene both majestic and tender, we have a combination, as Pauphilet showed, of three eucharistic themes.[2] The Divine Liturgy, that is, the participation of the Church triumphant and the heavenly host in the celebration of the mass, is responsible for the presence of Bishop Josephé, who had departed this life more than 300 years before, and of the angels who bring in the sacred objects. The Apostolic Communion, a re-enactment of the Last Supper, accounts for Christ Himself as the officiant and the addition of nine knights to the three elect in order to complete the number of the apostles. The miracle of Transubstantiation made visible was a matter of common belief and is illustrated first by the descent of an infant from the skies and his incorporation in the sacramental bread, and secondly by the emergence of the crucified Saviour from the holy vessel.

These sublime imaginings are set down in a prose precise, transparent, lacking colour and ornament—a style consonant with the Cistercian ideal of austerity. But in these scenes and in some of the dialogues and sermons one finds not only well-constructed periods but an animation and a fire which are not unworthy of the lofty themes. One may agree with Pauphilet that the author was more of an orator than a poet,[3] but his phrasing is capable of translating the rhythm and the glow of his passion for the ideal vision of the Holy Grail.

'La Mort Artu'[4]

After the deaths of Galaad and Perceval in the land of Sarras, Bohort returns to Camaalot, and his account of the adventures of the Grail is set down by scribes. Lancelot relapses into his old sin. Wounded while attending incognito a tourney at Winchester, he takes refuge at a house where the fair maid of Escalot, who nurses him, falls desperately in love. Rumours reach the court which persuade Arthur that Lancelot reciprocates her feeling, and Guenièvre is torn with jealousy. But one day a barge floats down to

---

[1] Queste, pp. 164 f.

[2] Pauphilet, Études, pp. 92–103. See also M. Lot-Borodine, 'Les Apparitions du Christ aux Messes de l'Estoire et de la Queste del Saint Graal', R, lxxii (1951), 202–23.

[3] Queste, p. xiii.

[4] Besides the edition of the Mort Artu in Sommer, op. cit. vi. 201–391, it has been edited by Bruce (Halle a. S., 1910) with elaborate notes, and twice by J. Frappier, with variant readings (Paris, 1936), and without (Geneva, Lille, 1954). See the review of the former edition by Lot in R, lxiv (1938), 123–30. General studies are: M. B. Fox, La Mort le roi Artu, Étude sur les manuscrits, les sources et la composition de l'œuvre (Paris, 1933), reviewed by Frappier in R, lix (1933), 572–7; J. Frappier, Étude sur la Mort le roi Artu (Paris, 1936), reviewed by Lot in R, lxiv (1938), 111–22, and by Trethewey in ZRP, lviii (1938), 698–710.

Camaalot, bearing the body of the maid and a letter ascribing her death to Lancelot's rejection of her love. Arthur's suspicions are renewed on a visit to Morgain's castle by the sight of Lancelot's paintings which depict the story of his guilty passion. The queen herself is unjustly charged with poisoning a knight and is only saved from the stake by Lancelot's victory in a judicial combat. When she and her lover are trapped together by Agravain and she is being led to the stake, Lancelot again comes to the rescue and carries her off to Joyeuse Garde, but kills Gaheriet, Gauvain's beloved brother, unwittingly in the fray. Arthur lays siege to Joyeuse Garde and finally through the intercession of the pope takes his wife back, while Lancelot crosses the sea to his kingdom of Gaunes.[1] Arthur follows him with an army, engages in indecisive battles, and only when Gauvain receives a severe wound in the head in a duel with Lancelot does the king withdraw to Meaux. Here he learns of the invasion of the Romans. Hardly has he triumphed over them and killed the emperor when news comes from Guenièvre that Mordret, who has been left as regent, has rebelled. Arthur sails back to England to punish the traitor, who is here represented as the king's son begotten in incest. After the landing at Dover Gauvain dies of his wound, but before expiring sends a message to Lancelot begging forgiveness. In spite of the most sinister prognostics Arthur advances against Mordret and after the battle Salisbury plain is covered with corpses. Arthur kills Mordret with his lance, but is himself mortally wounded in the head. However, the next day, accompanied by Giflet, he reaches the sea. Giflet, commanded by his lord to throw Escalibor into a lake near by, twice fails to do so and only the third time obeys, whereupon a hand rises from the water, brandishes the blade, and sinks back. A barge approaches by sea, full of ladies, including Morgain, and bears the king away. A few days later Giflet discovers his tomb in the Noire Chapelle and learns that his body had been brought there by ladies. His widow takes the veil and dies repentant. Lancelot and his friends return to Britain and kill the sons of Mordret in battle. This accomplished, they pass the rest of their lives as hermits. Lancelot's soul is borne skyward by angels; his body is interred beside that of his friend Galehaut at Joyeuse Garde.

No other prose romance of the Middle Ages offers a texture so tightly woven as the *Mort Artu*. In the first part the use of *entrelacement* is combined with a firm and precise chronology. Thereafter the action is simplified and moves uninterruptedly to the ineluctable catastrophe. If the composition of the *Lancelot* proper is loosely narrative, that of the *Queste* symbolic and didactic, that of the *Mort Artu* is dramatic. There is a chain of causes and effects. The ruin of the Round Table is caused ultimately by the sin of Lancelot and the queen. This initial cause produces a secondary cause, the death of Gaheriet at the hands of Lancelot and Gauvain's determination to avenge

---

[1] On Gaunes see Lot, *Étude*, p. 147, n. 8; Loomis, *Arthurian Tradition*, p. 190, n. 33.

his brother. This in turn causes Arthur's departure from Britain and provides the opportunity for Mordret, swayed by his lust for Guenièvre, to rebel against his father. Such a concatenation of events can only be the result of design.

The feat appears the more remarkable when one considers that the author has unified materials as distinct in nature and origin as the adulterous loves of Lancelot and Guenièvre, celebrated by Chrétien, and the downfall of Arthur through the treason of Mordret, rendered classic by Geoffrey. For the elaboration of the former theme he took over suggestions from Béroul's *Tristan* or some closely related version—the espials, the trapping of the lovers, the queen led to the stake, her rescue, and her restoration to her husband. He gives to these episodes a somewhat more courtly, a less barbaric, tone. Other situations and motifs were probably borrowed from the *Lancelot* proper:[1] the papal interdict,[2] the borrowed shield, the sleeve worn at a tourney, the damsel who loves the hero in vain. The boat bearing a corpse and a letter recalls the swan-drawn barge of the First Continuation of *Perceval*,[3] the boat which bears the body of Perceval's sister in the *Queste*, and perhaps the floating coffin of the wife of Apollonius of Tyre.

The latter part of the *Mort Artu* rests on the framework provided by Wace, but there are skilful changes. Mordret's love for the queen is not of long duration but springs up as the consequence of daily contact with her in the absence of Arthur. The Roman war is abridged and Arthur's triumph is timed to coincide with the arrival of the news of Mordret's treason, whereas Wace allowed a whole winter to intervene. The three battles described in the *Brut* are concentrated in the one battle on Salisbury plain. As for the departure of Arthur in the barge with his sister Morgain, the author could hardly have drawn on Geoffrey's *Vita Merlini*, since the differences far outnumber the few resemblances, but rather on those tales of the 'fabulosi Britones' about Arthur's kinswoman Morganis, who transported his body to the isle of Avalonia, which Giraldus Cambrensis mentioned about 1216 in the *Speculum Ecclesiae*[4] and which are also reflected in Layamon's *Brut* and the *Didot Perceval*.[5] It has already been pointed out in Chap. 10 that some unknown source, perhaps a scribal addition to the *Brut*, supplied both Layamon and the *Mort Artu* with the name of one of Mordret's sons, Melyon or Melehan.

Two themes which link the *Lancelot* proper with the *Mort Artu*, the incestuous birth of Mordret and the tell-tale paintings in Morgain's castle, I

---

[1] Frappier, *Étude*, pp. 206–10.

[2] Sommer, op. cit. iv. 72 f. Freymond and Bruce have urged that the papal intervention was suggested by the interdict imposed by Innocent III in 1200 on France to force Philip Augustus to take back his queen. *ZRP*, xvi (1892), 97, n. 1. *Mort Artu*, ed. Bruce, pp. 284–6.

[3] *Continuations of the Old French Perceval*, ed. Roach, i (Philadelphia, 1949), vss. 14119–432.

[4] E. K. Chambers, *Arthur of Britain* (London, 1927), p. 272.

[5] Frappier, *Étude*, pp. 177–83; *RES*, x (1934), 81. See Chaps. 7, 10 above.

would ascribe, not to borrowing on the part of the author of the later work, but rather to one whom I shall call the 'architect', and who blocked out the grandiose scheme which included both works.[1] The motif of the incestuous birth may have come, as Micha suggested,[2] from a legend about Charlemagne's begetting of Roland, preserved in the *Karlamagnus saga* and the Provençal *Ronsasvals*.[3] More probably it belongs to an almost universal tradition of heroes born in incest.[4] In either case, it remains to explain by what quirk of mind Arthur was charged with a sin so black, even though committed without knowledge of his sister's identity.[5]

As for the magnificent episode which relates the casting of Escalibor into the lake, there is again a rough correspondence with the Norse and Provençal versions of Roland's death,[6] but a more significant parallel lies in the celestial hand which removes the Grail and the lance at the end of the *Queste*.[7] And the whole situation, enveloped in mystery, seems like a natural outgrowth of the Celtic tradition, found in Geoffrey's *Historia*, that Caliburnus was forged in the isle of Avalon.[8] The sudden, violent rain which announces the arrival of the fays in their barge seems also an authentic touch of Celtic supernaturalism derived from some Breton *conte*.[9] The elements which go to make up the story of Arthur's passing may have diverse origins, but a feeling for poetic grandeur has assembled and arranged them.[10]

The author deserves praise for thus preserving and embellishing the ancient myth of Arthur's departure to Avalon for healing, although he has adopted a compromise, for instead of reaching Avalon, Arthur is entombed

---

[1] Frappier, *Études*, pp. 32–37; Bruce in *Medieval Studies in Memory of G. Schoepperle Loomis* (Paris, New York, 1927), pp. 197–208, argued that the *Mort Artu* was the source.

[2] *ZRP*, lxvi (1950), 371 f.   [3] Roques in *R*, lxvi (1941), 458–60.

[4] O. Rank, *Inzest-Motiv in Dichtung und Sage* (Leipzig, Vienna, 1912); J. A. MacCulloch, *Celtic Mythology* (Boston, 1918), pp. 25, 90, 201.

[5] The hagiographic tradition of St. Giles and the legend of the unspecified sin ascribed to Charlemagne shed no light on the subject. See Guillaume de Berneville, *Vie de St. Gilles*, ed. G. Paris, A. Bos, *SATF* (1881), pp. lxxii–lxxxv.

[6] See Bédier, *Légendes Épiques*, 3rd ed. (Paris, 1929), iii. 388, n. 1, and Roques in *R*, lxvi. 451–8, on the motif of the sword cast into the water. A close paralell to Giflet's unwillingness to obey Arthur's command, his false report that he had seen nothing, his casting in the sword and its reception by the waters has been discovered in a twelfth-century Persian text. *Athenaeum*, April 6, 1901, p. 434; *Mort Artu*, ed. Bruce, p. 297.

[7] *Queste*, ed. Pauphilet, p. 279.

[8] Faral, iii. 233. Early Irish parallels have been found for two elements in the story. When Fraech was wounded by a water-monster, he was borne away by his faery kinswomen to be healed. G. Schoepperle Loomis in *Vassar Medieval Studies*, ed. C. F. Fiske (New Haven, 1923), pp. 21 f.; T. P. Cross in *Manly Anniversary Studies* (Chicago, 1923), pp. 284–94. When Fergus mac Leite was wounded by a water-monster, he lay beside a lake and charged his people that his sword Caladcolg (the original of Escalibor) should be preserved till it could be given to a fitting lord. Compare this with Arthur's situation and his speech to Escalibor. Loomis, *Arthurian Tradition*, p. 425.

[9] On the connexion between the shower and the proximity of the faery world see A. C. L. Brown in *PMLA*, xx (1905), 677, n. 8, and *Perlesvaus*, ed. Nitze, ii. 102 f.

[10] Another poetic touch is the sun's ray which shone through the wound which Arthur's lance opened in the body of Mordret. Frappier, *Étude*, pp. 252 f.

by the fays in the Noire Chapelle—a concession to the discovery of Arthur's body at Glastonbury in 1191. This more prosaic and hallowed ending has its justification, for if Arthur were to be presented as waiting in elysium for the hour of his triumphant return, the circle of fatality would have been broken, and it is this sense of inexorable doom which makes one think of Greek and Elizabethan tragedy. The vision of Fortune and her wheel which precedes the battle of Salisbury and presages Arthur's downfall is a conventional motif, adopted also by the *Suite du Merlin* (*Huth Merlin*) and the Alliterative *Morte Arthur*. But it is more than mere decoration; it points the lesson and applies it to Arthur: ' "Mes tel sont li orgueil terrien qu'il n'i a nul si haut assiz qu'il ne le conviengne cheoir de la poesté del monde".'¹ (But such are the prides of earth that there is no one seated so high that he is not obliged to fall from mundane power.) The theological problem seems to be solved here as for Dante:² Fortune, promoted to the rank of angelic creatures, is delegated by Providence to control the vicissitudes of human life. Arthur is presented with a choice, whether to fight with Mordret and die or to renounce his vengeance and live, but the alternative is illusory. His death, announced by Fortune and by Merlin's inscription on the rock,³ is predestined. Thus, unconsciously, the author of the *Mort Artu* rediscovered the climate of Greek tragedy. In the realm of the spirit, however, man is still free, with the aid of divine grace, to work out his salvation.

Other passages reveal a preoccupation with the ironies of fate. When Mordret splits Yvain's skull, Arthur exclaims: ' "Ah, God! why do you suffer what I see? The worst traitor on earth has slain one of the worthiest men alive." ' Whereupon Sagremor comments: ' "Sire, these are the sports of Fortune." '⁴ The maid of Escalot, smitten with a hopeless passion for Lancelot, says to her brother: ' "Thus is it destined for me that I should die because of him." '⁵ In various ways the injustice and the power of fate are emphasized for effects of irony and pathos. There are ironic notes also in Arthur's outpouring of thanks for his victory over the Romans just before he is informed of treason at home,⁶ and in the scene where he forces Agravain at the point of the sword to tell him the truth, and then tries to escape the truth which no sword can kill.⁷

But the woes and calamities which evoke the protests of suffering humanity are not represented as wholly the work of an external power. A wilful blindness leads the heroes to their perdition. Throughout the first part the characters seem unaware of the black future which lies ahead. But after Lancelot's messenger at the siege of Joyeuse Garde has reminded Gauvain of his symbolic vision at Corbenic,⁸ there can be little doubt that he and the

---

¹ *Mort le Roi Artu*, ed. Frappier (1936), p. 201.   ² *Inferno*, vii, vss. 67–96.
³ *Mort le Roi Artu*, pp. 202 f.   ⁴ Ibid., p. 218.   ⁵ Ibid., p. 34.
⁶ Ibid., p. 184.   ⁷ Ibid., pp. 185–7.   ⁸ Ibid., p. 118.

other characters act in full knowledge of the consequences. This is brought out with special clarity by Arthur's joining battle with Mordret after a triple warning. Thus an interior fatality collaborates with Fortune to work man's doom.

With a psychological insight rare in his epoch the author adapted to his tragic pattern the characters bequeathed to him by the *Lancelot* proper and the *Queste*. Lancelot as he now appears is a personality both old and new. Relapsing into his former sin hardly a month after his return from the quest, he remains in spite of mishaps the most brilliant of earthly knights; but he is more reckless, and his secret becomes the common knowledge of all except the King. When Arthur, learning the truth at last, makes war on him for possession of the queen, Lancelot sacrifices his personal happiness and thus achieves a spiritual regeneration by parting from her whom he continues to love.[1] He exhibits a new clemency and magnanimity and says of his mortal foe Gauvain that 'he cannot ever hate me so much that I will not love him'.[2] In the words of Dante's *Convivio* he 'lowered the sails of his mundane labours',[3] ended his days as a hermit, and angels bore his soul to Paradise. Other characters develop in novel but not inconsistent ways. Gauvain becomes possessed by a vindictive rage. Guenièvre is ravaged by her jealousies. Arthur, tormented by suspicion, becomes pathetic. Even the secondary personages undergo a natural transformation. More complex but not the less realistic is the interplay of emotions revealed by the scene in which the queen discusses with Lancelot and his kinsmen Arthur's offer to take her back with honour; fear of public opinion, political interests, and weariness mingle with a pure passion and the spirit of sacrifice.[4] The characters of the *Mort Artu* are no longer the stylized types of the *Queste* but are creatures of flesh and blood.

The severe piety of the earlier book is relaxed. Religious observances are not stressed, and the hermits minister more often to the body than to the soul. The divine mercy spares not only Lancelot but also Guenièvre and Gauvain. Is this due merely to an easy-going tolerance? Adler has called attention to the affinities between the theological perspective of the *Mort Artu* and medieval Aristotelianism, which was asserting itself more and more against the Augustinian tradition in the early thirteenth century.[5] Every created being is something other than the sign or shadow of a divine archetype. The infinite variety of these creatures involves a combination of evil and good in each, so that a man's faults do not nullify irremediably his virtues. Thus the

---

[1] MS. Palatinus latinus 1967 tells of a last interview between Lancelot and the queen after she has taken the veil. Ibid., pp. 239 f., and *R*, lvii (1931), 214–22. This account passed into the Stanzaic *Morte Arthur* (see Chap. 37 below) and thence into Malory. See Malory's *Works*, ed. Vinaver, iii. 1251–3.

[2] Frappier, *Étude*, pp. 233–9; *Mort le Roi Artu*, ed. Frappier (1936), p. 162, ll. 7 f.

[3] *Convivio*, iv. 28.

[4] *Mort le Roi Artu*, ed. Frappier, pp. 129–31.   [5] *PMLA*, lxv (1950), 930–43.

nobility of Lancelot coexists with his sin, and Gauvain's almsgiving offsets his worldliness and hatred.[1]

Despite the limitations of his vocabulary and the monotony of his expression, the author of the *Mort Artu* commands a style dignified and at times vivacious and dramatic. But it is not adequate to the richness and beauty of the theme. This 'Twilight of the Gods' needs all the resources of an orchestra and the thunder-peal of organs; one has to be content with a flute.

'L'Estoire del Saint Graal'[2]

Though it may seem anomalous to treat last the *Estoire del Saint Graal*, which precedes the other parts of the Vulgate cycle, the work is in fact a retrospective sequel, as Pauphilet demonstrated,[3] due to a continuator whose talent was not equal to his pious intentions.

According to the prologue, this author, living a solitary life, received on Good Friday, 717 years after the Passion (A.D. 750), a vision in which Christ Himself gave him a book of which the *Estoire* was a faithful transcript. There follows a narrative which in the early part bears a marked resemblance to Robert de Boron's *Joseph*. It relates that Joseph collected the blood of the Crucified in a dish (*escuele*) used at the Last Supper. Imprisoned by the Jews, kept alive and consoled by the 'holy vessel', he was delivered after forty-three years by Vespasian. He was baptized and at the divine command departed with his wife, his virgin son Josephé, and a small company to preach the gospel. An ark was constructed to transport the holy dish. Arrived at Sarras (an imaginary city of the Saracens), Joseph succeeded in converting King Evalac and his brother-in-law, who received respectively the baptismal names of Mordrain and Nascien. Meanwhile Josephé had gazed on ineffable mysteries taking place within the ark and had been consecrated bishop by the Saviour Himself. Because of a moment's lack of zeal he was pierced in the thigh by the lance of an angel, and was later healed by a similar celestial intervention. The evangelization of the Orient proceeded, to the accompaniment of many miracles. The narrative then splits into three divisions dealing respectively with the trials of Mordrain, Nascien, and his son Celidoine; there are Mediterranean voyages, tempests, disappearances, searches, dreams, temptations, pirates, angels and demons. Solomon's ship carries chosen passengers from one island to another. Finally, a longer voyage brings Joseph to

---

[1] *Mort le Roi Artu*, p. 73, ll. 10–16. Gauvain's charity to the poor is mentioned in Chrétien's *Perceval* (ed. Hilka, vss. 9206–14), and is not forgotten in the *Lancelot* proper (Sommer, op. cit. iv. 358).

[2] Three editions have appeared: by E. Hucher, *Le Saint Graal* (Le Mans, Paris, 1875–8), vols. ii, iii; by F. J. Furnivall, *Seynt Graal or the Sank Ryal* (Roxburghe Club, 1861–3); by Sommer, *Vulgate Version*, i (Washington, 1909).

[3] *R*, xlv (1918–19), 524–7.

Britain on Josephé's shirt, together with those of his company who have refrained from lechery. In due time these are joined by Celidoine, Nascien, and Mordrain. By force or by preaching, the Christian faith is established. The Grail, token of God's covenant with the faithful, works its prodigies— the multiplication of bread and also of the fish which Alain, nephew of Joseph and twelfth son of Joseph's brother-in-law Bron, has caught. Moise, who dares to occupy the vacant seat at the Grail table, is rapt away by fiery hands. Joseph and his wife in their old age have a second son, Galaad de Galafort. At his death Joseph commits the vessel to Alain, first of the Fisher Kings, who takes it to the Terre Foraine, builds the castle of Corbenic, and there successive guardians of the relic await the coming of the Good Knight.

In this recital one recognizes easily an amplification of Robert's poem, an amplification rendered necessary by his silence regarding the conversion of Britain and by the void of 400 years between the time of Joseph and that of Arthur.[1] Heinzel and Lot held that the author filled this gap with material from the apocryphal *Acts of St. Simon and St. Jude* and the *Passio Matthaei*,[2] but Bruce threw doubt on this theory,[3] and the derivation of proper names from these sources is particularly questionable. Nevertheless, a general debt to the apocrypha cannot be denied. The *Tristan* is doubtless the source of the voyage of the wounded Pierre to Orcanie, where he is healed by the king's daughter.[4] The misadventures of Hippocrate were suggested by a similar fabliau of the beguiling of Virgil.[5]

Though most scholars seem to regard the *Estoire* as directly dependent on Robert's *Joseph* for the early part and for the concept of the mission to Britain, one cannot exclude the possibility that the longer work derived not from the *Joseph* but from a common source, the 'grant livre' containing the secrets of the Grail to which Boron referred in vss. 932–6. One should not overlook the fact that the *Estoire* does not make the error of confusing the *graal* with a chalice, as Robert does, and never uses Hebron, the alternative name which Robert gives Bron.[6] Moreover, R. S. Loomis and Helaine Newstead have tried to show that the episode of Moise's sitting at the Grail table and the marriage of the twelve sons of Bron except one, as well as the subsequent episode of the testing of Joseph's company by the Grail borne by Pierre, are cognate with, rather than derived from, the corresponding scenes in Robert's poem.[7] Vendryes has compared the vision which forms the prelude to the *Estoire* with the appearance of Fergus in the Irish saga, the *Cattle-Raid of Cooley*.[8]

[1] Lot, *Étude*, pp. 204 f.
[2] Heinzel, *Über die französischen Gralromane*, pp. 136 ff.; Lot, *Étude*, pp. 123–5, 206–11.
[3] See the long note 27 in Bruce, i. 386–90.
[4] Sommer, op. cit. i. 269–72.   [5] Ibid., pp. 171–82.
[6] Nitze in *Medieval Studies in Memory of G. Schoepperle Loomis*, pp. 135–45.
[7] Loomis in *MLR*, xxiv (1929), 420–3, 428–30; in *RR*, xxxiii (1942), 170–3; Newstead, *Bran the Blessed*, pp. 28–55. See also Marx in *MA*, lix (1953), 69–86.   [8] *EC*, v (1949), 117.

Much of the early history of the Grail and of the mission to Britain was influenced by the *Queste*, from which the genealogy of Lancelot, which makes him a descendant of Nascien, was taken. The construction of pedigrees is extended to other heroes; Gauvain is of the lineage of Pierre (Robert's Petrus), who became King of Orcanie by marriage to the daughter of King Orcan; Yvain, to our surprise, is descended from Joseph of Arimathea through his son Galaad of Galafort. Claiming such a saintly ancestry for Gauvain and Yvain exposes the author's failure to grasp the fundamental concept which in the *Lancelot* proper and the *Queste* limited such antecedents to the elect. A happier innovation is the elaborate account of the initiation of Josephé into the awesome mysteries of the eucharist and his consecration as the first Bishop of Christendom—a series of majestic tableaux, whose symbolism and theological implications Myrrha Lot-Borodine has expounded with precision.[1]

The author of the *Estoire* was surely not the author of the *Queste*, as a comparison of the structure, the powers of characterization, and the quality of mysticism in the two works would make plain.[2] The former is comparatively loose and aimless; the characters are crudely drawn; the religion tends to be dissipated in a wild romance of thaumaturgy, without the moral significance or the sublime atmosphere of the *Queste*. Though at the start the author refused to disclose his name,[3] interpolators attributed the work to Robert de Boron.[4] Bruce and Carman have urged that the name of the Grail castle, Corbenic, found in both the *Queste* and the *Estoire*, was suggested by the Benedictine monasteries of Corbie near Amiens and of Corbény between Laon and Rheims,[5] but the argument is not strong. Except that the *Estoire* was probably composed by an ecclesiastic, we have no clue to his identity.

Unity and Diversity in the Prose 'Lancelot'

The foregoing analyses seem to lead to two conclusions regarding the authorship of the trilogy made up of the *Lancelot*, the *Queste*, and the *Mort Artu*. First, it seems clear that these are the work of three separate authors; the possibility is not excluded that more than one hand had a share in the composition of the huge *Lancelot*, whereas the *Estoire* is a reworking by still another author of an older early history of the Grail. The second conclusion is that all of these elements (except the *Estoire*) form a unified structure, bound together by preparations and prognostics on the one hand and by backward references on the other. This diversity in unity presents us with

[1] Sommer, i. 32–42; *Neo*, xxxiv (1950), 65–79; *R*, lxxii (1951), 202–23.
[2] *Neo*, xxxiv. 71 f.; *R*, xlv. 524–7.   [3] Sommer, op. cit. i. 3.
[4] Ibid., pp. 195, 244, n., 280.
[5] Bruce in *MLN*, xxxiv (1919), 385–91; J. N. Carman, *Relationship of the Perlesvaus and the Queste del Saint Graal, Bulletin of the Univ. of Kansas, Humanistic Studies*, v, no. 4 (1936), 13 f.

a paradox. As Pauphilet has said:[1] 'There is no enigma in all medieval literature which forces itself so strongly on the mind and irritates it at the same
time.'

How is one to solve this enigma? Lot demolished the theory which attributes the Prose *Lancelot* to an indefinite number of authors.[2] The most
reasonable hypothesis, upheld by Brugger, Bruce, and Pauphilet,[3] which
would explain the cohesion between the parts as due to the patching of later
redactors and interpolators is not without weaknesses. It fails to take account
of the essential fact that Lancelot is the father of Galaad. This invention is
the keystone of the arch; it could not have been conceived except by one who
had the whole edifice in mind, or who, at least, saw the *Lancelot* proper and
the *Queste* as inseparable. Is such an idea merely the afterthought of a redactor? Are we not rather in the presence of the original and dominant
theme? The man who conceived it was the true creator of the *Lancelot-Graal*
and its unity. And the *Queste* itself looks forward to a sequel. In the middle,
the destruction of the order of the Round Table is predicted in veiled terms,
and before the end Lancelot and Bohort have returned to Camaalot to share
in its downfall.[4]

The case for unity was ably argued by Lot, but he went so far as to maintain that a single author composed the whole vast work in the space of four
or five years. He tried to account for the marked differences in art and spirit,
especially the contrast between the worldliness of the *Lancelot* and the mystic
asceticism of the *Queste*, by the argument that this antinomy was inherent in
medieval thought.[5] But even if one admitted the truth of this proposition, it
would not explain the variety of styles and the changing literary interests
which one meets in reading the Prose *Lancelot*.

The compromise solution which I set forth in my *Étude sur la Mort le
Roi Artu*[6] still seems to me plausible. In my opinion, a single man, whom I
have called the 'architect', conceived the trilogy and outlined the plan of the
whole. He was probably the author of the *Lancelot* proper, or at least the
greater part of it. Two other authors then wrote the *Queste* and the *Mort
Artu*, but in spite of their distinct personalities they conformed to the
original plan. The *Estoire* was a later addition which supplied a portico for the
edifice. Only one passage, near the beginning of the *Lancelot* (Sommer, op.
cit. iii. 29), which implies that Perlesvaus or Perceval, not Galaad, was destined to occupy the Siege Perilous, offers any difficulty. However, even
though it has been shown that this was the reading of the archetype of all the

---

[1] Pauphilet, *Legs du moyen âge*, p. 214.   [2] Lot, *Étude*.
[3] Brugger's articles entitled 'L'Enserrement Merlin', in *ZFSL*, xxix[1] (1905)–xxxv[1] (1909);
Bruce, i. 398 f.; Bruce in *RR*, ix (1918), 241 ff., 353 ff.; x (1919), 48 ff., 97 ff.; Pauphilet, *Legs du
moyen âge*, pp. 212–17.
[4] Frappier, *Étude*, pp. 141 f.   [5] Lot, *Étude*, p. 106.
[6] Frappier, *Étude*, pp. 122–46.

extant manuscripts,[1] it is contradicted by so many other pronouncements and is introduced so casually that one is justified in suspecting that the scribe of the archetype here asserted his independence from the author's copy and recorded the prevailing tradition that Perceval was the hero of the adventure, as in the *Didot Perceval*.

Such a mode of collaborative creation may seem foreign and improbable, but the erection of a medieval cathedral presents an analogy. One may imagine the Prose *Lancelot* as the product of a sort of literary atelier. Several clues discovered by Lot—the mention of Meaux and of the feast of the Magdalen—would indicate a localization in Champagne.[2] The Cistercian colouring of the *Queste* is not inconsistent with this view if we suppose that the author of that holy romance had attended the abbey school of Clairvaux, not far from Troyes. The period of composition must have extended over fifteen or twenty years, and it seems that the general consensus of scholarly opinion would place it between 1215 and 1230.[3] Unless future editors turn up more significant facts, it is unlikely that we shall ever know more of the circumstances which surrounded the making of this literary monument. It stands, nevertheless, like a cathedral of which the *Queste* is the spire, and bears mute witness to the genius of its architect.

Circulation and Influence of the Prose 'Lancelot'

From the time of its publication the Prose *Lancelot* enjoyed great fame. About a hundred manuscripts survive, in whole or in part, and there must have been many more. Those of the fifteenth century, though proportionately rare, bear witness by their superb calligraphy and decoration that they were destined for princely libraries. Seven printed editions appeared at Paris between 1488 and 1533, while an abridgement was published at Lyon as late as 1591. According to Lot, the Prose *Lancelot* was 'the best propagator of the conception which represented chivalry as an ideal of moral nobility, far removed from the reality in the brutal society of the Middle Ages'.[4]

---

[1] Lot, *Étude*, pp. 109–23; Bruce, ii. 145–50; Carman in *RP*, vi (1952–3), 179–86. Miss E. Kennedy, who has prepared a critical edition of the *Lancelot* proper, has kindly informed me that *Perlesvaus* (or *Perceval*) is the reading of the archetype.   [2] Lot, *Étude*, pp. 150 f.

[3] Bruce, i. 450–4; Lot, *Étude*, pp. 126–40; Lot in *R*, lvii (1931), 137–46; lxiv (1938), 119–22. Frappier, *Étude*, pp. 20, 133–8. Carman's attempt in his *Relationship of the Perlesvaus*, pp. 10–13, to fix the *terminus ad quem* for the *Estoire* at 1223 is not conclusive, for, granted that Helinandus wrote before 1223, he may not be referring to the *Estoire* in the oft-quoted passage (Migne, *Patrologia Latina*, ccxii, cols. 814 f.) concerning the Grail, but rather to a lost work intermediate between Boron's *Joseph* and the *Estoire*. Helinandus says that the 'historia de Gradali' was revealed to its author by an angel, whereas the *Estoire* pretends to be transcribed from a book received from Christ Himself. One may also ask whether Helinandus may not be referring to *Perlesvaus*, which begins: 'Li estoires du saintisme vessel que on apele Graal', and claims that it was put in remembrance by Josephes according to the voice of an angel (ll. 1–4). See also ll. 2158–60, where a priest invokes the testimony 'de Josep le bon clerc et le bon hermite par qui nos le savons, et il le set par l'anoncement del Saint Esperit et de l'angle'.   [4] Lot, *Étude*, p. 102.

The influence of the cyclic work on other romances was profound;[1] it was felt by the last continuators of Chrétien's *Perceval*, Gerbert de Montreuil and Manessier;[2] the so-called Pseudo-Robert de Boron cycle was a clumsy imitation.[3] In Italy it affected the *Tavola Ritonda* and the compilation of Rusticiano da Pisa;[4] in the Iberic peninsula, the Spanish and the Portuguese *Demanda* and *Amadís*;[5] in England, the Stanzaic *Morte Arthur* and Malory's book;[6] in the Netherlands, the huge *Lancelot*.[7] The *Queste* was translated into Irish and Welsh.[8] Perhaps the most intelligent use was made by the author of *Perceforest*, as Jeanne Lods has recently made clear.[9]

Added proof of the popularity of the Prose *Lancelot* is found in certain remarkable allusions. There are three in the *Divine Comedy*, two of them concerned with the famous rendezvous arranged by Galehaut.[10] Another, already mentioned, occurs in the *Convivio*, and Dante's eulogy of the 'ambages pulcerrimae Arturi regis' in the *De Vulgari Eloquentia* refers, we may assume, to the interlacing technique of the Prose *Lancelot*.[11] Chaucer was an amused and sceptical reader of 'the book of Launcelot de Lake, that wommen holde in ful greet reverence'.[12] Even in the sixteenth century Marot,[13] du Bellay, and Ronsard expressed their admiration for it, but it could not resist the wave of neo-classical taste, and though Chapelain offered a defence, it fell into oblivion. With the revival of medieval studies its true character has emerged, and no one has estimated its value more fairly than Lot when he wrote:[14] 'It is not the most perfect work of romance and mysticism which medieval France produced, but it was of a certainty the most powerful.'

---

[1] Bruce, i. 127; ii. 39–41.   [2] Ibid. i. 304–8.
[3] Ibid. i. 458–79. See pp. 327–32 below.
[4] E. G. Gardner, *Arthurian Legend in Italian Literature* (London, 1930), pp. 47–63, 152–74. See Chap. 27 below.   [5] See Chap. 31 below.
[6] See Chaps. 37 and 40 below.   [7] See Chap. 34 below.
[8] *Lorgaireacht an tSoidhigh Naomhtha*, ed. S. Falconer, with English translation (Dublin, 1953). Reviewed by R. Bromwich in *MedAev*, xxv (1956), 92–95. The Welsh translation is published (with English translation) in *Selections from the Hengwrt Manuscripts*, ed. Robert Williams, i (London, 1876). T. Stephens, *Literature of the Cymry*, 2nd ed. (London, 1876), pp. 419 f.
[9] Jeanne Lods, *Le Roman de Perceforest, Origines, Composition, Caractères, Valeur et Influence* (Geneva, 1951). See especially pp. 37–74.
[10] *Inferno*, v. 127–38; xxxii. 61 f.; *Paradiso*, xvi. 13–15. See E. G. Gardner, op. cit., pp. 136–51, and Chap. 32 below.
[11] *De Vulgari Eloquentia*, i. 10; Rajna in *Studi Danteschi* diretti da M. Barbi, i (Florence, 1920), 91–99.
[12] Chaucer, *Complete Works*, ed. F. N. Robinson (Boston, 1933), p. 242, vss. 3211–3.
[13] Marot, *Élégie*, xvi.   [14] Lot, *Étude*, pp. 8, 279.

23

THE VULGATE *MERLIN*

ALEXANDRE MICHA

IN Chap. 19 the work of Robert de Boron was surveyed; it was pointed out that his *Merlin* was clearly and firmly attached to his *Joseph*, but that it survived in complete form only in two prose redactions. The more faithful of these is incorporated in the so-called *Suite du Merlin* or *Huth Merlin*;[1] the other is incorporated in the Vulgate cycle and has been brought into harmony with the later portions of that monumental work.[2] The Vulgate *Merlin*, in fact, consists of two parts: the redaction of Robert's poem and a sequel. Let me first pass in review the events which derive from Robert.

The devils, infuriated by the descent of Christ into hell and his deliverance of the righteous Jews, plot to bring about the ruin of mankind by means of a prophet, half human, half devil. One of their number is given the task; he reduces a wealthy man to despair, corrupts two of his daughters, and cohabits with the third in her sleep. She, however, tells her confessor, is signed with the cross, and devotes herself to piety, so that, when a son is born, he has a hairy body and preternatural knowledge but not his father's will to evil. The infant is baptized as Merlin, and reveals his power by saving his mother from sentence of death; before he is two years old he dictates to the learned clerk Blaise the history of Joseph and the Grail and of his own birth. Rather unexpectedly we find that we are in the fifth century, and learn how Constant, King of Britain, is succeeded by his three sons. The first, Moine, is murdered by his barons, and his place is usurped by his seneschal Vertiger. In the civil war which follows Vertiger allies himself with the Saxons under Hangus (Hengist) and marries his daughter. He attempts to build a strong tower, and when it collapses time after time, he sends on the advice of his wise men for a fatherless child, whose blood will cause the foundations to stand. Merlin, now aged seven, is produced, and reveals the existence of the red and white dragons in a pool beneath the tower. The dragons fight each other, forecasting the struggle of the Britons with the Saxons; the Saxons under Constant's sons invade Britain, and Vertiger perishes in the flames of his own tower. Pandragon, Constant's second son, now reigns, the Saxons are persuaded to retire from Britain, and Merlin gives further proof of his

---

[1] Ed. G. Paris, J. Ulrich, *SATF* (Paris, 1886), i. 1–146.

[2] Ed. H. O. Sommer, *Vulgate Version* (Washington, 1908), ii. 3–88, l. 18. Cf. particularly the corresponding passages on the book of Blaise (ed. Paris, pp. 31 f.; ed. Sommer, pp. 19 f.) and on the three tables (ed. Paris, p. 98; ed. Sommer, p. 56).

uncanny wisdom. But the Saxons return, and in the great battle at Salisbury Pandragon is slain, whereupon his brother Uter assumes the throne, adopting the name of Uterpendragon. Merlin transfers the stones from Ireland to Salisbury as a monument to the fallen Britons. By his advice Uter causes the Round Table to be made. In a great Christmas feast at Carduel Uter falls in love with Ygerne and with the aid of Merlin's enchantments lies with her in the castle of Tintagel. Arthur is born, Uter is slain in battle with the Saxons, and his son by drawing the sword from the anvil proves himself the rightful heir. Though the barons remain unconvinced, he is finally crowned.

It is obvious that the *Merlin* is largely indebted to Geoffrey of Monmouth's *Historia* and *Vita Merlini*, but it is a disputed question whether Robert himself made the adaptation, or whether he found it already made in a work which certain manuscripts of the Vulgate *Merlin* attribute to an otherwise unknown Martin of Rouecestre, Rouain, &c.[1] The balance of probability favours the view that Robert himself was the chief architect of the *Merlin*, and the work does him credit. To be sure, there is an astounding perversion of Geoffrey's account of the kings preceding Arthur. Geoffrey names three brothers who reigned in succession: Constans, who became a monk, Aurelius, and Uterpendragon.[2] Robert substitutes Constant, his son Moine, and two other sons, Uter and Pandragon![3] It is hard to understand how anyone who consulted the *Historia* or Wace could have produced such a result. Gaston Paris suggested that this portion, at least, of the pseudo-history came to Robert in oral form.[4] It seems quite possible that if Wace's *Brut* had been read aloud to him, he might have reconstructed the rather complicated succession in this distorted form from memory. But on the whole the *Merlin* displays considerable intelligence in its adaptation of Geoffrey's material and in making the wizard the centre of interest.

Robert suppressed much that did not concern his hero Merlin, for example, the role of Vortimer and the wars of Aurelius with Hengist; he condensed the story of the marriage of Vertiger with Rowenne. If Pandragon and Uter die gloriously in battle, instead of being poisoned as in the *Historia*, it is because an inglorious death by treachery was not consonant with the protective care of Merlin for his royal protégés. At the same time Robert amplifies and adds, usually with happy effect. The council of the demons which opens the *Merlin* is admirably reported, is firmly fitted into the cosmic scheme of the struggle of God and the Devil for the souls of men, and its outcome provides a rational explanation of Merlin's somewhat impish humour and his nonhuman powers. The innocence of Merlin's mother, her saintly life, and the precautions she takes to convert her offspring into an agent of the powers not of hell but of heaven, all are emphasized in order to

---

[1] On this Martin see Bruce, i. 29, n. 59, and above, p. 94, n. 1.
[2] Faral, iii. 170.   [3] Ed. Paris, p. 33; ed. Sommer, p. 20 .   [4] Ed. Paris, p. x.

PLATE 7

MERLIN IN THE SHAPE OF A BOY
MERLIN BEARS THE DRAGON BANNER
Bib. Nat., fr. 95. *c.* 1290

clarify Merlin's benevolent role. The fidelity of Ygerne to her husband is also stressed, and when through no fault of hers Arthur is conceived out of wedlock, his legitimacy is ensured by her marriage to Uter soon after. After Arthur's birth, it is Merlin who puts him into safe fosterage with Antor and in due course brings about his coronation as the rightful heir of Uter.[1]

Inspired perhaps by the *Vita Merlini*, Robert has endowed the mage not only with extraordinary powers which affect the destiny of Arthur, but also with a puckish spirit. Merlin, from infancy to age, delights in pranks and mystifications, even sometimes at the expense of his friends. He has inherited from the *Vita* the prophecy of the triple death[2] and the ironic episode of the churl who a few hours before his death buys leather to mend his shoes,[3] but some of Merlin's other exhibitions of preternatural knowledge and his playful adoption of various disguises may be of Robert's invention.

Everything in the *Merlin* converges toward the supreme event, the establishment of the Table Round. Though, of course, this table had been mentioned by Wace as the subject of Breton tales, and by Chrétien as something already familiar to his readers, Robert introduced a daring and a felicitous conception. It is more than a romantic piece of furniture about which the greatest of Arthur's knights assemble on an equality. It is an exact replica of the table of the Grail fashioned by Joseph of Arimathea, which in turn was a replica of the table of the Last Supper; and the three tables form a symbol of the Trinity. The Round Table expresses the loftiest conception of chivalry; superior to the table of the Grail, it stands for an ideal of action, for the defence of the Church. The author, passing from the plane of mundane chronicle to the plane of transcendent significance, shows that for him 'the sacred history which precedes is not to be distinguished from the history of knightly prowess'.[4] With due deliberation he gave to the *Joseph* and its continuations the title 'Livre du Graal'.

Maistre Blaise, recognized by several scholars as the Maistre Blihis in the *Elucidation*,[5] authority for the assertion that nobody should tell the secret of the Grail, is the secretary of Merlin and records from his dictation the story of Joseph and his vessel, and later is informed of the unrolling of British history. His reward is to live in the society of those who behold the Grail, and his book, though lacking divine inspiration, nevertheless, so Merlin assures us, will guard its readers from sin.

The prose redactor has done an injustice to the poet. Behind the Prose

---

[1] For the incident of the sword in the stone see *R*, lxx (1948–9), 37–50.
[2] See above, Chap. 3, p. 26, n. 1; Chap. 8, p. 91, n. 5.
[3] See above, Chap. 8, p. 91, n. 6.
[4] See the excellent pages of P. Zumthor, *Merlin le prophète*, pp. 125 ff.
[5] E. K. Chambers, *Arthur of Britain*, p. 157; W. H. Schofield, *Mythical Bards and the Life of William Wallace* (Cambridge, Mass., 1920), pp. 182 f.; *Prophecies de Merlin*, ed. L. A. Paton (New York, 1926), i. 415–17; *MedAev*, xxv (1956), 184 f. See above, pp. 57 f., 208.

Merlin (and the Prose *Joseph* confirms it) there was an original in verse which was no better written than the metrical *Joseph* and was occasionally obscure, but the general conception was far from feeble and incoherent. In some respects a *fabliau*, in others a chronicle, and a work of edification to judge by the sermons scattered through it, the *Merlin* is at once the evangel of the Grail and the prelude to Arthur. As such it was fitted into the Vulgate cycle, and constitutes an irreplaceable part.

The prose redaction of Robert's *Merlin* was followed in the manuscripts of the Vulgate cycle by a continuation,[1] written probably after 1230, which Brugger aptly called the historical sequel, as distinct from the romantic sequel of the *Huth Merlin*. An anonymous author apparently felt the need for filling the gap between the youth and coronation of Arthur and his apogee. The pseudo-chronicle which he composed is long drawn out, but it is not without a plan. If we put aside certain episodes intended to break the monotony, such as Merlin in Rome and the cat of Lausanne, the rest of the narrative resolves itself into two long epics: the conflict of Arthur with his rebellious vassals, and the much more important conflict between Christian Britons and heathen Saxons. Arthur plays a conspicuous role as the ally of Leodegan; Gauvain, his brothers, and his cousins perform their youthful exploits. Unity is assured by the almost continuous presence of Merlin and also by the bonds of cause and effect. The refusal of the vassals to accept Arthur as king creates a situation which must be solved. Political motives, the danger of a common enemy, the admiration of Gauvain and his brothers for Arthur, all lead to the reconcilement of the king with his barons; and thus Arthur is in a position to destroy his two great foes, the Saxons in Britain and the Romans in Gaul. Ths history of Merlin, then, is the history of the rise of Arthur. The author employs the device of 'interlacing', pursuing one thread of interest for a few pages, then taking up another and another before returning to the first. The result is not altogether fortunate. The calendar of the sequel spreads the events over some three and a half years, and shows that the work is conceived not so much as symbolism or drama but as chronicle.[2]

One might expect that a book devoted to Arthur's youth would have drawn heavily on Wace's *Brut*, but this is not true of the Vulgate sequel, except for a few details and for the account of the war with the Romans. Here, however, the correspondence is very close.[3] But the author has transferred this supreme triumph from its place in the *Brut*, where it immediately precedes the final catastrophe, to a position of far less significance among the

---

[1] Ed. Sommer, *Vulgate Version*, ii. 88–466; Micha, 'La Suite-Vulgate du Merlin, Étude littéraire', *ZRP*, lxxi (1951), 33–59; F. Lot, *Étude sur le Lancelot en Prose, passim*.

[2] Micha, 'La Composition de la Vulgate du Merlin', *R*, lxxiv (1953), 199–220.

[3] Micha, 'L'Épisode de la Bataille des Romains', *R*, lxxii (1951), 310–23. Two-thirds of this part of the continuation are simply a prose version of Wace; in order to avoid the recurrence of the rime, the author has often changed the order of words.

various campaigns and romantic adventures of the young king. And the readjustment of these events to the whole course of Arthur's history has caused certain changes; for example, Keu and Beduier are not slain in battle but live on to reappear in the *Lancelot*. The fact that the Roman war and the combat with Frollo, which is also displaced, are the only elements in the Merlin sequel which reveal a close dependence on Wace, leads one to ask whether they were not written by a different pen.

The sources of the sequel are of four kinds.[1]

First, sources in historic fact. One may imagine that the reign of Philip Augustus furnished some suggestions: the coalition of insurgent vassals, including kinsmen of the king; the battle tactics; the break-up of the coalition through the intercession of a woman.

Second, sources in literature. The names of the Saxon chiefs are largely borrowed from the *chansons de geste*, as well as some details of combat. Familiar motifs of romance are introduced and accounted for: thus Arthur's generosity was inspired by the advice of Merlin; Sagremor owed his epithet *desréé* to his furious attacks on the Saxons; Arthur's custom of waiting for an adventure before eating was the result of a vow made at the Feast of the Assumption. The most influential romances are those of Chrétien, the *Didot Perceval*, and *Meraugis de Portlesguez*.

Third, sources in floating tradition. The episode of Merlin and Grisandole is one form of the oriental legend of a faithless queen who hides her lover or lovers in female costume and whose guilt is disclosed by a wild man with a mysterious laugh, captured by a young woman who serves the king in male disguise.[2] The theme of the squire who slaps his master in the face and the double metamorphosis by which a dwarf is restored to his original beauty while Gauvain is turned into a dwarf may be derived from folk-lore. The magic chessboard and Arthur's combat with the Chapalu seem ultimately to come from Wales, though the latter may already have been localized on the Mont du Chat in Savoy.[3]

Fourth, sources in other parts of the Vulgate corpus. From the Prose *Merlin* the explanation of Keu's discourteous speech, the transformations and the laughter of the prophet, and many other themes have been adapted, sometimes producing contradictions. Arthur's incest with his sister is retold in a different form.[4] The Round Table, instead of being established by Merlin at Carduel, is in the possession of King Leodegan and is given by him to Arthur as his daughter's dowry. Uterpendragon, instead of appearing as two persons, has resumed his single individuality as in Wace.

Since it is generally agreed that the Merlin continuation was the last part

---

[1] Micha, 'Les Sources de la Vulgate du Merlin', *MA*, lviii (1952), 299–345.
[2] L. A. Paton, in *PMLA*, xxii (1907), 234–76.　　　[3] See above, Chap. 2, p. 15, n. 4.
[4] Bruce in *Medieval Studies in Memory of G. Schoepperle Loomis* (Paris, New York, 1927), p. 207.

of the Vulgate corpus to be composed, it is natural to find that the *Lancelot*, the *Queste del Saint Graal*, and the *Mort Artu* have provided suggestions which have been developed in the *Merlin* continuation. The beguiling of Merlin by Viviane seems, indeed, to have been taken over from the *Lancelot*, transferred from the forest of Darnantes to that of Broceliande, and the enchanter's character has been rendered more sympathetic.[1] But more frequently the correspondences with the *Lancelot* take the form of preparatory episodes, and the author has arranged them with more care than his resumption of matters broached in the *Merlin* proper or in the *Estoire del Saint Graal*. There are no inconsistencies between the *Merlin* sequel and the *Lancelot* except in regard to the fate of the prophet, as just noted, and in the chronology, the former text extending the youthful exploits of Arthur and Gauvain over a longer period than the latter text permits. Of all the passages in the *Merlin* sequel which represent the development of themes suggested by the *Lancelot*—the amours of Morgain and Guiomar, the entombment of Merlin, the adultery of Ban, &c.—those of the marriage of Arthur and the birth of the false Guenièvre best exemplify the methods of our author.[2] The enchanter preserves his active role in thwarting the plot, but the attempted abduction of the true Guenièvre is treated differently. There is a more dramatic scene with the intervention of Ulfin and Bretel, and the recognition of the true Guenièvre is brought about through a birthmark of a crown on her hip—a familiar motif employed in the *Roman de la Violette* and *Guillaume de Dôle*. Finally, Bertholai is replaced as the instigator of the abduction by the kinsmen of the false Guenièvre.

The author of the sequel seems to have been influenced by the *Queste del Saint Graal*, as well as by the *Lancelot*, in his introduction of allegories and dreams, and by the *Mort Artu* in ascribing the birth of Mordret to Arthur's incestuous union with his sister.

The literary quality of the *Merlin* sequel is not great. The romancer is not skilled in the treatment of love; even the pages on the betrothal of Arthur and Guenièvre are banal. But the tale of Merlin and Viviane is more than an 'antifeminist fabliau', as Brugger described it. An inescapable fatality confers on these pages a real grandeur. Merlin is dominated by morbid passion; he succumbs to a destiny which he knows in advance; though endowed with foreknowledge, he accomplishes his own ruin. To be sure, the various wars do not escape the fault of monotony, and the narrative is not free from obscurities, improbabilities, and inconsequences; but here and there are incidents finely sketched, such as the arrival of Gauvain and his companions before the three kings, and many impressions of sound, light, and atmosphere are effectively conveyed.

---

[1] On the various forms of this legend see Zumthor in *ZRP*, lxii (1942), 370–86, and above, p. 261, n. 4.   [2] Sommer, op. cit., iv. 10–82; ii. 301–13.

24

THE *SUITE DU MERLIN* AND THE
POST-VULGATE *ROMAN DU GRAAL*[1]

FANNI BOGDANOW

THE prose redaction of Robert de Bor(r)on's *Merlin*, as was pointed out in the last chapter, was followed in the manuscripts of the Vulgate cycle by a continuation or sequel of a pseudo-historical nature, and in the so-called Huth manuscript (Brit. Mus. Add. 38117) by a romantic continuation. Though the latter has often been referred to as the *Huth Merlin*, it is now common practice among scholars to call it the *Suite du Merlin*. In 1945 Professor Vinaver discovered a far more complete version of the *Suite* in a fourteenth-century Anglo-Norman manuscript, now in the Cambridge University Library (Add. 7071).[2] A small fragment of the *Suite* preserved in an unnumbered thirteenth-century manuscript in the State Archives of Siena, Italy, has recently come to light.[3] The narrative contents of this romance are familiar not merely to specialists, but also to many lovers of *belles lettres* throughout the English-speaking world, since they are to be found, condensed, rearranged, and somewhat altered, in the first four books of Malory's work. A Spanish version of the *Suite*, derived from a text similar to the Huth manuscript, was embodied in the *Demanda del Sancto Grial*.[4]

This romance, after giving an account, based on the Vulgate *Merlin* sequel,[5] of Arthur's wars against the rebel kings,[6] continues with the early

---

[1] This chapter was originally assigned to Prof. E. Vinaver, but as I had prepared a thesis on the subject, under his direction, he kindly entrusted it to me. I cannot thank him enough for all his help and encouragement in its preparation.

[2] *Merlin*, ed. G. Paris, J. Ulrich, *SATF* (1886). The tale of Balain has been edited separately by M. D. Legge, with an introduction by E. Vinaver, as *Le Roman de Balain* (Manchester, 1942). For a detailed description of the Cambridge manuscript see Vinaver, *The Works of Sir Thomas Malory* (Oxford, 1947), iii. 1277–80, and Vinaver in *Mélanges . . . Hoepffner* (Paris, 1949), pp. 299 f.

[3] The fragment corresponds to Paris's edition, ii. 64–72. I first identified the fragment in February 1956. Micha's transcription, *R*, lxxviii (1957), 37–45, is marred, unfortunately, by a number of errors.

[4] Malory, *Works*, i. 1–180. On printed editions of the *Demanda*, see Chap. 31 below.

[5] Sommer, *Vulgate Version*, ii.

[6] The account of the rebellion of the kings is found only in the Cambridge manuscript and in Malory. It was omitted from the Huth manuscript and the Spanish *Demanda*, as Vinaver established in Malory, *Works*, iii. 1277–80, and in *Mélanges . . . Hoepffner*, pp. 295–300. R. H. Wilson maintained in *University of Texas Studies in English*, xxxi (1952), 13–26, that the rebellion section of the Cambridge manuscript was a late interpolation, but I have shown, ibid. xxxiv (1955), 6–17, that there is every reason to believe that the *Suite* originally included the kings' rebellion.

history of Arthur's reign, recounting Mordret's birth, the revelation of Arthur's parentage, his combat with Pellinor, the obtaining of Escalibor from the lake, the wars against Rion and Lot, the tragic tale of Balain, Arthur's marriage to Leodegan's daughter, the quests of Gauvain, Tor, and Pellinor, the story of Merlin and Niviene (Viviane), Arthur's wars with the five kings, Morgain's plots to destroy Arthur, and the triple adventures of Gauvain, Yvain, and the Morholt. The conclusion to the last set of adventures, missing in the Huth and Cambridge manuscripts, was discovered by Wechssler in a fifteenth-century compilation, MS. Bib. Nat. fr. 112,[1] and I have recently found in the same manuscript and in MS. Bib. Nat. fr. 12599 still other episodes which, although they do not join on to the *Suite du Merlin* immediately after the end of the triple adventures of Gauvain, Yvain, and the Morholt, clearly belong to the original form of the work.[2] The first of these episodes, Gaheriet's slaying of his mother, is foreshadowed in the fragment of the *Suite* discovered by Wechssler.[3] The account of Lancelot's madness, which follows, is modelled on the Vulgate *Lancelot*,[4] but is combined with fresh material, including the adventures of Erec, Gauvain's slaying of two of Pellinor's sons—Lamorat and Drian,[5]—the youth of Perceval,[6] and other episodes which are clearly attached to the theme of vengeance in the *Suite*.[7] The narrative ends with an account of Hector's meeting with Lancelot on the 'Isle de Joie' and Lancelot's return to court.[8]

The *Suite du Merlin*, which repeatedly claims Robert de Bor(r)on as its author, has given rise to a prolific literature about its relation to the other versions and has led to much speculation about a 'pseudo-Robert de Bor(r)on' cycle.[9]

---

[1] *Livre* ii, fols. 17b–58b. Published by Sommer in *Beihefte ZRP*, xlvii (1913), as *Die Abenteuer Gawains, Ywains und Le Morholts mit den drei Jungfrauen*. Malory and the Spanish *Demanda* conclude the narrative differently, the latter with an account of Merlin's death, Malory with a long passage which may be of his own invention. See Whitehead in *MedAev*, ii (1936), 199–216.

[2] The narrative in MS. 112 begins shortly before that of the 12599 fragment and continues beyond the point where the latter breaks off. Löseth in his *Roman en Prose de Tristan* (Paris, 1891) gives a summary of the 12599 fragment (p. 216, §§ 283a–291a), but does not suggest that it belongs to the *Suite du Merlin*. I am preparing a critical edition of this new portion of the *Suite*.

[3] See *Beihefte ZRP*, xlvii. 93: 'Et lors dist a Gaheriet: "Tu passasses de bonté et de valeur tous lez compaignons de la Table Ronde fors seulement deus, se ne fust la mort de ta mere que tu hasteras par ton pechié, et ce sera la chose qui plus abaissera ton pris." '

[4] Sommer, *Vulgate Version*, v. 378–83, 393–404.

[5] This account is adapted from the First Version of the Prose *Tristan* (Löseth, op. cit., § 307). The *Suite* announces at an earlier point that Gauvain will slay Pellinor and two of his sons in order to avenge the death of his father Lot, whom Pellinor killed (*Merlin*, ed. Paris, i. 261; Cambridge MS., fol. 259b).

[6] Adapted from the First Version of the Prose *Tristan* (Löseth, op. cit., § 308–12). The *Suite* refers clearly to this narrative as part of its composition: 'Et ceste aventure devise ceste ystoire anchois que on kieche a conter la vie de Percheval' (*Merlin*, ed. Paris, ii. 288).

[7] Some of the later episodes bring in the *Lait Hardi*, a knight whose adventures are announced in the *Suite*, but who does not appear elsewhere (*Merlin*, ed. Paris, i. 209).

[8] MS. 12599 breaks off before it reaches this point (Sommer, op. cit. v. 389–93, 404–98).

[9] See Wechssler, *Über die verschiedenen Redaktionen des Robert von Borron zugeschriebenen Graal-*

Gaston Paris, in his edition of the Huth text, held that the *Suite du Merlin* was independent of the Vulgate *Merlin* and formed part of a trilogy, of which the last part consisted of a *Queste* and a *Mort Artu* older than the Vulgate versions and now represented by the Portuguese *Demanda do Santo Graal*.[1] But since the Cambridge manuscript of the *Suite* contains an account of the rebellion of the kings adapted from the Vulgate *Merlin* sequel, the *Suite* must be later than the Vulgate.[2] Nor is there any doubt that the *Demanda Queste* and *Mort Artu* are also *remaniements* of the corresponding branches in the Vulgate cycle: they merely modify some of the Vulgate incidents, omit others, and add fresh material.[3]

Writing a few years after Gaston Paris, Wechssler produced an elaborate hypothesis concerning a cycle of which much had been lost in its original French form, but which could be reconstructed from various French and non-French adaptations. This he called the 'pseudo-Robert de Borron' cycle to distinguish it from the Vulgate or 'pseudo-Map' cycle. In its original form it was divided into six branches, corresponding to the *Estoire del Saint Graal*, *Merlin*, *Merlin* sequel, *Lancelot*, *Queste del Saint Graal*, and *Mort Artu* of the Vulgate. This form A, no longer extant, was cut down into two other hypothetical forms, B and C. The A version of the *Merlin* sequel was followed by Malory, who gives some proper names and other details missing from the Huth manuscript; the B version was the source of MS. Bib. Nat. fr. 112; the C version was represented by the Huth manuscript, while the Spanish *Demanda* of 1535, mainly based on C, retained traces of A, and of the *Conte del Brait*, which was supposed to consist of extracts from the original *Suite*. Similarly, various hypothetical versions of the Pseudo-Borron *Queste* survive in MS. Bib. Nat. fr. 112 and 343, in the Portuguese *Demanda*, and the Second Version of the Prose *Tristan*. Such was Wechssler's complicated scheme. Bruce accepted the theory of a 'pseudo-Robert de Borron' cycle and the three redactions, but he realized that the *Suite du Merlin* and the *Demanda* versions of the *Queste* and *Mort Artu* were dependent on the Vulgate, and therefore argued for the priority of the Vulgate over the 'pseudo-Borron' cycle.[4]

In a series of illuminating studies Vinaver has shown that the whole

---

Lancelot-Cyklus (Halle, 1895); R. Heinzel in *Denkschriften der kaiserlichen Akad. der Wissenschaften zu Wien*, phil.-hist. Kl., xl (1891), 162–71; Brugger, 'L'Enserrement Merlin', *ZFSL*, xxix (1906), 56–140; xxxiv (1911), 99–150; also *ZFSL*, xxx (1907), 169–239; xxxi (1908), 239–81; xxxiii (1910), 145–94; xxxv (1912), 1–55; Sommer in *R*, xxxvi (1907), 369–462, 543–90; *MP*, v (1907–8), 295–322; *ZRP*, xxxii (1908), 324–37; introd. to *Die Abenteuer Gawains*, pp. xiv–xxvi; E. Vettermann, *Beihefte ZRP*, lx (1918), 85–192.

[1] *Merlin*, ed. Paris, i, pp. l–lxix. The Portuguese *Demanda* was edited by A. Magne (Rio de Janeiro, 1944). On this text and the Spanish *Demanda* see below, pp. 409 f.
[2] See above, p. 261, n. 6.
[3] Pauphilet, 'La Queste du Saint Graal du MS. Bibl. Nat. fr. 343', *R*, xxxvi (1907), 591–609.
[4] Bruce, i. 458–79.

speculative fabric rests on an insecure premiss and that the variations in the surviving texts can be explained by quite a different theory. The *Suite du Merlin* is not the result of 'a process of regression and decay, but of a consistent evolution from simpler patterns to more coherent and comprehensive ones'.[1] The same can be said of the remodelled *Queste*.[2] Vinaver has further demonstrated that the details which distinguish Malory's text from the Huth and Cambridge manuscripts are not the relics of an older *Suite du Merlin*, but are Malory's own additions.[3] The fundamental error underlying Wechssler's theory is the assumption that a more attractive and more cogent reading is necessarily the original. That a scribe or redactor may try to eliminate discrepancies in his exemplar and add episodes to fulfil unrealized allusions is a possibility which seems to have been largely overlooked by generations of earlier scholars.[4] Not only the minor details peculiar to the *Demanda*, but all the episodes supposedly derived from the *Conte del Brait* can be explained as the inventions of the Spanish translator, who, meeting in the *Suite* with references to episodes told in a *Conte del Brait* ('Tale of the Cry'), supplied from his imagination the requisite narratives.[5] That the *Conte del Brait* is a phantasm is further proved by the fact that the *Queste* and *Mort Artu* sections of the *Demanda* likewise refer to it for incidents which they do not relate[6]—a manifest absurdity since the hypothetical *Brait* terminated with Merlin's death and did not cover the later events of Arthur's reign. Thus the 'pseudo-Borron' cycle and its three redactions do not deserve a place in literary history, and the whole question of the genesis and purpose of the *Suite du Merlin* may be examined afresh.

It requires no great perspicacity to realize that the *Suite* was composed to fit into a larger whole. Not only does it look back to the *Estoire del Saint Graal*,[7] but it anticipates many incidents in the *Queste del Saint Graal* and

---

[1] Vinaver in *Roman de Balain*, ed. Legge, pp. ix–xxii; Malory, *Works*, iii. 1265–73; *Mélanges*... *Hoepffner*, pp. 295–300.

[2] In my typewritten thesis for the Master of Arts degree, University of Manchester, I have suggested that the *Demanda Queste* and the Prose *Tristan* go back to a common source Y, a *remaniement* of the Vulgate *Queste*. Y was, on the one hand, incorporated into the Prose *Tristan*, and, on the other, considerably remodelled by another redactor. This *remaniement* of Y, which one may call FD, fragments of which have survived in MSS. Bib. Nat. fr. 112, 116, 340, 355, 1463, is the immediate source of the *Demanda*. Far from being shorter than the Prose *Tristan Queste*, it contained much additional material. I shall deal with this question fully in a study I am preparing.

[3] *Roman de Balain*, ed. Legge, p. x, n. 2; Malory, *Works*, iii. 1267, and notes to p. 78. 22–27, and p. 92. 14–21.

[4] How common this peculiar habit of mind was among earlier scholars was first pointed out by Vinaver in *Bulletin of the John Rylands Library*, xxxvi (1953), 237, n. 3.

[5] F. Lot pointed out in *Étude sur le Lancelot en Prose*, p. 13, that it is a common procedure in the prose romances for redactors to refer to an imaginary *branche* for incidents that they do not wish to relate. For a more detailed discussion see my doctorate thesis, *Le Roman du Graal: a Study of a Remaniement of the Vulgate Cycle of Arthurian Romances*.

[6] Portuguese *Demanda*, § 664. MS. Bib. Nat. fr. 343, fol. 101a.

[7] For instance, the *Suite* refers to Lambor and Varlan's battle in the *Estoire* (*Merlin*, ed. Paris,

the *Mort Artu*. It refers to the famous passage in the *Queste* in which Perceval's sister gives of her blood to heal a leprous damsel;[1] it predicts that Gauvain will slay Baudemagus[2] and alludes to the deaths of various characters in the *Mort Artu*: Lancelot is to give Gauvain his mortal wound after Gaheriet's death,[3] and Arthur, Sagremor, and Yvain are to die at the hand of Mordred.[4] Allusions which do not fit the Vulgate versions of the *Queste* and *Mort Artu* can be explained with the aid of the post-Vulgate versions of these works preserved in the Spanish and Portuguese *Demandas*, in certain manuscripts of the Second Version of the Prose *Tristan*,[5] and in MS. Bib. Nat. fr. 112 and 343. The *Suite* mentions the 'beste glatissant', 'the barking beast', and Merlin explains that it is 'one of the adventures of the Grail'.[6] The Vulgate *Queste* does not introduce the 'beste glatissant', but it appears several times in MS. 343 and in the Portuguese *Demanda*.[7] Again, the *Suite* announces that Gauvain will kill Erec and that Hector will accuse Gauvain of treachery before King Arthur's court, 'si com cist livres le devise apertement del Saint Graal', 'just as this book of the Holy Grail will clearly describe it'.[8] Now Erec plays no part in the Vulgate *Queste*, but the Portuguese *Demanda* fulfils the forecast of his death[9] and Hector's denunciation of Gauvain.[10] Similarly, the *Suite* predicts that Gauvain will slay Pellinor, Perceval's father,[11] and relates how Gauvain slew two of Perceval's brothers.[12] Now while in the Vulgate *Queste* Pellehen, not Pellinor, is Perceval's father, MS. 343 and the Portuguese *Demanda* agree with the *Suite* and frequently refer back to the death of Pellinor and his sons.[13] One of the most memorable scenes in the *Suite* describes the Dolorous Stroke which Balain, the knight with the two swords, dealt King Pellean.[14] In MS. 343 and the Portuguese *Demanda*, when Galaad heals Pellean, the latter says that it was the 'Chevalier

ii. 7 f.). It is unlikely that the *Estoire* which originally preceded the *Suite* differed much from the Vulgate *Estoire*. The Portuguese *Josep Abarimatia* contains a colophon stating that it is the first part of the *Demanda*. Except that it contains an allusion to Balain's Dolorous Stroke, the Portuguese *Demanda* does not differ markedly from the French *Estoire*.

[1] *Merlin*, ed. Paris, ii. 19.   [2] Ibid. i. 273.

[3] Ibid. ii. 59. Sommer, *Die Abenteuer Gawains*, p. 63.

[4] *Merlin*, ed. Paris, i. 147 f., 274; *Die Abenteuer Gawains*, pp. 78 f. This list of examples is by no means exhaustive. See my thesis referred to on p. 328, n. 5, chs. v, vi.

[5] The following manuscripts contain the *Tristan Queste*: Bib. Nat. fr. 97, 99, 101, 336, 349, 758, 772, 24400; Brit. Mus. Add. 5474, Egerton 989, Royal 20 D II; Dijon 527; Aberystwyth 5667; Chantilly, Musée Condé 317; Brussels, Bib. Roy. 9086; Vienna 2537, 2540, 2542; Morgan Library, New York, 41.

[6] *Merlin*, ed. Paris, i. 160.

[7] Portuguese *Demanda*, §§ 82 f., 97–102, 121–8, 193 f., 581–4, 604–9.

[8] Bib. Nat. fr. 12599, fol. 240a. Cf. also Bibl Nat. fr. 112, Livre iii, fol. 249a.

[9] Portuguese *Demanda*, §§ 280–352; Bib. Nat. fr. 112, Livre iv, fols. 101b–113d.

[10] Portuguese *Demanda*, § 625; Bib. Nat. fr. 772, fol. 417c.

[11] *Merlin*, ed. Paris, i. 261; ii. 11.

[12] Bib. Nat. fr. 12599, fols. 246d–250d; 112, Livre iii, fols. 254b–257a.

[13] Bib. Nat. fr. 343, fol. 93b; Portuguese *Demanda*, § 548.

[14] Cambridge Univ. Lib. Add. 7071, fols. 270^r–272^v.

as Deus Espees' who had caused the wound.[1] Moreover, the Holy Lance
and the Grail Chamber are described in almost identical terms in the *Suite*
and MS. 343. At another point, the *Suite* remarks that King Marc's death
will be related after Lancelot's.[2] Now the only extant version of the *Mort
Artu* which relates Marc's death is the one which follows the *Demanda
Queste*: it says that after the death of Arthur and Lancelot, Marc invaded
Logres and devastated the country, but was killed by a knight of Ban's line
when he attempted to murder the last survivors of Arthur's fellowship.[3]

In the passage where the author of the *Suite* refers to this event, he speaks
of his intention to write a *livre* divided into three equal parts, and states plainly
that the third part begins with the *Queste* and ends with an account of the
death of Arthur:[4]

> Et sacent tuit cil qui l'estoire mon signeur de Borron vaurront oïr comme il
> devise son livre en trois parties, l'une partie aussi grant comme l'autre, la premiere
> aussi grande comme la seconde, et la seconde aussi grant comme la tierche. Et la
> premiere partie fenist il au commencement de ceste queste, et la seconde el com-
> menchement dou Graal, et la tierche fenist il apriés la mort de Lanscelot, a chelui
> point meisme qu'il devise de la mort le roi March. Et cest[e] chose amentoit en la
> fin dou premier livre, pour chou que [se] l'*Estoire dou Graal* estoit corrompue par
> auchuns translatours qui aprés lui venissent, tout li sage houme qui meteroient lour
> entente a oïr et a escouter porroient savoir se elle lour seroit baillie entiere ou cor-
> rompue, et connisteront bien combien il i faurroit.

(And know all those who wish to hear the story of *mon signeur de Borron* how he
divides his book into three equal parts, one part as big as the other: the first part as
big as the second, and the second as big as the third. And the first part ends at the
beginning of this quest, and the second at the beginning of the Grail, and the third
finishes after Lancelot's death at the very point where it relates King Marc's death.
And he told you this at the end of the first book, so that if the story of the Grail is
broken up by later scribes, all wise men who would endeavour to hear and to listen
would be able to know if they have been given the story in its complete form or in a
fragmentary state, and they will know how much is missing.)

The author claims to have excluded the *Lancelot* from his composition because it would have made the middle portion of his book three times as long
as the other two. In referring to the ring which the Damoisele du Lac gave
Lancelot, he says:[5]

> Et cel anelet li avoit douné la damoisiele del lac, si coume la grant hystore de

[1] Portuguese *Demanda*, § 590; Bib. Nat. fr. 343, fol. 103b.

[2] *Merlin*, ed. Paris, i. 280.

[3] Portuguese *Demanda*, §§ 701–6; Spanish *Demanda*, chs. cccclii–ccclv. Bib. Nat. fr. 340, a
manuscript of Rusticien's compilation, contains at the end two fragments of the *Demanda Mort Artu*,
one of which relates Guenièvre's death and the other Marc's death (see Bib. Nat. fr. 340, fols. 205a–
207c).

[4] *Merlin*, ed. Paris, i. 280; Cambridge MS. fol. 263d.

[5] *Merlin*, ed. Paris, ii. 57; Cambridge MS. fol. 279c.

Lanscelot le devise, cele meisme ystoire qui doit estre departie de mon livre, ne mie pour chou qu'il n'i apartiegne et que elle n'en soit traite, mais pour chou qu'il couvient que les trois parties de mon livre soient ingaus, l'une aussi grant coume l'autre, et se je ajoustaisse cele grant ystore, la moi[ene] partie de mon livre fust au tresble plus grant que les autres deus. Pour chou me couvient il laissier celle grant ystoire qui devise les oevres de Lanscelot et la naissance, et voel deviser les neuf lignies des Nascions, tout ensi coume il apartient a la *Haute Escriture del Saint Graal*, ne n'i conterai ja chose que je ne doie, ains dirai mains assés que je ne truis escrit en l'ystoire dou latin.

(And the Damsel of the Lake had given him this ring, as the great story of Lancelot tells, the very story which has been removed from my book, not because it does not belong to it and deal with its subject matter, but because it is necessary that the three parts of my book be equal in length, the one as big as the other, and if I added this long story, the middle portion of my book would be three times as big as the other two. For this reason it is necessary to exclude this long story which relates the deeds and birth of Lancelot, and I will tell of the nine generations of Nascien, as befits the high story of the Holy Grail; nor will I ever relate more than I should, but will tell much less than I find written in the Latin story.)

Now MS. 343 and the Portuguese *Demanda* contain similar references to the tripartition of the romance and state clearly at one point that it *is* the third part of the 'livre de cil de Beron':[1]

Et Galahaz, quant il se fu partiz del chevalier, chevaucha puis mainte jornee and maintes aventures mist a fin, dont cil de Beron ne parole mie, car trop eust a faire se il voxist a celui point raconter toutes les merveilles del Grahal, *et la darraine partie de son livre fust trop grant avers les autres deus premieres.*

(And when Galahad had left the knight, he rode on for many a day and ended many adventures of which *de Beron* does not speak, for he would have too much to do if he wished at this point to relate all the marvels of the Grail, and the last part of his book would be too big in comparison with the first two parts.)

Furthermore, in referring to one of the events related in the *Estoire del Saint Graal*, MS. 343 remarks that the latter belongs to the 'first part of the book'.[2]

There can be no doubt, therefore, that the *Suite du Merlin* forms part of a larger work, not the imaginary one postulated by Wechssler and Bruce and entitled by them the 'pseudo-Robert de Borron' cycle, but a long romance beginning with the *Estoire del Saint Graal*, followed by the prose redaction of Robert de Boron's *Merlin*,[3] the *Suite* and the Post-Vulgate Versions of

---

[1] Bib. Nat. fr. 343, fol. 101a; Portuguese *Demanda*, § 581.

[2] Bib. Nat. fr. 343, fol. 98b.

[3] In my view, the *Suite du Merlin* was originally followed by a version of the *Queste* which represents the common source of the Prose *Tristan* and *Demanda Queste* (cf. p. 328, n. 2 above). This original *remaniement* of the Vulgate *Queste* was replaced by the *Demanda Queste* (see ch. iv of my doctorate thesis).

the *Queste* and *Mort Artu*. This composite but unified work we shall call the *Roman du Graal*.[1] The *Lancelot* proper formed no part of it. In order to provide a transition to the *Queste*, the author simply summarized certain *Lancelot* episodes which he interspersed with his own inventions. This is perfectly clear from the *Suite* fragment contained in MSS. Bib. Nat. fr. 112 and 12599. In fact, far from leading up to a *Lancelot* 'branch', the *Suite* compilation appears to be an 'anti-Lancelot'. The few episodes derived from the Vulgate *Lancelot* do not breathe the spirit of courtly love. In MS. 112 Gaheriet defends the murder of his mother as the punishment which a queen deserves 'qui par maleureuse luxure fait honte a ses enfans et a tout son lignage'.[2] The union of Gauvain and Arcade is denounced as a 'pechié grant et orrible'.[3] The Post-Vulgate *Queste* which follows the *Suite* belittles the relationship of Tristan and Yseut,[4] and the Post-Vulgate *Mort Artu* omits nearly all the scenes in which Lancelot and Guenièvre alone appear. Evidently the Post-Vulgate Grail romance or *Roman du Graal* was written to counteract the influence of the Vulgate *Lancelot* and *Mort Artu* by providing a substitute in which the famous story of adulterous love, though not ignored, was given little place, in which illicit amours were condemned as sin, and in which Arthur's downfall was the consequence of the incest which he unwittingly committed at the beginning of his reign.

Not only does the *Roman du Graal* differ in spirit and purpose from the great Arthurian cycle; its composition, too, is far more closely knit than that of the latter. The Vulgate, far from being a harmonious whole, consists in reality of three loosely joined romances—the *Estoire del Saint Graal*, the *Estoire de Merlin*, and the *Roman de Lancelot*.[5] Gaston Paris and Bruce thought that the *Suite* compilation was equally amorphous and condemned it as an agglomeration of disconnected episodes, a 'labyrinth of fantastic adventures'.[6] This is certainly not the case. The romance was conceived as an organic whole and is remarkable for its inner cohesion. The author was clearly interested in its general design and sought to produce a coherent and convincingly motivated narrative. But he did so, as Vinaver alone of critics realized, in a manner characteristic of thirteenth-century writers: not psychologically, but structurally, by supplying the antecedents of the stories which had to be elucidated.[7] Hence the early portion of the romance,

---

[1] The author of the *Suite* frequently refers to his book as the *Estoire dou Saint Graal* or the *Haute Escriture del Saint Graal* (see *Merlin*, ed. Paris, i. 280; ii. 57, 61, 173). It is significant that the *Demandas* refer to the whole work as the *Demanda del Sancto Grial*.

[2] Bib. Nat. fr. 112, Livre iii, fol. 215d.

[3] Sommer, *Die Abenteuer Gawains*, p. 32.

[4] Cf. Bib. Nat. fr. 343, fol. 83d.

[5] That is, the *Lancelot* proper, *Queste*, and *Mort Artu*.

[6] Bruce, i. 464. *Merlin*, ed. Paris, i, p. xlviii.

[7] See Vinaver in Malory, *Works*, iii. 1265–74; *Mélanges* ... *Hoepffner*, pp. 295–300; *Roman de Balain*, ed. Legge, pp. ix–xxii; *MedAev*, xxv (1956), 175–80.

the *Suite du Merlin*, far from being a perfunctory addition like the Vulgate *Merlin* sequel, forms an integral part of the whole: it consists to a large extent of long narrative sequences intended to prepare and foreshadow incidents related in the later portions. The initial episode of the *Suite*, the conception of Mordret, has its proper significance only if read in connexion with the particular account of the 'Death of Arthur' story in the Post-Vulgate *Mort Artu*, and the account of the inauguration of the marvels of Logres and the maiming of King Pellean finds its full resonance only in the version of the final scene at Corbenic as related in the Post-Vulgate *Queste*. Conversely, many features of the Post-Vulgate *Queste* and *Mort Artu* are comprehensible only in the light of certain events and ideas which occur in the *Suite*. The various sections, in fact, dovetail together and form an indissoluble whole.

All this helps to explain the references to the tripartition of the work. The suggested divisions cut across the traditional Vulgate branches, the first part ending in the midst of one of Balain's adventures. Gaston Paris thought that the desire to make the three parts equal in length was the determining factor and that the third part alone had a logical beginning. Sommer,[1] on the other hand, suggested that the scribe of the Huth manuscript deliberately displaced the beginning of the second part because, having used for the *Joseph* and the *Merlin* a different manuscript of the *Suite*, he could not retain the original divisions of the 'book'.[2] Wechssler, Brugger, and Bruce were likewise unable to find a reason for the division indicated in the Huth manuscript and took it to be purely arbitrary. But if we regard the *Roman du Graal* as a romance and get away from the idea of 'branches', and conceive of Arthur as the central figure, the work will fall logically into three parts corresponding to the three phases of the history of Logres. Arthur's kingdom is the *roiaume aventureux*, the land in which great adventures, those of the Grail, take place. The first part contains the story of Logres before the beginning of the *aventures* and naturally includes a history of the Grail,[3] for it is the Grail which produces the marvels of Logres; it ends when Balain sets out on the quest which is to lead him to the Grail chamber where, with the Holy Lance, he is to strike the Dolorous Stroke and so inaugurate the marvels of Logres. The second part of the story shows us Logres labouring under the spell which the *dolorous cop* has cast upon it, and we see the adventures arriving *espessement* in Arthur's land. The last part begins with the news of the arrival

[1] *Merlin*, ed. Paris, i, p. lxii f. Sommer in *ZRP*, xxxii (1908), 325 f.; *R*, xxxvi (1907), 380; *Die Abenteuer Gawains*, pp. xviii, xxi f.

[2] Sommer in *R*, xxvi. 377 f.; Brugger in *RF*, xxvi (1919), 150. Sommer's theory has been disproved by the discovery of the Cambridge manuscript, where the *Merlin* is preceded by the *Estoire del Saint Graal*, and the division between the first and second parts occurs at the same point as in the Huth manuscript.

[3] That is, the *Estoire del Saint Graal*.

of the Good Knight who will end the adventures of Logres, and includes not only the *Queste* proper but also an account of the destruction of the kingdom. Pre-Arthurian history—*l'Estoire del Saint Graal*—is, as it were, symmetrical to the account of the misfortunes which befell Logres after the death of Arthur and with which the Post-Vulgate *Mort Artu* ends.

Many of the difficulties raised by the romance are solved once we see it as a unified work with a single theme, the story of the *roiaume aventureux*, which is also that of the Grail. Even the *Estoire del Saint Graal*, which presumably had a separate existence before the later parts were written, is not thought of as a separate and detachable 'branch', but simply as the opening chapter of a longer story. And indeed the whole romance is often referred to in the *Suite* as *l'Estoire dou Saint Graal* or *la Haute Escriture del Saint Graal*, a title which adequately expresses the author's intentions.

There is no reason to suppose that the author had access to any sources other than the French verse and prose romances, although there are, according to R. S. Loomis, Irish 'analogues' for Balain's adventure in King Pellean's castle, and for the treacherous substitution of a counterfeit Escalibor, as well as Welsh 'analogues' for Niviene's galloping into Arthur's hall, and for Merlin's tale of the murder of Faunus by Diana and her huntsman paramour.[1]

The *Suite du Merlin* and the *Roman du Graal* or Post-Vulgate Grail romance of which it forms a part, though pretending to come from the pen of Robert de Bor(r)on, the author of the metrical *Joseph* and *Merlin*,[2] are actually anonymous. Since they made extensive use of the Vulgate cycle (written *c.* 1215–30) and the First Version of the Prose *Tristan* (written *c.* 1225–30),[3] the year 1230 can be considered a *terminus a quo*. On the other hand, one of the incidents of the *Suite*, the death of the Queen of Orkney, together with the whole of the first redaction of the Post-Vulgate *Queste*, were incorporated into the Second Version of the Prose *Tristan*, which probably belongs to the second half of the thirteenth century.[4] But the most important piece of chronological evidence is the fact that *Palamedes*, which was in existence by 1240,[5] contains a precise reference to the final episode of the Post-Vulgate *Mort Artu*, the destruction of Logres by Marc after Arthur's death. The relevant passage in MS. Brit. Mus. Add. 12228 (fol. 16d) reads as follows:

Et por ce que li rois Artus l' [i.e. Camalot] ama toute sa vie sor toutes les autres cytez qu'il avoit, la destruist puis tote et dessola li felons roi Marc de Cornoaille

[1] R. S. Loomis, *Arthurian Tradition*, pp. 106 f., 295, 380–2, 421–5.

[2] Robert de Boron died probably before 1210 (*Roman de l'Estoire dou Graal*, ed. W. A. Nitze, *CFMA* (1927), p. viii).

[3] E. Vinaver, *Études sur le Tristan en Prose*, p. 23. Gaston Paris, who did not realize that the *Suite* was dependent on the Vulgate, dated it as early as 1225–30 (*Merlin*, ed. Paris, i, p. lxix).

[4] Vinaver, *Études*, pp. 28–30.   [5] See Chap. 27 below, p. 348; Bruce, ii. 21.

aprés la mort li roi Artus. Missire Robert de Borron mi compaignon en comença a dire en son livre cele destrucion et celui desertement, et en comença a dire la descorde del roi Artus et de monseigneur Lancelot et de celui lygnage. . . .[1]

(And because Arthur loved all his life Camalot more than all his other cities, the treacherous King Marc of Cornwall destroyed it completely and razed it to the ground after the death of King Arthur. Missire Robert de Borron, my companion, began in his book to tell of this destruction, and began to speak of the discord between Arthur and Lancelot and his lineage.)

If, as seems reasonable, this allusion is to be regarded as the *terminus ad quem*, the *Suite du Merlin* and the larger work to which it belongs must have been written between 1230 and 1240.[2]

---

[1] Löseth, *Roman en Prose de Tristan*, p. 439, § 630. Bruce, i. 479, n. 70, took no account of the allusion in *Palamedes* to the Post-Vulgate *Mort Artu*, and placed what he called the 'pseudo-Robert' cycle between 1230 and 1250.

[2] The *Suite du Merlin* (*Huth Merlin*) is discussed in the following works not mentioned above: A. C. L. Brown, 'Balin and the Dolorous Stroke', *MP*, vii (1909), 203–6; 'The Bleeding Lance', *PMLA*, xxv (1910), 1–59; W. J. Entwistle, *Arthurian Legend in the Literature of the Spanish Peninsula* (London, 1925), pp. 133–81; L. A. Hibbard, 'Malory's Book of Balin', in *Medieval Studies in Memory of G. Schoepperle Loomis* (Paris, New York, 1927), pp. 175–95; Vinaver in *BBSIA*, vi (1954), 105 f.; Vinaver, 'King Arthur's Sword', *Bulletin of the John Rylands Library*, xl (1958), pp. 513–26; P. Zumthor, *Merlin le Prophète* (Lausanne, 1943), pp. 200–10, 217, 220 f., 232–4, 239 f., 250–6; and summary of my paper on 'The Post-Vulgate *Mort Artu*', *BBSIA*, vi. 106 f.

THE *LIVRE D'ARTUS*

FREDERICK WHITEHEAD AND ROGER SHERMAN LOOMIS

BESIDES the two continuations of the prose version of Robert's *Merlin* discussed in the previous chapters—the Vulgate sequel and the *Suite du Merlin* of the Huth and Cambridge manuscripts—there is still a third known as the *Livre d'Artus*,[1] though its principal hero is Gauvain. It is contained only in a late thirteenth-century manuscript, Bib. Nat. fr. 337, which begins with the Vulgate *Merlin* sequel, but branches off[2] and continues tirelessly through a series of battles, duels, spells, imprisonments, amours, and so forth till it breaks off abruptly as Gauvain comes to the aid of a lady who is being dragged by her hair.

H. O. Sommer, who published the *Livre d'Artus*, propounded the theory that the contents of MS. 337 were portions of a huge compilation beginning at a point before the Vulgate *Merlin* sequel starts and carrying on after MS. 337 breaks off.[3] Sommer dated this vast work, of which the episodes peculiar to MS. 337 constituted only a tiny portion, before the Vulgate cycle, and argued that the latter was developed out of the hypothetical work by providing a shorter pseudo-historical *Merlin* sequel, by substituting Lancelot for Gauvain as the principal hero, and by substituting Galaad for Perceval as the winner of the Grail quest.

Sommer's hypothesis has not won acceptance.[4] The facts on which he founded it can be better explained on the supposition that the episodes in the *Livre d'Artus* which are forecast in the Vulgate *Merlin* sequel which precedes it were invented to fulfil these anticipations, or borrowed from other sources for the same purpose. In fact, this is the explanation now generally accepted. The *Livre d'Artus* not only carries out these forecasts but continues the theme of Arthur's wars with the Saxons and reintroduces Merlin in characteristic roles. The author displays familiarity with the other branches of the Vulgate cycle. He copies the episode of the Isle Tournoyante from

---

[1] Ed. H. O. Sommer, *Vulgate Version* (Washington, 1913), vii. Freymond gave a full synopsis in *ZFSL*, xvii[1] (1895), 39–128. L. M. Gay criticized Sommer's text in *MP*, xiv. 430 ff. For comments see Freymond, loc. cit., pp. 1–38, and in *ZRP*, xvi (1892), 90–127; Bruce, i. 443–5; L. A. Paton, *Fairy Mythology of Arthurian Romance* (Boston, 1903), index I, *sub* Livre d'Artus.

[2] At the point in Sommer's edition of the Vulgate *Merlin*, p. 339, l. 4.

[3] Sommer, *Structure of the Livre d'Artus* (London, 1914).

[4] See criticism by Brugger in *ZFSL*, xlvii[2] (1925), 319–60.

the *Estoire del Saint Graal*.[1] But in the main he follows the chivalric pattern of the *Lancelot* proper, and at times appropriates whole incidents from it.

Thus the account of the two bridges into the land of Gorre built by Baudemagus is common to both romances.[2] So too are the stories of Morgain's establishing the Val sanz Retor and of the darkening of the castle of Escalon.[3] In the *Lancelot*[4] we are told how Gauvain was captured by the gigantic Carado and imprisoned in the Tour Douloureuse because he was alleged to have murdered the brother of Carado's mother. Lancelot, on his way to release Gauvain, rescued Driant le Gai from a coffer in which Carado's mother had confined him. All this is explained and elaborated in the *Livre d'Artus*.[5] We are told that Karacado was one of five Saxon brothers, that one of them had been slain by Gauvain and another by Driant le Gai, and that in revenge Driant had been placed in a coffer by Karacado's mother, and would not be set free except by the best knight in the world. Lucy Paton noted the skill with which the author of the *Livre* achieved a closer linking of these episodes than we find in the *Lancelot*. Let me quote:[6]

In the *Lancelot*, the object of the special adventure upon which Lancelot is engaged at the time when he went on his excursion into the Val sanz Retor is the release of Gawain from the Tour Douloureuse. The episode of the Val sanz Retor is merely incidental to this. The knight who can put an end to the enchantment of Ascalon le Tenebreus is he who will accomplish the adventure of the Tour Douloureuse. The knight who can perform the adventure of lifting from a certain river the bodies of two guiltless lovers who have been drowned there, is he who will be able to rescue Gawain from the Tour Douloureuse. In the *Livre d'Artus* it is said that only he can break the spell of the Val sanz Retor who has successfully accomplished the adventure of Ascalon le Tenebreus; and he who cannot perform the adventure of the valley will not succeed in taking from the water the bodies of the two guiltless lovers, nor in accomplishing the adventure of the Tour Douloureuse.

The Vulgate cycle was by no means the only source of the *Livre d'Artus*. The Giant Herdsman, arbitrarily represented as one of the shapes of Merlin, was taken from Chrétien's *Yvain*.[7] *Meraugis* furnished Gauvain's experience at the 'esplumeor Merlin',[8] and the *Vengeance Raguidel* supplied Lore de Branlant and her scheme to murder Gauvain with a sort of guillotine.[9] Probably Pellinor, the father of Perceval, was derived from the Prose *Tristan*. The lurid episode of the *Laide Semblance* (Hideous Image)[10] was an ingeniously elaborated version of the medieval Gorgon myth, which was variously reported by Walter Map, Gervase of Tilbury, the author of

---

[1] Sommer, *Vulgate Version*, vii. 299–303.   [2] Ibid. iv. 40 f.; vii. 144.
[3] Ibid. vii. 135 f.   [4] Ibid. iv. 87–138.
[5] Ibid. vii. 137.   [6] L. A. Paton, op. cit., p. 102.
[7] Sommer, *Vulgate Version*, vii. 124–6. Freymond in *ZFSL*, xvii.[1] 56, n. 1, and Zenker in *Beihefte ZRP*, lxx (1921), 245–7, think it is an independent tradition.
[8] See below, p. 374. Sommer, *Vulgate Version*, vii. 272.   [9] Ibid. pp. 94–107, 143.
[10] Ibid., pp. 150–62.

Mandeville's Travels, and others.[1] The author of the *Livre d'Artus* evidently noted in a manuscript of the Vulgate *Merlin* a brief reference to the *Laide Semblance* as a boundary mark which Judas (Maccabaeus?) had placed and which would not be removed till the adventures of the kingdom of Logres began to end.[2] Apparently the author recognized the reference and decided to use the legend on a big scale in his own work; he even prepared for it when he copied the Vulgate *Merlin* by substituting in a list of knights 'Greu the nephew of the Wise Lady of the Forest without Return' for the reading 'Agraveil the son of the Wise Lady of the Forest without Return'.[3] Now it is this Greu who in the *Livre d'Artus* is the hero of the elaborate adventure of the *Laide Semblance*, removes the death-dealing image from a river in Libya, marries the niece of the Wise Lady, and finally turns the fatal object over to Merlin, who drops it in the Gulf of Satellie.

Apart from this story the name Greu is unknown to Arthurian romance, and this suggests that it was taken over from some version of the medieval Gorgon story. Moreover, the geographical setting—Libya, Cyprus, the Gulf of Satalia—proves that the author knew the story as it was actually localized in the Levant. The Old French word for Greek is precisely *Greu* (nom. *Greus*); so it seems that the hero's racial designation was adopted, by error or design, as his name, and so a new Arthurian knight came into being.

Some scholars have claimed that other important elements are based on lost sources. Lucy Paton and R. S. Loomis see in the enchanted garden of the Queen of Danemarche a variation on the theme of Morgain's Val sanz Retor,[4] and Loomis argues for a relation between the Queen of Danemarche and the Queen of Meydelant in *Lanzelet*, since both enchantresses established a trap for the knights of Arthur's court in order to protect their sons. He also points out that the rescue of Floree from the giants by Gauvain, her restoration to her father, her love rivalry with Guingambresil's sister, and the hostility of Guingambresil to Gauvain correspond point for point to the story of Florete in *Floovant*.[5] Though *Floovant* belongs to the previous century, it does not seem a very likely source for the *Livre d'Artus*, and one may reasonably suspect a common origin in a lost Arthurian *conte*.

The author of the *Livre d'Artus* is to be credited with remarkably wide reading and no small literary talent in organizing his miscellaneous materials into a coherent narrative. Bruce noted as a characteristic trait the marked relish for sensual detail revealed in several scenes.[6] Evidently the romance was inspired by rather different motives from those which we detect in the *Suite du Merlin*.

---

[1] For references see *Mandeville's Travels*, ed. P. Hamelius, EETS 154 (London, 1923), ii. 34.
[2] Sommer, *Vulgate Version*, ii. 231.   [3] Ibid., p. 148.
[4] Paton, op. cit., pp. 81–84; Loomis, *Arthurian Tradition*, pp. 112 f., 163 f.
[5] Loomis, op. cit., pp. 82–84.
[6] Bruce, i. 445; Sommer, *Vulgate Version*, vii. 109 f., 190, 276.

THE PROSE *TRISTAN*

EUGÈNE VINAVER

THE French prose romance known in the Middle Ages as *Le Roman de Tristan de Léonois* has come down to us in an impressive number of manuscripts[1] and early printed editions.[2] The manuscripts fall into two main groups, the 'First Version', written between 1225 and 1235, which is relatively short, and an expanded 'Second Version' which belongs to the second half of the thirteenth century. The printed editions are based upon the second version.[3] The name of the author or authors is unknown. The first version is attributed in the manuscripts to Luce, lord of the castle of Gaut (Galt) near Salisbury, the second to Hélie (or Elie) de Boron described as a relative of Robert de Boron and, like the latter, a member of the Barres family in northern France. As early as 1886, however, Gaston Paris showed conclusively that the name of Hélie de Boron was fictitious.[4] As for Luce de Gaut, he may well have been a real person, but the attribution is at best doubtful.

The romance is, to all intents and purposes, a sequel to, and an elaboration of, the French Vulgate cycle. The similarities of style and manner are such that, but for the subject-matter, considerable sections of either work could have been incorporated in the other. Even the subject-matter is to some extent common to both. Tristan is a knight-errant of that peculiar variety of which Lancelot is the most notable example. The climax of his adventures is reached when he is solemnly received at the court of King

[1] For the most up-to-date list see B. Woledge, *Bibliographie des Romans et Nouvelles en prose française antérieurs à 1500* (Paris, 1954), pp. 122–5.

[2] See my *Études sur le Tristan en Prose* (Paris, 1925), pp. 58–62. The earliest edition appeared in 1489 at Rouen and the latest in 1586 at Paris. Since then the Prose *Tristan* has never been printed in full. For bibliography of critical works published before 1925 see my *Études*, pp. 62–89. Works published since that date include (besides those cited below) the following editions and critical studies: G. Bertoni, 'I "lais" del Romanzo in Prosa di Tristano', *SM*, n.s. ii (1929), 140–51; A. Hilka, 'Zum Fragment des altfranzösischen Prosaromans in der HS. Grenoble 866', *ZRP*, xlviii (1928), 483 f.; F. C. Johnson, 'An Edinburgh Prose *Tristan*: the *Bret*', *MLR*, xxviii (1933); E. S. Murell, 'The Death of Tristan from Douce MS. 189', *PMLA*, xliii (1928), 343–83; M. Pelaez, 'Un Frammento del Romanzo Francese in Prosa di Tristano', *SM*, n.s., ii (1929), 198–204; J. Séguy, 'Fragments mutilés du Roman de Tristan en prose', *BBSIA*, v (1953), 85–95.

[3] The most reliable guide to the text is E. Löseth's *Le Roman en prose de Tristan*, &c. (Paris, 1891), a remarkably accurate summary of the entire work as represented by the Paris manuscripts.

[4] *R*, xv (1886), 600–2; *Merlin*, ed. G. Paris, J. Ulrich, *SATF*, i, pp. xxviii–xxxvii.

Arthur and made a knight of the Round Table.[1] In the twelfth-century poems he owed allegiance to King Mark, and because he recognized King Mark as his overlord the fatal bond of love between him and Iseult was the cause of a conflict which death alone could resolve.[2] No such conflict exists in the prose romance outside the comparatively short passages borrowed from the poetical source. The character of Mark is altered: he is a villain and a traitor, an enemy of Arthurian knighthood, and it is Tristan's duty, not his misfortune, to act as his rival and keep him in check. In this Tristan has the wholehearted support of King Arthur and his knights, who look upon the rivalry between Mark and Tristan as a contest between a hero and a traitor. The tragic tale of unlawful love yields its place to a romance of chivalry with its characteristically simple scale of values, its exaltation of chivalric virtues, and its condemnation of all that lies beyond the narrow boundaries of the 'adventurous kingdom'.

The habit of expanding biographical romances by adding the lives of the hero's ancestors is reflected in a long preliminary section in which an attempt is made to trace the genealogy of the kings of Cornwall and of Léonois as far back as the first century A.D.[3] This is followed by the story of Tristan's birth, considerably embellished by new incidents—Merlin is introduced at this point as a rescuer of the newly born baby from his father's enemies—and by a significant reference to King Mark as the murderer of his own brother. Tristan's father, Meliadus, is murdered by two knights of the household of the Count of Norhout, and Tristan, accompanied by his tutor and servant Governal, goes to the court of Pharamont, King of Gaul. There he finds himself involved in an intrigue which threatens his life, and Governal takes him to the court of King Mark. From this point onwards the prose writer follows for a time the story as told in the poems, adding to it incidents and characters of a more strictly 'Arthurian' type. He seems to have known both the version used by Béroul and Eilhart (*l'estoire*) and the poem written by Thomas in the seventies or eighties of the twelfth century.[4] His indebtedness to the latter work is evident from the way in which he describes the last discovery of the lovers by King Mark[5] and from the episode of the abduction of Iseult by Palamède.[6] Another important link between the two versions is the treatment of the love-potion theme. Whereas in Béroul and Eilhart the separation of the lovers is made possible by the partial abatement of the potion,

[1] See Löseth, op. cit., p. 149.
[2] Thomas, *Tristan*, ed. Bédier, *SATF*, ii. 165 f.
[3] See Löseth, op. cit., pp. 3–16.
[4] On the poetical sources of the prose romance see my *Études*, pp. 8–20, and Löseth, op. cit., pp. xxv f. The passages containing the story as told in the poems were published in Bédier's edition of Thomas, ii. 321–95, from MS. Bib. Nat. fr. 103, and in part by Miss F. C. Johnson in *La Grant Ystoire de Monsignor Tristan* (Edinburgh, London, 1942).
[5] See Löseth, op. cit., § 284.
[6] Ibid., § 43.

in Thomas and in the prose romance they are allowed to part in spite of the supposedly unlimited efficacy of the magic drink.[1]

The agreement with the poetical tradition ends abruptly at a point which the author must have thought convenient for a long digression: Tristan's marriage to Iseult of the White Hands. One day as he is sailing with her and her brother Kahedin their boat founders upon a rock and they are forced to seek refuge in a strange country.[2] The adventures that follow have no connexion with the traditional love story apart from occasional references to Iseult of Ireland and her grief at the separation. She sees Tristan once more when he is brought back to court from the forest where he had been living as a fugitive, ill-treated by shepherds who had taken him for a madman and yet respected him for his strength and courage. At Tintagel the people run after him shouting, 'Veez le fol, veez le fol!' but he is recognized by his dog Houdenc and taken to Iseult, who restores him to health. Mark then orders him to leave Cornwall forever. He sails for Camelot, but refuses to appear at Arthur's court until he has won distinction as a knight-errant. When after a long series of adventures he is made a knight of the Round Table his name is found inscribed on the seat previously occupied by Le Morhout, whom he killed in single combat while still in Mark's service. We are reminded for the last time of the original Tristan romance in the story of the lovers' death. In one of the manuscripts, B.N. fr. 103, and in the early printed editions the story is told in much the same way as in the poems.[3] In all the other texts, however, it appears in a new form. The hero is not wounded by a poisoned arrow while fighting on behalf of his friend, Kahedin, in far-away Brittany, but killed treacherously by the King. As Tristan sits in Iseult's room singing a lay for her and playing it on his harp Mark rushes in with a poisoned lance in his hand and strikes him with it.

Gertrude Schoepperle thought that this ending was a survival of an early Celtic theme, 'a tradition, if not older than the poems, at least independent of them'. 'It is difficult to believe', she wrote, 'that it was written by a poet who was acquainted with the version of the poems. It represents a much simpler stage of the story, involving only three main characters—the husband, the wife, and the lover. The vengeance comes, as in the Celtic stories, from the injured husband [. . . .] It is hardly conceivable that this ending

---

[1] There is good reason to believe that in the primitive Tristan romance, as in Eilhart, the potion was meant to retain its full efficacy for a few years (4 in Eilhart, 3 in Béroul), during which the lovers could not live apart, and to abate partially at the end of that time so as to enable them to separate. Thomas must have suppressed this notion because he was less inclined to interpret events in terms of supernatural influences.

[2] See Löseth, op. cit., § 62. The name of the country is Servage; it is ruled by a giant Mabon, an enemy of the Round Table. Tristan defeats him and sets all the prisoners free. The country then receives the name of 'La Franchise Tristan'.

[3] Bédier, 'La Mort de Tristan et Iseut d'après le MS. 103 de la Bib. Nat. comparé au poème allemand d'Eilhart d'Oberg', *R*, xv. 481–510.

should have taken the place of the one we have in the poems after the tradition of Isolt's healing powers had become established by the incident of the
rudderless voyage, and after the second Isolt had come to constitute an element in the story.'[1] Kelemina thought likewise: the prose-writer's account
of the lovers' death was, in his opinion, a relic of an older version in which
there was no reference to Tristan's marriage.[2] It is conceivable, however,
that as long as Tristan's death was to occur at or near the court of King Mark
the author felt that he could easily dispense with the second Iseult whose
home was in Brittany. What calls for an explanation is not her absence from
the story, but the presence of King Mark, which causes the scene to be
shifted from Brittany to Cornwall. But in order to account for the part
assigned to King Mark all we need assume is that the author was anxious
to conclude the story with a final encounter between the hero and the villain
and so provide a fitting ending to a romance in which the hero was a victim
of the evil designs of a wicked king. There is no need to imagine behind this
version a primitive Celtic theme not previously used; it is enough to realize
the extent of the transformation which the story was bound to undergo at
the prose-writer's hands. Nor is this transformation so complete as to leave
no trace of the original tale. Grievously wounded, Tristan takes refuge in
Dinas's castle. He sends for Mark and begs him to let him see Iseult for the
last time. When she comes he has but a few hours to live, and all Iseult's
skill and care cannot save him. In this way the two characteristic traits of
the original theme are preserved: the separation which precedes the death
scene, and the fatal delay which prevents Iseult from using her healing
powers.

Another striking feature of the death-scene is the blending of the Tristan
tradition with the chivalric ideology of Arthurian romances. Tristan's first
thought is of chivalry. He asks Sagremor to bring him his sword and his shield
and says: 'Today I take leave of chivalry which I have loved and honoured.'
He then begs Sagremor to give his last greetings to his faithful fellow-knights,
Palamède, Dinadan, and Lancelot, and to take his armour to King Arthur:
'Farewell, my good sword, I commend you to God for I shall see you no
more', he says, kissing the blade. But his last thoughts are for Iseult: 'What
will you do when I am gone? Can Iseult live without Tristan?' And Iseult
replies, 'If suffering alone could kill I should have died a thousand deaths.'[3]
At this point there are some variations in the texts, but according to the
majority of manuscripts it is Tristan's last embrace which causes Iseult's
death: Tristan 'estraint la royne de tant de force que il li fist le cuer partir';

---

[1] G. Schoepperle, *Tristan and Isolt, A Study of the Sources of the Romance* (Frankfurt, London,
1913; reprinted Burt Franklin, New York, 1959), pp. 9 f., 439–42.

[2] J. Kelemina, *Untersuchungen zur Tristansage* (Leipzig, 1910), pp. ix, 71–78.

[3] See Löseth, op. cit., p. 387. 'S'il suffisait de la douleur, je serais morte plus d'une fois, car je crois
que jamais dame n'a été si affligée que je ne le sois encore davantage.'

the same manuscripts add, however, that both Tristan and Iseult died *par amour* and so restore to the scene its genuine meaning. As the people of Cornwall behold the two lovers lying dead they say that this is the greatest marvel that ever occurred in any land: 'li uns est finé par l'autre; bien ont mostré apertement que l'amours dont il s'entr' amoient n'estoit pas a gas; tant com li siecle durera sera parlé de cest amor'.[1] Even Mark, overcome by sorrow ('si dolanz que pou qu'il ne meurt de doulour'), recognizes the miracle of love: 'Et por ce qu'il s'entramoient tant en lor vie con je vous cont, les fist le roi Marc metre ensemble, por qu'ils fussent en lor mort aisié aussint con il furent en lor vie.'[2]

It is significant that passages such as these should have come from the same pen as the considerably longer 'Arthurian' portion of the work, its 'endless descriptions of jousts and tournaments, of knight-errant adventures and of love-affairs conducted in the fashion of a highly organized society'.[3] J. D. Bruce remarks that Tristan is more lifelike than Lancelot because 'as a lover, his fidelity is not above reproach'. Tristan's love intrigue with Segurade's wife is certainly the kind of diversion that would be unthinkable in a Lancelot romance. But the reason for such diversions is not so much the author's concern with realism as his lack of concern with any particular conception of a lover's duty towards his lady or, for that matter, with any doctrine of courtly behaviour. He shifts the interest from all such things to the adventurous mode of living of knights-errant. Emotional digressions are by no means absent, and there are even some fine examples of tragic lyricism. A new character, Palamède, is added, whose unrequited love for Iseult introduces a sombre note in an otherwise idyllic picture of chivalric life. Palamède is Iseult's faithful knight, doomed never to be loved in return, and yet invariably generous and loyal to his successful rival, Tristan. But while uttering many pitiful laments he never embarks upon sophisticated analyses of feeling in the true 'courtly' style. With him as with most of the other characters of the Prose *Tristan* the fantastic world of Arthurian romance is ever present, but not the doctrine of courtly love—the enchanted 'secret orchard' which the initiated alone were allowed to enter. Occasionally, even the Arthurian setting seems to break down, and we are introduced to incidents and situations totally unlike any romance of chivalry. The story of Tristan's grandmother, Chelinde, is a curious medley of themes drawn from classical antiquity, from the *fabliau* tradition, and from oriental fairy-tales, and it is no accident that Boccaccio included an adaptation of it in the

---

[1] 'They died for each other, and in doing so proved that their love was no light one. As long as the world endures, it will be on the lips of men.' See Löseth, op. cit., pp. 388 f.

[2] 'And because, as I have told you, they loved each other so deeply in life, King Mark decreed their burial in one tomb, so that they should have their desire in death as they had in life.' See Löseth, op. cit., p. 389.

[3] Bruce, i. 484 f., 489.

Decameron.[1] Tristan's own adventure with King Pharamont's daughter[2] strikes an equally unorthodox note. It belongs to a type of literature which, generally speaking, left little or no mark on Arthurian romance proper, and its presence in the Prose *Tristan* is an indication of the author's constant readiness to emancipate himself from traditional patterns. Perhaps the most striking example of his freedom from these is his attempt to ridicule Arthurian chivalry by introducing another new character, Dinadan, a friend and companion of Tristan's, noted for his happy and cheerful disposition, and yet determined to call in question the wisdom of the Arthurian world. Already in the 'first version' of the romance we find Dinadan in this unusual role: at the tournament of the Castle of Maidens he pokes fun at Tristan, who has just been thrown from his horse; and when the next day he is brutally punished for it he wonders whether the friendship of a knight-errant is not more dangerous than his enmity. Most of Dinadan's observations, however, occur in the second, or expanded, version—mainly in the long interpolation containing Mark's adventures in Logres.[3] His speeches would fill a small volume, but the gist of his criticisms may be summarized thus: 'A love that torments and murders its servants merely punishes them for their folly. . . . May God protect me against such a love! . . . The love that is in my heart gives me joy, delight and merriment. . . . It never deceives me because I never ask of it more than it can give. . . . And never do I lose my heart: ceul ci sont en trop fort prison qui pensent a dame et a damoiselle.' The chivalric code of duty, the rules of knight-errantry, and the peculiar etiquette of single combats provide occasions for equally caustic comments. Dinadan wonders why knights-errant always greet each other—most discourteously—by saying 'Sire chevalier, a jouster vous convient' before they know whether there is any reason why they should fight at all: 'Se Diex me saut, ce saluz n'est mie trop cortois.' The necessity of fighting battles simply in order to display valour is seriously questioned: 'Ma couardise me fet vivre, et vostre hardiment vos fet orendroit estre a pié.' Dinadan seeks the meaning of things—*le sens du monde*—and knows that none is to be found in the world to which he so unwillingly belongs.

Nor is it on the ideological plane alone that the Prose *Tristan* marks a departure from the conventional forms of Arthurian romance. Critics have not so far made any distinction between the structural peculiarities of the Vulgate cycle and those of its continuations, nor indeed any attempt to dis-

[1] Bruce, 'A Boccaccio Analogue in the Old French Prose Tristan', *RR*, i (1910), 384 ff.

[2] See Löseth, op. cit., § 26. 'Averti par Gouvernal, Tristan refuse l'amour de la princesse, qui s'en désespère. Un jour, elle l'embrasse; il repousse ses caresses; aux cris de la princesse on accourt. Elle l'accuse d'avoir essayé de lui faire violence.'

[3] In Löseth this section (210) begins on p. 152. For full text of Dinadan's criticisms of the manners and customs of Arthurian knights see my *Études*, pp. 91–98, and my edition of Malory's *Works* (Oxford, 1947), iii. 1462 f., 1475–83, 1493, 1498–1501, 1507.

cover whether the form of the cyclic romances developed in any way in the course of the thirteenth century.[1] In recent years some progress has been made towards a better understanding of the processes involved in the building up of the *Lancelot-Grail* which, as a result, has ceased to be regarded as an indiscriminate accumulation of episodic matter. The process described by Ferdinand Lot as *entrelacement*[2] has been found to represent something more than a gratuitous complication. But the analysis has not been extended to other works of the same kind, with the result that one of the fundamental aesthetic issues of thirteenth-century prose literature has remained to this day unexplored. Until some further progress has been made little more than the most general indications can be given. One thing, however, is certain: the Prose *Tristan* shows a gradual deterioration of the method of 'interweaving'. Typical of this method is the care with which narrative threads are picked up, sometimes after a long interval, lengthened, dropped again, and taken up after another interval. It is a method which can only be practised with success by an author capable of carrying the entire complex web of the narrative in his head and seeing as it were its various strands alternating upon a vast canvas. The risk of letting the whole fabric disintegrate increases as the work grows in size and complexity, and the Prose *Tristan* enables us to see what happens when the disintegration takes place. Loose threads are scattered everywhere: quests are undertaken and abandoned, interpolations occur that have no bearing on any of the earlier or later episodes, and the work as a whole tends to become a vast *roman à tiroirs*. One can find in it some complete romances which, once removed from their context, can be read as self-contained works. The experiment has been successfully tried with *Alixandre l'Orphelin*[3] and could be tried equally well with a number of other 'stories in a story'. A typical example of this type of narrative is a tournament involving a great number of knights and lasting several days.[4] From the nature of things, a tournament is primarily a game, a means of testing the skill and the valour of the knights who take part in it, and there is no reason why their encounters, whether in single combat or in a mêlée, should have any repercussions on their subsequent adventures. But while in the Prose *Lancelot* tournaments generally have some connexion with at least one of the themes of the story, in the Prose *Tristan* they are divorced from the general scheme of the work in much the same way as the pageantry of

---

[1] Until recently it has been common to describe the French prose romances as incoherent compositions devoid of any artistic value except perhaps that of their language. It was largely this assessment that led certain scholars, particularly of the German school, to regard the extant texts as corrupt versions of works which have not come down in their original form. See my introduction to *Le Roman de Balain*, ed. M. D. Legge (Manchester, 1942), pp. ix–xi.

[2] F. Lot, *Étude sur le Lancelot en prose* (Paris, 1918), pp. 17–28.

[3] See below, p. 353.

[4] The most conspicuous examples are the tournaments which take place at the Château des Pucelles (Löseth, pp. 100–9), at Sorelois (ibid., pp. 195–201), and at Louvezerp (ibid., pp. 272–5).

real tournaments at the close of the Middle Ages was divorced from real life. In both cases we witness a decline of a once powerful tradition: of chivalry as an institution and of the romance of chivalry as a form of narrative art. But because in the sphere of fiction form is perforce more fragile than matter and less easily adaptable to the changes of taste and fashion, long before the legends of Lancelot and of Tristan lost their appeal the elaborate technique of the cyclic compositions gave way to patterns suited to less refined tastes.

This was no doubt the reason why the prose romance of Tristan so easily superseded all the poetical versions of the legend. From the thirteenth century onwards it became the only recognized form of the Tristan story, and it is only in comparatively recent times that the names of Tristan and Iseult have come to be associated in the minds of European readers with the tragic love story told by medieval poets. As late as 1812 Creuzé de Lesser, the author of a poem in twenty cantos entitled *Les Chevaliers de la Table Ronde*, was unaware of the existence of the French poetical tradition and thought that it was his privilege to be the first French poet to deal with the theme in verse: 'Lancelot et Tristan sont dans tous les poèmes excepté dans les nôtres. Du moins j'aurai essayé de réparer cet oubli.'[1] Not that the medieval French poems were entirely unknown at that date: as early as 1804 Walter Scott had produced his edition of *Sir Tristrem* with 'a description and abstract of two ancient fragments of French metrical romances on the subject of Sir Tristrem', now known as the Douce fragments of the poem of Thomas;[2] but it was not until 1823 that Béroul's poem was revealed in volume II of von der Hagen's edition of Gottfried, and it was only in 1835 that the fragments of Thomas saw the light of day in print in Francisque Michel's *Recueil*.[3] The contrast between this slow discovery of the poems and the wide diffusion of the prose version is indeed striking. Throughout Europe the Prose *Tristan* was read and imitated, and its *rifacimenti* in the various European languages often became classics in the countries in which they appeared.[4] The most important of these imitations outside France was Sir Thomas Malory's *Book of Sir Tristram*, published by Caxton in 1485 as part of a volume entitled *Le Morte Darthur* (Books VIII–XII). Not only did Malory

---

[1] M. Creuzé de Lesser, *Les Chevaliers de la Table Ronde, Poème en vingt chants tiré des vieux Romanciers* (Paris, 1812), p. xviii.

[2] *Sir Tristrem, A Metrical Romance of the Thirteenth Century . . . edited from the Auchinleck MS.* by *Walter Scott* (Edinburgh).

[3] *Tristan, Recueil de ce qui reste des Poèmes relatifs à ses aventures*, &c.

[4] The Prose *Tristan* is the main source of *La Tavola Ritonda*, ed. Polidori (1864–5), of the German 'Volksbuch', *Die Histori von Herren Tristan und der schoenen Iso den von Irlande*, ed. Benz (1912), of the Spanish *Libro del Esforçado Cavallero Don Tristan de Leonis*, ed. Bonilla y San Martín (1912), of the Danish *En meget smuk Historie om den aedle og tappre Tristran*, ed. Rahbek (1830), and of the Russian *Trishchan i Izhotta* (see *R*, xviii. 312). The *Tavola Ritonda* is based on an Italian translation; see Parodi, *Il Tristano Riccardiano* (Bologna, 1896). For Malory's version see my edition of his *Works*, pp. 365–846.

succeed in preserving the story for English readers, but the impact of his version upon English poetry was such that in nineteenth-century England no other form of the legend attracted much attention. Hence the survival of many features of the French Prose Romance in Tennyson's *The Last Tournament* and Swinburne's *Tristram of Lyonesse*.[1] Perhaps, as Sir Edmund Chambers once said, 'Malory would have done better to have left the *Tristan* alone'.[2] For if he had, English poets might have sought their inspiration elsewhere, as Wagner did when he chose Gottfried von Strassburg's poem as his model. Of the original character of the Tristan poems, of the blending of magic and tragedy which had made the legend great, few traces remain in the prose romance and fewer still in its modern adaptations. But when all is said,

> La matière est si très notable
> Qu'elle amende tout le méfait.

[1] On Matthew Arnold's *Tristram and Iseult* see I. E. Sells, *Matthew Arnold and France* (Cambridge, Mass., 1933), pp. 140 ff.

[2] E. K. Chambers, *Sir Thomas Malory*, English Assoc. Pamphlet No. 51 (London, 1922), p. 5.

MISCELLANEOUS FRENCH PROSE ROMANCES

CEDRIC E. PICKFORD

Palamedes

PALAMEDES[1] was written after the first version of the Prose *Tristan*, in which the Saracen knight Palamedes first appeared, but before the second or cyclic version, which was itself influenced by *Palamedes*. MS. B.N. fr. 335 calls the romance 'Le Livre de Meliadus et de Guiron le Courtois et de Palamedes' (f. 65ʳ), but the title *Palamedes* was given to the work as early as 1240, witness the reference to the 'liber Palamidis' in a letter of 5 February of that year by the Emperor Frederick II.[2] From the thirteenth century onwards, however, the romance was often presented in two parts: *Meliadus*, named after the father of Tristan, who plays an important role in the first part, and *Guiron le Courtois*, named after the principal figure in the latter part. The author is unknown, though the prologue,[3] after mentioning the romances attributed to Gautier Map, Robert de Borron, Luce de Gast, and Gasse le Blond (doubtless Wace), says that *Palamedes* is the work of Elie de Borron, companion of Robert de Borron. Of course, none of these attributions should be taken seriously.[4]

The narrative opens with the arrival at Rome, of Esclabor, a pagan noble from Babylon, and his saving the life of the emperor. He travels on to Logres and reaches Camelot at the time of Arthur's coronation, where simultaneously Pharamont, King of Gaul and Arthur's enemy, also arrives. At the

---

[1] There is no modern edition of this work. A detailed summary was given by E. Löseth in his *Roman en Prose de Tristan . . . analysé critique d'après les manuscrits de Paris* (Paris, 1890), pp. iii–iv, 433–68, 475, 481–5, 487–91. He gives here a list of the Paris manuscripts, and of others in *Le Tristan et le Palamède des manuscrits français du British Museum*, pp. 1–2, 29–32, and in *Le Tristan et le Palamède des manuscrits de Rome et de Florence*, pp. 3 f., 6, 83–136. Other manuscripts are: Brussels, Archives générales, 1411; Modena, Bib. Est. 42; Marseilles, Bib. Mun. 1106; Turin, Bib. Mun. R 1622; Vannes, Arch. du Morbihan, I F; Venice, Bib. S. Marco, Fr. IX; Privas, Arch. de l'Ardèche, I (F 7); Geneva, collection Bodmer (formerly Phillipps 8344). Parts of the romance were printed under the titles of *Meliadus* and *Gyron le Courtois* in Paris in the first half of the sixteenth century. For discussion see Bruce, ii. 20–25.

[2] For text of letter see H. L. D. Ward, *Catalogue of Romances in the Department of Manuscripts at the British Museum*, i. 366.

[3] Quoted from various manuscripts in Ward, op. cit. i. 365; Paulin Paris, *Manuscrits françois de la Bibliothèque du Roi*, ii. 346; Hucher, *Saint Graal*, i. 156; Löseth, *Tristan . . . Rome et Florence*, pp. 83–85.

[4] *Merlin*, ed. G. Paris, J. Ulrich, i, pp. xxxiii–xxxvii.

Château du Pin au Géant the Kings of Northumberland and Ireland hold a tournament in the course of which Meliadus, King of Leonois, wounds his rival, Le Bon Chevalier Sans Peur, and abducts his mistress, the Queen of Scotland. The King of Scotland attacks Meliadus with the aid of Le Bon Chevalier and several kings, but at a critical moment Meliadus receives help from Guiron le Courtois.[1] Peace is then restored, the Queen of Scotland returns to her husband, and Meliadus sets out in search of his deliverer. Guiron meanwhile displays his prowess at two great tournaments, then rescues the wife of his friend Danain from King Lac, and in spite of her advances remains loyal to Danain. This does not prevent the latter from abducting Guiron's lady, but Guiron recovers her and a reconciliation follows. Separating from Danain at a cross-roads, Guiron and his lady are taken captive and she dies in prison giving birth to their son. The eventual liberation of Guiron and the child by Lancelot is forecast by the romancer, and is fulfilled in a fifteenth-century version.[2] Danain remains a prisoner in the valley of the two towers.

The romance concludes with the statement that this is the end of the first book, that the second will extend up to the beginning of the Grail quest, and the third will end after the death of Arthur. Though this suggests that *Palamedes* was intended to explain and elaborate the Prose *Tristan* and the Prose *Lancelot*, it fails to carry out this purpose. It consists mainly of ambushes, imprisonments, abductions, unrelated to any larger scheme. Meliadus, Guiron, and their friends are ready for any adventure of love or battle which comes their way, but seem to be guided only by whim. The lack of guiding principle and controlling pattern made it easy for scribes to omit, rewrite, or add episodes.[3] In one group of manuscripts there is a repetition in slightly different form of an earlier passage.[4]

There are many reminiscences of the *Lancelot* and *Tristan* and, in the later versions, of *Perceforest*. Though some figures, such as the Morholt and Palamedes himself, had already appeared in these texts, the dominant aim of the author was to make up out of whole cloth the romantic history of an older generation, the generation of Uterpendragon. Thus we have the stories of Lac, father of Erec, Meliadus, father of Tristan, Esclabor le Mescogneu, father of Palamedes, to name but a few of the knights of the 'Old Table', as they came to be called in the Italian romances.

Palamedes contains a few remarkable scenes, such as that in which Guiron, about to succumb to the amorous advances of Danain's wife, is reminded by the inscription on his sword-hilt of the glory of loyalty and the shame of treachery; or that in which Breus sans Pitié visits the cavern in which the

---

[1] Löseth, *Roman en prose de Tristan*, p. 447.   [2] MS. B.N. fr. 363; Löseth, p. 468.
[3] The confused state of the manuscript tradition is reflected in Löseth's analysis of the many variant versions.   [4] Löseth, p. 455.

ancestors of Guiron, kings of France, lie. Thus, in spite of its defects, *Palamedes* achieved a prodigious popularity, especially in Italy. As already noted, the emperor Frederick II acknowledged with thanks the receipt of a copy. Portions of it were incorporated by Rusticiano da Pisa in his compilation, as we shall presently see. The episode of the cavern was rendered into Italian verse with some changes in the first half of the fourteenth century, and has been published as *Febusso e Breusso*. *Palamedes* was the source of some of the best scenes in Boiardo's *Orlando Innamorato*, and was Ariosto's favourite among all the Arthurian romances.[1]

The Compilation of Rusticiano da Pisa

This work,[2] like *Palamedes*, is a confused patchwork of adventures narrated without regard to chronology. After the initial episode of the triumph of Branor le Brun (who was 120 years old and a knight of the 'Old Table') over the champions of Arthur's court, the author interpolates a version of the story of the rivalry of Tristan and Palamedes, and this leads up to the combat of Tristan with Lancelot at the Perron Merlin. Tristan mistakes Lancelot for his rival, but when the heroes recognize each other, Lancelot brings Tristan to Camelot to be installed as a knight of the Round Table.[3] This material derived from the Prose *Tristan* is followed by an earlier episode from the same source—Tristan's victory over thirty-six knights of Morgain.[4] The author goes on without a break to give a much later episode in which Palamedes frees his rival from prison.[5] An adventure of Galaad is inserted, to be followed by a tale of Erec and Enide.[6] The theme of the enmity between Palamedes and Habé le Renommé is introduced. More or less disconnected episodes conclude with the statement that the narrative will return to Branor le Brun, but instead the whole *Palamedes*, with its prologue, is added.[7] Some manuscripts end with the escape of the Bon Chevalier sans Peur from the Val de Servage and the renaming of the valley.[8] Other manuscripts[9] contain further exploits of Tristan, Lancelot, and Palamedes. They deliver several of their companions from prison, and all return to Camelot for the feast of All Saints. A damsel riding a white mule arrives and presents Arthur with a

---

[1] *Febusso e Breusso*, ed. Lord Vernon (Florence, 1847); P. Rajna, *Fonti dell' Orlando Furioso*, 2nd ed. (Florence, 1900); E. G. Gardner, *Arthurian Legend in Italian Literature* (London, 1930), pp. 269, 279; G. Bertoni, *Nuovi Studi su Matteo Maria Boiardo* (Bologna, 1904), ch. vii.

[2] There is no modern edition, but Löseth in his *Roman en Prose de Tristan* gives a summary on pp. 423–75, 487–91, and supplemented it in his study of the Brit. Mus. MSS., pp. 4, 30–32, and in his study of the Rome and Florence MSS., pp. 4, 83–136. Besides fragments in Florence, Bib. Laur. Ash. 123; B.N. fr. 12599, there are also complete MSS. B.N. fr. 340, 355, 1463, and Brit. Mus. Add. 23930. The second part only is found in B.N. fr. 357 and Arsenal 3478. For discussion see Bruce, ii. 26–28; H. L. D. Ward, *Catalogue of Romances*, i. 369–71. The two parts were printed in Paris as *Gyron le Courtoys* and *Meliadus de Leonnoys*.   [3] Löseth, *Roman en Prose de Tristan*, § 196–203.

[4] Löseth, § 108.   [5] Löseth, § 445.
[6] Löseth, § 448, 627.   [7] Löseth, p. 432.
[8] B.N. fr. 340; Arsenal 3478.   [9] B.N. fr. 340 and 355.

crown to place on the head of the knight who overthrew ten others at the Fontaine du Val de Pleurs. Meliadus receives the prize and surrenders it to the queen. Five days later each knight departs to his own country.

In his preamble the author announces that he translated his work from 'the book of Messire Edward, King of England, at the time that he passed beyond the sea in the service of our Lord God to conquer the Holy Sepulchre'.[1] In the epilogue he refers to other sources which he describes as 'pluseurs hystoires' and 'pluseurs croniques' from which he has made extracts at the request of King Edward.[2] He adds that the multiplicity of his models accounts for the incoherent nature of his compilation. It seems, therefore, that he was responsible for grouping the various extracts into a single work. Possibly his main source was a manuscript of *Palamedes*, or a cyclic version of the Prose *Tristan*, or a conflation of the two. The parts of the compilation which have not been traced to extant sources consist usually of rescues from prison or sumptuous festivities at Arthur's court. Of greater interest is the opening episode in which the aged Branor le Brun discomfits the knights of the Round Table. It emphasizes the glory of a mysterious past, as does the cavern scene in *Palamedes*. In fact, the author takes care to preserve the atmosphere of that romance in the narrative which he constructed around it.

The Italian author names himself Rusticien de Pise and is generally identified with the Rusticiano or Rustichello da Pisa who, when in captivity at Genoa in 1298, wrote down in French an account of the travels of his fellow prisoner, Marco Polo. The opening phrases of the prologues to both works are very similar.[3] The Arthurian compilation was doubtless the earlier work, for fragments of it survive in thirteenth-century manuscripts, and if any reliance may be placed on Rusticiano's statement that he worked at the request of Prince Edward, he probably began his task soon after acquiring the manuscript.[4]

Rusticiano's romance was expanded in MS. B.N. fr. 340, fo. 207^r, by the pathetic tale of the death of King Marc. The continuator, who calls himself 'cil de Borron', relates how, after the death of Arthur and Lancelot, Marc destroyed Joyous Garde and Camelot, and how, in search of the four surviving companions who were living as hermits, he was slain by a knight of the lineage of Ban, and none dared bury him in consecrated ground. Such a tale of catastrophe affords a powerful and not inappropriate ending to the downfall of Arthur and his fellowship.

---

[1] Löseth, pp. 423 f. Prince Edward of England set out on Crusade in Aug. 1270, succeeded to the throne in 1272, and returned to England in 1274. For Edward's interest in Arthurian matters see *Spec*, xxviii (1953), 114–27, and below, pp. 554, 558 f.   [2] Löseth, p. 472.

[3] P. Paris, *Manuscrits françois de la Bibliothèque du Roi*, ii. 355 ff.; Ward, *Catalogue of Romances*, i. 367 ff.

[4] For an interesting conjecture on the subsequent history of this codex see E. G. Gardner, *Arthurian Legend*, p. 154.

The popularity of Rusticiano's compilation is revealed in various ways. The opening incident of Branor le Brun was rendered into Greek iambic tetrameters about 1300.[1] A series of illustrations, of which eight scenes remain, was painted on the walls of the castle of St. Floret near Issoire about 1350.[2] The romance influenced the Italian *Tavola Ritonda*, the *Orlando Innamorato*, *Gyrone il Cortese*, and the Spanish *Don Tristán de Leonís*.[3]

'Les Prophécies de Merlin'

This work,[4] composed between 1272 and 1279, consists largely of prophecies placed in the mouth of Merlin, but his mysterious pronouncements refer chiefly to political events which occurred during the twelfth and thirteenth centuries in Italy and the Holy Land, and have little or nothing to do with Geoffrey of Monmouth's treatment of the wizard, or with the vast accumulation of prophecies in many languages attributed to Merlin.[5] It is attributed in the manuscripts to 'Maistre Richart d'Irlande', who, according to the prologue, translated the work from Latin into French at the command of the Emperor Frederick, the same, of course, who received a copy of *Palamedes*. Though there was a 'magister Ricardus' at Frederick's court, Lucy Paton demonstrated that the *Prophécies de Merlin* was written by a Venetian, probably a Minorite, who flourished at least two decades after Frederick's death and who referred to him in unflattering terms as one who would die in contumacy.

The prophecies are grouped in over 300 short conversations between Merlin and his scribes—Blaise, Maistre Antoine, Bishop Tholomer, the 'Sage Clerc', and Maistre Petronne. The fact that many of these conversations begin with similar phrases, such as, 'Je vueil que tu metes en escrit, ce dit Merlin', 'I wish that thou set down in writing, said Merlin', made rearrangement easy, with resultant confusion in some manuscripts. Nevertheless, there is certainly a plan, and the Italian copies make a division into five books:[6]

---

[1] The best edition is in A. Ellissen, *Nachtrag zum ersten Teil des Versuchs einer Polyglotte der europäischen Poesie* (Leipzig, 1846). See also Bruce, ii. 28, n. 24, for other editions.

[2] R. S. and L. H. Loomis, *Arthurian Legends in Medieval Art* (New York, 1938), pp. 57–61, figs. 92–95, 99–105.

[3] E. G. Gardner, *Arthurian Legend*, pp. 49, 154, 157 n., 277, 310; W. J. Entwistle, *Arthurian Legend in the Literatures of the Spanish Peninsula* (London, New York, 1925), pp. 109, 113 f.

[4] A classified list and description of the manuscripts, as well as a list of early printed editions, is given by Lucy Allen Paton in her edition, based on MS. 593, Bib. Mun., Rennes, published by the Mod. Lang. Assoc. (New York, London, 1926), i. 3–50. The manuscript described as a 'Text of Merlin's Prophecies' in *Spec*, xxiii (1948), 102 f., contains only a part of Geoffrey's *Historia*. Besides the comprehensive treatment in Miss Paton's edition, see Brugger's comments on the work in *ZFSL*, lx (1935–7), 213–23; lxi (1937–8), 321–62, 486–501; lxii (1938), 40–73; *ZRP*, lvi (1936), 563–603; *AR*, xx (1936), 359–448.

[5] R. H. Taylor, *Political Prophecy in England* (New York, 1911). P. Zumthor, *Merlin le Prophète* (Lausanne, 1943), pp. 49–114.   [6] *Prophecies*, ed. Paton, i. 6–8.

PLATE 8

MORGAIN LA FÉE AND ALIXANDRE L'ORPHELIN
Pierpont Morgan Library 41. *c.* 1468

LANCELOT AT THE PONT DE CORBENIC
Pierpont Morgan Library 41. *c.* 1468

A. Prophecies which Merlin delivered to Maistre Antoine (Paton, i, chs. i–cxx).

B. An account of the entombment of Merlin by the Dame du Lac, together with some prophecies which he gave her, and some earlier prophecies given to Maistre Antoine (Paton, i, chs. cxxi–cxxxvi).

C. Prophecies of the entombed Merlin to Meliadus; prophecies reported by Meliadus to Maistre Antoine and the 'Sage Clerc' (Paton, i, chs. cxxxvii–ccxxiv).

D. Illustrations of Merlin's wisdom reported to Perceval by the hermit Helias (Paton, i, chs. ccxxv–cclxvii).

E. The book of Merlin, entrusted to Helias for Perceval and delivered to the 'Sage Clerc' by Perceval; prophecies of Merlin to Meliadus (Paton, i, chs. cclxviii–cccxxviii).

The original purpose of the *Prophécies* was reform. The book inculcates obedience to the Church, but attacks the cupidity of the papal curia and the luxurious living of the friars. It takes advantage of the feverish contemporary interest in prophecies, whether those of Michael Scot or Joachim of Flora, to comment on events of the past and to predict apocalyptic wonders. The author realized the necessity of relieving the monotony of these solemn matters by varying the interlocutors as we have just observed, and the collection of anecdotes which Helias tells Perceval to illustrate the uncanny wisdom of Merlin—anecdotes similar to those in Geoffrey's *Vita Merlini* and the early French romances—is less weighty, more homely in tone. For instance, a merchant complains that he has been cheated by money-changers. The accused, summoned to court, deny having seen the merchant before. The judge, at a loss whom to believe, turns to Merlin, who fastens the guilt on the money-changers by showing foreign coin in their coffers.

Furthermore, the author of the *Prophécies*, who must have been himself steeped in the French prose romances, exploited their popularity and not only introduced well-known figures like Blaise, Perceval, Dinadan, and Meliadus as participants in the dialogues, but also retold famous tales such as that of the entombment of Merlin. In certain manuscripts other romantic histories were incorporated. That of Alixandre l'Orphelin, found also in a late version of the Prose *Tristan* (whence Malory derived it), is given at length.[1] The hero is a Cornish knight, a cousin of Tristan. His father was stabbed to death by King Mark, and Alixandre learns of this on the day of his knighting and swears revenge. Though the thread of his adventures is frequently interrupted by other episodes, we read how he met various knights in combat, defended a damsel, killed her persecutor, was imprisoned by the lustful Morgain, was released by the grateful damsel, and defended her lands, but fell in love with Aylies la Belle Pelerine. Also interwoven through the

---

[1] *Prophecies*, ed. Paton, i. 375–421; ii. 268–70, 275 f. Edited by H. O. Sommer in Malory, *Morte Darthur* (London, 1891), iii. 259–312, and by C. E. Pickford, *Alixandre l'Orphelin* (Manchester, 1951).

narrative fabric is the long account of the tournament held at Sorelois by Galehault, lord of the Loingtaines Isles,[1] which is likewise given in the Prose *Tristan* and Malory. Not only are these narratives bound together by the principle of *entrelacement*, but they are tied to the Prose *Lancelot* by referring them to the period when the false Guenièvre had supplanted the true, and are likewise tied to the romance of Palamedes by making its hero and his brother Saphar have a brush with Alixandre l'Orphelin and take part in the hurly-burly at Sorelois.

One curious feature of this medley is provided by the rivalry and the enchantments of Morgain and the other fays, Sebille, the Dame d'Avalon, and the Queen of Norgales, 'a company unequalled in *felonie*'.[2] Not only do they plot against Lancelot, Hector, and Lamorat, but they quarrel among themselves, and the Dame d'Avalon amuses herself by forcing the other fays by virtue of a magic ring to disrobe, and then mocks their shame.

A unique manuscript of the fifteenth century, Arsenal 5229, is a conglomerate of material from many sources.[3] Principally concerned with three brothers with the surname of Le Brun, it brings in a Saxon invasion, the mockeries of Dinadan, the enchantments of Morgain, Iseut in the role of an incendiary, the chase of the Beste Glatissant,[4] and copper automata operated by levers and a box of quicksilver! Needless to say, chronology counts for little in this chaos.

The *Prophécies*, even in its original form, possessed small literary merit. Ch.-V. Langlois described the style as 'une détestable logorrhée d'homme sans culture littéraire ni autre, qui s'adresse à des illettrés'.[5] Nevertheless, the work should not be dismissed too lightly. It went through a number of printed editions between 1498 and 1528 and was translated into Italian.[6] It must have had a strong appeal in its day, and as an expression of certain absorbing interests and prevailing fashions it is for us highly instructive.

The Compilations of Jehan Vaillant and Michel Gonnot

The desire of noble bibliophiles to acquire large, comprehensive collections of prose romance resulted in two productions. The first was made by Jehan Vaillant de Poitiers at the command of Louis II, Duc de Bourbon, and survives in longer form in B.N. fr. 358–63 and in a shorter form in the library of M. Bodmer of Geneva. Both were copied in the second half of the fifteenth century, but the latter bears the date 1391, when we may presume the compilation was made.

[1] *Prophecies*, ed. Paton, i. 376–86; ii. 251–76.
[2] *Prophecies*, ed. Paton, i. 402, 415–17, 421.
[3] *Prophecies*, ed. Paton, i. 28–35, 423–48.
[4] See *Perlesvaus*, ed. Nitze, ii. 134–44.
[5] Langlois, *Connaissance de la Nature*, nouv. éd. (Paris, 1927), p. 214.
[6] *Prophecies*, ed. Paton, i. 39–50.

The longer version provided a pseudo-historical setting, beginning with the story of the *Grantz Geanz* who inhabited Albion before the conquest by Brutus,[1] and a short history of the island up to Uther's reign, based on Geoffrey of Monmouth. The adventures of Guiron and the Le Brun brothers follow. Next we have the whole *Palamedes*, extracts from the *Prophécies de Merlin*, and an abridged version of the enfances and the first knightly deeds of Lancelot. We return to Guiron, and then proceed to extracts from the Prose *Tristan* and a prose redaction of Chrétien's *Erec* up to the marriage with Enide.[2] The episode of the false Guenièvre is followed by the tournament of Sorelois, and the long pastiche concludes with the final exploits of Guiron and his death as a hermit. Thus Vaillant produced a fairly complete fabulous history of Britain before the downfall of Arthur.

Some eighty years later a similar compendium was made by the tireless scribe Michel Gonnot for Jacques d'Armagnac, Duc de Nemours, in the form of a huge tome, B.N. fr. 112. It was finished in 1470 and illustrated by Evrard d'Espingues.[3] Though the manuscript lacks the first quarter, it includes the Prose *Lancelot* entire, sprinkled with extracts from the *Suite du Merlin* (*Huth Merlin*), a short form of the Prose *Tristan*, the stories of Alixandre l'Orphelin and the Tournament of Sorelois, and a version of the *Queste del Saint Graal*, expanded by the addition of conventional chivalric adventures. In spite of its miscellaneous character, the work is far from being a massive accumulation of contradictions and absurdities, as some have thought. It attempted in French what Malory at the same time carried out more successfully in England.

'Le Chevalier du Papegau'

This anonymous romance[4] differs from many of the other late prose tales as it does not form part of a cycle, and its hero is Arthur himself. The action begins at the court of the newly crowned Arthur, to which a damsel comes, as usual, to secure a champion to deliver her mistress from a knight who is oppressing her. The king, after putting his realm in the charge of Loth, sets out and meets with a number of banal adventures.[5] The author

---

[1] See P. Meyer in *Bulletin* of SATF, 1878, pp. 128 ff. G. E. Brereton, in her edition of *Des Grantz Geanz* (Oxford, 1937), does not list the version of B.N. fr. 358 among the various forms of the legend (p. xxxvi).

[2] Not the version published by W. Foerster in his 1890 edition of *Erec*.

[3] On this manuscript see P. Paris, *Manuscrits françois*, i. 151, and R. S. and L. H. Loomis, *Arthurian Legends in Medieval Art*, pp. 110 f., figs. 297, 298.

[4] Preserved only in B.N. fr. 2154, written in fifteenth century. There is no reason to suppose that the text is much earlier. Ed. F. Heuckenkamp (Halle, 1896). Rev. in *Archiv*, xcvii. 438. Comment in Bruce, ii. 31 f. G. Paris gives a synopsis in *Hist. Lit. de la France*, xxx. 103–10.

[5] One of his sources seems to have been a lost French romance, which was also used by Wirnt von Grafenberg in part of his *Wigalois*. See Heuckenkamp's introduction to the *Chevalier*, pp. xxviii–liv, and Saran in *Beiträge*, xxi (1896), 253 ff., and Chap. 33 below.

is not lacking, however, in inventive powers. Into a comparatively short space he has packed an unusually high proportion of wonderful, magical, and superhuman elements. The parrot which gives to the romance and to its hero, King Arthur, their titles, *Le Chevalier du Papegau*, is kept in a cage carried on the back of a horse. This cage is made of fine gold, with all varieties of birds and animals engraved upon it. At the corners of the cage are carbuncles whose brilliance lights up the night. The whole is covered with a richly embroidered silken cloth. In addition the parrot not only entertains the hero with its songs, but also encourages him in spite of its own cowardice.

Before Arthur meets the knight whom he has set out to punish, he encounters many adventures. Among the more noteworthy of his victories is his slaying of the Fish-Knight,[1] a creature dwelling in the sea, but of the form of a mounted and armed knight, but the whole, knight, horse, and even armour, form one living creature, so that when the shield is cut it drips blood. Arthur vanquishes several giants, and is led to his principal opponent by a beast which is the size of a bull, but has the neck of a dragon, the head of a stag surmounted by two long snow-white horns ringed with gold, and is bright red in hue. This is none other than the spirit of King Belnain, whose daughter, Flor du Mont, Arthur has set out to deliver. On his return, Arthur encounters a dwarf whose son, having been suckled by a unicorn, has grown to gigantic stature.

Although the author is interested in such wonders, he also seems to have a rather unusual interest in small practical everyday details. He states the income of a lady to be 300 silver marks annually, without counting the corn and the wine.[2] When Arthur sets out to meet the marshal who is oppressing Flor du Mont, he has to traverse a country where he will be unable to procure food. Flor du Mont, while providing the hero with a costly embroidered silken cloth to adorn his helmet, does not forget to have fixed to his saddle two barrels of wine together with meat sufficient for three days.[3] The approaches to the territory of the marshal are defended by a narrow bridge, in the centre of which is a whirling wheel. A friendly knight advises Arthur to cut all the moving parts he can see in a small hole in a pillar supporting the wheel. This will destroy the 'enchantment'.[4] When Arthur comes to the wheel he cuts the only moving part he can see, namely a metal thread.[5] Thus this terrifying enchantment is worked by wires!

Many of the elements of the story are borrowed from other romances. From the *Tristan* comes the motif of the hero narrowly escaping death from the poison of a dragon. It is more difficult to determine from precisely which

---

[1] Freymond in *Beiträge zur romanischen Philologie, Festgabe für G. Gröber* (1899), pp. 346–54, points out a connexion with the Chapalu.

[2] Ed. Heuckenkamp, p. 51.   [3] Ibid., p. 63.

[4] Ibid., p. 71.   [5] Ibid., p. 73. See Huet in *R*, xl (1911), 433–42.

romance the author drew the 'Sparrow-Hawk' theme: the prize in this case being of course a parrot. It is, however, interesting that it is Arthur himself who is the hero of this adventure, which in so many romances begins at his court but is achieved by other knights.[1] Arthur has all the characteristics of the chivalric hero: he is successful in his combats, indulges in love-affairs, and returns to his own court at Windsor with an honourable wound, bringing his prisoners with him, and it is the parrot who sings there of the king's exploits.

In this minor romance wonder follows wonder so rapidly, the petty adventures crowd upon each other to such an extent that the reader is bewildered. The atmosphere is familiar enough, but the names of most of the characters are new. Most of these names are descriptive, such as Lion Sans Mercy, Jaiant Sans Nom, or Dame aux Cheveux Blons. Some suggest that the author was using them to stress the unreal air of the story, e.g. Chevalier Amoureux du Chastel Saulvage. Their very vagueness underlines the lack of geographical precision in the story: Arthur sets out from Camelot, and after many days' journeying returns to Windsor, but the places through which he passes cannot be traced on a map. The chronology is equally vague, or even careless. Towards the end of the story, whose whole action cannot last more than a few weeks, a dwarf explains to Arthur that years ago, before the birth of his son who has now grown to be a young giant, he was travelling with his master to the court of King Arthur. And this conversation took place quite shortly after the coronation of the young king!

This tale,[2] of no very great literary value, was not popular in its own day.[3] It does, nevertheless, have the merit of bringing to the enchanted kingdom of Arthur a new wonder, a talking parrot whose advice to Arthur and to the dwarf who has charge of it, provides a welcome relief in this over-marvellous chronicle of adventures.

[1] K. G. T. Webster, *Guinevere, A Study of her Abductions* (Milton, Mass., 1951), pp. 83 f.

[2] In the manuscript B.N. fr. 2154 it is called *Le Conte du Papegaulx qui contient les premieres aventures qui avindrent au bon roy Artus*, which, although this title is in a later hand, does justify the use of the term 'tale'.

[3] Only two other manuscripts which may have contained the *Chevalier du Papegau* are recorded, and both are lost. See G. Paris in *Hist. Lit. de la France*, xxx. 103–10.

MISCELLANEOUS FRENCH ROMANCES IN VERSE

ALEXANDRE MICHA

Introduction

AFTER Chrétien de Troyes, Arthurian fiction in verse is represented, not only by the additions to his *Perceval*, certain Breton lais, Béroul's *Tristan*, and the work of Robert de Boron, but also by eighteen poems which extend from the time of Renaud de Beaujeu and Raoul de Houdenc, immediately succeeding Chrétien, to that of Froissart's *Meliador*, 200 years later.[1] In this period a tradition was formed, a gallery was created in which, though new heroes often occupy the foreground, other figures long established, such as Gauvain and Keu, appear again and again, and a number of familiar narrative themes are treated over and over, frequently with a monotonous effect.

The influence of the Champenois poet on most of these writers was great. Some, to be sure, offered a measure of resistance, but almost all were affected by it, borrowing situations, narrative techniques, stylistic features, and methods of character analysis. Of course, their use of certain materials of Celtic origin not found in Chrétien's work is not to be overlooked, but the vogue established by the earliest romancers must have impelled their successors to gather in their turn from the traditional Matter of Britain elements and details neglected by or unknown to the pioneers in the field.

It is not hard to draw up a list of the favourite motifs and situations, and here are some of those first used by Chrétien:

a tourney in which the hero plays his part incognito, often by changing his arms: *Cligès, Fergus, Floriant et Florete*;[2]

the heads of knights impaled on stakes: *Erec, Vengeance Raguidel, Meriadeuc, Yder, Le Bel Inconnu*;[3]

---

[1] Most of these romances have been summarized and discussed by G. Paris in *Hist. Lit. de la France*, xxx, and by Bruce, ii. 194–286.

[2] See Stith Thompson, *Motif-Index of Folk-Literature*, R222; L. A. Hibbard, *Medieval Romance in England* (New York, 1924), pp. 55, 152, 225 f., 229; J. L. Weston, *Three Days' Tournament* (London, 1902); Carter in *Haverford Essays* (Haverford, Pa., 1909), pp. 246 ff.

[3] *Studies and Notes in Philology and Literature*, iv (1895), 175–9; viii (1903), 137, n. 1; A. Taylor in *RR*, ix (1918), 21 ff.

the contest of which a sparrow-hawk is the prize: *Erec, Le Bel Inconnu, Meraugis, Durmart*;[1]

the besieged damsel: *Perceval, Meraugis, Durmart, Meriadeuc, Escanor, Claris et Laris*;[2]

the rebuffed seductress: *Lancelot, Yder, Fergus*;[3]

the abduction: *Lancelot, Durmart, L'Atre Périlleux*;[4]

Keu's ill success: *Erec, Lancelot, Yvain, Perceval, La Mule sans Frein, Vengeance Raguidel*, &c.[5]

There are also many motifs connected with Gauvain, not all of which are represented in Chrétien's work: Gauvain violently hated by a damsel: *Escanor, Vengeance Raguidel*; Gauvain unjustly accused of killing a knight by treachery: *Perceval, Escanor*; Gauvain loved by a woman who had never seen him: *Vengeance Raguidel, Hunbaut, Meriadeuc, L'Atre Périlleux*; Gauvain never refuses to tell his name: *Perceval, Vengeance Raguidel, Chevalier à l'Epée, L'Atre Périlleux*, &c.; Gauvain's strength increases until midday (or after midday):[6] *Meraugis, L'Atre Périlleux*, &c.; Gauvain's death is falsely reported: *Meriadeuc, L'Atre Périlleux*; Gauvain possesses a horse named Gringalet:[7] *Erec, Vengeance Raguidel, L'Atre Périlleux, Fergus, Escanor*, &c.

In spite of the unquestioned influence of Chrétien's work on most of these poems, it would be incautious to assume that the repetition of a motif first employed in French romance by him was derived necessarily from him. The abduction of Guenièvre, for instance, had already appeared before 1136[8] in Caradoc of Lancarvan's *Vita Gildae*, and was evidently a traditional theme; other recurrent themes are treated so differently that it would be rash to assume that Chrétien was the model. Still he was plainly responsible for much analysis of the emotions and the introduction of such conventional topics as love sickness, the arrow and the eye, the heart and the body, the monologue of complaint, and the monologue of deliberation.[9]

Two tendencies manifest themselves as we advance into the thirteenth century. In the first thirty or forty years the romancers contrive with more or less skill to maintain a kind of unity, and about the middle of the century

[1] Loomis, *Arthurian Tradition*, pp. 86–100.   [2] *PMLA*, lxiii (1948), 803-30.

[3] Loomis, op. cit., pp. 230–32. *Spec*, xx (1945), 186 f. See Chap. 39 below.

[4] G. Schoepperle, *Tristan and Isolt* (Frankfurt, London, 1913), ii. 528–40; T. P. Cross, W. A. Nitze, *Lancelot and Guenevere* (Chicago, 1930), pp. 20–62; K. G. T. Webster, *Guinevere, A Study of Her Abductions* (Milton, Mass., 1951).

[5] Loomis, op. cit., pp. 154 f., 202–4, 274 f.

[6] *Mort Artu*, ed. J. D. Bruce (Halle, 1910), pp. 287 f.; Loomis, op. cit., pp. 152 f.

[7] Loomis, op. cit., pp. 156–9.

[8] On date see Tatlock in *Spec*, xiii (1938), 139–52.

[9] Cross and Nitze, op. cit., pp. 79–98; Lowes, 'The "Loveres Maladye of Hereos"', *MP*, xi (1914), 491 ff.; Guyer, 'The Influence of Ovid on Crestien de Troyes', *RR*, xii (1921), 97 ff.; Reinhard in *RR*, xv (1924), 240–53.

the *Atre Périlleux* provides a good example of this control. But afterwards there are signs of decadence. The Prose *Lancelot* came to exercise a marked influence on the structure of the narratives; the romance made up of quests found favour, but the device was employed without the care for organization which characterized the great prose cycle or the *Meraugis* or Chrétien's *Lancelot*. The poet rambles on interminably because he can at will dispatch twenty or thirty questers over hill and dale. To this type *Meriadeuc* already belongs, and above all *Claris et Laris, Rigomer,* and *Meliador*. Except in the case of *Rigomer,* the reader is discouraged by the author's poverty of invention and the monotony of the adventures; the genre becomes etiolated; instead of composition we have compilation.

Another tendency which we can perceive in the course of the thirteenth century is toward realism. Not that the marvellous lost all its attraction; it was exploited up to the very end of Arthurian romance, but often in a clumsy fashion, particularly in *Claris et Laris*. But at the same time other romances shun the fantastic, reject giants, fays, monsters, enchanted castles, and concentrate on depicting the life of an ideal knight under more normal conditions, as in *Yder*[1] (1210–25), in *Durmart*[1] (1220–50), in *Fergus,* and in *Gliglois*. Romantic sentiment and the vicissitudes of love are also a major concern from *Meraugis* to the end of the century. Even the poets who indulge most freely in the marvellous are also drawn to the familiar aspects of courtly life; descriptions of banquets, of dressings and undressings, of arrivals and departures, impede the march of the action.[2] In these different ways the verse romances brought to flower what had first come to bud in the work of the Champenois master.

Since, like the First Continuation of *Perceval,* several of these poems celebrate Gauvain as their hero, let us occupy ourselves first with them.[3]

'Les Enfances Gauvain'

Only two fragments, totalling 712 lines, survive of a French romance recounting the birth, infancy, and youthful exploits of Gauvain.[4] The first tells how King Arthur's sister Morcades has a love-child by Lot, her page. The lovers give the infant to a knight named Gauvain le Brun, who, after baptizing it with his own name, places it in a cask which is set adrift on the sea. In the second fragment a fisherman rescues the child, learns from an accompanying letter the secret of his birth, and brings him to Rome, where in due time he is educated and knighted by the pope and makes a name for himself in tournaments. With the death of the emperor the fragment ends.

---

[1] Both *Yder* and *Durmart* avoid any grossness in the treatment of love and address themselves to the aristocracy: *Yder,* vss. 6762–9; *Durmart,* vss. 1–10.

[2] See W. Borsdorf, *Die Burg im 'Claris und Laris' und im 'Escanor'* (Berlin, 1890).

[3] On Gauvain's prominence and character see Whiting in *Medieval Studies,* ix (1947), 189–234.

[4] *R,* xxxix (1910), 1–32; Gelzer in *ZRP,* xxxviii (1917), 614.

Three other works have left an account of Gauvain's *enfances*:[1] first, a few lines in Wace's *Brut*, relating how Gauvain returned, a valiant and famous knight, from the Apostle St. Sulpice, who had given him arms;[2] second, a brief account in *Perlesvaus* resembling the *Enfances Gauvain*;[3] third, the Latin romance, *De Ortu Walwanii*.[4] These texts seem to represent variant versions of a common tradition. The *De Ortu*, which probably follows a French romance, calls Arthur's sister not Morcades but Anna, as do Geoffrey and Wace, and likewise gives the pope the name Sulpicius. Arthur's queen is called Guendoloena.[5] The child is not placed in the sea in a cask, but is confided by his mother to merchants and is stolen from their ship by a fisherman. There is no person corresponding to Gauvain le Brun, no name is given to the boy, and the emperor, instead of the pope, brings him up. *Perlesvaus* completes the scenario of the *Enfances Gauvain*, for it informs us that the hero was destined to be emperor himself, but refused lest he be taunted with bastardy.

R. S. Loomis has pointed out several links with other romances and lais.[6] Morcades appears in three Arthurian texts as the wife of Lot and in the First Continuation of the *Perceval* as a queen in the Castle of Ladies and as the mother of Gauvain. Curiously enough, the heroine of *Doon* is the mistress of the Castle of Maidens; she, like Morcades, sends her young son away with a ring as a recognition token; and this son, like Gauvain in the Vulgate *Merlin*, meets his father in combat incognito but recognizes him in time. Moreover, Morcades, the sister of Arthur, may be suspected of originating in Morgain la Fée, for Morgain was also the sister of Arthur, and was the mistress of a castle of maidens not far from Edinburgh, which was itself called the Castle of Maidens, and which lay in Lothian, King Lot's territory. The reader may judge whether these correspondences are due to accident or not.

The *Enfances*, in broad outline, reproduces the strange legend of the incestuous birth of Pope Gregory, as found in the *Gesta Romanorum* and elsewhere,[7] and this fact may explain the unexpected upbringing of Arthur's nephew at Rome by the pope, both in Geoffrey's *Historia* and in the stories of Gauvain's youth. The influence of the same pious legend may also be detected in the tales of Modred, who, according to the Vulgate cycle, was conceived through the incestuous union of Arthur and his sister, and according to the *Suite du Merlin (Huth Merlin)* was exposed on the sea and was

[1] The story of Mordret, son of Lot and Arthur's sister, saved by a fisherman after being exposed on the sea, shares only these two traits with the Gauvain fragments. *Merlin*, ed. G. Paris, J. Ulrich, SATF, i. 203–5.

[2] Wace, *Brut*, ed. I. Arnold, SATF, ii. 518 f.

[3] *Perlesvaus*, ed. Nitze and others (Chicago, 1932–7), i. 307 f.; ii. 327 f.

[4] See below, pp. 475 f. Bruce, in *Evolution*, ii. 57, n. 1, maintains that *De Ortu* and *Enfances Gauvain* had a common source, and that it was older than Chrétien's *Perceval*.

[5] *PMLA*, xliii (1928), 419.   [6] Loomis, *Arthurian Tradition*, pp. 111–13.

[7] See the abridged version in *R*, xxxiii. 42.

rescued by a fisherman.[1] There can be little doubt that the legend of Pope Gregory determined in large measure the shaping of the *Enfances Gauvain*.[2]

In conclusion, let it be noted that Paul Meyer dated the fragments early in the thirteenth century, and it is a remarkable fact that the author was totally unacquainted with Chrétien's *Lancelot*, for he not only calls Arthur's queen Guinemars, reflecting not Chrétien's Guenièvre, but a form close to the Guenhumara of the Bern MS. of Geoffrey's *Historia*, but he also represents her as an entirely devoted and faithful spouse.

'La Mule sans Frein'[3]

From the early years of the thirteenth century also comes a poem of 1,136 lines which its author, Paien de Maisières, called 'La Demoiselle à la Mure' (vs. 18) but which is usually cited as *La Mule sans Frein* (*The Mule without a Bridle*). As in so many other romances, a lady comes to Arthur's court to seek a champion. She is riding a mule without a bridle; if a knight will bring back to her this indispensable object, which someone has carried off, she will find happiness again. Keu comes forward and sets off, but the perils of the road prove too much for his courage and he returns. Gauvain accepts the adventure and at last brings back the bridle, which the lady's sister has been keeping in her castle.

Before this is accomplished, however, there are numerous trials to be undergone, and their fantastic nature is in the purest Arthurian tradition: a forest infested by wild beasts, which, however, bow down at the passing of the magic mule, lent by the lady to Gauvain; a valley of serpents; a narrow bridge over deep water, like that in Chrétien's *Lancelot*; a castle which revolves so that the mule's tail is cut off in entering, much as Yvain's horse was bisected by the portcullis; a churl who challenges Gauvain to play the beheading game; fights with two lions, with a knight, and with two dragons.

Paien's narrative, far from being prolix, is concise to the point of obscurity. Whether intentionally or not, he never lets us know why the damsel is so attached to her bridle, or why she fails to keep her promise to reward the successful hero with the enjoyment of her body. Fortunately, Heinrich von dem Türlin has preserved in *Diu Krône* (c. 1215) what is evidently a fuller version of the same romance.[4] When the knight Laniure dies, he leaves behind a bridle which is intended to serve his two daughters as a title-deed to their patrimony. The elder daughter, however, takes possession of the

---

[1] See above, p. 361, n. 1.

[2] For other opinions see below, pp. 436, 475 f.

[3] Ed. B. Orlowski (Paris, 1911); ed. R. T. Hill (Baltimore, 1911). Corrections of text by R. Levy in *MedAev*, iv (1935), 194–8; by Orr, ibid. v (1936), 77 f.

[4] L. L. Boll, *Relation of Diu Krône of Heinrich von dem Türlin to La Mule sans Frein* (Washington, 1929). G. Paris in *Hist. Lit. de la France*, xxx. 68 f., and Kittredge, *Study of Gawain and the Green Knight* (Cambridge, Mass., 1916), p. 251, derive the German poem from the French.

bridle and the inheritance, and this explains why her sister seeks out Gauvain to recover the bridle for her. Chrétien drew upon the same original story to bring about the combat between Gauvain and Yvain.[1] The younger daughter of the Sire de la Noire Espine (compare the name Laniure in *Diu Krône*) goes to Arthur's court to find a champion who will restore to her the estates which her sister has wrongfully seized. We must assume therefore a common French source for *La Mule sans Frein* and the episodes in *Diu Krône* and *Yvain*—a narrative which Paien has preserved in an abridged and obscure form.

The revolving castle is an authentic Celtic motif, to be compared with a similar fortress in two ancient Irish sagas, the *Voyage of Maelduin* and *Bricriu's Feast*;[2] in the latter as in the *Mule sans Frein* the fortress is said to revolve as swiftly as a millstone. Celtic also is the motif of the Beheading Test since two versions are given in *Bricriu's Feast*.[3] The pattern of disenchantment is also an old one; when Gauvain leaves the deserted castle with the bridle, the streets are filled with dancers, much as, when Erec defeats Mabonagrain in the enchanted *verger*, all the folk of Brandigan are filled with joy. The *Mule* also shares with *Erec* the motif of heads impaled on stakes, and the single stake awaiting the hero's head in case of his defeat.[4]

'*Le Chevalier à l'Epée*'[5]

Another short poem, written according to Armstrong before 1210, is the *Chevalier à l'Epée*, consisting of 1,206 lines in the dialect of the Ile de France. It tells how Gauvain, lost in a forest, accepts the invitation of a knight to visit his castle. The host precedes him, welcomes him on his arrival, and even offers him his beautiful daughter. When Gauvain has entered her bed and is about to take advantage of the offer, the damsel warns him of an enchanted sword suspended above them. Nevertheless he disregards the warning and is twice wounded slightly by the sword. In the morning the host is surprised to find Gauvain still alive, declares that by passing the ordeal his guest has proved himself the best of knights, and gives him his daughter in marriage. The wedded couple depart from the castle, but Gauvain leaves his bride for a short while to fetch her hounds. On his return, another knight is about to lead her away and demands that the lady be allowed to choose between him and Gauvain. She chooses the stranger. Her hounds, however, given a similar choice follow Gauvain. A combat ensues, Gauvain kills his rival, and when

---

[1] *Yvain*, vss. 4703–5106, 5810–6450.

[2] Huet in *R*, xl (1911), 235–42; *La Mule*, ed. Orlowski, pp. 78 f. The Welsh *ynys pybyrdor*, mentioned by Orlowski, does not mean 'ile de la Porte tournante' but 'island of the strong door'; Loomis, *Wales*, pp. 164 f.

[3] Kittredge, op. cit., pp. 9–19, 42–52.

[4] See above, p. 358, n. 3.

[5] Ed. E. C. Armstrong (Baltimore, 1900).

his bride wishes to return to him, he rebuffs her with sarcastic comments on the ingratitude of women.

The author was well acquainted with the work of Chrétien. He mentions him by name (vs. 19), echoes some of his phrases,[1] and of course calls to mind the episodes of the perilous bed in *Lancelot* and *Perceval* and the episode of the amorous hostess in the former romance. It is to be noted that the ordeal of the bed serves in each of these cases to designate the survivor as the best of knights. It is probable, though not certain, that the sword which functions as a protector of a woman's chastity may be a variant of the enchanted pillow of the *Tristan* romance, which possesses the same virtue.[2] The imperious host who demands that his guest go to bed with his daughter or wife re-appears in the *Carl of Carlisle* and *Wolfdietrich*, and, somewhat modified, in *Hunbaut* and *Gawain and the Green Knight*.[3] The incident in which the fidelity of greyhounds is contrasted with the infidelity of their mistress is a *fabliau* which has been variously preserved in the *Vengeance Raguidel* and the Prose *Tristan*, and most faithfully by a series of English miniatures of the early fourteenth century.[4]

The *Chevalier à l'Epée* resembles certain lais, *Doon*, *Melion*, and *Tyolet*, in combining two originally distinct tales, and the result is a serious in-consistency in the characterization both of the lady and of Gauvain. The lady in the first episode is described as 'preuz et sage', and she is so charmed by the 'bones mors' of the hero that she warns him several times of his danger; but in the second part she has become the typical loose female of *fabliau*. The author has sacrificed psychological realism to a satiric purpose. Gauvain, too, in the first episode conforms to the romantic pattern; he willingly tells his name to whoever asks, is careful of his reputation, and is always suscept-ible to the charms of the fair; but in the second episode he is deceived by his wife and adopts a philosophy of cynical resignation. The author himself draws a misogynist moral:

> Qui de les [les femmes] servir se painne
> Et plus lor fait bien et anor,
> Plus s'en repent au chef de tor.

(Whoever strives to serve women will find that the more he does for them and the more he honours them, the more he will repent in the end.)

But though the poem suffers from this dichotomy in tone and characteriza-

---

[1] Cf. *Chevalier*, vss. 598–601, with *Lancelot*, vss. 530–2, and *Chevalier*, vss. 160–3, with *Erec*, vss. 5716–21.

[2] Newstead, 'Kaherdin and the Enchanted Pillow', *PMLA*, lxv (1950), 290–312.

[3] *Chevalier*, ed. Armstrong, pp. 67–69; Kittredge, op. cit., pp. 85–104.

[4] *Chevalier*, ed. Armstrong, pp. 63–67; Kittredge, op. cit., p. 304; R. S. Loomis, in *MP*, xiv (1917), 751–5.

tion, the style is good and the dialogue between the lady and the two rivals for her favour is written with spirit.

'La Vengeance Raguidel'[1]

A certain Raoul composed about the same time, in the same dialect, and with a similar misogynist bias, a poem of 6,182 lines entitled *La Vengeance Raguidel (The Avenging of Raguidel)*. Gauvain is again the chief personage; it is he who near the beginning of the poem alone succeeds in drawing out from the corpse of the knight Raguidel the truncheon of a lance which must be used to avenge his death on his slayer, Guengasoain; and it is Gauvain who near the close of the poem employs the same truncheon against Guengasoain, and, though it fails him, nevertheless overcomes and beheads his foe. A secondary hero is Yder, who near the beginning draws five rings from the hand of Raguidel, and who at the close aids Gauvain in his combat with Guengasoain and marries Guengasoain's daughter, destined to wed only the slayer of her father. One may detect in these *dénouements* remote analogues to the slaying of Curoi mac Dairi with his own sword[2] and the marriage of Culhwch to Olwen, whose father he had slain.[3]

Inserted in this framework are two independent narratives. The first tells how the Pucele del Gaut Destroit (the Maid of the Narrow Wood) was infatuated with Gauvain, but when he scorned her, planned to decapitate him with a sort of guillotine set in the window of her castle. When he visited her, however, she failed to recognize him and discovered his identity only after his escape. The second narrative concerns a lady named Ydain, whom Gauvain saved from a would-be ravisher and won for his own mistress. But later when her lust was excited by another knight and she was given the choice of lovers, she deserted Gauvain. Gauvain killed his rival and took the faithless Ydain back under his protection, but only to turn her over to the dwarf Druidain (i.e. *dru Ydain*, lover of Ydain).

The author has not succeeded in giving a real unity to this combination of stories. He introduces details which slow down the action, repeats what has already been said (vss. 5016–308), and overworks the motif of an incognito. For instance, Gauvain goes unrecognized by the Noir Chevalier, Yder, the Pucele del Gaut Destroit, and Raguidel's lady.

The *Vengeance Raguidel* exposes cruelly the frailties of the fair sex. Ydain's fidelity suffers by comparison with that of her hounds;[4] the mantle test is catastrophic for the ladies of Arthur's court.[5] There are exceptions, to be sure. Raguidel's mistress, faithful to his memory, patiently awaits his avenger. There is the flawless but banal Tremionette and there is Marot,

---

[1] Ed. M. Friedwagner (Halle, 1909). Discussed by Bruce, ii. 214 f.
[2] *ZCP*, ix. 205, 216.   [3] Loth, *Mabinogion*, 2nd ed. i. 295 f., 345 f.
[4] See above, p. 364, n. 4.   [5] See Chap. 11 above and Chap. 35 below.

who saves Gauvain at considerable risk to herself. But it is the faithless and sensual Ydain that we do not readily forget.

Raoul's forte is realistic observation. He describes the kitchens of Arthur, a morning in the forest, a miniature guillotine.[1] He is interested in the life of a town and the wares exposed for sale, in the techniques of a siege, the inspection of the defences, the building of a 'castelet', and the repair of breaches.[2] When Arthur cannot sleep, he kicks off the quilt. Though the psychological analysis may be thin, what spirit there is in the scene when Ydain tries to ingratiate herself again with Gauvain after her desertion, in the dialogue when Gauvain asks his way of the cowherd to the castle of the Noir Chevalier, and most of all in the interview between Gauvain and the Pucele del Gaut Destroit! Many pages are tinged with irony.

The marvellous is limited to the opening scene,[3] when an enchanted boat brings the body of Raguidel to court and Gauvain alone succeeds in extracting the spear-shaft and Yder alone is able to remove the rings from the body, and both are thus designated as the avengers. The theme is an old one, for in the First Continuation of the *Perceval* Guerrehet draws the truncheon of a lance from the body of Brangemer, brought likewise by a boat to Arthur's court, and with the weapon avenges himself.[4] There are traces of primitive savagery, as, for instance, when Yder is obliged to fight a bear before he can attack Guengasoain.

Raoul was familiar with Chrétien. The hurried departure of Keu in quest of the murderer of Raguidel is perhaps an imitation of *Yvain*. Marot plays the role of Lunete. From *Erec*, perhaps, came the motifs of the heads impaled on stakes and the hunting of the white hart; and there are verbal resemblances between the description of the castle of Gaut Destroit and the description of Guingambresil's castle in *Perceval*.[5]

The attribution of the poem to Raoul de Houdenc has been long debated. In its favour Mussafia, Michelant, Paul Meyer, and Friedwagner have ranged themselves; Zingerle and Boerner on the other side.[6] Some scholars have imagined two authors, but without justification.[7] The language, the style, the versification, the spirit, and the rudimentary psychology seem in-

---

[1] Vss. 319–28, 3360 ff., 2120 ff.

[2] Vss. 1806–75, 2772–983.

[3] The mention of the brazen lion in vs. 4856, far from creating an atmosphere of fantasy, is too incongruous with the realism of the episode.

[4] The story of the marvellous ship is regarded by J. L. Weston in *R*, xlvii (1927), 349 ff., as an independent tale, but it is possible that Raoul knew it as it appears in the First Continuation of Chrétien's *Perceval*, or in the source of the Continuation.

[5] *Vengeance*, ed. Friedwagner, pp. clxviii–clxxi.

[6] Zingerle, *Raoul de Houdenc und seine Werke* (1880); O. Boerner, *Raoul de Houdenc, eine stilistische Untersuchung* (1884).

[7] Zenker, *Ueber die Echtheit zweier dem Raoul de Houdenc zugeschriebenen Werke* (1889); Kaluza, 'Ueber den Anteil des Raoul de Houdenc', in *Festgabe G. Gröber* (1900).

compatible with the ascription to the author of *Meraugis de Portlesguez*, Raoul de Houdenc.[1]

The *Vengeance* was alluded to by Etienne de Bourbon in *Les Sept Arts du Saint Esprit*, and was translated in abridged form in the Dutch *Lancelot*.[2]

'*L'Atre Périlleux*'[3]

This anonymous poem of 6,676 lines, written in the Norman dialect about 1250, owes its title, *L'Atre Périlleux* (*The Perilous Cemetery*) to one of a series of complicated adventures in which Gavain plays many of his characteristic parts. It opens with the abduction of Arthur's maiden cup-bearer by a knight whose name, as we learn later, was Escanor, who bore a red shield, and whose strength increased till noon and then waned. First Keu pursued Escanor, only to be unhorsed and wounded. Gavain, setting out after some delay, met three damsels mourning his own death at the hands of three villainous knights, who had thought they were killing Gavain. The hero did not reveal the mistake, but promised to avenge the victim. Spending the night in a cemetery, he learned the plight of a damsel imprisoned in a tomb by a devil. Of course, he beheaded the fiend, and the next day overtook and killed Escanor. Throughout these and subsequent adventures Gavain maintained his incognito and was referred to as 'cil sans non' (the nameless one). He forced a faithless knight, Espinogre, to return to his *amie*, and finally with his aid overcame the two knights who mistakenly claimed to have killed him and made one of them bring back to life the victim of the error. The poem ends with the wedding of Espinogre and two other knights to their *amies*.

The author claims (vss. 4728 f.) to have found the *conte* written in a book, but nothing is less certain, for he borrowed several heroes from known sources, Raguidel from the *Vengeance Raguidel*, Espinogre from *Meraugis*, and Codrovain from *Durmart*, and employed a large number of stereotyped features and incidents—Gauvain mistakenly believed to be dead; Gauvain loved for his reputation alone (First Continuation of *Perceval*, *Vengeance Raguidel*, *Chevalier aux Deux Epées*, *Hunbaut*); Gauvain willing, after his final victory, to reveal his name; Keu rashly attempting an adventure which ends in his disgrace; a knight whose strength waxes and wanes with the rising and the setting of the sun. The motif of a woman who promises to marry a suitor if he can get the better of Gauvain may have been derived from the *Chevalier aux Deux Epées*, and the incognito combat between friends may have been suggested by Chrétien's *Yvain*. The cemetery episode has no

---

[1] Micha in *R*, lxviii (1944–5), 333–60.

[2] See Chap. 34 below.

[3] Ed. B. Woledge, *CFMA* (1936); see Zingerle in *ZFSL*, xxxvi (1910), 274–93, and Woledge, *L'Atre Périlleux*, *Étude sur les Manuscrits, la Langue et l'Importance Littéraire du Poème* (1930).

counterpart in Arthurian romance[1] but resembles a scene in *Amadas et Ydoine*;[2] differences in treatment, however, exclude the derivation of one version from the other. Both versions involve also the theme of the Sleeping Beauty, which Krappe traced back to the Orient[3] but which here may have been contaminated by the Breton belief in a King of the Dead.[4] Gauvain's mother, Morcades, mistress of Lot and sister of Arthur, seems to have been in origin identical with Morgain la Fée.[5] As for the abduction of Arthur's female cup-bearer, there is a marked parallel with Chrétien's *Lancelot*.[6] In both versions an insolent knight arrives at Arthur's court and announces that he will await in a neighbouring wood a champion to dispute the possession of a woman; Keu behaves with arrogance and comes to grief; Gauvain undertakes the rescue of the woman and acquits himself better than the seneschal. If there is any connexion, as R. S. Loomis has proposed,[7] with the Irish saga of the abduction of Blathnat by Curoi, it is very remote.

In spite of the variety of the materials the narrative is unusually coherent. Only two episodes could be omitted without leaving loose ends, one of them, strangely enough, being the cemetery adventure which gives the poem its title. The false report of Gavain's death and the incognito which he so long maintains enable the author to achieve some piquant effects; as, for instance, when Gavain enters a castle demanding food for a famished damsel, the chatelaine declares that no one would have dared to make such a demand if Gavain had been alive. Moreover, the author exercises considerable ingenuity in rousing the reader's curiosity and leaving him in suspense. Thus the meetings of Gavain with Cadrovain and later with Raguidel introduce chapters which are concluded only after other adventures have intervened. His early meeting with the women who lament the death of one whom they believe to be Gavain is neatly balanced at the close by the defeat of the slayers, the resurrection of the victim, and the disclosure of Gavain's identity. Indeed this is not a *roman à tiroirs*, in which the episodes are separate and do not connect with each other; rather it is a *roman à tirettes*, constructed like a telescope, in which one event slides into another.

Gavain plays his customary part as a paragon of chivalry, but it is rather as a defender and comforter of ladies than as a lover. Indeed, he shows a tendency to sermonize, now giving a somewhat unexpected discourse on fidelity

---

[1] L. Hibbard Loomis proposes in *MLR*, xxvi (1931), 408 ff., a connexion between certain Arthurian tombs and cemeteries and megalithic monuments. On other tombs see *Perlesvaus*, ed. Nitze and others, ii. 220 f., 306–9.

[2] Reinhard in *RR*, xv (1924), 238 f.

[3] *R*, lviii (1932), 260 ff.

[4] Loomis, *Arthurian Tradition*, p. 168.

[5] Ibid., pp. 112–14.

[6] For verbal parallels cf. *Atre*, vss. 151 f., *Lancelot*, vss. 47 f.; *Atre*, vss. 156–9, *Lancelot*, vss. 49–51; *Atre*, vss. 174–9, *Lancelot*, vss. 58–62; *Atre*, vss. 183 f., *Lancelot*, vss. 72–77.

[7] Loomis, *Arthurian Tradition*, pp. 203 f.

in love (vss. 3304 f., 3493 ff.), now offering instruction on how to aid lovers in distress (vss. 3877 ff.)—a role in which he himself sets a good example.

In spite of some excessively long passages and some obscurities (one is not always clear as to the whereabouts of damsels who at one time or another have attached themselves to the hero), the romance makes agreeable reading. The style is easy, not padded. There are interesting pictures of indoor life, of which the most successful is a description of Gavain taking a bath, then supping, and spending the evening in the chimney corner of a hospitable burgess (vss. 1938–80). Though the *Atre Périlleux* never achieved wide popularity, its influence may be seen in the naming of Girard d'Amiens's hero, Escanor, and in the episode of the lady imprisoned by a devil in *Claris et Laris*.

'*Hunbaut*' [1]

A poem which calls itself 'De Gunbaut' is contained in a unique manuscript at Chantilly and stops, incomplete, at vs. 3618. Its author came from Hainaut and wrote between 1250 and 1275. In spite of its title the chief character is still Gauvain. He is sent by Arthur to the King of the Isles to demand submission, and is joined by Hunbaut. The two finally reach their destination, deliver Arthur's message, and manage to escape with their lives. On the return journey an adventure separates the two friends, Hunbaut rescues the father of a damsel from robbers and goes back to Arthur's court. Gauvain pursues those who have abducted the lover of the same damsel, then sets off in quest of his own sister, vanquishes her captor, and compels him to surrender himself to Arthur.

The adventures which mark the journey to the court of the King of the Isles and the return often remind us of Chrétien, mentioned with admiration in vs. 186, and of other earlier romances. We have an imperious host who commands Gauvain to kiss his daughter, but who orders his eyes to be put out when he kisses her four times; compare the *Chevalier à l'Epée*.[2] We have the Pucele del Gaut Destroit, who keeps an image of Gauvain beside her to make up for his absence; compare the *Vengeance Raguidel* and Thomas's *Tristan*.[3] We have an incognito combat between Gauvain and his brother Gaheriet, which derives added piquancy from the fact that Gauvain is forced to fight because he will not concede that he is the best knight at Arthur's court (vss. 2362–595). The author has made an amusing short story of the stereotyped situation where Gauvain compels a faithless lover to carry out his promise to marry. The lover is a realistic type, a conceited chatterer who boasts of his conquest to the first comer (vss. 1885–2113). In these two

---

[1] Ed. J. Stürzinger, H. Breuer (Dresden, 1914).
[2] See p. 364, n. 3.
[3] Thomas, *Tristan*, ed. Bédier, i. 310–14.

incidents the author displays a talent which one misses in the physical feats accomplished by the hero—plunging a man with an artificial leg into a moat, or cleaving a dwarf to the teeth. Hunbaut has a wearisome habit of informing his companion of the strange customs of the castles they pass and of the individuals they meet. One of these individuals is a churl who guards a bridge and who proposes to Gauvain the so-called Beheading Test. Gauvain accepts, takes the churl's axe, sends his head flying, but prevents the completion of the test by catching him by his clothes so that he cannot recover his head and so dies. This theme had already been treated in three French romances—the First Continuation of Chrétien's *Perceval*, the *Mule sans Frein*, and *Perlesvaus*—and was destined to receive its finest treatment in the Middle English poem, *Gawain and the Green Knight*.[1] Its Celtic origin was recognized by Gaston Paris as early as 1888 and by many scholars since.[2]

Hunbaut is on the whole a mediocre performance, but it shows some attention to stylistic effects. In the prologue the author calls attention to the quality of the rimes (vss. 36 f.):

> Or entendes con il asamblent
> Et con il sont a dire fort.

(Now hear how they harmonize and how strong they sound when they are spoken.)

Indeed the rimes occasionally come near to punning, for example in vss. 57 f., 'd'amor ot' with 'demorot'. The poem does not seem to have had many readers, however, though vss. 2414–640 were plagiarized in a rimed version of the *Chastoiement d'un Père à son Fils*.[3]

'Le Bel Inconnu' or 'Guinglain'[4]

The history of Gauvain's son is preserved in several forms, of which the earliest is found in the First Continuation of Chrétien's *Perceval*[5] and in a poem of 6,266 lines, composed between 1185 and 1190 in the dialect of the Ile de France, with some Walloon traits.[6] The latter poet was Renaud de Beaujeu, not necessarily a member of the great family of Beaujeu, for in *Guillaume de Dôle* he is referred to as a knight of the Raincien.

Le Bel Inconnu (*The Fair Unknown*) opens with the arrival of the damsel Hélie and her dwarf at Arthur's court, seeking a champion to deliver her mistress, the daughter of the King of Wales, who has been transformed into

[1] See p. 363, n. 3 above and Chap. 39 below.
[2] *Hist. Lit. de la France*, xxx. 71–78; Bruce, i. 88 f.; Kittredge, op. cit.; A. Buchanan in *PMLA*, xlvii (1932), 315–38; J. Marx, *Légende Arthurienne et le Graal* (Paris, 1952), pp. 75–77; M. Dillon, *Early Irish Literature* (Chicago, 1948), p. 18.
[3] Hilka in *ZFSL*, xlvii. 60 f.
[4] Ed. G. Perrie Williams, *CFMA* (1929).
[5] *Continuations of Old French Perceval*, ed. W. Roach (Philadelphia, 1949), i. 370–80.
[6] W. J. K. Bidder, *Ergebnisse von Reimuntersuchung und Silbenzählung des . . . Li Beaus Desconus des Renaut von Beaujeu für die Sprache des Dichters* (Coburg, 1913).

a serpent or dragon by two enchanters, Mabon and Evrain. Much to her disgust, the young and as yet nameless Guinglain is assigned to the task, but in spite of her scornful treatment of him, he accompanies her to the ruined city of Sinadon, vanquishes the enchanters, removes the spell on Blonde Esmerée, and finally weds her.

Renaud has filled in this frame with an assortment of adventures destined to become commonplace. Guinglain unhorses the guardian of a perilous ford; he kills two giants who are about to rape a maiden; he wins the contest for a sparrow-hawk against Girflet le fils Do; he is involved in a liaison with a fay; he is finally lured away from her by the proclamation of a tourney at the Castle of Maidens arranged by Blonde Esmerée.

The central theme of a hero summoned by a damsel to deliver her mistress from reptile form by a kiss is shared by three other romances—the English *Libeaus Desconus*, Pucci's *Carduino* (1350–1400), Wirnt von Gravenberg's *Wigalois* (*c.* 1210).[1] The relationship between these four texts has been discussed several times,[2] and the most probable view is that the French and English versions are independent retellings of an older tale. *Libeaus Desconus* makes the visit of Guinglain to the fay of the Ille d'Or only a minor episode and does not bring him back to her after he has broken the spell on Blonde Esmerée. In *Carduino*, too, the fay has only an incidental part, and *Wigalois* is still further removed from the common pattern.

The theme of the transformation of a dragon by a kiss, known commonly as the 'Fier Baiser', was regarded by Gaston Paris as of Eastern origin, because in 'Mandeville' it is localized in the island of Cos and attached to the daughter of Hippocrates. But, as R. S. Loomis has shown,[3] we have here an Arthurian motif (represented abundantly in modern folk-lore)[4] which 'Mandeville' transferred to the Mediterranean, just as the Celtic Avalon came to be identified with Mongibel (Mount Etna) in Sicily.[5] The oldest versions of the 'Fier Baiser' are found in *Lanzelet* (1194–1203) and in *Le Bel Inconnu*. The latter reveals a knowledge of the Roman ruins of Segontium near Carnarvon under the name of Sinadon,[6] and in this 'gaste cité' it places the eerie adventure of the dragon kiss. All these versions of the 'Fier Baiser' were derived from an Irish tradition of which the earliest extant form is a poem composed before 1024, entitled the *Adventures of the Sons of*

---

[1] See below, Chaps. 32, 33, 37.

[2] G. Paris in *R*, xv (1886), 12 ff.; *Libeaus Desconus*, ed. M. Kaluza (Leipzig, 1890), pp. cxxxi–cxlv; A. Mennung, *Der Bel Inconnu des Renaut de Beaujeu in seinem Verhältnis zum Lybeaus Desconus, Carduino und Wigalois* (Halle, 1890); review in *R*, xx. 297–302; W. H. Schofield, *Studies on the Libeaus Desconus, Studies and Notes in Philology and Literature*, iv (Boston, 1895).

[3] *SM*, nuova serie, xvii (1951), 104–13; Ulrich von Zatzikhoven, *Lanzelet*, trans. K. G. T. Webster (New York, 1951), pp. 224–6.

[4] Stith Thompson, *Motif-Index of Folk-Literature*, D735; E. Frank, *Der Schlangenkuß, Form und Geist*, ix (1928).   [5] See Chap. 7 above.

[6] Loomis in *Spec*, xxii (1947), 520–30; reprinted in Loomis, *Wales*, pp. 1–14.

Eochaid Mugmedon.[1] The Irish tradition differs from the Arthurian mainly in the fact that it is not a dragon but a monstrous hag who is metamorphosed into a figure of radiant beauty and that she represents allegorically the Sovereignty of Ireland. Still another Celtic feature is the name of the enchanter Mabon, doubtless the Mabon of Welsh texts, though cast in a very different role.[2]

The influence of Chrétien's *Erec* is certain. Schofield made a collection of Renaud's borrowings—rimes, phrases, and passages reproduced with little or no change.[3] Philipot, however, was justified in distinguishing these certain signs of Chrétien's influence from the similarities in subject-matter,[4] for the sparrow-hawk contest and the heads impaled on stakes are features of the English *Libeaus Desconus* and therefore were derived from a common source, as we have already seen. And the same must be said of the relation of the giant Mauger le Gris to the fay of the Ille d'Or, even though it reminds one of the relationship of Mabonagrain to his mistress.

Renaud's poem, in spite of a few incidents which could be discarded as unessential, is remarkable for the firmness and unity of its structure. The mission on which Guinglain sets out in the opening scene is duly brought to completion at the close when the wedding bells ring for his marriage with Blonde Esmerée. The affair with the enchantress introduces a well-motivated complication, while the passage in which she teases Guinglain with nightmarish illusions introduces a welcome element of comedy.[5] The waste city of Sinadon, with its fallen towers and deserted streets, the palace lit with a thousand candles, where the minstrels utter their ominous welcome, provide exactly the right atmosphere for the disenchantment of the serpent-maiden. Skilfully the poet brings himself into his own work, which was undertaken, he tells us, to touch the heart of one who has him in her 'baillie', and he promises, if she will look graciously on him, to reunite Guinglain at last with his faery mistress.[6] The merits and the meaning of *Le Bel Inconnu* are clear to all who read, and it seems quite unnecessary to discover deep symbolisms in the most trivial details, as a recent critic has done,[7] in order to appreciate the author's purpose and his artistry.

'Meraugis de Portlesguez'[8]

Meraugis, like *Le Bel Inconnu*, is one of the best of the French romances and gives us the name of its author. It was composed by Raoul de Houdenc

[1] *Eriu*, iv (1910), 91–111. See Marillier in *Revue de l'Histoire des Religions*, xl (1899), 75 f.
[2] *R*, xxiv (1895), 321 f.; xxv (1896), 284; Schofield, op. cit., pp. 125 f.
[3] Schofield, op. cit., pp. 60–134.   [4] *R*, xxvi (1897), 290 ff.
[5] Krappe in *R*, lviii (1932), 426–30, compares this scene with an Irish folktale.
[6] Vss. 6247–66. Cf. *Partenopeus de Blois*.
[7] A. Fierz-Monnier, *Initiation und Wandlung*; review in *ZRP*, lxx (1954), 148 ff.
[8] Ed. M. Friedwagner (Halle, 1897). For corrections to text see G. Paris in *R*, xxvii. 307–18; Ebeling in *ZRP*, xxiv. 508–44, and *Archiv*, ciii. 403–30.

(probably Houdan, Seine-et-Oise) early in the thirteenth century and runs to 5,938 lines.

The chief theme is the rivalry between the two friends, Meraugis de Portlesguez and Gorvain Cadrut for the love of Lidoine, daughter of the King of Cavalon. Intertwined with this theme are many variations on familiar situations: a tournament is held at Lindesores, of which the prize is a sparrow-hawk; a court of ladies decides that Meraugis, who loves Lidoine for her courtesy, is more deserving than Gorvain, who loves her for her beauty; Gauvain goes in search of the Sword of Strange Hangings (*Renges*); Meraugis goes in quest of Gauvain, accompanied by Lidoine and a dwarf; Laquis de Lampadaiz (or Lampagres) defends a ford, riding bareback without bridle or spurs; the victor in a tournament has the right to choose husbands for marriageable damsels; Gauvain, incognito, defends an island and its lady against all comers; he fights with Meraugis, his friend, for some time before he recognizes him; his strength increases after midday; Meraugis enters an enchanted garden and is forced by a spell to join a group of dancers; though in the guise of a fool, with head shaved, he is recognized by Lidoine.

Raoul interweaves these various strands with much skill. Meraugis undertakes the search for Gauvain, not merely for the excitement but to prove his valour to Lidoine, and he must prove his valour in order to deserve her more than Gorvain. Thus a series of feats spring out of the initial situation. Characters who drop out of the narrative for a moment return and resume their activities in a natural way. The jealous hostility between Meraugis and Gorvain, which breaks out into a duel early in the romance, is felicitously concluded by Meraugis's victory at the end and by mutual reconciliation.

As a disciple of Chrétien, Raoul displays a delicate psychological feeling and unravels with a fine skill the interplay of emotions in the hearts of his characters. Besides the long monologues in which one perceives the methods of the master (note Meraugis's rhapsody over the springtime, vss. 4357–401), and the short monologues which express grief or mark decisions, dialogue and narrative also are employed to illuminate the inner life, as in the quarrel between Gorvain and Meraugis (vss. 519–653), and in the scene where Lidoine pretends with consummate art to accept Belchis's proposals (vss. 3682 ff.). Analysis, too, is not uncommon, as when Meraugis's state of mind after he has kissed Lidoine (vss. 1170–239) is explicated. This interest in psychology is accompanied by an equally marked taste for preciosity in thought and expression; Raoul juggles with the words *tort* and *droit* (vss. 1884–98), he indulges in puns (vss. 1979–81), he treats the problems of sentiment with the logic of scholasticism (vss. 1016 ff.).

To Chrétien's influence may also be ascribed the introduction of some of the motifs already mentioned,[1] though whether he was the direct source may

---

[1] See Friedwagner's edition, pp. lxxvii–lxxxi, for detailed comparison.

be doubted because of marked differences in handling. *Erec* may have supplied the episode of the sparrow-hawk contest,[1] and the trio of riders consisting of the hero, the heroine, and a dwarf. *Lancelot* may have suggested the role of Gauvain as the hero's friend and the quest for him, while *Yvain* could have provided the incognito combat between friends, and *Perceval* the Sword with Strange Hangings. Celtic origin has been argued for the Ile sans Nom,[2] whence no one returns and where a knight, under the spell of an enchantress, fights all comers; and also for the enchanted carole or dance which causes all those who are drawn into it to forget everything—a theme which Lot rightly compared with the island of the black weepers and the isle of the laughing men in the *Voyage of Maelduin*.[3] Lot also maintained that the name Gorvain was derived from the name borne by one of Arthur's warriors in *Culhwch*, Gwrvan; while the surname Cadrut may well represent the Welsh adjective *cadrauc*, meaning 'strong, mighty'.[4] Gaston Paris pointed out that Portlesguez probably referred to St. Brieux.[5] The duel between Meraugis and Gauvain, in which the latter, after recognizing his friend, agrees to let himself be beaten and left for dead in order to deceive a lady, may, like a similar episode in the First Continuation of *Perceval*, be derived ultimately from Cuchulainn's agreeing to flee before his foster-father Fergus in order to deceive Queen Medb, as related in the *Cattle Raid of Cooley*.[6]

More problematic is the meaning of the incident, the *esplumeor* (cage of) *Merlin*.[7] Meraugis arrives before a tall rock, on the summit of which twelve prophetic damsels sit. When he asks where he may find the *esplumeor* of Merlin, one of them replies, 'Lo, here it is' (vs. 2703). Is the rock then Merlin's abode, or the abode of fays whom he has instructed in the mantic art? Was the idea derived from the *Didot Perceval*,[8] which tells briefly of Merlin's departure to his *esplumeor*, or from some popular tradition? These are puzzles to which as yet scholarship has found no clear answer.

In spite of certain artificialities of expression and an excessive fondness for enjambment, *Meraugis* must have had a fair number of readers, as is attested not only by the survival of three complete manuscripts and two fragments but also by its apparent fascination for later writers. It was imitated in *Durmart*, in Robert of Blois's *Beaudous*, and, less clearly, in Guillaume le Clerc's *Fergus*,[9] while the incognito combat of Gauvain and Meraugis on

[1] Morgain, daughter of the King of Avalon, was originally the heroine of this adventure, as R. S. Loomis has shown in *Arthurian Tradition*, p. 86.   [2] Philipot in *R*, xxv. 267 ff.

[3] *R*, xxiv. 325 ff. See also *ZFSL*, lvii (1933), 156–62.

[4] *R*, xxiv. 326; *MedAev*, xxv (1956), 181 f.   [5] *Hist. Lit. de la France*, xxx. 223, n. 3.

[6] Loomis, *Arthurian Tradition*, pp. 329–31.

[7] Vss. 2633 ff. See discussion by Nitze in *Spec*, xviii (1943), 69–79; Loomis in *BBSIA*, 1957, pp. 79–83; Brugger in *ZFSL*, xxxi¹ (1907), 245 ff.

[8] Ed. W. Roach, pp. 111 f., 278 f. See above, p. 261, n. 4.

[9] C. Habeman, *Die literarische Stellung des Meraugis de Portlesguez in der altfranzösischen Epik* (Göttingen, 1908); Huet in *R*, xli (1912), 518 ff.

the island may have suggested the tragic encounter of Balaain and Balaan in the *Suite du Merlin* (*Huth Merlin*).[1]

'*Yder*'[2]

There is in the University of Cambridge Library a unique manuscript of a poem concerned with the fortunes of Yder, composed between 1210 and 1225, in western France, perhaps in the department of the Manche. Defective at the beginning, the poem runs to 6,769 lines. The author, a man of some learning,[3] addressed himself to aristocratic circles.

He told how Yder, born out of wedlock, left his mother and grandmother at the age of seventeen to seek his father Nuc. At Caruain he fell in love with a certain Queen Guenloie, and to prove himself worthy of her he set off on a career of adventure. He killed two assailants of a knight who turned out to be King Arthur, but when Arthur proved ungrateful, Yder decided to go to the aid of Talac de Rogemont, whose castle Arthur was besieging. Guenloie was present, witnessed her lover's deeds of prowess, and when he was treacherously wounded by Quoi (Kay), nursed him, and had him cured by a physician. Visited by Arthur, he was persuaded to join the Round Table, and rendered a service to Guenièvre by killing a bear which had entered her chamber. Returning to Rogemont, he engaged at a damsel's request in combat with a knight, who turned out to be his father Nuc. Father and son went to Arthur's court. Arthur became violently jealous of Yder when Guenièvre admitted that if she were to marry again she would choose Yder, and the king sought his death. But Yder succeeded, nevertheless, in killing two giants and bringing back their knife—a feat which Guenloie had imposed as the condition of marriage. Accordingly Yder made her his bride and, shortly after, his birth was legitimized by the wedding of his mother with Nuc.

In this poem Yder is exalted at the expense of Quoi (Kay) and Arthur. Quoi is a traitor, a coward, a murderer. Overthrown by Yder three times at the siege of Rogemont, he takes a cowardly vengeance. He crouches in terror when he sees the giants, but when Yder has vanquished them, he gives the victor poisoned water. Even Arthur is presented in an odious light. He forces Guenièvre to confess an interest in Yder, and thereafter tries to rid himself of his rival.

This jealous role seems to have been forced on Arthur by an old tradition that Yder was once represented as the lover of Guenièvre, a tradition alluded to in the Berne *Folie Tristan*.[4] Even Yder's affair with Queen Guenloie may be a second echo of this tradition since there is reason to believe that the name

[1] *Merlin*, ed. Paris and Ulrich, SATF, ii. 46–56.

[2] Ed. H. Gelzer (Dresden, 1913). Corrections to the text in *R*, xliii (1914), 246–52, and *ZRP*, xxxvii (1913), 466.

[3] He knew the *Metamorphoses* and *Heroides* (list of female victims of love, vss. 2564–70) and derived *amis* from *amor* (vs. 2718).   [4] Ed. E. Hoepffner, vss. 232–5.

Guenloie is a substitute for Guenièvre.[1] The fight with the giants finds a cognate version interpolated in William of Malmesbury's *De Antiquitate Glastoniensis Ecclesiae*,[2] where we read that Ider son of Nuth, after being knighted by Arthur at Caerleon, killed three giants near Glastonbury, but died of his wounds; and the king, feeling responsible for his death, richly endowed the abbey. Obviously this interpolation is a pious fraud which sought to glorify the abbey by adapting a Welsh or Anglo-Norman story, the same as that which was used by the author of *Yder*. The fact that in the *Vengeance Raguidel* also Yder is credited with killing a bear suggests that this exploit too was traditional.[3]

The influence of Chrétien is not to be denied, even though Cligès is depicted as an insolent and brutal knight, the antithesis of his original self. The *Enéas* is another influence; vss. 2695–9 of *Yder* offer a variation on the famous lines in which Lavinia utters the name of Enéas between three sighs (vss. 8551 ff.).

On the whole the romance follows *Cligès* in the trend toward realism. Though giants were not commonly to be encountered in ordinary life, though Yder is a type of the ideal knight and perfect lover, and Guenloie is ready to commit suicide when she despairs of finding her lover again, there is a penchant for less romantic situations. For instance, the duel between Yder and his father is brought on by the fact that Nuc, though middle-aged, is philandering with a damsel without revealing his name, and that she implores Yder to force the name out of him.[4] In the same realistic vein is the departure of Yder's squire Luguein from his father's home, where he has suffered from inactivity in spite of his parents' affection. Realism reaches downright brutality in the scene where Yder meets the amorous advances of King Ivenant's wife by a well-directed kick in the stomach.

Highly significant is the contrast between the poet's attitude toward the monastic and the secular life. He launches an attack against the Benedictines and Cistercians (vss. 3677–717), in the manner of the nearly contemporary satirists Hugues de Berzé and Guiot de Provins, and lashes out at the avarice and carnality which reigned in the monasteries. On the other hand, there is the true lover, 'le vrai amant', and there is the true religion: 'Ço est droite religion que haï tote vilanie.' A true lover is assured of salvation by his sincerity, and if he receives in dying the kisses of his lady love, he has made the best confession and obtained the most efficacious of viatica.

---

[1] *Medieval Studies in Memory of G. Schoepperle Loomis* (New York, 1927), p. 222.

[2] Faral, ii. 451–7; E. K. Chambers, *Arthur of Britain* (London, 1927), pp. 117 f., 267.

[3] *Yder*, ed. Gelzer, p. lvi.

[4] The recognition scene is less touching than in *Milon*, but is brought about very naturally; Yder's scrip is cut in the course of the combat with his father, falls to the ground, and Yder tries to pick it up because it contains half of the ring which his father left with his mother. On these combats between father and son see Loomis, *Arthurian Tradition*, pp. 326–8.

'Fergus'[1]

Two authors calling themselves Guillaume le Clerc flourished in the Middle Ages; one wrote the *Bésant de Dieu*, the other a poem of 6,894 lines in the dialect of Namur or Dinant entitled *Fergus* (*c.* 1225). The latter avoided a common defect of Arthurian romance by focusing the interest on one, rather than two or three heroes, and is unique in representing that hero as the son of a peasant. One day, when Fergus is following the plough, Arthur and a hunting party come by. Though dazed at first by their splendour, the youth leaves his home and is eventually knighted at Carduel (Carlisle). Setting out, he meets at the castle of Lidel the fair Galiene, Lady of Lothian, and though he is smitten by her beauty, he rejects her favours till he has achieved the perilous adventure of Nouquetran. This he accomplishes by removing a horn and a wimple from an ivory lion and killing their guardian, the Black Knight. But when he returns to Lidel, Galiene has vanished. In the course of a long search for her, he performs sundry exploits and wins a magic shield from a giantess at Dunostre. Finally he learns that Galiene is being besieged at Roceborc and, though keeping the secret of his identity, he overcomes the king who is conducting the siege and then disappears. Arthur proclaims a tournament at Gedeorde; Fergus takes part incognito but is recognized by Galiene, and thus the poem ends with the nuptials of Fergus and the Lady of Lothian.

It has been proposed that Fergus belongs to a group of four romances which celebrate the winning of a lady of Lothian and which are all derived from an oral tradition of the *conteurs*.[2] Malory's book of Gareth and Dame Lyones (Lothian)[3] shares with *Fergus* the scene where the heroine comes, inflamed by love, to the hero's bed by night, the hero's spectacular performance incognito at a tournament organized by Arthur, and Arthur's awarding the hero, as a consequence, to the heroine in wedlock. Malory's tale of Dame Lyones presents in turn some peculiar resemblances to Chrétien's tale of *la dame* Laudine, daughter of Duke Laudonet (Lothian), particularly the roles of Lynet and Lunete, the estrangement between the hero and heroine, and the hero's wandering half crazed as a result of his lady's rebuff. There is also an elaborate correspondence between Chrétien's tale of Laudine and the story of the fountain fay of Calatir, that is, Calder in Lothian, as related in the lai of *Desiré*. What is one to make of these curious links between the four tales of a lady of Lothian? Though in my opinion they do not prove a common ultimate origin, they do raise the question. It is certain, at any rate, that Chrétien's *Yvain* was not the common source.

Nevertheless, the influence of the Champenois master on *Fergus* is

---

[1] Ed. F. Michel (1841); ed. E. Martin (Halle, 1872); corrections of text in *ZRP*, xliv, 102–5.

[2] Loomis, *Arthurian Tradition*, pp. 115 f., 291, 301–5, 365 f., and *Proc. of the Soc. of Antiquaries of Scotland*, lxxxix, pp. 11–13.   [3] Brugger in *MP*, xxii (1924), 159–91; Bivar in *MP*, l (1953), 162–70.

unquestionable.[1] The opening scenes of the romance are skilful variations on
Chrétien's *Perceval*: the hero is brought up in rustic surroundings, is moved by
the spectacle of Arthur's knights to leave his home, arrives at Arthur's court,
is mocked by Keu, and so forth. Galiene is a more aggressive Blancheflor, and
possibly Fergus's quest for the shining shield was suggested by the quest of
the shining Grail. There seems to be imitation of *Cligès* in a monologue of
Galiene (vss. 1798–862); of *Yvain* in the motif of a maiden seeking a champion for her mistress; of *Erec* in the portrait of the heroine (vss. 1511–81).
Even more evident is the impress of Chrétien on the phrasing and style.

Several of the Celtic elements, such as the chase of the white hart, were
probably borrowed from earlier romances, and this is surely true of the plot
of the besieged lady, though it may ultimately be derived from the *Sickbed
of Cuchulainn*.[2] Other motifs, such as the serpent guardian of treasure, the
sounding of a horn to summon an adversary, are mere commonplaces of
medieval fiction, and the fountain which miraculously restores strength is
probably a reminiscence of the Fountain of Youth.

A distinctive feature of *Fergus* is the connexion with southern Scotland.
It may in fact have been written under the patronage of Alan of Galloway
(ob. 1233), descendant of a Fergus of Galloway and a Somerled, lord of the
Hebrides,[3] though in that case it is odd that the poet represented his hero's
father Soumilloit (i.e. Somerled) as a farmer. His Scottish geography is
remarkably accurate.[4] He not only mentions but places correctly Liddell,
Jedburgh, Roxburgh, Melrose, Trimontium (Mont Dolerous), Edinburgh
(Castiel as Puceles), Queensferry (Port le Reine), and Dunottar. In the
whole range of Arthurian romance there is no instance of a more detailed,
more realistic geographical setting.

Humour is present, though restricted mainly to caustic speeches and ironic
jests,[5] and on the whole the tone is too courtly to permit the conclusion that
Fergus marks the beginning of a cynical trend which culminated in *Petit
Jean de Saintré*. Moreover, Jordan's characterization of Guillaume le Clerc
as a democrat and a rationalist is open to challenge. *Fergus*, to be sure, is the
son of a peasant, but a peasant who owns three castles and is married to a
lady of high birth. Guillaume's purpose was not to describe how a plough-boy
became a knight, but rather to show that nature is stronger than nurture.
The poem does not herald the dawn of democracy.

---

[1] W. Marquardt, *Der Einfluss Kristians von Troyes auf dem Roman Fergus des Guillaume le Clerc*
(Göttingen, 1906).

[2] H. Newstead, 'The Besieged Ladies in Arthurian Romance', *PMLA*, lxiii. 803–30.

[3] M. Schlauch in *PMLA*, xliv (1929), 360–76; J. Greenberg in *PMLA*, lxvi (1951), 524–33;
M. D. Legge in *Transactions of Dumfriesshire and Galloway Natural History and Antiquarian Soc.*,
xxvii. 163–72.

[4] See preceding note and E. Brugger in *Arthuriana*, ii (1930), 7–19; in *Miscellany of Studies in
Honour of L. E. Kastner* (Cambridge, 1932), pp. 94–107; Loomis, *Arthurian Tradition*, pp. 109 f.

[5] Mussafia in *Literarisches Centralblatt*, 1872, p. 364; Jordan in *ZRP*, xliii. 154 f.

It seems to have enjoyed a slight popularity. The adventure at Dunostre was imitated in *Huon of Bordeaux*,[1] and the whole was translated into Dutch in the fourteenth century as *Ferguut*.[2]

'Le Chevalier aux Deux Epées' or *'Meriadeuc'*[3]

This poem of 12,352 lines was composed in the language of the Ile de France in the first half of the thirteenth century and survives in a single manuscript. The core of the plot is this:

Meriadeuc, whose name is not revealed till the end of the romance, was called 'le Chevalier aux Deux Epées' from the fact that he won a second sword when he alone at Arthur's court was able to unfasten the belt of a sword which Lore, Lady of Garadigan, wore about her waist. After this feat he disappeared, and Lore declared that she would have no other husband than the nameless hero. We learn that some time earlier she had obtained the sword and the belt from the corpse of Bleheri, father of Meriadeuc, when it had been brought for burial to the Gaste Chapele (Ruined Chapel). Meriadeuc, after performing various feats of arms, came by chance to the castle of his mother, who discovered his identity and revealed the circumstances of his father's death: Brien de la Gastine had by a trick obtained the services of Gauvain in his war with Bleheri, and Gauvain had unwittingly slain him, but Bleheri before expiring had declared that his son must avenge his death. This Meriadeuc accomplished; he became reconciled, however, to Gauvain, returned to Arthur's court, and was married to Lore by the Archbishop of Canterbury.

The main plot of a vendetta carried out with the slain man's own sword is combined with a long-drawn-out sub-plot in which Gauvain is the principal figure. He is sent by Arthur in search of Meriadeuc, is treacherously attacked by Brien des Illes and left for dead, recovers, survives other attempts on his life, champions a lovely damsel, fights incognito with Meriadeuc, overcomes Brien, delivers Meriadeuc's mother from siege, who then pardons him for her husband's death and reconciles him with her son. When Meriadeuc is wedded to Lore, Gauvain consummates his long-delayed union with the damsel whom he has championed earlier and who has to be convinced that he is indeed Gauvain before she will accept him as her lover.

Other adventures are introduced with more or less skill. At the beginning there is the eerie incident of the horse-chain, left by Lore on the altar of the Ruined Chapel—an incident which leads up somewhat artificially to her appearance at Arthur's court with the girdle which only the hero can unloose. There is also the motif of a sword which will heal the wound which

---

[1] Brugger in *MLR*, xx (1925), 158–75.   [2] See Chap. 34 below.

[3] Ed. W. Foerster (Halle, 1877). Criticism by Mussafia in *Zts. f. österreichische Gymnasien*, 1877 pp. 197–213.

it has itself inflicted, reminding one of the healing of the Maimed King in the *Queste del Saint Graal* by the blood from the lance. The author borrows from Chrétien and Raoul de Houdenc the technique of holding the reader in suspense. We do not learn till late in the poem that the Knight of the Two Swords is named Meriadeuc and that the Lady of Garadigan is named Lore.

There are other reminiscences of earlier romances.[1] Gauvain saves the damsel from an unwelcome suitor, much as Yvain saves Lunete from Harpin de la Montagne. The episode in which Brien des Illes figures is modelled in large part on that of the Black Knight, Maduc, of the *Vengeance Raguidel.* The passage in which King Ris sends a messenger to Arthur demanding his beard[2] and the allusion to the loves of Uter and Igerne demonstrate a familiarity with Wace's *Brut.*

The style is easy, the versification smooth, and the descriptions are rich in realistic detail. The importance attached to male and female dress makes several pages read like a *jardin des modes* of the time. Military tactics are elaborately developed in connexion with the siege of Tygan, the castle of Meriadeuc's mother. But the linking of episodes is clumsy, particularly in the middle of the poem, and the frequent use of enjambment makes one think of the acrobatics of Verlaine; for instance in vss. 10998 f.:

> Un jor avint que ains couchant
> Soleil les murs ot mout mal mis.

The *Chevalier aux Deux Epées* seems to have contributed to the *Suite du Merlin (Huth Merlin)* the scene where the damsel arrives at Arthur's court demanding that a knight unloose the sword-belt from her waist.[3] Likewise its influence is apparent in the *Atre Périlleux* (vss. 5080 ff.), where two damsels demand as the price of their favours the defeat of Gauvain.

'Durmart le Gallois'[4]

Written between 1220 and 1250 in the dialect of the border between Normandy and Picardy, this poem of 15,998 lines tells the following story. Young Durmart, son of the King of Ireland and Denmark, has an affair with the wife of his father's seneschal, but, seeing the error of his ways, he decides to make amends and to render himself worthy of the Queen of Ireland, whose beauty has been described to him by a peasant. Not long after he meets her and wins the sparrow-hawk for her as a prize of beauty, but without recognizing that she is the object of his devotion. When he

---

[1] R. Thedens, *Li Chevalier as Deus Espees in seinem Verhältnis zu seinen Quellen* (Göttingen, 1908).

[2] *Brut*, ed. Arnold, vss. 11563 ff. A somewhat similar treatment of this motif is found in the *Suite du Merlin. Merlin*, ed. Paris and Ulrich, i. 202.

[3] *Merlin*, i. 213–23.

[4] Ed. E. Stengel (Tübingen, 1873). Corrections of text in A. Stoericko, *Über das Verhältnis der beiden Romane Durmart und Garin de Montglane* (1888).

learns her identity he sets out in search of her, rescues Guenièvre from the power of Brun de Morois, and wins the tournament of the Blanches Mores. At Glastonbury he is welcomed by Arthur and Guenièvre, but refuses to join the Round Table until he has found his lady. He comes to a land wasted by war, which turns out to be Ireland, and proceeds to the town of Limeri (Limerick), where the queen is being besieged by Nogant. Though Nogant summons Arthur to his aid and accuses the queen, whose name we now learn is Fenise, of atheism, he prudently escapes on a dromedary rather than meet Durmart in trial by combat. Of course, when Durmart asks for her hand in marriage she readily grants it. There is a pious conclusion in which the hero founds abbeys, makes a pilgrimage to Rome, and delivers the holy city from a pagan army.

The romance is cast in the mould of the 'quest'. Durmart goes in search of a lady whom he has never seen, meets her without recognition, loses her, finds her again and marries her. Though one is reminded of Jaufré Rudel and his 'princesse lointaine', the motif is far too common and is treated so differently by the two poets that no connexion can be assumed.[1] The abduction of Guenièvre and her rescue, it has been suggested by R. S. Loomis, may be related to the scene carved over the portal at Modena.[2] From the *Didot Perceval* may come the 'siege perilous' which Durmart occupies on his arrival at Arthur's court. The episode of the sparrow-hawk seems to blend the versions of this same theme in *Meraugis*[3] and the *Bel Inconnu*. The two visions of a candle-lighted tree elaborate a motif found in the Second Continuation of the *Perceval*.[4] The giant knight whom Queen Fenise had relied on to win the sparrow-hawk for her but who shows the white feather may represent the type of Handsome Coward discussed by Brugger.[5]

The author knew his Chrétien well.[6] The heroine owes her name Fenise to her counterpart in *Cligès*. The participants in the tourney of Blanches Mores include Erec, Yvain, Perceval, Lancelot, Greoreas, &c. When Keu in vss. 13088–90 'verse jus Si que les deux janbes en vont A reversées contremont', we recall the somersault of Calogrenant near the beginning of *Yvain*. The successive monologues in which the lovers analyse their feelings and employ the motif of two hearts in one body, the scene in which Fenise is obliged to hide her love during Durmart's combat (vss. 12384 ff.), and the scene in which the lovers, finally united, hide their joy, these all bear witness

---

[1] See Stengel's introduction.
[2] *Medieval Studies in Memory of G. Schoepperle Loomis*, p. 223.
[3] L. Kirchrath, *Li Romans de Durmart le Galois in seinem Verhältnis zu Meraugis de Portlesguez und den Werken Chrestiens de Troyes* (Marburg, 1884), compares *Durmart* with *Meraugis* from the point of view of tendencies and techniques.
[4] See above, p. 214, n. 3.
[5] Brugger in *ZRP*, lxi. 1–44; lxiii. 123–73, 275–328; lxv. 121–92, 289–433.
[6] See above, n. 3.

to the admiration of the poet for the Champenois master. The influence of *Erec* is manifest, particularly in the passage (vss. 15377 ff.) where Fenise thinks that if Durmart loves 'de bone fine amor', he should 'guard his good name (*pris*), to honour both himself and me, and may God grant him to guard it so well that no one can reproach him in any way'.[1]

The romancer, though he repeatedly condemns prolixity, is nevertheless repeatedly guilty. Twenty times or more he tells us how the hero retires to bed, rises, dresses, and takes his meals. He is very slow in winding up the story after Durmart's marriage. But he is successful in maintaining unity, keeping his hero constantly in view. The coward knight already mentioned does not disappear from the romance but reappears under the name of Nogant to continue his discreditable activities. The intimate picture of manners and customs has more than a documentary value. Psychological realism is seen at its best in the affair with the seneschal's wife and its termination, though it shows neither party in an admirable light. The lady declares that if Durmart is going to give her up, she does not propose to go mad (*derver*), and his response, 'Lady, you will say all you want to say', is brutally frank (vss. 691 f.).

Gaston Paris went too far in comparing *Durmart* with *Télémaque* or the *Cyropédie*,[2] but the medieval poet does show a moralistic strain. The affair with the seneschal's wife is a sort of exemplum, a warning. There are numerous 'chastoiements' enjoining the virtues of prowess, generosity, and energy,[3] and the last part, with its account of Durmart's pious works and the vision of the child in the tree, symbolizing the Christ and the world,[4] is plainly intended for the reader's edification. The romance has been handed down only in the unique manuscript at Bern; it was imitated by the author of *Garin de Montglane*,[5] and Christine de Pisan alludes to it in her *Débat des Deux Amants*.

'*Gliglois*'[6]

The same realistic tendency observable in *Durmart* is even more pronounced in *Gliglois*, a poem of 2,942 lines written in Picardy in the first or second quarter of the thirteenth century. The supernatural is entirely lacking. The young hero comes to Arthur's court, finds a rival in Gauvain, and

---

[1] This passage and vss. 15451–60 may enlighten us as to the much discussed meaning of *Erec* since they form an indirect commentary by an admirer of Chrétien.

[2] *Hist. Lit. de la France*, xxx. 114.

[3] This is forcefully repeated: vss. 10365 ff., 12825 ff., &c.

[4] For the origin of this episode, derived directly from the Second Continuation of the *Perceval*, see the *Didot Perceval*, ed. W. Roach (Philadelphia, 1941), pp. 73–76; E. S. Greenhill in *Traditio*, x (1954), 323–71.

[5] See p. 380, n. 4.

[6] Ed. C. H. Livingston, *Harvard Studies in Romance Languages*, viii (1932); reviewed by E. G. Gardner in *MLR*, xxviii (1933), 117 f.; by Langfors in *R*, lviii (1932), 450–3; Nitze in *MP*, xxx (1932–3), 323–5; discussed by Schofield in *Studies and Notes in Philology and Literature*, iv. 180–2.

is wedded at Carduel, but otherwise *Gliglois* might well be regarded as a society romance, like the poems of Jean Renart or *Amadas et Idoine*, rather than as a representative of the Matter of Britain. To be sure, there is a tournament of which the prize is a falcon and in which the hero participates incognito, but otherwise the imitation of Chrétien is limited to a few touches reminiscent of *Cligès*.

The plot is very simple. Gliglois, the son of a German noble, is sent by his father to Arthur's court and enters the service of Gauvain as a squire. Both master and squire fall in love with Beauté, a handmaid of Guenièvre. Beauté rejects them both, but secretly favours the youth. When he has sufficiently demonstrated his devotion and his valour, he is rewarded by his lady's hand in marriage. Despite the banal plot and other conventional features, the poem does not lack freshness and felicity of treatment. Twice, when the young squire is carving at table, he becomes entranced and cannot take his eyes off his beloved. One morning, when Beauté descends into her garden, she finds Gliglois feeding his master's falcons. She has trouble in lacing up her chemise, engages the squire's assistance, leads him on to a confession of love, only to banish him from her presence in feigned dudgeon. She plays again the cruel coquette when Gliglois procures for her an escort to a great tourney, follows her with bleeding feet, and never murmurs when she forbids her escort three times to share his mount with her suffering lover.[1]

These episodes display originality and sensitive observation. Dialogue, too, is handled with naturalness, as in the provost's welcome to the hero and in the conversation of Guenièvre and Gauvain. Realism, however, is suffused with courtly idealism and romantic optimism. Gliglois wins Beauté because he accepts humiliation and suffering, and the poet emphasizes the moral in the concluding lines:

> Or sachies qui volentiers sert
> Que biens en vient u tost u tart.

(Now understand that he who willingly serves will have good reward sooner or later.)

It is strange that a poem of such excellence has left no trace in foreign literatures and is not alluded to even by the French.

'Floriant et Florete'[2]

This biographical narrative of 8,278 lines was written by a poet of eastern France or northern Burgundy, in a dialect of the Ile de France with Picard features, between 1250 and 1275. Of the author we can infer only that he

---

[1] Several passages exalt the virtue of Largess: vss. 2055 ff., 2186 ff.

[2] Ed. H. F. Williams, *Univ. of Michigan Pub., Lang. and Lit.* xxiii (1947); F. Michel, Roxburghe Club (1873). Corrections of text in *Zts. für österreichische Gymnasien*, xxvi. 538–46, and *R*, iv. 511. Discussed by I. P. McKeehan in *PMLA*, xli (1926), 785–809.

probably visited Sicily, for he knew Monreale, Palermo, and the legend of Morgain's palace of Mongibel (Etna).

The hero, Floriant, was the posthumous son of a king of Sicily, murdered by his treacherous seneschal. Morgain la Fée carried off the new-born child to Mongibel, had him baptized, trained in the seven arts and in chivalry, and in due time sent him in a magic boat to Arthur's court at Cardigan. Preceded by the fame of numerous exploits, he arrived, only to be recalled by the plight of his mother, besieged by the false seneschal at Monreal. Arthur took up his cause, brought an army to Sicily, and began operations against the seneschal and his suzerain, the Emperor of Constantinople. In the ensuing battles Floriant performed brilliantly, fell in love after a glimpse of the Emperor's daughter, Florete, vanquished the seneschal in trial by combat, and married the lady. Some time later, overhearing criticism of his inactivity, he undertook a second journey to Britain, this time assuming the name of 'Li Biaus Sauvages' and accompanied by Florete. Passing through Calabria and Apulia he proved his prowess against a dragon and against a sultan who was besieging Rome. Hardly had he arrived in London and been welcomed by Arthur when he was recalled to the East. He settled down in domestic felicity at Palermo and the years went by till, one day, he chased a white stag, which brought him to Morgain's castle. Thither Florete was also conveyed by three fays in Morgain's service, and, though the conclusion is lost, we may feel sure that she and her Floriant enjoyed the immortality of Morgain and Arthur.

The biography is admirably constructed. The hero carries out the obligation to avenge his father's murder and his mother's wrongs and in the process woos and wins a bride. As in Chrétien's *Erec*, a second series of adventures is motivated by the slur on the hero's knightly reputation. The conclusion brings him back under the sheltering care of his foster-mother and forecasts a future of endless bliss for him and his bride.

The sources are unusually diverse. The virtuous woman who rebuffs a hateful suitor and as a consequence suffers tribulation is a familiar character in medieval fiction; the villainous suitor is a seneschal not only in *Floriant* but also in *Doon de Mayence*, *Joufrois*, *Macaire*, and *La Reine Sibille*. Floriant's birth and childhood resemble those of Lancelot in the prose romance but even more those of Lanzelet in Ulrich's poem, who was abducted at birth by a fay of the sea, was brought up by her in an island castle, presented with a horse and arms, and sent out into the world in a boat.[1] There is also a remarkable parallelism between the *enfances* of Floriant and those of Maugis d'Aigremont—a parallelism which seems due to a common source and which extends to the Sicilian background.[2] Arthur's expected arrival at

[1] Ulrich von Zatzikhoven, *Lanzelet*, trans. Webster, pp. 27–30.
[2] *Revue des Langues Romanes*, xxx. 76–84.

Morgain's palace of Mongibel reflects the tradition recorded by Gervase of Tilbury, Caesarius of Heisterbach, and Jean d'Outremeuse in his *Myreur des Histors*, while in the *Chevalier du Papegau* Morgain is called 'la fée de Montgibel'.[1] Some of the names, even those of the hero and the heroine, reveal the influence of the *chansons de geste*; so also do the deliverance of Rome from the Saracens and the handling of other sieges and battles. Though some of the monsters which Floriant meets in the course of his travels belong to standard types, not so are the 'sardinnas' or 'sathenas' with their huge ears, nor the Pellican which devours a girl a day! The love-affair is treated in the tradition of *Enéas* and *Cligès*.[2] Otherwise the influence of Chrétien is not discernible, save in certain verbal echoes of *Perceval*[3] in the description of Guingambresil's castle and, as noted above, in the motivation of Floriant's return to chivalric adventure.

The author takes an evident delight in elaborate description; for example, read the passages on the curtain of Morgain's boat, embroidered with scenes from the Troy and Aeneas legends (vss. 843 ff.), on Floriant's rich girdle (vss. 5131 ff.), on the bridal dress of Florete (vss. 5921 ff.). The ceremony of knighting, the wedding festivities, and the siege operations are reproduced for us in remarkable detail. Though far from original in content, the poem skilfully combines the diverse elements; and though the transitions follow a monotonous formula ('A tant laissons', 'De . . . vous conterons'), the style is easy and flowing. The manuscript in the New York Public Library is unique, but the romance was popular enough to be retold in fifteenth-century prose, and a passage on the value of reading romances (vss. 6231–40) was paraphrased in *Claris et Laris*.

'*Les Merveilles de Rigomer*'[4]

A certain Jehan, a *trouvère* of the region about Tournai and Cambrai, composed in the last third of the thirteenth century the *Merveilles de Rigomer*, a poem which, though incomplete, extends to 17,271 lines. The title refers to a castle situated in 'un regort de mer' (a bay of the sea); hence the name Rigomer. It is imagined as somewhere in Ireland, but the author's

---

[1] See Chap. 7 above, and Williams's edition, p. 4, n. 5. Wolfram von Eschenbach twice refers to 'dem berc ze Famorgan', evidently meaning Etna. See E. Martin's edition of *Parzival*, ii, p. lix, and notes to 56, 18; 400, 8; and 496, 8; *Ly Mireur des Histors*, ed. S. Bormans (Brussels, 1877), pp. 50–58.

[2] Cf. the nocturnal monologues of Florete and Floriant with those of Soredamor and Alexandre. Florete watches the combats from her window, as Lavine does in *Enéas*. The sojourn of Enéas at Carthage and his arrival in Lombardy are among the subjects which are depicted on the curtain of Morgain's boat, as well as scenes from the *Roman de Troie*. For other evidence of the author's reading see Williams's edition, pp. 26–38.

[3] Cf. vss. 797–800 and 1377 f. with *Perceval*, vss. 3272–5 and 3327 f.

[4] Ed. W. Foerster, H. Breuer (Dresden, 1908–15). On text see Foerster in *ZFSL*, xxxii. 81 ff., 219 ff.; Brugger in *ZFSL*, xxx². 129–56; Schultz-Gorra in *ZRP*, lv (1935), 663–7.

knowledge of the Emerald Isle seems limited to the names of a few districts, Brefny, Connaught, and Desmond. The fauna which the heroes encounter has never been observed in these or any other Irish locality, and it is safe to conclude that the geographical setting is a bluff.

In the opening scene a maiden sent by the mistress of Rigomer appears at Caerleon and invites the knights of Arthur's court to remove the spell from the castle and its mistress, Dionise. About 4,500 lines are devoted to the journey of Lancelot, who surmounts many perils, performs many exploits, but on his reaching Rigomer a magic lance deprives him of physical power; a ring steals his mental faculties, and he becomes a scullion. It is now the turn of Gauvain and others to seek Lancelot, and they too meet with many marvels. Gauvain, though trapped at first in the castle of Gaudionet, is delivered through the efforts of his mistress, Lorie, and at last reaches Rigomer. All the enchantments which had proved too much for Lancelot lose their power; the maiden with the lance predicts Gauvain's success and the maiden with the rings flees before him. He delivers Lancelot and the other prisoners, but refuses the hand of Dionise and returns to Arthur's court. A second quest[1] begins with the appearance of a second maiden messenger, seeking a champion for the heiress of Quintefuele, who has been robbed of her heritage. This time Arthur himself sets out, accompanied by Lancelot, and after some remarkable adventures, carries out the mission by killing the usurper in a duel. The conclusion is missing.

The poem is not notable for unity, refinement, or narrative skill. The quest of Arthur and Lancelot has nothing to do with the 'merveilles de Rigomer', and some scholars have argued, though without success, that originally it formed a separate poem. In the earlier part Lancelot with monotonous regularity seeks harbourage, is received by a host who asks his name and errand and warns him against proceeding farther. Monotonously these warnings are reinforced by the arrival of one knight after another suffering from the wounds he has received at Rigomer. When at last Gauvain reaches the enchanted castle, his triumph is something of an anticlimax, since the enchantments cease to operate, the anticipated terrors melt away.

In spite, however, of the monotony and the staleness of many incidents, the author has invented some novel and uncanny features. There is the polyglot bird Willeris, which leads Gauvain to a castle where his adversaries multiply as he kills them. There is the panther of the Male Gaudine (the Evil Wood), which breathes forth flames. There are the cats which surround a bier, attack Lancelot savagely, and have to be driven away with a blazing brand. There is the falcon which makes its diet exclusively of human heads. Among the creatures which bar the way to Rigomer are dog-headed men

---

[1] Ed. E. Stengel, *Die Turiner Rigomer-Episode* (Greifswald, 1905); E. Pessen, *Die Schlußepisode des Rigomerromans* (Heidelberg, 1907). See Bruce, ii. 246, n. 11.

and monsters which run swiftly on one foot, derived ultimately perhaps from Pliny. The charming episode of the lady rapt away from her lover during a storm and later discovered by Engrevain in a cave which opens only at night, in the company of feasting and singing knights and damsels, sounds like a fairy-tale. Probably Welsh in origin is the chess-board with pieces which move of themselves,[1] and also the hideous hag whose eyelids are so heavy that they have to be propped up, for she has a counterpart in *Culhwch*, the giant whose eyelids had to be supported by forks.[2]

The author of *Rigomer* doubtless knew Chrétien, Raoul de Houdenc,[3] and the Prose *Lancelot*. When Arthur claims that he has in Gauvain the best knight in the world, the queen rouses his anger by remarking that she knows one just as good, meaning Lancelot.[4] There are echoes of the Grail romances; for example, the Maimed King is evidently the model for the aged and wounded knight who is kept alive by the visits of strangers. Gauvain, it is worth noting, has taken on something of the messianic character of Perceval and Galaad. Though his mission is entirely secular, he is the chosen one, the liberator, the healer, the restorer of a land blighted by spells. The poem provides in the episode of 'l'Atre Maleïs' (the Accursed Cemetery) a superior version to that which Chrétien tells of Lancelot's visit to the cemetery.[5] At least, in Jehan's account the tombs which Cligès sees filled with corpses and the empty one awaiting an occupant have a rational function; the empty tomb is destined for Cligès himself, should he be slain in the ensuing combat. No such plausible explanation is supplied by Chrétien; Lancelot inspects the tombs, learns for whom they are destined, and departs.

'Claris et Laris'[6]

The tendency to egregious length is again illustrated by a poem of 30,370 lines begun in 1268 by a professional minstrel of Lorraine.[7] As the title, *Claris et Laris*, suggests, the work is devoted to the fortunes of two friends and is divided into two parts.

The first half is mainly concerned with Claris, who is smitten with love for Lidoine, wife of the aged King of Gascony, and it leads up to their marriage after her husband's death. Meanwhile the two friends embark on a series of adventures, in the course of which Claris confides the secret of his

---

[1] *RF*, xlv (1931), 69, n. 2; Loth, *Mabinogion*, 2nd ed. ii. 114, n.

[2] S. Singer, *Germanisch-romanisches Mittelalter* (Zürich, 1935), pp. 178 f.; Loth, op. cit. i. 299.

[3] See Foerster and Breuer's ed., ii. 142–69; H. Kuhse, *Der Einfluß Raouls von Houdenc auf den Roman Les Merveilles de Rigomer* (Göttingen, 1914).

[4] Loomis, *Arthurian Tradition*, pp. 134 f.

[5] Ibid., pp. 233 f.

[6] Ed. J. Alton (Tübingen, 1884).

[7] Jordan in *AR*, ix (1925), 5–33, shows that the text belongs to the valley of the Moselle.

passion to Laris, who promises his aid. But Laris is carried off in his sleep and imprisoned by a fay, Madoine. Only after he has been sought for a long time by Claris and eleven other knights is he discovered and freed.

In the latter half of the poem the affair of Laris with Marine, sister of Yvain, is the principal theme. Her father, King Urien, besieged by King Tallas of Denmark, who wishes to marry Marine by force, applies to King Arthur for aid. The two friends respond to the appeal, and thanks to their feats of prowess and those of Gauvain and Yvain, Tallas is vanquished, but Laris is taken prisoner. An interminable series of quests now begins, conducted by thirty knights, divided into groups of ten. Merlin himself takes a hand and reveals to Brandaliz the whereabouts of Laris and the means to liberate him.

Between the two parts there is a marked symmetry. The two friends aid each other in their amours and use the same methods: Laris, for instance, revives Claris from a swoon by means of a kiss from Lidoine; Claris later revives Laris by asking Lidoine to kiss him, impersonating the absent Marine. In the first half of the romance the Britons deliver Lidoine, after her husband's death, from Savari l'Espagnol, who was endeavouring to force her into marriage; likewise in the second half the Britons triumph over Tallas, who had the same designs upon Marine. Each half ends with the marriage of one of the protagonists.

The author employs in the first half the technique of 'entrelacement', setting each knight off on a quest, then interweaving the threads of their adventures. But he fails to hold the reader's interest because of the staleness and the sameness of his stock: brigands killed, giants and dragons destroyed, tournaments won, helpless damsels avenged. Many knights lie captive in dungeons for shorter or longer periods, to be freed singly or *en masse*. The author retells one of the most poetic of medieval themes, that of the fay who falls in love with a mortal and keeps him beside her in her paradise.[1] It is the theme of the Val sans Retour, of the 'Paradis de la Reine Sibille', and of *Tannhäuser*, but in this romance it has been robbed of most of its poetry. Claris and Laris enter the forest of Broceliande, destroy the enchantments of the Château Périlleux, are lured on by siren voices, find themselves captives in Morgain's sensual paradise, and are finally able to escape through the friendly aid of Morgain's companion, Madoine, who is enamoured of Laris. Thus Madoine is moved by jealousy to intervene several times in the story with intent to thwart the marriage of Laris and Marine.

A complete catalogue of the probable sources of the poem has been made

---

[1] P. S. Barto, *Tannhäuser and the Mountain of Venus* (New York, 1916), pp. 18–57; L. A. Paton, *Fairy Mythology of Arthurian Romance* (Boston, 1903), pp. 49–103; H. R. Patch, *The Other World* (Cambridge, Mass., 1950), pp. 261–90; F. Desonay, *Antoine de la Sale, Le Paradis de la Reine Sibylle* (Paris, 1930). There is a certain resemblance between the story of Morgain's paradise in *Claris et Laris* and that in Antoine de la Sale's book. See below, p. 426.

by Klose.[1] Among them are Chrétien's works (though *Lancelot* seems to have affected only the style), the continuations of his *Perceval*, many of the romances listed in this chapter, and *Perlesvaus*. The invasion of Britain by Romans under the emperor Thereus, constituting an entirely separate episode of 1,300 lines, derives from Wace, or more probably from the final section of the *Didot Perceval*. Merlin too appears as an old man before a fire, the sage 'qui tout set, tout fet et tout voit' (vs. 22236); there is a rapid summary of Robert de Boron's *Merlin*.

The most original passages are characterized by an anti-chivalric humour. Dodinel avoids a dangerous combat by using his wits, and escapes imprisonment by passing himself off as a minstrel. Keu expresses himself like Sancho Panza (vss. 10098 ff.):

> 'Que il n'a en cest mont terrien
> Si sote gent con chevalier,
> Car querant vont lor encombrier. . .
> Or ne sui je pas en Bretaigne,
> A la cour le roy mon seignor,
> Ou je prenoie le meillor
> Et le plus bel en la cuisine.'

('For there are no people in this earthly world so foolish as knights, for they go hunting for trouble. . . Now am I no longer in Britain at the court of my lord Arthur, where I used to take the best and daintiest food in the kitchen.')

Is this the voice of the author speaking, or is it a sign of the times?

'*Escanor*'[2]

Girard d'Amiens, author of *Meliacin* and the compilation *Charlemagne*, wrote *Escanor* about 1280, and may have presented it in 1279 to Eleanor of Castile, wife of Edward I of England, on the occasion of her visit to Amiens.[3] It comprises nearly 26,000 lines, without allowing for several gaps in the unique manuscript. In this long-winded performance two main plots, as in *Claris et Laris*, are intertwined, but without any attempt at chronological sequence. One is the story of Keu, who at the tourney of Banborc (Bamborough), organized by Canor of Northumberland, to discover a valiant husband for his daughter, distinguished himself in the eyes of young Andrivete and fell in love with her. But he retired to Carlion without daring to confess his passion. After her father's death the girl's uncle tried to marry her to a man of low degree so as to gain possession of the kingdom, but she escaped from his clutches; his plot to discourage Keu by a lying letter was foiled, and he was forced to raise the siege of Banborc. The other story tells

---

[1] M. Klose, *Der Roman von Claris und Laris in seinen Beziehungen zur altfranzösischen Artusepik*, *Beiheft zur ZRP*, lxiii (1916).

[2] Ed. Michelant (Tübingen, 1886). Corrections of text by Tobler in *ZRP*, xi. 421 ff.

[3] On date see forthcoming article by Brault in *BBSIA*, 1959.

how Gauvain was unjustly accused by Escanor le Beau of the murder of his cousin. When he showed some hesitation about defending his honour, young Galantivet, brother of Gifflet, anticipated him by meeting the accuser on the road and leaving him half dead. The accuser's uncle, Escanor le Grand, tried to capture Gauvain, but succeeded only in taking Gifflet, and sent him as a prisoner to the queen of the town of Traverses. Arthur besieged the town. Gauvain won a victory over the younger Escanor in a duel, and they were reconciled.

As usual, these bare outlines are filled in with numerous incidents, of which a goodly proportion belong to the common stock of Arthurian romance. Girard knew the cycle better than some commentators have allowed.[1] He probably took the name Escanor from *L'Atre Périlleux*, though in the form Esquanors it is found in the *chansons de geste*.[2] There is little novelty in the formula of a tournament attended by the hero in arms of varying colours, as Keu does at Banborc, or in the false accusation of murder directed at Gauvain, or in the bitter denunciation of Arthur by a damsel, or in the combat at the *perron* of Merlin, already told in the Prose *Lancelot* and the Prose *Tristan*.[3]

But the author does depart from established conventions in several ways and not always with a happy result. Gauvain, after playing at first his normal heroic role, reveals an unexpected streak of cowardice at the prospect of a duel with Escanor le Beau. Keu is strangely presented as a bashful lover, though at the same time he retains his old habit of insolent raillery. To the reader's surprise Escanor le Beau ends his days as a hermit, and the Virgin Mary and a company of angels attend his burial. His grave is revealed to his uncle through the nocturnal visions of an abbot. The poem concludes in an atmosphere of sanctity which palely reflects the *Queste del Saint Graal*.

Other novelties introduced by Girard are more happily inspired. There is the story of how Gauvain won his famous steed Gringalet from Escanor le Grand in combat, but found that, parted from its old master, the noble animal would not eat or drink. A beautiful damsel, Felinete, provided a remedy by removing a bag of powder from Gringalet's ear, and its appetite returned. There is the fay Esclarmonde, who learned the art of necromancy from Vergil, was successively the mistress of Escanor le Bel and of Briant des Illes, bestowed the steed Gringalet on the former, and for the latter prepared a chamber painted with scenes from the legend of Troy. She is a double of Morgain la Fée, the pupil of Merlin, the promiscuous paramour, the bestower of the steed Galatée on Hector of Troy, and noted for the mural decorations of her castle.[4]

---

[1] *Hist. Lit. de la France*, xxxi. 168.   [2] In the *Prise d'Orange*.
[3] This *perron* is 'lez la fontaine, sous le pin' (vs. 13017); cf. *Yvain*, vs. 414.
[4] Loomis, *Arthurian Tradition*, pp. 157 f.; *Wales*, pp. 105–15.

On the other hand, the trend toward realism is also perceptible. There is the charming scene where the faithful seneschal of Andrivete rises and leaves the table with his wife in order that Andrivete may enjoy a *tête-à-tête* with her guest and lover Keu (vss. 9580 ff.). There is even a note of cynicism in the remarks which Dinadan, a character borrowed from the Prose *Tristan*, utters on the subject of chivalry (vss.11780 ff.). For, like Dodinel in *Claris et Laris*, he is frankly disdainful of the noble art of fighting. But far too much of Girard's psychological interest takes the form of rather dull conversations and tedious monologues, in imitation of Chrétien but without his delicacy of perception.

'Meliador'[1]

Not only is *Meliador* the last and the longest of the French Arthurian romances in verse, but we know more about its author and the circumstances of its composition than in the case of any other French work of the cycle in verse or prose. Jean Froissart of Hainaut was attached to the royal household of England from 1361 to 1368, and regarded King Edward III as a second Arthur and Queen Philippa as the greatest queen since Guenevere. In 1365 he visited Scotland, was cordially received by David II, and accompanied him on a tour of the country—an experience reflected in the geography of *Meliador*. After Philippa's death in 1369 Froissart enjoyed the patronage of Wenceslas, Duke of Luxembourg, who often entertained the poet at his sumptuous court at Brussels and commissioned him to compose the *Meliador*, inserting in it seventy-three lyrics of the Duke's own composition. During the winter of 1388–9 Froissart read the poem aloud to Count Gaston de Foix at Orthez night after night. No one dared speak during the reading, and after it was finished the count was pleased to discuss the poem and to reward its author with draughts of wine.

Meliador has come down to us in two versions, the first only in fragments, the second, though incomplete, extending to 30,771 lines. The dates of these versions are disputed, Longnon putting the first before 1370 and the second before 1388; Kittredge putting the first after 1373 and the second after 1388.[2] In favour of Kittredge's dating is the remarkable likeness between the somnambulistic behaviour of Camel described in the second version and that of Pierre de Béarn described in Froissart's *Chronique*. Since sleep-walking is not a commonplace in medieval literature, it seems probable that the poet introduced this unusual feature into his second redaction after he had learned of the case of Pierre de Béarn, and that was in 1388.

In outline this redaction tells the following story. In the early years of Arthur's reign, Hermondine, daughter of the King of Scotland, is vigorously wooed by Camel, a knight of Northumberland. But, learning of

[1] Ed. A. Longnon, *SATF* (1895–9).
[2] Ibid. iii. 363 ff.; Kittredge in *ESt*, xxvi (1899), 321 ff.

his nocturnal habits, just mentioned, she puts him off by vowing to marry only the knight who displays the greatest prowess over a period of five years. News of this reaches Meliador, son of the Duke of Cornwall, at Arthur's court at Carlion; he is smitten with yearning for the unseen princess and sets out to win her. He encounters and kills Camel; disguised as a jewel merchant, he has a glimpse of his beloved at Aberdeen; he completes his five years of loyal service by winning a tournament at Roxburgh against a field of 1,566 knights, and weds the princess Hermondine. The missing conclusion apparently recounted the victory of Sagremor at the tourney of Camalot and his marriage to Sébille.

Of course, Meliador had many rivals, who like him suffered blows for Hermondine, succoured distressed ladies, and married them in the end. Tournaments indeed occupy so large a part of the narrative that one might divide it into books, each centring round a great passage of arms. On the other hand, love scenes are few, and those hurried over. One happy exception is the interview between Sagremor and the *ingénue* Sébille, in which Sagremor declares his passion, the girl takes fright, but when he comes to announce his departure, she gives him a glance which remains in his memory throughout the hardships which ensue. Froissart takes a surprising interest in the friendships of his female characters. Not only Hermondine and her cousin Florée, but other damsels, too, exchange confidences and seek together a solution to their predicaments.

There are many signs of the poet's familiarity with Arthurian fiction in its later stages, such as references to Guiron and Melyadus and the adoption of the principle of 'entrelacement' on a grand scale. He takes over a few names without change from the Matter of Britain: Loth, Florée, Lionnel, Carlion, Clarence (a broad river in Ireland!); other names he alters slightly: Meriadoc becomes Meliador; Carmelide, Carmelin; Sinaudon, Signandon. The last he identifies with Stirling on the basis of information received there in 1365.[1] One detects the conscientious chronicler in the fact that, having once dated his romance at the beginning of Arthur's reign, he excludes all those heroes later destined to achieve fame, Perceval, Lancelot, and so forth; also in the effort to keep his geography somewhat close to reality. For the same reason almost nothing is left of Celtic magic except a single episode in which Sagremor, pausing to rest in an enchanted forest, is carried off on the back of a stag and finds himself plunged into a lake, there to meet with three ladies clad in white, who have thus contrived to bring him to their presence.

Though Paris called *Meliador* 'a literary anachronism', and though its length has evidently frightened off readers both medieval and modern, it has, apart from its romantic interest, a good deal of light to shed on Froissart's artistry and on contemporary tastes and manners.

---

[1] Froissart, *Chroniques*, ed. S. Luce and others (Paris, 1869–1931), i. 348 f. See above, p. 371, n. 6.

THE TROUBADOURS

RITA LEJEUNE

THE influence of the Arthurian legend on Provençal literature presents a complicated problem. For more than half a century certain critics have accused Fauriel of exaggerating the interest of the troubadours in 'Breton' subjects,[1] and have tended to minimize its extent. As recently as 1945 the great provençalist, Jeanroy, pronounced this laconic verdict: 'The romances of the Table Round seem to have enjoyed only a moderate degree of favour with high society in the South; the only work which has any connexion with them in the thirteenth century is *Jaufré*, and even that was written for a foreign court.'[2] It is to the credit of Joseph Anglade that fifteen years earlier he had collected the many allusions to the Matter of Britain in the work of the troubadours, but his monograph, *Les Troubadours et les Bretons*,[3] ended with a conclusion which, strange to say, contradicted the results of his researches: 'Works belonging to the "Breton" cycle are few; allusions to the same are equally rare. This scarcity betrays an almost complete indifference to the prevailing literary opinion of the time.'[4]

The reason for this attitude is easy to understand. The so-called 'positivist' criticism of the late nineteenth and the early twentieth century refused on principle to believe that any texts had ever existed except those which have survived. Now, compared with the very large number of Arthurian romances preserved in the *langue d'oïl*, only two are preserved in the *langue d'oc*, *Jaufré* and *Blandin de Cornouailles*! The conclusion followed that these two were isolated narrative works, late and uninteresting, accidental 'sports' in a literature essentially lyrical.

Nevertheless, there is reason to believe that some prose romances in the *langue d'oc* have been lost. Two pages of a beautiful thirteenth-century manuscript, containing passages from the loves of Uter and Ygier and from the episode of the sword in the anvil, have been found in a binding.[5] In the middle of the fourteenth century the writers of the *Leys d'Amor* and the *Flors*

---

[1] Fauriel, *Histoire de la poésie provençale* (Leipzig, Paris, 1847), iii.
[2] A. Jeanroy, *Histoire sommaire de la poésie occitane* (Toulouse, Paris), p. 94. A printer's error has substituted 'XIIᵉ siècle' for 'XIIIᵉ'.
[3] *Publ. Spéciales de la Société des Langues Romanes*, xxix (Montpellier, 1929).
[4] Ibid., p. 89.
[5] Ed. Chabaneau in *Revue des Langues Romanes*, xxii. 105–15, 237–42.

del Gay Saber allude to the story of the *Sant Grazal* in prose.[1] Two 'romans de Lancelot' listed in an inventory drawn up in 1351 at the castle of Ozon may possibly have been written in Provençal.[2] And there is the doubtful statement of Tasso that Arnaut Daniel wrote a *Lancelot* in prose.[3]

Far stronger evidence as to the early familiarity of Southern poets with the Matter of Britain is provided by certain works of instruction. The first of these was composed before 1170 by the Catalan nobleman, Guiraut III de Cabrera, who in the form of a list of subjects with which his *jongleur* should be familiar, mentions, together with personages famed in pious, classical, or Old French epic literature, a gallery of Arthurian figures—Artus himself, Erec, Tristan, Iseut, Gualvaing, who without companion hunted so many a quarry, and Dovon, father of Jaufré.[4] He knows also tales of Viviane and Cardueil, and implies clearly by the manner of his allusion that these themes were not novelties. Thus at the very moment when Chrétien was at work on *Erec*, the knights of the Round Table were already celebrated in far-away Catalonia. And the art of the Breton minstrels was rated so highly that Guiraut reproached his *jongleur* that he did not know how to end his recital with the 'tempradura' (a musical term) of a Breton.

It was probably between 1160 and 1170 that Arnaut-Guilhem de Marsan, a noble from the Landes in Gascony, in his *Ensenhamen del Cavalher* recommended as models of behaviour, not only Paris, Aeneas, and Apollonius, but Arthurian heroes as well.[5] 'Imitate Tristan then, who far excelled Paris. By Heaven, there was never a lover who better practised the art of love!' 'Of Yvain, the king's son, you must learn why he was more pleasing than any other living man; for he was the first to wear furs, and he had a brooch and a clasp on his mantle, and a girdle for his robe, a clasp for his spurs, and a boss on his shield. Yes, he had all that, we know, and the first gloves too.' 'You should know, too, about King Arthur; you will be all the worthier for it. For he did not die, and he never committed a fault and will not commit one as long as the world endures. Always he lived for love with joy and honour, for he knew all that appertained to love and all that God has revealed of the matter.' How different these silhouettes of Yvain and Arthur are from those to which the literature of Northern France has accustomed

---

[1] *Leys d'Amor*, ed. Gatien-Arnoult (Toulouse, 1842), i. 12; *Las Flors del Gay Saber*, ed. Anglade (Barcelona, 1926), p. 10.

[2] *Revue des Sociétés Savantes*, ii. 165–7. Chabaneau (see p. 393, n. 5 above) remarks that the forms 'del Lac' and Ginnievra suggest that the romances were written in the *langue d'oc*.

[3] In spite of much controversy, the latest editor of Arnaut Daniel thinks that Tasso was not mistaken. R. Lavaud, *Poésies d'Arnaut Daniel* (Toulouse, 1910), pp. 125–32.

[4] M. de Riquer, *Los Cantares de Gesta Franceses* (Madrid, 1952), pp. 358–406. I. Cluzel, 'A propos de l'Ensenhamen du troubadour catalan G. de C.', *Boll. de la Real Ac. de buenas lettras de Barcelona*, xxvi (1954–6), 87–93.

[5] K. Bartsch, *Provenzalisches Lesebuch* (1855), pp. 132–9. I am preparing a new edition, from which the translation has been made. On date of *Ensenhamen* see my article in *SM* (1939), pp. 160–71. Recent works have established the date as prior to 1170.

us! Yvain, the first model of fashion! Arthur, the prototype of amorous courtesy!

Between 1195 and 1200 Guiraut de Calanson, like Guiraut de Cabrera, composed an *ensenhamen* for his *jongleur*, which contains the lines: 'Apren, Fadet, de Lansolet, com saup Islanda conquerir.'[1] (Learn, Fadet, of Lansolet, how he was able to conquer Iceland.) It is to be noted that the name of Lancelot is given a form which approaches that employed by Ulrich von Zatzikhoven about the same time,[2] and that in view of several hints in Arthurian romance that Lancelot was connected with Ireland[3], it is possible that 'Islanda' is a scribal error for Irlanda.[4] Here again is an Arthurian hero presented in a role foreign to the contemporary literature of the North.

Still a third poem of instructions to a *jongleur* is that which Bertran de Paris en Rouergue dedicated to a countess of Rodez in the first quarter of the thirteenth century. In it occur the following references to the Matter of Britain:[5] 'You do not know as much about Arthur as I do, nor about his court, where there was many a *soudadier* (knight who served for pay).' 'Nor do you know the *novas* (stories) of Tristan, nor of King Marc, nor of the handsome Apsalon.' 'Nor do I think that you know of Ivan, who was the first to tame birds.' 'You do not know anything to tell about the English Merlin, how he lived or what he did.'

Finally, about 1250 Peire de Corbian speaks in his *Thezaur*[6] of several Arthurian characters, 'of Merlin the Wild,[7] who uttered obscurely prophecies about all the English kings; I know of the death of Artus, for there is no doubt of it, of the adventures of his nephew Galvan, and of the deceitful cleric and by what calumnies he broke the marriage of King Mark and her (Iseut?)'.

Thus the eighty years which followed 1170 and which saw the flowering of Arthurian literature in Northern France also witnessed, unless the testimony of contemporaries is to be rejected, the establishment of a similar vogue in the South.

---

[1] Ed. W. Keller in *RF*, xxii (1906), 151, 200–2.

[2] Ibid., p. 201; *Lanzelet*, ed. K. A. Hahn (Frankfurt a. Main, 1845), vs. 4913, &c.

[3] *Queste del Saint Graal*, ed. A. Pauphilet (Paris, 1949), p. 136; R. S. Loomis in *R*, lxxix (1958), 58–61. Thus in Arthurian romance we have Lancelot, great-grandson of the King of Ireland; his grandfather, also named Lancelot, son-in-law of the King of Ireland; Lanceor the King of Ireland's son; in *Culhwch and Olwen* Llenlleawc the Irishman, a warrior who accompanied Arthur on an expedition to Ireland.

[4] See Bruce, ii. 229, 252, for two cases in Arthurian texts where Islande has probably been substituted for Irlande.

[5] Ed. V. de Bartholomaeis, vss. 9–42. On date see F. Witthoeft, *Sirventes Joglaresc* (Marburg, 1889), p. 37, notes 19–21. Jeanroy in *Poésie lyrique des troubadours*, i. 351, mistakenly assigned Bertran de Paris to the last quarter of the thirteenth century.

[6] Ed. Bertoni and Jeanroy in *Annales du Midi*, xxiii.

[7] Note that 'Merlin le suvage' appears as the title of a lai (or romance) in a thirteenth-century list. *MLR*, xlv (1950), 40–45.

The lyrics of the troubadours amply corroborate the conclusion to be drawn from the didactic poems. Though under no compulsion to allude to the personages of the Arthurian cycle, the poets of the *langue d'oc* make even more frequent mention of them than do the poets of the *langue d'oïl*. Needless to say, such passing allusions imply an intimate acquaintance on the part of the public with the persons alluded to; otherwise the point of the allusion is lost. The chart giving the number of references to Arthurian characters by troubadours of the South, compared with the number of references by the *trouvères* of the North, is eloquent.[1]

Arthurian person	Trouvère citations	Troubadour citations
Arthur . . .	5	24
Guenièvre . .	1	1
Iseut . . .	7	22
Tristan . . .	21	37
Gauvain . .	2	15
Ivain . . .	2	5
Perceval . .	0	7
Lancelet . .	1	3
Keu . . .	1	2
Erec . . .	0	7
Enide . . .	0	3

Let us examine some of these references more closely and especially the oldest ones. About 1137, on the death of William VIII of Poitou, Marcabru declared in his elegy: 'Since the Poitevin has left me, I shall be lost like Artu.'[2] Between 1135 and 1145 Cercamon, cursing his fickle mistress, contrasted the unfaithful one with 'the heart of Tristan', that is, a heart of exemplary fidelity.[3] There is a possible allusion to the *Cour de l'Epervier* at Le Puy in a poem by Bernart Marti, dated about 1150, and this would reflect the popularity of contests for the prize of a sparrow-hawk in Arthurian literature.[4] About 1154 Bernard de Ventadour, mourning the absence of Eleanor of Poitou, complained that his lot resembled that of Tristan without Iseut.[5] In three other poems he employed Tristan as a *senhal*,[6] while in still another he referred with scorn to the 'Breton hope' of Arthur's return.[7] Before 1160, apparently, Rigaut de Barbezieux compared himself to Perceval.[8] 'Just as

---

[1] This chart is based on Anglade's *Les Troubadours et les Bretons* and his *Onomastique des troubadours* and on H. P. Dyggve's *Onomastique des trouvères* (Helsinki, 1934).

[2] Dejeanne, *Bibliothèque méridionale* (Toulouse, 1909), no. iv, vss. 60 f.

[3] Cercamon, ed. Jeanroy, *CFMA* (1922), no. iv, vs. 38.

[4] Bernart Marti, ed. E. Hoepffner, *CFMA* (1929), no. iii, vss. 51 f. The allusions to the 'Cour de l'Epervier' at Le Puy are numerous enough to justify this interpretation of 'del Pueg' as a reference to Le Puy. On connexions of sparrow-hawks with the Matter of Britain see R. S. Loomis, *Arthurian Tradition*, p. 92.

[5] 'Tan ai mon cor ple de joya.'

[6] 'Amors queus es'; 'Lo rossignols'; 'Quan vei la lauzeta'.   [7] 'La douss' aura.'

[8] *Revue des Langues Romanes*, 1920, p. 20. On date see my study, 'Le troubadour Rigaut de Barbezieux' in *Mélanges István Frank* (Universität des Saarlandes, 1957).

Perceval, when he was alive, was lost in wonderment at the sight, so that he could never ask what purpose the lance and the Grail served, so I likewise, *Mielhs de Domna*, for I forget all when I gaze on you.' About 1169 Raimbaut d'Orange addressed to his lady a song which is a tissue of references to the Tristan legend, to the love philtre, and to the clean shirt, symbol of her virginity, which Iseut gave to her lover.[1] There is no mention of this shirt in any extant romance of Tristan, except for a possible allusion in Eilhart's version.[2]

These early allusions of the troubadours to the Matter of Britain lead us again and again to the court of Poitou or to the domains of Eleanor, Countess of Poitou and Duchess of Aquitaine. It was her father, William, who was the subject of Marcabru's elegy. He was also the patron of Cercamon. To Eleanor herself Bernard de Ventadour addressed the lyrics in which Tristan is named. She was the suzerain of Rigaut de Barbezieux, and it was she, probably, who was celebrated under the *senhal Mielhs de Domna*. From her lands in Auvergne, visited frequently by Raimbaut d'Orange, it was easy for the Arthurian legend to pass down the Rhone to Provence and the territories of Alfonso II of Aragon, situated north of the Pyrenees. And several of these great houses of the South—Orange, Montpellier, Barcelona—were bound by ties of blood or policy to the dynasty of Henry II and Eleanor of Poitou, his queen.

What is the significance of all this? Perhaps most striking is the evidence that Arthur was known in Poitou when Geoffrey of Monmouth was finishing his opus at Oxford, and that by 1170, the date of Chrétien's *Erec*, the Matter of Britain had conquered Catalonia. This precocious diffusion south of the Loire links up with the appearance of Arthur and his knights on the portal of Modena Cathedral and the christening of boys of Padua with the names of Artus and Walwan in the early years of the twelfth century.[3] And though there has been no systematic search for such names in south-western France, we find in the second half of the twelfth century a *jongleur* named Arthur, attached to the Dauphin of Auvergne, and a poetess of the Cevennes named Iseut.[4] Is it likely that her aristocratic parents chose for her this ominous and un-Christian name after reading a North-French romance, or after listening by chance to a charming *conteur*?

[1] Walter T. Pattison, *Life and Works of the Troubadour Raimbaut d'Orange* (Minneapolis, 1952), no. xxvii. On date of poem see ibid., p. 44.

[2] On this subject see Thomas, *Tristan*, ed. Bédier, SATF, i. 161; ii. 47, 241; Sudre in *Rom.* xv. 546; Pattison, op. cit., pp. 163 f.

[3] R. S. Loomis in *SM*, nuova serie, ix (1936), 1–17; R. S. Loomis, *Wales*, pp. 198–213; J. Frappier, *Le Roman Breton, Les Cours de la Sorbonne* (Paris, 1949), p. 39; O. Brattö, *Studi di Antroponimia Fiorentina* (Göteborg, 1953), pp. 130 f., cites forms like Galganus, Galvagnus, Gualvagnus from Pisa in 1130, from Lucca in 1146, from Volterra in 1150, from Florence in 1174, and concludes that these names are due to the prestige of Gawain, knight of the Round Table.

[4] On Iseut de Chapieu see *Annales du Midi*, xxviii. 462–71.

A second striking fact is the attestation by Southern poets to the existence of themes which have not survived in the literature of Northern France, though one cannot prove, of course, that they were never known there. Here are some of these curiosities: Yvain as the first falconer (Bertran de Paris); Yvain as the originator of masculine fashions in dress (Arnaut-Guilhem de Marsan); Yvain, composer of a lai (*Flamenca*, vs. 602); Keu imprisoned by a person unmentioned in Northern story (*Flamenca*, vss. 684–7); lais of *Cabrefoil* and of *Tintagoil* (*Flamenca*, vss. 599 f.),[1] whether in northern or southern dialect, who knows?—though the form *Cabrefoil* would suggest the latter; Gualvaing described as one who, without a companion, made such a good chase (Guiraut de Cabrera); Galvaing in combat with 'the fair, unfortunate Stranger' (Uc de Saint-Circ).[2]

It is true, of course, that no literary texts existing today (except *Chèvrefeuil*) supply us with further information about the topics thus alluded to. But did they never exist? I leave the reader to cope with this problem. But I would ask him not to be hypnotized, like many critics of the past fifty years, by the well-known statement of Raimon Vidal de Besaudun, made in the early thirteenth century: 'The French language is better and more suitable for the composition of romances, *rotrouenges*, and *pastourelles*, but the language of the southern regions is better fitted for the composition of poems, songs, and *sirventes*.'[3] Before accepting docilely this remark as conclusive proof that romances, Arthurian or otherwise, were seldom attempted in the Provençal language, it might be well to submit it to a preliminary investigation and to ask when it was written, by whom, and what degree of credence it deserves. I have limited myself to noting down the scraps of wreckage in the form of allusions to Arthurian tales (let me emphasize the word 'tales') which have been cast up on the shores of the twentieth century. They prove beyond doubt that the Matter of Britain enjoyed great favour with the cultivated society of the Midi, even before the time of Chrétien and Thomas, and they prompt two groups of questions.

First, did a literature as sophisticated and mature as the lyrics of the troubadours refer thus regularly to a literature undeveloped and almost entirely oral? Or, on the other hand, is it possible that at least some of the *contes* of Arthur and his knights, as certain allusions suggest, had acquired firm outlines and a fixed form, for example, that of the *novas* of Tristan mentioned by Bertran de Paris en Rouergue ?

Second, the Arthurian legend of the twelfth century, whether in spoken or written form, to which the troubadours made such frequent allusion—was

---

[1] *Flamenca*, ed. P. Meyer (Paris, 1901). Though C. Grimm, *Étude sur le Roman de Flamenca* (Paris, 1930), dates the poem no earlier than 1272, it is probable that it was really composed shortly after the period of the action, late in the twelfth century.

[2] Uc de Saint-Circ, ed. Jeanroy and Salverda de Grave (Toulouse, 1913), no. i, vs. 35.

[3] C. Appel, *Provenzalische Chrestomathie*, 4th ed. (Leipzig, 1912), p. 196.

it treated in the highly cultivated courts of Aquitaine, Auvergne, Provence, Toulouse, Montpellier, Narbonne, and Catalonia in the native language of King Louis VII and of Abbot Suger? Or was it treated in the language of the great families of these regions, the *langue d'oc* of the troubadours?

Once more, it is for the reader to reflect and to draw his own conclusions.

30

JAUFRÉ

PAUL REMY

JAUFRÉ is of great interest as the unique example of Arthurian romance in the *langue d'oc*.[1] In the course of 10,956 octosyllabic lines it introduces several personages familiar to readers of Chrétien de Troyes, and its hero, Jaufré son of Dovon, is generally recognized as Chrétien's Giflet fils de Do.

According to the latest editor, Brunel, the author originated either in Catalonia or just north of the Pyrenees.[2] As to his character, it is impossible to draw any safe conclusions from conventional expressions of piety or from allusions to Daniel, Susanna, and like characters.[3] Some critics, to be sure, have argued that there were two authors,[4] mainly on the basis of the last twelve lines, which may be translated as follows: 'Now let us pray together to Him who was born to save us all, that He should deign, if He will, to pardon him who began this romance, and to let the one who finished it so live in this world as to merit salvation. Now say "Amen" with one voice. This good book is finished. God be thanked for it forever.' There are also two dedications at vss. 59–84 and 2616–30. Riquer maintains that the theory of dual authorship would solve the puzzle presented by the conflicting evidence as to date, and that the poem, as we have it, is the revised version by a second author of an earlier original.[5]

It does not seem necessary, however, to postulate two authors, for the same style and manner are preserved throughout, and there is a coherent, unified structure.[6] After the hero has set out from Arthur's court and engaged in some introductory combats, he arrives in the garden of Monbrun and becomes involved in two trains of events. He hears cries of lamentation, which we later learn were provoked by the injuries inflicted on Melian de Mon-

---

[1] Ed. H. Breuer, *Gesellschaft für romanische Literatur*, xlvi (Göttingen, 1925); ed. C. Brunel, *SATF* (Paris, 1943). The latter has been reviewed by J. Melander in *Studia Neophilologica*, xviii (1945–6), 125–30; P. Remy in *RB*, xxiv (1945), 248–55.

[2] Ed. Brunel, i, p. xlii. Brunel also suggests that the author was a *jongleur* who recited his poem before a crowd in the public square, but the opening verses do not prove more than that he intended it to be read. Cf. Chrétien's *Yvain*, vss. 149 f.

[3] Cf. A. Stimming in *ZRP*, xii (1888), 323–47.

[4] For example, A. Thomas in *Annales du Midi*, i (1889), 559; P. Meyer in *R*, xix (1890), 616 f.; A. Pontecorvo in *AR*, xxii (1938), 400.

[5] *Recueil de travaux offert à M. Clovis Brunel* (Paris, 1955), ii. 435–61.

[6] This view is also taken by Stimming, loc. cit., p. 324; Lewent, in *ZRP*, xlviii (1928), 581 f.; Jeanroy in *Annales du Midi*, liii (1941), 365; Brunel, op. cit. i, pp. xxxv–xxxvii.

melior by Taulat de Rogimon, who had affronted Arthur at the beginning of the romance and whom Jaufré now has a double duty to punish. And it is at Monbrun also that Jaufré is brought before the mistress of the castle, Brunissen, and rouses in her the sentimental feeling which, though long concealed, leads to their union. Thus the two major themes of retribution and love dominate the scheme, and the minor episodes provide colour and amplitude. There is also a symmetry between the first and second meetings between Jaufré and Melian, and the adventure of Arthur with a monstrous bird forms a pendant to his misadventure with a bull. Thus the structural harmony of *Jaufré* makes one question the theory of the dual authorship of the poem.

The problem of authorship is tied up with the problem of date, which I have discussed elsewhere.[1] The dedications make it clear that the poem was written to please a king of Aragon, who is described as the father of Valour, the son of Largess, the lord of Happiness—in short, a model of all the chivalric and Christian virtues. He loves and fears God, and in return is loved and honoured by God. Only two statements are more specific: he was crowned when young; he vanquished in his first battle those who did not believe in God (cel per qe Deu es descresutz, vs. 74). On the basis of this last statement Gaston Paris proposed[2] that *Jaufré* was written in the reign of Jaime I, between 1225 (the siege of Peñiscola, held by the Moslems) and 1228 (the conquest of Majorca), and this dating has been accepted by Breuer, Jeanroy, and Brunel,[3] reinforced as it is by the fact that Jaime was only five years old at the time of his coronation.

Lewent and Mme Lejeune have noted,[4] however, in the poems of Peire Vidal and Guiraut de Borneil references to a certain Jaufré, and have maintained that this Jaufré is the hero of our romance. Peire Vidal in a love lyric declared: 'If some day I see her disrobe before me, I will behave better than the lord of Eissidolh, who maintains his honour when another proves recreant; and I know no more than that Jaufré has as much.'[5] These lines are interpreted as alluding to the happiness of Jaufré when united at last with Brunissen in the nuptial chamber. Guiraut de Borneil wrote: 'I go to one who does not call me, and I ask him for what he has not to give. As for good manners, I am of the same opinion as Jaufré, for I know how to do what I ought: I rise when I ought to lie down, and I sing when I should weep.'[6] There are occasions in the Provençal romance when the hero goes to sleep

---

[1] *RB*, xxviii (1950), 1349–77.

[2] *Histoire Littéraire de la France*, xxx (1888), 215 f.

[3] *Jaufré*, ed. Breuer, pp. 365, 377; A. Jeanroy, *Anthologie des Troubadours* (Paris, 1927), p. 13; Jeanroy in *Annales du Midi*, liii (1941), 364. Jeanroy, *Histoire sommaire de la poésie occitane* (Paris, Toulouse, 1945), p. 94; *Jaufré*, ed. Brunel, I, p. xxxviii.

[4] *MP*, xliii (1946), 153–69; *MA*, liv (1948), 267–70, and *RB*, xxxi (1953), 719 f.

[5] *Poésies de Peire Vidal*, ed. J. Anglade, *CFMA* (1923), p. 58.

[6] *Sämtliche Lieder des Trobadors Giraut de Bornelh*, ed. Kolsen (Halle, 1909), i. 334.

when he should wake and when he insists on asking questions with disastrous results. Now both troubadours flourished in the last quarter of the twelfth century and could not have read a romance composed as late as 1225. Mme Lejeune therefore dates *Jaufré* about 1180,[1] in the reign of Alfonso II of Aragon: Alfonso came to the throne in 1162 at the age of ten, and in 1169 he commenced a victorious war against the Moors. He thus meets two of the requirements set by the dedications of *Jaufré*. Riquer, accepting the identification of the poet's patron with Alfonso, would date the first redaction of the poem, however, as early as 1169–70,[2] since it would be absurd to mention only his earliest triumph, 'la primera bataila', after the king had won even greater victories.

Let us be prudent in the interpretation of the passages which allude to a certain Jaufré. The application to the hero of our romance is by no means clear and conclusive, and for myself I do not believe that either Guiraut de Borneil or Peire Vidal had read it. Even if it were true that they had in mind an Arthurian figure named Jaufré, they might have heard of him through other channels.[3] As the preceding chapter has shown, references to Arthurian personages occur in Provençal lyrics before the time of Chrétien, but they do not imply the existence of literary romances at this early date, any more than do the Arthurian names carved over the Modena portal and the laudatory mention of Gauvain (Walwen) by William of Malmesbury in 1125.[4]

Though Alfonso II meets the requirements set by the dedications, should one ignore the possibility that the royal dedicatee was his successor, Pedro II, who probably mounted the throne at the age of nineteen? One is not old at that age. He did not win his first battle against the Moors, but why must the phrase, 'cel per qe Deu es descresutz', or 'mescresutz', MS. B (vs. 74) refer to Moslems? The first author of the *Chanson de la Croisade contre les Albigeois* employs the participles *mescrezant* and *mescrezu(d)a (gent)* to designate the heretics.[5] And Pedro II swore at the time of his coronation in 1204 to put down the Albigenses; the next year he forced a group of them to surrender near Albi, and took possession of the castle of Escuria.[6] Though later, faithless to his vow of 1204, he sided with the Count of Toulouse, in the first years of his reign he could justly be called 'the new knight of God' (vs. 69), and the dedication might have been written in 1205 or shortly after.

This may seem a frail hypothesis, but it meets one difficulty which a date earlier than 1182 must overcome, for it is certain that the author of *Jaufré*

[1] *MA*, liv. 257 f.
[2] *Recueil de travaux offert à M. Clovis Brunel*, ii. 447.
[3] Remy in *RB*, xxviii. 1361 f.
[4] See Chap. 6 above and R. S. Loomis, *Arthurian Tradition*, pp. 15–20.
[5] Ed. P. Meyer (Paris, 1875), vss. 72, 76, 2199; Remy in *RB*, xxviii. 1359, 1361.
[6] F. Soldevila, *Historia de Catalunya* (Barcelona, 1934), i. 174 f.

displays a thorough familiarity with the works of Chrétien de Troyes. For he not only mentions such traditional figures as Galvain, Tristan, and Quec (Keu), who might well have been derived through other media than Chrétien, but in vss. 102–6 he lists together Lancelot del Lac, Ivan, Erec, Perceval, Calogranan, and Cligès—a collocation of names which could have had no other source than a collection of Chrétien's poems. 'Lucans lo boteilliers' and Taulat seem to be borrowed from *Erec*. In vss. 7610–12 there is a specific allusion to the burial of Fenice alive and to the passion of Cligès, and these personages do not belong to the traditional Matter of Britain but were the creations of the Champenois poet. Riquer has also pointed out in vss. 6640 f. (MS. A) an allusion to the incident in the First Continuation of the *Perceval* in which Keu is struck with a roasted peacock on a spit.[1]

The impact of Chrétien on *Jaufré* is apparent, moreover, in some of the incidents. Many resemblances, to be sure, between the work of the two poets are too vague to prove the dependence of one on the other; other similarities may be of the inevitable kind when two narratives treat similar material; still others may be due to a common dependence on the tales of professional *jongleurs*. But the correspondences between *Jaufré* and *Yvain* are too many and too specific to be attributable to such causes. Both poets, for example, represent the king or the queen rebuking Quec (Keu) for his raillery;[2] both employ the image of the key of love.[3] There is likewise a community of ideas. In *Yvain* one reads (vss. 24–26): 'Now love is turned into a fiction (*fable*) because those who feel it not say that they love; but they lie.' In *Jaufré* one finds (vss. 7872–5): 'Courtesy is lost, and love is turned into nothing. One who says he loves lies and only makes a pretence of what is not.' These are only a few out of many parallels.

Chrétien's *Perceval* has also left its traces. The resistance which Jaufré, waked from sleep, puts up against three attacks, recalls the combats in which Perceval engages when roused from his contemplation of the blood drops on the snow.[4] It is highly probable that the wounded knight, Melian, whom Jaufré finds stretched on his couch, is a prosaic imitation of Chrétien's Fisher King.[5] To these more or less obvious borrowings of names and incidents may be added the imitation by the Southern poet of Chrétien's monologues and analyses of mental and emotional states. And a wider range of reading is indicated by allusions to the death of Eneas, the loves of Floris and Blancaflor, and the madness of Tristan.[6] The 'fada del Gibel', that is, Morgain la Fée, her subaqueous home, and her marvellous tent are derived from a source or

---

[1] *Recueil de travaux offert à M. Clovis Brunel*, pp. 452 f.
[2] *Yvain*, vss. 86–91; *Jaufré*, vss. 618–26.
[3] *Yvain*, vs. 4632; *Jaufré*, vs. 7842.
[4] *Perceval*, ed. Hilka, vss. 4194–319; *Jaufré*, vss. 3171–479.
[5] *Perceval*, vss. 3068–87; *Jaufré*, vss. 4918–41.
[6] *Jaufré*, vss. 7601–20.

sources which, though lost in the form which the author of *Jaufré* knew, are attested by the appearance of cognate traditions in other romances of the cycle.[1] The strange form given to the name of the queen (Guilalmer) suggests the possibility of an unknown source.[2]

Though deeply indebted to sources oral and written, our poet was not a plagiarist without talent. He may be naïve, but he is not dull, and he has a marked bent toward humour. The opening scene, which illustrates this bent, seems entirely original. Arthur is carried off on the horns of a bull, is dropped from a cliff, and is saved by his knights from multiple fractures by the ingenious device of making a pile of clothes at the spot where he was due to fall. Without suggesting that we have here the verve of Ariosto or the irony of Cervantes, there is no doubt that this and several other episodes were written with tongue in cheek. It is a sign, moreover, of the poet's independence that in the age and in the territory of the troubadours he did not depict his ideal lady as an imperious tyrant nor his ideal love-affair as refined adultery. Jaufré is no Lancelot. The highly realistic treatment of the lepers (vss. 2251–819), as I have tried to demonstrate elsewhere,[3] seems to be an original combination of popular, medical, and biblical ideas about the unhappy victims of this disease.

Written perhaps in northern Catalonia, addressed to a king of Aragon, *Jaufré* naturally found its most receptive audience in Spain. The chronicler Muntaner, early in the fourteenth century, declared that every exploit of the knights who debarked in Calabria would make a better romance than *Jaufré*.[4] Pedro IV of Aragon in 1352 directed that a chamber in the Aljaferia of Saragossa, adorned with scenes from the same poem, should be restored.[5] In 1513 there was printed at Toledo a chronicle of *Tablante de Ricamonte y de Jofre hijo del Conde Donason*, a free rendering of the adventures of Taulat and Jaufré, to which Cervantes referred with ironic enthusiasm.[6] And it is enough to open a modern edition of the *Libros de Caballerias* to realize that the medieval romance still remains popular south of the Pyrenees. From the presses of the north there issued in the early sixteenth century several editions of the *Hystoire de Giglan*, in which an Antonine friar named Claude Platin combined a version of the story of Gauvain's son with that of Jaufré and complicated things still further by confusing Dovon, father of Jaufré, with Doon de Mayence of the Carolingian epic.[7] The strangest

[1] R. S. Loomis, *Arthurian Tradition*, pp. 306 f.

[2] P. Remy in *Recueil de travaux offert à M. Clovis Brunel*, ii. 412–19; *RB*, xxix (1951), 1356 f.

[3] *MA*, lii (1946), 195–242.

[4] *Chronik des edlen En Ramon Muntaner*, ed. K. Lanz, *Bibliothek des literarischen Vereins in Stuttgart*, viii (1844), 214.

[5] A. Rubió y Lluch, *Documents per l'historia de la cultura Catalana migeval* (Barcelona, 1908), i. 159 f.; R. S. and L. H. Loomis, *Arthurian Legends in Medieval Art* (New York, 1938), p. 26.

[6] *Don Quijote*, ed. F. Rodríguez Marín (Madrid, 1927), i. 450 f.

[7] *Jaufré*, ed. Brunel, i, pp. xlviii–liii.

descendant of the Provençal romance, however, is a Philippine version in 408 alexandrine quatrains in Tagalog dialect entitled the *History of Tablante de Ricamonte and of the pair, Jofré and Bruniesen, in the realm of Camalor in the reign of King Artos and Queen Ginebra.*[1] Thus while philologues edit, discuss, and speculate, the Filipinos take a simple pleasure in listening to a belated redaction of the sole surviving Arthurian romance in Provençal.

[1] D. S. Fansler in *Journal of American Folk-lore*, xxix (1916), 217–22.

ARTHURIAN LITERATURE IN SPAIN AND PORTUGAL

MARÍA ROSA LIDA DE MALKIEL

The Literary and Historical Background

IT has been pointed out in Chap. 29 that about 1170 the troubadour Guiraut (or Guerau) de Cabrera expected his *joglar* to be familiar with Arthurian themes, which are mentioned as the current literary fashion,[1] and reproached him for being unable to end his recital with the 'tempradura' (a musical term) of a Breton. Cabrera was a Catalan, and his is the earliest recorded allusion in Hispanic literature to the new vogue. The first known date of a translation is 1313, found at the end of the Portuguese *Josep Abaramatia*.[2] In the interval several events occurred which had a bearing on the diffusion throughout the Peninsula of the Matter of Britain. In 1170 Alfonso VIII of Castile married Eleanor of England, whose father and mother, Henry II and Eleanor of Poitou, seem to have encouraged Arthurian literature. The earlier version of *Jaufré* (*c.* 1170) was written at the court of Alfonso II of Aragon; his successor, Pedro II (1196–1213), was likened to King Arthur; contact with the English court was renewed through the marriage of Alfonso the Learned's sister to Edward II.

During this period sundry facts illustrate the Arthurian vogue. The Catalan troubadour Guilhem de Berguedan addressed one of his poems to 'mon Tristan' (1190);[3] Arturus was used as a Christian name in Salamanca (1200);[4] Guilhem de Cervera, who wrote between 1259 and 1282, referred to Tristan in his *Proverbis*, and to Tristan, Lancelot, Perceval, and Ivain in his lyrics. After the example of Provençal and Catalan troubadours, poets using Galician-Portuguese displayed a knowledge of these legends, for instance, Alfonso X, in a love poem included in the *Cancioneiro de Lisboa*

---

[1] M. Milá y Fontanals, *De los trovadores en España, Obras complétas* (Barcelona, 1889), ii. 272 ff. See Chap. 29 above and R. Menéndez Pidal, *Poesía juglaresca y juglares* (Madrid, 1924), pp. 159 f.; J. Rubió Balaguer, 'Literatura catalana', *Historia general de las literaturas hispánicas* (Barcelona, 1949), i. 658 f.; and M. de Riquer, *Los cantares de gesta franceses* (Madrid, 1952), pp. 378 ff.

[2] P. Bohigas Balaguer, *Los textos españoles y gallego-portugueses de la Demanda del Santo Grial* (Madrid, 1925), pp. 76 f., 148; W. J. Entwistle, *Arthurian Legend in the Literatures of the Spanish Peninsula* (London, 1925), pp. 136 ff. (referred to hereafter as Entwistle).

[3] M. de Riquer, 'El trovador Guilhem de Berguedan y las luchas feudales de su tiempo', *Boletín de la Sociedad Castellonense de Cultura*, xxix (1953), 219 ff., 247 ff.

[4] M. García Blanco, 'Sobre los nombres épicos', *Revista de Filología Española*, xxi (1934), 280.

and in several *Cantigas*; more precise and numerous are the allusions in the poetry of his grandson Diniz and of the latter's contemporary Estevam da Guarda and Fernand' Esquio. The historiographers increasingly made use of Britain's fabulous history, beginning with the *cronicón* added to the *Fuero de Navarra* (1196), which records the battle of Camlann, presumably on the basis of Geoffrey of Monmouth's *Historia*, and this entry is repeated in the *Anales Toledanos Primeros* (1217). Half a century later, Alfonso X's *General estoria*, Parts II–IV, consist of a translation from Geoffrey, Book I. 3–III. 8. Pedro, Count of Barcelos, great-grandson of Alfonso, composed early in the fourteenth century his *Nobiliário* and included a brief summary of the *Historia*, based, it would seem, on a Castilian abstract.[1]

Catalonia preceded the rest of the Peninsula in familiarity with the Arthurian matter, because of its closer linguistic and literary ties with France and Provence. The troubadours Cabrera and Berguedan were noblemen, and the earliest signs of an Arthurian vogue point to a restricted aristocratic group, able to understand the new works without translation. Conversely, Berceo's religious poems and the *Fernán González* epic, written for burghers, are silent about the British heroes.[2] From the late twelfth to the early fourteenth century, Arthurian literature took root in the courtly milieu alone.

Translations from Arthurian texts belong to a later period. The Portuguese *Josep Abaramatia* of 1313 has already been mentioned, and the Castilian *Tristán* may be slightly earlier.[3] Then we have the *Gran conquista de Ultramar*, with its allusion to the Round Table (ch. xliv), and the *Sumas de historia troyana*, which combine the Trojan with British themes. Not much later comes the old Pamplona romance of Lancelot and Bors, a manuscript of which belonged to Carlos III of Navarre (1387–1425). The first Catalan Arthurian text is mentioned by Pedro IV in 1362; the Catalan *Storia del Sant Grasal* is dated 1380. Elsewhere translations allow us to gauge the diffusion of the romances among burghers not conversant with French; the translation of the Portuguese *Josep Abaramatia*, already mentioned, we owe significantly to the archdeacon João Sanchez. The tardy spread of the romances from the court to the middle class may be due, at least in part, to the persistent popularity of the Oriental didactic tale and, in Castile, to the hold of the folk epic.

[1] Milá y Fontanals, op. cit. ii. 308; Entwistle, pp. 80 ff.; Bohigas Balaguer, op. cit., pp. 98, 100 f. For Arthurian sources of the *Nobiliário*, see L. F. Lindley Cintra, *Crónica General de Espanha de 1344* (Lisbon, 1951), pp. cv f.

[2] Witness the *Libro de Alexandre*, which translated the *Alexandreis*, vii. 412, 'Arthuro Britones [superbiunt], Cuémos preçian mucho por Artús los bretones.' The unintelligible wording was mutilated in the two known manuscripts. See *Revista de Filología Hispánica*, vii (1945), 47 f.

[3] The *post quem* date is 1258, when the golden *doblas* mentioned in chap. xxxviii were first coined. The *ante quem* date is 1343, when the *Libro de buen amor*, which refers to the *Tristan* in quatrain 1703ab, was written. From these facts a date in the early fourteenth century may be inferred.

Texts and Sources

The texts preserved convey no accurate idea either of the variety or of the number of Arthurian narratives once extant. The three lais ascribed to Tristan at the beginning of the *Cancioneiro de Lisboa* seem to derive from a version of the Prose *Tristan* different from that used by the Hispanic translators.[1] The *Zifar* (*c.* 1300), the oldest surviving book of chivalry in Castilian, refers in chap. cv to Arthur's combat with the Cath Palug in the form which it takes in the Vulgate *Merlin* as the fight with the Cat of Lausanne. In chap. ccvi 'the story of don Yván, son of King Orián' is extolled, and an epitome is given of its content.[2] The history of Britain related in G. Díez de Games's *Victorial* (*c.* 1450), though indirectly descended from Geoffrey's *Historia*, implies intermediate stages. Only the title is left of what seems to have been a Castilian rendering of Chrétien's *Perceval*.[3]

On the other hand, we possess in whole or in part a number of redactions from the French prose romances which may be grouped under three heads: I. Merlin and the Holy Grail; II. Lancelot; III. Tristan. Let me list them before proceeding to discuss their literary characteristics.

I. *Merlin and the Holy Grail.* A certain Brother Juan Vivas translated a cyclic work, formerly known as the 'Pseudo-Boron' cycle and consisting of the *Estoire del Saint Graal*, the *Merlin* and *Suite du Merlin* of the Huth version, and the *Queste del Saint Graal*, followed by a brief *Mort Artu*.[4] This translation has not been preserved in its complete form but in various redactions of the separate parts.

1. The translation of the *Estoire del Saint Graal* exists in two forms, known as the *Libro de Josep Abarimatía* and the *Livro de Josep Abaramatia*. The former is a Castilian fragment showing an earlier Leonese layer, and is found in a manuscript dated 1469.[5] The latter, already mentioned, was written in Portuguese, and survives in two copies, one of which was dedicated to João III (1521–57), but reproduces a manuscript some two centuries older.[5]

2. Vivas's redaction of the *Merlin* and the *Suite du Merlin* has come down

---

[1] Bohigas Balaguer, op. cit., pp. 17, 39, 103 f.; Entwistle, pp. 40 ff., 70 f.

[2] The name Yván suggests the hero of Chrétien's poem, while the narrative corresponds to Marie de France's *Lanval* and to *Graelent*. Could the source have been something like the lai of *Desiré*, which at the start calls to mind Chrétien's *Yvain* and at the end *Lanval*? See R. S. Loomis, *Arthurian Tradition*, pp. 271 f., 304 f. The name of Yván's spouse, 'la Señora del Parescer' (the Lady of Appearance), recalls Urganda's epithet in *Amadís*, 'la Desconocida', and hints at her multiple shapes. Both are more than likely to have been derived from the ever-changing Morgain la Fée. Nothing is known of the 'estoria de Belmonte', mentioned in *Zifar*, chap. ccx, probably another chivalric romance.

[3] A. Bonilla, *Las leyendas de Wagner en la literatura española* (Madrid, 1913), p. 48.

[4] Bohigas Balaguer, op. cit., pp. 68–80. See for a new account of this cycle Chap. 24 above.

[5] K. Pietsch, *Spanish Grail Fragments* (Chicago, 1924), i. 3–54.

[6] Now being edited by A. Magne, Rio de Janeiro. See M. Martins, *O Livro de José de Arimateia da Torre do Tombo* (Lisbon, 1952), p. 13.

in three forms. The *Estoria de Merlín* is found in the same manuscript as the *Libro de Josep Abarimatía* and displays the same linguistic features.[1] The second and third forms are both entitled *Baladro del sabio Merlín con sus profecías* (*The Cry of the Wise Merlin, together with his Prophecies*) and consist of a Castilian text printed at Burgos in 1498 and another text printed at Seville in 1535 as part of a *Demanda del Sancto Grial* (*Quest of the Holy Grail*).[2] Bohigas Balaguer assumes that the two *Baladros* derived from a common source, the lost *Estoria de Merlín* translated from the French.[3] The earlier text provides prologues and an epilogue absent from the later, while the later concludes with several obscure prophecies dealing with Spanish politics before the year 1467.

3. The *Queste del Saint Graal* and *Mort Artu* are represented by three Hispanic texts. The first consists of three fragments, derived from the *Mort Artu* and entitled by the scribe *Lançarote* because of the prominence of this personage, which are included in the same manuscript as the *Libro de Josep Abarimatía* and *Estoria de Merlín*.[4] A second text in Portuguese, entitled *Demanda do Santo Graal*, was copied between 1400 and 1438,[5] and a third in Castilian, entitled *Demanda del Sancto Grial con los maravillosos fechos de Lançarote y de Galaz su hijo*, was printed at Toledo in 1515 and at Seville in 1535.[6] Both editions suffer from the loss of about a third of the narrative through omission of lines, paragraphs, and even folios. On the other hand there is a considerable interpolation from the Vulgate *Queste*. All three Hispanic texts are traceable to a single translation of the *Queste* and *Mort Artu* of the Pseudo-Boron cycle.

What was the language of this archetypal translation by Brother Juan Vivas? The safest approach is through the analysis of the oldest extant text and the collation of parallel texts. Pietsch in his articles and vol. II of his edition completed the first task, pointing out the underlying Leonese stratum. The second problem has not yet been seriously tackled. Throughout the Middle Ages the Castilian-Portuguese linguistic frontier was not nearly as sharp as it became later, largely owing to the preservation of the transitional Leonese dialect. A passage in *Josep Abaramatia*, which mentions the Leonese town of Astorga, and stresses occurrences of equal concern to Portugal and Castile, suits the cultural and political role of León, and matches the dialectal flavour of Pietsch's fragments. About 1250 Leonese developed a short-lived literary activity known through derivative, often strongly

---

[1] Pietsch, op. cit. i. 57–81.
[2] The prologues, table of contents, and epilogue of the Castilian *Baladro* were printed by G. Paris and J. Ulrich in *Merlin* (Paris, 1886), i. lxxxi–xci. The Seville edition of 1535 was reprinted by A. Bonilla (Madrid, 1907).
[3] Bohigas Balaguer, op. cit., pp. 35–52. See above, p. 328.
[4] Pietsch, op. cit. i. 83–89.   [5] Ed. A. Magne (Rio de Janeiro, 1944).
[6] The Seville edition was reprinted by Bonilla (Madrid, 1907).

Castilianized versions, for example, the *Estoria del rey Guillelme*. In this setting one may fit Juan Vivas's translation of Arthurian stories. This hypothesis would explain the mixed dialect of Pietsch's fragments and occasional 'Western' features in the Castilian *Demanda*. It would further account for the similarity (not identity) of content between the two *Demandas*,[1] and for the fact that the Portuguese *Demanda* claims no descent from a French version and the question of its filiations is obscure.

Besides these redactions of the Pseudo-Boron *Queste*, there is a *Storia del Sant Grasal* in Catalan based on the Vulgate *Queste*.[2] The manuscript, completed in 1380 probably by a Majorcan, is not the original. There is, of course, no verbal correspondence with the preceding romances of the Grail, not even with the interpolation mentioned above.

II. *Lancelot*. As with Vivas's rendering of the Pseudo-Boron *Merlin*, *Queste*, and *Mort Artu*, so with the Hispanic *Lancelot*; it has survived only in later and sometimes fragmentary redactions. There is a Galician-Portuguese *Lançarote* in a manuscript of about 1350, containing thirteen short chapters based on Part II of the Vulgate *Lancelot*.[3] There is also a single folio from a late fourteenth-century manuscript which originally contained the Catalan text of Parts I and II.[4] A copy of this text may be the subject of the request by Pedro IV for the return of a manuscript of 'Lançalot en catalá'.[5] The National Library at Madrid possesses a sixteenth-century manuscript of *Lançarote de Lago* copied from a manuscript of 1414 and probably going back to an early fourteenth-century text.[6] It contains Parts II and III of the French *Lancelot*, beginning with the departure of Galehaut for Sorelois and ending with tales which Gawain, Bors, and Gariet told of their adventures. To this the author has added a link intended to introduce a *Libro de Tristán*.

III. *Tristan*. There are two redactions of the French Prose *Tristan*. The first is represented by a single late-fourteenth-century folio in Castilian and a slightly modernized *Tristán de Leonís* printed in 1501, 1528, and 1534.[7] The publisher inserted two stanzas composed by Alonso de Córdova for Juan de Flores's *Grimalte y Gradissa*, and borrowed from that romance the

---

[1] Entwistle, pp. 166, 172. For other explanations see Bohigas Balaguer, op. cit., pp. 56, 81 ff., and M. Rodrigues Lapa, *A Demanda do Santo Graal, Prioridade do Texto Português* (Lisbon, 1930), and review by Bohigas Balaguer, *Revista de Filología Española*, xx (1933), 180 ff.

[2] Ed. V. Crescini, V. Todesco (Barcelona, 1917).

[3] Ed. M. Serrano y Sans, *Boletín de la Real Academia Española*, xv (1928), 307–14.

[4] Ed. A. Rubió i Lluch, M. Obrador in *Revista de Bibliografía Catalana*, iii (1903), 5–25; Entwistle, pp. 95 ff.

[5] Entwistle, p. 94, n. 1.

[6] Portions have been published in *ZRP*, xxvi (1902), 202–5; in Bonilla, *Las leyendas de Wagner*, pp. 73–106; in *Revista de Filología Española*, xi (1924), 292–7; Entwistle, pp. 193–6.

[7] The fragment was edited by Bonilla, *Anales de la literatura española* (Madrid, 1904), pp. 25–28, and the editions of 1501 and 1528 were reprinted by Bonilla in 1912 and 1907.

description of a tomb. He also amplified rhetorically the end, as witness the description of the beauty of Isolt.[1] We have also two manuscripts of the late fourteenth century. The first, entitled *El cuento de Tristán de Leonís*, was composed originally in the Aragonese dialect, which is preserved in its purity by one scribe and is discernible through the Castilian disguise of others.[2] The second, in Catalan, entitled *Tristany de Leonis*, consists of only four folios.[3]

These Hispanic *Tristans* coincide as to content, though not verbally nor in the matter of proper names and other details. They seem to have descended from a common archetype, which was not based on any known French version but corresponded rather to the Italian texts, particularly the *Tristano Riccardiano*. Entwistle, mindful of the French origin of other Peninsular Arthuriana and of the late impact of Italian literature, postulated a French source for the mutually independent Italian and Hispanic texts. Northup, after comparing the southern versions as to motivation of the plot and proper names, was inclined to derive the Spanish from the Italian and the latter from a lost French version. Bohigas Balaguer, recognizing the early relations between Aragon and Italy, held that the Aragonese *Tristán* was a direct outgrowth of the Italian text, while the Castilian version was adopted through the Catalan intermediary.[4]

The popularity of the Matter of Britain south of the Pyrenees is also illustrated by five lyrics preserved in the *Cancioneiro de Lisboa*, and dating from the late thirteenth or early fourteenth century.[5] Though called *lais de Bretanha*, they are, of course, quite distinct from the narrative poems treated in Chap. 11. Nos. 1, 3, and 4 are free translations of lyrics in the French Prose *Tristan*. The second, 'O Marot haja mal-grado', has not been traced to a French lyric, but was perhaps suggested by a sentence in the French *Suite du Merlin*: 'elles dient que mal gre en ait le Morholt'. Similarly the fifth lai, 'Ledas sejamos ogemais!', has a refrain which echoes the statement in the Vulgate *Lancelot* that its hero was 'li mieldres chevaliers del monde'.

---

[1] The portrait was added after the completion of the main text, as its late linguistic features show. Entwistle, p. 120, recalled that Brunetto Latini, the guest of Alfonso X about 1260, attributed to Tristan a rhetorical description of Isolt. *Li Livres dou Tresor*, ed. F. J. Carmody, pp. 331 f.

[2] Ed. G. T. Northup (Chicago, 1928).

[3] Ed. A. Duràn i Sanpere, *Estudis Romànics* (Barcelona, 1917), pp. 284–316.

[4] Entwistle, pp. 112 f., 115 ff.; *El cuento*, ed. Northup, pp. 13 ff.; Bohigas Balaguer in *Revista de Filología Española*, xvi (1929), 284 f.; P. H. Coronedi in *AR*, xvi (1932), 172 ff.

[5] Entwistle, pp. 64–71; ed. C. M. de Vasconcelos, *Cancioneiro da Ajuda* (Halle, 1904), ii. 479–525, and *Revista Lusitana*, vi (1900), 1 ff. Senhora de Vasconcelos inferred the existence of an earlier Galician-Portuguese *Tristan*. But since that language, until well into the fourteenth century, was the vehicle of lyric in most of the Peninsula, Entwistle, p. 68, argues that the prose of the 'earlier' text may have been written in another dialect. Why not credit the versifier with directly translating the originals of lais 1, 3, and 4, and with borrowing from the prose lais 2 and 5? The only conclusion the lais justify is that their author knew a *Tristan* different from the one adopted by the preserved translations.

Lancelot is also the hero of two narrative ballads. The first has no known source but tells how the hero fought and killed the Orgulloso, who had boasted that he would win the love of Guenevere.[1] The other is a variant form of the chase of the stag with the white foot, discussed in Chaps. 11 and 34.[2] Finally, a third ballad, 'Herido está don Tristán', preserved in four late-fifteenth- and early-sixteenth-century versions, describes the death of Tristan and Isolt in accordance with the Castilian romance.[3]

Literary Purposes and Values

Measured by the standards of excellence attained by its models and counterparts in French, English, German, Dutch, and Italian, the Arthurian literature of the Spanish Peninsula is unoriginal and of scant literary value. It fails to stress the supernatural adventures typical of the Matter of Britain, or the irresistible force of love, or the mystic mood of the Grail romances. Hence its choice of the Pseudo-Boron cycle, in which external action prevails over delineation of character, passion, and symbolic meaning.

These flaws stand out in the Grail texts, particularly in the Castilian *Demanda* with its preference for duels and knightly deeds. Moreover, the additions are singularly awkward, leaving the narrative shot through with inconsistencies. The mania for piling up mere feats of chivalry produces a slovenly structure and leaves little scope for characterization. Such vivid personalities as Galahad, Perceval, Lancelot, and Gawain lose their individuality. Only the Portuguese *Demanda*, faithful at least to Pseudo-Boron, maintains a certain coherence in matter and differentiates the characters. The same work and the Castilian *Baladro* of 1498, polished by its publisher, rise in style above the mediocrity of the mainly literal translations from the French. In fact, all things considered, the Portuguese *Demanda* is the work of highest literary merit in the *Merlin-Grail* series. The second and fifth 'lais de Bretanha', which belong to this branch of the Arthurian cycle, conform to the conventional pattern of the 'cantiga d'amor'.

The romances based on the French Vulgate *Lancelot* are superior to the Castilian *Demanda*; they translate a superior model in a plain style, with no sham elegance. In contrast to the Carolingian cycle, the Arthurian inspired few ballads, but of marked merit. The Lancelot ballads referred to above possess spirit and charm. The first especially is a typical creation of the *Romancero* and was a favourite with Cervantes, who quoted it three times.[4] The second must have contained originally the complete story; through a

---

[1] Entwistle, pp. 199 f.; Bonilla, *Anales*, pp. 29 f.
[2] Entwistle, pp. 203–9; ed. *MLR*, xviii (1923), 435–48.
[3] Ed. Bonilla, *Tristán de Leonís*, pp. 393–401; Entwistle, pp. 111 f.
[4] *Quixote*, Part I, chaps. xii, xlix; Part II, chap. xxxi.

process not uncommon in ballads with romantic plots, the poem begins at a high point in the story.

The Hispanic *Tristan* texts, like their French source, are inferior to the poems of Thomas and Béroul. Love is either grossly sensual or is almost lost from sight in the turmoil of fights and tournaments. Nevertheless, the Castilian version is not without distinction of style. The three 'lais' translated from the French lyrics are sentimental complaints in abstract, discursive language. But the ballad on the death of Tristan is a masterpiece of poignancy and compression. It condenses the end of the Spanish romance, borrows picturesque phrases from other ballads, and ends with the folk-lore theme, a magic herb which springs from the lovers' tombs.

Circulation and Influence

The mass of translations in manuscript must have extended the knowledge of Arthurian legends to a wide circle of readers, which was to grow even larger with the invention of printing. From 1350 on, political propaganda dictated new prophecies of Merlin with every new king. Arthurian subjects are referred to more and more frequently and begin to appear in various artistic media, examples of which, unfortunately, have not been preserved, except for a few miniatures.[1] Most important is the influence which these translations had on original romances of chivalry composed in the Peninsula, an influence sometimes superficial and slight, sometimes penetrating to the very core.

It has already been pointed out that the Castilian *Zifar* contains allusions to the Arthurian cycle, and there are also certain debatable signs of influence.[2] Literal correspondences have not been found. However, two interrelated episodes, although loosely linked to the rest of the romance, show Arthurian colour. Both episodes, that of the Bold Knight (chaps. cix–cxvii) and that of the Fortunate Isles (chaps. cciv–ccxv) involve supernatural adventures, the former in a land under the waters of a mysterious lake; the latter in distant, magic islands. In both the respective heroes, after ephemeral love affairs with the queens—both of whom give birth to a renowned knight—are violently

---

[1] On Arthurian names see p. 406, n. 4 above, Entwistle, pp. 15, 19, and Bohigas Balaguer, *Los textos españoles*, pp. 99 f. Hawks named Lanzarote and Galván belonged to the Infante don Enrique, who died in 1304, and the Infante don Juan named a hound Merlín (1372); Entwistle, pp. 18, 92. For Arthurian themes in the fine arts see R. S. and L. H. Loomis, *Arthurian Legends in Medieval Art* (New York, 1938), pp. 23–27, 92 f.; Bonilla, *Anales de la literatura española*, pp. 25–28.

[2] Wagner in *Revue Hispanique*, x (1903), 23, suggested that Zifar's feigning madness in order to enter a beleaguered city (chaps. lxiii f.) is an imitation of the Bern *Folie Tristan*, vss. 127 ff., but his second suggestion, that it was based on 1 Kings xxi. 10–15, carries greater conviction. Wagner also suggested that Marie de France's *Eliduc* influenced the theme of the man with the two wives in chaps. lxxxvii, cxviii f., but there seems to be a closer connexion with *Bueve d'Hantone*, which has affected other episodes in *Zifar*. See E. von Richthofen, *Studien zur romanischen Heldensage des Mittelalters* (Halle, 1944), pp. 51 f.

dismissed. A. H. Krappe attempted to dissolve the first episode into its motifs, pointing out parallels with universal folk-lore in an effort to disprove its Celtic origin.[1] Krappe's analysis does not carry conviction; the author of the *Zifar* in inserting other extraneous stories does not freely combine individual motifs, but on the contrary adheres in each instance to a single continuous source. For the second episode, Krappe assembled several Oriental versions which relate all the essentials in the same sequence.[2] Here the author, it seems, started out from an Oriental story which, unlike many others in the *Zifar*, he embellished with Arthurian touches (the magic boat, the Fortunate Isles, the sovereign loath to laugh) and also with classical echoes (*Heroides*, vii). Aside from these episodes, the *Zifar* clashes with the Arthurian narratives. Its religion is robust and by no means mystical; its protagonists are moral and middle-class, with stray gleams of humour. Not even in the last part, a trifle less pedestrian and didactic, are there traces of courtly love or of pure chivalric honour.

The famous *Amadís* contains several allusions to Arthurian legends, principally to *Tristan* (I. i and x; IV. xlviii; perhaps also I. iv). Arthurian influence, though hardly exclusive, prevails in proper names, epithets, and titles.[3] Coincidences of wording are numerous; for example, the keywords with which Amadís dedicates himself to Oriana's service are modelled on Lancelot's. Besides identical themes and even adventures, in many episodes the same motifs occur in the same order, which proves that the *Amadís* imitates the Arthurian stories that have come down to us. Thus, Amadís reminds King Lisuarte, who has reared him, of his wish to be knighted: Lisuarte stresses the hardships of knighthood and suggests a waiting period; since the youth insists, the king acquiesces and makes all the requisite preparations; at the proper moment, Oriana asks King Perión to knight Amadís, and the request is granted: these incidents, strung in identical sequence, are told of Lancelot, the Lady of the Lake, and King Arthur. Also, Amadís dispatches Gandalín as his messenger; Oriana shows him a low window facing the orchard; Amadís retires for sleep, then rises again, enters the orchard and through the grating grasps Oriana's hands; she insists on the secrecy of their love: here the *Amadís* combines in a single assignation two of Lancelot's. In Books III and IV, reworked by G. Rodríguez de Montalvo, there are also episodes imitated from the Arthurian cycle, some indirectly through those of the first Books.

[1] *Bulletin Hispanique*, xxxv (1933), 107–25.
[2] Ibid. xxxiii (1931), 97–103.
[3] G. S. Williams, 'The *Amadís* Question', *Revue Hispanique*, xxi (1909), 40 ff.; 'El desenlace del *Amadís* primitivo', *RP*, vi (1953), 283–9, confirmed by the recently found *Amadís* fragment; cf. A. Rodríguez Moñino, 'El primer manuscrito del *Amadís de Gaula*', *Boletín de la Real Academia Española*, xxxvi (1956), 199 ff. For influence of Chrétien's *Lancelot*, see R. J. Michels in *Bulletin Hispanique*, xxxvii (1935), 478 ff.

One still more important imitation has been observed by Bohigas Bala-guer:[1] the central plot of *Amadís* coincides with that of *Lancelot*. In both an unknown youth of royal descent is accepted at the court of a king, whom he serves loyally, except that he falls in love with the sovereign's wife or daughter. There are two main vicissitudes in the course of this love-affair: first, the knight rescues his lady from an abductor, thus earning her love or promise of love; second, the lady, jealous on account of a false report, rejects the knight, who loses (or comes close to losing) his mind and lives in solitude. The chief accomplishment of both heroes is the conquest of a marvellous abode—the Joyeuse Garde or the Ínsula Firme—to which they take their ladies in moments of peril. In both romances an important role is played by a group of noblemen, kinsfolk of the protagonist or of the king. Some magicians protect the monarchs and their knights, others are hostile to them; at the end, the Romans appear as vanquished enemies. No less significant is the same exaltation of adventure, honour, and love, the same indifference to other ways of living, in sharp contrast to fourteenth- and fifteenth-century romances native to the Peninsula. One cannot overstress the importance of the *Amadís* imitation. It offers a synthesis of the distinctive features of a typical Arthurian romance, and channels chivalric literature in this direction down to Cervantes's parody: presumably the leave-taking of the Knight and the Infanta, much like the cruel practical joke of Maritornes (*Quixote*, Part I, chaps. xiii, xliii), can be traced, through the first meeting of Amadís and Oriana, to the scene in which Lancelot touches Guenevere's hands through the grating.[2]

Between 1360 and 1370 the Majorcan Guillem Torroella (or Torrella) composed a poem, *La Faula* (*The Tale*), in Provençalized Catalan, with French insertions,[3] and told how he had been carried on the back of a whale to a faery island far to the East. There he saw a palfrey whose harness was adorned with the story of Tristan and Isolt and other lovers; its silver bells played the tune to one of Tristan's lais. Reaching a palace, he was welcomed by Morgain and beheld paintings of many heroes of the court of Arthur. When she held up her ring, the poet perceived Arthur gazing at his sword, and inquired whether he was that King Arthur 'expected by the Bretons', since

---

[1] 'La novela caballeresca, sentimental y de aventuras', *Historia general de las literaturas hispánicas* (Barcelona, 1951), ii. 222 f.

[2] On Cervantes's knowledge of Arthurian legends, see Entwistle's excellent remarks, pp. 250–3. Two scenes in the *Quixote* possibly burlesque situations in Arthurian romance: Don Quixote in the cart (end of Part I) and his fight with the cats (Part II, chap. xlvi); cf. Lancelot's, Gawain's, and Bors's adventures in the shameful cart, and Arthur's fight with the Chapalu (Bruce, i. 41, n. 9). For stray Arthurian reminiscences in the episode of Montesinos's cave (Part II, chap. xxiii) and in *Persiles and Sigismunda*, book iii, chaps. xvi f., see *RP*, ix (1955), 156 ff.

[3] J. Massó Torrents, *Repertori de l'antiga literatura catalana, La Poesia* (Barcelona, 1932), i. 501–11. Note the Majorcan origin of the *Lançalot* fragment and probably of the *Storia del Sant Grasal* (ed. Crescini and Todesco, pp. liii f.).

he had read in 'the authors who wrote about the feats of the Britons' that Arthur had died on the battlefield. Arthur explained how, though mortally wounded, he had been cured by Morgain by bathing in the paradisal waters of the Tigris and was now preserved in youthful vigour by the annual visit of the Grail. When the poet sought to learn the cause of the king's melancholy, he was told to look at the royal sword where he saw figured blindfolded misers and men of courage tied hand and foot by poverty. This localization of Arthur's palace on a Mediterranean isle relates *La Faula* to other traditions of Arthur's survival dealt with in Chap. 7. With these the author must have been familiar, and has treated them with a free fantasy.

The anonymous author of *Curial e Güelfa* (1443–60) reveals a familiarity with Arthurian fiction. At the beginning of Book II he refers to the Catalan *Tristan* and *Lancelot*. When the ladies laugh at sight of Curial wearing his beloved's shirt, he identifies himself as the 'donzell de la cota mal tallada', a figure unknown to the Hispanic *Tristans* and presumably suggested by a reading of the French prose romance.[1] Among the dancing couples seen in Güelfa's dream appear Tristan and Isolt, Lancelot and Guenevere.[2] Other references, however, are hostile in tone, and the most quoted Arthurian personage is the cruel Brehus-sens-pietat (Brehus sans Pitié). Tristan and Lancelot are represented as enjoying an easy renown for courage since they were never called on to match the Aragonese knights.[3] The attitude toward adventure and love is far removed from the Arthurian ideal. Realism, in fact, prevails over romance, and the literature of classical antiquity and of Italy is preferred to the Matter of Britain.

The Catalan romance of *Tirant lo Blanc* of about 1460 displays a more sympathetic feeling. The characters extol the Round Table,[4] and the hero himself is descended from a captain of Uther Pendragon—a common aspiration among noblemen of the period, as Riquer points out in his introduction.[5] The walls of the palace at Constantinople are adorned with portraits of Arthurian lovers and scenes from the Grail quest,[6] as were the walls of Aragonese and Catalan castles of the day. Guenevere and Isolt actually attend a festival held by the Emperor of Constantinople.[7] Morgain la Fée arrives in search of Arthur, with her maidens, Honour, Chastity, Hope, and Beauty. The emperor informs her that he has in his court a knight whose name is unknown but who possesses a marvellous sword.[8] Morgain recog-

---

[1] *Curial e Güelfa*, ed. R. Aramon i Serra, i. 176. Cf. E. Löseth, *Roman en Prose de Tristan*, § 66 ff.
[2] *Curial e Güelfa*, iii. 230.   [3] Ibid. ii. 101.
[4] M. de Riquer, *Tirant lo Blanc* (Barcelona, 1947), chaps. xxxiv, lxxxiv, cxiv, clxxxii, cccxliv.
[5] Ibid., p. 63.   [6] Ibid., chaps. cxviii f.
[7] Ibid., chaps. clxxxix–ccii.
[8] Arthur is accompanied by the aged Fe-sens-pietat, whom Riquer (*Tirant*, pp. 1255 f.) identifies with Brehus sans Pitié. Perhaps there has been an association with the aged knight Branor le Brun of Rusticiano da Pisa's compilation (see Chap. 27), since Brehus is at times called Brun : the *Tirant*, known for its partiality to high sounding names, retains the epithet but changes the name.

nizes in him her brother and listens to an elaborate moral discourse. When she lifts her ring to his eyes, Arthur comes out of his trance, greets the emperor, and all join in a dance. This narrative evidently describes a typical courtly interlude, and shows how the British king had invaded even the field of dramatic pageantry.

The reader will perceive, however, that many features of this interlude were suggested by *La Faula*—Morgain and her allegorical maidens, the role of the ring, and Arthur's moral discourse. Likewise a ballad about Tristan, sung by the empress,[1] seems to have been suggested by the extant Castilian ballad.[2] Riquer has pointed out that the title, the Count of Joiosa Guarda, may well have been derived not from the castle of Lancelot but from Jacme March's poem (1370) on the allegorical city of Joiosa Guarda, the refuge of loyal lovers. Thus it appears that, in contrast to *Amadís*, direct influence of Arthurian romance on *Tirant* was slight. There are no verbal borrowings, no sustained imitation, and the atmosphere is totally different, down-to-earth and humorous, as Cervantes observed with understandable sympathy (*Quixote*, Part I, chap. vi).

As a final example of the impingement of Arthurian matter on the literature of the Peninsula one may cite an episode, *Estoria de dos amadores*, inserted by Juan Rodríguez del Padrón in his *Siervo libre de Amor* (*c.* 1440), the first Castilian sentimental novel.[3] Ardanlier, son of the King of Mondoya, flees from his father, who is opposed to his love for Liessa, and lives with her in a palace hewn out of the rock. Seven years later, when he is out hunting, his father recognizes his hounds, rushes to the palace, and kills Liessa. Ardanlier, on his return, commits suicide, and a friend builds a sumptuous monument for the lovers. The palace remains under an enchantment until the Galician troubadour Macías arrives. Here there seem to be reminiscences of the House of the Sage Damsel in *Tristan*[4] and of an incident in the *Suite du Merlin* (*Huth Merlin*),[5] probably adapted to the Inés de Castro legend. Curiously enough, the version of this latter incident in the *Baladro del Sabio Merlín*, as published in 1535, seems to show traces of Rodríguez del Padrón's recasting.[6]

By way of conclusion, it may be observed that the career of the Arthurian legends in Spain and Portugal is typical of Hispanic literature. Initially introduced in French forms, they became fashionable with an aristocratic *élite*. They were absorbed at a later date into the vernacular literature and adapted to the taste and temper of the people; mysticism was minimized and action

---

[1] *Tirant*, chap. cclxiii.
[2] Riquer in *Revista de Filología Española*, xxxvii (1953), 225–7.
[3] Ed. A. Paz y Mélia, Madrid, 1884, pp. 54–74.
[4] Ed. Bonilla, chaps. xxxv f.; ed. Northup, chap. lxxviii f.; Löseth, § 52.
[5] *Merlin*, ed. Paris and Ulrich, ii. 192.
[6] *Nueva Revista de Filología Hispánica*, viii (1954), 19 ff.

emphasized. Thus acclimatized, they stimulated the creation of original works.[1] At the end of the fifteenth century, when the medieval strain blended with that of the Renaissance, the old-fashioned, stylized representation of life in these romances was affected by the vigour and artistry of the new movement. *Tirant*, Montalvo's *Amadís*, and *Palmerín* with its sequels attained an immense vogue, and started a new fashion of romance throughout Europe. Apart from its signal influence on the modern narrative and drama, this literary fashion left a significant vestige in the toponymy of the New World: the names of California and Patagonia seem to be traceable to episodes of the *Esplandián* and *Primaleón*, the respective continuations of the *Amadís* and the *Palmerín*.[2]

[1] Derivative Arthurian literature composed or translated in Spain: *Historia del rey Canamor y de Turián su fijo* (Burgos, 1509): reprinted by Bonilla (Madrid, 1908) and ascribed by Bohigas Balaguer, 'La novela caballeresca', *Historia general de las literaturas hispánicas*, ii. 200, to the late fifteenth century; *Crónica de los nobles cavalleros Tablante de Ricamonte y Jofré, hijo de don Assón* (Toledo, 1513): reprinted by Bonilla (Madrid, 1907) and traceable to the Provençal *Jaufré*, probably through a French fourteenth-century prose translation; and the *Corónica de don Tristán de Leonís y del rey don Tristán de Leonís el joven* (Seville, 1534): Part I reproduces the Castilian *Tristan* plus an interpolation paving the way for Part II, entirely the work of the sixteenth century author (P. de Gayangos, *Libros de caballerías* [Madrid, 1857], pp. xiv–xv, and E. G. Gardner, *Arthurian Legend in Italian Literature* [London, 1930], pp. 295 ff.). In the sixteenth century, aside from the *Amadís* and *Palmerín* continuations, the following romances are noted for their authors' distinction: Gonzalo Hernández de Oviedo's *Claribalte* (1519); João de Barros's *Clarimundo* (1522); Antonio de Torquemada's *Olivante de Laura* (1564); Jerónimo de Urrea's *Clarisel de las Flores* (first printed by J. M. Asensio, Seville, 1879); and Jorge Ferreira de Vasconcelos's *Memorial da Segunda Távola Redonda* (1567, possibly written fifteen years earlier). Cf. H. Thomas, *Spanish and Portuguese Romances of Chivalry* (Cambridge, 1920), pp. 119 ff., and M. Moisés, *A Novela de Cavalaria no Quinhentismo Português* (São Paulo, 1957).

[2] For California, see R. Putnam and H. I. Priestley, *California: the Name*, *University of California Publications in History*, iv (1917), 293–365; I. A. Leonard, *Books of the Brave* (Cambridge, Mass., 1949), chap. iv. For Patagonia, see 'Para la toponimia argentina: Patagonia', *Hispanic Review*, xx (1952), 321 ff.

ARTHURIAN INFLUENCES ON ITALIAN LITERATURE FROM 1200 TO 1500

ANTONIO VISCARDI

EARLIER chapters of this book have called attention to various signs of the powerful influence which the Matter of Britain exercised on the Italian imagination during the Middle Ages. In Chap. 6 there was mention of the Modena sculpture and the Otranto mosaic, proving the circulation of tales, elsewhere unrecorded, in widely separated parts of the peninsula even in the twelfth century. The same chapter and the next introduce the famous legend, so thoroughly studied by Arturo Graf, of Arthur's abode in the cavernous depths of Mount Etna, a legend already established by 1200. Chap. 7 records the references by Boncompagno da Signa and Godfrey of Viterbo, both dated about 1200, to the expectation of Arthur's return. Chap. 22, in dealing with the Prose *Lancelot*, discusses the significant references to that work by Dante. Chap. 27 is devoted in part to two works composed in French prose by Italians between 1272 and 1279, the compilation of Rusticiano da Pisa and the *Prophécies de Merlin*. Other evidences of the same vogue are the ceiling paintings at Palermo, three Sicilian bed-quilts, and several extant French texts illuminated in Italy.[1] We possess a Hebrew *Mort Artu* of the year 1279, which was translated, as the forms of the proper names indicate, from an Italian, probably a Tuscan, source.[2]

As for the Italian texts themselves—the prose romances relating the adventures of the knights of the Old Table and the New, the loves of Tristano and Isotta, the quest of the Grail, the downfall and the passing of Arthur; the several *cantari* on the same or similar themes; the great adaptations of this material by Boiardo and Ariosto—these have been treated in such comprehensive and masterly fashion by Edmund G. Gardner in *The Arthurian Legend in Italian Literature*,[3] on the basis of the work of Parodi, Rajna, Bertoni, and Levi, that it seems hardly necessary to cover the ground again

[1] R. S. and L. H. Loomis, *Arthurian Legends in Medieval Art* (New York, 1938), pp. 21–23, 29, 61–65, 114–21; Rajna in *R*, xlii (1913), 517 ff.; E. Gabrici, E. Levi, *Lo Steri di Palermo e le sue Pitture* (Milan, Rome), tav. 59 f., 63 f., 73 f., 99–101; pp. 93–104.

[2] Gaster in *Archiv*, cxxii (1909), 51–63; in *Folk-lore*, xx (1909), 272–94.

[3] E. G. Gardner, *Arthurian Legend in Italian Literature* (London, New York, 1930). Hereinafter referred to as Gardner. See also his 'Notes on the "Matière de Bretagne" in Italy', *Proc. Brit. Acad.*, xv.

in this book. Accordingly, the following pages will depart from the plan adopted in the preceding chapters and will be devoted not so much to a survey of the texts themselves, their problems, and influences, as to the scattered references and the adaptations in non-Arthurian Italian literature between 1200 and 1500 which afford us another measure of the pervasive power of the *Materia di Bretagna*.

The references in the lyrics of the early thirteenth century examined by Gardner, when they are specific enough to determine the source, lead us to the poems of Thomas and Chrétien de Troyes.[1] The notary Giacomo da Lentino, the founder of the Sicilian school, has two mere allusions to the Tristan theme—'Lovelier you seem to me than Isolda the blonde', 'Tristano and Isalda . . . did not love so deeply',—but he has a third which seems clearly inspired by a motif in Thomas's *Tristan*. It is in the canzone 'Meravilliosamente':

> Having a great desire, I painted a portrait, fair one, resembling you, and when I do not see you, I look upon that figure and it seems that I have you before me.[2]

One may recognize in these lines an echo of those in which Thomas defined Tristan's purpose in carving an image of the absent Isolt.

> For this reason he made that image, for he wished to speak his heart to it, his good thought, his foolish error, his pain, his joy in love, for he knew not to whom to reveal his will or his desire.[3]

Another line, from Guittone d'Arezzo, 'You are my God and my life and my death', recalls the famous couplet which Gottfried von Strassburg took over from Thomas: 'Isolt ma drue, Isolt m'amie, En vus ma mort, en vus ma vie.'[4] A passage in Guittone d'Arezzo's canzone 'Amor tant' altamente' makes a clear reference to Chrétien's *Perceval*.[5] The poet asserts that it is a fault when a good servant dares to ask a reward for his long service, and hence he does not ask for one, but remains silent. Yet he hopes that it will not go with him as it did with Prenzevallo (Perceval), whose fault it was not to ask. It is evident that Chrétien's famous description of the passage of the bleeding lance and the shining grail before the silent hero has become a living part of Guittone's culture so that he uses the situation naturally to convey an impression of his own dilemma.[6] An anonymous sonnet (no. 274 of the Canzoniere Laurenziano Rediano) contains the line: 'I am yours more than

[1] Gardner, pp. 21–43.

[2] E. Monaci, *Crestomazia Italiana dei Primi Secoli* (Bologna, 1926), p. 46.

[3] G. Bertoni, *I Cantari di Tristano* (Modena, 1937); Thomas, *Tristan*, ed. Bédier, SATF, i. 317.

[4] Gardner, p. 28; *Rime di Fra Guittone d'Arezzo*, ed. F. Pellegrini, p. 93; Thomas, *Tristan*, ed. Bédier, i. 258.

[5] *Rime di Fra Guittone*, p. 341; Gardner, pp. 29–31.

[6] A. Viscardi, *Letteratura d'Oc e d'Oil* (Milan, 1952), pp. 254–7.

Erecche was Enida's.' Since in the French cyclical romances and in the Italian derivatives Erec does not figure as the lover of Enide, it is plain that the reference is to Chrétien's elaborate story of their passion. In the allegorical poem, *L'Intelligenza*, composed about 1300, the pair are listed as the subject of sculptures, together with a multitude of other lovers famous in medieval story.[1] Among them are eight of those celebrated by Chrétien: Ginevra and Lancilotto, Rosenna d'Amore (Soredamors) and Allessandro, Ivano and Analida (Laudine), Erecco and Enidia. Between 1350 and 1368 Fazio degli Uberti described in his *Dittamondo* a fanciful tour which he had made of Arthurian lands under the guidance of the geographer Solinus, and declared: 'I saw the castle where Arech lay with his Nida.'[2] This is presumably the castle of Penevric, or Pointurie, where Erec recovered from his wounds and the lovers forgot their pains.

A survey of these scattered references in the Italian poets of the thirteenth and fourteenth centuries proves that, besides being familiar with the prose compilations in French or in their own vernacular which they possessed, they had also read the older poems of Thomas and Chrétien.[3] From them they derived some of their themes and the formal aspects of their technique.

Highly significant too is the reception given to the ideal figures of Arthurian story by scholars and rhetoricians writing in Latin. Lancelot and Tristan take their places beside the great figures of biblical and historical literature and the characters of Ovid, Vergil, Lucan, and Statius, and represent a synthesis of the refined, loyal lover of troubadour lyrics with the mighty warrior of the *chansons de geste*. Thus already at the end of the twelfth century the classicizing poet, Arrigo da Settimello, placed beside such typical sufferers of antiquity as Tantalus and Niobe, 'Tristanus qui me tristia plura tulit'.[4] And as Tristan has become a type of the tragic hero, Arthur exemplifies human grandeur and felicity. Not long after (*c.* 1205), Boncompagno da Signa, professor of rhetoric at Bologna, assumed in his *De Amicitia* that the beauty of Isolt was as much a matter of common knowledge as that of Helen, asserting that he who is blinded by love can make no distinctions and transforms a hunchbacked or wry-nosed woman into a Helen or an Isolt.[5] Just as the verses of the troubadours were placed on an equal plane with academic Latin poetry by the cultivated classes of Italy, so also the Matter of Britain was adopted into the historical manuals along with the narratives of the Bible and of pagan antiquity.[6] As a result we find Arthur, Lancelot, Isolt, Guenevere,

---

[1] Gardner, pp. 107–10; *L'Intelligenza*, ed. V. Mistruzzi (Bologna, 1928); ed. Petronia (Bari, 1952), st. 72–76, 287.

[2] Gardner, p. 226; Fazio degli Uberti, *Il Dittamondo e le rime*, ed. G. Corsi (Bari, 1952), I. iv. 23.

[3] A. Viscardi, A. Pompeati, *La Letteratura Italiana* (Milan, 1951), pp. 70 ff.

[4] Gardner, p. 8; *Henrici Septimellensis Elegia*, ed. A. Marigo (Padua, 1926), vss. 97 f.

[5] Gardner, p. 10; *Amicitia di Maestro Boncompagno da Signa*, ed. S. Nathan (Rome, 1909), p. 71.

[6] Viscardi, *Letteratura d'Oc e d'Oïl*, pp. 70 f.

Tristan, and Perceval beside Esther, Joshua, Judith, Caesar, Alexander, Piramus, Thisbe, Achilles, and Antigone.[1]

We have already noted that Fazio in the *Dittamondo* claims to have seen the very castle where Erec lay with his Enide, but this was only one of many sights of Arthurian interest which he observed on his tour through Little and Great Britain.

> I was in Gannes, where the death of Dorens and the tale of the damsel who left the greyhounds to the King of the Desert are still believed. I was there, too, where they say that Arthur killed Froles in combat. . . . We were in London and I saw the tower where Ginevra defended her honour, and also the Tamis, that flows close by. I saw the fair castle which brave Lancilotto took by force with the aid of three shields during the second year that he engaged in deeds of prowess. I saw the wasted, ruined Camelotto, and I was there where the maid of Corbenich and she of Scalotto were born. . . . I saw the plain and the fountain by the pine.[2]

We detect in these lines allusions to episodes and persons of the Prose *Lancelot*, to the kingdom of Bohort, to the slaying of Dorin, son of Claudas, by young Bohort and Lionel and their transformation into greyhounds, to Arthur's combat with King Frolle, to Guenièvre's taking refuge from Modred in the Tower of London, to Lancelot's capture of the Douloureuse Garde, to King Pelles's daughter and the Maid of Escalot, to Hector des Mares, who guarded a fountain beneath a pine.[3] Fazio claims to have visited also the site of the calamitous battle of Saglibiere (Salisbury), described in the *Mort Artu*, and the sites of two great combats between Aroan (Ariohan) and Meliadus of Leonois, and between Danain and Guron lo Cortois, both told in *Palamedes*.[4] Two other stanzas refer to the island where Tristano killed Amoroldo, to Tintoille (Tintagel), where an ivy sprang from Tristano's tomb, and to a valley which the same hero won in combat with a giant—the last a reference to *Palamedes*.[5]

The Prose *Lancelot*, as is well known, made a great impression on the imagination of Dante, three detailed references appearing in the *Commedia* and one, somewhat more general, in the *Convivio*. The first is the famous passage in the *Inferno*, canto v. In the circle of lovers, which includes Tristan, Francesca's spirit relates the circumstances of her fall.

> 'Noi leggevamo un giorno per diletto
> Di Lancelotto come amor lo strinse. . .
> Quando leggemmo il disiato riso
> Esser baciato da cotanto amante,
> Questi, che mai da me non fia diviso,

[1] Viscardi, *Le Origini*, 2nd ed. (Milan, 1950), pp. 451–6.
[2] Fazio degli Uberti, op. cit. 1. iv. 22, 23.   [3] Fazio, op. cit. 1. iv. 23, 26.
[4] Gardner, pp. 223–6.   [5] Fazio, op. cit. 1. iv. 22, 23.

La bocca mi baciò tutto tremante:
Galeotto fu il libro e chi lo scrisse.'

('We were reading one day for our delight of Lancelot, how love bound him.
. . . When we read how the longed-for smile was kissed by so great a lover, he
who shall never be divided from me, kissed me on the mouth all tremblingly.
Galeotto was the book and he who wrote it.')

Here Dante recalls the tender scene in which Galehaut brings about a
meeting between the bashful hero and the amorous queen, and in which she,
taking the initiative, gives him a long kiss. This act may be taken, like the
queen's sending to Lancelot the sword of knighthood, as a sort of investiture.
Dante, however, seems to assign the initiative to Lancelot, and some students
have surmised that he had read another redaction of the romance than any
known to us.[1] It is far more probable that the change was intentional and
conformed to the poet's ideal of feminine modesty.

An earlier moment in this same scene is reflected in the *Paradiso*, canto
xvi, where the smile which Beatrice turns upon Dante when he begins to
address Cacciaguida with the honorific *voi* is compared to the cough which
the Dame de Malehaut gives when Lancelot avows his love for the queen.
The resemblance is by no means obvious, and this uncertainty has given rise
to various conjectures.[2] Did Dante take both the smile and the cough to
be signs of encouragement? The cough, however, had exactly the opposite
effect and reduced Lancelot to silence.[3]

The Vulgate *Mort Artu* finds two echoes in Dante. Among the traitors
of the *Inferno*, canto xxxii, is 'he whose breast and shadow were cleft at
a single stroke by the hand of Arthur'. This recalls the battle of Salisbury,
in which Arthur is described as driving his lance so fiercely through Modred's
body that when it was withdrawn a ray of sunlight shone through.[4] A moving
passage in the *Convivio* likens the approach of the soul to the end of its earthly
career to the approach of a vessel to harbour. 'The knight Lancelot wished
not to enter with hoisted sails, nor our own most noble Guido da Montefel-
tro. Truly, these noble men lowered the sails of their mundane labours.'[5]

This solemn recalling of Lancelot's entry into religion at the close of his
life combines with the other very specific references to the Prose *Lancelot*
and with the familiar compliment in the *De Vulgari Eloquentia* to the 'Arturi
regis ambages pulcerrimae' to reveal with what attention and what respect

---

[1] V. Crescini, 'Il bacio di Ginevra e il bacio di Paolo', *Studi Danteschi* iii (1921); G. Bertoni,
Studi su vecchie e nuove poesie e prose d'amore e romanzi, 2nd ed. (Modena, 1927), pp. 175–81; Gardner,
pp. 139–45. Note also the influence of the Prose *Tristan* on the Paolo and Francesca episode.
P. Toynbee, *Dante in English Literature*, ii. 521.

[2] P. Rajna, *Dante e i romanzi della Tavola Ritonda*, pp. 232–4.

[3] Sommer, *Vulgate Version*, iii. 261, ll. 13–17.

[4] Gardner, pp. 147 f.; Sommer, op. cit. vi. 377, ll. 2–6.

[5] Gardner, p. 148; *Convivio*, iv. 28; Sommer, op. cit. vi. 387.

the greatest poet of the Middle Ages read the Prose *Lancelot* in the original. In fact, it seems clear that it was on the basis of this romance that Dante assigned to the *langue d'oïl* the primacy as the language of prose narrative.

In the course of the fourteenth century a degeneration set in, which reduced the tone of Arthurian composition in Italy to monotony and triviality. This tendency had already manifested itself in the previous century in the French Prose *Tristan* and in the compilations in which the amours of various lovers are interspersed with the quest of the Grail.[1] The heroes lose their distinguishing characters. Tristan is identical with Lancelot, and Lancelot with Perceval, and all spiritual rapture and significance disappears from the adventures of Galaad. The Prose *Tristan* was the source of many versions in Italian and bequeathed to them its banality. Besides the compilation of Rusticiano in French, there are the *Tavola Ritonda*, the *Tristano Riccardiano*, the *Tristano di Vienna*, and the *Tristano Corsiniano*. These prose romances, together with the *Storia di Merlino*, composed by the Florentine Pierino Pieri early in the *trecento*, formed a part of the cultural baggage of the bourgeois writers after 1300. Moreover, the Matter of Britain tended to lose something of its individuality and charm through contact with and assimilation to the other great bodies of historical or legendary narrative. The knights of the Round Table, the paladins of Charlemagne, the heroes and heroines of the Bible, the warriors of Greece and Troy and Rome—all lost their characteristic outlines and melted into each other.

A striking example of this unification of materials from every source may be found in the *Storie Nerbonesi* of Andrea da Barberino.[2] Guillaume d'Orange gave orders that a *piazza* in Paris should be hung with tapestries illustrating scenes drawn from the four religions of the world, Jewish, pagan, Saracen, and Christian; and the subjects of the hangings are systematically listed. In the fourth series appear not only scenes from the New Testament but also from the Carolingian cycle and *Bovo d'Antona* (Bevis of Hampton), and the stories of Giuseppe di Baramanzia (Joseph of Arimathea), of the Old Table and the New, of Lancelot, Tristan, and their ladies, and of the Holy Grail.

French literature of the thirteenth century as represented in *Huon de Bordeaux* actually fused the Carolingian and Arthurian cycles, retaining the theme of the strife between Charlemagne and the rebel barons as the main plot but interjecting characters and adventures reminiscent of the Matter of Britain. In Italy the fusion of the two cycles was carried out with extraordinary fervour and fecundity. A Paduan poet of the late thirteenth or early fourteenth century launched this movement with the Franco-Italian poem,

---

[1] See Chaps. 24, 26 above, and G. Bertoni, *Il Duecento*, 3rd ed. (Milan, 1939), pp. 365 ff.; N. Sapegno, *Il Trecento*, 2nd ed. (Milan, 1938), pp. 610 ff.

[2] *Storie Narbonesi*, ed. I. G. Isola (Bologna, 1887), pp. 339–58.

L'Entrée d'Espagne.[1] Roland leaves Charlemagne involved in the war in Spain and sets out on a career of adventure in the Orient, where, forgetful of Aude and of his obligation to his country and his faith, he draws inspiration for his exploits from the eyes of a Saracen beauty. The saintly and austere Roland of the French epic has been transfigured into a knight of the Round Table.

In the *Entrée* and in its continuations and redactions, *La Spagna in Rima* and *Li Fatti di Spagna*,[2] we come upon many motifs characteristic of the Matter of Britain: the marvellous fountain, the search undertaken to find the hero, the wild forest inhabited by giants, the fight with a hideous witch, enchanted arms, a sword left by the hero as a token for his unborn son.

No less interesting is the adoption and adaptation of Arthurian themes and sentiments by Andrea da Barberino in his prose works. *Aspramonte*, an elaboration of the *Chanson d'Aspremont*, deals with the invasion of Italy by the Saracens and the youthful exploits of Rolando.[3] At sight of Alda (Aude) the hero is consumed with love, and, like the young Lancelot in the presence of Guenièvre, dares not raise his eyes to her again. When at last he has won her favour by his prowess and receives her from the hand of her brother Ulivieri (Oliver), he swears that he will conquer Spain and crown her queen. Thus it is for her sake, not in the cause of religion or through fealty to Charlemagne, that he takes the road of St. James. The names and the geography of the Carolingian cycle remain, but the spirit is forgotten.

The *Storie Nerbonesi*, already mentioned,[4] draws its material from the cycle of Guillaume d'Orange, Vivien, and Aimeri de Narbonne. But how completely the atmosphere has changed when we read that it is his love of 'donna Tiborga' (Guiborc), the wife of his uncle, which sustains Beltramo in his combat with the terrible King of Numidia, mounted on a serpentine charger. In the *Reali di Francia* Andrea combines with the Carolingian material assembled in a Franco-Italian manuscript (marciano franc. xiii) other adventures suggested by Byzantine fictions and the romances of Alexander the Great and still others reminiscent of the Matter of Britain.[5]

In *Guerino il Meschino* (1391) Andrea turned away from the Old French epic.[6] The hero is the son of a king of Apulia and Calabria and his beautiful

---

[1] *L'Entrée d'Espagne*, ed. A. Thomas, SATF (1913), introd. A. Viscardi, *Letteratura Franco-italiana* (Modena, 1941), with bibliography.

[2] *La Spagna*, ed. M. Catalano (Bologna, 1940), with excellent introduction and indexes; *Li Fatti d'Espagna*, ed. R. M. Ruggieri (Modena, 1951).

[3] A. da Barberino, *L'Aspromonte*, ed. M. Boni (Bologna, 1950).

[4] See above, p. 424, n. 2.

[5] A. da Barberino, *I Reali di Francia*, ed. G. Vandelli, G. Gambarin (Bari, 1947). See also the phototype edition by P. Rajna (Florence, 1925), introd.; Viscardi, *Letteratura d'Oc e d'Oïl*, pp. 360 ff.

[6] There are no good editions of *Guerino il Meschino*, and one must go back to fifteenth- and sixteenth-century editions. See G. Osella, *Il Guerrino Meschino, Pallante*, ix, x (1932); Antoine de la Salle, *Le Paradis de la Reine Sibylle*, ed. F. Desonay (Paris, 1930), pp. xcix–cx.

Arab wife, but, ignorant of his parentage, he is sold as a captive and, after proving his valour in tourney and battle, he sets out as a knight errant to discover the secret of his birth. He crosses rivers and seas, enters deep caverns, slays giants and monsters, excites the passions of lovely damsels, and arrives at last in the land of the tree of the sun, where a voice informs him of his royal descent. More combats, more wanderings follow. Guerino visits the realm of Prester John and dwells for a time in the subterranean palace of the enchantress Alcina and there learns from her the name of his father. He weds the princess Antinesca and is reunited with his parents. When they and his wife are dead, he plans to retire from the world and do penance for his sins. One cannot help being reminded of the fact that Lancelot in the French prose romance was long ignorant of his royal parentage, stirred the hearts of various charming damsels, and at last became a hermit; that 'le Bel Inconnu' was informed of his parentage by a mysterious voice;[1] and that Claris and Laris were imprisoned in a palace of Morgain la Fée which resembled that of Alcina in several striking features.[2]

The *Cento Novelle Antiche* contains four Arthurian tales:[3] the combat of Lancelot with a knight of Sansogna (Saxony) at a fountain; the magnanimity of King Meliadus, who delivered his mortal enemy, the Knight without Fear, from hanging; the assignation of Tristano and Isotta at the fountain beneath the pine; the arrival of the Maid of Scalot (Astolat) in the barge at Camelot. The far more famous collection of stories, Boccaccio's *Decameron*, bears the sub-title, *Principe Galeotto*, presumably a reference to Galehaut's role in the Prose *Lancelot* as a friend of lovers.[4]

The *cantastorie*, reciters and singers who catered to crowds in the *piazze*, composed *cantari* in *ottava rima* and thus served to bring the loves and adventures of the Arthurian heroes to the attention of the masses.[5] One of the earliest, *Febusso e Breusso* (1320–5), retells the episode in *Palamedes* where Breus, cast into a cavern by a treacherous damsel, learns the story of Febus from the grandfather of Guiron.[6] *La Pulzella Gaia* (1350–75) deals with the love of the Gay Maiden, daughter of 'la Fata Morgana', for Galvano.[7] Certain names seem to derive from the *Tavola Ritonda*, but the main plot is clearly related to the Breton lais of *Graelent*, *Lanval*, and *Desiré*, in which

---

[1] Renaut de Beaujeu, *Le Bel Inconnu*, ed. G. P. Williams, *CFMA* (1929), pp. 98 f.

[2] *Claris et Laris*, ed. J. Alton (Tübingen, 1884), vss. 3587–4073. See *R.*, lxxx (1959), 337–67.

[3] Bertoni, *Il Duecento*, 3rd ed., p. 385; Gardner, pp. 88–95.

[4] Gardner, p. 238; Barbi in *Studi di Filologia Italiana*, i (1927), 53 f.

[5] Sapegno, *Il Trecento*, 2nd ed., pp. 618 ff.; E. Levi, *I Cantari Leggendari del Popolo Italiano*, *GSLI*, Supp. xvi; Gardner, pp. 239–41; V. Branca, *Il Cantare Trecentesco e il Boccaccio del Filostrato e del Teseida* (Florence, 1936).

[6] Gardner, p. 269; *Il Febusso e Breusso*, ed. Lord Vernon (Florence, 1847).

[7] *Fiore di Leggende*, ed. E. Levi (Bari, 1914), pp. 31–58; *GSLI*, Supp. xvi, pp. 36–45; *Annales de Bretagne*, lvi (1949), 213 f.; L. A. Paton, *Fairy Mythology of Arthurian Romance* (Boston, 1903), p. 100, n. 1; Gardner, pp. 241–47.

a faery mistress grants her favour on condition that her lover keep the secret, and withdraws it when he breaks his vow, but comes to his aid when he is condemned to die.[1] One may recognize other familiar motifs: the fay is in love with Galvano before she meets him; she assumes the form of a dragon; she is punished by being obliged to sit in water.[2] *Carduino* (1360–80) combines themes from the *enfances* of Perceval—his upbringing by his widowed mother and the obligation to avenge his father's murder on the sons of Lot—with the adventures of Guinglain as told in *Le Bel Inconnu, Libeaus Desconus,* and *Wigalois.*[3]

The Florentine poet, Antonio Pucci[4] (1318–88), composed a *canzone* which, though it lacks the Arthurian cast of characters, is undoubtedly cognate with the story of the imperious host in the English *Carl of Carlisle,* described below in Chap. 37, of which the hero is Gawain.[5] He also devoted two *cantari* to the adventures of Gismirante,[6] who succeeds in slaying 'un uomo selvaggio' with an external heart in much the same way as in many modern Irish folk-tales the hero succeeds in putting an end to the giant with an external soul.[7] The resemblance is indeed startling, and Gardner may have been right in suggesting that the 'porco troncascino', which guards the wild man's heart, was connected with the 'porcus Troit' of Nennius and the Twrch Trwyth of *Culhwch and Olwen.*[8] Pucci is also credited with the *cantare Bruto di Bretagna,* a fairly close retelling of the Arthurian *conte* which Andreas Capellanus included in his *De Amore* and which may have been brought to Pucci's attention by a previous translation into Tuscan.[9]

There are two Tuscan *cantari* of the same century concerned with Tristan: *La Morte di Tristano* and *La Vendetta che fe meser Lanzelloto de la morte di miser Tristano.*[10] The first follows with slight variations the account in the Prose *Tristan* of the murder of the hero as he was harping before Iseut.

---

[1] See Chap. 11 above; also *Lays of Desiré, Graelent and Melion,* ed. E. M. Grimes (New York, 1928), pp. 12–23.

[2] On this punishment see *L'Atre Périlleux,* ed. B. Woledge, CFMA (1936), p. 218; *Beihefte ZRP,* lxiii. 285 ff.; A. Dickson, *Valentine and Orson* (New York, 1929), pp. 83 f.

[3] Gardner, pp. 252–8; P. Rajna, *Poemetti Cavallereschi* (Bologna, 1873); W. H. Schofield, *Studies on the Libeaus Desconus* (Boston, 1895), pp. 2–53, 183–97; C. Strucks, *Der junge Parzival* (Leipzig, 1910); Loomis, *Arthurian Tradition,* pp. 400 f.

[4] Sapegno, op. cit., pp. 404–22.

[5] G. L. Kittredge, *Study of Gawain and the Green Knight* (Cambridge, Mass., 1916), pp. 85–106, 304 f.; *Sir Gawain and the Carl of Carlisle,* ed. A. Kurvinen, *Annales Academiae Scientiarum Fennicae* (Helsinki, 1951), pp. 80–84.

[6] *Fiore di Leggende,* ed. Levi, pp. 171–98; GSLI, Supp. xvi, pp. 91–113; Gardner, pp. 247–50.

[7] R. S. Loomis, *Celtic Myth and Arthurian Romance* (New York, 1927), pp. 18–20; Kittredge, op. cit., p. 150, n. 1.   [8] Gardner, p. 250, n. 2. See Chaps. 1, 4 above.

[9] *Fiore di Leggende,* pp. 201–13; GSLI, Supp. xvi, pp. 101–13; Gardner, pp. 250–2; S. Battaglia, *Il De Amore di Andrea Cappellano, con una Versione Toscana* (Napoli, 1946), pp. 869 ff. See on Andreas, Chap. 36 below.

[10] Gardner, pp. 262–5; G. Bertoni, *I Cantari di Tristano* (Modena, 1937); N. Sapegno, *Poeti Minori,* pp. 938 ff.

The *Vendetta* relates how Lanzelotto led 107 knights in black mourning garments to Tintagel to avenge Tristano, how they laid siege to the castle, how Marco, for once represented as a brave and formidable knight, sallied forth and performed prodigies of valour before he was beheaded by Lanzelotto. A short *cantare* of the late fourteenth century, *Tristano e Lancielotto*, is based on an episode in Rusticiano's compilation.[1] Tristano encountered his rival Palamede in combat, and when interrupted by Lionello arranged to continue the battle eight days later. Arriving at the rendezvous and finding Lancielotto, he mistook him for Palamede and the two fought to the point of exhaustion. Only when Tristano revealed his name, did mutual embraces take the place of blows. The latest and the longest of the *cantari* is called *Lancellotto*[2] (1380–1405); it consists, in fact, of seven *cantari* and covers, with some transpositions and additions from the Prose *Tristan*, the events narrated in the Vulgate *Mort Artu*.

In the preceding survey I have tried to show how early in the thirteenth century the Matter of Britain was known in Italy mainly in the sophisticated and aristocratic poems of Chrétien and Thomas; how it affected profoundly the Italian adaptations of the Matter of France; how it filtered down into the literature of the lower social strata, the *novelle* and the *cantari*. But a reversal took place in the second half of the fifteenth century, strangely enough at a time when the new humanism was all the fashion. It achieved favour once more with the aristocracy, particularly at the court of the Este family at Ferrara, one of the very few old dynasties which was still flourishing in the high Renaissance. There, as we learn from a document of 1476, a large library including French chivalric romances had been accumulated,[3] and there Boiardo and Ariosto were able to enter the magic world of adventurous knights and courtly ladies. Even though depending themselves mainly on the desiccated versions of the Prose *Tristan* and *Palamedes*, these patrician writers poured into their poems a new vitality and a lofty sentiment. Like Andrea da Barberino they chose the geography and the personages of the Carolingian epic, but the adventures and the idealisms are those of Arthurian romance. The title of Boiardo's masterpiece, *L'Orlando Innamorato*, gives the clue and sets the tone.

> Ne tante prove più mai fece Orlando
> Quante nel tempo che de amor si accese.[4]

(Never did Orlando perform so many feats as when he was afire with love.)

---

[1] Gardner, pp. 260–2; Rajna, *Poemetti Cavallereschi*, pp. 45 ff.

[2] Gardner, pp. 265–9; *Li Chantari di Lancellotto*, ed. E. T. Griffiths (Oxford, 1924).

[3] G. Bertoni, *La Biblioteca Estense e la Coltura Ferrarese* (Turin, 1903), pp. 85 ff.; Gardner, p. 274. For the Gonzaga library see *R*, ix (1880), 497 ff.; xix (1890), 161 ff.; R. S. and L. H. Loomis, *Arthurian Legends*, pp. 120 f.

[4] Bk. II, canto iv. A. Viscardi, A. Pompeati, *La Letteratura Italiana* (Milan, 1951), pp. 243 ff.

In a highly significant prelude to one of his cantos, Boiardo asserted the superiority of the Matter of Britain over the Matter of France.

> Fo gloriosa Bertagna la grande
> Una stagion per l'arme e per l'amore,
> Onde ancora oggi il nome suo si spande,
> Si che al re Artuse fa portare onore. . .
> Re Carlo in Franza poi tenne gran corte,
> Ma a quella prima non fo sembïante. . .
> Perchè tiene ad Amor chiuse le porte,
> E sol se dette alle battaglie sante,
> Non fo di quel valore e quella estima
> Qual fo quell' altra che io contava in prima.[1]

(One time Britain the great was glorious for arms and for love, wherefore still today its name is spread abroad, so that it brings honour to King Arthur. . . . Later King Charles held high court in France, but it was not like that first one. . . . Because it kept the gates closed to love and devoted itself only to holy battles, it was not of such worth and such fame as was the other of which I spoke first.)

Thus revived and rehabilitated by Boiardo, the old, fantastic matter of Arthurian romance and the amorous idealism of the Round Table enjoyed an amazing triumph even in the age of Bembo, Aretino, and Machiavelli.

---

[1] Bk. II, canto xviii. On Boiardo see Gardner, pp. 273–82; Bertoni, *Nuovi Studi su Matteo Maria Boiardo* (Bologna, 1904); G. Razzoli, *Per le Fonti dell' Orlando Innamorato* (Milan, 1901).

33

HARTMANN VON AUE AND HIS SUCCESSORS

HENDRICUS SPARNAAY

THE *Erek* of Hartmann von Aue may be accepted as the first Arthurian romance in German,[1] unless Eilhart von Oberge's *Tristrant*, which is probably earlier, is to be reckoned Arthurian. To be sure, Lachmann[2] suggested the possibility of lost poems belonging to the cycle as current in the Rhineland before Hartmann's day, and Zwierzina[3] and Singer[4] supported him with rich material; but there is only one piece of incontestable evidence, the reference to 'Keiî der kâtspreche' in *Erek*, vs. 4664,[5] a Lower Rhenish form which Hartmann could not have invented. The names ending in -ân and -în are open to another interpretation. Wintwaliten, the name of Gawan's horse as it appears in *Erek*, vs. 4714, does not occur in the Dutch poems. Even the very early recording of Arthurian names,[6] such as Iwan in a Freising document between 764 and 784, Tristan in a document from Lake Constance of 807, and Parcival de Caldes dating from 1007, proves nothing since we cannot be sure that they are borrowed from Arthurian poems. More noteworthy is Steinmeyer's[7] demonstration that the use of certain epithets like 'klâr, wert, kluoc' first appears in High German with Wolfram von Eschenbach, while these words are employed far earlier by religious poets in the Rhineland. That Wolfram borrowed them form religious poetry is not probable, and one thinks rather of secular epics as a source. Nevertheless, these are still conjectures, not proofs.

It is therefore the prevailing opinion that Hartmann composed the first German Arthurian romance, *Erek*, and until a few years ago the generally accepted date was about 1190, or, more precisely, between 1190 and 1192. This assignment is based on the mention of 'Connelant' in vs. 2003, where Hartmann contradicts his source, as he never does elsewhere, and introduces under this form a new geographical name, Conne-Iconium, a sultanate in

---

[1] F. Piquet, *Étude sur Hartmann d'Aue* (Paris, 1898), regards *Iwein* as older than *Erek* because the former is more faithful to its source.

[2] *Zu Iwein*, vs. 925.

[3] *ZDA*, xlv (1901), 322 ff. [4] *Aufsätze und Vorträge* (Tübingen, 1912), pp. 154 ff.

[5] Haupt's reading. Leitzmann gives: 'Keiîn der quâtspreche.' The reading 'Keiîn der arcspreche' occurs twice in *Lanzelet*.

[6] For Iwan see *ZDA*, xii. 357; for Tristan see Hertz's translation of Gottfried's *Tristan*, 4th ed., p. 483; for Parcival de Caldes see *Germania*, i (1856), 294.

[7] E. Steinmeyer, *Über einige Epitheta der mittelhochdeutschen Poesie* (Erlangen, 1889).

Asia Minor with a capital of the same name. Iconium acquired fame in Europe, and particularly in Germany, when Frederick Barbarossa won a brilliant victory at the gates of the city shortly before his death by drowning. This was in 1190, and the news reached Germany in the late autumn and produced such excitement that it was natural for Hartmann to mention Connelant, though his statement that it produced the best sable fur makes it clear that he himself could not have taken part in Barbarossa's Crusade.

This, the commonly accepted explanation of the reference to Connelant, seems far more probable than that put forward a few years ago by F. Neumann,[1] who pointed out that in 1179 an embassy from Iconium appeared at the imperial court with a proposal of marriage. But it is not clear why this particular embassy should have made a strong impression on Hartmann; other diplomatic missions came from the Near East in Barbarossa's time, among them one from Saladin, a far more famous potentate than the sultan of Iconium.[2] Neumann's purpose was to push back the beginnings of Arthurian romance in Germany,[3] and he therefore dated *Erek* between 1185 and 1188. But why not 1179 or 1180, immediately after the embassy? Moreover, it is impossible to base any calculations on the speed with which the poet worked. Whether he required eleven or sixteen years to write the 14,000 lines which followed *Erek*, no man can say.

That such a reconstruction of Hartmann's biography has found favour with certain readers may be accounted for by the recent demand for a 'neues Hartmannbild'. If the new concept of the poet sprang from a better interpretation of the text or a deeper knowledge of his genius or a recognition of historical relationships hitherto ignored, it would be welcomed by everyone. But when long-established conclusions are pushed aside and their place is taken by contradictory hypotheses based on subjective intuitions, it seems that scholarship has given way to the desire for novelty. There are certain plain facts and inferences which must be taken into account in forming a true picture of Hartmann, and which remain valid until proved otherwise. To these belongs what the last 'Crusader's Song' (218. 5) reveals, namely, that Hartmann went on Crusade for the first time after Saladin's death in 1193, that he chose the sea-route (218. 18), as we know was in fact that of the Crusade of 1197, whereas Barbarossa went by land in 1189.[4] It is also established

---

[1] F. Neumann in *Studien zur deutschen Philologie des Mittelalters, Festschrift Fr. Panzer* (1950), p. 65; in W. Stammler, *Die deutsche Literatur des Mittelalters; Verfasserlexikon* (Berlin, Leipzig, 1933–53), v. 322–31.

[2] R. Grousset, *Histoire des croisades et du royaume franc de Jérusalem* (Paris, 1934), especially vol. ii *passim*. See index under Quilij Arslân II.

[3] Sievers made the first attempt to date *Erek* earlier by the 'Querindexmethode' in *Festgabe P. Strauch, Hermaea*, xxxi (1932), 53 ff. According to his 'Querindex' *Erek* would be dated about 1165. See Sparnaay in *Neo*, xxix (1943–4), 107 ff.; in *Deutsche Vierteljahrsschrift*, xxvi (1952), 162 ff.

[4] See also in *Deutsche Vierteljahrsschrift*, xxvi. 162 ff., references to the relevant literature.

that when Hartmann in 1195 or shortly after composed his lament of a widow he was seeking to emulate Reinmar. Those who have denied his authorship of these songs have resorted to the most arbitrary measures.[1]

A fertile cause of error is neglect of the results of comparative literary studies. When, for instance, it has been shown that much that Hartmann tells us of the fay Morgane finds no counterpart in Chrétien's *Erec* and that, on the contrary, almost every detail is to be found in earlier descriptions, for instance, in Geoffrey of Monmouth's *Vita Merlini*,[2] it is idle to assert that Hartmann's *Erek* is dependent solely on Chrétien. When, moreover, it is shown that the same poem corresponds in many specific points to other Erec poems, as against Chrétien, then one can only conclude that Hartmann had other sources.[3] To say, as H. Kuhn[4] and H. de Boor[5] have done, that nothing compels us to postulate such sources, is to shut one's eyes to the facts, and De Boor himself concedes that Hartmann may have *heard* the details not found in Chrétien, implying that there were oral versions.

There is therefore no good reason for abandoning the following positions: Hartmann began his poetic career with *Erek* in 1190; his masterly 'Crusader's Song' was composed shortly before he went on the Crusade of 1197, so that the narrative and the lyric poems are not long separated in time; the *Gregorius* cannot be assigned, as is sometimes done, to the eighties, because after Gerd Krause's[6] work no one can deny that the French model (whether direct or indirect) was not composed until the last decade of the century.

Since the French *Erec* has already been discussed in Chap. 15, it is unnecessary to treat it except in its relation to Hartmann's redaction. But since that relationship has often been over-simplified through neglect of the results of comparative research, some attention must be paid to this matter. I have mentioned already that what Hartmann says about Fâmurgân cannot be derived either from Chrétien or purely from his own imagination, but must have another traditional source. Likewise, while Chrétien's Keu is consistently a ridiculous boaster, Hartmann introduced a passage in praise of the seneschal in *Erek* (vss. 4632 ff.) and in *Iwein* (vss. 2565 ff.), though in spite of this his opinion coincides with that of Chrétien.[7] Now Keu is held up to

---

[1] See Bech in his first edition, followed by W. Greve, *Leben und Werk Hartmanns von Aue* (Fellin, 1879), and by G. Eis in *Euphorion*, xlvi (1951), 276 ff.

[2] Sparnaay in *Neo*, xvi (1930–1), 255 ff.; R. S. Loomis in *Spec*, xx (1945), 183–203.

[3] H. Sparnaay, *Hartmann von Aue, Studien zu einer Biographie* (Halle, 1933), i. 63–125; Zenker in *ZFSL*, xlv (1917–19), 47 ff.; xlviii (1925–6), 1 ff., 386 ff.

[4] H. Kuhn in *Annalen der deutschen Literatur*, ed. H. O. Burger (Stuttgart, 1952), p. 123; in *Der Deutschunterricht*, 1953, Heft ii, pp. 11 ff.

[5] *Geschichte der deutschen Literatur* (Munich, 1955), ii.[2] 69.

[6] The Cambrai manuscript of the Old French *Vie de Saint Grégoire, Romanistische Arbeiten*, xix (1931). The ninth edition of *Gregorius* by H. Paul, A. Leitzmann (1955) mentions the Cambrai manuscript only in an additional note.

[7] Likewise Wolfram's *Parzival*, 296, 13 ff., which does not derive from Hartmann's *Erek*, as Piquet, op. cit., p. 33, asserts.

admiration in later French works—the *Livre d'Artus*, *Escanor*, and a manuscript of Chrétien's *Perceval*. Can one believe that Hartmann knew nothing of this tradition, especially when we know from Welsh sources that Kei was originally a great hero?[1]

In many places Hartmann agrees with the Welsh *Gereint* against Chrétien.[2] It is hard to believe that in each instance he substituted the Welsh account, which he could not have read, or that he followed a manuscript of the French poem of a type which varied widely from those which have come down to us. I will limit myself to describing some of Hartmann's variations. When Erek has parted from the queen, both Hartmann and the Welsh author relate first his experiences and afterwards those of the queen. Chrétien, however, first tells how the queen returned to the court and asked Arthur to postpone the kiss until Erec had come back—an irrational request since no one could foresee that Erec would bring with him a lady worthy of the kiss. There are many contradictions, especially in Hartmann, in the description of the poverty and the arms of Enide's father. Hartmann's account of the combat for the sparrow-hawk coincides in many details with the Welsh version; so also with the narrative of the adventurous journey. The motive which the Welsh author assigns for Gereint's harsh treatment of Enid, suspicion of her fidelity, is suggested in the other versions.[3] Finally let me point out the significant fact that the German and Welsh texts omit the coronation at Nantes, which Chrétien describes at length. The only reasonable conclusion is that, as Chrétien himself remarks in vss. 19–22, the story of Erec was told in various forms, and that Hartmann knew others besides the poem of Chrétien. Whether these were written or oral remains uncertain.

Though many of Hartmann's variations from Chrétien's text seem to have been suggested by these secondary sources, there are others which are to be regarded as original.[4] Often the German poet developed a long excursus out of a brief remark of Chrétien's, of which practice we have an instructive example in the long description of Enite's sorrow when Erek lay lifeless at her feet (vss. 5739–6115). The French text devotes only a few lines to the subject, but Hartmann goes into a full description of her anguish; she tears her hair, beats her breast, shrieks, and storms against the Divinity. She calls on the wild beasts to devour her, offers herself to Death as a bride, and at last seizes Erek's sword with intent to commit suicide. Indeed, by contrast with

---

[1] For the literature about Keie see Zenker in *ZFSL*, xlviii (1925–6), 13 ff.

[2] Zenker in *ZFSL*, xlv (1917–19), 47 ff.; xlviii. 1 ff.; Sparnaay in *ZRP*, xlv (1925), 53 ff.; Sparnaay, *Hartmann von Aue*, i. 72 ff.

[3] The double motivation of Erek's adventurous ride, in which certain passages imply that Enîte has been unfaithful, and others merely serve to prove Erek's unimpaired strength, furnishes an argument in favour of the episodic construction of the romance which it is impossible to evade. Sparnaay, *Hartmann von Aue*, i. 79 ff.; in *ZRP*, xlv. 61 ff.; Loomis, *Arthurian Tradition*, pp. 120–9.

[4] Schönbach discusses many passages in *Über Hartmann von Aue* (Graz, 1894), pp. 472 ff.

Chrétien's realistic sobriety, Hartmann's extravagant portrayal has almost a comic effect. The poet has not yet learned to value the courtly 'mâze' and decorum which dominates his later *Iwein*.

In *Erek*, as in all his greater works, Hartmann is concerned with the expiation of a sin. He conceives of the hero and his bride as neglecting, in the ardour of their love, their duties toward courtly society, and this leads to their estrangement. Whereas Chrétien tends to excuse, if not justify, Enide's behaviour, Hartmann says explicitly (vss. 3007, 3811) that she too is at fault. Thus he not only justifies Erek's severity, but also is more consistent, more thorough, in his application of the thesis that suffering is the penalty and the atonement for sin.

Though more original in handling than his later work, *Erek* is immature in style and must be ranked lower than his second Arthurian romance. This poem, *Iwein*, is generally dated about 1202 and its history is far simpler than that of *Erek* since it is derived from Chrétien's *Yvain* alone. A comparison of *Iwein* and its source reveals that the additions and expansions are due not to borrowing from variant versions but to deliberate modification and emphasis. The German poet is at pains to furnish a moral foundation for events. The incidents are built into an organic whole and assume a symbolic value. The hero, who at first is an embodiment of conceited audacity, is educated by experience to the ideal of 'saelde und êre', to happiness and honour (see vss. 3 and 8166). More clearly than its French counterpart and source, *Iwein* is designed as a story of education. Hartmann calls Iwein's behaviour to his vanquished enemy undisciplined and shameless (vss. 1056, 2589), and maintains that his love for Laudine is chiefly sensual lust (vss. 1331 ff.). When Iwein fails to keep his promise to return to his wife, he is not only rebuked by her messenger as in Chrétien's poem, but Hartmann adds that the king will no longer tolerate a dishonourable man at court.

As in *Erek*, Hartmann does not exempt his heroine from blame, though he treats her more leniently and without the ironic tone employed by Chrétien. He represents her at first as reluctant to take Iwein as a husband, though ready to retain him as guardian of the spring. Only when Lunete has convinced her of the impracticability of this plan does she yield to the sway of Frau Minne, the goddess of love. Thus she as well as Iwein come under Hartmann's condemnation, for both have offended against the laws of love by the excess of their passion.

The theme of education and expiation is continued through the poem. Even after Iwein has saved Lunete from the pyre in a trial by battle, his penance is not ended. Laudine still will not acknowledge him since his unworthiness stands in the way (vss. 5512–20). Only when he appears at last at the fountain, when his guilt has been atoned for and both he and his bride

have achieved the maturity and honour which are requisite for the attainment
of happiness and a position of power, does the poem end.[1]

Other changes which Hartmann made in his redaction of *Yvain* reveal his
preoccupation with chivalric manners and morality. Of the many comparative studies of the two poems few are satisfactory. The earliest[2] efforts
usually concluded that Hartman provided better motivation or declared that
he failed to understand his source.[3] The latest[4] commentators have discussed
the ideas expressed by the two poets but too often ascribe to them notions
which would have been utterly remote from their minds. Hartmann in re-
writing *Yvain* in another language revised it to conform to his concept of
'mâze', self-control, and decorum. Too realistic detail and violent emotion
he suppressed,[5] and he put into the mouth of Kâlogrêant a little lecture to the
Giant Herdsman on knightly honour (vss. 527 ff.). He would not allow
Arthur to take sides in the quarrel between the daughters of the Sire de la
Noire Espine before the case had been settled by combat, and so omitted the
passage (Chrétien, vs. 5928). Significant is his opinion that Lunete would have
been a courtly damsel 'hete sî sich niht verclagt' (vs. 1154), that is, if she had
not bemoaned her fate too loudly. If we compare this judgement with Hartmann's earlier description of Enite's wild outburst, we may see clearly how
far he has moved toward an ideal of restraint. This ideal of knightly conduct
is most fully and strikingly exemplified in the climactic combat in which
Iwein proves himself the equal of that paragon of chivalry, Gawein, not only
in physical prowess but also in courtesy and honour. Indeed, Hartmann's
alterations sometimes assume a polemic character. In this same combat as
described by Chrétien, the knights continued to fight on horseback after they
had broken their spears, but Hartmann makes them both dismount in order
that they may avoid the 'boorish' practice (vs. 7121) of conducting a sword-
duel in their saddles.[6]

Thus we see that in *Iwein* Hartmann not only strove like Gottfried von
Strassburg to employ the 'cristallînen wortelîn', the crystal-clear word, and

---

[1] The connexion with *Parzival*, which I have often pointed out, has not been sufficiently recognized by scholars. Parzival, too, is cast out into the world as a sinner and returns after years of purification to the Grail castle.

[2] C. Rauch, *Die walisische, französische und deutsche Bearbeitung der Iweinsage* (Berlin, 1869);
F. Settegast, *Hartmanns Iwein verglichen mit seiner altfranzösischen Quelle* (1873); G. Gärtner,
Vergleich des Hartmannschen Iwein mit dem Löwenritter Chrétiens (1896); A. Güth in *Archiv*, xlvi
(1870), 251 ff.

[3] J. Firmery, *Notes critiques sur quelques traductions allemandes de poèmes français au Moyen Âge*
(1901).

[4] R. Putz, *Chrestiens Yvain und Hartmanns Iwein nach ihrem Gedankengehalt verglichen* (Erlangen,
1927); A. Witte in *Beiträge*, liii (1929), 65–192; H. Drube, *Hartmann und Chrétien, Forschungen zur
deutschen Sprache und Dichtung*, ii (1931).

[5] For examples see Sparnaay, *Hartmann von Aue*, ii. 55 ff.

[6] Both practices are described in the romances of chivalry: Gottfried, *Tristan*, vs. 6868; Wolfram,
Parzival, 263, 23, describe the sword combat on horseback.

to avoid the coarse locution, but also to express in every detail a high ideal of courtly conduct.

A third poem by Hartmann, *Gregorius*, is usually classified as the life of an apocryphal saint, and there can be no doubt that it is largely and ultimately derived from a pious legend of Oriental origin. But there are also clear parallels in secular romance. Gregorius delivers from siege a princess who dwells in a castle by the sea. This motif we find in Chrétien's *Perceval*, in the Belacâne episode[1] in Wolfram's *Parzival*, and with slight variations in *Partonopeus de Blois*,[2] Heinrich von Neustadt's *Apollonius*,[3] and the cycle of the Knight with the Sleeve,[4] especially *Richars li Biaus* and the *Ridder metter Mouwen*, where the child is ignorant of his parentage. That this motif was not borrowed from the legend of Pope Gregory is indicated by the fact that Hartmann's version gives evidence that the motif of the besieged princess has been lifted out of its original context, for soon after the infant had been exposed his mother was forced to flee to a castle and was there besieged by a foreign prince, and yet when, fifteen years later, Gregorius appears as a young knight, the situation has not changed; his mother is still besieged. There is, moreover, a remarkably elaborate resemblance between the *enfances* of Gregory and those of Gawain, and the latter are not only related in three romances drawn from a common source but seem to have been known to Geoffrey of Monmouth as early as 1136. Though the pious elements in the Gregory legend doubtless came from the Orient, the romantic element of the deliverance of the princess from siege, common to the Gregory and Gawain stories, seems to have been introduced first in the latter tradition. Bruce's[5] belief that the Gregory legend was the source of the *enfances* of Gawain reverses the true relationship.

'Lanzelet'

Lanzelet is an early romance of adventure, the work of an uninspired translator of an uninspired original. Because of its crude composition and archaic diction it must be ranked far below Hartmann's *Erek*. Its chronological position was long debated till W. Richter, after a careful study of its style and vocabulary, proved that the author used *Erek* but not *Iwein*.[6]

---

[1] L. Grimm, *Wolfram von Eschenbach und die Zeitgenossen* (Leipzig, 1897), i. 46.

[2] R. Palgen, *Der Stein der Weisen* (Breslau, 1922), pp. 54 ff.

[3] Singer in *ZDA*, xliv (1900), 342.

[4] Sparnaay, *Verschmelzung legendarischer und weltlicher Motive in der Poesie des Mittelalters* (Groningen, 1922), pp. 45 ff.; Sparnaay, *Hartmann von Aue*, i. 172 ff.; in *Neo*, v (1919–20), 26 ff. See also Chap. 34 below.

[5] J. D. Bruce, *Historia Meriadoci and De Ortu Walwanii* (Göttingen, Baltimore, 1913), pp. xli–lv. See also discussion of *De Ortu Walwanii* in Chap. 36 below.

[6] W. Richter, *Der Lanzelet des Ulrich von Zatzikhoven* (Frankfurt, 1934), surveys the older literature; so also Campion in *MLN*, xxxii (1917), 416–21. Though Wallner attempted in vain to invalidate Richter's results in *Anzeiger für deutsches Altertum*, liv (1935), 171 ff., he dated *Lanzelet* correctly, 1194.

Whether he used *Gregorius* is not settled. Most of the passages cited by Leitzmann in *Beiträge zur Geschichte der deutschen Sprache und Literatur*, lv. 293 ff., to show an acquaintance with certain books of Wolfram's *Parzival* are susceptible of another explanation, and the possibility of a lost German poem on Lanzelet may be considered. On the other hand, there can be no doubt that Wolfram displays in *Willehalm* a knowledge of the extant *Lanzelet*.[1]

The date is also fixed by what the author tells us of the circumstances which led to his undertaking the poem. At the end he asserts that Hûc de Morville gave him a French (*welschez*) book, which, at the urging of his friends, he turned into German. This Hugh de Morville was one of the hostages whom Richard Lion-heart was forced to send to Duke Leopold VI of Austria and who were transferred in 1194 to the custody of the emperor Henry VI. This year, then, furnishes a *terminus a quo* for our poem. The simple, old-fashioned diction and the disregard of dialectal differences and of courtly fashions of speech suggest that the poem was finished soon after. The author, Ulrich von Zatzikhoven, is presumably to be identified with a 'capellanus Uolricus de Cecinhovin', who according to a deed of 1214 was residing in the Swiss canton of Thurgau.

Ulrich's story of Lancelot differs widely from Chrétien's, most patently in the fact that it is a biographical and not an episodic narrative. The contents may be sketched as follows:

Carried off when less than two years old by a water fay, Lanzelet grew up among women till the age of fifteen, ignorant of his name and his royal birth. After leaving the isle of maidens, he was instructed in horsemanship and the use of weapons by a young knight and set out on a career of adventure. Three times in succession he arrived at a castle, killed its lord in combat, but nevertheless inspired the lord's daughter or niece with an ardent passion. Two of these ladies soon after disappear from the story; the third, Iblis, though we hear of no wedding ceremony, is assumed to be his wife and so remains. The third combat, which somewhat resembles the fountain adventure in *Iwein*, is followed by the receipt of a message from Lanzelet's foster-mother, announcing his name and his kinship to King Arthur. Welcomed at Arthur's court, he championed Queen Ginover against Valerin in combat. He next won a new mistress, the Queen of Pluris, and then deserted her. By contrast, the fidelity of Iblis to her fickle spouse was proved by a mantle test. Valerin abducted the queen, and it was only by securing the aid of the wizard Malduc that King Arthur recovered her. Finally, after Lanzelet had by a kiss restored to her true shape a damsel in the form of a dragon, he returned with Iblis to his own kingdom, there to live happily ever after.

[1] Richter here follows Singer, who in *Aufsätze und Vorträge* (1912) p. 147, places *Lanzelet* after *Wigalois* and after Book XIII of *Parzival*, in spite of the fact that Ulrich did not know *Iwein*.

The correspondence between the Swiss poem and Chrétien's *Lancelot* is restricted to the fact that the hero in both poems fights a duel as champion of the queen, and that in both the queen is abducted and recovered. But there is no hint of an adulterous love-affair, Lanzelet is not the agent of the queen's recovery, there is no cart, while on the other hand there are many themes of which Chrétien shows no knowledge. Hugh de Morville's book, therefore, represents an entirely different branch of Lancelot tradition from that represented in the French poem. So far as the parentage and the *enfances* are concerned it represents the same tradition as the French Prose *Lancelot*, but even here the divergences are such as to suggest a common origin not in written but in oral sources.[1]

Many of the elements in *Lanzelet* have their counterparts in the corpus of European literature. The hero's fosterage by a fairy queen, his athletic training by mermen, his ignorance of his name, and even the dragon kiss R. S. Loomis would derive ultimately from legends of the Irish god Lug.[2] The chastity test which Iblis undergoes is found in French and English forms. The tempting of the hero by Galagandreiz's daughter and his combat with her father[3] is closely paralleled in *Wolfdietrich*.[4] There is an analogue to the combat with Iblis's father in Hartmann's *Iwein*—wonder-garden, gong, and so forth; but no direct influence can be detected. A common ancestry may safely be predicated of Lanzelet's visit to Schatel le Mort, the Limors adventure in Chrétien's *Erec*, and an elaborate story involving the Countess of Limos in the *Livre d'Artus*.[5]

As the foregoing remarks suggest, the loose episodic construction of the poem may be accounted for by an early stage in its history when it formed part of the repertory of a professional story-teller. Each section would correspond to the material chosen for a single sitting, and the narrator would aim at a self-contained unit. Whether this explanation is correct or not, it is obvious that the composer of Ulrich's source did not have the ambition or the capacity to organize his miscellaneous incidents into a coherent pattern as Chrétien had done in *Erec*. Another flaw in his art is the lack of emotional

---

[1] The most important treatments of the source problem are: Märtens in *Romanische Studien*, v (1880), 557 ff.; G. Paris in *R*, x (1881), 471 ff.; Chrétien de Troyes, *Karrenritter*, ed. W. Foerster (Halle, 1899), pp. xx ff.; W. Foerster, *Kristian von Troyes, Wörterbuch* (Halle, 1914), pp. 76* ff.; S. Singer, *Aufsätze und Vorträge*, pp. 144 ff.; Carter in *Haverford Essays* (Haverford, 1909), pp. 248–55; Ulrich von Zatzikhoven, *Lanzelet*, trans. K. G. T. Webster, introd. and notes. On the relationship between *Lanzelet* and French Prose *Lancelot* see Richter, op. cit., pp. 47 ff.

[2] *Lanzelet*, trans. Webster, pp. 15–18, and notes 10, 14, 18, 178, 228; *R*, lxxix (1958), 57–62.

[3] See Chap. 39 below. Ade often declares that her uncle will bestow her on no other man. Singer in *Aufsätze und Vorträge*, p. 144, infers from vss. 4150 ff., 4162 ff. that Iblis lived with her father in an incestuous relationship. If this was the case, Ulrich was not aware of it, for he allows Iblis alone to triumph in the mantle test.

[4] For the literature of the subject see *Lanzelet*, trans. Webster, n. 37; H. Schneider, *Die Gedichte und die Sage von Wolfdietrich* (Munich, 1913), pp. 287 ff.

[5] Loomis, *Arthurian Tradition*, pp. 163 ff.

subtlety and noble purpose. Though it is true that Lanzelet possesses the virtue of courage, axiomatic in a medieval hero, and is capable of loyalty, sacrifice, and liberality, he takes life much as it comes. He has no conscience in love; religion is as foreign to him as it was presumably to the author of Morville's book. His biography is an Arthurian romance in its most elementary stage.

Various manuscripts and fragments of a German prose romance of Lancelot have gradually come to light. It was evidently written shortly after its French original, as the Amorbach fragment (*c.* 1225) indicates. Only the first part, corresponding to the *Lancelot* proper, has been published,[1] but it is followed by the *Queste del Saint Graal* and the *Mort Artu*. Very significantly it lacks the *Estoire del Saint Graal* and the *Merlin*, and thus confirms F. Lot's contention that these were later additions to the Vulgate cycle. Traces of a second German prose version have been noted.

'*Wigalois*'

Wigalois was composed by the East-Frankish Wirnt von Grafenberg in the first decade of the thirteenth century.[2] In vss. 8063 f. there is reference to the 'vürste von Meran', that is, Duke Bertold IV, who died in 1204. From the mention in vs. 6343 of Wolfram von Eschenbach one infers a knowledge of the first six books of *Parzival*, and, from that point on, the influence of Wolfram is traceable, though Wirnt as a disciple of Hartmann never abandons the simple, clear style. His organization is less casual and crude than that of *Lanzelet*, but there are many loose joints. He manifests a didactic purpose in the prologue and in many moral reflections. He stresses the unity of the divine and the secular and illustrates by example the thesis that the best knights are those who do God's will. None the less, the poem is essentially a romance of adventure, with an abundance of phantoms and enchantments. Perhaps in imitation of Wolfram, the author introduces Oriental features; the Queen of Persia invites Wigalois to go home with her, and his betrothed Larie rides with him to Arthur's court on an elephant!

The hero's name is apparently a compound of Gui and the adjective *galois*, though the similarity of many of his adventures to that of Guinglain, the hero of Renaud de Beaujeu's *Le Bel Inconnu*, suggests that this was the true origin. Schofield proved, however, that Renaud's poem could not have been the source, since *Wigalois* agrees frequently with the cognate versions, *Libeaus Desconus* and *Carduino*, against Renaud.[3] There are striking resemblances also between the German poem and the *Chevalier du Papegau*; in

---

[1] *Lancelot I*, ed. R. Kluge, *Deutsche Texte des Mittelalters*, xlii (1948). Reviewed by Ranke in *Anzeiger für deutsches Altertum*, lxiv (1948–50), 109 ff.

[2] On *Wigalois* see Stammler, op. cit. iv, 1027–32.

[3] See Chap. 28 above, p.371, n. 2, and F. Saran in *Beiträge*, xxi (1896), 253 ff.; xxii (1897), 151 ff.; F. Heuckenkamp, *Chevalier du Papegau* (Halle, 1897), introd.

both, for instance, the prize of the beauty contest is not a sparrow-hawk but a parrot. R. S. Loomis would derive the account of the hero's birth, his arrival at Arthur's court, and his taking the perilous seat from ultimate Irish sources.[1] On the other hand, Wigalois's encounter with knights bearing flaming lances in a purgatorial castle is unique in Arthurian romance, and is presumably one of Wirnt's original and most macabre additions. The popularity of his work is attested by the survival of thirty-five complete or fragmentary manuscripts and the illustrative paintings at Schloss Runkelstein in the Tyrol.[2]

'Diu Krône'

About a decade after *Wigalois* the first Austrian romance appeared, *Diu Krône*, the work of Heinrich von dem Türlin of Kärnten.[3] The title is explained in vss. 29890 ff., where the incidents in the poem are compared to the jewels in a crown which the author has made in honour of noble women. The incidents are indeed numerous and evince an extensive knowledge of Arthurian literature both in French and German. But the poem suffers from a lack of design and coherence, and the same motif may be repeated. The author also lacks a sense of the profound meaning of the Grail scenes in Wolfram, with the result that the unasked question and the choice of the Grail King are reduced to banality.

The romance falls into two parts. Arthur at first takes the leading role, but before long Gawein comes to the fore and in the second part is the principal figure. Many of the stories deal with familiar themes but present fresh and sometimes startling differences of detail. A chastity test forms the opening scene, but the testing cup is brought to Arthur's court by a knight covered with fish-scales and mounted on a winged horse. The nocturnal combat of Arthur and Gasozein near a ford presents a strong likeness to a combat between Arthur and Walwanius in *De Ortu Walwanii*. As in *Lanzelet*, there is a knight who claims to have been Ginover's husband before Arthur, but the circumstances of her abduction differ widely in the two poems. *Diu Krône* furnishes an independent treatment of the story of *La Mule sans Frein*. Much of the second part is based on the Gawain adventures in Chrétien's *Perceval* and in Wolfram's *Parzival*; a few features found in neither of these poems suggested to Martin the possibility of a second French source (Kyot?).[4]

Heinrich tells of two visits to the Grail castle. On the first occasion Gawein was the witness of hair-raising sights, differing strangely from those described by other medieval authors. On the second he arrived with two com-

---

[1] Loomis, *Arthurian Tradition*, pp. 237 ff. For other influences see ibid., pp. 47, 90–92.
[2] R. S. and L. H. Loomis, *Arthurian Legends in Medieval Art* (New York, 1938), pp. 79–81, 134 f., figs. 171–83, 371–4.   [3] On *Diu Krône*, see Gülzow in Stammler, op. cit. ii. 352–5.
[4] *Parzival*, ed. E. Martin, ii, pp. xlvi ff.

panions, beheld a vessel in the form of a reliquary containing the sacramental bread, of which his host partook, asked concerning the mysteries, and thus ended the enchantment. Certain scholars have seen in the two visits adaptations of the account given by the First Continuator of Chrétien's *Perceval* (Pseudo-Wauchier),[1] but neither offers a close resemblance. The whole treatment reveals how inadequate Heinrich was to the problem of endowing the subject with real significance.

The nomenclature of *Diu Krône* is interesting. The poet assigns to well-known characters names found in no other text; for example, the knight who claims to have been Ginover's lover is not Valerin as in *Lanzelet*, but Gasozein; the enchanter with whom Gawein plays the so-called beheading game is not Bercilak as in *Gawain and the Green Knight*, but Gansguoter; an anonymous figure in Chrétien's *Perceval* is called Karadas. One may suspect that Heinrich, like Wolfram, sometimes coined names arbitrarily, but one should observe that Laniure, the father of the quarrelling sisters in the story of the Mule without a Bridle bears simply a truncated and corrupt form of his title in Chrétien's *Yvain*, 'li sire de *la Noire* Espine'. On the whole, one gets the impression that Heinrich created very little out of whole cloth, that much of his material came from lost sources, but that he made his own combinations and exercised considerable freedom in the invention of detail.

'Wigamur'

There is little of interest or novelty in *Wigamur*, composed about 1250. The upbringing of the hero by a water fay was plainly suggested by *Lanzelet*, and for his subsequent career the poet has drawn on *Parzival*, *Iwein*, and *Wigalois*. Though Singer and Webster[2] clung to the possibility of a French source, there is no proof. G. Sarrazin[3] ascribed the unpolished, uncourtly style to the influence of minstrel poetry.

Other Arthurian Romances

German literature includes a whole series of romances of the decadent period in which Arthurian elements can hardly be separated from those of different origin. Der Stricker's *Daniel vom blühenden Tal*,[4] which though composed about 1215, already bears the marks of the epigone. It is a confused miscellany of adventures, to which Hartmann, Ulrich von Zatzikhoven, and

---

[1] R. Heinzel in *Denkschriften der k. Akad. der Wissenschaften zu Wien*, xl (1892), 25 f.; W. Golther, *Parzival und der Gral* (Stuttgart, 1925), pp. 215 ff.

[2] Singer, *Aufsätze und Vorträge*, pp. 158 ff.; Singer in *Sitzungsberichte der k. Akad. der Wissenschaften zu Wien*, clxxx (1916), 125; *Lanzelet*, trans. K. G. T. Webster, pp. 162 ff. For the literature on *Wigamur* see C. von Kraus, *Mittelhochdeutsches Übungsbuch*, 2nd ed. (Heidelberg, 1926), pp. 287 f.

[3] G. Sarrazin, *Wigamur, Quellen und Forschungen*, xxxv (1879).

[4] Ehrismann, *Literaturgeschichte*, Schlußband, pp. 14 ff.

Wirnt stood as godfathers, and the legends of classical antiquity brought their gifts. In imitation of Lamprecht's *Alexander* the poet appealed to the authority of Alberich of Bisanze, but his success was meagre. About fifty years later another imitator of Hartmann, Der Pleier,[1] reworked the *Daniel* in his *Garel vom blühenden Tal*, but retained little that is Arthurian except a few well-known knights, the Round Table, and the abduction of Arthur's queen by Meljacanz. Equally slender is the Arthurian connexion of Der Pleier's other poems, *Meleranz* and *Tandareis*. The *Trojanerkrieg* of about 1300 not only retells the Troy story but blends it with fictitious adventures from the Matter of Britain and the saga of Dietrich von Bern. Heinrich von Neustadt of Vienna, familiar with the work of Hartmann, Wolfram, and Wirnt, incorporated Arthurian motifs in his version of *Apollonius of Tyre*. In the second half of the fourteenth century the Swabian, Konrad von Stoffeln, showed the influence of Wolfram, Gottfried, and Wirnt in his *Gauriel von Muntabel*,[2] a rehandling of the Breton theme of *Lanval* and *Graelent*.

Besides these complete romances there are fragments of German poems, apparently modelled on French originals: *Segremors* (from *Meraugis de Portlesguez*), *Blanchandin* (from *Blancandin et l'Orgueilleuse d'Amour*), *Edolanz*, and *Manuel und Amande*. The last preserves a remarkable version of Arthur's fight with a monster cat,[3] his apparent death, and his return to reign. Contemporary notices of lost romances with Arthurian content refer to German versions of *Cligès*, Bligger's *Unbehanc*, a romance by Gotfrid von Hohenlohe, and Heinrich von Linouwe's *Wallaere*.[4]

Ulrich Füetrer, who wrote his *Buch der Abenteuer* in the last quarter of the fifteenth century, brings us to the end of our period.[5] He was primarily a disciple of Wolfram, but we are indebted to him also for an adaptation of *Iwein*[6] in 297 *Titurel*-stanzas, as well as of *Wigalois* and *Diu Krône*. His *Lantzilet*, however, is based on the German prose romance. To the same period belong the South German Shrovetide farces on the theme of the chastity test mentioned below on p. 559.

---

[1] Ehrismann, *Literaturgeschichte*, Schlußband, pp. 58 ff; Hartl in W. Stammler, op. cit. iii. 903–9.

[2] Hartl in W. Stammler, op. cit. ii. 908 ff.

[3] See above, p. 15, n. 4.

[4] Ehrismann, op. cit., Schlußband, pp. 98 ff.; Stammler, op. cit., under names of authors.

[5] *BBSIA*, no. 3 (1951), p. 105.

[6] A. Carlson, *Ulrich Füetrer und sein Iban* (Riga, 1927), with complete bibliography; J. Boyd, *Ulrich Füetrer's 'Parzival', Material and Sources* (Oxford, 1937).

34

THE DUTCH ROMANCES

HENDRICUS SPARNAAY

SEVERAL Arthurian romances have come down to us in Middle Dutch, some of them not known in Old French or elsewhere. Dutch literary historians commonly refer to them as 'British romances of chivalry', as distinct from 'French romances of chivalry', by which term they understand the French national epic.[1] Two reasons in particular contributed to this confusion. First, the conception 'courtly' appears in a far less sharply defined form in Middle Dutch than in Middle High German or Old French. Secondly, the Arthurian romances were translated into Dutch at roughly the same time as the Carolingian epic and the romances on classical themes, with the result that there is in Middle Dutch no distinctive period of Arthurian romance. Te Winkel[2] goes so far as to call it an 'accident' that the 'classical romances of chivalry', though later in date in France than the 'Frankish romances', were translated into Dutch at an earlier time. Arthurian romance in the Netherlands attained its flower in the second half of the thirteenth century, though it is often difficult to date the texts.

For several of these we still have only the editions of Jonckbloet, which came out about the middle of the last century and were in fact already out of date when they appeared. Jonckbloet excused himself[3] for not having followed Lachmann's methods of textual criticism in a work of more than 100,000 verses. Doubtless the chief reason was that, in spite of Grimm's *Grammatik*,[4] research in the Middle Dutch language and metre had not yet developed far enough to make this possible. Verdam's and te Winkel's editions, which appeared a few decades later, and Overdiep's *Ferguut* show an improvement.

There were no outstanding poets, such as Chrétien de Troyes and Wolfram von Eschenbach, among the Dutch Arthurian romancers, but several

---

[1] This term, 'Ritterroman' was also applied by K. Simrock to his adaptation of *Loher und Maller* (1868).

[2] J. te Winkel, *De Ontwikkelingsgang der Ned. Letterkunde* (Haarlem, 1922 et seq.), i.[2] 215.

[3] *Roman van Lancelot* ('s Gravenhage, 1846), i, pp. lxviii f.

[4] There have appeared since, among others, J. Franck, *Mittelniederländische Grammatik* (Leipzig, 1883; 2nd ed. 1910); M. Schönfeld, *Historiese Grammatika van het Nederlands* (Zutphen, 1921 et seq.); M. J. van der Meer, *Historische Grammatik der niederländischen Sprache* (Heidelberg, 1927), i; C. G. N. de Vooys, *Geschiedenis van de Nederlandsche Taal* (Groningen, 1931 et seq.). On metric see G. S. Overdiep, *Beknopte Nederlandsche Versleer* (Zwolle, 1933), and in *Tijdschrift voor Nederlandsche Taal- en Letterkunde*, 1917, pp. 107 ff.; and the introduction to J. van Mierlo's *Letterkunde van de Middeleeuwen* (Brussels, 1940), pp. 3 ff.

works are important for their relation to versions in other languages, while some have survived only in the Dutch version. It is these last on which we shall concentrate our attention in this chapter.[1]

A General Survey

The greater part of the Dutch Arthurian romances have come down to us in two great cycles, best designated as the *Joseph-Merlin* Cycle and the *Lancelot* Cycle. Apart from these, *Walewein* and *Ferguut* have been transmitted as independent romances, while a few fragments allow us to infer the existence of an earlier more extensive Arthurian tradition.

The *Joseph-Merlin* Cycle corresponds in part to the French so-called *Pseudo-Robert de Boron* Cycle, the main difference being that in the Dutch a version of the *Livre d'Artus* is substituted as Part 3 for the *Suite du Merlin* (*Huth Merlin*). I shall discuss this later. The *Lancelot* manuscript, however, in the form in which we have it, has an entirely different content from the Vulgate Cycle, although we must admit the possibility that the *Lancelot* proper was at one time preceded by an *Estoire del Saint Graal* and a *Merlin*, the numerous individual romances being clearly later insertions; so that the whole manuscript may have originally contained an exact reproduction of the Vulgate. I shall say more on this point later. The manuscript known to us consisted of two parts, the first of which is lost. The second part consists of Books 2, 3, and 4. Book 2, which covers more than half of the surviving part, contains a metrical version of the final section of the French Prose *Lancelot* and a great part of Chrétien's *Perceval*, and *Moriaen*. Book 3 begins with a versification of the Vulgate *Queste*, followed first by *De Wrake van Ragisel*, second, by two poems of episodic character where the chief role is assigned to Lancelot, third, by *De Ridder metter Mouwen*, fourth, by two shorter poems, *Walewein ende Keye* and that to which Gaston Paris gave the title *Lancelot et le Cerf au Pied Blanc*, and finally by *Torec*. Book 4, the last, contains a metrical version of the Vulgate *Mort Artu*. Everyone must see at a glance that the *Lancelot* manuscript as it has been transmitted to us is not a unity. It contains some Vulgate texts mingled with various independent romances, and in many cases no attempt has been made to establish any connexion between them. Still the Dutch *Lancelot* manuscript is not a miscellaneous manuscript in the ordinary sense. The hand of the compiler is more visible than in Füetrer's *Buch der Abenteuer*, though less so than in Malory's *Morte Darthur*. In this chapter I propose first to consider the three parts of

---

[1] For bibliography of Dutch Arthurian literature up to 1910 see L. D. Petit, *Bibliographie der Middelnederlandsche Taal- en Letterkunde* (Leiden, 1888–1910), i. 57–63; ii. 37–40. For the later period see *Jahresberichte über die Erscheinungen auf dem Gebiete der germanischen Philologie*, and the bibliographies of Parry and of *BBSIA*.

the *Joseph-Merlin* Cycle, then the *Lancelot* Cycle, finally casting a glance at *Walewein* and *Ferguut*.

The Joseph-Merlin Cycle[1]

This includes three works, two of which are by the poet Jacob van Maerlant, the *Historie van den Grale* and *Merlijns Boeck*. This last merges without any external mark of distinction into its continuation, which has been recognized as a version of the *Livre d'Artus*, added in 1326 by Lodewijk van Velthem.

The *Historie van den Grale* was rendered into verse from the prose version of Robert de Boron's *Joseph* by Maerlant about 1261. We notice that Maerlant's activity falls about sixty years earlier than Velthem's *Boec van Coninc Artur*, so that it seems questionable whether Velthem had the original text of Maerlant before him. The rendering of the *Joseph* is very free; not only does Maerlant omit various matters but in several places he even attacks his original. The fanatical attachment to truth which Maerlant displays in other writings is also apparent here. Where Robert in his work differs from Scripture, Maerlant never fails to represent him as a liar. When Robert says that Judas retained a tithe of the money received by Jesus, Maerlant declares him a thief (John xii. 6). Maerlant omits the washing of the feet, clearly because Robert adds there a long discussion on the power of priests, themselves also sinful men, to forgive the sins of others, just as dirty water can still wash the feet of later comers. The emperor, called Titus by Robert, is by Maerlant correctly called Tiberius. The translator does not believe that Jesus was taken prisoner in Simon's house or that Joseph received the blood of Our Lord in a bowl found by a Jew, but he adds that he found this in his French source. In describing Joseph's release from prison Maerlant follows the *Gesta Pilati*, not Robert. In introducing Veronica he does not, like Robert, follow the *Vindicta Salvatoris*, but presumably the *Mors Pilati*.[2] Maerlant refuses to accept Joseph's liberation by Vespasian and he rejects Robert's assertion that Vespasian was a Christian. After vs. 641 two leaves are missing from the Steinfurt MS., containing presumably 312 verses. After this gap Maerlant keeps closer to his original, evidently because he has no other sources.[3]

Maerlant's *Historie van den Grale* ends with the sentence, cut to a known pattern, 'Aldus so endet dat ierste boeck' (vs. 1926). The poet then without a break continues with a translation of the French prose version of Robert's

---

[1] Ed. J. van Vloten under the misleading title *Jacob van Maerlants Merlijn* (Leiden, 1880). The *Historie van den Grale* extends as far as vs. 1926; the *Merlin* as far as vs. 10399; the *Livre d'Artus* as far as 36218. There are two fragments in N. de Pauw, *Middelnederlandsche Gedichten en Fragmenten* (Ghent, 1903), ii. 66 ff.

[2] J. te Winkel in *Tijd*. i. 339, 344.

[3] P. Paris in *Hist. Litt. de la France*, xxii. 412 ff.

Merlin. Maerlant follows his source fairly faithfully, but inserts a new section (vss. 2013–900), the so-called *Masceroen.* The version of the Trial of Satan, where Mascaron or Belial appears as Devil's advocate, is well known in medieval Latin literature. In Middle Dutch we know besides Maerlant's an independent version of the theme,[1] which doubtless goes back to the same Latin original.

The Royal Library in Brussels possesses, bound up with a copy of the *Cronycke van Vlaanderen int Corte* (Antwerp, 1539), two quires of a sixteenth-century Dutch version of the *Merlin,* which differs considerably from Maerlant's and all other versions of the *Merlin.*[2] The fragment first describes the coronation of Vortiger and some of his experiences (the building of the tower, &c.) before coming to the birth of Merlin. It has been compared to the English *Arthour and Merlin,* but cannot be derived from it.

At vs. 10398 Maerlant's *Merlin* breaks off. It closes with the information that Arthur 'lange hilt' the land 'met groten vreden' (Fr. et tint la terre de Logres en pez). The continuator, Lodewijk van Velthem, changed 'vreden' to 'onvreden' and then added nearly 26,000 verses, bringing the work to a close in the year 1326. This continuation corresponds to the *Livre d'Artus* (Bib. Nat. fr. 337).[3] Velthem in his translation has greatly abbreviated, though changing little of the contents. As a poet he is far inferior to Maerlant. The weakness of his talent is particularly striking in the verse structure and in the great increase in the number of patchwork verses.

The 'Lancelot' Cycle

We now turn to the *Lancelot* romance proper. The Hague manuscript[4] originally consisted of four books, the first of which, apart from inconsiderable fragments, is lost.[5] Jonckbloet inferred the contents from the Paris MSS. 7185 and 6939 (old number),[6] and placed the French text before Book 3 in his edition, vol. ii, pp. vi ff. We do not know if the poet made any alterations, nor do we know whether Book 1, like Books 2 and 3, also contained works of another kind, such as independent Arthurian romances.

One possibility must be left open. The lost first portion of the manuscript

---

[1] F. A. Snellaert, *Nederlandsche Gedichten uit de 14e Eeuw van J. Boendale, H. van Aken* (Brussels, 1869), pp. 493 ff.

[2] M. E. Kronenberg in *Tijd.* xlviii. 18 ff.

[3] Freymond in *ZRP,* xvi. 90 ff. and in *ZFSL,* xvii. 1 ff. See above, Chap. 25.

[4] *Roman van Lancelot,* ed. W. J. A. Jonckbloet ('s Gravenhage, 1846–9). See M. Draak in *Mededelingen der Koninklijke Nederlandse Akademie van Wetenschappen, Afd. Letterkunde,* N.R. xvii, no. 7, pp. 193–242.

[5] C. P. Serrure, 'De Ridder met de Kar', *Vaderlandsch Museum,* iv (1861), 309 ff.; M. de Vries in *Tijd.* iii (1883), 59 ff. See also J. te Winkel, *Jacob van Maerlants Roman van Torec* (Leiden, 1875), pp. xxxviii ff.

[6] See for the section dealing with the Knight of the Cart, G. Hutchings, *Le Roman en Prose de Lancelot du Lac, Le Conte de la Charrette* (Paris, 1938).

may have contained not merely the first book of the *Lancelot* proper, but also a version of the Vulgate *Estoire del Saint Graal* and the Vulgate *Merlin*. If this were so, then the whole series of Vulgate texts would have been translated into Middle Dutch. We cannot say that there was no room in the first part of the manuscript for the *Estoire* and the *Merlin*, especially if we consider that Book 2 contained no less than 47,262 verses. The *Estoire* and *Merlin* cannot have been omitted for the reason that the Pseudo-Robert de Boron cycle already contained a *Joseph* and a *Merlin*, for this cycle must be later than the *Lancelot* compilation, as is shown by the numerous passages where Pseudo-Robert depends on *Lancelot*.[1] Jonckbloet reckons in his *Geschiedenis der Nederlandsche Letterkunde* (Groningen, 1884), ii. 97, that the first book, judging by the French source, must have contained about 48,000 verses. If we can assume that the lost first section of the Hague manuscript contained the same amount as the preserved section, there was still room in the first section for about 36,000 verses, that is approximately the length of the missing portions of the Vulgate. This reckoning assumes that the first book contained no inserted pieces.

Book 2 has first the *Lancelot* continuation in 36,947 verses. Its divergences, mostly trivial, from the French prose romance, are collected by Jonckbloet in the introduction to his edition, vol. ii, p. ccix. The Dutch translator added a prologue of sixteen verses. Between fol. 99 and fol. 100 there is a hiatus, where clearly several leaves are missing. Jonckbloet fills the gap (vol. ii, pp. cxlii–cxlvii) by supplying the relevant section from the French prose romance. After this hiatus there follow parts of the *Perchevael* and the *Moriaen*, to be discussed later.

Book 3 contains the *Queste* (11,160 verses) and a string of Arthurian romances and fragments of romances, some known elsewhere and some not otherwise surviving. To these we shall return. Jonckbloet has already called attention to the fact[2] that only the *Queste* shows traces of a corrector's hand and contains references to earlier books. Both these features are absent in the accompanying romances, but they reappear in Book 4. This proves that the series of romances was inserted later, when the *Lancelot* proper was already completed in provisional form. The same may be true of the insertions in the second book, where the language of the *Moriaen* differs markedly from that of the *Lancelot*.

Book 4, after a prologue which has no basis in the French text, tells the story of Arthur's death, according to the Vulgate *Mort Artu*, in 13,054 verses. But vss. 9683–10128 derive from another source, Maerlant's *Spiegel Historiael*, iii, chaps. 50–54. After Book 4, vs. 10427, the *Lancelot* manuscript has a hiatus of several hundred verses, which the editor supplements

---

[1] J. te Winkel, *Ontwikkelingsgang*, i. 500, n. 8.
[2] *Roman van Lancelot*, ii, p. clxxiv.

from Paris MSS. 6792–4, and another shorter gap after vs. 3382 (*Roman van Lancelot*, II. clxxx ff., ccxiii).

The *Lancelot* manuscript closes with the words:

Hier indet boec van Lancelote,
dat heren Lodewijcs es van Velthem.

From this we might conclude that Lodewijk van Velthem was the compiler of the whole collection. But the difference in style between this work and the writings which are certainly his excludes the possibility of his being the translator of the whole. It has also been doubted, and rightly, whether he included the *Moriaen*. In the light of what has been said on the relation of the French Vulgate to the Dutch *Lancelot* Cycle, one might conjecture that Velthem found a complete translation of the Vulgate already in existence. He supplemented this by introducing other romances independent of the Vulgate and was either unable or would not take the trouble to establish any internal connexion between them. Possibly it was he who divided the whole into four books, of which Book 1 was lost later. The cycle must have come into existence before 1326, as Velthem himself says that he finished his version of the *Livre d'Artus* on Maundy Thursday in that year, and as several passages in the *Merlin* Cycle depend on the *Lancelot* Cycle, so that the latter must be earlier. So the *Lancelot* compilation must have been made in the first quarter of the fourteenth century, and the *Joseph-Merlin* Cycle, at least in its final form, some time later.

'*Perchevael*'

Lancelot, Book 2, vss. 36948–42546, contains long extracts from Chrétien's *Perceval*. Nevertheless, it is by no means always clear which manuscript the compiler had before him; and various episodes are included to which nothing in Chrétien's work corresponds.[1] The version begins with the appearance at Arthur's court of the loathly damsel, who scolds Perchevael as dishonourable and recreant. Certain passages must be regarded as additions:

Vss. 37584–8231: Keye and Acgravein have been imprisoned and are freed by Perchevael. The three then free Iwein and Gariet, who have been imprisoned in a castle. Mordret and Griflet are also taken prisoner and Walewein frees them (vss. 38681–9140). The game is repeated once more; the three last named are saved from great danger by Perchevael. Vss. 40786–1420 describe experiences of Keye, Lancelot, and Perchevael which are missing in the French romance. The adventure of Perchevael and others described in vss. 41660–844 is also missing in the French. But Perceval's meeting with the penitents and his visit to the hermit are omitted from the Dutch version.

---

[1] J. te Winkel, *Roman van Moriaen* (Groningen, 1878), introd., pp. 4 f. See, however, *Catholic Univ. of America, Studies in German*, xiv (Washington, D.C., 1939).

The great bulk of the *Perchevael* in the *Lancelot* manuscript consists, then, of the adventures of Walewein. He, and not Perceval, is the chief figure, so that in the *Merlin* (vs. 24656) the romance is actually referred to as the '*Gaweine*'. The reason why the Perchevael sections were for the most part omitted is probably that they had already found, to be sure in variant form, a place in the *Lancelot* proper (vss. 35827–6702),[1] and the translator could hardly contradict himself by describing the experiences of the young Perceval immediately afterwards from a different source. The narrative in the Dutch *Lancelot* manuscript is closely related to that of some manuscripts of the French Prose *Lancelot* and Prose *Tristan*, to which Hilka called attention.[2] The knight Aggloval, while seeking Lancelot, accidentally comes back to his mother. Here he finds his fifteen-year-old brother Perchevael. In spite of the mother's urgent prayers—she would like to keep him away from the world of chivalry—Perchevael goes with Aggloval to Arthur's court, where the king knights him. A maiden who up to this time was thought to be dumb addresses him and allows him to sit down in the place next the Siege Perilous; this indicates that Perchevael has a part to play in the quest for the Grail, but is not destined to complete it himself. Provoked by Keye's scornful words he leaves the court.[3] The entrance of Aggloval helps to prepare the connexion with the *Moriaen*.

It can be proved incidentally that Chrétien's whole romance was translated into Dutch, for we possess four small fragments, altogether nearly 1,100 verses, of a Dutch translation of *Perceval*.[4] Te Winkel demonstrated (loc. cit.) that this is the same text which Velthem had before him. The compiler has greatly abbreviated, particularly in the details, and on occasion as we have seen has also introduced new matter, but his manuscript is shown by various turns of phrase to have been identical with that from which the fragments come. So Chrétien's whole Grail romance once existed in Middle-Dutch. It is impossible to decide whether the first and second and perhaps also Manessier's continuation were translated.

The case of the *Perchevael* tells us much about Velthem's method of work, as in the fragments we probably have the text which he had before him. We see from this that Velthem changed little of the content, but often shortened the work drastically, sometimes reducing whole sections to a few lines, but on the whole worked not unskilfully, though his poetic talent was meagre. We recognize the same technique in his greatly abbreviated version of the *Chronicle* of Jan van Heelu in the fifth book of the *Spiegel Historiael*.

---

[1]   *Tijd.* x (1891), 161 ff.   [2]   *ZRP*, lii. 513 ff.

[3]   The Prose *Tristan* is closer to Chrétien. Perceval has been reared in ignorance of the world. He meets his brother Agloval and other knights in a forest. Attached to this is the episode of the blood drops in the snow, followed by Perceval's defeat of Gauvain.

[4]   F. van Veerdeghem in *Bull. de l'Acad. Roy. de Belgique*, 3 série, xx (1890), 637 ff.; J. te Winkel in *Tijd.* xiii (1894), 24 ff.; N. de Pauw, op. cit. ii. 73 ff.; J. te Winkel, *Ontwikkelingsgang*, i. 285, n. 3.

G g

'*Moriaen*'[1]

This romance, which is one of the best of its type, has for its main theme the quest of a son for his father—one of the most popular motifs of the Matter of Britain, occurring in the *Ridder metter Mouwen*, *Yder*, *Historia Meriadoci*, as well as in the non-Arthurian *Richars li Biaus*, *Sir Degare*, and *Gregorius*. What strikes one in particular is the correspondence with the story of Feirefîz in Wolfram von Eschenbach's *Parzival*. A Christian knight has a love-affair with a black princess and leaves her before or shortly after the birth of his son. As soon as he is grown up, the youth sets out to seek his father or to avenge his death. Feirefîz is the son of Gahmuret, therefore Parzival's half-brother. In the *Moriaen*, where, as te Winkel has shown in his edition, pp. 22 ff.,[2] Perchevael is originally the father, he has taken over the role of Gahmuret. So Perceval meets the Black Man in both works. In *Parzival* he is his brother, in *Moriaen* his father. The relationship between Feirefîz and *Tyrol und Fridebant* has been pointed out by J. Grimm.[3] It may further be remarked that, dimly in Chrétien and Wolfram and more clearly in the English *Sir Perceval*, the young hero sets out to avenge his father's death. I have shown this in detail in an earlier work.[4]

The poet of *Moriaen* has skilfully interwoven this main theme with others. A wounded knight who has been defeated by Perchevael appears at Arthur's court. Walewein and Lancelot now set out in search of Perchevael. On the way they encounter Moriaen, whom they do not yet know but who is likewise seeking Perchevael. At a cross-ways the three choose different paths. The adventure of each is recounted in detail. The most interesting to us is that of Walewein—his freeing of a maiden, his visit to the lord of the castle whose son Walewein has killed, and finally his liberation by Moriaen —because in part it agrees word for word with sections of *Walewein*, vss. 3676–4352 and 8713–9176. The poet of *Moriaen* must have combined these passages independently or have known their sources. So the question here arises as to the models of *Walewein*—their content, date, and language.

Moriaen's adventure has meanwhile miscarried. He has learned from a

---

[1] Edited by Jonckbloet in *Roman van Lancelot*, bk. 2, vss. 42547–7262, and by J. te Winkel (Groningen, 1877); trans. by J. L. Weston (London, 1901). Lot in *R*, xxiv. 336 ff., derives the name Morien from the Welsh name Mor. It is certainly connected with Lat. *Maurus*, Old Fr. *Mor*. *Moriaen* is still used in Dutch in a number of phrases with the meaning 'black man'.

[2] The compiler of the Lancelot manuscript was aware that Perchevael must remain a virgin. Agglovael is not so rare a character in Arthurian romance as te Winkel and others believe. See Hilka in *ZRP*, lii. 513 ff.

[3] *ZDA*, i. 7 ff. Singer in *ZDA*, xliv. 321 ff., showed that not only the early but also the later Books of *Parzival* are related to other versions of the Grail legend.

[4] *Verschmelzung legendarischer und weltlicher Motive in der Poesie des Mittelalters* (Groningen, 1922), pp. 73 ff. On pp. 44 ff. I show that almost all the romantic elements in the legend of Pope Gregory are derived from the Arthurian tradition. See also my *Hartmann von Aue* (Halle, 1933),i. 172 ff., and R. S. Loomis, *Celtic Myth* (New York, 1927), pp. 331–7.

hermit that his father is in Ireland, but the sailors who are to convey him across the sea have mistaken him because of his colour for the Devil and fled in terror. He returns to Walewein, who is still with the hermit. Walewein's brother Gariet arrives and informs Moriaen that Arthur has been captured by the Saxons and his realm conquered by the Irish, all but one castle, now being defended by the queen. Moriaen with the help of Gariet finds his father, who is ready to marry his old love and who now joins them. Meanwhile Walewein has made ready to seek Lancelot. Lancelot has killed a monster and secured a claim on the hand of a princess, but a traitor declares himself the victor; he is unmasked and killed by Walewein.

This theme of the false claimant appears again in the Dutch *Lancelot* (Book 3, vss. 22271–3125) in the episode of the stag with the white foot, and has numerous analogues in Arthurian literature and elsewhere.[1] The version in the lai of *Tyolet* is closer to the original form, but it does not seem to be the source of either of the Dutch versions. The offering of the stag's head or foot is a very old hunting custom. When Queen Juliana of the Netherlands attended a hunt in France in 1952, she was offered a forefoot of the slaughtered stag. The end of the romance follows the inevitable course. The five knights meet again at the hermit's cell, set out to rescue King Arthur, free him, drive off the Saxons and Irish, and Perchevael celebrates his belated wedding with the black queen.

It is difficult to answer the question whether *Moriaen* was originally Dutch or French. The former view is held as far as I know only by Dutch scholars. The fact that a French source cannot be shown proves nothing. We must give due weight to the fact that many episodes, among them the main motif, are clearly related to French poems, so that nobody would be surprised if a French original were to turn up. On the other hand, we have to consider that the poet of *Moriaen* is highly gifted, so that one might feel inclined to allow him, equally with any Frenchman, the creative power to construct an independent poem out of known—in any case French—motifs, and it must strike us that there is never any mention of a French composer of a *Moriaen*, whose gifts would presumably have been widely recognized. And yet there are no specifically Dutch traits in the *Moriaen*.

It is often assumed that *Moriaen* was included in the *Lancelot* compilation later than the other romances. An investigation of the language which might make a decision possible has yet to be made.

'De Wrake van Ragisel'

Book 3 of the *Lancelot* manuscript contains not only a close rendering of the French *Queste del Saint Graal*[2] (vss. 1–11160) but also a series of

---

[1] G. Paris in *R*, vii. 568; viii. 45; ix. 379 ff.; *Hist. Lit. de la France*, xxx. 113 ff. See Chap. 11 above.   [2] The discrepancies are noted by Jonckbloet in his edition, vol. ii, pp. ccxii ff.

romances. The first of these, *De Wrake van Ragisel* (The Avenging of Ragisel) occupying vss. 11161–4136, is obviously an abridgement from a longer translation which Velthem had before him.[1] This more detailed version could not have been directly dependent on the French poem, the *Vengeance Raguidel*, as we know it, but presupposes a fuller version. It is disputed whether this was an independent redaction, or merely a divergent manuscript.[2]

The French *Vengeance*, though it contains only a little over 6,100 lines, is really a compilation, bringing together various adventures of Gauvain. The considerably shorter Dutch version includes other matters, yet the narrative remains fairly coherent and lucid. The moral tone, however, and the contemptuous treatment of women make it far less agreeable reading than *Moriaen* and *Ferguut*.

Velthem opens the *Wrake van Ragisel* with a preface (vss. 11161–234) in which he links the story to the preceding *Queste* and explains how the maiden of Galestroet (Fr. Gautdestroit)[3] fell in love with Walewein. This affair is continued in vss. 11424–12268 and is concluded in vss. 13181–586 by the marriage of the maiden to Maurus (Fr. Maduc le Noir). The most remarkable interpolation, however, is the section entitled 'How Walewein wanted to learn the thoughts of women (vrouwengepens)', which occupies vss. 12635–13054. This section is itself a composite of several stories. The meeting of Walewein with the dwarf huntsman, who announced himself as a king, transformed Walewein into his own shape, and invited him to his castle bears a striking resemblance to the opening incident in the mabinogi of *Pwyll*, and is probably related in some way to it. The sequel in which Walewein in the form of a dwarf seduced his mistress Ydeine, received from her a ring which he had previously given her, and when, the next day, having returned to his proper form, he asked about the token, received the explanation that it had fallen by accident into the moat and been swallowed by a fish, is a variant of the Ring of Polycrates motif, which is also found in the Irish saga, *The Cattle-Raid of Fraech*, and in Joceline's Latin *Life of St. Kentigern*.[4] A third element, the dwarf king's faithless wife, who was condemned to eat her meals in a room alone, finds its closest analogue in the

---

[1] Eight fragments of the longer version, 104 verses in all, have been edited by F. Deycks, *Carminum Epicorum Germanicorum Saeculi XIII et XIV Fragmenta* (1858), pp. 15 ff., and by te Winkel in *Tijd.* xiii. 116 ff. Other fragments have been edited by Moltzer in *Tijd.* xiv. 232 ff., and by Franck, ibid. xix. 1 ff.

[2] See also te Winkel in *Tijd.* xiii. 116 ff., and *Vengeance Raguidel*, ed. M. Friedwagner (Halle, 1909), p. cc. See Chap. 28 above.

[3] Friedwagner in his edition, p. cclv, considers the Dutch form of the name older than the French. See also Brugger in *ZFSL*, xxix. 103. Velthem's derivation of the name from Galaat (vs. 11184) cannot be right.

[4] K. Jackson in *Studies in the Early British Church* (Cambridge, 1958), 322–4, 350–7; R. S. Loomis, *Celtic Myth*, pp. 333–6; R. E. Bennett in *Spec.* xiii. 68–75, and bibliography p. 72, n. 1.

Latin romance of *Arthur and Gorlagon*,[1] but also bears most complex relationships to Oriental tales, Breton lais, and modern Irish folk-tales.

The *Wrake van Ragisel* is separated in the *Lancelot* manuscript from the *Ridder metter Mouwen* by two independent chapters. The first of these episodes (Chap. 28) is a kind of continuation of the *Ragisel*. Arthur's queen having failed in the mantle test, Lancelot in consequence was seized by a senseless fury against all wearers of mantles. Seeing a knight whose mistress wears a mantle, he at once attacks him and after a long fight has to be told by Bohort that his opponent is his friend Ydier, with whom he is then reconciled.

Chapter 29 is no doubt new, although the adventure described could occur in any Arthurian romance of the second rank. Some wicked knights have tied a maiden to a tree. Whoever tries to release her is attacked and slain by the culprits, who are summoned by the sound of a bell. The knight Dodineel nearly suffers the same fate, but escapes just in time and meets Lancelot and Bohort in the wood. These two now release the maiden and kill the wicked knights. This episode is connected with the preceding episode by a discussion of the mantle test.

'De Ridder metter Mouwen'[2]

This romance, which might better be called *Miraudijs en Clarette* after the chief characters, borrows its title from the *dit* of the *Chevalier a la Mance*,[3] which has come down to us in a Turin manuscript, together with *Richars li Biaus*.[4] The Dutch romance owes little to the former, much to the latter. Almost all the motifs of the Dutch *Knight of the Sleeve* recur in *Richars*; so Jonckbloet's view that the *Ridder metter Mouwen* is an independent Dutch work must be modified. But since the order and linking of the incidents is completely different from that of *Richars*, the editress goes decidedly too far when she asserts that *Richars* is the source of the *Ridder metter Mouwen*. It is probably a free adaptation of the French romance or of a closely connected work.

The *Ridder metter Mouwen* was composed about 1300. It shows considerable discrepancies in style and language from the other parts of the Lancelot compilation and has nothing to do with the main content; so the presumption that it, like *Moriaen*, was included later is doubtless correct.

The *Ridder metter Mouwen*, together with *Richars*, *Moriaen*, *Gregorius*, and others, belongs to a group of narratives which combine the following

---

[1] See Chap. 36 below and Bennett, loc. cit.

[2] *Roman van Lancelot*, ed. Jonckbloet, bk. iii, vss. 14581–18602. Also ed. by B. M. van de Stempel (Leiden, 1914).

[3] *Dits et Contes de Baudouin de Condé et de son Fils Jean de Condé*, ed. A. Scheler (Brussels, 1866), ii, no. 23.

[4] Ed. W. Foerster (Vienna, 1874).

motifs: exposure of hero, often following a secret or incestuous birth; search for father or parents; freeing of a lady, usually in a besieged castle by the sea, the lady often turning out to be the mother of the hero; as a consequence further incest. The *Ridder metter Mouwen* keeps fairly closely to this type. The hero is a foundling, who has attended a monastic school for ten years, but then comes to Arthur's court and is knighted by the queen. With the sleeve of his beloved, Clarette, on the tip of his lance, he passes through many adventures, conquers knights, giants, a dwarf, and a lion, until he is wounded and taken into his own monastery. When a tournament is proclaimed at Arthur's court, with Clarette's hand as prize, he in his monk's cowl comes off victor. At the wedding a strange queen is present, who recognizes the Knight of the Sleeve as her son. This duplication of ladies enables the poet to avoid introducing incest. In the second part of the romance the hero finds his father also and comes with him after various adventures to the castle of his mother, who of course is being besieged. I do not need to call attention to the numerous reminiscences of other Arthurian romances, which every reader will recognize.

The short romance of *Walewein ende Keye (Gawain and Kay)*[1] is another which has been transmitted only in Dutch. It is impossible to decide whether a French original ever existed. In any case any poet reasonably familiar with the Arthurian material could have constructed a short work of this kind. Though Kay's glorious past was still known to poets like Hartmann von Aue, Wolfram von Eschenbach, Heinrich von dem Türlin, and in France to Chrétien de Troyes and the composers of the *Livre d'Artus* and *Escanor*,[2] our Dutch poet knew nothing of all this, and his only aim was to make the seneschal ridiculous. Keye is introduced declaring that Walewein once boasted of having passed in one year through more adventures than all the other knights of the Round Table together. Although nobody believes the slanderer, Walewein leaves the court. He has a variety of splendid but disconnected adventures, conquers giants and a dragon, frees maidens, overcomes many knights, and sends all his defeated opponents to Arthur's court. But the court recognizes that even if Walewein had spoken the boasting words which Keye attributed to him, it would have been no exaggeration. Keye is scorned as a liar and makes his escape, the king telling him to go to the Devil. This last vulgarity shows how little the poet understood the courtly spirit of Arthurian romance.

Definitely superior is the short poem, *Lanzeloet en het Hert met de Witte Voet (Lancelot and the Stag with the White Foot)* (vss. 22271–3126).[3] We do not know of a direct source, but we do know of several kindred

[1] *Roman van Lancelot*, ed. Jonckbloet, bk. iii, vss. 18603–22270.
[2] Zenker in *ZFSL*, xlviii. 16 ff.; G. Paris in *Hist. Lit. de la France*, xxx. 50 ff.
[3] *Roman van Lancelot*, bk. iii, vss. 22271–3126. Ed. also by A. M. E. Draak (Zwolle, 1953).

versions,[1] of which the closest is found in the lai of *Tyolet*, discussed in Chap. 11. Except that Lancelot takes the place of the hero, there is little difference between the two variants, but this difference requires a different ending, and Lancelot, instead of marrying the lady whom he has won by procuring the stag's white foot, declines the honour out of loyalty to the queen. The plot is made up of two familiar elements. The first is what Ehrismann called the *Verlockungsmotiv* and is particularly common in Irish folk-tales. A fay sends a messenger to entice a mortal to her, so that after proving his worth by overcoming great dangers he may enjoy her love. The first to attempt the enterprise is a coward and dares not cross the river, which represents the boundary of the Other World. The hero, of course, is successful. The second element is given in its earliest form by Pausanias. The King of Megara promises his daughter to the man who will deliver the land from a terrible lion. Alkathoos kills the monster and cuts out the tongue. So when a traitor falsely claims credit for the feat, Alkathoos produces the tongue as proof of his own claim, exposes the traitor, and marries the princess. This motif of the false claimant became a favourite with the medieval romancers, and has already been noticed in Chap. 12. The substitution of the stag's foot for the dragon's tongue seems to show the influence of an old hunting custom which I have noted in discussing *Moriaen*.

Torec, which occupies vss. 23127–6980 of Book 3, is likewise known to us only in Middle Dutch.[2] But the poet professes to have translated the story from the French (vs. 23178), and we know that a *Torrez* in rime existed in the library of the Louvre in 1392.[3] Moreover, Maerlant informs us in the *Historie van Troyen* (vs. 59) that he has translated *Torec* into Dutch, and scholars have tried to see his characteristic tendencies in the didactic portions. The poem is dated about 1255 or 1265. The workmanship is careless and the plot is full of obscurities,[4] but because of the many unusual features it may be summarized more fully than the conventional narratives. King Briant of the Red Island sees a beautiful maiden, Mariole, with a golden circlet perched on a tree in a forest. He determines to marry her. But the circlet is stolen by Bruant, her sister's beloved. No doubt in consequence of this loss Mariole becomes poor, her husband dies, and she casts out on the sea (why?) the little daughter Tristouse, born after his death. The child is kindly received in the land of King Ydor, and on attaining maturity becomes the bride of her

---

[1] See p. 451, n. 1 above.

[2] *Roman van Lancelot*, bk. iii, vss. 23127–6980; ed. by te Winkel, *Jacob van Maerlants Roman van Torec* (Leiden, 1875).

[3] G. Paris in *Hist. Lit. de la France*, xxx. 269.

[4] For example, in the names Briant, Bruant, Briade. In vss. 3 and 17 Briant and Briade are identical, but cf. vs. 83. Is the second sister meant to give up once more at vss. 123 f. the ring which her lover Bruant has just stolen? The latter part of the story contradicts this. Does Torec really marry his grandmother's sister, who is still after forty years the loveliest maiden in the world?

foster-father. Of this marriage Torec is born, and at his birth his mother laughs for the first time. When he is twenty years old, she shows him the letter which came with her as a foundling and tells him of the stolen circlet. The young man at once decides to set out in search of the circlet, and his mother then laughs for the second time. Torec finds and conquers Bruant, but the circlet is now in the possession of his sister-in-law, Miraude, the loveliest maiden in the world. She is ready to marry Torec if he can over-come all the knights of the Round Table. He achieves this, as Walewein obligingly persuades his comrades to cut the girths of their saddles so that they are all unhorsed at the first shock. Arthur, who himself takes part on this occasion, is victorious, but this does not prevent the nuptials. At the wedding feast Miraude wears the golden circlet. Then Tristouse laughs for the third and last time and soon afterwards dies, as does her husband also, and Torec ascends the throne.

The story thus extends over three generations. We recognize easily that the role of Tristouse has little to do with the main theme. It is, in fact, borrowed from some version of the *Manekine* of Philippe de Beaumanoir, in which also a maiden by the name of Tristouse is exposed as a child.[1] The maiden in the tree and the maiden who would not laugh appear elsewhere in medieval fiction. Miraude, who eventually becomes Torec's wife, though represented as his grandmother's sister, must have been in origin a healing fay. Hence her timeless beauty and her contempt for Arthur's world.[2]

Torec contains some interesting minor features. There is Mariole's brother, who goes invisible and fights with his grand-nephew Torec three times. There is Cleas van den Briele, who is under a spell which causes him to feel three times a day as if his head were being cut off. There is the voyage of Torec himself in the Ship of Adventure, which bears him off to a marble castle. There he is led into the Chamber of Wisdom and listens to knights and ladies disputing on all manner of moral questions, only to wake up on the fourth day at the place where he had embarked. This voyage seems alien to the Matter of Britain, and scholars have suggested that it is to be classed with the Eddaic Ship of the Dead.[3]

Thus with *Torec* the third book of the Dutch *Lancelot* comes to an end. The fourth book is mainly a translation of the Vulgate *Mort Artu*, but with gaps and the inclusion of a passage from Maerlant's *Spiegel Historiael*, as already stated.

    [1] G. Paris in *Hist. Lit. de la France*, xxx. 268. *Œuvres Poétiques de Philippe de Remi*, ed. H. Suchier (Paris, 1884), i. J. Bolte, G. Polívka, *Anmerkungen zu den Kinder- und Hausmärchen der Brüder Grimm* (Leipzig, 1913), i. 299.
    [2] Cf. the lais of *Graelent* and *Lanval*. Maerlant shows in the introduction to his *Spiegel Historiael* that he knew the latter.
    [3] J. te Winkel, *Ontwikkelingsgang*, i. 310 ff.

'Walewein'

Apart from the poems embedded in the long cycles, the Netherlands produced two separate Arthurian romances in verse, *Walewein* and *Ferguut*. The first of these offers several surprises in both structure and content and therefore deserves a fuller summary than usual.[1]

As Arthur is sitting surrounded by his knights, a splendid chessboard is wafted into the hall and presently disappears. In order to obtain it for the king, Walewein follows the mysterious object through a cleft in a mountainside, which then closes behind him. He kills four young dragons and their dam, crosses a deep river, and finds himself in the castle of King Wunder, owner of the chessboard. But the king will not surrender it unless Walewein brings him the sword with Two Rings, which is in the possession of King Amoraen. Setting out on this new quest, the hero meets a squire and lends him the famous steed Gringolet to ride in a trial by combat. When others unfairly join in the fight, Walewein takes the part of the squire and proves victorious.

The next day he arrives at the castle of King Amoraen and obtains the Sword with Two Rings, which ensures victory,[2] but only on condition that he bring with him on his return the maiden Ysabele. Leaving the castle he saves a damsel from rape and kills the offender, but not before he has promised him Christian burial, and this promise he keeps. After long wanderings he reaches a boiling river, crossed by a bridge as sharp as a ploughshare. He takes a nap but is waked by a fox named Roges, who has tried to steal his magic weapon. He gives Roges a blow with his fist and elicits from him the information that he is actually a prince who has been reduced by his stepmother to this vulpine shape until the day when he shall see brought together King Wunder, his son, Walewein, and Ysabele. Roges also reveals that the boiling river is purgatory and that souls, plunged into it in the form of black birds, emerge white.

Guided by the fox, Walewein follows a passage under the river and penetrates ten metal doors, each guarded by eighty men, but at the eleventh is encountered by King Assentin, who strikes the magic sword from his hand, and places him in the custody of his daughter, Ysabele. In the course of the night the damsel and Walewein are discovered in an amorous situation and are thrust into a dungeon. Providentially the ghost of the knight to whom Walewein had given Christian burial is mindful of his debt, releases the pair, and leads them back to Roges. Walewein recovers his sword.

After being involved in several dangerous situations on account of Ysabele, he comes back to King Amoraen, only to find that the king has just died.

---

[1] Penninc en Pieter Vostaert, *Roman van Walewein*, ed. Jonckbloet (Leiden, 1846–8). G. S. Overdiep, *Fragmenten van den Roman van Walewein* (Zwolle, 1924).

[2] An inference from the fact that only the perfect knight can bear it.

Thus he is free to keep both Ysabele and the magic sword. Though she is stolen from him on his return journey, Roges wakes him in time for him to overtake and defeat the abductor, who turns out to be his good friend Estor. After more perils, Walewein and Ysabele arrive at King Wunder's castle, where they find the king and his son. Thus the conditions for the disenchantment of the fox are fulfilled and he resumes human shape. The magic sword is delivered in exchange for the chessboard, the first object of quest, and Walewein returns with it to Arthur's court, the starting-point of the story. The poet adds that though he has read in his source that Walewein married Ysabele and later became Arthur's successor, he will not vouch for these statements.[1]

One recognizes, of course, many recurrent motifs of the Matter of Britain —sword-bridge, under-water passage, magic sword,[2] Gringolet, chessboard,[3] lady abducted and rescued, amorous custodian of hero,[4] duel between friends,[5] and so forth. On the other hand, the theme of the Grateful Dead, widely scattered through medieval fiction, occurs in no other Arthurian romance, and the chessboard which floats through the air is a novelty. The plot structure is also, I believe, unparalleled in the medieval French romances and their derivatives, consisting as it does of a series of interlocking quests, ultimate success being dependent on the fulfilment of earlier quests. And the enchanted fox is a unique figure in the Matter of Britain.

W. P. Ker first proposed that *Walewein* was based on the fairy tale of the *Golden Bird*,[6] which is No. 57 in Grimm's *Kinder- und Hausmärchen* and is represented by variants all over the world. This tale is also constructed on the principle of interdependent quests and contains a friendly fox, who is restored in the end to human shape. Unfortunately for this theory, the differences outweigh the resemblances. Walewein is far from being a *Dümmling*; none of the quests correspond; the disenchantment of the fox is accomplished by entirely different means. Then, too, there is no proof that the *märchen* existed in the thirteenth century. One cannot deny that *Walewein* is distinguished by some features drawn from folk-tales, but a specific dependence on the *Golden Bird* has not been demonstrated. Even less convincing is the thesis of S. Eringa, who would have us believe that the Dutch romance is derived from an Indian myth.[7]

---

[1] See the ballad 'The Wedding of Sir Gawain' discussed by G. Paris in *Hist. Lit. de la France*, xxx. 97, and in Chap. 37 below.

[2] Cf. *Chevalier as Deus Espees*, ed. W. Foerster (Halle, 1877).

[3] Bruce in *RR*, ix. 375; Weinberg in *PMLA*, l (1935), 25–35.

[4] R. S. Loomis, *Arthurian Tradition*, pp. 80 f., 254–8.

[5] Ibid., pp. 328–31; M. A. Potter, *Sohrab and Rustem* (London, 1902). pp. 207–9; F. Lot, *Étude sur le Lancelot en Prose* (Paris, 1918), p. 264.

[6] *Folk-lore*, v. 121 ff.; Bolte, Polívka, op. cit. i. 511; A. M. E. Draak, *Onderzoekingen over de Roman van Walewein* (Haarlem, 1936), *passim*.

[7] *Tijd.* xliv. 51 ff.

It seems likely that *Walewein* represents the expansion of a lai which told a rather simple tale of a hero who accomplished a series of interlocking quests for a chessboard, a sword, and a maiden, with the aid of a fox, finally won the maiden for his bride, and paid the debt of gratitude by releasing the fox from a spell.[1] This lai would then have been lengthened by the addition of several well-worn Arthurian motifs and episodes. If such was the history of *Walewein*, it would correspond to what we can clearly see happening in the development of the romance of *Ile et Galeron*[2] from the lai of *Eliduc*,[3] and of *Galeran de Bretagne*[4] from the lai of *Le Fresne*.[5] Both romances agree with the respective lais in basic conception and plot but differ in elaboration and in adaptation to courtly ideology.

Was the plot of *Walewein* a product of Dutch inventive skill or was it taken over directly from a French source? The question seems to be answered by the following considerations. We know that the poem was written in part (vss. 1–7843) by Penninc, and in part (vss. 7844–11198) by Pieter Vostaert. Now there is such consistency and continuity in the narrative that it is hard to believe that Vostaert's portion originated in his own imagination, and the hypothesis that Penninc left an outline for his continuator to follow cannot be proved. Until some kind of certainty is afforded by an investigation of the language and the style, such as that undertaken by Singer into the style of Wolfram von Eschenbach,[6] we are bound to conclude that *Walewein* derives from a French romance. The date of composition may be set about 1250, perhaps a little later, at all events earlier than the *Ridder metter Mouwen* and *Moriaen*.

'Ferguut'

We can deal more briefly with *Ferguut*,[7] since the French *Fergus* by Guillaume le Clerc[8] is extant and has been treated already in Chap. 28. The Dutch redactor, an East Fleming, follows manuscript A of the French text

---

[1] The editor of this book points out to me that *Walewein* is like *Culhwch and Olwen* in that it is composed in a similar manner out of similar materials. In the Welsh tale too the hero is a relative of Arthur and wins a bride in the end by a series of interdependent quests. Here too the bride's father is hostile to the hero. Here too one of the objects procured is a sword. The hero has helpful companions, two of whom, at least, take the form of a bird. There is also a king who has been transformed into a boar, and a stag which acts as a guide. Though no one would claim that *Culhwch* was the source of *Walewein*, we know that it was written down before 1100 and presents other analogies to Arthurian romance. See *Mabinogion*, ed. J. Loth, 2nd ed. i. 243–346, and Chap. 4 above.

[2] Ed. W. Foerster (Halle, 1891).

[3] *Die Lais der Marie de France*, ed. K. Warnke, 3rd ed. (Halle, 1925), pp. 186–224.

[4] Jean Renart, *Galeran de Bretagne*, ed. L. Foulet (Paris, 1925).

[5] *Die Lais*, &c., ed. Warnke, pp. 54–74.

[6] S. Singer in *Sitzungsberichte der kaiserlichen Akad. der Wissenschaften zu Wien.*, phil.-hist. Kl., clxxx (1916), Abh. 4.

[7] Ed. E. Verwijs (Leiden, 1882); J. Verdam (Leiden, 1908), rev. by G. S. Overdiep.

[8] Ed. E. Martin (Halle, 1872); F. Michel (Edinburgh, 1841). See L. Jordan in *ZRP*, xliii (1923), 154 ff.

as far as vs. 2592. He then suddenly works more freely. There are omissions and additions, and though the content is not greatly changed[1] there are signs of independence. Altogether vss. 3229–6990 of the French texts are reduced to vss. 2593–5596 in the Dutch; the innovations are sometimes clumsy or childish; and certain homely ideas and expressions creep in.[2]

Various opinions have been offered as to the change which takes place in the Dutch romance at vs. 2593. Verwijs suggested that there were two translators, one careful, the other careless. Overdiep wondered whether the second part was not based on a different French text, which diverged from MS. A as much as MS. P does. Overdiep also considered the possibility that after writing vs. 2592 the Dutch redactor had to part with his French source corresponding to MS. A, and wrote the second half from memory. In that case, however, would it not be natural for him to procure another manuscript to work from? And there is a strong argument in favour of a second French text, namely, the substitution in the second part of new names, e.g. Macedone for Artofilas, Lunette for Arondele, and in the addition of many new ones where MS. A has none.

Epilogue

Ferguut brings to an end the series of Middle Dutch Arthurian romances. But there are other works, which, although they do not belong to the genre of Arthurian romance, are related to it in technique and subject-matter. To this group belongs in the first place *Flandrijs*,[3] which has come down to us in a very fragmentary form, and then the *Roman van Heinric en Margriete van Limborch*.[4] The former work is probably somewhat older and belongs to the first decade of the fourteenth century. The name of the poet of *Flandrijs* is disputed; the composer of *Limborch* is probably Hein van Aken. We leave many problems unsolved and stick to Franck's chief conclusion, that *Flandrijs* is a compilation. The editor succeeds in tracing the sources of nearly all its motifs, mainly episodes in Dutch romances, like *Walewein*, *Moriaen*, *Ferguut*, *Ragisel*, *Lancelot*, *Torec*—a clear indication of the Dutch origin of *Flandrijs*. Similar resemblances occur between *Limborch* on the one hand and *Lancelot*, *Merlin*, *Torec*, *Ferguut*, and perhaps *Tristan* on the other, while *Flandrijs* and *Limborch* frequently agree. Both romances are certainly of Dutch origin and show to what degree the matter and the technique of the Arthurian romance overlapped into related fields.

The lively interest felt in the Netherlands in the Arthurian world is shown by a longish section in Lodewijk van Velthem's continuation of the *Spiegel*

[1] Introd. to Overdiep's ed., pp. vii ff. G. Kalff, *Geschiedenis der Nederlandsche Letterkunde* (Groningen, 1906), i. 114 ff.
[2] Verdam's ed., introd., p. xxxvii.
[3] Ed. J. Franck (Strassburg, 1876).
[4] Ed. R. Meesters (Amsterdam, Antwerp, 1951).

Historiael,[1] to which R. S. Loomis has called attention.[2] It is a detailed description of a 'Round Table'; how King Edward I of England, who took an eager interest in Arthur and his knights, held a Round Table meeting where everything took place exactly as at one of Arthur's festivals, where Lancelot, Gawain, Perceval, Bohort, Kay, &c., were represented by Edward's knights, where the big-mouthed Kay was hurled from his saddle, and so on. Velthem connects the feast with Edward's marriage to Eleanor of Castile and makes several errors of historical fact, but Loomis makes it probable that Velthem describes an actual 'Round Table', held in connexion with his second marriage in 1299. King Edward was well known in the Netherlands owing to his kinship to the ducal house of Brabant and was in high esteem there, and this is no doubt the reason why Velthem devoted so much attention to him in the *Spiegel Historiael*.

[1] *Lodewijk van Velthems Voortzetting van den Spiegel Historiael*, ed. H. van der Linden, W. de Vreese (Brussels, 1906), i. 295–321.

[2] *Spec*, xxviii (1953), 118–21; Huet in *MA*, xxvi (1913), 173–97. See Chap. 41 below.

35

SCANDINAVIAN LITERATURE

PHILLIP M. MITCHELL[1]

THE medieval Scandinavian literary works which are wholly or partly Arthurian may be listed as follows:[2]

(a) *Merlínusspá*, a poem by Gunnlaug Leifsson, based on Book VII of Geoffrey of Monmouth's *Historia*.

(b) *Breta sögur*, a translation of Geoffrey's *Historia*, excluding Book VII.

(c) *Tristrams saga ok Ísondar*, a Norwegian version of Thomas's poem, and a late Icelandic redaction.

(d) *Ívens saga Artuskappa*, a condensation of Chrétien's *Yvain*.

(e) *Möttuls saga*, a free version of *Le Mantel Mautaillié*.

(f) The *Skikkju rímur*, derived from *Möttuls saga*.

(g) *Erex saga*, a condensation of Chrétien's *Erec*.

(h) *Parcevals saga*, which together with

(i) *Valvers þáttr* constitutes a free rendering of Chrétien's *Perceval*.

(j) *Janual's lióð* and *Geitarlauf*, translations from Marie de France's lais of *Lanval* and *Chèvrefeuil*.

(k) One of the Swedish 'Eufemiavisor', *Herra Iwan*, and its Danish translation.

(l) Certain Icelandic, Norwegian, Danish, and Faroese ballads concerned with Tristan and Ivan.

It must be borne in mind that the Scandinavians and especially the Icelanders were already in possession of a rich literary tradition when the Arthurian legends and other courtly romances came to the North, and that the thirteenth century, when this foreign penetration took place, was the great age of saga writing. It was the period when Snorri Sturluson compiled the Edda, providing a key to the ancient mythology of Scandinavia and an introduction to the intricacies of Old Norse-Icelandic poetry; it was the century when the same Snorri wrote the *Heimskringla*, the monumental history

---

[1] I am indebted to my colleague Prof. W. D. Paden for valuable assistance and to Dr. N. Lukman of the University of Copenhagen for several suggestions which have been incorporated in the footnotes.

[2] The best general treatments of the subject are to be found in H. G. Leach, *Angevin Britain and Scandinavia* (Cambridge, Mass., 1921), pp. 129–234, 382–5; and R. Meißner, *Die Strengleikar* (Halle, 1902).

of the Norwegian kings, and when the great prose epics, such as *Njáls saga* and *Egils saga*, were composed. At the beginning of the same century Saxo Grammaticus was fabricating in Latin a glorious history of the Danish past. There was no great void which the foreign importations were introduced to fill. The legends of Arthur, like those of Charlemagne and of Dietrich von Bern, were welcomed in the north, not because of the poverty of the indigenous culture, but, on the contrary, because of its vitality and the desire to extend its range to more exotic themes.

In spite of the proximity of the British Isles and the various forms of intercourse which linked them to the Scandinavian countries in the twelfth century,[1] there is no evidence that the Matter of Britain crossed the North Sea at this or at any later stage in the form of oral tales. Even if we admit that Saxo and Snorri show a knowledge of Geoffrey of Monmouth in the *Gesta Danorum* and the *Heimskringla*, as H. G. Leach has suggested,[2] this does not prove any familiarity with popular traditions. And the earliest treatment of Arthur in Northern literature is derived from Geoffrey's *Prophetiae Merlini*, which later became Book VII of the *Historia*.[3]

This work, *Merlínusspá* (*The Prophecy of Merlin*),[4] was written, as already noted, by Gunnlaug, an Icelandic monk who died in 1218. It is metrically similar to the *Völuspá*, and the translator displayed typical medieval freedom by adding several stanzas of new material. Even though it may have been well known, the poem seems to have inspired no imitators, and the figure of Merlin failed to excite the Scandinavian imagination if we may judge by the fact that the prophet makes no later appearance in Northern literature. The compiler of the Icelandic miscellany known as the *Hauksbók* inserted the *Merlínusspá* in the prose translation of Geoffrey's *Historia*, the *Breta sögur*.[5] Leach argued from this insertion of an Icelandic poem that the *Breta sögur* itself was written in Iceland,[6] but other scholars do not accept the argument, since Old Icelandic and Old Norwegian litera-

---

[1] Leach, op. cit., pp. 25–113.

[2] The influence of Geoffrey of Monmouth on Saxo has been discussed by Leach, op. cit., pp. 139–48, and most recently by Lukman in *Historisk Tidsskrift*, 10. R. vi (1943), 593–607, and in *Classica et Mediaevalia*, vi (1944), 72–109. On Snorri see Leach, op. cit., pp. 145–8.

[3] On *Prophetiae* see Chap. 8 above.

[4] Discussed by Leach, op. cit., pp. 137–9. Lukman points out a possible, if tenuous, connexion between a twelfth-century Danish manuscript and Gunnlaug's poem: In Wilhelm of Æbeltoft's *Genealogia Regum Danorum*, dated 1194, occurs the earliest Scandinavian reference to Arthur. See *Scriptores Minores Historiæ Danicæ Medii Ævi*, ed. M. C. Gertz (Copenhagen, 1917–18), i. 177. Wilhelm probably knew the Sorø MS. (burnt in 1728), which contained the chronicle of Adam of Bremen, and which Steinnes has tried to prove in (Norsk) *Historisk Tidsskrift*, xxxiv (1946), 1 ff., 59 ff., was known to the cleric from Norway or the Orkneys who wrote the *Historia Norwegiae* between 1190 and 1202. The *Historia* cites the 'prophetia Merlini'. *Monumenta Historica Norwegiæ*, ed. G. Storm (Kristiania, 1880), p. 91.

[5] *Hauksbók*, ed. F. Jónsson (Copenhagen 1892–6), pp. 193–226. Discussed by Leach, op. cit., pp. 132–6.

[6] Leach, op. cit., p. 133.

ture were often intermingled, and they believe that the translation of the *Historia* was made at Bergen in Norway. In either case, Leach is correct in pointing out that it is less faithful to the original than Gunnlaug's poem, and shows many additions, omissions, and changes. The classical deities are supplanted by the Scandinavian in a homely effort at elucidation. Arthur is said to have been conveyed to Assysla island, where he died, and his corpse to have been buried at Christ Church in Canterbury. The date of the *Breta sögur* is hard to fix, but the work is so different from literature based on French and Anglo-Norman models which King Hákon Hákonsson of Norway commissioned in 1226 and later that it must have been at least an independent undertaking and was probably earlier.

The series of translations which are associated with Hákon was begun by 1226, for in that year a Brother Robert composed for him the *Tristrams saga*.[1] Hákon had been elected king in 1217, when he was only thirteen years old, and it is likely that this task was, if not the first, then one of the first, literary commissions executed for him. His name appears as the instigator not only in this saga but in *Ívens saga* and *Möttuls saga*. Since Brother Robert translated *Elie de St. Gille* and the Breton lais (*Elis saga* and *Strengleikar*) it seems likely that his royal patron was responsible, indirectly if not directly, for these and perhaps other translations—*Erex saga*, *Parcevals saga*, and *Flores saga ok Blankiflur*—which were made during the same reign.

What were the motives which led King Hákon to promote this literary activity? Two may be suggested, and both may be correct. The first is that assigned by Abbot Robert (presumably the same as Brother Robert) for the composition of *Elis saga*, namely 'til skemtunar', 'for amusement'.[2] The second may be inferred from the nature of Hákon's reign.[3] It was his ambition to end the isolation of Norway and to obtain recognition for the country and for himself as its representative among the monarchs of Europe. He strove zealously to establish the general ecclesiastical culture of Europe, with its learning, architecture, and arts, and to introduce also the secular and courtly culture of France and England. In this effort he used all the power of the throne, convinced, as the *King's Mirror* (an anonymous treatise composed near the end of his reign) puts it, that 'the king represents divine lordship: for he bears God's own name and sits upon the highest judgment seat upon

---

[1] Ed. by E. Kölbing (Heilbronn, 1878) with German translation. Discussed by Leach, op. cit., pp. 174–84.

[2] Paul V. Rubow has argued in 'Den islandske Familieroman', *Tilskueren*, 1928, 347 ff., and more fully in *Smaa kritiske Breve* (Copenhagen, 1936) that Robert's work stimulated the composition of the Icelandic family sagas of the thirteenth century, and describes him as in all probability the founder of Old Norse fiction. See also the revised statement in English of Rubow's views, *Two Essays* (Copenhagen, 1949). His aesthetic approach to the sagas is generally regarded as sound, but his theory of Robert's impact on Icelandic literature has not been accepted.

[3] On King Hákon see Leach, op. cit., especially pp. 49–56, 149–57.

earth.[1] It was typical that when Hákon was to be crowned in 1247, he requested the pope to send a cardinal to perform the ceremony, and that the *Hákons saga* gives an ornate, elaborate description of the coronation which seems very French.

In following these broadening, pro-foreign policies, Hákon showed no scorn for the native culture of Scandinavia. We learn that on his death-bed he had first Latin, then Old Norse works read to him, and that the saga of King Sverri was the last to which he listened.

The translations made during his reign from French and Anglo-Norman were all in prose. Apparently Scandinavian metrics did not seem suitable to the task. Moreover, the translators displayed a tendency to omit the detailed descriptions and the subtleties of emotion in order to get forward with the plot. This emphasis on narrative content would seem to have satisfied the king and his court and reveals a failure to appreciate some of the essential qualities of the literature which he sought to introduce into Norway.

In this respect *Tristrams saga ok Ísondar* is representative, for it is a condensed redaction of the Anglo-Norman *Tristan* of Thomas,[2] and is preserved only in Icelandic manuscripts. It is of no high literary quality. The earlier part, so far as one can judge in the absence of Thomas's complete text, was fairly faithful to its source, but in the latter parts, where we can compare them with the original French, we find that conversations have been cut and scenes have been abridged. Nevertheless, Brother Robert deserves our gratitude since he has handed down to us the best redaction of Thomas's masterpiece which we possess.

The strong appeal of the Tristan legend to the Scandinavians, exceeding that of any other branch of the Matter of Britain, is demonstrated by the popular songs which it later inspired in Danish, Icelandic, and Faroese.[3] Two Danish ballads, both presumably composed in the fifteenth century, are entitled 'Tristram og Isodd',[4] but one of them preserves no more of the famous legend than the names, and adds to these that of Kriemhold, which has of course been borrowed from the Nibelungen-Volsung cycle. The Icelandic *Tristrams kvæði*,[5] like the Faroese *Tistrams Táttur*,[6] is concerned only with the death of the hero. It is a matter of conjecture whether these ballads are direct descendants of the saga tradition, or have some other source. Incidentally, the Faroese version was not written down till 1847.

Ívens saga Artuskappa (The Saga of Iven, Arthur's Champion) was trans-

---

[1] *The King's Mirror*, trans. from Old Norwegian by L. M. Larson (New York, 1917), p. 247.

[2] On relation of *Tristrams saga* to Thomas's poem see above Chap. 13 and Thomas, *Tristan*, ed. Bédier (Paris, 1902–5), ii. 64–75.

[3] On Tristan ballads see Leach, pp. 195–8; for bibliography, ibid., p. 399.

[4] *Danmarks gamle Folkeviser*, ed. S. Grundtvig and A. Olrik (Copenhagen, 1905), viii. 34 f.

[5] *Íslenzk Fornkvæði*, ed. S. Grundtvig, J. Sigurðsson (Copenhagen, 1854–85), i. 188 ff.

[6] Ibid., and V. Hammershaimb, *Færøsk Anthologi* (Copenhagen, 1891), pp. 216 ff.

lated from Chrétien's *Yvain* for King Hákon, by whom we do not know, and is preserved only in Icelandic manuscripts.[1] Like *Tristrams saga*, it follows the French text closely at the beginning, but becomes more hurried, less detailed, and less accurate as the story progresses. While it is conceivable that Robert was the author, it is unlikely he was responsible for the colophon, 'Here concludes the saga of Sir Iven, which King Hákon the Old had translated from French into Scandinavian.' For Hákon would not have been referred to as 'hinn gamli', 'the Old', during his lifetime.

The style, being very different from the terse and dramatic prose of the *Íslendingasaga*, is suggestive of the French original. Take, for example, chap. vi. 1:

> Nú lætr mærin svá fyrir frú sinni, sem hon hefði eptir sent herra Íven. Hon gerði honum hvern dag laug, þvær honum ok kembir ok bjó honum ríkan gangara af nýju skarlaki ok gullsylgju, setta dýrum gimsteinum, ok belti gort einkanligri gullsmíð með margháttuðum hagleik; beltispúss gullofin með svá smágerðu starfi, sem kvenna hagleiks kunnasta finnr vildast at gera.

(Now the maid pretended to her mistress that she had sent for Sir Iven. The maid prepared a bath for him every day, washed him and combed his hair, and clothed him in a costly garment of scarlet with a golden brooch. She adorned him with costly jewels and an extraordinary belt very skillfully worked in gold. A pouch attached to the belt was interwoven with gold and as carefully made as a knowledge of women's handicraft finds most agreeable.)

French *kurteisi* has affected the blunt native prose. Take also chap. vi. 19–20:

> Frú, kvað hann, engi nauðsýn er svá oflug sem sú, er mik nauðgar, svá at gera, at hlýðaz er til alls þess, þér þú vill mér bjóða svá gersamliga um allt. Þat, er þér vel líkar, skal ek gjarna gera, ok eigi óttumz ek, þóat enn mesti háski á liggi. En ef ek mætta bæta dauða þess, er ek drap ok ek misgerða við, þá skylda ek svá vel þat gera, at engi skyldi at mega telja.

('Madam,' he said, 'no necessity is so great as that which makes me listen to you for the sake of whatever you will bid me do. That which you desire I will do gladly and I shall not be afraid though it involves the greatest danger. And if I could atone for the death which I have caused and for the misdeed I have thereby committed, I should indeed do so, so that no one could rebuke me.')

A comparison of the Norwegian ballad *Ivar Erlingen og Riddarsonen*[2] with the Faroese *Galians Kvæði* demonstrates that both are related to the Yvain legend.[3] The connexion of the Norwegian poem with the saga or with the original French poem is very tenuous, but the Faroese song provides a link.

---

[1] *Riddarasögur*, ed. E. Kölbing (Straßburg, 1872), pp. 73–136, and *Ívens saga*, ed. E. Kölbing, Halle, 1898 (*Altnordische Saga-Bibliothek*, Heft 7). Quotations from the latter edition.

[2] N. B. Landstad, *Norske Folkeviser* (Christiania, 1853), pp. 157–68.

[3] Comparison made by Kölbing in *Germania*, xx (1875), 396 f.

Though the extant forms of these folksongs are probably not medieval, they do represent an offshoot of the Yvain romance comparable to the songs about Tristan.

Möttuls saga (*The Tale of the Mantle*),[1] which was translated from the French at the command of King Hákon, is in the opinion of G. Cederschiöld 'sans doute la plus importante de toutes pour la connaissance du fabliau même; car c'est une traduction assez fidèle et soignée d'un manuscrit français perdu qui a ressemblé en général au meilleur des manuscrits conservés'.[2] Again the saga is preserved only in Icelandic manuscripts. Concerned with the popular theme of a chastity test by means of a mantle, it has a tenor very different from that of Tristan and Yvain romances, and was apparently undertaken 'til skemtunar' (for amusement) and for no didactic purpose. Much later, probably in the fifteenth century, this waggish tale was turned into verse in the so-called *Skikkju* (Mantle) *rímur*.[3] The *ríma* is a peculiar Icelandic development of the medieval ballad which has been popular since the fourteenth century. In this form foreign material acquired a Scandinavian garb, inasmuch as the alliterative pattern of Old Norse poetry was preserved. Otherwise the pattern consists of four-line stanzas of riming couplets, with four stresses to a line, / ∪ / ∪ ∪ / ∪ /. The *Skikkju rímur* are a free treatment of *Möttuls saga*, with a moralizing supplement of two stanzas in which Arthur commands the embarrassed ladies to leave his court. Cederschiöld points out[4] that there is a relatively large number of foreign words which can be found neither in earlier indigenous literature nor in other translations, and their presence has not been satisfactorily explained.

Erex saga, a condensation of Chrétien's *Erec*,[5] is the work of an unknown author, who wrote about 1230, but it is preserved only in a seventeenth-century Icelandic manuscript. Despite a number of changes in detail, the translator followed Chrétien somewhat more closely than Robert had done, though like him, the translator made many omissions and shortened many lengthy passages. Some of his additions seem to indicate a clerical background. As Cederschiöld has pointed out, the translator is especially prone to condensation where Chrétien's verses possess aesthetic value. The fine quality of French verse could not be reproduced in a prose translation; as a consequence, the Norwegian translator felt no need to translate passages of poetic virtuosity which delay the unfolding of the plot. The fact that

[1] *Versions Nordiques du Fabliau Français 'Le Mantel Mautaillié'*, ed. G. Cederschiöld, F. A. Wulff (Lund, 1877); *Saga af Tristram ok Ísönd samt Möttuls saga*, ed. G. Brynjúlfsson (Copenhagen, 1878), pp. 217–42. On other versions of the mantle test see O. Warnatsch, *Der Mantel* (Breslau, 1883), pp. 4–7, and above, pp. 115 f., below, p. 518.

[2] *Versions Nordiques*, p. 46.

[3] Ibid., pp. 51 ff. Edited from a better manuscript by Finnur Jónsson, *Rímnasafn* (Copenhagen, 1913–22), ii. 326 ff.

[4] *Versions Nordiques*, p. 77.

[5] Ed. G. Cederschiöld (Copenhagen, 1880).

Erex saga occasionally resembles Hartmann von Aue's *Erek* indicates no dependence of the one on the other, but rather the possibility that both drew on a common French version which is not now extant.

Chrétien's *Perceval* is the source of both *Parcevals saga* and *Valvers þáttr*,[1] two works which presumably were translated in Norway, but are preserved only in Icelandic manuscripts. The date of the translation is uncertain; judging on the basis of style and vocabulary one might conclude that these were written several decades later than the translations previously discussed. There seems to be no reason for the division of Chrétien's *Perceval* into two separate works. The major and central portion of *Parcevals saga* was, for the time, a careful rendering of Chrétien's poem. The translator added an introduction and a conclusion, no doubt in order to round out, as Wolfram did, what he felt to be the defective parts of the original. He caused Parceval to marry Blankiflur,[2] but he did not bring him back to the Grail castle, to pass the question test and to heal the Fisher King. Indeed, he seems to have been baffled by the word *graal*, which, as we know, was often misunderstood even by Frenchmen. He describes[3] the entrance of a fair maiden, carrying in her hands a thing 'því líkast sem textus væri; en þeir í völsku máli kalla braull; en vér megum kalla ganganda greiða' (most like as it were a *textus*; and they call it in the foreign [i.e. Old French][4] language *braull*, and we may call it 'ganganda greiða'). Twice at the end of the saga the mysterious object is again referred to as 'gangandi greiði'. Modern scholars are as much perplexed by the Norseman's interpretation as he was by Chrétien's passage.[5]

Valvers þáttr, which corresponds to vss. 6519–9098 of the *Perceval*, opens with Gauvain's (Valver's) meeting Orgueleuse de Logres and Greoreas, and closes abruptly with his dispatching a squire to Arthur's court. The redactor of the two sagas used a manuscript of a type unlike any preserved,[6] added a number of Scandinavian proverbs, but in general condensed his material, particularly the descriptions and dialogues.

Two of the Norse lais (*Strengleikar*),[7] *Januals lióð* and *Geitarlauf*, are Arthurian since they are translations from Marie de France's *Lanval* and

---

[1] *Riddarasögur*, ed. Kölbing, pp. 1–71.   [2] Ibid., p. 53.

[3] Ibid., p. 30.   [4] On meaning of *völsku* see Leach, op. cit., p. 153.

[5] See Heinzel in *Denkschriften der kaiserlichen Akad. der Wissenschaften zu Wien*, xl (1892), 6 f.; J. Fourquet, *Wolfram d'Eschenbach et le Conte del Graal* (Strasbourg, 1938), pp. 63 f. The substitution of *braull* for *graal* may well have been made by the Icelandic transcriber as Fourquet asserts; and the scribal confusion of initial *b* and *g* is a common phenomenon. See *MP*, xvi (1918), 348; *MedAev*, xxv (1956), 187. Heinzel made the ingenious suggestion that the Latin word *textus*, which Ducange defines, 'Liber seu Codex Evangeliorum . . . auro gemmisque ut plurimum exornatus', was employed to interpret the word *graal* through a confusion with *grael*, 'graduel, livre d'église', which was also spelled *graal*.

[6] *Percevalroman*, ed. Hilka, p. xlvi.

[7] *Strengleikar eða Lioðabok*, ed. R. Keyser, C. R. Unger (Christiania, 1850). Discussed by Leach, op. cit., pp. 199–226.

Chèvrefeuil.[1] *Geitarlauf (The Honeysuckle)* is a fairly careful rendering of the French, but the other is marred by the omission of details.[2]

All the translations so far treated, from *Tristrams saga* through the *Strengleikar*, reveal a natural effort to adapt the narratives to the new audiences. Not only is French verse turned into Old Norse prose, but there is a distinct tendency toward alliteration and the use of stereotyped phrases.[3] Often explanatory terms are employed to describe or define unfamiliar concepts and objects, but not always, as we have seen, with complete success. On the other hand, foreign words have crept in. In *Ívens saga*, for instance, we find *kastali, skarlak, leoparð, kapella, smaragd, silkikult, hertugadæmi, barón, herimiti.* The fact that words like *kurteisi,* which is to be met in *Laxdæla saga,* one of the great masterpieces of Icelandic literature, came into common use in the thirteenth century may be a result of their occurrence in these translations.[4] But it is dangerous to be positive in this matter, for they may have been adopted into the spoken language, just as many English words are *à la mode* today in Scandinavian countries.

New motifs, new codes of conduct, and a new style combined to remould the native literature, as all the later sagas bear witness. Two of them, *Vilmundar saga Viðutan* and *Blomsturvalla saga,* as Margaret Schlauch suggested in her fascinating study, *Romance in Iceland,*[5] were patterned after Chrétien's *Perceval* or after *Parcevals saga.* Likewise, Leach has shown how two other sagas seem to have been affected by the Arthurian cycle;[6] *Harald Hringsbani* borrowed from the *Tristan* the betrothal by proxy, the substituted bride, and the quest for healing, while *Samsons saga Fagra* has for its hero a son of Arthur, otherwise unknown, and echoes several typical Arthurian themes. There are casual references to the British king and his knights in works which have no connexion with the Matter of Britain. In chapter 21 of *Elis saga* a champion is mistakenly identified as 'Arthur, King of Britain, the famous and victorious'. The Swedish chronicle of Duke Erik

---

[1] See Chap. 11 above.

[2] R. Meissner, *Die Strengleikar,* p. 273, has tried to account for this omission. Dr. Lukman feels that the Old Norse titles may reflect knowledge of lost English versions of the lais. Vs. 115 of *Chèvrefeuil* states, '"Gotelef" l'apelent Engleis', while the Old Norse translator calls the lai *Geitarlauf.* William of Malmesbury calls Gawain 'Walwen' (see Chap. 6 above), while in Old Norse Gawain is called Valver. The form Tristram employed by Brother Robert is also used by Malory and approximates the spelling of the Middle English *Sir Tristrem.* Leach in his *Angevin Britain,* pp. 152 f., believes that the translations of romances and lais into Old Norse were a direct product of Hákon's friendship with England and the English, and that internal evidence shows that the originals were Anglo-Norman or Middle English, not continental.

[3] G. Cederschiöld, *Fornsögur suðrlanda* (Lund, 1884), pp. xxii ff.

[4] A. T. Laugesen, *Om de germanske folks kendskab til fransk sprog i middelalderen (Studier fra Sprog- og Oldtidsforskning,* ccxvii, 1951), pp. 46 ff.

[5] (New York; London, 1934), pp. 165–7.

[6] Leach, op. cit., pp. 189–95, 232 f. See also Leach and Schoepperle in *Publications of the Soc. for the Advancement of Scand. Study,* ii. 264 ff.

mentions Gawion and Persefall. The so-called rhyme about Alexander the Great, written in Sweden about 1320, mentions together in vss. 11, 12 'tidrik van berna oc percefal herra gawain oc ektor',[1] i.e. Dietrich von Bern, Perceval, Sir Gawain, and Hector. As in other parts of Europe, especially in Italy, the various cycles tended to assimilate and to lose their distinctive character. Chronological gaps and cultural barriers were ignored. The *Breta sögur* form a continuation of the *Trojumanna saga*, and relate that when Hengist and Horsa landed in Britain, they were accompanied by a Didrik, whom we may presume to be Dietrich von Bern.[2] In *Ívens saga* Arthur himself is styled 'keisari yfir Rómaborg', 'emperor over Rome-town', and is compared to Charlemagne.[3]

It has already been pointed out, and it should be stressed, that the early prose translations of Arthurian romance were made in Norway, but have been preserved only in Iceland, the great storehouse of Germanic antiquity. Thus we are indebted to the island for preserving much medieval literature which has disappeared from the Scandinavian peninsula. We do not know precisely when the Arthurian translations made their way across the ocean, but the transfer must have taken place before the fourteenth century.

About 1300 the Arthurian tradition took on a new life in the North. For the first time since the days of Gunnlaug the monk, it took the form of verse. Eufemia, the German-born queen of King Hákon V of Norway, had three poems composed between 1300 and 1312, namely *Herra Iwan*, *Hertig Frederik*, and *Flores ok Blankiflur*. These so-called *Eufemiavisor* have been the subject of a long and learned debate, most of it provoked by the fact that the language of these poems as they have come down to us is Swedish.[4] Various possibilities have been suggested. According to one theory the poems were first translated for Eufemia into Old Norse, and these versions were lost, but not before they had again been translated into Swedish. A theory which counts more adherents proposes that the queen intended the poems for the edification of a Swedish nobleman who became her son-in-law. A recent view is that the three poems were not the work of one author, and that the association with Eufemia is apocryphal.[5]

Whatever the answer to these puzzles, it is with only one of the three we are here concerned, since obviously the loves of Flores and Blanchefleur have no connexion with Arthur, and the adventures of Duke Frederick of

---

[1] G. Storm, *Sagnkredsene om Karl den Store og Didrik af Bern hos de nordiske Folk* (Kristiania, 1874), pp. 136 f.
[2] It should be noted that the *þiðriks saga* was compiled in Norway between 1200 and 1250.
[3] *Ívens saga*, ed. Kölbing (1898), p. 1.
[4] O. Klockhoff, *Studier öfver Eufemiavisorna* (Upsala, 1880).
[5] A. Nordfelt, 'En svensk riddardikt och dess original' (in *Studier i modern språkvetenskap*, Nr. 7, Uppsala, 1920); P. Wieselgren, 'Hertig Frederiks Datering', *Arkiv för Nordisk Filologi*, lxii (1947), 1 ff.

Normandy have very little.[1] For this one poem, *Herra Iwan* or *Herr Ivan Lejon-Riddaran* (*Sir Ivan, the Knight of the Lion*), the testimony of the text itself is quite explicit. It was translated in 1303 at the command of Eufemia 'aff valske tungo ok a vart maal' (from the foreign tongue into our language) —the usual form of reference to a French source.[2] Though there are several passages which closely resemble the text of *Ívens saga* and suggest a direct connexion, yet one may say that *Herra Iwan* comes closer to its French model in content, spirit, and form than any other Scandinavian treatment of Arthurian themes. It is, in fact, a translation, in the modern sense of the word, of Chrétien's *Yvain*. It reproduces the metrical scheme of the original, rimed couplets with four accents to each line—a verse-form which subsequently became fashionable in Scandinavia, replacing the metrical patterns inherited from Germanic antiquity. Moreover, the poem has a literary quality superior to that of the earlier redactions of Arthurian romance in prose.

The *Eufemiavisor* must have enjoyed a wide popularity, for six manuscripts have survived, and the collection was translated, though perhaps from a different archetype, into Danish.[3] But from the fifteenth century onwards, there appears, as elsewhere in Europe,[4] a tendency for the romances to descend in the social scale, to adapt themselves to humbler, less sophisticated audiences, as is evidenced by a completely confused retelling of Brother Robert's *Tristrams saga*.[5] There are, finally, the chapbooks of the sixteenth and seventeenth centuries, based not on the older translations from French romance but representing a new influx from the South.

[1] Thorstenberg gives a synopsis of *Hertig Frederik* in *MP*, vii (1910), 395–415, and claims it as Arthurian, but as Bruce, ii. 307, remarks, the connexion is very slight.

[2] See above, p. 468, n. 4.

[3] Ed. by C. J. Brandt, *Romantisk Digtning fra Middelalderen*, i (Copenhagen, 1869).

[4] See especially Chap. 32 above.

[5] Ed. G. Brynjúlfsson in *Annaler för Nordisk Oldkyndighed*, 1851, pp. 1–160. Discussed by Leach, op. cit., pp. 184–6.

36

THE LATIN ROMANCES

ROGER SHERMAN LOOMIS

B ESIDES many treatments of Arthur in the Latin chronicles and a few
in the saints' lives, there are four narratives in the same language with
an Arthurian setting which may loosely be called romances. To be
sure, one of them is not longer than a Breton lai and is incorporated in a work
of instruction, while another is characterized by an acid misogyny which is
hardly romantic. But all four are more closely akin to Chrétien de Troyes
than to Geoffrey of Monmouth. These Latin texts are: (1) a chapter in
Andreas Capellanus's *De Amore*; (2) *Historia Meriadoci*; (3) *De Ortu Walwanii*; (4) *Arthur and Gorlagon*.

Andreas, who seems to have had intimate knowledge of the courtly circle
of Marie de Champagne, wrote his extraordinary and influential work in
1184–5,[1] ostensibly to reveal to his friend Walter how fleshly love may be
sought and won in accordance with etiquette, and then how it leads to
perdition. Though the book offers difficult problems of interpretation, it
obviously reflects the absorbing interests of the time. It is therefore significant
that Andreas chose to insert both an incident based on a Breton lai[2] and a
miniature Arthurian romance. The latter serves the all-important function of
introducing a code of thirty-one laws laid down by the King of Love himself—laws which provide the most specific formulation of *amour courtois*
which we possess.

In brief,[3] Andreas relates how a Briton knight met in a forest an equestrian fay, who permitted him to boast of her love and instructed him how to
achieve his quest for a hawk at Arthur's court. After surmounting various
perils, he arrived at Arthur's golden palace, found the hawk on a golden
perch and, attached to the perch, a scroll with the laws of love. He successfully maintained in combat his claim to the possession of the most beautiful
mistress, and brought away in triumph the bird and the scroll.

How much originality Andreas exercised in composing the little romance

---

[1] Andreas Capellanus, *De Amore*, ed. E. Trojel (Copenhagen, 1892); ed. A. Pagès (Castellon de la
Plana, 1929). Trans. J. J. Parry, *Art of Courtly Love* (New York, 1941). For date cf. *Spec*, xiii (1938),
308.

[2] This is the *Lai du Trot*. Cf. W. A. Neilson in *R*, xxix (1900), 86; E. M. Grimes in *RR*, xxvi
(1935), 313–21.

[3] Andreas, *De Amore*, bk. ii, chap. viii.

is impossible to say, but it is certainly a medley of familiar Arthurian motifs. The chance meeting with a faery mistress who presents the hero with her own steed is matched in the English *Sir Launfal*.[1] In *Le Bel Inconnu* and *Wigalois* this meeting with the fair equestrian leads on to a combat for the prize of a bird,[2] and Nitze has listed[3] a number of other romances, including *Erec*, in which the contest for a sparrow-hawk is a picturesque feature. The crossing of a partly submerged suspension bridge is probably a variation on the motif of the Water Bridge, in Chrétien's *Lancelot*.[4] Others besides Andreas have told how a knight came on a table sumptuously spread, sat down to a solitary meal, and was interrupted by a giant forbidding him to eat.[5] A study of the handling of these motifs suggests that Andreas did not derive any of them from extant texts, nor can any successors be proved to have borrowed this episode from him, except in the obvious case of the Italian *cantare*, *Bruto di Bretagna*.[6] Why did he introduce them at all? The answer seems to be that such bizarre fantasies formed the favourite entertainment of a public wearied by the piety and bellicosity of the Carolingian epics, and that, thanks to Geoffrey of Monmouth and Wace, Arthur's court was established as the standard for refined manners and true love.

Historia Meriadoci and *De Ortu Walwanii* are biographical romances like Chrétien's *Perceval*.[7] Both came from the same pen, for both display a fondness for the same unusual words, both use the same four synonyms to translate 'horse', both contain *sententiae* (apophthegms) and other florid stylistic features; in fact, the author refers to his 'composito eloquencie stilo'.[8] Take, for instance, this speech of the Black Knight of the Black Glade:[9]

'Multas cum multis congressiones inii, et nunquam me forciorem nec eciam mei parem usque hodie reperire valui. Tui autem impulsus impetus omnis me protinus pristina virtus reliquit, nec alterius modi mihi tua est experta impulsio, quam si celi et terre una adinvicem, me medio existente, fieret collisio.'

Note the balance, alliteration, like endings, and hyperbole.

The ascription of the two romances to Robert of Torigni, abbot of Mont St. Michel, who died in 1186, is absurd, as Bruce made clear.[10] As for date, the *terminus a quo* is in all likelihood 1277, the year in which Edward I besieged Llywelyn, the last native prince of Wales, in his fortress of Snowdon

---

[1] R. S. Loomis, *Arthurian Tradition*, pp. 87 f.

[2] Ibid., pp. 86–90.   [3] *MP*, xi (1914), 450, n. 1.

[4] H. Newstead, *Bran the Blessed in Arthurian Romance* (New York, 1939), pp. 135–42.

[5] Ibid., pp. 70–76.

[6] E. Levi in *GSLI*, Supplemento 16 (1914), p. 105. For text of *Bruto*, cf. Levi, *Fiore di Leggende* (Bari, 1914), pp. 201–12; *Poeti Minori del Trecento*, ed. N. Sapegno (Milan, 1952).

[7] Both texts ed. by J. D. Bruce, *Hesperia*, Ergänzungsreihe, ii (Göttingen, Baltimore, 1913). For discussions cf. Bruce, *Evolution*, ii. 33–38; P. Rajna in *Medieval Studies in Memory of G. Schoepperle Loomis* (New York, 1927), pp. 1–16; E. Brugger in *ZFSL*, xlvi (1923), 247–80, 406–40.

[8] *Hesperia*, loc. cit., pp. viii–x, 93; Rajna, loc. cit., pp. 6–14.

[9] *Hesperia*, loc. cit., p. 21.   [10] Ibid., pp. x–xv.

and starved him into surrender,[1] for just so Arthur is described as starving out Griffinus in the same region. Edward's sensational triumph served as a model for Arthur's. The one solid *terminus ad quem* is the date of the Cotton manuscript, authoritatively set early in the fourteenth century, but the three mentions of the nose-guard (*nasus cassidis*) suggest an earlier date for the texts. Oddly enough, nasals appear for the last time in English art, so far as I know, in the Painted Chamber at Westminster, completed in 1277,[2] the very year of Edward's success at Snowdon.

Though interested in things Welsh, the author was not of Welsh blood, for, if he had been, he would never have said that Snowdon was the Cambrian name of the mountain: 'Kambrice Snaudone resonat'.[3] Such common personal names as Ivorius, Griffinus, Caradocus, Meriadocus could easily have been picked up by one who had no knowledge of the Welsh language, whereas other names purporting to be British, such as Walwanius and Gwendoloena, are not close to Welsh forms.[4] The stories themselves, though incorporating much that is of ultimate Celtic origin, do not represent direct borrowings from Wales, even though the author's familiarity with the river and the town of Usk and with the fact that Caerleon (Urbs Legionum) is near by shows that he himself must have known the neighbourhood.[5] Presumably, then, he was a cleric of English or Norman blood, who lived on the marches of South Wales about 1280.

His interests extended, however, far outside the usual range of Arthurian fiction, for he sends Meriadocus to the Rhine and Walwanius to Jerusalem. Though he exploits the marvellous elements, he displays a strong tendency toward realism. He represents Meriadocus as a mercenary soldier seeking service under the Emperor of Germany for pay—a motivation quite alien to a Lancelot or a Galahad. He anticipates Defoe in his detailed explanations of contrivances and concoctions; he tells how Ivorius prepared meat in a forest without fire or cooking vessels, how Arthur besieged Griffinus in his Snowdonian stronghold with machines, a ditch, and barricades; he devotes three whole pages to the manufacture of Greek fire, which required not only pitch, sulphur, and petroleum, but also the blood of a red-headed man and water-snakes fed on a human cadaver!

Doubtless these passages were largely original, not to be found in his literary sources. As to the latter, Geoffrey of Monmouth's *Historia* is certainly one,[6] and probably Gregory of Tours supplied the Frankish names,

[1] J. E. Lloyd, *History of Wales*, 3rd ed. (London, New York, 1939), ii. 759.

[2] E. W. Tristram, *Medieval English Wall Painting, Thirteenth Century* (London, 1950), Text, p. 97; Plates, pl. 22–25; *Burlington Magazine*, vii (1905), 260.

[3] *Hesperia*, loc. cit., pp. xxv, 1.

[4] Loomis, *Arthurian Tradition*, pp. 146–51; *Annales de Bretagne*, xv (1899–1900), 533 f.

[5] *Hesperia*, loc. cit., pp. 85–87.

[6] Geoffrey's influence is seen in the names of Anna, Pope Sulpicius, and Gormundus. Ibid., pp. 54,

Gundebaldus, Guntrannus, and Moroveus.[1] The incidents, however, are drawn from the common stock of romance. *Historia Meriadoci* incorporates the following: (1) The faithless guardian orders his royal wards to be murdered; they appeal to his pity, and are allowed to live. This sequence is found in the Havelok legend and may be derived from it.[2] (2) The combats with the Black Knight of the Black Glade, the Red Knight of the Red Glade, and the White Knight of the White Glade are surely related to Gareth's encounters, in Malory's Book VII, with the Black Knight of the Black Launde and the Red Knight of the Red Launde. In both texts we have the recurrent theme of the fight at a ford, which has Welsh and Irish antecedents.[3] (3) Arthur refuses to begin a banquet till some adventure is announced—a common motif, which may also be of Irish origin.[4] (4) As in Chrétien's *Lancelot*, a lord of the land whence no one returns, abducts a woman; the same or another woman in due time provides the hero with a horse which enables him to vanquish the abductor.[5] (5) A marvellous palace appears where none had been seen before.[6] (6) The steward of this palace, who answers no questions but mocks the hero, may well be derived from the silent but mocking inhabitants of the Isle of Joy in the *Voyage of Bran*.[7] (7) The square island in the Rhine shares several peculiarities with an island described in *Sone de Nausay*.[8]

De Ortu Walwanii contains at least five traditional elements. The first, which deals with the parentage, birth, and early history of Gawain, has complex relationships. As Bruce recognized,[9] the fragmentary French poem, *Les Enfances Gauvain*,[10] also tells of Lot's liaison with Arthur's sister, the birth of Gawain, his discovery by a fisherman, and his adoption by a pope. These tales had a common Welsh source in the *enfances*, related in *Pwyll*, of Gwri of the Golden Hair, whose alternative epithet, Gwallt-a(d)vwyn, 'Bright Hair', became first Galvagin (on the Modena relief), then Galvain, then Gauvain.[11] Bruce also pointed out a remarkable similarity between the

58, 79. Cf. Geoffrey of Monmouth, *Historia Regum Britanniae*, ed. A. Griscom (New York, 1929), pp. 427 f., 447, 515. The description of Caerleon (*Hesperia*, loc. cit., p. 85) is taken verbatim from Geoffrey (ed. Griscom, p. 291).

[1] *ZFSL*, xlvi. 261 f. Brugger (ibid., pp. 250–79) refutes Bruce's thesis that these names were suggested by the Prose *Tristan*.

[2] M. Deutschbein, *Studien zur Sagengeschichte Englands* (Cöthen, 1906), pp. 134 ff.; *Hesperia*, loc. cit., p. xxx.

[3] *MP*, xliii (1945), 63–71; Loomis, *Arthurian Tradition*, pp. 127–33; J. R. Reinhard, *Survival of Geis in Mediaeval Romance* (Halle, 1933), pp. 76–79.

[4] Reinhard, op. cit., pp. 182–93.

[5] *Spec*, xx (1945), 187 f.

[6] Loomis, *Arthurian Tradition*, p. 385. Cf. J. Loth, *Mabinogion*, 2nd ed. (Paris, 1913), i. 159 f.

[7] T. P. Cross, C. H. Slover, *Ancient Irish Tales* (New York, 1936), pp. 594 f.

[8] *Hesperia*, loc. cit., pp. xxxiv f.; *Sone von Nausay*, ed. M. Goldschmidt (Tübingen, 1899), vss. 17131–90.

[9] *Hesperia*, loc. cit., pp. xlv–xlvii.   [10] *R*, xxxix (1910), 1 ff. See above, pp. 360–2.

[11] Loth, op. cit. i. 106–16; Loomis, *Arthurian Tradition*, pp. 146–51.

enfances of Gawain and those of Pope Gregory.[1] Whether this was due to the influence of the Gregory legend on that of Gawain, or whether the Gregory *enfances* themselves were derived from a combination of the Gwri story and the Coptic story of the grandson of Armenios is still an unsettled question,[2] but I incline to the latter view. A second traditional element is the hero's going under a nickname till at last his true name is revealed. Similar mystery surrounds the youthful Perceval, Lancelot, and Guinglain, and the motif can be traced back to Irish legends of Finn and Lug.[3] A third tradition tells how the hero plotted with a woman to obtain the sword with which her abductor was fated to be killed, and how this was brought about. Any Irish scholar will recognize in this the essence of the *Violent Death of Curoi*.[4] A fourth tradition, discussed by Bruce,[5] is the combination of the queen's taunt (found in *Diu Krône* and *Arthur and Gorlagon*) with the nocturnal fight at the ford (found in *Diu Krone* and *Le Lai de l'Espine*). A fifth tradition is the relief of the Castle of Maidens, which had been officially identified as Edinburgh since 1142.[6] Of this equation the author was aware since he located the castle in North Britain, but he seems ignorant of the uncanny associations which Chrétien and his continuators knew.[7] Rather we have a commonplace battle, which reminds us of the deliverance of the Queen of Maydenland in the Middle English *Sir Perceval of Galles*.[8] It seems that in spite of its late date and its idiosyncrasies, *De Ortu Walwanii* preserves a good deal of the old story of Gawain.

Very different is *Arthur and Gorlagon*, edited by Kittredge from the same early fourteenth-century manuscript which contained the two previous romances.[9] The style is unpretentious, and the cynical portrayal of womankind links it to the Breton *Lai du Cor* and *Lecheor* rather than to typical tales of chivalry. The date of composition is unknown, but, thanks to Kittredge, Krappe, Gruffydd, Malone, and Roger Bennett,[10] we are able to trace the strange history of this piece of fiction far in time and space.

[1] *Hesperia*, loc. cit., pp. xli–lv.

[2] R. S. Loomis, *Celtic Myth and Arthurian Romance* (New York, 1927), pp. 331–41; H. Sparnaay, *Verschmelzung legendarischer und weltlicher Motive* (Groningen, 1922), pp. 44 ff.

[3] *Hesperia*, loc. cit., p. lv, n. 1; W. J. Gruffydd, *Math Vab Mathonwy* (Cardiff, 1929), pp. 71, 88–91, 102–5, 120–7; Loomis, *Arthurian Tradition*, pp. 338, 406; *BBSIA*, no. 3 (1951), 71.

[4] *JEGP*, xlii (1943), 156–8; Loomis, *Celtic Myth*, pp. 12–15; R. Thurneysen, *Die irische Heldenund Königsage* (Halle, 1921), pp. 431–44.

[5] *Hesperia*, loc. cit., pp. lvii f. Cf. Loomis, *Arthurian Tradition*, pp. 128–38, 277, n. 16; *JEGP*, xlii. 170–6.

[6] Loomis, *Arthurian Tradition*, pp. 109–11.

[7] Ibid., pp. 442–59; *R*, lix (1933), 560–2.

[8] *Hesperia*, loc. cit., pp. lviii f.; H. Newstead in *PMLA*, lxiii (1948), 811–15.

[9] *(Harvard) Studies and Notes in Philology and Literature*, viii (1903), 149–275.

[10] Ibid.; *PMLA*, xliii (1928), 397–446; Gruffydd, op. cit., pp. 277–91; *Spec*, viii (1933), 209–22; xiii (1938), 68–75. *Arthur and Gorlagon* was translated by F. A. Milne in *Folk-lore*, xv (1904), 40–60; notes by A. Nutt, ibid., pp. 60–67.

The opening scene at Caerleon, when Arthur is taunted by his queen with his ignorance of feminine psychology, and his departure with Kai and Walwain to discover the secret are plainly paralleled by the opening of the ballad of *King Arthur and King Cornwall*,[1] and by a passage in the Dutch *Lancelot*.[2] Presumably, therefore, these features, including the search for some occult knowledge about women, were standard Arthurian material. So, too, was Arthur's riding his horse into a banquet-hall. The story which King Gorlagon told Arthur about his transformation by a treacherous wife into a werewolf constitutes the rest of the romance, and connects it with the Breton lais of *Bisclavret* and *Melion*. All this is quite normal, and suggests immediate French and Breton sources.

But in general outline *Arthur and Gorlagon* presents a strange resemblance to a group of modern Irish folk-tales:[3] (1) A hero set out to learn a story about women. (2) He visited a king and was sent on to another person. (3) This man reluctantly related that he had been changed by his wife with a magic wand into the form of a wolf. (4) When hunted by dogs, he had leapt on to the saddle of a friendly king and had been sheltered in his household. (5) Accused falsely of having devoured the king's child, the werewolf had revealed where the living child was hidden.

Since it is almost out of the question that the modern Irish tales were descended from a medieval Latin romance which survives in a unique manuscript, there must have been a common source. Kittredge believed this source to be Old Irish,[4] but it is unlikely that a saga which left so many offshoots not only in Irish folk-lore but also in Breton and Arthurian fiction should be unrepresented in the ample remains of older Irish literature. May it not be that in this instance the normal transmission of Irish saga material to Britain and the Continent[5] has been reversed, and that the common source of the Irish tales, *Arthur and Gorlagon*, and the episode in the Dutch *Lancelot*, *Bisclavret*, and *Melion* was Breton? This would not be wholly exceptional, for it has been shown that parts of the Irish stories of the *Slothful Gillie* (*In Gilla Decair*) and the *Great Fool* were borrowed from Arthurian romance.[6] And though Kittredge affirmed that *Arthur and Gorlagon* was based directly on a Welsh text, his evidence consisted mainly of questionable etymologies of names,[7] and Gruffydd pointed out the closer affinity to non-Welsh romances.[8]

---

[1] *English and Scottish Popular Ballads*, ed. H. C. Sargent, G. L. Kittredge (Boston, 1904), pp. 49 f. See below, p. 498.

[2] *Spec*, xiii. 68–71. Cf. also the quest for some secret knowledge about women in the *Wife of Bath's Tale* and its cognates. Sigmund Eisner, *A Tale of Wonder* (Wexford, 1957), pp. 57–59.

[3] *Studies and Notes in Philology and Literature*, viii. 162 ff.

[4] Ibid., pp. 261–4.   [5] Ibid., p. 266; *MP*, xxxiii (1936), 225–38.

[6] R. Zenker, *Ivainstudien, Beihefte ZRP*, lxx (1921), 41–83; S. J. McHugh in *MP*, xlii (1945), 197–211.

[7] *Studies and Notes in Philology and Literature*, viii. 200–9.

[8] Gruffydd, op. cit., p. 279 and n. 98. 'The Arthur of *Arthur and Gorlagon* is the later Arthur of

The odds, then, favour an elaborate Breton story as the source both of the medieval texts mentioned and of the modern Irish folk-tales.

However this may be, the ultimate source of this West European narrative type must be sought in the Orient, for Krappe and Malone found so many variants of the general plot in Yugoslavia, Turkey, Persia, and Upper Egypt that no other explanation seems possible. Though most of the recorded Oriental analogues are late, one at least, incorporated in the *Forty Viziers*, takes the tradition back to the fifteenth century.[1] In one or more of the Eastern tales the following parallels to *Arthur and Gorlagon* occur: (1) At a woman's instigation, the hero set out to learn a secret about women or a story about a woman. (2) He met and consulted three persons who sent him from one to another. (3) He wrung out of a reluctant king the story of his faithless wife. (4) She had learned from the king how he could be turned into an animal. (5) In this shape the king had won the confidence of another monarch, and saved his son. (6) He was restored to human form, and punished his wife by forcing her to eat in the presence of her paramour's severed head.

Just how this and other stories of feminine treachery were carried from the East to the West has not been established, and, of course, more than one route is possible. If the earliest Western forms of this particular story were the Breton lais, it seems likely that Breton *conteurs*, following their patrons on the First or the Second Crusade,[2] added it to their repertory. Whatever the channel of transmission, the fact remains that not only the *fabliaux* and the *exempla* but also the romances pillaged the resources of the East for farcical and melodramatic fiction.

The four Latin texts treated in this chapter raise one final question: to whom were they addressed?[3] For Andreas the answer is easy: he wrote for

---

the Continent.' 'The only evidence that I can find which might lead one to suppose that *Arthur and Gorlagon* is a translation of a Welsh original is the use of the word *diviciae*... for "dominions", "realm", .exactly like the Welsh *cyvoeth*.'   [1] *PMLA*, xliii. 428, n. 15.

[2] Robert Curthose, Duke of Normandy and one of the heroes of the First Crusade, was a liberal patron of 'mimi', that is, professional story-tellers. Cf. *Comptes Rendus de l'Académie des Inscriptions*, 1890, p. 208; William of Malmesbury, *Gesta Regum Anglorum*, ed. W. Stubbs, Rolls Series (London, 1889), ii. 461, n. 6.

[3] Three other Latin texts should be noted. One is an exemplum of Italian provenience, which Kittredge in *A Study of Gawain and the Green Knight* (Cambridge, Mass., 1916), pp. 93–97, showed was related to the theme of the imperious host in the Middle English poem. Another is an anecdote given by Pierre Bercheur in his *Reductorium Morale*, relating Gawain's visit to a subaqueous palace, where he saw a man's head on a platter. See Kittredge, op. cit., pp. 181 ff.; Helaine Newstead, *Bran the Blessed*, pp. 76–85. The third piece is Walter Map's story of Sadius and Galo in *De Nugis Curialium*, dist. iii, cap. ii (trans. F. Tupper, M. B. Ogle [London, 1924], pp. 131–55). Though neither the nomenclature nor the setting is Arthurian, Roger Bennett has demonstrated in *Spec*, xvi (1941), 34–56, that the plot follows in numerous details the stories of Gawain and Bran de Lis and of the shaming of Guerehes in the First Continuation of Chrétien's *Perceval*; that it is also related to the plot of *Amicus and Amelius*; and that it derived some of its material from the Irish saga of Fingal Ronain.

the court circle.[1] The romances of Meriadoc and Gawain were composed largely as a rhetorical exercise, and though the author may have hoped for a large group of sophisticated readers among the clergy, he evidently did not have the influence and the wealth to multiply and distribute copies. The same was probably true of the author of *Arthur and Gorlagon*, who professed to reveal the inner nature of the female sex, for, though his theme should have guaranteed him a public, the language stood in his way. If these entertaining works had been offered in French, they might well have enjoyed a limited vogue; but, as it is, they merely enjoy an obscure immortality in the stacks of great libraries and on the shelves of a few scholars.

[1] W. T. H. Jackson in *RR*, xlix (1958), 243–51.

ENGLISH RIMED AND PROSE ROMANCES

ROBERT W. ACKERMAN

THE Arthurian legend is profusely represented in Middle English literature. Nearly one-fourth of the hundred and more English romances, including several of the longest and most elaborate vernacular writings of the period, belong to the various branches of the cycle. Moreover, since a half-dozen of the Arthurian stories are extant in from two to seven copies differing at least slightly from each other in content, date, and sometimes in dialect, one may see that the bulk of the Middle English Arthuriana is considerable.[1] Malory's work and the poems composed in alliterative long lines and in rimed alliterative stanzas will be discussed later.[2] Here we are concerned with the prose romances, other than Malory's, and with the many poems written in couplets, tail-rime stanzas, and ballad metre. In the comments on those English romances the French originals of which are treated in earlier chapters, summaries of plot and reference to remoter sources are curtailed or omitted altogether.

The twenty-three separate Arthurian tales making up the group with which we are concerned have come down to us in more than thirty copies. In the order of supposed dates of composition, these tales are as follows: *Arthour and Merlin* (1250–1300), *Sir Tristrem* (*c.* 1300), *Libeaus Desconus* (before 1340), *Sir Perceval of Galles* (before 1340),[3] *Sir Launfal* (before 1340),

---

[1] The standard bibliographical guide to Middle English literature is J. E. Wells, *Manual of Writings in Middle English, 1050–1400* (New Haven, 1916) (hereafter referred to as 'Wells'), followed by nine supplements, carrying the bibliography through 1945. For the Arthurian romances (except Malory) cf. pp. 27–82 of the 1916 volume and ch. i, secs. 16–48 in the supplements. A completely revised bibliography under the editorship of J. Burke Severs is in preparation. See also *Cambridge Bibliography of English Literature*, ed. F. W. Bateson, i (1941), 130–40; v (1957), 111–13. Critical comments may be found in the late Dorothy Everett's fine essay, 'A Characterization of the English Medieval Romances', *Essays and Studies by Members of the English Association*, xv (1929), 98–121, and in Kane's *Middle English Literature* (London, 1951). In the present chapter names are spelled according to the form they most frequently assume in Middle English literature. See my *Index of the Arthurian Names in Middle English*, Stanford University Publications, University Series, x (1952). Quotations from Middle English are normalized to this extent: *i* is substituted for the 'long *i*'; 3 is represented by *gh* or *y*; þ by *th*; and the vowel often spelled *v* by *u*.

[2] See the next two chapters.

[3] The usual dating of *Sir Perceval* is 1350–1400 (Wells, p. 72), but the possibility that the romance was included in a lost portion of the Auchinleck MS. (which must have been completed before 1340) has led to the dating given here. See Laura H. Loomis in *Essays and Studies in Honor of Carleton Brown* (New York, 1940), pp. 111–28, especially pp. 116 f.

Ywain and Gawain (*c.* 1350), *Arthur* (1350–1400), Chaucer's *Wife of Bath's Tale* (1392–4), Stanzaic *Morte Arthur* (*c.* 1400), *The Carl of Carlisle* (*c.* 1400), *The Avowing of King Arthur* (*c.* 1425), Lovelich's *Holy Grail* and *Merlin* (*c.* 1430), *The Gest of Sir Gawain* (*c.* 1450), *The Wedding of Sir Gawain* (*c.* 1450), Prose *Merlin* (*c.* 1450), *Lancelot of the Laik* (1482–1500), *King Arthur's Death* (*c.* 1500), *The Green Knight* (*c.* 1500), *The Turk and Gawain* (*c.* 1500), Prose *Joseph of Arimathea* (early 16th century), *King Arthur and King Cornwall* (early 16th century), *The Boy and the Mantle* (16th century).[1]

A large number of the romances, Arthurian and otherwise, may be shown to be adaptations or fairly close translations of extant Old French romances and lais, and still others are properly regarded as derivatives of French or Latin models no longer known to us. At least a half-dozen of the French originals may have been the work of Anglo-Normans.[2] Only a small handful of the English romances, then, tell stories which could plausibly have originated with an English poet. Yet, in their adaptations and often in their translations as well, the English writers, who were addressing a later audience, tended to create a type of romance quite distinct from the French. An adequate study based on the departures of English romances from their French antecedents is yet to be made, but it would undoubtedly result in a sounder understanding of the genre of English romance than we now possess.[3] Whatever one may think of the aesthetic criticism of medieval literature exemplified in the work of a number of present-day European scholars,[4] it would seem that the extraordinary dependence of the English romances on French literature renders serious attention to source studies inescapable. Certainly, it is not irrelevant to inquire whether the author was merely attempting a translation of a French work, or whether he was striking out with a free and independent adaptation of a traditional story.[5]

Rimed couplets, various stanzaic patterns, and prose are represented in the

[1] The following stories exist in more than one version: *Arthour and Merlin* is represented in five separate forms; *Libeaus Desconus* in six manuscripts; *Sir Launfal* in six; *Sir Gawain and the Carl of Carlisle* in two; *The Wedding of Sir Gawain* in two; *Lancelot of the Laik* in two; and *Joseph of Arimathea* in two early sixteenth-century prints in addition to the alliterative version. Chaucer's *Wife of Bath's Tale*, which is listed separately from *The Wedding of Sir Gawain*, although it tells the same story, exists in numerous manuscripts, of which no account need be taken here. Some interesting observations about the time lag between the original composition and the writing down of English romances appear in H. S. Bennett, 'The Production and Dissemination of Vernacular Manuscripts in the Fifteenth Century', *The Library*, 5th ser. i (1946–7), 171–2.

[2] J. Vising, *Anglo-Norman Language and Literature* (London, 1923), pp. 45 ff.

[3] See D. Everett's essay, cited in n. 1, p. 480.

[4] Recent works in this vein are R. R. Bezzola's *Le Sens de l'Aventure et de l'Amour*, Ingeborg Dubs's *Galeran de Bretagne: Die Krise im französischen höfischen Roman*, and Hildegard Emmel's *Formprobleme des Artusromans und der Graldichtung*. See the critique by H. Newstead in *RP*, iv (1950), 68–76.

[5] Kane's study (cf. n. 1, p. 480) seems occasionally to be limited by a failure to take into account the debt which the English romances owe to their sources.

romances studied here. Two of the earliest, *Arthour and Merlin* and *Ywain and Gawain*, are in couplets of four-stress lines, and the same metre is employed in *Arthur*, *Lancelot of the Laik*, and Lovelich's two translations. One early poem, *Sir Tristrem*, is in a curious eleven-line stanza, not met with elsewhere, in which all the lines are of three stresses except for the ninth, normally an iamb. *Le Morte Arthur* is in eight-line stanzas made up of alternately rimed four-stress lines, and the four-stress lines of *The Gest of Sir Gawain* are in six-line stanzas. Two of the pieces are ballads of a fairly late date, and prose is used only in a mid-fifteenth-century translation of the Vulgate *Merlin* and several late summaries of *Joseph of Arimathea*. The remaining poems, consisting to a large extent of Gawain romances, are in tail-rime stanzas ranging from six to sixteen lines in length.

The tail-rime poems are all notably shorter than the works composed in lines of uniform length, with the exception of the versified chronicle known as *Arthur*. This consideration, together with the fact that tail-rime would seem to be well adapted to public recitation, suggests that such works are minstrel versions. Because of its stanzaic pattern, *Sir Tristrem* might also be so regarded.[1] Furthermore, the variations, particularly minor differences in plot and in name forms, to be observed among multiple copies of the same romance (the copies of *Sir Launfal* provide an example) are not infrequently of the sort which could be ascribed to the faulty memory of professional singers. It is true that Thomas Chestre's *Sir Launfal* and also *Libeaus Desconus*, which is often ascribed to the same writer, seem somewhat too sophisticated in execution to be classed with *The Turk and Gawain* and *The Avowing of King Arthur*, yet both romances probably lent themselves quite as readily to minstrel rendition. On the other hand, the couplet poems and the Stanzaic *Morte Arthur* could very well be the work either of serious poets or of translator-versifiers, poor hacks one notch above the scribes, who earned their bread in the manuscript shops.

Some support for the distinctions just made between minstrel work and the other romances is to be found in studies of the famous Auchinleck manuscript by Laura Hibbard Loomis and of the Chaucer manuscripts by Manly and Rickert, for these have made us aware that much vernacular literature was composed in manuscript shops and that the translator-versifiers in these shops seem to have specialized in couplet rather than tail-rime romances.[2] In Lovelich's two translations from the French, we apparently have an imitation of the products of the professional hacks.[3] On the other

[1] A. C. Baugh, 'The Authorship of the Middle English Romances', *Annual Bulletin of the Modern Humanities Research Association*, 1950, pp. 16 f.

[2] L. H. Loomis, 'Chaucer and the Auchinleck MS'; also *SP*, xxxviii (1941), 14–33; *PMLA*, lvii (1942), 595–627; J. M. Manly and E. Rickert, *Text of the Canterbury Tales* (Chicago, 1940), i. 604 f.

[3] *PMLA*, lxvii (1952), 473–84.

hand, the poems themselves yield little internal evidence as to authorship. Because virtually all popular literature was meant to be recited or read aloud, including that which was not executed by or for the minstrels, such characteristics of oral delivery as the constant repetition of set phrases and epithets are to be found everywhere.[1] Even the common 'Listeneth, lordings!' invocation and requests to the audience to keep quiet are scarcely proof of minstrel origin, inasmuch as remarks of this kind occur in poems like the alliterative *Morte Arthure*, which seems to be of clerical authorship, if one may judge by its display of learning and of piety.[2]

But, whether serious poets, hacks, or minstrels, the authors of most English Arthurian romances, though not all, must have been humble men to whom anonymity seemed normal and appropriate. At any rate, with the noteworthy exceptions of Malory, Henry Lovelich, and Thomas Chestre,[3] they withhold their identity from us. Such modesty suggests that few could take pride in the mention of their own names, as could the knightly Wolfram von Eschenbach or Hartmann von Aue. One is further tempted to conclude, from the dearth of such dedications as occur in Chrétien, Wace, and Froissart, that not many of the English works could have been written at the behest of an illustrious patron.[4]

In this chapter the romances are not treated in chronological order of composition, but are grouped by subject as in Wells.[5] First are discussed those romances setting forth what Wells calls 'The Whole Life of Arthur'; second, those confined mainly to 'Merlin and the Youth of Arthur'; third, 'Launcelot and the Last Years of Arthur'; fourth, 'Gawain'; fifth, 'The Holy Grail'; and finally, 'Miscellaneous Heroes'.

THE WHOLE LIFE OF ARTHUR

'Arthur'

The poem *Arthur*,[6] which is interpolated in a fragmentary Latin chronicle belonging to the Marquis of Bath,[7] is worth only the briefest notice here.

---

[1] Ruth Crosby in *Spec*, xi (1936), 88–110; and *Spec*, xiii (1938), 413–32.

[2] Baugh, loc. cit., pp. 22 f., 27.

[3] In addition, there is the enigmatic Tomas in *Sir Tristrem*.

[4] It is true that a direct reference to a poet's patron, Humphrey de Bohun, occurs in *William of Palerne* (EETSES, i, vss. 165–9, 5530), as H. S. Bennett has noted in *English Books and Readers, 1475–1557* (Cambridge, 1952), p. 4. I know of no other English romance, however, in which a clear statement about the poet's patron may be found. I feel, therefore, that Bennett's remark in the work just cited (p. 4), to the effect that many English romances were composed for noble patrons, is open to question. The dedication to the Duke of Berry and Auvergne in the English *Melusine* (EETSES, lxviii, p. 1) has been carried over from the French source.

[5] pp. 27–82.   [6] Ed. F. J. Furnivall, EETS, ii (1864).

[7] The Latin chronicle occupies fols. 35b–54, and the English poetic interpolation appears on fols. 42b–46a. See *Third Report of the Royal Commission on Historical Manuscripts* (London, 1872), p. 182. An index incorporated in the manuscript (fol. 3a) is dated 1428. On dialect see *University of Michigan Publications, Language and Literature*, xiii (1935), 51.

After a fourteen-page recital of pre-Arthurian history, the Latin breaks off and the 642-line English poem begins, summarizing what might well be Wace's account of the begetting and birth of Arthur, the duel with the Giant of Mont St. Michel, and the last battle. A completely disproportionate amount of space is given to an enumeration of Arthur's chief vassals.

The simplest explanation which may be offered for the Bath chronicle and the English poem it embodies is that the writer functioned merely as a copyist until he came to the Arthurian section, whereupon he was inspired to translate the Latin text before him into English verse. The poem is written in four-stress rimed couplets; the dialect is Southern;[1] and the date is presumably the second half of the fourteenth century.[2] Not even in recounting the passing of Arthur is the poet, who may well have been a cleric, capable of breaking away from the crude monotony of his verse.

'King Arthur's Death'

Another brief sketch of Arthur's career in ballad metre is to be found in the Percy Folio manuscript,[3] and consists of two distinct poems as has long been recognized.[4] The first 96 lines are given over to a first-person recital by Arthur himself of his begetting and some of his conquests, and the king then speaks sorrowfully about Mordred's treason and the ensuing battle in which all his followers were slain—'alas that woefull day!'[5] The remaining 155 lines set forth again, this time in the third person, the events of the last battle. The final stanza, in which it is stated that Arthur reigned as king for twenty-two years, has been shown to be the misplaced conclusion of the first of the two pieces and thus to belong after line 96.[6]

The language and metre of both poems suggest late composition, possibly the end of the fifteenth century. The first poem, in which Arthur gives his autobiography, sounds like the speech of a character in a play or pageant. The second piece is a fairly straightforward synopsis of the version of the last battle given by the Stanzaic *Morte Arthur* and Malory, with emphasis on the negotiations of the emissaries and the incident of the adder. It is conceivable that a scribe in copying the first poem was moved to append

---

[1] Two rimes based apparently on Kentish pronunciation have been noted by Bülbring in *Quellen und Forschungen zur Sprach- und Culturgeschichte der germanischen Völker*, lxiii (1889), 1–140.

[2] Wells, p. 35.

[3] *Bishop Percy's Folio Manuscript*, ed. J. W. Hales and F. J. Furnivall (London, 1867–8), i. 497–507. This edition is hereinafter referred to as 'Hales and Furnivall'.

[4] For an independent copy of the first half of the Percy Folio poem see C. B. Millican in *PMLA*, xlvi (1931), 1020–4.

[5] Ed. cit., vs. 96.

[6] Millican, loc. cit., p. 1021.

[7] See *Le Morte Arthur*, ed. J. D. Bruce, EETSES, lxxxviii (1903), vss. 3168 ff.; Malory, *Works*, ed. Vinaver, iii. 1227 ff.; also Vinaver's note, iii. 1634. But it is Lukin, Duke of Gloucester, not Bedivere, who disposes of Arthur's sword.

one of his own which would provide a more detailed account of the passing of the king.[1]

MERLIN AND THE YOUTH OF ARTHUR

The development of the Merlin legend has been traced in earlier chapters, and it is hardly necessary to say that it became well known in England, first through Geoffrey of Monmouth and Wace, later through the French romances, and lastly through English renderings from the French. The Latin chroniclers naturally make reference to the mage and his mantic powers,[2] and Robert Mannyng translated Wace's *Brut* as the first part of his *Story of England*, which he completed in 1328, and vss. 12884–19961 retell the Merlin story.[3] There are four English versions derived from French romances: besides Malory's, which is reserved for treatment in Chap. 40, they are *Arthour and Merlin*; Lovelich's poem; the Prose *Merlin*.

'Arthour and Merlin'

This romance is best preserved in the famous Auchinleck manuscript,[4] where it runs to 9,938 lines, and extends from the death of Constans to the defeat of Rion immediately after the betrothal of Arthur and Guenevere. It was composed probably in Kent during the middle years or the third quarter of the thirteenth century.[5] Though the story is obviously developed with care, there is a change of pace beginning with the events following Arthur's coronation (vs. 3133). The crown is placed on young Arthur's head by Bishop Brice (Dubricius)[6] in the presence of the great lords, and at the feast the new king rises to distribute gifts and receive homage. At this juncture, Nentres, Lott, and other kings voice their bitter objections to the crowning of Arthur, whereupon Merlin is moved to explain just as he had done only a few lines earlier (vss. 3021–40) that Arthur is indeed their legitimate ruler. This abrupt transition, involving some doubling back of the story, introduces Arthur's struggle with his rebellious vassals, which is the most important theme in the remainder of the poem. With few relieving touches, the second part is given over to detailed accounts of single combats and of general *mêlées*.

[1] Hales and Furnivall, i. 497.
[2] L. Keeler, *Geoffrey of Monmouth and the Late Latin Chroniclers, 1300–1500, Univ. of California Publications in English*, xvii, no. 1, Index *sub* Merlin and Prophecies of Merlin; R. H. Fletcher, *Arthurian Material in the Chronicles* (Boston, 1906; reprinted New York, 1958), Index *sub* Merlin.
[3] Robert Mannyng, *Story of England*, ed. F. J. Furnivall, Rolls Series (1887).
[4] Ed. E. Kölbing, *Altenglische Bibliothek*, iv (1890), 1–272. A variant version of *Arthour and Merlin* is represented, in whole or in part, by four manuscripts; Hales and Furnivall, i. 419–21.
[5] Ed. Kölbing, pp. lix f.
[6] See explanation of this name in my *Index of the Arthurian Names in Middle English*, 'Dubris'.

As Kölbing argued, the source of the Auchinleck poem must have embodied two distinct stages in the development of the history of Merlin. The first portion, up to the coronation, represents the pre-Robert story expanded from the chronicles; and the remainder the Vulgate sequel.[1] Despite the gaps and the monotonous details of battle in the last two-thirds of his work, the Auchinleck poet tells his story clearly and in the second portion, at least, he abridges considerably and to advantage. Further, the four May songs and the other nature descriptions sprinkled throughout are probably his own, whether or not one sees in them evidence that the same poet also wrote *Kyng Alisaunder* and *Richard Coer de Lyon*.[2] The nature lyrics are conventional, to be sure, yet they illustrate the smooth handling of the four-stress couplet which characterizes the entire poem.[3] The poet is self-conscious about presenting his tale in English. He observes that children who have been set early to their books have the advantage of knowing Latin and French well. As for him, he knows many an English noble who understands only English, and he will, therefore, tell his tale in that language:

> Right is, that Inglische understond,
> That was born in Inglond.[4]

(It is proper that he who was born in England understand English.)

Lovelich's 'Merlin'

Henry Lovelich's poem[5] of 27,852 lines, enormous as it is, represents only about 50 per cent. of the French *Vulgate Merlin*, of which it is a translation.[6] As already pointed out, Lovelich is one of the few writers of English romance whom we know by name, and he is unique in that he seems to have been, not a professional purveyor of romances, but rather a solid man of affairs. At least, the available evidence suggests that he was a member of the London Company of Skinners and wrote his prodigious *Merlin* and *Holy Grail* as a compliment to a fellow gildsman of no small importance in his day, Harry Barton. By choosing to emulate in his work the products of the poor translator-versifiers in the manuscript shops, Lovelich all too plainly reveals his level of literary sophistication.[7]

It is possible that Lovelich's original intention was to turn into English the whole of the Vulgate *Estoire del Saint Graal*, *Merlin*, and *Queste*.[8] He suc-

---

[1] Ed. Kölbing, pp. cxi ff. See above, pp. 322–4. [2] Ibid., pp. lx ff.
[3] Ed. cit., vss. 6595–600. [4] Ed. cit., vss. 21 f.
[5] On correct form of this name see *MLN*, lxvii (1952), 531–3.
[6] See Hales and Furnivall, i. 419; Kölbing's ed., pp. xviii–xix, &c.; *Merlin*, ed. H. B. Wheatley, EETS, cxii (1899), lxiii–lxix, especially p. lxix, n. 1.
[7] *PMLA*, lxvii (1952), 473–84.
[8] At the conclusion of his *Holy Grail*, Lovelich states that he must now begin another branch of the legend dealing with the 'Prophet Merllyne', for that too belongs to the story of Sank Ryal. He does not specifically allude to the quest story itself, however. *The Holy Grail*, ed. F. J. Furnivall, EETSES, xx, xxiv, xxviii, xxx (1874, 1875, 1877, 1878), chap. lvi, vss. 509–20.

ceeded in completing the first portion carrying the story up to the life of King Launcelot, grandfather of Launcelot de Lake, in his work entitled *The Holy Grail* (which might more accurately be called *Joseph of Arimathea*). Whether Lovelich ever completed the last half of the *Merlin*, which is lacking in our single copy, and whether he then went on to translate the Grail story proper must remain open questions. The manuscript preserving both poems is wanting some ten leaves at the beginning, and it is conceivable that a great many more leaves have been lost at the end. On the other hand, if one takes seriously the poet's lugubrious complaints about his poor eyesight and about the vast size of his appointed task, one might conclude that we have as much, or nearly as much, as Lovelich was able to produce.[1]

The exact form of the French *Merlin* which Lovelich turned into English seems not to be available, yet a comparison with Sommer's text of the Vulgate[2] indicates that he probably followed his source as closely as the exigencies of versifying permitted. The principal discrepancies between the French and English seem to arise from the poet's failure to grasp the meaning of a word or a passage in his source. Several egregious blunders of this sort are represented in Lovelich's proper names. Thus, he creates a spurious character, Sir Ambroy Oyselet, out of a French phrase, 'oiseaus au brai', 'birds in the net'; and still another knight, Sir Raynes, owes his name and his existence to Lovelich's failure to understand a phrase containing the word *roines*, 'queens'. These errors, and many more like them, would provide a devastating comment on Lovelich's ability to read French were it not that his *Holy Grail* presents no such evidence of incompetence. Perhaps we must assume that the skinner-poet had grown weary of his task before he was well into his second work and that he was content with a hurried and uncritical rendering of the French original.[3]

Literary historians are accustomed to dismiss Lovelich's poems as 'monuments of dullness', when they mention them at all.[4] There can be no doubt about the poor quality of his poetry, as a few lines from the first of his *Merlin* suffice to demonstrate:

> So as aftyrward longe beffelle,
> To gederis they conseilled, the develis, ful snelle
> And token hem to gederis in parlement,
> The maister-develis be on assent,
> And seiden: 'What mester man is he, this,
> That doth us here al this distres?'[5]

[1] *PMLA*, lxvii (1952), 483 f.
[2] *Vulgate Version of the Arthurian Romances*, ed. H. O. Sommer (Washington, 1908), ii.
[3] *PMLA*, lxvii (1952), 473–84.
[4] See, for example, Kane, op. cit., pp. 16–17. See also *PMLA*, lxvii (1952), 477.
[5] Ed. cit., vss. 9–14.

(And so it befell long afterwards that the devils gathered together very quickly in parliament to take council, and the chief devils, of one assent, said: 'What sort of man is he who causes us all this woe?')

Only a man with no ear whatever could rest content with such ragged metre and with such rimes as *he this* | *distres*. Moreover, he consistently expresses himself with the utmost awkwardness. On the other hand, one can scarcely condemn Lovelich because he could not write as well as the author of the Alliterative *Morte Arthure*.

The Prose 'Merlin'

Because the English Prose *Merlin*[1] is a fairly literal translation from the French Vulgate it requires only brief comment here.[2] The English translator is unknown, but the work is thought to have been composed about 1450, not long before Malory's *Morte Darthur*. It exists in a single manuscript, Cambridge University Library, Ff III 11.

There is a remarkably close agreement between Lovelich's poem and the prose translation, yet in certain details, especially in the forms of the proper names, the variations are sufficiently great to demonstrate that the English writers worked with different French manuscripts.[3] Further, as already indicated, the two works differ in their state of completeness. The author of the prose work achieved a better translation of his original than Lovelich, although it is by no means free from error. Brandis of the Dolorous Tour, for example, is once called Ladris.[4] What is one to think of the attentiveness of an author who allows two entirely different characters to be called by the same name? Thus, an English knight and one of the heathen invaders of Britain are both called Pynados, and the name Brangore applies both to a king of South Wales and to a heathen Saxon king.[5]

Certain faults of Lovelich's *Merlin* and also of the prose work are due to their source, a congeries of themes by no means well fitted together. The transition from one course of action to the next is more often than not disconcertingly abrupt, being signalized in the Prose *Merlin* by some phrase such as 'Now, seith the booke', or 'But now resteth to speke of hem at this time and telleth of King Arthur'.[6] At the same time, the style of the *Merlin* is far from contemptible, as a comparison with Malory shows, though one will search in vain for the subtle rhythms and the deep feeling which are in large measure responsible for the vitality of *Le Morte Darthur*. If, by chance, it had been the manuscript of the Prose *Merlin* rather than Malory's book, which was printed by William Caxton in response to the demand of 'many

---

[1] Ed. H. B. Wheatley, EETS, x, xxi, xxxvi, cxii (1865, 1866, 1869, 1899).
[2] Ibid., cxii, pp. lviii–lxii; and Kölbing's ed., pp. xix f.
[3] Ed. Wheatley, EETS, cxii, pp. lxii–lxix.   [4] *PMLA*, lxvii (1952), 482.
[5] See my *Index of the Arthurian Names in Middle English*, 'Pinados', 'Pynados', 'Brangore', and 'Brangue'.   [6] Ed. Wheatley, EETS, cxii, pp. ccxlii–ccxlvi.

noble and dyvers gentylmen of thys royame of Englond', we would have had a far more systematic narrative of the career of Merlin than Malory affords, yet we would also be immeasurably the poorer for the substitution.[1]

LAUNCELOT AND THE LAST YEARS OF ARTHUR

The career of Launcelot was not treated in English, so far as we know, till late, but then it had the good fortune to be taken up by two accomplished writers—the author of the Stanzaic *Morte Arthur* about 1400 and by Malory, some fifty to sixty years later. About the time of the publication of Caxton's Malory, 1485, appeared the Lowland Scots *Lancelot of the Laik*, a much inferior work, and still later, a Lancelot ballad of which we have only an imperfect copy.[2]

A separate chapter of the present volume is devoted to Malory's *Morte Darthur*, but a brief comment on the Launcelot material embedded in it may be permitted here. In that work, Launcelot is easily the most important personage next to Arthur himself. But his eminence is not surprising when one considers that, of the twenty-one books into which Caxton divided the *Morte Darthur*, more than half were drawn, at least in part, from various sections of the great French Prose *Lancelot*. The last four books in particular contain much Launcelot material. The tale of the poisoned apple, in which Launcelot saves Guenevere from a false charge of murder, and the account of the Maid of Astolat were both derived from the French *Mort Artu*, although strong claims for Malory's use here of the English Stanzaic *Morte Arthur* have been advanced.[3] The first chapters of Book XX were apparently taken from some debased form of Chrétien's *Lancelot*,[4] but the rest of Book XX and also Book XXI, recounting the war resulting from the adultery of Launcelot and Guenevere, the treason of Mordred, and the passing of Arthur, reveal Malory's occasional dependence on the English *Morte Arthur*.[5]

'Le Morte Arthur'

The Stanzaic *Morte Arthur*,[6] then, influenced some of Malory's greatest passages, but it deserves attention also on the score of its own merits. Though marred by faults typical of the minstrel style, it tells a moving story vividly and swiftly.

[1] For example, cf. Prose *Merlin* (EETS, x, p. 108) with the corresponding passage in Malory (*Works*, ed. Vinaver, i. 17).

[2] See Hales and Furnivall, i. 84–87; and A. J. App, *Lancelot in English Literature, His Role and Character* (Washington, 1929), pp. 1–90.

[3] R. H. Wilson, 'Malory, the Stanzaic *Morte Arthur*, and the *Mort Artu*', *MP*, xxxvii (1939–40), 125–38; Malory, *Works*, ed. Vinaver, iii. 1572–8; and E. T. Donaldson, 'Malory and the Stanzaic *Le Morte Arthur*', *SP*, xlvii (1950), 460–72.   [4] Vinaver's ed. iii. 1578–81.

[5] Wilson, loc. cit.; and Vinaver's ed. iii. 1600–12.

[6] Ed. J. D. Bruce, EETSES, lxxxviii (1903).

The first of the eight-line stanzas in which the poem is composed is the usual invocation of the minstrel:

> Lordingis that ar leff And dere,
> Lystenyth and I shall you tell
> By olde dayes what aunturs were
> Amonge oure eldris that by-felle:
> In Arthur dayes, that noble kinge,
> By-felle Aunturs ferly fele,
> And I shall telle of there endinge
> That mykell wiste of wo and wele.[1]

(Lords, beloved and dear, listen while I tell you what adventures took place in the old days among our forefathers: in the days of Arthur, that noble king, wondrously many adventures befell, and I shall tell you of the ending of those who knew much of weal and woe.)

Two separate episodes of Launcelot's career are skilfully interwoven in the tale that ensues: first, the hero's entanglement with the Maid of Astolat and his championship of the queen when she is falsely accused of the poisoning of an Irish or Scottish knight; and second, the discovery of the adulterous union of Launcelot and Guenevere and its tragic sequel—the siege of Benwick and the death of Arthur.

The source of the romance, which was composed about 1400 in the Northwest Midlands,[2] is apparently the French *Mort Artu* in a version somewhat different from the one known to us;[3] we cannot, therefore, be sure how literally the poet has rendered his original. In the single manuscript containing the English poem, Brit. Mus. Harley 2252, a leaf is missing, and the loss of seven pairs of lines in other portions of the work is revealed by irregularities in the stanza form. The narrative is so closely knit, however, that the reader can guess accurately the sense of the missing passages. The lines on the lost leaf, for example, must have dealt with the honourable burial given the Maid of Astolat. The story is told economically in 3,969 lines, rimed alternately, two riming sounds each to the eight-line stanza. The metre is regular, and though many of the common romance clichés appear, they generally advance the action rather than serve as mere line-fillers.

As Kane observes, we have here none of the rich imagery of the Alliterative *Morte Arthure* or of *Gawain and the Green Knight*. Though a man of less imagination than his two near-contemporaries, the composer of *Le Morte Arthur* nevertheless succeeds by the strength of humbler virtues—his good taste, his sense of proportion, and his sound ear.[4] If a sense of Launcelot's moral obloquy—in particular, the hero's brazen assertion of innocence on the

[1] Ed. cit., vss. 1-8.   [2] Bruce's ed., pp. xx ff.
[3] *Mort Artu*, ed. J. D. Bruce (Halle, 1910). See preface, especially pp. viii ff.
[4] Kane, op. cit., pp. 65-69.

part of Guenevere and himself—ever crossed the English poet's mind, he resisted the temptation to criticize Launcelot or to bring the ethics of courtly love into question.[1] He knew a good story when he heard one, and without much doubt he considerably enhanced the tale by his direct, uncomplicated retelling of it. No wonder that Malory followed him closely in his narrative of the last battle, the passing of Arthur, and Launcelot's last interview with Guenevere.

'Lancelot of the Laik'

The late fifteenth-century Scots *Lancelot of the Laik*[2] is the sole Arthurian work in the English language which refers to the contemporaneous political scene. Only in this respect is the romance of much interest, for otherwise it is a badly conceived rehandling of the first portion of the French Prose *Lancelot*.

The prologue of 334 lines, evidently original with our poet, opens with a welcome to spring:

> The soft morow ande The lustee Aperill,
> The wynter set, the stormys in exill,
> Quhen that the brycht & fresch illumynare
> Uprisith arly in his fyre chare. . . .[3]

(The soft morning and lusty April, the winter past, the storms in exile—the time when the bright and fresh luminary rises early in his fiery chariot.)

Even more clumsily reminiscent of Chaucer than the introductory lines is the succeeding passage in which the poet, who is also a lover, dreams that a bird sent by the God of Love is offering advice to him:

> 'Sum trety schall yhoue for thi lady sak,
> That wnkouth is, als tak one hand and mak,
> Of love, ore armys, or of sum othir thing.'[4]

('You shall also take in hand and compose for the sake of your lady some treatise hitherto unknown about love, or arms, or some other subject.')

The dreamer all too accurately protests his lack of skill in rhetoric, and even his inability to read French well; nevertheless, he decides to translate a portion of a French story he has heard concerning Arthur, Galiot the son of the Fair Giant, and Launcelot.

Because the romance is incomplete in our single copy, the main drift of the story which follows becomes clear only when we fill it out from the French.[5] In general, it concerns a war between Arthur and a rival, King Galiot

---

[1] See App, op. cit., pp. 41–45.
[2] Ed. W. W. Skeat, EETS, vi (1865); and Margaret M. Gray, *Scottish Text Society*, ii (1912). Quotations are from the latter edition. [3] Ed. cit., vss. 1–4.
[4] Ed. cit., vss. 145–7. [5] See Sommer, *Vulgate Version*, iii. 244–63.

(Galehaut). Launcelot, fighting first on one side, then the other, is instrumental in arranging a truce. Galiot brings about a meeting of the hero and Guenevere, from which the fateful love affair is born. At the height of the fighting, just before the truce, the poet pauses to describe a long conversation between Arthur and a clerk named Amytans. This wise man arrives in Arthur's camp to warn the king that he has lost the esteem of God and the hearts of his people because he attends only to his own pleasure and does not protect the poor. Upon Amytans's insistence, Arthur then confesses humbly to a priest. Almost at once, two noble messengers announce Galiot's willingness to grant a truce of one year, and Amytans is not slow to point out to the king the reward he has received for his penitence. The wise man then launches into a lengthy discourse on the duties of a virtuous prince. After listening to this flood of excellent counsel, the king acknowledges that his heart is now at ease. Throughout the ensuing year, he is careful to govern according to Amytans's precepts.

In the French the wise man, to whom no name is assigned,[1] continues his speech to Arthur for only a few lines beyond the interruption caused by Galiot's messengers.[2] The extended form of Amytans's discourse in the English suggested to Skeat the possibility that the poet meant to hint at the turbulent conditions prevailing under James III of Scotland (1460–88), a monarch who, like Arthur, was in the habit of consulting astrologers.[3] A later study develops this thesis and explains the medieval political doctrine embodied in Amytans's advice.[4] The probability of historical allusions is strengthened by the fact that in *Lancelot of the Laik*, just as in *Golagros and Gawain* and certain other Arthurian works of Northern origin, a prominent theme is the demand for homage. Such an emphasis may well reflect the concern of many Scots of this period over relations with the English.[5] Galiot's voluntarily rendered homage to Arthur in the poem is conceivably an expression of one attitude prevailing in the North on this subject. It is easy, then, to imagine that the poet was presuming to offer good advice to a reigning monarch of the character of James III.

Largely on the basis of the Amytans passage, the composition of *Lancelot of the Laik* is placed between 1482 and 1500. The confusion of dialect forms in the single copy, Cambridge University Library Kk I 5, indicates that an English scribe tampered with the original Scots.[6] The poem is written in decasyllabic rimed couplets, but the metre is notably irregular and rough. The major theme, in keeping with the dream-vision framework, is the dawning love of Launcelot and Guenevere. Instead, however, of subordinating

[1] See B. Vogel, 'Secular Politics and the Date of *Lancelot of the Laik*', *SP*, xl (1943), 4–5.
[2] See Sommer, *Vulgate Version*, iii. 215–23.   [3] Skeat's ed., pp. xi f.
[4] Vogel, loc. cit., pp. 1–13.
[5] Gray's ed., pp. xiii f.
[6] See Skeat's ed., pp. xiv–xix; and Gray's ed., pp. xx–xxiii.

the other elements to the development of this theme, the poet actually expands them considerably, particularly the Amytans incident. It is true, as Kane notes, that the attempt to write in 'aureate' English had an unfortunate effect on the poet's style,[1] yet the primary defect seems rather to lie in the endeavour to combine love and politics.

GAWAIN

More than one critic has remarked that Gawain is probably more fully represented in English literature before Malory than Arthur himself.[2] At least, he is omnipresent in the role of an important knight in Arthur's household, and in no fewer than seven of the romances he is indisputably the hero. One peculiarity of the English Gawain poems is that, as a group, they are far more independent of earlier French literature than the English works devoted to other heroes. This circumstance supports the belief that Arthur's nephew was a perennial English favourite. Indeed, the Stanzaic *Morte Arthur*, Malory's *Morte Darthur*, and possibly *The Gest of Sir Gawain* are the only English works extant in which the hero appears in the degraded state to which he is reduced in the later French romances.[3]

The relationships binding the Gawain poems together are puzzling and, despite a full century of inquiry,[4] they are far from settled today. Jessie Weston, noting in the First Continuation of Chrétien's *Perceval* parallels to a few of the English adventures of Gawain, put forward the hypothesis that the English Gawain poems are survivors of a large body of such episodic tales which have otherwise vanished completely.[5] The Weston theory provoked Bruce's severe critique in his chapter entitled 'Miss Weston's Gawain-Complex'.[6] But study of the recurring motifs and of their combinations continues.[7] The Gawain romances will be treated in three groups: those in which one of the chief characters is decapitated; those concerned with the performance of vows or boasts; those which connect Gawain with a Loathly Lady.[7] *The Gest of Sir Gawain*, which falls into none of these groups, will be discussed after *The Avowing of Arthur*.

'The Carl of Carlisle'

This poem provides an interesting example of a tale, composed of traditional matter, which was converted, although imperfectly when compared

[1] Kane, op. cit., p. 17.   [2] J. L. Weston, *Legend of Sir Gawain* (London, 1897), pp. 2 ff.

[3] On Gawain's reputation see Whiting's thorough study in *Medieval Studies*, ix (1947), 189–234.

[4] Sir Frederick Madden's great anthology, *Syr Gawayne, A Collection of Ancient Romance Poems by Scotish and English Authors*, was published in 1839.

[5] J. L. Weston, *Legend of Sir Perceval* (London, 1906, 1909), i. 282–97, 323.

[6] Bruce, ii. 91–103. Note Roach's view in *Romans du Graal dans la Littérature des XIIe et XIIIe Siècles* (Paris, 1956), pp. 88, 117.

[7] *BBSIA*, no. 9 (1957), pp. 128–31; Frappier in *RP*, xi (1958), 331–44.

with *Gawain and the Green Knight*, into a sort of tract on knightly virtues. The full story of the enchanted Carl of Carlisle may be recovered only by consulting both of the extant versions—the fourteenth- or early fifteenth-century poem in the Porkington manuscript and the much later text in the Percy Folio manuscript.[1]

The adventures take place in the hall of a terrible giant, the Carl of Carlisle, where Gawain, Kay, and Bishop Baldwin take shelter after a day of hunting. Having successfully undergone certain tests of bravery, courtesy, and obedience, imposed upon him by his host, Gawain relieves the Carl from 'all false witchcraffte' by striking off his head. Now transformed into his normal human shape (in the Porkington version the change comes abruptly and without the disenchantment), the Carl promises to forsake his evil life and to build a chantry wherein priests will pray continually for the souls of his victims. Gawain and the Carl's daughter are then married by the bishop and rich gifts are exchanged. Arthur himself is summoned to a great feast at the castle, after which he knights the Carl, confers on him the lordship of Carlisle, and makes him a member of the Round Table.

No single source for *The Carl* is known. Although the tempting of Gawain by the Carl's wife and the beheading are strongly reminiscent of the experiences of the same hero in the country of the Green Knight, the parallelism is not so close that one may assume direct dependence upon *Gawain and the Green Knight*. And the scattered analogues that have been noted in *Le Chevalier à l'Epée*, *Hunbaut*, and in Irish literature[2] are probably the result of independent treatments of the same basic themes. One recent critic thinks that the frame-story belongs to the type known as the Imperious Host.[3] But, even if one concedes the presence of this motif, the analysis advanced by Kittredge and others is still to be preferred. According to this theory, *The Carl* represents fundamentally a combination of the type of the Giant's Daughter (a special form of the temptation such as we find in *Gawain and the Green Knight*) and the Beheading Game or Champion's Bargain of the Irish *Bricriu's Feast*.[4] In any case, it seems clear that the composer of the first romance version, whether he wrote in French or English, was seeking to celebrate the knightly courtesy and bravery of Gawain.

The Porkington and the Percy Folio versions of *The Carl* differ widely in form. The first consists of 660 lines arranged in twelve-line stanzas riming

[1] For the Porkington MS. poem, see my edition, *University of Michigan Contributions in Modern Philology*, no. 8 (1947). For the Percy Folio version, see Hales and Furnivall, iii. 275–94. A parallel-text edition of both poems by Auvo Kurvinen has appeared more recently: *Sir Gawain and the Carl of Carlisle in Two Versions*, *Annales Academiae Scientiarum Fennicae*, Ser. B, tom. 71, 2 (Helsinki, 1951). Quotations are taken from my edition.

[2] Kurvinen's ed., pp. 80–111.

[3] Ibid., pp. 86 ff.

[4] G. L. Kittredge, *Study of Gawain and the Green Knight* (Cambridge, Mass., 1916), pp. 9 ff. See also the discussion of the relation of *The Carl* to Curoi's Castle in *PMLA*, xlvii (1932), 331–4.

aabccbddbeeb. The couplet-lines are of four stresses as a rule, and the tail-lines of three. The Percy Folio poem of 500 lines is in couplet form, but the lines are irregular in length. The fact that a significant number of those lines of the Folio version which correspond to the short tail-lines of the Porkington text are of only three stresses suggests that the common source of both was a tail-rime poem. On this basis, it is argued that the tail-rime Porkington romance is somewhat closer to the lost original than the other. There is general agreement on placing the composition of the earlier poem about 1400 and localizing it in or near Shropshire.[1] The later version is thought to have been written in Lancashire during the first half of the sixteenth century.[2] Both versions are crude, and the scene in which the Carl puts Gawain to bed with his wife is scarcely treated with finesse:

> To the bede he went full sone,
> Fast and that good spede.
> For softnis of that ladys syde
> Made Gawain do his wyll that tyde,
> There of Gawain toke the carle goode hede.
> When Gawain wolde have donn the prevey fare,
> Then seyd the carle, 'whoo there!
> That game i the for-bede'.[3]

(He went to bed promptly and with good speed. The softness of the lady's side incited Gawain to do what he wished on that occasion, but the Carl took good heed of Gawain. When Gawain would have done the secret act, then the Carl said, 'Whoa there! I forbid that game to you!')

The contrast between this passage and the finely wrought scenes in *Gawain and the Green Knight* is a measure of the respective taste of the two poets. Kane's charge that the poetry is 'technically poor, cheap, and coarse fibred' applies with sufficient accuracy to both versions, but his further characterization of the romance as a 'burlesque' is questionable.[4] Possibly the feeling that the poet overdoes the clownish aspects of the Carl, whose wine flagon holds nine gallons, has led to this dictum. Yet, the term 'burlesque' normally implies more literary sophistication than one may seriously impute to the author of *The Carl.* The poet, in fact, seems to have been a simple man, perhaps a minstrel, who intended little if any humour in his portrayal of the dreadful Carl and whose compliment to Gawain as the knight of courtesy is almost painfully sincere.

'The Turk and Gawain'

The Turk and Gawain,[5] a tail-rime poem written in the North or North-west Midlands and, roughly speaking, about 1500, has much in common

---

[1] Ackerman's ed., p. 13; Kurvinen's ed., pp. 51, 53.
[2] Kurvinen's ed., p. 63.
[3] Ed. cit., vss. 461–8.
[4] Op. cit., p. 53.
[5] Hales and Furnivall, i. 88–102.

with *The Carl* besides its external form and its place of origin. So mutilated, however, are the pages of the Percy Folio containing the only known copy that we can only guess at the nature of several important episodes. Approximately 288 lines or nearly one-half of the poem are lost, having been written on pages that were partially torn out to light the fires by maids in Sir Humphrey Pitt's household.[1]

The early part of the story and the concluding incident, involving a challenge and the beheading of the challenger (a Turk or dwarf) by Gawain, are obviously connected in some way with the beheading in *The Carl* and *Gawain and the Green Knight*. But the adventures in which the Turk acts as Gawain's guide and assistant, not duplicated elsewhere in English,[2] parallel rather closely certain episodes in the twelfth-century *Pèlerinage de Charlemagne*.[3] That is, the lifting of the brass tennis ball by the Turk corresponds to William of Orange's feat with the huge *pelotte* in the *Pèlerinage*, the tossing of the giant into the cauldron is reminiscent of the boast of Ernalt to the effect that he can sit in a bath of molten lead, and the Turk's invisible garment is similar in function to Aimer's 'chapel' or cap. Moreover, the role of the Turk in this series of tasks is roughly the same as that of the angel in the *Pèlerinage*.[4] Still other elements of the French epic seem to be mirrored in the ballad, *King Arthur and King Cornwall*, which is to be discussed next.

The fact that *The Turk* and *King Arthur and King Cornwall* embody different elements which are found in the *Pèlerinage* suggests that the Charlemagne story, more or less in its present form, served as a source for both Arthurian pieces. But other theories are not lacking, chief among which is the possibility that the account of a king who visits the marvellous, or Otherworld, palace of a rival monarch was earlier associated with King Arthur, and that the Charlemagne epic is itself derived from the now lost Arthurian *conte*. This view receives support from the fact that several Arthurian romances, including Heinrich von dem Türlin's *Krône*, Ulrich von Zatzikhoven's *Lanzelet*, and *Arthur and Gorlagon*, contain quite clearly related episodes.[5] It has further been shown that the themes of the reproving wife, the Otherworld visit, and the gab are of Celtic provenance, occurring in such Irish sagas as the tenth-century *Second Battle of Moytura*.[6]

The exact relationship between the version of the beheading in *The Turk* and those in *The Carl* and *Gawain and the Green Knight* cannot be established with any certainty because of the absence of intermediate documents. It is

---

[1] Hales and Furnivall, i, p. xii.   [2] Kittredge, op. cit., pp. 123 ff.

[3] Ibid., pp. 118 ff.; and K. G. T. Webster in *ES*, xxxvi (1906), 357–60.

[4] Kittredge, op. cit., pp. 123 ff.; and J. R. Hulbert, 'Syr Gawayne and the Grene Kny3t', *MP*, xiii (1915–16), 703 ff.

[5] Kittredge, op. cit., pp. 274 ff.; and Hulbert, loc. cit., pp. 697 ff.

[6] Webster, loc. cit., pp. 348 ff.; and J. R. Reinhard, 'Some Illustrations of the Mediaeval *Gab*', *University of Michigan Publications in Language and Literature*, viii (1932), 38–57.

clear, however, that *The Turk* is closer than *The Carl* to *Gawain and the Green Knight* in at least two respects: first, the fact that Gawain must journey to a far country to receive a return blow, and second, the suggestive detail that the Turk lives in or near a hollow hill.[1] We can probably assume, then, that the first portion of *The Turk* represents a free adaptation of a tale fairly close to the original source of both *Gawain and the Green Knight* and *The Carl*, and that the remainder, as already suggested, comes from a story about a king's visit to his rival's palace which had already, perhaps, been attached to Arthur. In combining his two sources, however, the poet changed the be-spelled knight, the challenger, from the monster required by the original beheading tale to a helpful attendant.

Even after making allowances for the mutilated state of the manuscript, one is likely to conclude that the story related in *The Turk* is much less satisfying than that of *The Carl*. Moreover, the rhymester who wrote it shows himself incapable of rising above doggerel.

> he [Gawain] drew forth the brand of steele
> that in battell bite wold weele
> & there stroke of his head,
>
> And when the blood in the bason light,
> he stood up a stalwortht Knight
> that day, I undertake,
>
> & song 'Te deum laudamus,
> worshipp be to our lord Jesus,
> that saved us from all wracke !'[2]

(He drew forth the sword of steel, which would bite well in battle, and struck off his head. And when the blood poured into the basin, he stood up, a stalwart knight, that day, I declare, and sang '*Te Deum Laudamus*, praise be to our Lord Jesus, who saved us from all destruction'.)

'*The Green Knight*'

This romance of 516 lines in tail-rime stanzas is found in the Percy Folio.[3] It tells essentially the same story as the great masterpiece, *Gawain and the Green Knight*, and it seems to be a condensation of the earlier poem based on a very hazy memory and composed by a minstrel of the South Midlands about 1500. In the process all the mystery, suspense, and power have evaporated. It is noteworthy that the Green Knight's home is located at Castle Hutton in the West Country, presumably Hutton Manor in Somersetshire, and that

---

[1] Kittredge, op. cit., pp. 123 ff.; Hulbert in *MP*, xiii (1915–16), 703 ff.
[2] Ed. cit., vss. 286–94.
[3] Hales and Furnivall, i. 56–77. See Kittredge, op. cit., pp. 125–36, 282–9, 296. Wells, op. cit., ch. i, no. 32.

Arthur's court seems to be placed both at Carlisle and at an unidentified Castle of Flatting in Delamere Forest, Cheshire. Gawain accepts from his temptress not a green 'lace', as in the earlier romance, but a white, and this token of his delinquency is adopted as the badge of the Order of the Bath. As a matter of fact, a shoulder-knot of white silk was worn in the fifteenth century by new members of the order, not to be removed until some doughty deed had been performed.

'King Arthur and King Cornwall'

King Arthur and King Cornwall[1] is a ballad which had the misfortune to be copied in the same damaged part of the Percy Folio as *The Turk and Gawain*, and the 301 lines preserved represent no more than one-half of the original text. Enough is left, however, to reveal a strong resemblance in plot to the *Pèlerinage de Charlemagne*. It is true that the gabs and the deeds actually performed do not match exactly those ascribed in the *chanson de geste* to Charlemagne and his peers, and, in fact, may show the influence of a traditional tale about a magical horse, horn, and sword.[2] Nevertheless, in their nature and in their sequence, a number of the chief events agree so closely with the story of the *Pèlerinage* that one may be readily persuaded to assume direct dependence of the English ballad upon the French poem, or at least, as Gaston Paris has suggested, upon one of the two independent stories making up that work—namely, the story of the king who visits his rival.[3] But, before one may accept this relationship, one must acknowledge the existence of such Arthurian analogues as are cited in the discussion of *The Turk and Gawain*. Again, one must note that a combination of the pilgrimage motif with a visit to the palace of a great king appears in Arthurian works like *Golagros and Gawain*.[4] On the whole, then, it seems more probable that the author of *Arthur and Cornwall* joined together certain motifs which he found already associated with Arthur than that he converted some form of the *Pèlerinage* into an Arthurian tale.[5]

The story of *Arthur and Cornwall* probably once existed in romance form, although to detect signs of its earlier character in the impersonal language and manner of the sixteenth-century ballad is difficult. But the ballad maker, so far as one can judge from the mutilated text, retold the tale swiftly and naturally in accordance with conventions of that popular type.

[1] Hales and Furnivall, i. 59–73; F. J. Child, *English and Scottish Popular Ballads* (Boston, New York, 1883–98; reprinted New York, 1956), i. 274–88. Hereafter referred to as Child.

[2] Child, i. 282 n.

[3] *Histoire Littéraire de la France*, xxx (Paris, 1888), 110 f.

[4] Webster, loc. cit., esp. pp. 338 f., n. 3. Here Webster seeks to answer the argument advanced by W. D. Briggs in *JEGP*, iii (1901), 342–51, to the effect that the palmer's garb mentioned in *Arthur and Cornwall* is convincing evidence of the dependence of the English poem on *Le Pèlerinage*.

[5] See above, p. 477; p. 496, n. 6, and Loomis, *Arthurian Tradition*, pp. 134–8.

'The Avowing of King Arthur, Sir Gawain, Sir Kay, and Baldwin of Britain'

The *Avowing*[1] is placed among the Gawain poems arbitrarily since the principal character is actually the somewhat obscure figure, Baldwin of Britain.[2] Though the title might suggest that the plot resembled that of the other boasting poem, *Arthur and Cornwall*, yet there is little similarity in content, tone, or form. The action deals with the performance of certain vows made by Arthur and his three knights after they have met a huge boar in Inglewood Forest.[3] Arthur promises to slay 'yon Satanas', Gawain to watch all night at the Tarn Wadling, and Kay to patrol the forest until dawn and kill anyone who opposes him. These vows rise naturally enough out of the situation, and conform well to the knightly practice celebrated in such poems as the *Voeux du Paon*.[4] Baldwin's threefold promise, however, is quite unrelated to the boar hunt or to the perilous wilderness in which it takes place; he will not be jealous of his wife or any fair woman, nor refuse food to any man, nor fear any threat of death. He seems to feel no obligation to make good on these statements,[5] but Arthur sees to it that he is put to the trial. When he comes through the three tests successfully, he tells of three experiences which have led him to adopt these principles of conduct. The tale told to prove the futility of jealousy, far from being a pious or chivalric exemplum, is an ultra-cynical *fabliau* of the type known as the Woman Wrongly Accused.[6] The characters are more than mere stereotypes and possess individuality. Not only is Arthur adventurous and brave, but he has a flair for practical jokes, and has a bluff, comradely way with his knights. Kay is the irrepressible and shameless scoffer, Baldwin a disillusioned, wordly-wise old man.

The *Avowing* survives only in a single manuscript, and, though composed probably in the North about 1425, has been copied by a scribe of the West Midlands.[7] The tail-line stanzas rime *aaabcccbdddbeeeb*. There are a few stanzas which are linked by the repetition of one or more words at the end of one stanza in the first line of the next; and the pious opening line, 'He that made us on molde [earth]', is echoed in the last.[8] The author handles both

---

[1] *Three Early English Metrical Romances*, ed. J. Robson (London, 1842), pp. 57–93; *Middle English Metrical Romances*, ed. W. H. French, C. B. Hale (New York, 1930), pp. 607–46. Quotations are from the latter edition.

[2] Not to be confused with Bishop Baldwin in *The Carl of Carlisle*, on whom see *Sir Gawain and the Green Knight*, ed. I. Gollancz, EETS, ccx (1940), p. 99.

[3] This is the same district in which *The Marriage of Gawain* and *The Awntyrs of Arthur* are laid.

[4] See E. A. Greenlaw, 'The Vows of Baldwin', *PMLA*, xiv (1906), 575–636, especially p. 577, n. 1; and Reinhard, loc. cit., pp. 27–57, especially pp. 37 f.

[5] Greenlaw, loc. cit., pp. 578–9.   [6] Ibid., pp. 579–636.

[7] Mary S. Serjeantson in *RES*, iii (1927), 319–31; and L. C. Tihany in *Summaries of Doctoral Dissertations, North-western University*, iv (1936), 5–7.

[8] M. P. Medary, 'Stanza-Linking in Middle English Verse', *RR*, vii (1916), 243–70; A. C. L. Brown, 'Origin of Stanza-Linking in English Alliterative Verse', ibid., pp. 271–83.

the intricate rime-scheme and the metre with competent craftsman-
ship.

'The Gest of Sir Gawain'

The Gest of Sir Gawain[1] is of far less interest than the other Gawain
poems. The hero's dalliance with a beautiful lady in a pavilion is interrupted,
first by her father, and then, in turn, by each of her three brothers. Gawain
easily defeats the first three of the outraged knights in combat, but the fourth,
Brandles, proves to be so doughty a fighter that the duel is broken off on the
understanding that it will be resumed 'even there as ether other may fynde'.
Sir Brandles then beats his erring sister black and blue, after which she
wanders off never again to be seen. The poem ends on a strangely unheroic
note; Gawain and Brandles never met again; 'Full glade were those
knyghtes therfore.' The poet does not explicitly censure Gawain for the
seduction nor does he seem aware of the tragedy in the young girl's situation.
The only trace of an uneasy conscience he allows to Gawain is the hero's
admonition to each of his adversaries that 'ye do no harme unto the mayde'.

The source of the romance is to be found in two passages in the First
Continuation of Chrétien's Perceval.[2] In the first, the seduction is described,[3]
and in the second, Gawain, called upon to explain his alarm at finding himself
in Brandles's castle, gives a quite different version in which he confesses the
crime of rape.[4] Brandles and Gawain thereupon engage in their second duel
and cease only upon the pleas of the young woman of the pavilion who
appears with the child, Ginglain, whom she has borne to Gawain. Whether
the English poet was acquainted with the full account of the siege of Branlant, of which the Brandles tale forms only an interlude in his French source,
cannot be determined with certainty. Yet, the emphasis laid upon two features
of The Gest—the complete discarding of the girl after the beating and the
express denial that Gawain and Brandles ever met again—suggests that the
poet was consciously altering his original in order to write a short romance
with a well-defined conclusion.

The manuscript, Douce 261 at the Bodleian Library, is almost unique
among English manuscripts of romance in providing illustrations, crude
drawings, most of which depict Gawain in combat. The poem, defective at
the beginning, consists of 541 lines in six-line stanzas riming aabccb, and was
composed in the South or South Midlands sometime during the middle or
later years of the fifteenth century. On the whole, the versification is smooth

---

[1] In Syr Gawayne, ed. Madden, pp. 207–23.
[2] Ibid., pp. 348–51; JEGP, xxxiii (1934), 57–63.
[3] Continuations of the Old French Perceval, ed. W. Roach (Philadelphia, 1949), i. 69–81.
[4] Ibid., pp. 265–84. For an explanation of the inconsistency see Frappier in RP, xi (1958),
pp. 336–9.

and the narrative, as the synopsis suggests, well knit. The basic fault, of
course, is the poet's callous indifference to the pathos implicit in the tale.

'The Wedding of Sir Gawain and Dame Ragnell' and Chaucer's 'Wife of Bath's Tale'

The wide appeal of the tale of the Loathly Lady Transformed is attested
by its appearance in numerous literary works in Irish, French, Old Norse,
and other vernaculars.[1] In English alone, the pattern is found in several
forms: in addition to a romance, *The Wedding of Sir Gawain and Dame
Ragnell*, we have Chaucer's *Wife of Bath's Tale*, Gower's *Tale of Florent*,[2]
and three ballads, *The Marriage of Gawain*, *King Henry*,[3] and *The Knight
and the Shepherd's Daughter*.[4] Of these six treatments, only the three in which
the characters have Arthurian names are discussed here—namely, *The
Wedding of Gawain*,[5] *The Marriage of Gawain*,[6] and *The Wife of Bath's
Tale*.[7]

The stories related in *The Wedding* and *The Wife's Tale* agree in general
outline. In both, a man's life depends on his finding the right answer to the
question, What do women most desire? There are, nevertheless, significant
differences in detail. In *The Wedding*, the man whose life is at stake is King
Arthur, and the hero, the bridegroom, is Gawain. The offence which brings
Arthur into jeopardy is his alleged bestowal of lands belonging to Gromore
Somyr Joure on Gawain. In Chaucer, the roles of Arthur and Gawain are
combined in one man, an unnamed bachelor of Arthur's court. This man is
guilty of rape, for which crime he is tried, convicted, and sentenced to death.
On Queen Guenevere's petition, however, he is offered life and freedom pro-
vided he can find in one year the answer to the fateful question. The correctness of the forest hag's solution, which is whispered into the knight's ear and
dramatically withheld until he appears before the court, is acknowledged by
Guenevere and her ladies. The marriage follows soon thereafter, as in *The
Wedding*, but here it is a secret affair rather than a great state occasion. Also,
the alternatives put to the bridegroom on the wedding night differ somewhat.
In *The Wedding*, the hag asks whether her husband wishes her fair by day
or by night, but in *The Wife's Tale*, he must decide whether he will have
her fair and promiscuous or ugly and faithful. The outcome is happy in both
versions, however, because in the former she becomes beautiful day and
night, and, in the latter, virtuous as well as beautiful. Finally, Ragnell, in
The Wedding, recovering her proper shape after Gawain's heartfelt kiss,

[1] G. H. Maynadier, *The Wife of Bath's Tale* (London, 1901), pp. 23 ff.
[2] Gower, *Works*, ed. G. C. Macaulay (Oxford, 1901), ii. 74–86.
[3] Child, i. 297–300.   [4] Ibid. i. 457–77.
[5] Ed. Laura Sumner, *Smith College Studies in Modern Languages*, v, no. 4 (1924).
[6] Hales and Furnivall, i. 103–18; Child, i. 288–96.
[7] Chaucer, *Works*, ed. F. N. Robinson (Boston, 1933), pp. 101–6.

reveals that she had been rendered ugly by a spell cast on her by her step-mother, and that her release depended on marriage to the best man of England and also on his meek acceptance of her sovereignty of 'all his body and goodes'. In Chaucer, the metamorphosis is preceded not only by a kiss but also by the lady's long, learned lecture on 'gentilesse', poverty, and true worth. On the other hand, no mention whatever is made of evil spells. The lady seems to resume her fair form of her own volition after satisfying herself as to her husband's submissiveness.

The *Marriage of Gawain* tells the same story as the 852 lines of the romance[1] with minor differences, one of them being that Arthur does not bother to consult Gawain before promising him to the Loathly Lady as her husband.

Bearing in mind Chaucer's unequalled narrative skill, one could readily imagine that *The Wife's Tale* is his own rather free reworking of *The Wedding* or its immediate source. Such a conclusion gains force, indeed, from verbal similarities in the passages of the two works in which the various objects of women's desires are enumerated.[2] Although Chaucer could have been influenced, in such passages at least, by knowledge of an earlier form of *The Wedding*, a glance at the several analogues suffices to indicate that he was following a development of the tale quite different from that represented in the romance. The rape story with which *The Wife's Tale* opens, for example, is probably not Chaucer's innovation since it belongs to the version of the Loathly Lady legend set forth in the ballad, *The Knight and the Shepherd's Daughter*. Still another feature which this ballad has in common with *The Wife's Tale* is that a queen acts as arbiter of the hero's fate.[3]

It is possible that Chaucer's treatment of the rape motif and of the scene in which Guenevere and her ladies sit in judgement reflects, if somewhat hazily, the courtly love tradition. That is, Guenevere's rather casual attitude toward the hero's act of rape is reminiscent of the view expressed by Andreas Capellanus to the effect that the forcing of a peasant woman, such as the maiden in *The Wife's Tale* appears to be, is not a heinous offence, although scarcely a recommended form of behaviour. Again, the solemn judgement of the 'lusty bacheler' by the queen's court, with Guenevere herself 'sittynge as a justise', may be reminiscent of the court of love of Eleanor of Aquitaine.[4] More clearly innovative is the wedding-night choice which, in *The Wife's Tale* only, consists of the alternatives of ugliness and chastity or beauty and infidelity in place of the simpler choice between beauty by day or by night, which Chaucer probably met in his source. Although another explanation

[1] Sumner's ed., pp. xx–xxii
[2] Sumner's ed., vss. 408–13; and Robinson's ed., vss. 925–8.
[3] Maynadier, op. cit., pp. 111 ff.
[4] G. R. Coffman in *Spec*, xx (1945), 43–50.

has been advanced,[1] it seems altogether likely that Chaucer was moved to make this substitution by the debates on marriage to be found in the same anti-feminist, patristic sources he had just used in developing the opinions and character of the Wife in the prologue to her tale.[2]

The background of the Loathly Lady legend may be only sketchily traced here. The existence of very satisfactory analogues in certain Irish tales of early date, particularly *The Adventures of the Sons of Eochaid Mugmedon*, suggests that the nucleus was an Irish story about a hero whose fitness for the kingship of Ireland is tested by his willingness to lie with or kiss a supernatural woman in the shape of a loathsome hag. Two themes introduced relatively early into the basic tale were the choice of beauty by day or night and the posing of a question on the answer to which the hero's life depends. In this completed form, the legend was absorbed by the Gawain cycle. The division of the functions of the hero, which we find both in *The Wedding* and *The Marriage*, may have been the result of an effort to celebrate Gawain's loyalty to Arthur. Of course, one must further assume that, at some point, the theme of winning the Sovereignty of Ireland, which appears in Celtic literature, was reduced to the notion of domestic sovereignty.[3] In a close analysis of the *Fier Baiser* and the enchantment theme as a whole, R. S. Loomis has shown that the hag not only had her prototype in the Sovereignty of Ireland, or Eriu, but also, farther back, in the bride of Lug, a Celtic sun god. The primitive tale, then, he conceives of as a nature myth in which the land of Ireland was transformed into a flowery loveliness by the embrace of the sun. This view makes the *Fier Baiser* an integral part of the basic story rather than an addition to some variant of the Fairy Mistress tale;[4] and it also provides an explanation for the parallels between the Loathly Lady stories and *Le Bel Inconnu*, in which the lady, transformed into a serpent, must be disenchanted by a kiss.[5]

Very possibly, the two anonymous English poems, *The Wedding* and *The Marriage*, have a common English source, although there is some slight evidence suggesting that the latter represents the older tradition.[6] Chaucer's tale, however, stems from a different and necessarily earlier branch in which the hero's functions are not divided and in which a queen acts as judge. *The Knight and the Shepherd's Daughter*, agreeing with Chaucer in these respects,

---

[1] B. F. Huppé in *MLN*, lxii (1948), 378–81.

[2] M. Schlauch in *PMLA*, lxi (1946), 416–30.

[3] Miss Schlauch believes that the difficulty of deriving the concept of domestic sovereignty from a story dealing with the kingship of Ireland suggests that Chaucer's source was much less directly influenced by the Irish story than by patristic discussions of marriage; loc. cit., pp. 426 f. See also Sumner's ed., pp. xiii–xxvi; Maynadier, op. cit., pp. 110 ff.

[4] Maynadier, op. cit., p. 31, n. 1, and p. 37, n. 1.

[5] R. S. Loomis, 'The Fier Baiser in Mandeville's Travels, Arthurian Romance, and Irish Saga', *SM*, xvii (1951), 104–13. See also S. Eisner, *A Tale of Wonder* (Wexford, 1958).

[6] Sumner's ed., pp. xxiii–xxv.

must be an independent development of the same source, and Gower's *Tale of Florent* is also closely related. On the other hand, *King Henry*, embodying as it does the so-called 'hag-visiting' theme, is the sole English survivor of a still more primitive stage of the legend.[1]

The author of *The Wedding of Sir Gawain*, who wrote in the East Midlands about 1450,[2] shows meagre talents both as a story-teller and as a poet. There is no subtlety or refinement of feeling, nothing to suggest the depth of his hero's repugnance at the thought of marrying the hideous forest hag. Indeed, Gawain's reaction is merely one of fixed determination:

> 'Ys this alle?' then sayd Gawen,
> 'I shalle wed her and wed her agayn,
> Thowghe she were as foulle as Belsabub.'[3]

In contrast, Chaucer's knight expresses profound shock when the marriage is forced upon him:

> 'For Goddes love, as chees a newe requeste!
> Taak al my good, and lat my body goo.'[4]

('For the love of God, choose a new request. Take all my property and let me go free.')

It is true that any comparison with one of Chaucer's most successful works is likely to prove invidious, yet one can scarcely deny either the inferior narrative art of *The Wedding* or the fumbling metre.

Because of the mutilation of the Percy Folio manuscript, *The Marriage of Gawain* is known to us only in seven fragments totalling 217 lines, perhaps 60 per cent. of the original. Enough remains to permit us to see that here the story, stripped of much detail, is told swiftly in the usual ballad idiom. But it is not an especially effective ballad, lacking as it does the powerful succinctness and the tragic overtones of other ballads dealing with transformed women, such as *Kempy Kay*[5] and *Kemp Owyne*.[6]

In narrative outline, as has been indicated, *The Wife of Bath's Tale* is almost certainly a close version of its original, although Chaucer may well be responsible for such details as those noted above. Nevertheless, Chaucer succeeds in making the tale entirely his own, not only by his individual treatment of the rape motif and of the choice which the Loathly Lady offers her husband, but also through his insertion of two rather lengthy passages. The first of these, Ovid's tale of Midas's barber (vss. 951–82), which the Wife relates *in sua persona* by way of reproving her sex for talking too much, is a delightful exposure of her own garrulity. The second passage is the wedding-

---

[1] Maynadier, op. cit., pp. 129–46; and Sumner's ed., pp. xxv–xxvi.

[2] Sumner's ed., pp. vii–xii.   [3] Ed. cit., vss. 342–4.

[4] Ed. cit., vss. 1060 f.   [5] No. 33 in Child, pt. 2, 300–6.

[6] No. 34 in Child, pt. 2, 306–13.

night discourse on 'gentilesse' (vss. 1109–218), in which the hag replies at great length to her husband's complaint about her presumed low birth. So carried away does the Wife of Bath become with the digression on true nobility that she returns to her main tale almost reluctantly and then finishes it off abruptly in no more than 50 lines. In these passages, together comprising nearly one-half the entire tale, Chaucer's mature expertness in the use of rhetorical principles—here, he employs two devices of amplification, *exemplum* and digression—is well demonstrated.[1] By such means he makes the whole story into an extension of the more direct characterization given of the Wife both in the General Prologue to the *Canterbury Tales* and the Prologue to the *Wife's Tale* itself. Further, the interpolations and the other innovations have a direct bearing on the place which the tale holds in the so-called Marriage Group. It was a happy chance which brought to Chaucer's hand the tale of the Loathly Lady, and a happy inspiration which led him to assign it to the Wife, relegating her original tale to the Shipman.[2]

THE HOLY GRAIL

Though we have seen in Chap. 20 that the Grail romance of *Perlesvaus* was read in England and was prized in Wales, the legend of the sacred vessel in this form has left no impress on the vernacular literature of England. Only the *Estoire* and the *Queste del Saint Graal* of the Vulgate cycle have survived in Middle English renderings, and the *Queste*, curiously enough, only in Books XIII through XVII of Malory's *Morte Darthur*, which will be the subject of brief comment in Chap. 40. The pre-Arthurian history of the Grail as related in the *Estoire del Saint Graal* became known in England shortly before 1250, as appears from an interpolation in William of Malmesbury's *De Antiquitate Glastoniensis Ecclesiae*, and was gradually accepted, though with modifications, by the monks of Glastonbury, as was shown in Chap. 21. Perhaps for this very reason five versions of the early history in English were made and have come down to us from late medieval and early Tudor times.[3] The earliest of these is the fragmentary alliterative *Joseph of Arimathea* of the mid-fourteenth century, which because of its verse-form will be considered in the next chapter. Three others, based, as Skeat has proved,[4] on the *Nova Legenda Angliae* of Capgrave, who died in 1464, were printed in early Tudor times. The last of these, a poetic life of Joseph published by Pynson in 1520, seems to have been written to encourage

---

[1] J. M. Manly, 'Chaucer and the Rhetoricians', *Proceedings of the British Academy*, xii (1926), 110 ff.

[2] B. J. Whiting, 'The Wife of Bath's Tale', in *Sources and Analogues of Chaucer's Canterbury Tales*, ed. W. F. Bryan and G. Dempster (Chicago, 1941), p. 223.

[3] All these pieces are edited by W. W. Skeat, EETS, xliv (1871).

[4] Skeat's ed., pp. xx–xxiii.

pilgrimages to the shrine of St. Joseph at Glastonbury. Finally, there is Lovelich's lengthy production.

Lovelich's 'Holy Grail'

Because of the loss of some ten leaves at the beginning of MS. Corpus Christi (Cambridge) 80, in which both of Lovelich's works are preserved, the opening episodes are missing from the English poem. Lovelich's poem[1] probably began, like the French *Estoire del Saint Graal*, with the tale of a hermit who 717 years after the Passion has a vision in which he is instructed by Christ to make a copy of the sacred book of the Grail.

Although twice printed by Furnivall, Lovelich's *Holy Grail* has never been provided with an adequate commentary.[2] A perusal of the parallel French and English texts reveals that the English work is a very close translation, the discrepancies being infrequent and trivial. One passage which may be original with Lovelich—at least, it is absent from the French text published by Furnivall—is to the effect that 'Brut' says nothing about Sir Piers (French Pierre), a relative of Joseph of Arimathea, and in fact that chronicle appears to know nothing of the history of the Grail.[3] Lovelich omits a description of the Turning Isle[4] and a few other passages,[5] but these deletions form no clear pattern; in fact, they may well be the result of *lacunae* in the French manuscript. Except for the autobiographical interpolations in which he groans over his arduous task,[6] Lovelich may scarcely be said to reveal a distinctive personality in this poem. At best, he is capable of conveying a sense of sincerity and warm feeling, for example, in his account of the meeting of Nascien and young Celidoine on an island.

> And so be hym A-wook ful swetely,
> And his Eyen he upe Caste ful softely:
> thanne whanne he sawh his sone it was,
> Ful gret Joye he Made In that plas;
> And up he stirte thanne riht Anon,
> And abowtes his Nekke his Armes he leide son,
> & him clipte & kyste An hundred Sithe,
> So Joyful he was, so glad and So blithe,
> that bothe for Joye & pyte he wepte.[7]

---

[1] Ed. by Furnivall, EETSES, xx, xxiv, xxviii, xxx. Also edited in parallel with the French prose in *Seynt Graal or the Sank Ryal* (London, 1861, 1863). Quotations from Lovelich's *Holy Grail* are from the EETS edition; those from the French text are from the parallel text edition.

[2] Dorothy Kempe's 'General Introduction', EETSES, xcv, deals mainly with broad aspects of the Grail legend.

[3] Ed. cit., chap. lii, vss. 1061–70.

[4] Ed. cit., chap. xxvii. Cf. with the French text, Furnivall's parallel ed. i. 347–9.

[5] Alice R. Nutis, 'The History of the Holy Grail', chap. ii, unpublished M.A. thesis, New York University, 1947.

[6] *PMLA*, lxvii (1952), 473 ff.

[7] Ed. cit., chap. xxxiv, vss. 139–47. Cf. with the Old French, Furnivall's parallel ed. i. 483.

(And so beside him [Nascien] woke very sweetly, and cast up his eyes very tenderly. Then, when he saw it was his son, he felt great joy in that place, and up he jumped at once and soon put his arms about his neck and embraced and kissed him a hundred times. So joyful, so glad, and so happy was he that he wept for both joy and pity.)

Passages of this sort are rare. One can only conclude that Lovelich lacked nearly every qualification for his task.

MISCELLANEOUS HEROES
'Ywain and Gawain'

In spite of its title, based on vs. 4, *Ywain and Gawain*[1] relegates Gawain to a subordinate role, and is in fact a fourteenth-century redaction of the French *Yvain*—the only Middle English redaction of a work by Chrétien that we have. But the excellence of *Ywain and Gawain* is due not simply to its being a version of one of the best of all medieval romances.[2] Rather, it must be ascribed to the fact that the composer possessed a literary mind of rare independence and made the tale he was translating his own.

Comparative studies reveal that the English poem, which contains only 4,000 lines as opposed to the 6,800 of Chrétien's work, departs from its source in such important respects as the emphasis placed on certain plot elements, the social tone of the discourse, and even the conception of the hero's character.[3] Indeed, a number of Chrétien's details are severely abridged or entirely suppressed by the English poet. For example, the search of the messenger of the Disinherited Maiden for the Knight of the Lion is a much simplified version of the same episode in Chrétien's poem.[4] But a significant number of the English poet's omissions occur in passages in which Chrétien discourses, *in propria persona*, or through one of his characters, on the right way of listening to a story, or the conflict between *amor* and *haïne*, or on Gawain's likeness to the sun and Lunete's to the moon.[5] The poet further shows little interest in Chrétien's fanciful or playful comments and elaborate descriptions of states of mind.[6] And, not infrequently, the elegant generalities and epic similes of French romance are replaced by more homely English expressions and sometimes by proverbs and saws.[7] Thus, the writer avoids a direct translation of the following:

[1] Ed. G. Schleich (Oppeln, Leipzig, 1887).
[2] See above, pp. 180–4.
[3] Schleich's ed., pp. i ff.
[4] *Yvain*, vss. 4821–5059.
[5] Ibid., vss. 142–74, 2397–414.
[6] For an account of the differences between *Ywain* and *Yvain*, see J. L. Weston in *Modern Language Quarterly* (London), ii (1889), 98–107; iii (1900), 194–202.
[7] B. J. Whiting, 'Proverbs in Certain Middle English Romances in Relation to their French Sources', [Harvard] *Studies and Notes in Philology and Literature*, xv (1933), 115–18.

> Vint d'ire plus ardanz que brese
> Li chevaliers a si grant bruit
> Con s'il chaçast un cerf de ruit.[1]

(Burning with wrath more than a live coal, the knight came with a noise as great as if he were pursuing a rutting stag.)

Here, the English poem reads:

> And sone he saw cumand a knight
> Als fast so the fowl in flyght.[2]

(And soon he saw a knight coming as fast as a bird in flight.)

But there are also a few details appearing neither in the French *Yvain* nor in Hartmann von Aue's adaptation which are quite clearly represented both in *Ywain* and in the Welsh *Owein*. For example, *Owein* and *Ywain* agree in describing Alundyne's hair as fair, and, much more significantly, in reporting in very similar phraseology a remark by the maiden who heals Ywain of madness by applying a magic ointment.[3] The inference to be drawn from such correspondences is that the English poet, although writing a more or less literal translation of his original, nevertheless had knowledge of a version akin in some respects to the Welsh tale—and that he adopted a number of minor details from this source. The alternative explanation—namely, that all these small points appeared in a now lost text of Chrétien's *Yvain*, despite the fact that they are missing in the half-dozen or so surviving manuscripts—seems somewhat less credible.[4]

In total effect, the English *Ywain* differs rather markedly from the French *Yvain*. The suppression of Chrétien's musings on his characters or on the action, the use of English proverbs, and, in general, the shunning of the French poet's high style—all combine to produce a more colloquial story in which the characters, somewhat more simply motivated, seem to act with greater directness and vigour. Knightly idealism is not lost because of the poet's reticence, but, especially in the duel between the hero and Gawain, it is allowed to express itself in actions rather than in words. Moreover, the English Alundyne is much less passionate of expression than her French counterpart. In the opinion of one critic, all these alterations are the result of a conscious and generally successful effort on the part of the English poet to improve upon Chrétien,[5] but it seems more likely that at least some of the

---

[1] *Yvain*, ed. cit., vss. 812–14.

[2] Ed. cit., vss. 629–30. Cf. Chaucer's *Canterbury Tales*, General Prologue, ed. cit., p. 21, vs. 190: 'Grehoundes he hadde as swift as fowel in flight.'

[3] The fair hair is referred to in *Ywain*, vs. 823, and the comment about the ointment, vs. 1898. See above, p. 507, n. 6.

[4] *Modern Language Quarterly*, iii (1900), 201 f.

[5] P. Steinbach, *Über den Einfluß des Crestien de Troies auf die altenglische Literatur* (Leipzig, 1885), pp. 7–27.

deletions in *Ywain and Gawain* are due to *lacunae* in the copy of the French poem available to him or simply to his desire for brevity[1] rather than to his critical judgement. Whether or not the English writer was capable of appreciating the *sens* of Chrétien's *Yvain*—that is, the ironic comment on certain tenets of courtly love[2]—it is certain that, in his version, the reflections of courtly love are much attenuated and that, perhaps for this reason, a more forthright and uncomplicated romance of adventure is the result.

The poet to whom we are indebted for *Ywain* did his work between 1300 and 1350. The language of the poem in our single copy, Brit. Mus. Galba E IX, is Northern, but there are a few indications, such as the appearance of *o* alongside *a* for OE *ā*, that the composer himself wrote a somewhat more southerly dialect.[3] The four-stress couplets are not notable for their metrical precision, but the use of run-on lines is as effective as Chaucer's:

> By the hand sho toke the knyght
> And led him unto chamber right
> Byfore hir lady (es nought at layne),
> And of that come was sho ful fayne.[4]

(She took that knight by the hand and led him directly into the chamber before her lady—it is not to be denied—and she was very glad of his coming.)

The diction is simple, and the poet seems, far better than most English romance writers, to have resisted the temptation to translate the French by borrowed forms of the same words. Kane speaks of the constant appropriateness of the writing in *Ywain* and of the achievement of the poet in composing the work which most perfectly fulfills the idea of romance.[5] There is much truth in this generalization if one understands 'idea of romance' to mean the popularized, virile, straightforward type which is specifically English.

'*Sir Perceval of Galles*'

The fourteenth-century tail-rime romance, *Sir Perceval of Galles*,[6] has seldom been discussed as a work of literature although many studies have been made of its relationship to the great Perceval-Grail cycle. As the only Middle English account of the career of Perceval outside of Malory's *Morte Darthur*, it deserves more critical attention.

The connexions of *Sir Perceval* with the Perceval-Grail romances in

---

[1] Schleich's ed., pp. xxxix–liv.
[2] T. P. Cross, W. A. Nitze, *Lancelot and Guenevere: A Study on the Origins of Courtly Love* (Chicago, 1930), p. 69.
[3] B. von Lindheim, *Wiener Beiträge zur englischen Philologie*, lix (1937), 65–71.
[4] Ed. cit., vss. 1125–8.
[5] Kane, op. cit., pp. 78 f. Most of the other features of which Kane speaks, such as the creation of 'a delicate fantasy of escape' (p. 66), could with more justice be ascribed to the source of the English poem, Chrétien's *Yvain*.
[6] Ed. J. Campion, F. Holthausen, *Alt- und Mittelenglische Texte*, v (1913).

other languages have to a great extent been clarified. Although the Grail as such figures not at all in the English poem, the career of the hero as given there up to the slaying of the Red Knight—that is, to the second part of the story—runs parallel to the *enfances* in Chrétien's *Perceval*, Wolfram von Eschenbach's *Parzival*, the Welsh *Peredur*, and the Italian *Carduino*.[1] The older view that the English romance is to a greater or lesser extent dependent on Chrétien[2] has been disputed by Jessie Weston[3] and later scholars. Indeed, Strucks has shown that *Sir Perceval*, *Carduino*, and Wolfram's *Parzival* drew upon forms of the story distinct from Chrétien's poem.[4] The English version seems to preserve some early traits; for example, it agrees with *Carduino* and contradicts Chrétien by bringing Perceval and his mother together again at the conclusion of his great adventures.[5]

Various theories about the background of the Perceval legend have been advanced by A. C. L. Brown[6] and Griffith.[7] The most convincing arguments lead one to believe that the *enfances* of the hero are derived from Irish accounts of the boyhood of Cuchulainn and Finn.[8] In fact, the correspondence between the story of Perceval's youth and *The Boyhood Exploits* of Finn is striking, as has long been recognized, and it is now established that the Irish tale was in existence when the earliest Perceval romance was composed.[9] *Sir Perceval* has in common with the saga two features not found in Chrétien: the hero's ability to catch wild animals and the king's half-recognition of his nephew.[10] It seems possible that the legend in its first shape concerned a youth of divine descent whose true name and lineage were not revealed until he had accomplished a great feat.[11]

---

[1] Campion and Holthausen's ed., pp. xii–xiii.

[2] Steinbach, op. cit., pp. 35–41; W. Golther, 'Chrestiens Conte del Graal in seinem Verhältniss zum wälschen Peredur und zum englischen Sir Perceval', *Sitzungsberichte der philosophisch-philologischen und historischen Classe der k. b. Akademie der Wissenschaften zu München*, 1890, part ii, pp. 174–217; Golther, *Parzival und der Graal in der Dichtung des Mittelalters und der Neuzeit* (Stuttgart, 1925), pp. 118–19. A convenient survey of opinion on this matter appears in R. H. Griffith, *Sir Perceval of Galles, A Study of the Sources of the Legend* (Chicago, 1911), pp. 7–11.

[3] *Legend of Sir Perceval*, i. 76 ff.

[4] C. Strucks, *Der junge Parzival* (Leipzig, 1910), pp. 70, 74 f.

[5] Ibid., p. 142.

[6] A. C. L. Brown in *MP*, xviii (1920–1), 201–28; xxii (1924–5), 113–32.

[7] Op. cit., pp. 116 f. In his reconstruction of the original tale, Griffith depended to some extent on *The Lay of the Great Fool*, a folk-tale which has been shown to be itself derived in part from Arthurian legend, specifically from the story represented in *Libeaus Desconus*. Modern tales also underlie Griffith's discussion of the Red Knight–Witch–Uncle theme. See S. J. McHugh in *MP*, xlii (1944–5), 197–211.

[8] For a summary of *The Boyish Exploits*, see F. C. J. Los, *Das Keltentum in Wolframs Parzival* (Amsterdam, 1927), pp. 85–89. Earlier notices about the Irish tales dealing with the boyhood of Finn and Cuchulainn are to be found in *Folklore Record*, iv (1881), 1–44; *GGA*, 1890, pp. 519–20; Griffith, op. cit., pp. 17, 22, &c.; *MP*, xviii (1920–1), 227 f. See also Loomis, *Arthurian Tradition*, pp. 335–40.

[9] R. B. Pace in *PMLA*, xxv (1917), 598–604.

[10] Ibid., pp. 602–4.

[11] Los, op. cit., pp. 102 f.

As already indicated, the immediate source of *Sir Perceval* is not known.
We infer, however, that the lost work must have resembled rather closely
the source of the Italian *Carduino*. The English poet, who may have been a
minstrel, probably found the uncourtly flavour of his original much to his
taste. His dialect is Northern, although Midland forms occur within some
lines, and he wrote during the first forty years of the fourteenth century.
A number of the 16-line tail-rime stanzas depart from the basic rime-scheme,
aaabcccbdddbeeeb, and a few are lacking a line or so. For the most part, the
stanzas are bound together, as in *The Avowing of Arthur*, by repetition of
the final line of the preceding stanza.[1] The metre is occasionally rough, and
the diction and tone are by no means refined.

> Now he strykes for the nonys,
> Made the Sarazenes hede-bones
> Hoppe als dose hayle-stones,
>   A-bowtte one the gres.[2]

(Now he lays about him and causes the skull-bones of the Saracens to hop about on the
grass like hail-stones.)

As Dorothy Everett suggested, *Sir Perceval* is a crude romance designed
to gratify popular interest in marvels for their own sake.[3] The poet, however,
shows some talent in pointing up the grotesque aspects of the burning of the
witch and the terrible duel with the giant. The *naïveté* of the young Perceval
is also well brought out in his quaint use of the exclamation 'Petir!', in his
misinterpretation of his mother's injunction to be a man 'of mesure', and in
his attempt to burn the Red Knight out of his armour. Chaucer makes an
amusing allusion to the youth's simplicity in his burlesque description of
Sir Thopas:

> Hymself drank water of the well,
> As dide the knyght sire Percyvell
> So worthy under wede.[4]

(He drank water from the well, as did the knight Sir Perceval, so brave under his
armour.)

Kane's characterization of the story as 'Innocence confronted with the
conventions', and his further comments about the human sympathy and the

---

[1] Campion and Holthausen's ed., pp. x–xi. See also Medary, loc. cit.
[2] Ed. cit., vss. 1189–92.
[3] Everett, op. cit., pp. 110 f.
[4] Chaucer, ed. cit., p. 200, vss. 915–17. The parodied passage in *Sir Perceval* reads as follows:
> His righte name was Percyvell,
> He was fosterde in the felle,
> He dranke water of the welle,
>   And yitt was he wyghte. vss. 5–8,

ironic wisdom to be found in the work[1] surely bespeak a far too generous appraisal of the poet's inventiveness and sophistication.

'Libeaus Desconus'

That *Libeaus Desconus (The Fair Unknown)*[2] was highly esteemed by English audiences is made clear not only by the six manuscripts that have come down to us but also by allusions in Chaucer's *Sir Thopas* and Skelton's *Philip Sparrow*.[3] In France, however, the son of Gawain seems not to have received great acclaim, since only a single copy of *Le Bel Inconnu*, to which *Libeaus Desconus* is closely related, is known.[4] Although not provable, it is altogether possible that Thomas Chestre, the composer of *Sir Launfal* and, perhaps, *Octovian*, was also the author of *Libeaus Desconus*. At least, the three poems, all of which appear in MS. Brit. Mus. Caligula A II, were written at the same period, the second quarter or middle of the fourteenth century, and in the dialect of south-eastern England.[5]

In no other English work do we find the story of Ginglain's career, although his youth, as described in *Libeaus Desconus*, is reminiscent of the *enfances* of other heroes, including Perceval, and certain of his adventures are paralleled in Malory's stories of La Cote Mal Taile and Gareth.[6] The true analogues, however, are in other languages: Renaud de Beaujeu's *Le Bel Inconnu* (c. 1190), the Middle High German *Wigalois* (c. 1210), and the Italian *Carduino* (c. 1375). Of these, only the Old French poem could possibly have been known to the English poet, yet careful studies show that direct dependence upon *Le Bel Inconnu* is most unlikely. The incidents in the first 3,428 lines of *Le Bel Inconnu* correspond in general to those in the English romance, but there are differences in detail and wide variations in the forms of the proper names. Moreover, in the French work, Guinglain's extended dalliance with La Dame d'Amour takes place after the hero has effected the disenchantment of the Lady of Sinadoune rather than before. So fully does Renaud develop this delaying action, as well as other episodes, that his poem runs to nearly three times the length of the English romance.[7]

---

[1] Kane, op. cit., p. 77.

[2] Ed. M. Kaluza, *Altenglische Bibliothek*, v (1890). This edition is composite; that is, Kaluza has pieced together passages from the several texts.

[3] Also, the poem was printed before 1600. Kaluza's ed., pp. ix–x. For a list of allusions, see W. H. Schofield, *Studies on the Libeaus Desconus*, [Harvard] *Studies and Notes in Philology and Literature*, iv (1895), 241 f.

[4] See *Le Bel Inconnu*, ed. G. P. Williams, *CFMA* (Paris, 1929), p. iii; and G. Paris in *Hist. Litt. de la France*, xxx. 196.

[5] See Kaluza's ed., pp. clviii–clxv, but more especially Kaluza's later article, *ES*, xviii (1893), 185–7; and D. Everett, 'The Relationship of Chestre's *Launfal* and *Libeaus Desconus*', *MedÆv*, vii (1938), 29–49.

[6] The parallels are most fully developed by Schofield, op. cit., pp. 146 ff.; and the associations with Malory's *Morte Darthur* are discussed by R. H. Wilson in *PMLA*, lviii (1943), 1–21.

[7] Schofield, op. cit., pp. 4–144.

Differences such as these are best explained by assuming *Libeaus Desconus* and *Le Bel Inconnu* to be independent adaptations of an earlier French, or Anglo-Norman, source.[1] It has been further surmised that this lost original was a fusion of two Breton tales, one of them dealing with the dragon kiss, a form of the *Fier Baiser*.[2]

The remoter background of the Fair Unknown has been variously explained. The leading view, however, is that the starting-point was the *Fier Baiser*, combined with the widespread motif of a woman transformed into a serpent.[3] Schofield sought to demonstrate that the nucleus was a form of the Unpromising Youth type, closely related to the Perceval legend.[4] The Irish source of the *Fier Baiser*, as has recently been suggested, provides a precedent for the fact that Libeaus, after bringing about the disenchantment, wins simultaneously a bride and a kingdom.[5] Among the subsidiary adventures, the sparrow-hawk episode appears to have been taken from Chrétien's *Erec*, despite certain puzzling differences.[6] Moreover, R. S. Loomis has shown that, in depicting the mysterious castle of Sinadoune, the *cité gaste*, the composer of the romance drew upon a legend developed by Breton *conteurs* about the ruined Roman fort of Segontium near Caernarvon, and that the two necromancers, Maboun and Irain, may possibly be traced to another Welsh tradition about the sons of Urien.[7]

In his 'Essay on Ancient Metrical Romances', Bishop Percy discusses *Libeaus Desconus* as a specimen of the skill of English romance writers in

distributing and conducting their fable, by which it will be seen that nature and common sense had supplied to these old simple bards the want of critical art, and taught them some of the most essential rules of Epic Poetry.[8]

If one understands this favourable, if condescending, judgement to apply only to a clear and efficient presentation of the story, one may accept it as reasonably accurate. In fact, Thomas Chestre, if that was the poet's name, proceeds from the recitation of one adventure to the next with the ease of a practiced hack, although occasionally there are crude transitions, such as the following:

---

[1] R. S. Loomis in *SM*, xvii (1951), 106.

[2] In *Le Bel Inconnu*, Elene states that the hero must accomplish the adventure of the *Fier Baiser*: 'et qui le Fier Baissier feroit.' Ed. cit., vs. 192.

[3] H. R. Patch, *Other World* (Cambridge, Mass., 1950), pp. 269 f.; G. Paris in *Hist. Litt. de la France*, xxx. 191.

[4] Schofield, op. cit., pp. 146 ff. See also the adverse criticism by Philipot in *R*, xxvi (1897), 296–300.   [5] R. S. Loomis in *SM*, xvii. 109.

[6] Schofield, op. cit., pp. 60–106, and 111–32. Very likely, the quarrel over Otes de Lile's hunting dog was not taken from *The Lay of the Big Fool*, as was once thought. Rather, this theme appears to have developed in Arthurian stories which served as a source for a part of *The Lay*. McHugh in *MP*, xlii. 203 ff.

[7] See above, p. 371, n. 6.

[8] In *Reliques of Ancient English Poetry* (Edinburgh, 1858), iii, p. xxii.

Nou reste we her a while
Of sir Otes de Lile
And telle we other tales.[1]

But Chestre is interested in his characters only as puppets in the marvels he hastens them through, and he seldom pauses to visualize his story in any satisfactory way. The following account of Libeaus's joust with Lambard is exceptional in its particularity of detail:

His schaft brak with greet power;
Libeaus hitte him in the lanier
  Of his helm so bright,
That pisaine, ventaile and gorgere
Fliye forth with the helm in fer,
  And sir Lambard upright
Set and rokked in his saddell,
As a child doth in a cradell,
  With oute main and might.
Ech man tok other by the lappe
And lough and gonne her hondes clappe,
  Baroun, borgais and knight.[2]

(His lance broke with the great shock; Libeaus hit him in the strap of his bright helm so that the pisane, aventaile, and gorget flew off together with the helm, and Sir Lambard sat back in his saddle and rocked like a child in a cradle, bereft of strength. The spectators seized each other by the hem of the robe and laughed and clapped their hands, baron, burgess, and knight.)

The above passage illustrates the *aabaabccbddb* rime scheme of the 186 stanzas of Kaluza's edition, but fourteen stanzas display irregularities.[3] The undoubted success of *Libeaus Desconus* must be laid to the sensational and marvellous elements in the narrative rather than to the art of the author.

'Sir Tristrem'

The tale of Tristan and Isolt was certainly well known in medieval England despite the fact that the only version in the vernacular, outside Malory, is a late thirteenth-century romance. For English audiences could well have known not only the English *Sir Tristrem*,[4] but also such Anglo-Norman works as the *Tristan* of Thomas, the Oxford *Folie Tristan*, and perhaps Marie de France's *Chèvrefeuil* as well. Artistic representations of the

---

[1] Ed. cit., vss. 1297–9.   [2] Ed. cit., vss. 1705–16.
[3] Kaluza, pp. xlii ff., notes variations in the metrical pattern.
[4] Ed. G. P. McNeill, Scottish Text Society, viii (1885–6); and E. Kölbing, *Die nordische und die englische Version der Tristan-Sage*, Zweiter Teil (Heilbronn, 1882). Quotations are from McNeill's edition.

story, such as the pavement tiles dug up at Chertsey Abbey, give further evidence of the wide popularity of the legend.[1]

Despite the fragmentary state of the twelfth-century romance of Thomas,[2] it is clear that the English poem, like Gottfried von Strassburg's *Tristan* and the *Tristrams saga*, is derived from that work.[3] Kölbing's minute analysis reveals further that the English work is a drastic condensation, at times little more than an abstract, of its original, although it contains virtually every incident.[4] The contrast between one of the fragments of Thomas and the corresponding passage in *Sir Tristrem* is instructive. In the English poem, Tristrem's marriage to Ysonde of the White Hand is described as follows:

> The forward fast he band
> With ysonde, that may
> With the white hand,
> He spoused that day.
> O night, ich under stand,
> To boure wenten thai
> On bedde.
> Tristrem ring fel oway,
> As men to chaumber him ledde.[5]

(He concluded the agreement firmly with the maiden Ysonde of the White Hand. He wed her that day. At night, I understand, they went to their bower to bed. Tristrem's ring fell off as he was led to the chamber.)

In fact, the marriage is disposed of in about forty lines (vss. 2672–706) with very little dialogue or analysis of emotion, but in the first Sneyd fragment Thomas expends 800 lines on the same story. The difference is caused largely by the omission of the hero's debates with himself whether he shall consummate his marriage to Ysonde of the White Hand.[6] Kölbing's plausible conclusion is that *Sir Tristrem* was written down from memory by a rhymester who was too intent on carrying out his intricate and difficult verse form to tell his tale effectively.[7]

In five different passages (vss. 2, 10, 397, 412, and 2787), the poem speaks of one 'Tomas' as the narrator ('As Tomas hath ous taught', vs. 2787). Whether the English poet is here giving his own name rather than that of the author of his French source, and whether, if the English poet's name Tomas is to be identified with one Thomas of Kendale, as Kölbing thought,[8]

---

[1] R. S. and L. H. Loomis, *Arthurian Legends in Medieval Art* (London, New York, 1938), pp. 42–69.

[2] In *Les Fragments du Tristan de Thomas*, ed. Bartina H. Wind (Leyden, 1950).

[3] Kölbing's ed., pp. xviii ff.; and McNeill's ed., p. xix.

[4] See introduction to *Tristrams Saga ok Ísondar* in Kölbing, *Tristan-Sage*, Erster Teil (1878), pp. xvii–cxlvii.

[5] Ed. cit., vss. 2676–84.

[6] Wind's ed., pp. 66–97.

[7] Introduction to *Tristrams Saga ok Ísondar*, p. cxlvii.

[8] Kölbing's ed., pp. xxvi–xxxii.

or with the well-known Thomas of Erceldoune, as Sir Walter Scott and McNeill held,[1] must still be regarded as moot points. The mixed nature of the language has always been explained by competent philologists such as Kölbing as the result of the copying by a Southern scribe of a romance written in the North, the home of Thomas the Rhymer and, possibly, Thomas of Kendale.[2] The contrary theory that the poet wrote a basically South-east Midlands dialect has been only sketchily developed,[3] yet it must be given more careful evaluation[4] before one may accept Thomas of Erceldoune or any other Northern poet as the author of *Sir Tristrem*.

In any case, the poem is a crude version of its courtly original. It is full of awkward inversions, and the transitions are frequently disconcerting in their abruptness. If the author felt any sympathy for the tale he was telling, it is hard to detect.[5] The strange eleven-line stanza, riming *abababababcbc*, is in three-stress lines except for the ninth, which is of two syllables only.[6] Lines as short as these would certainly make for a jerky, staccato effect in oral delivery, yet the style suggests that we have here a minstrel product.

'Sir Launfal'

Thomas Chestre's *Sir Launfal*, or *Launfal Miles*,[7] as it is entitled in our single manuscript copy, sets forth an especially interesting form of the Fairy Mistress story. In addition to Chestre's poem, which was written about 1350, the story exists in five later English texts, some of them fragmentary. Although based on the same source as Chestre's romance, together they represent an independent development.[8] A tale so frequently reproduced probably enjoyed more than passing popularity, but Launfal himself seems never to have become a well-established Arthurian hero. The cause may be found either in the supposition that the name Lanval was an arbitrary choice by Marie de France and was not traditionally associated with Arthur's circle, or in the fact that she so limited Lanval's career by sending him and his mistress off to Avalon that no additional adventures were possible.[9]

Chestre's story is considerably longer than that recounted in *Landavall*, *Lambewell*, and the other three Middle English pieces.[10] Although it is quite

---

[1] McNeill's ed., pp. xxxii–xlvii.   [2] Kölbing's ed., pp. lx–lxxviii.

[3] *JEGP*, xl (1941), 538–44; xli (1942), 478–81.

[4] *Year's Work in English Studies*, xxii (1941), 72.

[5] Kane (op. cit., p. 20) speaks of the insensitivity and unresponsiveness of the poet.

[6] Kölbing's ed., pp. lii–lx.

[7] Ed. Kaluza, 'Thomas Chestre, Verfasser des Launfal, Libeaus Desconus and Octovian', *ES*, xviii (1893), 165–90; also in *Middle English Metrical Romances*, ed. French and Hale, pp. 345–80. Quotations are from the latter edition.

[8] Wells, pp. 131–4.

[9] In *Vier Lais der Marie de France*, ed. Karl Warnke (Halle, 1925), pp. 86–112.

[10] *Landavall*, MS. Rawlinson C 86, in 'Launfal', ed. G. L. Kittredge in *American Journal of Philology*, x (1889), 1–33; *Sir Lambewell*, Percy Folio MS., ed. Hales and Furnivall, i. 142–64; Malone and Douce fragments, ibid. i. 521–33; *Sir Lamwell*, a fragment in MS. Cambridge Univer-

clear that *Sir Launfal* must be derived from the same English translation, now lost, which underlies the five later poems, the additional material in Chestre must be explained otherwise.[1] Some of the expansions are undoubtedly original with the poet. The tournament at Caerleon in which the hero engages soon after acquiring his fairy wealth (vss. 433–92) and his duel with Valentine in Lombardy (vss. 505–612) are commonplaces of which any romance composer would have been capable. The English work describes more circumstantially than Marie the great state maintained by Launfal and his open-handed liberality. On the other hand, the fact that, in *Sir Launfal*, it is the queen rather than Arthur who refuses gifts to the hero has led to the belief that Chestre's version was influenced more or less directly by the lai of *Graelent*,[2] a closely related form of the Fairy Mistress tale; and this belief is strengthened by the suffering which Launfal endures while awaiting the gifts of the fay.[3] In another way, too, *Graelent* may have affected the Launfal story, for it is suspected that Marie used that work as the basis for her *Lanval*, adding to it Arthurian material from Wace's *Brut*.[4]

That Marie's lai is superior as a work of literature to Chestre's romance is immediately obvious. Her story is of Celtic provenance, as the parallels adduced by Cross amply demonstrate. The fay's ready acceptance of Launfal as her paramour, the *geis* she lays upon him, and the fairy gifts all appear in Irish legend.[5] Again, the rivalry between the fairy mistress and the queen and certain other features represent a variation on the conflict between Morgan le Fay and Guenevere in the Prose *Lancelot*.[6] By her delicacy of touch and her avoidance of sensual detail, Marie provided a perfect atmosphere for the Celtic love story of a supernatural woman and a mortal. It is probably unfair to say that Chestre destroys completely the fairy tone of the original story in his version. Yet, the net effect of the changes he introduces is that his hero stands far less in the shadow of his Other-world mistress. One feels, in fact, that the interpolation of stock chivalric exploits and the addition of various mundane details lay bare the poet's conscious intention of transforming the lai into a typical episodic romance. The theme which he evidently wished to emphasize is Launfal's largess:

sity Library Kk V 30, in *Captain Cox, His Ballads and Books*, ed. F. J. Furnivall, Ballad Society, No. 7 (1890), pp. xxx–xxxii.

[1] *American Journal of Philology*, x. 6 ff.

[2] *Lays of Desiré, Graelent and Melion*, ed. E. M. Grimes (New York, 1928), pp. 76–101.

[3] For other parallels between *Graelent* and *Sir Launfal*, see A. Kolls, *Zur Lanvalsage* (Berlin, 1886), pp. 66, &c. See also Kittredge, 'Launfal', pp. 6 ff.; Grimes, op. cit., pp. 18–21; and R. S. Loomis, 'Morgain la Fée and the Celtic Goddesses', *Spec*, xx (1945), 189–92.

[4] W. C. Stokoe, Jr. in *PMLA*, lxiii (1948), 392–404; and Grimes, op. cit., pp. 18–21. For a different view see Schofield, 'The Lays of Graelent and Lanval, and the Story of Wayland', *PMLA*, viii (1900), 121–80.

[5] T. P. Cross, 'Celtic Elements in Lanval and Graelent', *MP*, xii (1914–15), 585–644.

[6] R. S. Loomis in *Spec*, xx. 191 ff.

> For hys largesse and hys bounté,
> The kynges stuward made was he
> Ten yere, y you plyght;
> Of alle the knyghtes of the Table Rounde,
> So large there nas noone yfounde,
> By dayes ne by nyght.[1]

(For his largess and his generosity, he was made steward of the king for ten years, I assure you. Of all the knights of the Round Table, there was none found so open-handed, by day or night.)

His possession of this chivalric virtue seems to be responsible at least in part for the favour which Launfal finds in the eyes of his fairy mistress, and perhaps of his author too. Chestre, in short, although revealing a kind of technical competence, shows in this poem a shrewd appreciation of the popular taste for run-of-the-mill fiction rather than true insight and poetic talent.

'The Boy and the Mantle'

The Percy Folio contains a ballad entitled The Boy and the Mantle,[2] which Kittredge described as 'an exceedingly good piece of minstrelsy'. The scene is laid in Arthur's court at Carlisle, and the hero is a 'little boy' named Craddocke, old enough, however, to boast of a wife. It has long been recognized that Craddocke is the Caradoc Briebras of the French romances, and the story of the testing of his wife, together with the other ladies of the court, by means of a magic mantle is the theme of the Mantel Mautaillié, the Möttuls saga, and an incident in the Swiss Lanzelet.[3] Not only does Craddocke's lady triumph in the test, but the boy himself, alone of all the knights, is able to carve a boar's head with his knife and to drink from a horn in proof that he is no cuckold. This last feat is ascribed to Caradoc in Biket's Lai du Cor and in the First Continuation of Chrétien's Perceval.[4]

In this connexion it is pertinent to notice the ballad of The Queen of Scotland,[5] which, though it names no Arthurian character and though it was recorded as late as the nineteenth century, contains another episode in Caradoc's history. As Miss Harper discovered sixty years ago,[6] the hero of the

---

[1] Ed. cit., vss. 31–36.

[2] Hales and Furnivall, ii. 301–11; Child, i. 257–74.

[3] See Chaps. 11, 33, 35 above. Ulrich von Zatzikhoven, Lanzelet, ed. K. A. Hahn (Frankfurt, 1845), vss. 5746–6140; trans. K. G. T. Webster, pp. 103–9, 211 f.; O. Warnatsch, Der Mantel (Breslau, 1883), pp. 58 ff.; Loomis, Arthurian Tradition, pp. 95–100.

[4] See Chaps. 11, 15 above, and Warnatsch, op. cit., pp. 66–69; Continuations of the Old French Perceval, ed. Roach, i. 231–8; ii. 370–7; iii. 194–205. There is a cynical poem, The Cuckold's Dance, of about 1450, which also localizes the horn-test at Arthur's court. C. H. Hartshorne, Ancient Metrical Tales (London, 1829), pp. 209–21. Ed. H. Hedenus, Erlangen diss., 1904.

[5] Child, v. 176–8. First published by P. Buchan, Ancient Ballads and Songs of the North of Scotland (Edinburgh, 1828), i. 46.

[6] MLN, xiii (1898), 417 ff. See also R, xxviii (1899), 214 ff. Lot's argument (ibid., pp. 568 ff.) that the tale of Caradoc and the serpent originated in Scotland and thence found its way

ballad, Troy Muir,[1] like Caradoc, is delivered from a serpent who has fastened itself to him by the sacrifice of a maiden who cuts off her breast. While this incident in the poem may well be derived from the First Continuation of the *Perceval*,[2] the earlier part is even more remarkable, for it seems to draw from a remote common source a tradition also embedded in the Prose *Lancelot*. In the thirteenth-century text we read of Morgain la Fée's vain effort to seduce young Lancelot, and of the mural paintings which Arthur saw when he visited his sister's castle in the neighbourhood of Edinburgh (Taneborc).[3] In the Scottish ballad we read of the queen's vain effort to seduce young Troy Muir, of her residence in 'Reekie's towers' (Edinburgh castle), and of the 'pictures' set round her bower. Though not strictly Arthurian, the ballad seems to preserve two Arthurian legends which had been kept alive in popular Scottish tradition for at least six centuries.

The heterogeneous group of twenty-three Arthurian romances treated in this chapter is susceptible of no generalization. They represent a great variety of media. They range in artistry from the plodding dullness of Lovelich and the sheer doggerel of the *Turk and Gawain* to the metrical perfection, the quizzical humour, and the robust vitality of the *Wife's Tale*. In tone they vary from the extreme of chivalric honour represented by *Ywain and Gawain* to the extreme of brutal license represented by the *Gest of Gawain*. It is a curious fact that Gawain himself exemplifies in his conduct both extremes! The only definite trend one can observe is the tendency of the later romances (except those concerned with the Grail) to indulge increasingly in buffoonery. But Malory, making skilful use of the Stanzaic *Morte Arthur* as well as of the Alliterative, was destined to restore the level of Arthurian fiction.

through northern England and Wales into French literature ignores the Breton place names in the *Perceval*, and the fact that only French speakers would have invented the story in order to explain the sobriquet Briebras, 'Short-arm'.

[1] Probably a corruption of the name Triamour, the hero of a Middle English romance.

[2] *Continuations of the Old French Perceval*, i. 169–231; ii. 296–370; iii. 164–95.

[3] Sommer, *Vulgate Version*, v. 218, ll. 13 f.; vi. 234, l. 34–239, l. 2. See R. S. Loomis, *Arthurian Tradition*, pp. 112 f., 157; *Proceedings of the Soc. of Antiquaries of Scotland*, lxxxix. 9 f.

THE ENGLISH ALLITERATIVE ROMANCES[1]

J. L. N. O'LOUGHLIN

WHILE in the South of England and the East Midlands various forms of rimed verse were employed by the writers of romance, as we have seen in the last chapter, in the West Midlands, in the North, and even up in Scotland, there was a powerful revival of alliterative forms. These, of course, go back as a narrative vehicle to the great days of Anglo-Saxon poetry, but though Layamon was still writing in the old tradition, with some admixture of rime and assonance, as late as the end of the twelfth century, the dominance of French models and fashions so discouraged the use of alliterative verse that it went out of fashion completely in the South and most of the Midlands. But in regions remote from the capital and less affected by intercourse with France, and especially where the Scandinavian element was strong, the four-beat line with three and often more alliterating words continued to enjoy favour. Not, of course, with the French-speaking upper classes but with a humbler public, at least a public which could not or would not pay for the recording of these longish poems on parchment. The result is that between 1200 and 1350 there is a gap in the tradition as it has come down to us.

But there can be no doubt that the tradition was alive and vigorous. For when things specifically English regained favour and those who spoke English grew more literate and wealthy, the poets of the West Midlands and the North found patrons who could afford to pay for copies of their effusions— no small matter if the poem ran to 14,000 lines; and after 1350 two of the greatest English poets of the Middle Ages, Langland and the anonymous author of *Gawain and the Green Knight*, used this ancient English heritage as a natural medium of expression. The best of the alliterative poets possessed a rich and racy native vocabulary and showed little or no trace of French influence on their style. We can only conclude that they were inspired, not by the reading of Old English codices, but by several generations of poets their predecessors, whose works, though not preserved in manuscript, were memorized and recited before appreciative audiences.

Probably the earliest of the Arthurian romances produced in the alliterative tradition is *Joseph of Arimathea*,[2] a fragment of 709 lines, lacking a

---

[1] For bibliographical references to Middle English romances see above, p. 480, n. 1.
[2] *Joseph of Arimathie*, ed. W. W. Skeat, EETS, xliv (1871).

beginning. Since it is preserved in the Vernon manuscript in the Bodleian Library, it must have been composed before 1375. Skeat thought that the ruggedness of the metre was evidence of an early date,[1] but this defect could be due to other causes. The imperatives in -*s* suggest a Northern origin, and, if they are original, then the trisyllabic weak preterites, to which Luick called attention,[2] would indicate a date well before 1340. The dialect of the manuscript, on the other hand, is South-west Midland.

The alliterative *Joseph* parallels closely the content of pp. 18–75 of Sommer's edition of the *Estoire del Saint Graal*,[3] beginning with Joseph's release from prison and ending with his departure from Sarras. There has been drastic curtailment, however, particularly of the speeches. The most effective part of the poem is the description of the battle (vss. 489–614), done in the typical alliterative style, but as a whole the piece is hardly more than competent learner's work.

The Alliterative *Morte Arthure*[4] is a romance of far higher quality, is, in fact, one of the masterpieces of the alliterative revival. Preserved in a manuscript (Lincoln Cathedral A 5. 2) in the hand of Robert of Thornton, Yorks., it runs to 4,346 lines in the stricter metre. The latest possible date for its composition is set by the handwriting and watermarks as 1430–40. Sources which the author must have used—the *Voeux du Paon* (*c.* 1310), *Somer Soneday* (*c.* 1327)—fix the earliest limits, and Eagleson's study of the costume brings the poem down to about 1360.[5] This date would accord with the spirit of the work and its echoes of English expansionism at the time of the Treaty of Brétigny (1360). On this point the study of the language offers little help, since the author made use of archaic forms.[6]

As to his identity there has been much and largely sterile controversy. Andrew of Wyntown, writing the *Orygynale Cronykil of Scotland* about 1425, remarked of a poet named Huchown that

> He made the gret Gest off Arthure
> And the Awntyre off Gawane
> The Pystyll als off Swete Susane.[7]

---

[1] Ibid., p. x.   [2] *Anglia*, xi (1889), 572.
[3] See Chap. 22.

[4] The text is most accurately reproduced in Brock's edition for the EETS. Mrs. Banks's edition has useful notes but has been superseded by Björkman's. The discovery of the Winchester manuscript of Malory and the progress of knowledge render a new edition necessary, and the present writer has one nearly ready. Branscheid's sketch of the sources in *Anglia Anzeiger*, viii. 179–221, has been supplemented and corrected by Imelmann, *Laʒamon: Versuch über seine Quellen*, and by Griffith, 'Malory, Morte Arthure, and Fierabras', *Anglia*, xxxii. 389–98. Neilson's *Huchown of the Awle Ryale* contains useful material for the historical background. Vinaver gives a detailed comparison with Malory's Book V in his edition of the *Works*, iii. 1360–97. See also Chap. 40 below, pp. 548 f. Boyle's translation in *Morte Arthur: Two Early English Romances*, Everyman's Library, is of value only to give a general idea of the story.

[5] *PMLA*, xlvii (1932), 345. See also *MedAev*, iv (1935), 167.
[6] *Anglia*, xi (1898), 593.   [7] v. xii. 4324.

(He composed the great historical poem of Arthur and the Adventure of Gawain and also the Epistle of Sweet Susanna.)

The last-named poem still exists in several manuscripts, and it was argued that Huchown was the author not only of the *Pistill of Susan* but also of a corpus of poems including the *Morte Arthure*, identified as 'the gret Gest off Arthure'. The evidence adduced for common authorship consisted of resemblances in phraseology; but these formed part of the common stock of alliterative verse of the period, and the very obvious differences between the poems ascribed to Huchown render the attribution to a single man out of the question. A second theory identified Wyntown's Huchown with a Scot, Sir Hew of Eglinton, mentioned by Dunbar. These two theories were critically examined and rejected by H. N. McCracken;[1] indeed the bare mention of 'Scathyll Scotlande' (Baneful Scotland) in the *Morte Arthure*, vs. 32, should have destroyed any claims for Scottish authorship. The vocabulary, too, is that of the North-west Midlands, sharing many expressions with the poems of MS. Brit. Mus. Nero A x (*Pearl, Patience, Purity, Gawain and the Green Knight*), and Luick has also pointed out metrical similarities.[2] But there are several features which suggest that the original poem was composed not in Lancashire or Derbyshire but farther to the north and east, namely in West Yorkshire. Certain words survive in the dialects of the latter district, and the reference to Catterick as a halting place on the route from Carlisle to the south points the same way.

In the course of transmission the original North-west Midland dialect has been modified first by a Southern scribe and secondly by the Yorkshire forms of Robert of Thornton. More than that, there is clear evidence that, like other romances in the Thornton manuscript, the *Morte Arthure* has been reconstructed from memory. Internal evidence and a comparison with Malory's redaction in the Winchester manuscript show that whole passages of the Alliterative *Morte* have been transposed, half-lines have been substituted from other contexts, names altered or introduced from other romances,

---

[1] *PMLA*, xxv (1910), 507. The problem of authorship was not solved, however, by McCracken. The long series of Arthur's conquests cited by Wyntown in his account of Huchown is derived, not, as McCracken said, from a *Brut* tradition, but from the conquests of Alexander, and these recur in *Morte Arthure*. Wyntown lists eighteen countries, five pairs of which alliterate and all of which are in *Morte Arthure*, mainly in vss. 30–47, and *Morte Arthure* borrows frequently from the French Alexander poems. McCracken declined to identify Huchown's *Gest* with *Morte Arthure* because Wyntown wrote: 'bot of his dede and his last ende / I fonde na wryt couythe mak it kende', whereas *Morte Arthure* has a circumstantial account of Arthur's death and burial; but the passage means, 'But as to his death and his final end, I found no document to make it authentic'. See *NED*, ken v. 18. In other words, Wyntown found confirmation for most of the details in his summary of Arthur's career as related by Huchown, but he could find no support for the *Gest*'s account of Arthur's death. What Wyntown meant by 'of the Awle Ryale' is a matter for speculation. Probably it signified 'of the royal court', but it would be strange to find such verse being composed for the king's court, where the language would have been almost incomprehensible and the techniques alien to southern taste.   [2] *Anglia*, xi. 597.

words and phrases changed to the detriment of metre and sense, passages omitted or clumsily patched over. All this should be borne in mind in judging the poet's competence and in tracing his literary relationships.

The Arthurian connexions are clearly with Geoffrey of Monmouth and, to be more exact, with a text of Wace closely related to that which Layamon used.[1] The poet's use of *Somer Soneday* shows that he could handle his sources with intelligence and independence, so that we are under no obligation to suppose that he followed his French 'cronycles' very closely. He was strongly affected by the Alexander cycle, particularly by the late romances, the *Voeux du Paon* (*Vows of the Peacock*) and the *Fuerre de Gadres* (*Foraging Expedition of Gadres*).

Even when unaffected by these literary influences the poet dealt freely with his version of Wace. He linked the tale of Arthur's vengeance on the giant of Mont St. Michel with the tale of the giant who collected the beards of kings—tales treated quite separately by Wace. It is evident that he wished to emphasize the role of Arthur when he assigned to the king, not to Sir Bedwer as in the earlier texts, the encounter with the old woman who relates the rape and murder of Hoel's niece. In other ways, by extending Arthur's conquests, comparing him favourably with other heroes, and attaching to him exploits traditionally ascribed to his knights, the romancer emulated and exceeded Geoffrey of Monmouth. It would be rash to identify Arthur and Gawayne with Edward III and the Black Prince, but there can be little doubt that these historic figures and their deeds stirred the poet's imagination and patriotic ardour. Edward's campaigns and the sea-battle of Winchelsea, otherwise known as Les Espagnols sur Mer, are reflected in specific detail by certain lines in the *Morte Arthure*.

The poem is firm in structure; events follow each other with a natural logic. After an elaborate minstrel prelude, the story opens with a recapitulation of Arthur's conquests, derived from Wace and the Alexander cycle. Then, in accordance with convention, the king is about to begin a banquet when messengers arrive from Lucyus, Emperor of Rome, and summon him to do homage. The British knights, however, promise Arthur their support and, as in the *Voeux du Paon*, each vows to perform a deed of valour in battle against the Romans. The messengers are splendidly entertained at a banquet, details of which are supplied by Walter de Bibbesworthe. After hurling

---

[1] It was Imelmann's view (op. cit.) that an expanded version of Wace lay behind Layamon and *Morte Arthure*. J. S. P. Tatlock in his *Legendary History of Britain*, pp. 479–82, threw doubt on Imelmann's evidence, and though it is probable that the Wace text known to Layamon and the poet of *Morte Arthure* included variants which do not appear in the known manuscripts, they seem to be too few to justify the term 'expanded Wace'. The occurrence of the otherwise unrecorded word *lothyn*, 'shaggy', in *Morte Arthure*, vs. 1095, and at the corresponding point in Robert Mannyng's translation of Wace may possibly indicate that Mannyng was the source rather than the French text of the *Brut*.

defiance at the emperor and sending back the messengers, Arthur prepares to sail for France. In a dream he sees a dragon, himself, defeat a bear, Lucyus—a combination of themes derived from Wace and the prophecies of Merlin. Landing in Brittany, he kills the giant of Mont St. Michel. Lucyus, meanwhile, has gathered his vassals from Europe and the Orient, the list being made up from Wace and the Alexander cycle. In a battle which bears some resemblance to the victory at Crécy the British knights perform their vows and defeat Lucyus.

The author now takes the opportunity to make large additions to Wace's narrative. Arthur kills the emperor and on the way to Rome lays siege to Metz. The details of the siege and of a foraging expedition led by Gawayne are suggested by the *Fuerre de Gadres*. On the other hand, Gawayne's encounter with a heathen knight, ending in the latter's conversion, is modelled on the *chanson de geste*, *Fierabras*.[1] After the capture of Metz Arthur descends into Italy, following an itinerary which reveals an accurate knowledge of geography,[2] and in Viterbo receives the submission of the Romans. That night he has a dream of Fortune's wheel—a borrowing from the Vulgate *Mort Artu*—and on the wheel he sees eight of the Nine Worthies or great conquerors, as listed in the *Voeux du Paon*.

The events now follow Wace's outline, though with obvious deviations and elaborations. Sir Craddoke (Caradoc) arrives with the news of Mordred's treason and Gaynour's adultery. Arthur, hastening back to Britain, defeats Mordred's navy at sea; here there are reminiscences of the battle of Winchelsea.[3] In the course of the landing Gawayne is killed by Mordred, who laments his death in a passage based on the *Fuerre de Gadres*. Arthur then gives battle, his forces are victorious, but though he slays Mordred, he receives a fatal wound. Instead of passing to Avalon, he is carried to Glastonbury, dies, and is buried with due solemnity.

The late R. W. Chambers classed the Alliterative *Morte Arthure* with *Beowulf* and *Paradise Lost* in the line of English epics, and as epic it should be judged. Two obstacles, however, stand in the way of adequate recognition: first, the richness and strangeness of its Northern vocabulary, which make it incomprehensible except to specialists, and secondly, the corruption of the text. Once these have been surmounted, the poem emerges as a masterpiece of narrative art on a large scale. It portrays the rise of a noble, valiant king, and his fall brought about by the Aristotelian *hamartia* of his begetting of Mordred. It has an aristocratic appeal which separates it from the bourgeois romances of the Auchinleck manuscript and the even humbler style of *Havelok* and *King Horn*. Arthur's threnody for Gawayne is one of the most moving passages in Middle English literature (vss. 3949–68).

---

[1] Griffith in *Anglia*, xxxii (1909), 389–98.   [2] Parks in *JEGP*, xlv (1946), 164–70.
[3] G. Neilson, *Huchoun of the Awle Ryale* (Glasgow, 1902), pp. 59–62.

Than gliftis the gud kyng: and glopyns in herte,
Gronys full grisely: wyth gretande teris,
Knelis down to the cors: and kaught it in armes,
Kastys upe his umbrere: and kyssis hym sone,
Lokes one his eyeliddis: that lowkkide ware faire,
His lippis like to the lede: and his lire falowede.
Than the corownde kyng: cryes full lowde,
'Dere kosyn o kynde: in kare am I levede.
For nowe my wirchipe es wente: and my were endide.
Here es the hope of my hele: my happynge of armes.
My herte and my hardynes: hale one hym lengede,
My concell, my comforthe: that kepide myn herte.
Of all knyghtes the kynge: that undir Criste lifede,
Thou was worthy to be kyng: thofe I the corown bare.
My wele and my wirchipe: of all this werlderiche
Was wonnen thourghe Sir Gawayne: and thourghe his witt one.
Allas!' said Sir Arthure: 'now ekys my sorowe.
I am uttirly undon: in myn awen landes.
A, dowttouse derfe dede: thou duellis to longe!
Why drawes thou so one dreghe?: Thow drownnes myn herte!'

(Then the valiant king looked and was sad at heart, groaned dreadfully, with tears of grief, knelt down by the dead body, and caught it up in his arms, lifted up his visor, and kissed him quickly, looked on his eyelids that were tightly closed, his lips like lead, and his pale countenance. Then the royal monarch cried aloud, 'Dear kinsman by blood, I am in sorry plight. For now my honour has departed and my struggle is ended. Here lies the expectation of my well-being, my success in battle. My courage and my valour stemmed wholly from him, my counsel, my succour that sustained my spirit. The king of all knights in Christendom, thou wert worthy to be king, though I wore the crown. My good fortune, my good name on earth were gained through Sir Gawayne, and through his wisdom alone. Alas,' said Arthur, 'now my sorrow increases. I am utterly destroyed in mine own land. Ah, treacherous, cruel Death, thou lingerest too long! Why dost thou hold back? Thou overwhelmest my spirit!')

The poet delights in descriptive passages which call into play his technical virtuosity and the abundant resources of his vocabulary. Noteworthy are his accounts of Arthur's dreams (vss. 760–805, 3230–391), and of the arming of Arthur (vss. 900–15), the description of the giant (vss. 1074–103) and of the sea-battle (vss. 3652–705). In vss. 920–32 and 2506–12 he shows himself capable of a more pastoral note, and his sober account of the king's funeral (vss. 4328–41) brings the epic to a quiet and impressive close. Though there is less subtlety of characterization than in *Gawain and the Green Knight*, there is no mean skill displayed in the portrayal of Gaynour (vss. 697–716), in the bluff behaviour of Sir Cayous, in the *flyting* of the knights before battle, in the unwillingness of Mordred to accept the regency (vss. 679–88), and in the contrast between the odious Lucyus and his pagan allies on the one hand and the Christian chivalry of Arthur and Gawayne on the other. Though the author was aware of the unfavourable light in which certain late French romances represented Gawain and Lancelot, he remained faithful to the earlier tradition which kept their names unsullied.

The *Morte Arthure* must once have enjoyed a considerable circulation though surviving in only one manuscript. There are signs that the description of the giant (vss. 1078–90) influenced that of Nebuchadnezzar in *Purity* (vss. 1689–96). There is unmistakable evidence that the prophecies in the *Awntyrs of Arthur* (vss. 287–312) are based on the Alliterative *Morte*. 'Blind Harry' in his *Wallace* proves that our poem was known in Scotland, and so, perhaps, does Wyntown's reference to the 'Great Gest of Arthur'. Malory's paraphrastic summary of vss. 1–3217 in Book V of his compilation has long been noted. Though it is generally assumed that Malory postponed the tragic doom and brought Arthur back in triumph from Rome, thus contradicting the poem as we have it, there is some evidence that he followed a version which ended in this way. For the prelude of the poem (vss. 16–24) promises no more, and the closing passage in Malory where he diverges from the Thornton manuscript contains phrases which seem to be drawn from an alliterative poem.

The *Awntyrs of Arthur*, referred to above, seems to have borrowed not only from the *Morte Arthure* but also from *Gawain and the Green Knight*, and consequently may be dated after 1375, and the five manuscripts are all of the fifteenth century.[1] The setting of the first part is the Tarn Wadling (now drained) in Cumberland, and the poet's familiarity with this region and the Scottish Lowlands simplifies the problem of provenance. As noted in the last chapter, this lake seems to have had strong Arthurian associations, and Ritson in his *Life of King Arthur* mentions a local legend of a castle in its depths. Dunbar's reference to a Clerk of Tranent who made 'the anteris of Gawane' cannot apply to this poem for linguistic reasons,[2] even though the chief character is in fact Gawain rather than Arthur.

Beginning with the description of a hunt, partly derived from *Gawain and the Green Knight* (vss. 1139–77), the poem recounts the appearance of the ghost of Gaynour's mother to Arthur's hunting party and her appeal for thirty masses to be said for the release of her soul from torment. The source of this macabre scene is the legend of the trental of St. Gregory, which appears elsewhere in Middle English. At vs. 339 the narrative is transferred to Arthur's court. A Scottish knight, Sir Galeron, whose lands Arthur has alienated, rides up to the high table as a banquet is about to be served, and challenges one of the knights to combat. Gawain accepts and is on the point

---

[1] Only the first four manuscripts are dealt with in *Scottish Alliterative Poems*, ed. F. J. Amours, Scottish Text Soc. (1897). See Hooper in *Leeds Studies in English*, iii (1934), 37–43.

[2] Hooper in *Leeds Studies in English*, iv (1935), 62–74.

of winning when the king halts the combat, and Galeron resigns his claim, but is made a knight of the Round Table. The source of this episode is unknown, but Sir Galeron of Galway (i.e. Galloway in Scotland) is apparently the same as the 'Galerantis li Galois' (the Welshman) of Chrétien's *Erec* (MS. A). He is also mentioned in the Alliterative *Morte Arthure*, the *Carl of Carlisle*, and in Malory, Book XII, chap. xiii.

The coupling of two such unrelated themes is certainly naïve, but in other respects the poem displays a not inconsiderable art. The difficult stanza, combining long alliterative lines riming *abab-abab* with an alliterating wheel riming *cdddc*, is well handled. As in the other poems of the Northern school, the descriptions are notable for their vigour and realism.

Somewhat similar in character and verse form is *Golagros and Gawain*, preserved only in the Chepman and Myllar print in the National Library of Scotland.[1] It consists of 105 stanzas combining long alliterative lines riming *ababcbcbb* with a wheel riming *ddb*. The language is literary Middle Scots, and the traces of aureate diction suggest a date not long before 1500.[2]

The content of the romance derives from two unrelated episodes in the First Continuation of Chrétien's *Perceval*, and Kettrick has shown that the author must have worked from a manuscript similar to that used for the prose paraphrase printed at Paris in 1530.[3] The first episode is based on Kay's foraging expedition and his visit to the castle where his surly behaviour earns him a buffet. The second is concerned with the Riche Soudoier and the siege of Chastel Orguellous. The author dealt somewhat freely with his source. He substituted the name Spinagros for Brandelis, and invented, apparently, the name Golagros for the anonymous Soudoier. Battles take the place of tournaments, and the love interest is discarded. Thus we hear nothing of Gawain's affair with the sister of Brandelis, nor of the love-trance of the Soudoier, and Gawain surrenders to the Soudoier out of disinterested chivalry, not for the satisfaction of the Soudoier's lady.

The alliterative romances discussed in this chapter provide a fair sampling of this North Midland and Northern school, and illustrate its masculine force, its fondness for action and realistic detail, and its occasional disregard of unity. They hardly prepare us for the perfection of plot, the delicacy of feeling, and the sensitiveness to beauty which distinguish that masterpiece of the alliterative school, *Gawain and the Green Knight*, the subject of the next chapter.

[1] *The Chepman and Myllar Prints . . . A Facsimile*, ed. W. Beattie, Edinburgh Bibliographical Soc. (1950), pp. 7–52.

[2] O. Noltemeier, *Über die Sprache des Gedichtes, 'The Knightly Tale of Golagros and Gawane'* (Marburg, 1889).

[3] P. J. Ketrick, *Relation of Golagros and Gawane to the Old French Perceval* (Washington, 1931); *Tresplaisante et Recreatiue Hystoire du Trespreulx et Vaillant Chevalier Perceual le Gallois*.

GAWAIN AND THE GREEN KNIGHT

LAURA HIBBARD LOOMIS

THE hero of *Gawain and the Green Knight (GGK)*[1] is likened to a pearl beside a pea (vs. 2364), and so might the poem itself be reckoned among its contemporaries. It moves over an almost flawless structure as smoothly as supple skin over the bones of the hand. With the exception of Chaucer's *Troilus and Criseyde*, no other Middle English romance approaches its artistic and spiritual maturity, its brilliant realism, its dramatic vigour, its poetic sensitivity to nuances of word and mood, its humour, its nobility of spirit.

This treasure of Middle English poetry exists in only one manuscript (British Museum, Cotton Nero A X), dated by the handwriting of its one scribe and the costumes of its rather crude illustrations about 1400.[2] The romance has 2,530 lines written in stanzas running from twelve to thirty-eight long lines of unrimed alliterative verse, each stanza concluding with a 'bob and wheel' of five short riming lines.[3] The author's mastery of alliterative phraseology predicates a close acquaintance with antecedent alliterative poems, but the extent of his indebtedness to earlier English verse or of his own influence on later verse is still largely undetermined.[4] His poetic pre-

---

[1] All references to *GGK*, unless otherwise indicated, are to the edition by Sir I. Gollancz, re-edited by M. Day and M. S. Serjeantson, EETS (1940); bibliography, pp. lxvii–lxxii. Other editions are by J. R. Tolkien and E. V. Gordon (T & G, Oxford, 1925, 1930, 1936); and by E. Pons (Paris, 1946, with French translation). For recent renderings into modern English see T. H. Banks (New York, 1929); K. Hare (London, 1946, 1948); M. R. Ridley (London, 1950, 1955); Gwyn Jones (London, 1952).

[2] A facsimile of the manuscript was published with an introduction by Sir I. Gollancz, EETS, 1923. For description of manuscript see *GGK*, pp. ix ff., and R. S. and L. H. Loomis, *Arthurian Legends in Medieval Art* (New York, 1938), pp. 138 f., with illustrations of miniatures (figs. 389–91). On scribal matters see Greg in *Library*, xiii (1933), 188–91, and Oakden, ibid. xiv. 353–8.

[3] J. P. Oakden, *Alliterative Poetry in Middle English*, i (Manchester, 1930), pp. 177 f., 218, 251–5, 266. See *GGK*, p. lxviii; T & G, pp. 118–21.

[4] Oakden, op. cit. ii, *passim*. For relation to Alliterative *Morte Arthure* and *Awntyrs of Arthur* see Chap. 38 above; to *Carl of Carlisle* and *Turk and Gawain* see Chap. 37 above. For theories about relation of *GGK* to *The Green Knight* see G. L. Kittredge, *Study of GGK* (Cambridge, Mass., 1916), pp. 125–35, 282–9; Hulbert in *MP*, xiii (1915–16), 49 ff., 461 f.; O. Löhmann, *Die Sage von GGK*, *Albertus Univ. geisteswissenschaftliche Reihe*, xvii (1938), 24–36. For relation to *Wars of Alexander* see *GGK*, pp. xiii–xviii; for connexion of *GGK*, vss. 2414 ff., with *King Alisaunder* see King in *MLR*, xxix (1934), 435 f. For possible influence of *GGK* on Chaucer's *Squire's Tale* see Chapman in *MLN*, lxviii (1953), 521–4; Whiting in *Medieval Studies*, ix (1947), 230 ff. For the influence of *GGK* on a poem by Humphrey Newton (d. 1536) of Cheshire, see Robbins in *MLN*, lviii (1943), 361–6; *PMLA*, lxv (1950), 249–81; Cutler in *JEGP*, li (1952), 562–70.

eminence, however, his outstanding artistry, have been searchingly studied and praised since 1839 when, in his *Syr Gawayne*, Sir Frederick Madden first published the poem.

The manuscript contains three other poems which, because of close similarities in vocabulary, phrasing, style, and spirit to *GGK*, have led to a general belief in their common authorship.[1] From different interpretations of the exquisite, elegiac-seeming *Pearl*, the homiletic *Patience* and *Purity* (*Cleanness*), and *GGK*, conjectural biographies and personalities have been built up for the poet, and several identifications have been proposed.[2] None of them, however, has won acceptance, and the identity of the 'Master Anonymous' remains a mystery. Was he a monk, a minstrel, a learned clerk, an official in some lordly household, or himself a man of rank and wealth?[3] In any case he wrote as one familiar with courtly life, its pleasures, luxuries, arts, and ways.[4]

The realistic references in *GGK* to North Wales, Anglesey, and the wilderness of Wirral in Cheshire (vss. 697–701) are unusual. The scenic descriptions, the extensive use of words of Scandinavian origin, the dialect, all place the author's home in the North-west Midland area.[5] The detailed account of the so-called Green Chapel and the great castle near by have suggested even more precise localizations.[6] The architecture, the costume, the armour, so accurately described, are appropriate to a date between 1360 and 1400, and of the four poems in the manuscript *GGK* is considered the

---

[1] *GGK*, pp. x–xiii; *Purity*, ed. R. J. Menner (New Haven, 1920), pp. xix–xxvii; Oakden, op. cit. i. 72–87, 251–3; ii. 88–93, 393 ff.; D. Everett, *Essays on Middle English Literature* (Oxford, 1955), pp. 68–96. The attribution to one author has been questioned for reasons more ingenious than convincing by J. W. Clark in *JEGP*, xlix (1950), 60 ff.; *MLN*, lxv (1950), 232 ff.; *MLQ*, xii (1951), 387 ff.

[2] For proposed identifications see *GGK*, pp. xviii f. For notably perceptive comments on the poet's nature, learning, background see *Pearl*, ed. C. Osgood (Boston, 1906), pp. xlvii–xlix; H. L. Savage, *The Gawain-Poet* (Chapel Hill, 1956), ch. i.

[3] Despite the poet's piety and knowledge of biblical and theological matters, his secularity has been increasingly emphasized. See *Pearl*, ed. Osgood, pp. lii–liv; T & G, p. xx. Oakden, op. cit. i. 257–61, thought him a retainer of John of Gaunt; Savage, op. cit., pp. 206–13, would assign him to the household of John's French brother-in-law, Enguerrand de Coucy, of whose chivalric character and English experiences, 1363–77, Savage (pp. 99–117) thought he detected some reflections in *GGK*. But the content and genesis of the poem seem best accounted for by the literary sources.

[4] For the poet's knowledge of music see Chapman in *PMLA*, xlvi (1931), 177–81; for courtly manners and sports see discussion below.

[5] Southern Lancashire, Cheshire, and Derbyshire have been suggested for the poet's home. For bibliography see *GGK*, p. lxviii, and Menner in *PMLA*, xxxvii (1922), 503–26; Serjeantson in *RES*, iii (1927), 327 f.; Oakden, op. cit. i. 82–87; Savage, op. cit., pp. 128–33.

[6] Tolkien and Gordon (p. 94), following Madden, accepted Volsty Castle and the neighbouring Chapel of the Grene, Cumberland. Oakden, op. cit. i. 257 f., proposed John of Gaunt's castle of Clitheroe, Lancs. Mabel Day (*GGK*, p. xx) identified the Green Chapel with a small, rocky 'cave projecting from a hillside' at Wetton Mill, Staffs., but confused it with Thor's cave (Thursehouse), a huge cavern in a cliff a mile away, which could not possibly fit the poet's description (vss. 2178–83). The supposition that the Green Chapel was a megalithic barrow (*GGK*, note to vs. 2172) is questioned by Brewer in *Notes and Queries*, cxciii (1948), 194 f.

latest.[1] Though no one has succeeded in connecting the green girdle worn as a baldric by the knights of Arthur's household (vss. 2515 ff.) with any historic order of chivalry, Gawain's wearing a costume like that of a knight of the Garter (vss. 1928 ff.) and the insertion of the Garter motto after the close of the poem have tempted some to think that the author wrote under the patronage of a knight of that order, renowned for chivalry and possessed of estates in the North-west Midlands, where the poet was at home.[2]

The romance, according to vss. 31–36, was heard 'in toun', but was also known to the author in a book (vs. 690). He proposes to tell it in 'letteres loken', that is, in alliterative verse.

Sources and Analogues

The main framework of the plot is known as the Challenge or the Beheading Game, and into this has been skilfully fitted a second major element called the Temptation. The earliest version of the Challenge is found in *Bricriu's Feast* (*BF*), a composite Irish saga of the eighth century extant in a manuscript antedating 1106.[3] The saga contains, in fact, two variants of the Challenge (*BF*, p. 99) and refers to other book versions. The first, or 'Terror', version is shorter and more archaic; the second, the 'Champion's Bargain', is more elaborate. In each a shape-shifting enchanter challenges Cuchulainn and two other Ulster heroes, likewise contending for the championship, to exchange with him a decapitating blow. Twice the challenger is decapitated but walks away with his head and returns the next day, his head restored to its place. Cuchulainn alone keeps his part of the bargain, and after receiving one or more pretended blows from the challenger's axe, he is acclaimed the champion. When this legend passed out of Ireland, it lost its most primitive and savage elements, and, somewhat rationalized and simplified, it passed eventually into several Arthurian romances. Of these, *GGK* has preserved by far the largest number of features which go back to some form of the Irish saga.[4]

In a fundamental study Kittredge summarized the Challenge as it appeared in these romances.[5] The earliest extant French version forms part

[1] *GGK*, p. xiii; T & G, pp. xx–xxii; Brett in *MLR*, xxii (1927), 451–8; Savage, op. cit., pp. 8, 141 f., 222.

[2] Connexion of the poem with the Order of the Garter was maintained by I. Jackson in *Anglia*, xxxvii (1913), 393–423; Cargill and Schlauch in *PMLA*, xliii (1928), 118–23; and by Savage, op. cit., *passim* (see especially pp. 146 ff. for a list of Garter knights with West Midland holdings). For those opposed to the Garter connexion see Menner, *Purity*, pp. xxvii ff.; Hulbert in *MP*, xiii. 710–18; T & G, pp. xx, 117.

[3] *Fled Bricrend* or *Feast of Bricriu* (*BF*), ed. G. Henderson (London, 1899), with English translation; Kittredge, op. cit., pp. 9–26.

[4] A. Buchanan in *PMLA*, xlvii (1932), 328 f.; R. S. Loomis, *Wales*, pp. 77 f.

[5] Kittredge, op. cit., pp. 26–74. See also Chap. 20 above for *Perlesvaus*; Chap. 28 for the *Mule sans Frein* and *Hunbaut*; and Chap. 37 for the *Carl of Carlisle* and the *Green Knight*. Kittredge's argument that the 'Champion's Bargain' was the sole source of the Challenge was refuted by Alice Buchanan, loc. cit., pp. 316–25.

of the so-called *Livre de Caradoc*,[1] included in the First Continuation of Chrétien's *Perceval*, and treated above in Chap. 17. Though the hero of the Challenge is Caradoc, not Gawain, it presents the closest correspondence to *GGK*. Both poems transform the court of Ulster into that of Arthur, and refer to his custom of waiting for a marvel to happen;[2] alike they mention the queen's presence and describe the challenger, not, as in the Irish, as a huge and hideous churl (*bachlach*), but as a tall knight who rides into Arthur's hall. Both offer parallels to the Irish challenger's grim proposal, his taunting the courtiers with their hesitancy, his decapitation, and his departure. Both tell how the challenge is accepted, not by three successive heroes as in the Irish, but by one, who is described as Arthur's nephew and who modestly speaks of himself as the most foolish of knights. Both romances remark that anyone accepting such a challenge would be mad; both speak of the grief of the knights and ladies for the hero; both add to the Irish hero's protest against the challenger's delay in striking a taunt as to his cowardice ; both change the interval of a day between the challenger's decapitation and his return to a year. Long before the Irish antecedents of the Challenge had been discovered the likeness between the episode in the *Livre de Caradoc* and *GGK* led to the belief that this French romance was the immediate source of *GGK*.[3] But Kittredge's conclusion that they were independent versions of a lost French story seems justified, for only thus could those Irish features which are found exclusively in one poem or the other be accounted for.

Among the Irish elements to be found in *GGK* but not in *Caradoc*, Kittredge (pp. 32–34) and others have noted the following: the challenger's size, his fierce eyes, silence as he enters the hall, his great axe (in *Caradoc* a sword), his high praise of the court, his exit carrying his head, not, as in *Caradoc*, replacing it on his shoulders. To these Irish elements, still preserved in *GGK*, another may well be added. In *GGK* alone the Challenger is named Bercilak (vs. 2445); as the Green Knight he plays the *same role*, is the *same character*, as the Challenger in the 'Champion's Bargain'. There he is repeatedly called a *bachlach* (churl), a trisyllabic word in Irish.[4] Changed in

---

[1] For texts of the Challenge see *Continuations of the Old French Perceval*, ed. W. Roach (Philadelphia, 1949–55), i. 89–97; ii. 209–19; iii. 141–56.

[2] Sixteen romances tell of this custom. Chrétien's *Perceval*, ed. Hilka, p. 668; J. R. Reinhard, *Survival of Geis in Medieval Romance* (Halle, 1933), pp. 182–95. The reference in *Caradoc* may well have been borrowed from a more original part of the *Perceval*. See *Continuations*, ed. Roach, i. 232; ii. 371; iii. 196.

[3] M. C. Thomas, *Gawain and the Green Knight, A Comparison with the French Perceval* (Zurich, 1883), pp. 34–68. See criticism in *R*, xii. 376; J. L. Weston, *Legend of Sir Gawain* (London, 1887), pp. 88 ff.

[4] Hulbert established in *Manly Anniversary Studies* (Chicago, 1923), pp. 12–19, the manuscript reading as Bercilak, and identified the name with that of Bertelak, Bercelai, emissary of the False Guenièvre in the Prose *Lancelot*. The reading was accepted by T & G, p. 114. R. S. Loomis in *Celtic Myth and Arthurian Romance* (New York, 1927), found its origin in Irish *bachlach*. Roland Smith in *JEGP*, xlv (1946), 16 ff., questioning this derivation, proposed a hypothetical Irish form *Bresalach*,

transmission, its meaning lost, the Irish common noun seems to have survived in the English name and best explains its origin.

Though so much in *GGK* was thus ultimately derived from the 'Champion's Bargain', other elements came from the 'Terror' version, also found in *Bricriu's Feast*.[1] In this tale the hero and his two rivals are not tested at the royal court but, journeying into a wild region, stop at a house and receive a guide from their host. They go to Terror, a shape-shifter, who proposes the head-cutting test. Three times, like the Green Knight, he makes a feint with his axe at the hero's neck. The corresponding features in *GGK*, especially the placing of this testing episode away from Arthur's court, establish the influence of the 'Terror' version upon the romance.

Besides the *Livre de Caradoc*, only one other French text provides a version of the Challenge which is significant for *GGK*, namely *Perlesvaus*,[2] discussed in Chap. 20. The Challenge is here set not in a palace hall, but in a Waste City, and its hero is Lancelot. Though differing widely in other respects from *GGK*, it offers three noteworthy resemblances: the challenger whets his axe with a whetstone (l. 6674) as the hero approaches to fulfill his bargain; the hero shrinks from the blow; he is sharply rebuked.[3] These parallels, supplemented by resemblances in phrase, again argue for literary borrowing, whether directly by the English poet or through a French intermediary.[4]

Thus we have three closely related Arthurian versions of the Challenge or Beheading Game. Since they do not agree as to the name of the hero, there is no certainty as to whether Caradoc, Lancelot, or Gawain was the first of Arthur's knights to meet a head-cutting challenger. It is remarkable that the challenger in no version antedating *GGK* appears as a green giant, clad in green and riding a green horse.[5] Explanations for this greenness have been

meaning contentious, and sought to relate the Green Knight to figures outside the Ulster cycle and without any connexion with the head-cutting episode.

[1] Kittredge, op. cit., pp. 97–101; D'Arbois de Jubainville, *Cours de Littérature Celtique*, vi (Paris, 1892), pp. 132–5.

[2] *Perlesvaus*, ed. Nitze and others, i. 136–8, 284–6; discussed ii. 281–3.

[3] Kittredge, op. cit., pp. 52–61, noted the weakening in this episode of the supernatural element.

[4] See *GGK*, pp. xxxi ff., for phrasal parallels. Nitze noted (*Perlesvaus*, ii. 3) that the Bodleian manuscript of *Perlesvaus* was once owned by Sir Brian Fitzalan of Bedale, Yorks. Possibly this very manuscript was read by the *GGK* poet.

[5] No extant French text before the prose *Perceval* printed in 1530 (Roach, *Continuations*, i, p. xxxii) supports Kittredge's belief (pp. 32, 140) that the challenger wore green in an early form of the *Livre de Caradoc*. For him, as for Hulbert (*MP*, xiii. 456 ff.), the challenger was green because in folk-lore green is often a fairy colour. R. S. Loomis in *Arthurian Tradition*, p. 279, n. 7, explains the colour as due to the ambiguity of the Irish and Welsh adjective *glas*, meaning either grey or green, and points out that Curoi, the Irish prototype of the Green Knight, was repeatedly referred to as 'the man in the grey mantle', though the word *glas* is not the word chosen. See Buchanan in *PMLA*, xlvii (1932), 327–30. No historic person seems to have been called the Green Knight. But two fourteenth-century Englishmen, Sir Ralph Holmes and Simon Newton, were known as the Green Squire. See Braddy in *MLN*, lxvii (1952), 240 ff.; Highfield in *MedAev*, xxii (1953), 18–23. Highfield studies an important West Midland family of Newtons of the type which might have produced the author of *GGK*. See above, p. 528, n. 4, for the Cheshire Humphrey Newton (1536) who used *GGK*.

sought in mythology, folk ritual, and folk-lore,[1] but since the ultimate sources of the Challenge—the two tales incorporated in *Bricriu's Feast*—provide no support in the way of hints of vegetation rites or concepts, and since in *GGK* the Green Knight and his other self, Bercilak, have only mid-winter associations,[2] his greenness there can hardly be due to vegetable traits.

Fitted into the framework of the test by decapitation is another test—the three successive temptations to which Gawain is subjected by the wife of the Green Knight. Though the finesse with which these scenes were developed was the poet's own contribution, yet the situation itself, the aggressive wooing of a reluctant young man in bed by a lovely lady—was already employed by romancers in the twelfth century. It is easily recognizable in the *Lanzelet* of Ulrich von Zatzikhoven,[3] which, as noted in Chap. 33, he translated from the Anglo-Norman shortly after 1194.

Lanzelet and two companions are welcomed at the castle of Gala-gandreis, a rich forester. Their host's daughter arrays herself sumptuously and at night tempts each of the three knights in turn in the most wanton manner. The story anticipates *GGK* in its emphasis on her elaborate dress and her young beauty, in the way she sits beside each sleeping knight and wakes him, in her offer of a gold ring and its rejection, in her urgent plea to hear talk of love, and in her frank proposals. The outcome of the temptation scenes differs from that in *GGK* since, though Lanzelet's companions repel the lady's advances, Lanzelet himself is easily persuaded. None the less, the lady's behaviour and conversation are similar enough to those of Bercilak's wife, though on a much lower level, as to suggest that the two poems were following the same original pattern. The Anglo-Norman source of *Lanzelet* also anticipated *GGK* in making Galagandreiz, like Bercilak, a notably human figure; despite warnings of his cruelty, he performs kindly services for his guests, and has almost nothing of the supernatural, gigantic, or imperious

---

[1] E. K. Chambers in his *Medieval Stage* (Oxford, 1902), i. 117, 185, and Nitze in *MP*, xxxiii (1936), 351–65, derive the Challenge from vegetation ritual or myth. Speirs in *Scrutiny*, xvi (1949), 270–300, urged that a ritual underlying the story and 'the poet's belief in its value as myth is what gives the poem its life'. This ignores both the power of individual genius and the evidence of the Irish stories of the Challenge, the sources of *GGK*, which are not easily susceptible to interpretation as vegetation ritual. Even more reckless is the statement of Francis Berry in *The Age of Chaucer* (Pelican Book, 1954, p. 158) that the poet's awareness of 'the generic forces of life . . . realizes itself in the Green Knight; . . . his reckless vigour and amorality of life . . . testify to an assumption that moral behaviour . . . is subservient to and dependent on something more primary—creative energy. Gawain and his society humbly come to terms with the Green Knight.'

[2] Loomis, *Arthurian Tradition*, pp. 208 ff., 230 ff., 280 ff., derived certain episodes in Arthurian romance from Irish texts preserving mythic concepts of sun and storm gods. These sometimes survived as dramatic or picturesque features, but it is to be doubted whether the French authors or the *Gawain*-poet who introduced such elements were conscious of their mythical origin and significance.

[3] Ulrich von Zatzikhoven, *Lanzelet*, trans. K. G. T. Webster (New York, 1951), pp. 34–43, and notes 37, 43.

qualities of other notable hosts in Arthurian romance.[1] Of special interest is the challenge which he issues to Lanzelet the morning after the temptation scenes—a challenge to throw knives at each other in alternation. It is as truly a *jeu parti* as the beheading by alternation in *GGK* and *Bricriu's Feast*,[2] and provides the earliest instance of the combination of the Challenge theme with that of the Temptation.

The *Lanzelet* version did not include the strange feature which Kittredge (pp. 79 ff.) pointed out in other Arthurian romances as well as in *GGK*, namely, that the temptress was the wife of the host and that she wooed at her husband's wish.[3] One of these, *Yder*, offers a striking parallel, representing the lady of the castle as making violent love, at her husband's order, to the hero as he lies in bed in the hall.[4] In other analogues cited by Kittredge her role is passive; she is constrained by her husband or father to admit the guest to her bed in order to test him. This situation presents, as Mabel Day has remarked, but a shadowy likeness to *GGK*. Equally remote from it are two repellent Temptation tales in Latin and French versions of the *Vitae Patrum*.[5]

A significant analogue to the Temptation occurs in the Vulgate *Lancelot* and has been proposed as perhaps 'the immediate cause for the insertion of Morgain la Fée into the English poem'.[6] This enchantress, who in the course of the French narrative thrice attempts to seduce Lancelot in vain,[7] sends her damsel, a younger self as it were, to effect the same end. Three times the girl employs her amorous arts on the recumbent hero. From this episode, with the instigating background figure of Morgain and the foreground figure of the young, active seductress, it is but a step to the two figures in *GGK*, the aged Morgain,[8] prime mover in the plot, and the agent of temptation, Bercilak's young wife. She was, no less than Bercilak, a servitor

---

[1] For these figures, see Kittredge, op. cit., Index, Imperious Host; Loomis, *Arthurian Tradition*, chap. xlvii.

[2] Kittredge, op. cit., pp. 21–23, 219–21, mentioned the combat in *Lanzelet* only as an instance of duelling by alternation and said nothing of the related Temptation.

[3] Kittredge summarized (pp. 83–101) analogues to the Temptation in *Ider*, *Carl of Carlisle*, *Chevalier à l'Epée*, *Hunbaut*.

[4] *Iderroman*, ed. H. Gelzer (Dresden, 1913), vss. 185–510, and p. lv.

[5] E. von Schaubert, 'Der englische Ursprung von *GGK*', *ES*, lxii (1923), 330–446. These tales have been widely but uncritically quoted as true analogues. The author's low estimate of the English poet's skill is almost unique. See *YWES*, iv (1923), 52.

[6] Hulbert in *Manly Anniversary Studies*, p. 18.

[7] H. O. Sommer, *Vulgate Version*, iv. 123–8; v, 91–93, 215–18; *Spec*, xx (1945), 186.

[8] Kittredge (pp. 131–5) and Hulbert in *MP*, xiii. 454, regarded Morgain as a late and poorly integrated element in *GGK*, mainly because she, though a supernatural person, failed in her purposes and did not foresee her failure. But in medieval romance enchanters and enchantresses often suffer defeat. Baughan in *ELH*, xvii (1950), 241–51, defended Morgain's role by the untenable argument that she had sent the Green Knight to purge Arthur's court of moral evil, and that the Beheading Game was 'an apotheosization of chastity'. Likewise unrealistic is the conclusion of J. F. Eagan in *The Import of Color Symbolism in GGK* (St. Louis, 1949), p. 83.

of the resident goddess who sat highest at their table (vs. 1001), who had already forced him to enact the Green Knight's cruel part, and who, presumably, also forced him to order his wife to tempt their guest (vss. 2446–63). No wonder that the young wife was at heart Gawain's 'enmy kene' (vs. 2406). Despite his moral sensitivity, the poet imputes no moral obloquy to the lordly pair who yet were helpless in the power of that malignant goddess. The might of Morgan le Fay (vs. 2446) was, for Gawain himself, a sufficient explanation and exculpation for all that he had endured and made him able to part from the Green Knight on most friendly terms.

The concept of Morgain as an evil enchantress, a witch, had appeared in Hartmann von Aue's *Erek* by 1190; her origin in Celtic mythology and the amazing diversity of her roles in medieval romance have been studied by Lucy Paton and R. S. Loomis.[1] Her wanton traits reappear in many amorous and related Arthurian figures; as we have seen, there are the temptresses in *Lanzelet* and *Yder*, and the splitting of Morgain's personality into two selves in the Vulgate *Lancelot*. The author of *GGK*, apparently familiar with this older dichotomy, has effectively contrasted the goddess, grown old and wrinkled, with the young beauty who is at once Morgain's other self and agent,[2] but who has also a personality of her own.

The earliest example surviving in medieval fiction of a Temptation approximating in curious ways that in *GGK* is to be met in the *mabinogi* of *Pwyll*, attributed to the eleventh century.[3] Arawn, a huntsman and an Otherworld king, like the Green Knight himself (vs. 992), arranged that Pwyll should be lavishly entertained in his absence in his palace and lie with his own wife as a test of his chastity and loyalty.[4] At the year's end Pwyll, like Gawain, was required to meet a supernatural enemy at a river-crossing. The differences between *Pwyll* and *GGK* forbid any thought of direct literary connexion, but undeniably *Pwyll* offers the oldest example of a traditional story pattern in which carnal temptation, whether passively or

[1] L. A. Paton, *Studies in the Fairy Mythology of Arthurian Romance* (Boston, 1903), chap. vii, on the Chapelle Morgain in the Val sans Retour; R. S. Loomis in *Spec*, xx (1945), 183–203; reprinted in *Wales*, pp. 105–30; Loomis, *Arthurian Tradition*, index *sub* Morgain; Hulbert, in *Manly Anniversary Studies*, pp. 16 ff.; T & G, notes on vss. 2452, 2460.

[2] *Sire Gauvain et le Chevalier Vert*, ed. E. Pons (Paris, 1946), p. 74, on Morgain as a foil to Bercilak's wife.

[3] *Mabinogion*, trans. G. and T. Jones, Everyman's Lib., pp. 1–9; for date see p. ix. In *JEGP*, xlii (1943), 170–81, and in *Wales*, chap. vi, R. S. Loomis detected in *Pwyll* four features also combined in *GGK*: the royal huntsman-host; the hero's resistance to the temptation presented by the host's fair wife with the latter's connivance; the anniversary combat; its localization at a river crossing. For other cases of the influence on Arthurian romance of traditions in *Pwyll* see Loomis, *Arthurian Tradition*, index *sub* Pwyll.

[4] These are precisely the virtues tested in *GGK*. In *Pwyll* Arawn's wife, on learning that it was her husband's friend, not her husband, who had slept chastely beside her, said to Arawn: 'Strong hold hadst thou on a comrade for warding off fleshly temptation and for keeping faith with thee.' Cf. Gawain's fears (vss. 1775 f.) that 'he should commit sin [i.e. lechery] and be a traitor to that man'.

actively offered, and a Hospitable Host who constrains wife or daughter to tempt a guest, are recurrent themes. It not only anticipates the conjunction of these and other elements in *GGK* and its analogues, but it at least suggests, as they do not, in its mysterious figure of Arawn and in the Welsh folk-lore connected with him, a clue to the mid-winter associations of Bercilak and his connexion with Morgain la Fée.[1] In *Pwyll* the still half-mythic Arawn hunts with fairy hounds, wears grey wool, and engages in annual combats with Havgan (Summer-White)—an apparent reminiscence of the strife of summer and winter. In Welsh folk-lore Arawn was also identified with that Wild Huntsman who, in Welsh as in European folk-lore, rode with his dogs on the winter winds. As late as 1276 it was remembered by Adam de la Halle that Morgain la Fée had once had for lover Hellekin, chief of the 'chasse furieuse', 'le gringneur prinche qui soit en faerie'. Before this date, then, the wanton Morgain was associated with a wild huntsman of whom, perhaps, some faint traditional trace remains in the wintry world of Bercilak, in the fury of his three hunts, in the occasional wildness of his manner (vs. 1087). But in any case Bercilak as regal host and mid-winter huntsman, as tester, through his own wife, of a hero, as a shape-shifter, finds an ancient prototype in the Welsh Arawn.

The Challenge and the Temptation, then, originated as entirely distinct stories. Who was responsible for their fusion into one of the best plots in medieval fiction?[2] We have seen that both elements appear combined in *Lanzelet*, and that this form of the Temptation, if read in the Anglo-Norman source of *Lanzelet*, may even have provided some suggestions for the *Gawain*-poet. But in other respects *Lanzelet* differs so widely from the English poem (and from *Bricriu's Feast*, with its early versions of the Challenge) that it cannot be regarded as the model for the combination in *GGK*. It is, therefore, still an open question whether the English author derived the Challenge and the Temptation from separate lost French texts (as well as the *Caradoc* version of the Challenge and the *Perlesvaus* version of the Temptation) and fitted the two stories together; or whether he found this highly artistic combination ready made by some French poet of unusual talent. Even if the latter alternative could be proved correct, one can hardly doubt that the English poet found large scope for his own genius in the adaptation of the plot to his special purposes and ideals.

He may well, indeed, have provided the one plot element which is completely non-Celtic in origin. The mutual promise of Bercilak and Gawain, to give each other what each has won at the end of each day, motivates a whole series of consequences. The motif of an Exchange of Winnings, as

---

[1] *JEGP*, xlii. 181–3; Loomis, *Wales*, pp. 81–85.

[2] See A. C. Baugh, *Literary History of England* (New York, 1948), pp. 236–8; G. Kane, *Middle English Literature* (London, 1951), pp. 73–76; *Sire Gauvain*, ed. Pons, p. 15.

Hulbert demonstrated,[1] appeared in a medieval Latin poem known as the *Miles Gloriosus*. A poor knight becomes the partner of a rich citizen; they agree to exchange their winnings. The citizen's faithless wife becomes the knight's mistress and gives him of her husband's treasure. The husband, suspicious, tries thrice to trap the knight, but is ultimately driven forth from his own home. This *fabliau*, now thought to have been written about 1175 in the Loire valley,[2] could have contributed nothing but the exchange idea to *GGK*. No other Arthurian narrative makes any use of the motif, and the deftness with which it is integrated into *GGK* bespeaks the English poet's skill in design and his sensitive perception of character. Gawain, facing the deadly head-cutting test, keeps the protective girdle given him by Bercilak's wife. He breaks his promise and presently suffers deep shame and remorse. The poet, aware of weakness even in the noblest, thus saves his hero from a 'schematic perfection' and humanizes him by his fault and his pain. This treatment of the Exchange motif can hardly be due to anyone but the Englishman who so deliberately fashioned his whole story to a 'fine issue' and a finer end.

Literary Art

The artistry which is revealed in the construction and style of *GGK* is exceptional. Kittredge noted (p. 4) passages which must be considered, because of their individuality, the poet's own. They include the traditional yet original passage on the seasons; the elaborate account of Gawain's arming, so precise and so contemporaneous in detail; the spirited hunting scenes equally exact and expert; the courtly dialogues between Gawain and his temptress, which reveal such delicacy of characterization. This sophisticated familiarity with varied aspects of aristocratic life and thinking prompts the question whether it was due to observation only or came from the intimate awareness of one who had been born to high estate and 'gentilesse'.[3]

The poem bears witness not only to the author's acquaintance with earlier romances in French and English,[4] but also to his awareness of literary types. He speaks of his creation as a 'laye' (vs. 30). The decapitation of the Green Knight is compared to the playing of an interlude (vs. 472), a short dramatic performance introduced between the courses of a banquet.[5] Indeed, *GGK*

[1] *MP*, xiii. 699 f. The text of the *Miles* is published by G. Cohen, *La Comédie Latine en France au XIIe Siècle* (Paris, 1931), i. 181–210.

[2] E. Faral, *Les Arts Poétiques du XIIe Siècle et du XIIIe* (Paris, 1924), pp. 3–6; F. J. Raby, *History of Secular Latin Poetry in the Middle Ages* (Oxford, 1934), ii. 65 ff.

[3] G. Mathew, 'Ideals of Knighthood in Late-Fourteenth Century England', *Studies in Medieval History Presented to F. M. Powicke* (Oxford, 1948), pp. 354–62, notes similarities between the Chandos Herald's characterization of the Black Prince and that of Gawain in *GGK*.

[4] Hulbert noted in *Manly Anniversary Studies*, pp. 16–19, that with two exceptions all the names in *GGK* occur in the French *Vulgate* romances. See also C. O. Chapman, *Index of Names in Pearl, Purity, Patience, and Sir Gawain* (Ithaca, N.Y., 1951).

[5] L. B. Wright in *MLN*, xl (1926), 96–100, and below, p. 538, n. 3, on interludes at banquets. For Arthurian dramatics see Chap. 41 below.

seems to interfuse the well-knit, romantic matter of the former type with the dramatic manner of the latter. It keeps the unified structure of the Breton lais, and, like them, concerns itself with marvels and an exclusively aristo-cratic world.[1] But in preserving their pattern, the *Gawain*-poet transformed their fragile charm. Almost alone among poets before 1400, he told of winter with all its harsh rigours, its freezing rain and snows, its howling winds. He conjured up the sense of cold with an intensity hardly matched till Keats wrote the *Eve of St. Agnes*. He laid his scene realistically in the English north country, on heath and crag and in tangled forests of hoar oaks, hazel, and hawthorn. He swept through this wilderness three great hunts that seem transcripts from life. He breathed into courtliness the naturalness of fine, happy people, rejoicing, even joking together. Here, in truth, and at its best, is 'merry England', splendid, stalwart, joyous, with its great Christmas and New Year feasts and frolics, inspirited by wine and mirth.

The *Gawain*-poet not only made of his romance a lai but also, in its dramatic effectiveness, something of an interlude, with which, as his own reference shows, he was familiar. Scenes are sharply set; speeches reveal character; gestures and bearing are indicated with lively verisimilitude. The Green Knight, enacting the role of the Challenger, does so with all the gusto of an accomplished mummer. He rolls his red eyes, wags his great beard, boasts and taunts derisively, makes, after his decapitation, a tremendous, noisy exit.[2] Though at first he seems almost gigantic (*half etayn*, vs. 140), actually he towers only by a head or so over other men (vs. 332). Apart from his green hue and separable head, he is represented as a fine, handsome, human figure. Later, at the Green Chapel, when he has finished his final testing of Gawain, he drops on the instant his role of magic horror and becomes again the gallant, benevolent Bercilak, full of warm goodwill. Though no moment in medieval romance surpasses in eerie terror that in which he held up his severed head and its eyes opened on Arthur's stricken court (vs. 446), he is primarily described, not as a supernatural being, but as a man acting a part. The gruesome incident of his decapitation is dismissed by Arthur himself, as no more than a play, the device of an interlude (vs. 472). Like Chaucer in the *Franklin's Tale* (vs. 1140),[3] similarly indulging in a bit of rationalizing over the dramatic illusions of skilful magicians, the *Gawain*-poet was in-clined to minimize marvels. He jokes a little about those Gawain encountered on his terrible journey; it would be too 'torc' (hard, vs. 719) to tell a tenth of them; anyway the fighting with giants and trolls was not so bad as the winter

[1] Garrett, 'The Lay of *GGK*', *JEGP*, xxiv (1925), 125–34.

[2] Elizabeth Wright in *JEGP*, xxxiv (1935), 157–63.

[3] For illustration of an *entremets* presented at the French court in 1378 see L. H. Loomis in *Spec*, xxxiii (1958), 242–55. The illumination accords with Chaucer's description (*Franklin's Tale*, vss. 1140–51) of the arts of 'subtile tregetours'.

weather! He derisively pictured Morgain la Fée, though he called her a goddess, only as an ugly, squat, old lady.

As an artist the *Gawain*-poet had the habit of close visual observation and an exceptional sense of form, proportion, and design. As a connoisseur familiar with costly things and courtly taste and custom, he pauses to describe exquisite trifles of embroidery or jewellery, rich fabrics, fine armour. He dwells on the architectural details of the great castle that Gawain first sees shimmering through the distant trees, then in all the glory of its chalk-white, many-towered magnificence. The poet accents social sophistication; manners are polished, talk is an art. The conversations between Gawain and the lady suggest the advances, the retreats, of a courtly dance. Within the set pattern of perfect courtesy, wit meets wit; a gracious comedy of manners is enacted. Temptation is offered to Gawain and refused largely in the tone of light social badinage. One has but to read other society romances[1] in Middle English to recognize the difference between them and the greater elegance, the more assured touch, of the *Gawain*-poet. Moreover, in this romance, unlike many others, there is no inchoate rambling, no waste. The episodes move directly from cause to consequence and individual act and character are finely linked. Situations are repeated, but with skilful, deliberate variety and contrast. Court scenes at royal Camelot are different from those at Bercilak's castle; the three temptations of Gawain have subtle differences of tone and temper; the three hunts, whether they have allegorical significance or not, are as different from each other as are the hunted beasts; each hunt implies expert familiar knowledge.[2] The rich indoor revels, whether at Arthur's court or Bercilak's castle, are effectively alternated with cruel winter realities without, and so is the gay fellowship indoors with Gawain's stark loneliness as he goes by desolate crags to seek his death.

The romance has superlative art in its fashioning; it is mature, deliberate, richly seasoned by an author who never suggests minstrel servility or even compliment to those who hear him.[3] He wrote in his own way and apparently for his own delight in a provincial dialect and in the alliterative verse which belonged to that same north country which he pictured with such startling vigour.

But above all else the romance has a quality of spiritual distinction com-

[1] S. F. Barrow, *Medieval Society Romances* (New York, 1924), Appendix. The English *William of Palerne*, though commissioned by Humphrey de Bohun, Earl of Hereford, has, in comparison with its French original, a homely tone. L. A. Hibbard, *Medieval Romance in England* (2nd ed., New York, 1960), pp. 214–23. Even Chaucer's *Troilus* is less consistently courtly than *GGK*.

[2] Savage in *JEGP*, xxvii (1928), 1–15; Savage, *The Gawain-Poet*, pp. 13, 32–48, 224.

[3] There are references to a listening audience in vss. 30, 624, 1996. For Chaucer's use of such minstrel tags as 'I yow telle' and 'be stille', see *Sources and Analogues of the Canterbury Tales*, ed. Bryan and Dempster (Chicago, 1941), pp. 496–503. Like Chaucer, the *Gawain*-poet may well have expected his work to be read aloud. Such expressions may echo a minstrel convention, but they do not prove minstrel authorship.

parable to that in the *Pearl*. Piety, devotion, purity of thought, are natural to it. Gentle meditations occur, on Troy's vanished glory, on the swift passing seasons with all their yesterdays, on the pentangle[1] as symbol of the endless interlocking of the knot of truth. Richly informed about the lovely things of life, the poem is without asceticism or intolerance. It has no mysticism; Gawain is called the Virgin's knight (v.1769), but he sees no vision, goes on no holy quest. Its deep concern is not with evil, but with good. In this Gawain, the blithe young embodiment of chivalry at its best,[2] goodness is made manifest and radiant, but not, as in Galahad of the Grail romances, a supernatural virtue touched by a mysterious divinity. The 'fine issue' of his story is not that he fell into vulgar sin, but that he failed to keep goodness perfect. Moral earnestness could hardly go farther.[3] Gawain's confession of his fault in breaking his word to save his life reveals a deep sense of Man's responsibility for his every act, no matter how deadly the betraying circumstance. For the author, as for William of Wykeham, 'Manners [in the sense of morals] maketh Man'. Integrity knows no compromise. Wholeheartedly Gawain recognizes this rigorous truth and contrition overwhelms him. Unlike other Arthurian heroes, he returns to Arthur's court, not in conventional glory, but in self-confessed shame. Yet, as noted above, that shame gave him new grace, and the Round Table achieved a new nobility by its act of compassionate fellowship. Henceforth all the knights will wear as a baldric the green girdle that was, to Gawain, the mark of his shame.[4] No other medieval poet, save Wolfram von Eschenbach, has so transformed traditional romantic materials by the grace of his own spiritual insight, or given them more enduring significance.

[1] On the pentangle see Hulbert in *MP*, xiii. 721–30; R. S. Loomis in *JEGP*, xlii. 167–9; Savage, *Gawain-Poet*, pp. 158–68; Ackerman in *Anglia*, lxxvi (1958), 254–65.

[2] Cf. B. J. Whiting, 'Gawain, His Reputation, His Courtesy, and His Appearance in Chaucer's *Squire's Tale*', *Medieval Studies*, ix (1947), 189–254.

[3] Mabel Day in *GGK*, p. xxxv, thought the story 'the vehicle of a great moral lesson'. Baugh strangely remarked (op. cit., p. 236) that it was 'in no sense a story told to enforce a moral'.

[4] Kittredge, op. cit., pp. 139 f., rejected the girdle as a feature of Celtic origin, but see R. S. Loomis in *JEGP*, xlii. 149–55.

SIR THOMAS MALORY

EUGÈNE VINAVER

THE identity of the man to whom Arthurian romance owes its survival in the English-speaking world was first established over sixty years ago by G. L. Kittredge in a short article entitled 'Who Was Sir Thomas Malory?'[1] Much additional evidence has since come to light to confirm the identification; but such knowledge as we now have of Malory's life has little bearing on our understanding of his literary character. Nothing would in fact be lost if he were still allowed to enjoy the advantages of his former obscurity, avoiding the indiscretions of literary biographers and the now fashionable disquisitions about 'the man and his work'.

Sir Thomas Malory's father, John Malory, held various offices in Warwickshire, was M.P. for his county in 1413, and died in 1434. Sir Thomas, born in the early years of the century, succeeded on his father's death to his estate in Warwickshire, served in the train of Richard Beauchamp, Earl of Warwick, at the siege of Calais in 1436[2] and was M.P. for Warwickshire in 1444 or 1445. About that time, however, his career appears to have taken a less conventional turn. Already in 1443 he was charged with an assault on property; little more is known of the case, but from 1451 the records become quite explicit. They allege that on 4 January 1450 Malory lay in ambush 'with other malefactors' in the woods of Combe Abbey for the purpose of murdering the Duke of Buckingham; that on the 25 May of the same year he broke into the house of Hugh Smyth at Monks Kirby and forced his wife Joan; that ten weeks later he repeated this last offence; that in June and July 1451 he led extensive cattle raids at Cosford and at Caludon; and that on two occasions he extorted money by threat. On 23 July, on the strength of these and other charges, he was arrested and committed to the Sheriff of Warwickshire at Coleshill. Five days later, having in the meantime escaped by swimming the Coleshill moat, he is alleged to have broken into the Cistercian abbey of Combe, to have stolen money and valuables from two of the abbot's chests, and on the next day to have repeated the assault with the help of numerous accomplices, broken eighteen doors, insulted the abbot, and stolen more money. Nine months or

---

[1] *Studies and Notes in Philology and Literature*, v (1896), 85–106.
[2] On the date of the siege of Calais see E. K. Chambers, *English Literature at the Close of the Middle Ages* (Oxford, 1945), p. 200.

more elapsed before he was rearrested; repeated postponements of his trial ensued, during which he was variously held by the Sheriffs of London, the King's Marshal, or the Constable of the Tower. In May 1454 he was released on bail and settled for a time in north Essex. There, with the help of a friend and accomplice, John Aleyn, he plotted an attack on the property of William Grene of Gosfield. The attack failed, but on 16 October Malory was committed to the keeper of the jail at Colchester. On 30 October he broke out of jail 'armed with swords, daggers and halberds', was recaptured on 18 November, and committed to the Marshal. In February 1456 he was released on the strength of a royal patent of pardon, but shortly afterwards was imprisoned again, this time at Ludgate, and, with occasional intervals of freedom, remained a prisoner for the next five or six years. The last of his recorded arrests took place in January 1460, when he was sent to Newgate.[1]

How much there was of truth or falsehood in the charges brought against Malory we shall probably never know. In the preface to Hicks's study of Malory's career Kittredge pointed out that indictments were only accusations, not evidence, and that there is no record of a trial and conviction—a point brought out also by Altick in his *Scholar Adventurers*. All we know is that from 1450 onwards Malory was alternately a fugitive from the law and a 'knight-prisoner', as he calls himself in the last lines of his *Tale of King Arthur*. His name occurs in the list of knights who accompanied Warwick the King-maker on an expedition to Northumberland in November 1462.[2] Warwick was at that time a loyalist, and the purpose of the expedition was to raise the royal standard of Edward IV against the forces of Henry VI and Margaret of Anjou. As a Warwickshire man Malory must have followed the shifting policies of Warwick, and later, when Warwick turned against Edward and joined the Lancastrians, Malory probably did so too;[3] but this does not explain why in 1468 he was excluded from two general pardons granted by Edward to the Lancastrians. He died on 14 March 1471, and the fact that he was buried in the church of the Grey Friars near New-gate suggests that he died a prisoner. The last of his romances, *The Tale of the Death of King Arthur*, is concluded, like some of his earlier works, by a colophon combining an appeal for release from prison with expressions of piety and contrition:

[1] The available records have been published by Kittredge (see p. 541, n. 1); by E. E. Hicks, *Sir Thomas Malory: His Turbulent Career* (Cambridge, Mass., 1928); and by A. C. Baugh in *Spec*, viii (1933), 1–29. See also E. K. Chambers, *English Literature*, pp. 199–205; my edition of the *Works* (Oxford, 1947), i, pp. xiii–xxvii; R. D. Altick, *Scholar Adventurers* (New York, 1950), chap. iii. In a review of Chambers's book in *MLQ*, viii (1948), 496, Laura H. Loomis questions the validity of using unproved charges against Malory for biographical purposes.

[2] *Brief Notes of Occurrences under Henry VI and Edward IV from MS. Lambeth 448 (Three Fifteenth Century Chronicles, &c.)*, ed. J. Gairdner, Camden Soc. (1880), p. 157.

[3] E. K. Chambers, *English Literature*, pp. 203 f.

I praye you all, jentylmen and jentylwymmen that redeth this book of Arthur and his knyghtes from the begynnyng to the endynge, praye for me whyle I am on lyve that God sende me good delyveraunce, and whan I am deed, I praye you all praye for my soule. For this book was ended the ninth yere of the reygne of King Edward the Fourth, by Syr Thomas Maleoré, Knyght, as Jesu helpe hym for Hys grete myght, as he is the servaunt of Jesu bothe day and nyght.

The ninth year of the reign of King Edward IV began on 4 March 1469. The work—or works—completed in that year were transcribed several times before they appeared in print. When William Caxton published them on 31 July 1485[1] he described them in the Preface as 'a book of the noble hystoryes of [. . .] kynge Arthur and of certeyn of his knyghtes', and in the colophon as 'the noble and joyous book entytled *Le Morte Darthur*'. He also said that the book was set up from a 'copye' ('after a copye unto me delyverd') which 'Sir Thomas Malorye dyd take oute of certeyn bookes of Frennsshe and reduced it into Englysshe'. For four and a half centuries Caxton's edition and its various adaptations and reprints contained the only known text of the work,[2] but when in the summer of 1934 a more authentic text was found by W. F. Oakeshott in a fifteenth-century manuscript in the Fellows' Library of Winchester College,[3] it became possible to separate Malory's text from Caxton's. Caxton claimed to have printed his 'copye' 'after the symple connynge that God had given' him and to have divided the entire work into twenty-one books and each book into chapters.[4] We now know that the liberties he took were considerably greater. Not only did he rephrase the text, depriving it of some of its original flavour, but he tried to make his readers believe that the volume he published was a single work.[5] To make it appear more homogeneous he gave it a general title, *Le Morte Darthur*, which has since become traditional,[6] deleted the colophons at the end of each of Malory's

[1] Only two copies of this edition are known. One, in the Morgan Library, New York, is complete but for the blank leaf (Sig. i). The other, in the John Rylands Library, Manchester, wants 11 leaves which were supplied in facsimile from the Morgan copy before it left the British Isles.

[2] Five editions appeared in the 150 years following Caxton's *Morte Darthur*, none in the following 182 years, seven between 1816 and 1889, and a much greater number since then. The years 1889–92 saw the publication of H. O. Sommer's faithful reprint of the original Caxton. Most of the editions published between 1892 and 1947 are based on this reprint.

[3] For details of the discovery see *The Times*, 23 July 1934 ('A Malory Manuscript' by W. F. Oakeshott), and the *Times Literary Supplement*, 27 Sept. 1934 ('The Text of Malory' by the same). On the critical value of the manuscript see my edition of Malory's *Works*, i, pp. lxxxvi–xci. The manuscript does not entirely supersede Caxton's text; the latter helps to emend a number of scribal errors and supplies all the missing parts (a gathering of 8 leaves at each end and 4 leaves in the body of the text).

[4] 'And for to understonde bryefly the contente of thys volume I have devyded it into twenty-one bookes and every book chapytred.'

[5] See my article in *BBSIA*, iii (1951), 75–82.

[6] The first editor to use it after Caxton was Haslewood (1816). Southey (1817) and Dent (1893–4) abandoned it, but all the other modern editors have reproduced it, with occasional attempts to correct the gender of *mort*.

romances except the last,[1] and ironed out certain stylistic inconsistencies.[2] Even the division into books and chapters would seem to have been prompted by the desire to present the whole matter as a single composition. In his last colophon Malory makes an important distinction between two well-defined concepts, that of a *series* of works and that of a single *tale* such as his own *Tale of the Death of King Arthur*:

Here is the ende of the hoole book of Kyng Arthur and of his noble knyghtes of the Rounde Table, that whan they were holé togyders there was ever an hondred and forty. And here is the ende of *The Deth of Arthur*.

The 'whole book' is the collection which grew up by means of successive additions of romances often unconnected with each other. Recent critics have tried to revert to the notion of the organic unity of the collection as a whole, only to find themselves ignoring not only Malory's explicit statements and Caxton's implied admissions (such as the use of the plural in his references to Malory's works in the Preface), but the fact that the whole of the middle portion—pp. 289–787—is unrelated to any of the themes which occur before or after.[3] There is no more 'unity' about the series than about Balzac's *Comédie Humaine*, although in both cases there is a certain consistency in the setting, in the atmosphere, and even in the choice and treatment of characters.

The first of Malory's romances—placed second by one of his early copyists—was *The Tale of King Arthur and the Emperor Lucius*,[4] a condensed adaptation of the Alliterative *Morte Arthure* (Caxton's Book V). His first work based upon a French romance was *The Tale of King Arthur* (Caxton's Books I–IV), 'drawn from' the *Suite du Merlin*. The colophon preserved in the Winchester manuscript suggests, however, that at the time when he completed this work he had no further project in mind and no more material at hand.[5] When, after an interval the length of which is unknown, he resumed his task he must have gained access to a manuscript of the French Prose *Lancelot*. With the help of three short fragments selected from this vast composition he wrote his *Noble Tale of Sir Launcelot du Lake* (Caxton's Book VI) and followed it up by *The Book of Gareth* (Caxton's Book VII), the source of which is unknown. Soon afterwards he embarked upon the

---

[1] See my edition of the *Works*, i, pp. xxx f.

[2] I refer particularly to Malory's adaptation of the Alliterative *Morte Arthure* (Caxton's Book V), so archaic in language that Caxton rewrote it almost completely, shortening it by half. See E. V. Gordon, E. Vinaver, 'New Light on the Text of the Alliterative *Morte Arthure*', *MedAev*, vi (1937), 81–98.

[3] For a more detailed account of the problem see my edition of the *Works*, i, pp. xxiv f. Among the more recent studies D. S. Brewer's article 'Form in the *Morte Darthur*', *MedAev*, xxi (1952), 14–24, is of particular interest.

[4] On the priority of this work see the *Works*, i, pp. xxxvi–xxxviii. The case does not seem to have been disposed of by J. A. W. Bennett's criticisms in *RES*, xxv (1949), 164.

[5] 'Who that woll make ony more latte hym seke other bookis of Kynge Arthure or of Launcelot or Sir Trystram' (*Works*, i. 180). Cf. *infra*, p. 552.

most unwieldy of all thirteenth-century romances of chivalry, the Prose
Tristan, the source of his longest and least attractive book, *Sir Tristram de
Lyones* (Caxton's Books VIII–XII).[1] He then returned to the Arthurian
cycle proper. *La Queste del Saint Graal* and *La Mort Artu* supplied him with
material for his *Tale of the Sankgreal* (Caxton's Books XIII–XVII), *The
Book of Sir Launcelot and Queen Guinevere* (Books XVIII and XIX), and his
last romance, *The Tale of the Death of King Arthur* (Books XX and XXI),
for which he used, in addition to the *Mort Artu*, the English stanzaic *Le
Morte Arthur*. There is undoubtedly in this collection of works a certain
unity of manner and style; there is no unity of structure or design. Walter
Scott was wrong in thinking that Malory's romances had been 'extracted at
hazard, and without much art and combination, from various French prose
folios',[2] but George Saintsbury was no nearer the mark when he said that
Malory, 'and he alone in any language, had made of this vast assemblage of
stories, one story and one book'.[3] The method Malory used was both more
subtle and more drastic. With great consistency, though with varying degrees
of success, he endeavoured to disentangle from his sources a series of self-
contained stories. The enterprise was the more hazardous because most of the
'French prose folios' were not, as Saintsbury thought, an 'assemblage of
stories', but a delicate and elaborate fabric in which the various threads of
the narrative were carefully interwoven with one another.[4] A narrative so
arranged did not lend itself either to a reduction to a single theme or to a
mechanical division. Malory set himself the task of unravelling the threads
and placing each of them separately upon the canvas. In this he instinctively
conformed to the principle of 'singleness' which underlies the rhythmical
structure of any modern work of fiction.[5] Often he failed; but his successes
redeemed most of his failures. In his *Book of Launcelot and Guinevere* he succeeded in producing two continuous sets of episodes, *The Poisoned Apple* and
The Fair Maid of Astolat, and to do this he had to alter the entire structure
of the French narrative.[6] In *The Tale of the Death of King Arthur* he achieved

---

[1] E. K. Chambers, *Malory*, English Assoc. Pamphlet No. 51 (1922), p. 5.

[2] *Sir Tristrem*, ed. W. Scott (Edinburgh, 1804), p. lxxx.

[3] G. Saintsbury, *English Novel* (London, 1913), p. 25.

[4] On this aspect of the cyclic romances see my edition of the *Works*, pp. xlviii–lii, and F. Lot, *Étude
sur le Lancelot en Prose* (Paris, 1918), pp. 17 ff.

[5] Malory applied this method not only to the larger sections of the cycle such as the *Lancelot*
proper, but also to some of the smaller narrative units. *The Tale of King Arthur* provides the earliest
examples of the way in which he tried to separate the interwoven threads from each other. See
Works, i, pp. lii–lv.

[6] C. S. Lewis in his *Allegory of Love*, p. 300, suggests an interesting comparison with Boiardo.
'His [Boiardo's] method is that of the interlocked story. The formula is to take any number of
chivalrous romances and arrange such a series of coincidences that they interrupt one another every
few pages. The English reader will be apt to think of Malory or Spenser. But Malory so often leaves
his separate stories unfinished or else, if he finishes them, fails to interlock them at all (so that they
drop away from the rest of the book as independent organisms) and is so generally confused that he is

the same effect by telling the story in such a way that the action, freed from links with the other branches of the cycle, no longer depended for its effect upon the reader's memory of earlier episodes. The clash of loyalties, the exuberance of the noble passions that once made Arthurian chivalry great, causes the downfall of Arthur's kingdom: the tragic irony of it is intelligible without any reference to the rest of the cycle, and the central theme, disengaged from all concomitant elements, draws its whole power from its own emotional content.[1]

Comparisons of Malory's text with that of the sources he used reveal many other important facets of his genius. But it is well to remember that such comparisons, however fruitful and instructive in themselves, are subject to serious limitations. It is too often assumed that literary history is a matter of assessing the exact extent of the influence of one work upon another. A timely warning has recently been sounded in the modern field by a critic 'assailed by doubts' about the reliability of the method. 'The quest', he writes, 'tends to operate in one direction only—away from the masterpiece. Yet the effort to retrogress towards the source remains largely gratuitous if the procedure is not inverted and pressed forward to appreciate the point at which source and influence are subsumed in the final synthesis. Considered in its full implication the problem of literary influence is an integral part of the problem of literary creation, and this can never be differentiated—not to say solved— until what a writer of genius does with his material becomes the object of a more intuitive type of scholarship than is common to-day.'[2] A vast amount of work has been done in the last quarter of a century on Malory's indebtedness to his sources, with the avowed object of separating all that is creditable to him from whatever he may have borrowed; but it has too often been assumed that these two ingredients of the work are in fact separable. A better understanding of the complexities of assimilation and growth in a literary composition is needed to restore the balance and arrest the fatal 'flight from the masterpiece'. The separable elements are generally those which matter least, such as the author's ideas, his prejudices, his conscious tendencies. It has been shown beyond dispute that Malory took a sceptical view of the supernatural,[3]

---

not a good parallel. Boiardo keeps his head: we have no doubt that if he had finished his poem, all the threads would have been neatly tied up.' Malory is not 'a good parallel' because he is trying something new, and his refusal to interlock the stories is, by his own standards, a measure of his success, not, as C. S. Lewis seems to think, of his failure. He, too, 'keeps his head', perhaps more consistently than Boiardo, but with a different object in mind.

[1] The motivation 'from within' is not entirely absent from the French romance, but there is nothing there comparable to the emphasis placed on it in Malory's version.

[2] P. Mansell Jones, *Background of Modern French Poetry* (Cambridge, 1951), pp. vii–ix.

[3] For examples of this see my *Malory* (Oxford, 1929), pp. 51 f. The case of Tristram, who, instead of being put in a rudderless boat which takes him to Ireland, is told 'plainly' where to go, is matched by that of the Lady of the Lake, who, instead of walking over an invisible bridge, tells Arthur and Merlin to take a boat and fetch the sword from the middle of the lake. Cf. also the curious trans-

that he had no sympathy with the French courtly tradition,[1] and that he had a practical, matter-of-fact conception of chivalry.[2] But to say this is to describe certain aspects of his mind, not the nature of his work. And because so many critics have evaded the latter issue we seem to be on the whole better informed about the author's ambitions and idiosyncrasies than about his ultimate achievement. To give but one example, it has never been properly explained how it comes about that while in Malory there are fewer marvels and more realistic detail, the feeling of the marvellous is not lessened, but intensified. In the story of Balin, which forms part of his *Tale of King Arthur*,[3] there is evidence of the suppression of some of the supernatural elements;[4] and yet not only is the essential magic of the tale retained, but its poetic meaning is brought home to us the more clearly because the story is relieved of some of its fairy-tale trappings. The same discrepancy between the author's attitude to his material and the impression left by his work on the reader's mind occurs in *The Tale of the Sankgreal*. Malory had little use for the doctrine of grace, upon which the whole elaborate edifice of the French *Queste del Saint Graal* rested. He consistently cut out the long theological disquisitions which to the French author mattered at least as much as the story itself.[5] And although attempts have been made by some critics to credit Malory with other doctrines,[6] it is doubtful whether he would have acknow-

formation of the 'terre foraine' into a castle not far distant from the Thames, 'seven miles of West-minster' (Malory's *Works*, p. 1581).

[1] Ibid., pp. 1355 f., 1580 f., and my *Malory*, pp. 48 f.

[2] Malory's *Works*, i, pp. xxvi f.

[3] Ibid. i. 57–92.

[4] Cf. my *Malory*, pp. 52–53.

[5] Cf. ibid., pp. 78 f., 155–88; Malory's *Works*, pp. 1522 f.

[6] Two of these attempts deserve special notice: C. S. Lewis's review of E. K. Chambers's *Sir Thomas Wyatt and Some Collected Studies* in *MedAev*, iii (1934), and E. M. W. Tillyard's review of my edition of Malory's *Works* in *Cambridge Review*, 25 Oct. 1947. C. S. Lewis writes as follows: 'I cannot share Sir Edmund Chambers' suspicion that Malory does not "see his way clearly through the queer spiritual tangle" of courtly love. Malory is simply in agreement with Andreas Capellanus' double doctrine; that on the one hand, *nullum in mundo bonum vel curialitas exercetur nisi ex amoris forte derivetur*, while on the other, love is a mortal sin [. . .] The apparent inconsistency results from the fact that the mediaeval writers are using a triple scale of values where their modern critics are using only a double one [. . .] Malory has a three-storeyed mind—a scale of bad–good–best (Mark, Launcelot, Galahad) which, if read backwards, becomes of course good–bad–worst. It will be seen that the middle term may appear sometimes as "good" and sometimes as "bad" without any inconsistency. He is thus perfectly serious about the nobility of Launcelot and of courtly love—the "old love" so much more faithful and patient than "love nowadays"; and he is equally serious about the yet higher law which cuts across the courtly world in the Grail books.' Tillyard says simply that 'Malory reconciles the code of love and the code of the Church' and quotes in support of this statement the famous passage on the month of May: 'and therefore all ye that be lovers call unto your remembrance the month of May, like as did Queen Guinevere for whom I make here a little mention, that while she lived she was a true lover, and therefore she had a good end.' It is the second *therefore* in this sentence that expresses, according to Tillyard, the author's own doctrine: 'it is because she (Guinevere) had been strict according to the courtly code (imperfect as that code was by religious standards) that she is allowed to end her days in monastic sanctity.' If C. S. Lewis's exegesis is over-subtle, E. M. W. Tillyard's seems to me to be based on a somewhat anachronistic view of the 'code of the Church'.

ledged these more readily than the one which he found fully stated in the French *Queste*. Without any thought of doctrinal interpretation he lets the story speak for itself. He leaves unaltered both the tale of Galahad, the son of Lancelot, and 'the divine irony whereby Lancelot's begetting of that son was at once his main offence against the courtly code and, on the divine plane, his sole *raison d'être*'.[1] Hence the irresistible sense of the approaching ruin of earthly values and the apprehension of that 'piercing moment' when, as Charles Williams says, 'the spiritual bids its implacable farewell to the natural'. The economy of expression, the consistent 'reduction into English' gives point and emphasis to such things. 'Lorde, I thanke The, for now I se that that hath be my desire many a day. Now, my Blyssed Lorde, I wold nat lyve in this wrecched worlde no lenger if hit myght please The, Lorde.'[2] How many readers suspect that these words, through which so much of the meaning of Galahad's destiny is conveyed to us, are a literal translation of some twenty French words gleaned from a passage about five times as long?[3] A subtle process of selection brings out with renewed vigour the deeper sense of the original with the result that the text as it stands represents both the genius of the story and the genius of the author. In the spacious world of Malory's books there is ample room for both. To quote a recent critic, 'we should approach him not as we approach Liverpool Cathedral, but as we approach Wells Cathedral. At Liverpool we see what a particular artist invented. At Wells we see something on which many generations laboured, which no man foresaw or intended as it now is, and which occupies a position half-way between the works of art and those of nature. . . . Here is a Middle-English crypt, there an Anglo-Norman chapel, a late French bit, and bits that are almost pure Malory.'[4]

The 'Middle-English crypt'—the alliterative *Morte Arthure*—is the only part of the structure which, apart from stylistic simplification, has undergone no change at Malory's hands: it belongs to the English epic tradition, and it is not a 'book' or a 'tale', according to Malory's terminology, but a 'romance'. His 'books' and 'tales' are all adaptations from the French, and if there ever was an 'Anglo-Norman chapel' it has been absorbed in later French accretions. Sometimes the sources of these accretions are not extant; some may yet come to light. And wherever Malory happens to tell a story which is other-

---

[1] See the front-page article in *The Times Literary Supplement* of 7 June 1947.

[2] Malory's *Works*, p. 1034.

[3] Here is the corresponding passage in the French *Queste* (I have italicized the words which Malory selected for his rendering): '*Sire, toi* ador *ge* et *merci* de ce que tu m'as accompli mon desirrier, *car ore voi ge* tot apertement ce que langue ne porroit descrire ne cuer penser. Ici voi ge la començaille des granz hardemenz et l'achoison des proeces; ici voi ge les merveilles de totes autres merveilles! Et puis qu'il est einsi, biax dolz Sires, que vos m'avez accomplis mes volentez de lessier moi veoir *ce que j'ai touz jors desirré*, or vos pri ge que vos en cest point ou je sui et en ceste grant joie *soffrez que je trespasse* de ceste *terriene vie* en la celestiel' (ed. Pauphilet, p. 278).

[4] See n. 1 above.

wise unknown, but for which he is clearly not responsible, 'retrogression towards the source' becomes a legitimate method. He is the only author to have preserved what must have originally been a French prose romance of Gaheret—Gawain's favourite brother of whom the Prose *Lancelot* says that he was 'le plus gratieus de touz les freres . . . et hardis et legiers et gens . . . et ot le brach destre plus lonc que l'autre'.[1] This last remark explains why in Malory's *Book of Gareth* Kay calls the hero *in mockery* 'Beaumains'; the nickname, as the hero's mother, the Queen of Orkney, says, is metaphorically true, for Gareth is the most generous (the 'largest-handed') man that ever lived.[2] Another text which has not survived except in Malory is the last of the three *Lancelot* fragments which constitute his *Noble Tale of Sir Launcelot du Lake*; one of the episodes recorded in this fragment is reminiscent of a passage in *Perlesvaus*,[3] but there is no extant French account of Lancelot's encounters with Gawtere, Gylmere, and Raynolde, of his rescue of Melyot de Logres, of his victory over Phelot who had framed a plot against him, or of his unsuccessful attempt to rescue a lady from Sir Pedyvere who, in a moment of anger, cut off her head, then did penance in Rome, and finally became 'an holy man and an hermyte'. There are also some Arthurian romances which have come down to us in copies distinctly more corrupt than the ones Malory used. His *Tale of the Sankgreal* is a case in point, based as it is upon a text more closely related than any one of the extant manuscripts to the lost original version of the French *Queste del Saint Graal*.[4] Similarly, the source of *The Tale of King Arthur* must have been a more authentic version of the French romance than either the *Huth Merlin* or the recently discovered Cambridge manuscript of the *Suite du Merlin*;[5] and finally *The Noble Tale of King Arthur and the Emperor Lucius* is 'drawn' not from the unique surviving copy of the alliterative *Morte Arthure*, but from an earlier version of the poem.[6]

The bulk of his work, however, consists of 'late French bits' for which reliable versions of his sources are available. A careful comparison of his text with the French makes it possible to discover a number of passages creditable to his own invention. But if the 'pure Malory' were limited to such passages it would be difficult to say anything positive about his art of writing. There are some significant disquisitions on love and marriage in his *Noble Tale of Sir Launcelot* and in the *Book of Sir Launcelot and Queen Guinevere*;[7] there

---

[1] MS. Add. 10293, fol. 250ʳ, col. 2.

[2] For a different and in my view extremely unlikely explanation of the origin of Beaumains's name see R. S. Loomis in *PMLA*, liv (1939), 656–68. See also *MLN*, lxx (1955), 326.

[3] Ed. Nitze and others (Chicago, 1932), i, ll. 8156–82.

[4] See my *Malory* (1929), pp. 141–7.

[5] See my article, 'La Genèse de la Suite du Merlin', in *Mélanges de Philologie romane et de Littérature médiévale offerts à Ernest Hoepffner* (Strasbourg, 1949), pp. 295–300.

[6] See *MedAev*, vi. 81–98.

[7] Malory's *Works*, pp. 270 f., 1119 f.

are examples of genuine lyricism in the *Book of Sir Tristram*;[1] and there are elaborate comments everywhere on the art of chivalry and the duties of those who belong to the 'High Order of Knighthood'.[2] Yet the additions which help us to see most clearly Malory's special characteristics as a writer occur in a story in which there is no room for such digressions, *The Tale of the Death of King Arthur*.[3] Malory's main concern here is to reinterpret the traditional tale in terms of Lancelot's devotion to the ideals upon whose conflict the fortunes of Arthurian chivalry must break—the two ideals symbolized by Guinevere and Gawain—and the reinterpretation is achieved by means of a subtle phrasing of some of the scenes, by a skilful expansion of soliloquies and dialogues, and by the sheer power of the words spoken by the characters.

It is in examining additions of this kind that one comes to realize where Malory's real originality lies and what the phrase 'pure Malory' should mean. The pure Malory is the prose-writer whose language has given new life to a dying tradition. Exactly how this happened we shall never know: but there is in Malory's prose the same aesthetic principle at work as in his method of composition. Both the literary English of his time and the language of his French Arthurian books were, like the books themselves, reminiscent of a woven fabric. Alternating themes, cross-links and overlappings were characteristic of the language of some of the best among his sources. More than that: there is much the same contrast between their style and Malory's as between the two types of structure: the same kind of structural evolution leads to a break with the traditional forms of writing. Hence Malory's natural falling back into the even tenor of familiar discourse and the characteristically haunting 'elegiac tone or undertone which never fails in romance or homily to bring its sad suggestions of the vanity and transience of all things, of the passing away of pomp and splendour, of the fall of the princes'.[4] What makes his prose live is his way of subordinating his verbal material to a rhythm all his own, his instinctive discovery of a new stylistic pattern. The smooth symmetry of the French *période* disappears and in its place we find a succession of abruptly divided clauses, some of them strikingly brief and compact, and all of them spoken rather than written:

And Sir Launcelot awok, and went and took his hors, and rode al that day and al nyght in a forest, wepyng. And atte last he was ware of an ermytage and a chappel stode betwyxte two clyffes, and than he harde a lytel belle rynge to masse. And thyder he rode and alyght, and teyed his hors to the gate, and herd masse.[5]

This is a slow movement—a *largo*—often used in description. Elsewhere, in the more dramatic scenes, when the situation calls for an utterance without

---

[1] Cf. Malory's *Works*, p. 502.   [2] See my *Malory* (1929), pp. 60–64.
[3] Cf. Malory's *Works*, pp. 1604–9.
[4] W. P. Ker quoted by E. K. Chambers, *English Literature*, p. 198.
[5] Malory's *Works*, p. 1254.

a pause, the rhythmical units tend to become shorter and the *tempo* is quickened:

> So hit felle uppon a daye, in hervest tyme, sir Launcelot loked over the wallys and spake on hyght unto kynge Arthure and to sir Gawayne.[1]

Here the effect approximates that of an *allegro*; but there are passages which convey a sense of tension without any acceleration of the movement, merely by a careful timing of each phrase, as in the opening phase of the 'wicked Day of Destiny':

> And so they mette as their poyntemente was, and were agreed and accorded thorowly. And wyne was fette, and they dranke togydir. Ryght so cam oute an addir of a lytyll hethe-buysshe, and hit stange a knyght in the foote. And so whan the knyght felte hym so stonge, he loked downe and saw the adder; and anone he drew hys swerde to sle the addir, and thought none othir harme. And whan the oste on bothe partyes saw that swerde drawyn, than they blewe beamys, trumpettis, and hornys, and shoutted grymly, and so bothe ostis dressed hem togydirs. And kynge Arthur toke hys horse and seyde, 'Alas, this unhappy day!' and so rode to hys party, and sir Mordred in lyke wyse.[2]

The author's own voice may not always be as audible as it is in these majestic lines, but it asserts itself often enough to sustain the pathos of the entire narrative. It is invariably heard in the speeches of the characters whenever dialogue replaces a straightforward account of the events:

> Than seyde that man, 'Truly, sir Gaherys and sir Gareth he slayne.'
> 'Jesu deffende!' seyd sir Gawayne. 'For all thys worlde I wolde nat that they were slayne, and in especiall my good brothir sir Gareth.'
> 'Sir,' seyde the man, 'he is slayne, and that ys grete pité.'
> 'Who slew hym?' seydé sir Gawayne.
> 'Sir Launcelot,' seyde the man, 'slew hem both.'
> 'That may I nat belive,' seyde Sir Gawayne, 'that ever he slew my good brother sir Gareth, for I dare say, my brothir loved hym better than me and all hys brethirn and the kynge bothe.' . . .
> 'Veryly, sir,' seyde the man, 'hit ys noysed that he slew hym.'
> 'Alas,' seyde sir Gawayne, 'now ys my joy gone!'[3]

The two voices—that of the mysterious, nameless 'man' uttering, like the blind Tiresias, the simple and yet unbelievable truth, and the passionate voice of Gawain seeking to disbelieve it—are here contrasted in a song of despair, in a tragic lament 'heard in the future'. For the first and perhaps the last time in the history of Arthurian literature the power of language raises the story to the level of tragic action.

In concluding his first adaptation of a French romance, *The Tale of King Arthur*, Malory wrote these words (not to be found in Caxton's edition):

---

[1] Ibid., p. 1187.   [2] Ibid., p. 1235.   [3] Ibid., pp. 1184 f.

'Who that woll ony more lette hym seke othir bookis of kynge Arthure or sir
Launcelot or sir Trystrams; for this was drawyn by a knyght presoner sir
Thomas Malleorré, that God send hym good recover.' The obscure 'knight-
prisoner' had certainly done as much as any man could to 'draw' Arthurian
romance from the enchanted frame of medieval fiction, and no one since his
day has succeeded in 'making any more'. Yet his own book was to become
the starting-point of a great tradition of imaginative prose and poetry, and
there are signs that the discovery of a more authentic text of his writings in
Winchester will add still further to their appeal.[1] After a recent broadcast of
the *Quest of the Holy Grail* Mr. Lionel Hale expressed what was no doubt in
the minds of most English listeners: 'Such knights, such ladies in distress,
such single combats, such fiends, such vows! The chivalry went briskly
by, with their own beauty and their own simplicities of bravura, and never
even relapsed into a dog-trot. . . . But the triumph was Malory's. What tales
and what a teller!'[2] Now that we know something of the complexities of
Arthurian romance and of Malory's place in its development we also know
that he alone in any language could thus have poured into the modern
mould the sentiment which the Middle Ages had created.

[1] The following should be added to the bibliography given in Malory's *Works*, pp. 1652–8: E. K.
Chambers, *English Literature at the Close of the Middle Ages*, pp. 185–203; M.-M. Dubois, Introd.
to Sir Thomas Malory, *Le Roman d'Arthur et des Chevaliers de la Table Ronde* (Paris, 1948); M. E.
Dichmann, 'Characterization in Malory's Tale of Arthur and Lucius', *PMLA*, lxv (1950), 877–95;
E. T. Donaldson, 'Malory and the Stanzaic Le Morte Arthur', *SP*, xlvii (1950), 460–72; D. S. Brewer,
article cited in n. 3, p. 544; R. H. Wilson, 'Malory's Early Knowledge of Arthurian Romance',
Texas Studies in English, xxix (1950), 33–50; Wilson, 'Malory's "French Book" Again', *Com-
parative Literature*, ii (1950), 172–81; Wilson, 'Notes on Malory's Sources', *MLN*, lxvi (1951),
22–26; Wilson, 'The Prose Lancelot in Malory', *Texas Studies in English*, xxxii (1953), 1–13;
P. E. Tucker, 'The Place of the Quest of the Holy Grail in the "Morte Darthur"', *MLR*, l
(1955), 490–2; Malory, *The Tale of the Death of Arthur*, ed. Vinaver (Oxford, 1955); R. T.
Davies, 'Malory's Lancelot and the Noble Way of the World', *RES*, N.S., vi (1955), 356–64;
Davies, 'Malory's Vertuouse Love', *SP*, liii (1956), 459–69; C. Moorman, 'Malory's Treatment
of the Sangreall', *PMLA*, lxxi (1956), 496–509; R. S. Loomis, 'Onomastic Riddles in Malory's
"Book of Arthur and His Knights"', *MedAev*, xxv (1957), 181–90; R. M. Lumiansky, 'The
Relationship of Lancelot and Guinevere in Malory's "Tale of Lancelot"', *MLN*, lxviii (1953),
86–91; Lumiansky, 'Malory's Tale of Lancelot and Guinevere as Suspense', *Medieval Studies*, xix
(1957), 108–22; Lumiansky, 'The Question of Unity in Malory's Morte Darthur', *Studies in English*,
v (1955), 29–40, Tulane University, New Orleans. The complete text has been translated into German by Hedwig Lachmann (*Der Tod Arthurs*, Leipzig, 1923), and into Turkish by Mina Urgan
(*Arthur 'ün Ölümü*, Istanbul, 1948). There is an excellent French translation of selected passages
from Malory's works in M.-M. Dubois, op. cit.

[2] The *Observer*, 25 Oct. 1953.

ARTHURIAN INFLUENCE ON SPORT AND SPECTACLE

ROGER SHERMAN LOOMIS

OSCAR WILDE's paradox that 'Life merely holds the mirror up to art' has seldom been better exemplified than in the reflections of Arthurian literature in the practices and pageantries, as well as the plays, of our medieval ancestors.[1] Kings presided at Round Tables and founded orders modelled on Arthur's fellowship; great lords adopted the names, the blazons, and the roles of Gawain, Lancelot, and Palamedes; young merchants caught the same fever, and in south Germany apprentices enacted Shrovetide plays, burlesquing Arthur's court. These mimicries of the Matter of Britain are recorded from Acre in the East (1286)[2] to Dublin in the West (1498),[3] and from Valencia (1269)[4] to Prague (1319).[5]

On purely *a priori* grounds one might assume that the earliest essays of this kind would have taken place in Britain as a result of Geoffrey of Monmouth's authority, or in France under the influence of Chrétien de Troyes. No procedure could be more hazardous. As with the Modena sculpture, the facts belie such facile assumptions. The first recorded evidence for the imitation of Arthurian figures comes from Cyprus under the date 1223.[6] When the lord of Beirut celebrated the knighting of his eldest sons, 'there was much giving and spending; there were *bohorts*,[7] the adventures of Britain and the Round Table were enacted (*contrefait*), and there were many other amusements (*jeus*)'. A continuation of the same chronicle tells how in 1286, when Henry II of Cyprus was crowned King of Jerusalem at Acre,

---

[1] On this general subject cf. R. S. Loomis, 'Chivalric and Dramatic Imitations of Arthurian Romance', *Mediaeval Studies in Memory of A. K. Porter* (Cambridge, Mass., 1939), i. 79–97. On Arthurian tournaments cf. Sandoz in *Spec*, xix (1944), 389–420; Cline in *Spec*, xx (1945), 204–11; Keeler in *Univ. of California Publications in English*, xvii (1946), no. 1, pp. 131–7.

[2] *Gestes des Chiprois*, ed. G. Raynaud (Geneva, 1887), p. 220.

[3] S. J. D. Seymour, *Anglo-Irish Literature, 1200–1582* (Cambridge, 1929), pp. 122–5. This was probably a 'riding'.

[4] Mila y Fontanals, *Obras Completas* (Barcelona, 1895), vi. 233; Ramon Muntaner, *Chronicle*, chaps. 23, 155, 173.

[5] E. Fricken, *Johann von Böhmen* (Göttingen, 1932), pp. 40 f.

[6] Philippe de Novare, *Mémoires*, ed. C. Kohler (Paris, 1913), pp. 7, 134.

[7] *Bohorts* apparently differed from tourneys in that precautions were taken against serious injuries. A. Schultz, *Das höfische Leben zur Zeit der Minnesinger*, 2nd ed. (Leipzig, 1889), ii. 113 f.; F. Niedner, *Das deutsche Turnier im XII. und XIII. Jahrhundert* (Berlin, 1881), pp. 15, 35.

there was a splendid festival, including *bohorts*, imitations of the Round Table, and impersonations (*contrefirent*) of Lancelot, Tristan, and Palamedes.[1]

From 1223 far into the fourteenth century a similar combination of jousting, feasting, dancing, known as a Round Table, was one of the most fashionable diversions of Christendom.[2] Instances are attested in Britain for the years 1252, 1259, 1279, 1281, 1284, 1302, 1328, and 1345.[3] That of 1284 was held at Nevin to celebrate Edward I's conquest of Wales, and the last was the consequence of Edward III's vow in 1344 to found an order of 300 knights in imitation of King Arthur.[4] This order later turned into the Order of the Garter, and for some unknown reason all Arthurian associations were dropped. Across the Channel Round Tables were held at Hesdin in 1235;[5] at Bar-sur-Aube in 1294,[6] when Duke John of Brabant was fatally wounded; at Bruges in 1300,[7] attended by the King and Queen of France; and at Paris in 1332.[8] *Tables rondes* are mentioned in Adam de la Halle's *Jeu de la Feuillée* (1262)[9] and in the *Livre du Chevalier de la Tour Landry* (1372).[10] When Edward I arranged for the marriage of his daughter to Alfonso III of Aragon at Oloron in Gascony in 1287, there were Round Tables and dancing.[11]

Such celebrations were at this time peculiarly favoured by the kings of Aragon, for we read of them in Muntaner's chronicle as being held at Valencia, probably in 1269, at Saragossa in 1286, at Barcelona in 1290, and at Calatayud in 1291.[12] On the last occasion the great Catalan admiral, Roger Luria, had a wooden castle built at the end of the lists, which served as his station. When he was challenged by a knight from Murcia, umpires brought the two combatants two pointless shafts, the challenger took his choice, and Luria the other. In the encounter Luria's shaft struck his opponent's helm, crushed his nose, and covered his face with blood. The Round Table was then halted for fear of quarrels.

While on the one hand Edward III, as we have seen, founded a short-lived Arthurian order, and while John of France in rivalry set up another

[1] See p. 553, n. 2.

[2] *Mediaeval Studies in Memory of A. K. Porter*, i, pp. 81 f.

[3] *Annales Monastici*, ed. Luard (Rolls Series), i. 150; ii. 402; iii. 313; iv. 445, 477, 491; W. Rishanger, *Chronica*, ed. Riley (R. S.), p. 94; *Flores Historiarum*, ed. Luard (R. S.), iii. 62; Fordun, *Chronica*, ed. Skene (Edinburgh, 1871), i. 308.

[4] W. H. St. John Hope, *Windsor Castle* (London, 1913), i. 111 f., 122 f.; Adam of Murimuth, *Continuatio Chronicarum*, ed. E. M. Thompson (R. S.), pp. 155 ff., 231 f.

[5] Albericus Trium Fontium, *Chronicon* (Hanover, 1698), p. 555.

[6] *Spec*, xxviii (1953), 117 f.; *Annales Monastici*, iii. 388.

[7] Giovanni Villani, *Cronica*, lib. viii, chap. 32; Moke, *Moeurs, Usages, Fêtes et Solennités des Belges* (Brussels, n.d.), ii. 172–9.

[8] C. Leber, *Collections des Meilleurs Dissertations* (Paris, 1838), xii. 163 f.

[9] Vss. 720–4.   [10] Ed. A. de Montaiglon (Paris, 1854), p. 55.

[11] Ramon de Muntaner, *Chronicle*, ch. 166.

[12] Ibid., chaps. 23, 155, 173, 179.

to attract knights to his banner,[1] other kings forbade tournaments and King Henry III specifically banned Round Tables in 1232 and in 1251.[2] Popes and prelates thundered against these costly, dangerous, and sometimes licentious frivolities, and denied Christian burial to those who took part.[3] But even the threat of hell fire does not seem to have deterred Western chivalry from breaking their bones and risking their lives in a pastime which enjoyed the prestige of King Arthur's patronage.

Though many notices of these passages of arms provide little detail, others provide too much for more than brief summary. Ulrich von Lichtenstein, a forerunner of Don Quixote, tells in his *Frauendienst* how he set out in 1240, assuming the role of King Arthur, challenging all knights whom he met to a joust, and admitting those who broke three spears on him without missing into the order of the Round Table.[4] The knights whom he met were given names such as Lanzilet, Ywan, and Segremors, and some of them joined his train. The Prince of Austria sent him a messenger, thanking him for coming from Paradise to his land—a reference to the Breton belief—and soon after brought a number of knights to swell the company. Near Neustadt a Round Table was held, tents were pitched, banners set up, and to the music of flutes, pipes, and sackbuts there were individual encounters which lasted for five days. On the sixth there was a general *mêlée* between two sides, broken off by the prince's order. The only damage mentioned, it is pleasant to relate, was a dislocated thumb.

The *bourgeoisie* were caught by the craze. In 1281 a burgher of Magdeburg sent invitations to the merchants of Goslar, Brunswick, &c., to come and try their knightly prowess, and he who excelled the rest was to receive as a prize a woman called Dame Feie.[5] Troops of young men came to Magdeburg and were met by two 'constables' with spears outside the town. A 'gral', consisting of tents and a tree hung with the shields of the local champions, was arranged in a marsh. To touch one of these shields with a spear was a challenge to its owner. Somewhat inexplicably an old merchant from Goslar won Dame Feie, and magnanimously gave her so much money that she was able to leave her wild life for a respectable husband. Similarly in 1330 the

---

[1] Jean le Bel, *Vraies Chroniques*, ed. M. L. Polain (Brussels, 1863), ii. 173.

[2] C. V. Langlois, *Règne de Philippe III* (Paris, 1887), pp. 196–9; T. Rymer, *Foedera*, ed. A. Clarke, F. Holbrooke (London, 1816), i. 205; R. C. Clephan, *Tournament* (London, 1919), p. 13.

[3] R. de Kellawe, *Registrum*, ed. T. D. Hardy (London, 1873), i. 495; L. Gautier, *Chevalerie*, nouv. éd. (Paris, 1884), pp. 681–4; G. R. Owst, *Preaching in Medieval England* (Cambridge, 1926), pp. 301, 322, 326, 332–6.

[4] Ulrich von Lichtenstein, *Frauendienst*, ed. R. Bechstein (Leipzig, 1888), ii. 173–231; *Studien zur deutschen Philologie des Mittelalters F. Panzer* (Heidelberg, 1950), pp. 131–52; map of *Artusfahrt* in P. Piper, *Höfische Epik* (Stuttgart, n.d.), iii. 900; R. Becker, *Ritterliche Waffenspiele nach Ulrich von Lichtenstein* (Düren, 1887).

[5] P. S. Barto, *Tannhaüser and the Mountain of Venus* (New York, 1916), pp. 114 f.; translated pp. 9 f.; A. Schultz, *Deutsches Leben im XIV. und XV. Jahrhundert*, ii. 445 f.

burghers of Tournai formed a society of the Round Table and sent out invitations for the next year to Valenciennes, Bruges, Paris, &c.[1] The members of the society took the names of kings, such as Gallehos, Pellez du
Castel Périlleux. There was the usual procession of combatants, and the
jousts took place in the market square. The prize was a golden vulture.

One of the most famous of these passages of arms was that of St. Ingelvert,[2]
described by Froissart. The Maréchal de Boucicaut and two other French
knights sent out in 1390 a challenge to all comers from England, Spain, and
Germany to meet them in the plain near Calais. Any foreign knight who
wished to joust would approach a large elm on which each of the challengers
had hung two shields, blow a horn, touch either the shield of peace or the
shield of war, and the combat would accordingly take place with either
pointed or blunt spears. A large pavilion was provided for the visitors to arm
or repose in, and there was an abundant supply of wines and food for their
entertainment. Among the English knights who came to the jousting were
the half-brother of Richard II, John Holland, and the future Henry IV.
Somewhat similar in character was the Pas de la Belle Pélerine held between
Calais and St. Omer in 1449.[3] It was so called for the alleged reason that a
fair lady had set out with her company on a pilgrimage to Rome, had been
attacked by robbers, and delivered by a knight, who promised to escort her
to the Holy City as soon as he had fulfilled his vow to guard a pass at the Croix
de la Pélerine. This knight was Jean de Luxembourg, lord of Haubourdin,
who presented all who accepted his challenge with a pilgrim's staff (*bourdon*)
of gold set with a ruby, in allusion to the lady's pious vow and his own title.
The accounts vary widely as to what happened, but it appears that Jean
assumed the role of Lancelot, his shield blazoned with the charge of that
hero, argent a bend gules, and that the Duke of Burgundy presided.

King René of Anjou in 1446 organized near Saumur jousts according to
the terms established by the knights of the Round Table, had a wooden castle
called 'Joyeuse Garde' constructed; and introduced into the pageantry lions,
tigers, and unicorns (?) from the royal menagerie.[4] There were kings of
arms, judges of the field, a dwarf dressed like a Turk, bearing the royal shield,
and a lovely damsel leading the king's horse. This like other jousts was
stopped because of a fatal injury. René caused a painting to be made of the
jousts and in 1451–2 composed his *Livre des Tournois*.[5]

---

[1] Moke, *Moeurs, Usages, Fêtes et Sollenités des Belges*, ii. 173–9.

[2] Froissart, *Oeuvres*, ed. Kervyn de Lettenhove (Brussels, 1872), xiv. 197 ff.; *Collection des Mémoires*, ed. M. Petitot (Paris, 1819), vi. 424–31.

[3] Mathieu d'Escouchy, *Chronique*, ed. Du Fresne de Beaucourt (Paris, 1863), i. 244–63; Olivier de la Marche, *Mémoires*, ed. H. Beaune, J. d'Arbaumont, ii (Paris, 1884), 118–23.

[4] Mathieu d'Escouchy, op. cit. i. 107; A. Lecoy de la Marche, *Roi René* (Paris, 1875), ii. 75, 146 f.; Vulson de la Colombière, *Vray Théatre d'Honneur* (Paris, 1648), pp. 82–106.

[5] Ibid., pp. 39, 49.

One of the latest and most elaborate of the festivals which followed Arthurian precedent, held in 1493 at the castle of Sandricourt, near Pontoise, was described by the Herald of Orléans.[1] There were on successive days combats on foot at the Barrière Périlleuse, a general tourney at the Carrefour Ténébreux, individual jousts at the Champs de l'Espine. The climax of the last day was the Adventures of the Forest Desvoyable. The participating knights rode out of the castle accompanied by their ladies, and were presented with lances and swords at the Pin Vert, where knights of the Round Table had formerly resorted in search of adventure. Proceeding separately along the forest paths, they would couch their spears when they met and batter each other. Servants were on hand to provide wine and refreshments for the weary. At eve the knights repaired to the castle to banquet and to relate their adventures on oath. Followed dances and farces lasting till two in the morning. Orléans estimated that nearly 2,000 persons including armourers, saddlers, and leeches were entertained at the castle for eight days, and declared that never since the time of Arthur and his order, which comprised Lancelot, Gawain, Tristan, and Palamedes, had there been a *Pas d'Armes* which approximated more closely the deeds of the knights of the Round Table.

As we have seen, impersonation of Arthurian characters had been a recurring feature of these festivals from the very beginning, and there were occasional efforts to adopt their heraldic charges and to emulate their deeds of arms. We have records of two occasions when the imitation of the romances went farther in the direction of drama, both from the last quarter of the thirteenth century when the vogue of Round Tables was at its height. The first is elaborately described by Sarrasin in his *Roman du Hem*[2] and probably took place at Hem-Monacu, near Péronne, in the year 1278.[3] The principal role of the Chevalier au Lion was taken by Robert II, Count of Artois and patron of the dramatist Adam de la Halle; while the part of Guenièvre was played by the sister of Aubert de Bazentin, one of the organizers of the tournament.[4]

Apparently the entertainment began with Guenièvre seated at supper with her court, when Soredamors rode in on a hackney led by a dwarf, to demand succour for her imprisoned lover. Keu remarked that any knight who imperilled himself for her sake ought to be tonsured. When, however, all the knights present asked the queen for the privilege, Keu claimed it as his right, and on the arrival of the knight who kept Soredamors's lover in prison arranged to meet him next morning in the field. It would seem that immediately thereafter seven knights, taken captive by the Chevalier au Lion, presented themselves, accompanied by a lion which made itself at home by

---

[1] Vulson de la Colombière, op. cit., pp. 147–70.
[2] Sarrasin, *Roman du Hem*, ed. A. Henry (Paris, 1939).
[3] *Romania*, lxii (1936), 386 ff.   [4] Sarrasin, op. cit., pp. liii, lxi.

resting its muzzle on the table. Keu once more indulged in his mockery, but the queen accepted the surrendering knights into her service, and dancing followed. The next day Keu, while waiting for his opponent, was unmercifully teased by the ladies and finally retorted with a wish that a flame would burn their tongues. The joust which followed left both combatants unhurt. The Knight of the Lion arrived with several rescued damsels, and a dark-complexioned handmaiden who announced their coming elicited some ironic compliments from Keu, which caused the queen to remark that it was futile to teach an old cat. The rest of the day was occupied with a series of jousts, the arrival of another distressed maiden, more comedy furnished by the lion and Keu, and with supper. The influence of Chrétien's work on the proceedings is obvious, and one wonders whether Adam de la Halle may have had something to do with a dramatic performance in which his patron played the chief heroic role.[1]

A somewhat similar affair seems to have celebrated the marriage of Margaret, daughter of Marie de Brabant, to the sixty-year-old Edward I of England in 1299.[2] It is described by the Brabançon priest, Lodewijk van Velthem,[3] and though he mistakenly assigns it to the occasion of Edward's first marriage to the Spanish princess Eleanor, it is fairly clear that it consisted of a tournament and three interludes[4] recalling Edward's triumphs over the Welsh, the Scots, and the barons.[5] At sunrise the Round Table began with a *mêlée* in which the knights who had taken Arthurian names had the best of their opponents, except Keye, whose saddle-girths had been cut—in fun of course—and whose consequent tumble evoked roars of laughter. When the company adjourned to the banquet hall, after the first course a page disguised as a squire rode in, spattered with blood, and called for vengeance on the Welsh, which the knights of the Round Table promised to wreak. After the second course and a pause a second squire rode in on a sumpter, his hands and feet tied, and after being released by Lanceloet delivered a challenge to him from the King of Irlant—doubtless an error for Scotland. The third course was followed by the entrance of the Loathly Damsel on a bony nag, charmingly made up with a nose a foot long, a goitre

---

[1] H. Guy, *Essai sur la Vie et les Oeuvres Littéraires du Trouvère Adam de la Hale* (Paris, 1898), p. 153.

[2] *Spec.* xxviii (1953), 118–21.

[3] Continuation of *Spiegel Historiael*, ed. Vander Linden and De Vreese, i (Brussels, 1906), 198–320; Huet in *Moyen Age*, xxvi (1913), 173–97; Chotzen in *BBCS*, vii (1935), 42–54.

[4] On the word interlude, meaning a play between the courses of a banquet, cf. *MLN*, xli (1926), 98–100. For a miniature depicting an interlude before Charles V of France, the Emperor Charles IV, and Wenceslas in 1378 cf. C. W. Previté-Orton, *Shorter Cambridge Medieval History* (Cambridge, 1952), ii. 851, and especially L. H. Loomis in *Spec.*, xxxiii (1958), 242–55.

[5] Though the wedding occurred at Canterbury according to the best authorities, Walter de Hemingburgh in his *Chronicon*, ed. H. C. Hamilton (London, 1849), ii. 185, placed it at London, and Lodewijk also assigned the wedding festivities to London.

on her neck, and teeth projecting a finger's length from her wry mouth. She called on Perchevael to win the castle of Leicester from its lord (Simon de Montfort), and bade Walewein ride to Cornuaelge (doubtless a corruption of Kenilworth, a stronghold of the rebel barons) to end the strife between commons and lords. While the squire who impersonated the Loathly Damsel slipped out to remove his make-up, a date was set for the campaigns which had been undertaken. It will be noted that, together with the Round Tables of 1279, 1284, 1287, and 1302, this makes the fifth such festival which Edward attended, and, according to Lodewijk, he was personally active in the arrangements.

In 1336 and at intervals thereafter, the Nine Worthies, the supreme warriors of pagan, Jewish, and Christian history, were represented in pageants, displaying their heraldic shields, and boasting of their exploits. Arthur, Charlemagne, and Godfrey de Bouillon formed the Christian trio, and several versions of Arthur's speech have come down to us.[1]

The only dramatic pieces which may be called medieval and of which the texts have survived are far removed in tone and in the circumstances of their performance from any of the spectacular displays thus far noted. They are three South German farces of the second half of the fifteenth century, which were presented at Shrovetide by groups of apprentices who went from house to house collecting money and enjoying refreshments.[2] All three deal with the theme of the chastity test at Arthur's court, of which the earliest literary form is Robert Biket's *Lai du Cor* of the twelfth century and one of the latest is the ballad of *The Boy and the Mantle*. The immediate sources of these *Fastnachtspiele* were the *Meisterlieder*. In one play the discriminating talisman is a drinking horn,[3] in the second a mantle,[4] and in the third we have an innovation, a crown which when donned by a cuckold causes antlers to sprout on his head.[5] All were calculated to provoke ribald guffaws at the expense of female virtue, deceived husbands, and the idealistic chivalry of King Arthur's day.

[1] *Parlement of the Thre Ages*, ed. I. Gollancz (London, 1915), preface and appendix; *MP*, xv (1917), 211–19.
[2] Creizenach, *Geschichte des neueren Dramas*, 2nd ed. (Halle, 1911), i. 410 ff.
[3] *Bibliothek des literarischen Vereins in Stuttgart*, xlvi (1858), 183–215.
[4] Ibid. xxix (1853), 664 ff.
[5] Ibid., pp. 654 ff.

EPILOGUE

No one would claim that the many and complex problems involved in the rise and flourishing of the vast literature which centred about the figure of Arthur have all been solved in this book, or that the purposes of the Arthurian authors have all been successfully probed, or that in every instance their achievements have been appraised at their right value. That, needless to say, is an impossible goal, and we make no apologies for failing to achieve it. Many opinions here expressed will be questioned, and in time new facts will be dug up, new manuscripts discovered, which will render certain parts obsolete.

Whatever conclusions one may come to as to the origins of the Matter of Britain, whether in the cranium of Geoffrey of Monmouth, or in the fancy of Chrétien de Troyes, or in the myths and hero tales of the Celts who preceded them, the chief causes of its popularity are not hard to discern. The twelfth century was an adventurous period in the thought and the arts of Europe; it was the age of Abelard, of the troubadours, and of the beginnings of Gothic architecture. The search for the strange and exotic which found satisfaction in the marvels of the Alexander legend took delight also in the wonders which had once abounded in the land of Logres, the Out Isles, and the fay-haunted forest of Broceliande—turning castles, testing horns, enchanted springs. Here were to be met the Questing Beast, the Dwarf King, the Green Knight, the Loathly Damsel, who needed but a kiss to be transformed into a radiant beauty. So, too, the new interest in the various manifestations of love, which was first exploited by the authors of *Enéas* and the *Roman de Troie*, found larger scope in the amorous adventures of Gawain, the tragic fate of Tristan and Isolt, the imperious whims and the jealousy of Guenevere, and the agonies of Lancelot. The Grail quest, so tantalizing in its contradictions and obscurity, led to ponderings on the mysteries of religion, while profound lessons of morality could be extracted from the history of Parzival. No wonder that these themes attracted some of the greatest geniuses of the Middle Ages and enthralled their readers. Enveloping and framing these diverse tales of love, adventure, comedy, and high emprise was the grandiose scheme of the rise and fall of King Arthur's Round Table. Here was food for all appetites, here were themes adapted to all moods, from naïve astonishment and broad humour to idealistic passion and awed speculation on the duties and destinies of Man.

The vogue of this cycle of story persisted, as the preceding pages have shown, well into the sixteenth century. The emperor Maximilian, who died in 1519 and was called 'the last of the knights', caused the well-known statue of the

British king to be cast by Vischer and placed near his tomb at Innsbruck. In England the Tudor dynasty upheld the fame of their predecessor on the throne, so that it was natural for the poet Spenser to represent Prince Arthur as the beloved of Gloriana and the perfection of all the virtues, magnificence. But we have also observed many signs of the vulgarization of Arthurian literature and the decline in the prestige of its heroes: and of this trend there is no more striking index than Shakespeare's irreverent mention of Merlin and Camelot, and his assigning a clown's part to Launcelot Gobbo. These were names, apparently, to make the unskilful laugh.

What causes can we discover for this *Götterdämmerung*? We all know that literary fashions, like others, have their day, and this, though it lasted for nearly 500 years, even if we exclude an earlier development in Wales and Cornwall, could not escape inevitable doom. Moreover, the sceptics finally triumphed over Geoffrey of Monmouth. While William of Newburgh had challenged his credibility in the twelfth century and Higden in the fourteenth, both in vain, Caxton in the late fifteenth bore witness that 'divers men hold opinion that there was no such Arthur, and that all such books as be made of him be but feigned and fables'. By the sixteenth century chroniclers were becoming increasingly doubtful about Geoffrey's reliability, and John Leland, the antiquary, was forced to fight a rearguard action in his defence. More effective than the cold scrutiny of historians in cooling the popular enthusiasm for Arthurian story were certain momentous events and powerful tendencies which we all recognize as signalling the close of the Middle Ages and the beginnings of the Renaissance and the Reformation. Feats of arms accomplished by spear and sword must have seemed quaint in a period when the arquebus and the cannon had proved more deadly weapons. New worlds of enchantment were opened up by the discovery of America, and as a consequence El Dorado and Florida acquired the magic associations which had clung so long to Avalon and Broceliande. Neo-classicism subjected the episodic structure of the romances to standards of rationality and coherence which they could not meet. Protestantism found the Grail legends not only lacking in scriptural authority, but also tainted with monkery, relic-mongering, and the hocus-pocus of the Mass. It is no wonder that, overwhelmed by such an array of hostile forces, the chivalry of the Round Table went down to defeat in a second Camlann, and the tales about them were forgotten, not, however, without contributing notably to the ideal of a gentleman and to the concept of romantic love.

But, as we know, the wheel of Fortune kept on turning, and Arthur, who had been consigned to obloquy and oblivion, rose again in majesty. A new line of geniuses—Wagner, Tennyson, Swinburne, Arnold—as well as many lesser men, took up the themes left by the Middle Ages and gave them new life. Even now, when the papers are filled with the exploits of spacemen, there are plenty of readers who turn with delight and profit to read T. H. White's *The Once and Future King*, a best-seller of the year 1958. Chrétien de Troyes seems to have been right after all when he wrote in *Yvain* concerning 'the King whose fame was such that men still speak of him far and near': 'I agree with the opinion of the Bretons that his name will live on for evermore.'

INDEX

(Page numbers in italics indicate main treatments.)

PRINTED IN GREAT BRITAIN
AT THE UNIVERSITY PRESS, OXFORD
BY VIVIAN RIDLER
PRINTER TO THE UNIVERSITY